God of Abraham

God of Abraham

L. E. Goodman

New York Oxford
OXFORD UNIVERSITY PRESS
1996

Oxford University Press

Oxford New York
Athens Auckland Bangkok
Calcutta Cape Town Dar es Salaam Delhi
Florence Hong Kong Istanbul Karachi
Kuala Lumpur Madras Madrid Melbourne
Mexico City Nairobi Paris Singapore
Taipei Tokyo Toronto

and associated companies in
Berlin Ibadan

Published by Oxford University Press, Inc.
198 Madison Avenue, New York, New York 10016

Goodman, Lenn Evan, 1944–
God of Abraham / L. E. Goodman.
p. cm.
Includes bibliographical references and index.
ISBN 0-19-508312-1
1. God (Judaism)—History of doctrines. 2. Monotheism.
3. Philosophy, Jewish. I. Title.
BM610.G66 1996
296.3'11—dc20 94-36970
CIP

Printing (last digit): 9 8 7 6 5 4 3 2 1

Printed in the United States of America
on acid-free paper

Hear me, ye who pursue justice, ye who seek the Lord.
Look to the rock whence ye were hewn,
To the quarry whence ye were dug—
Look to Abraham your father, and to Sarah, who bore you. . . .

Isa. 51:2

Preface

Late Monday night, November 23, 1654, Blaise Pascal, mathematician, naturalist, skeptic, and bon vivant, underwent a religious experience that profoundly changed his life. On a piece of parchment, later found sewn into his clothing, he wrote: "From about half past ten in the evening until half past midnight. Fire. 'God of Abraham, God of Isaac, God of Jacob,' not of the philosophers and scholars. Certainty, certainty, heartfelt joy, peace."[1] Yet things are never quite so simple. In Jewish tradition, the God of Abraham *is* the God of the philosophers and scholars, and Pascal's dichotomy between simple faith and reasoned inquiry is a false one. Just as the same mind that felt this fire could devise the barometer and confirm Torricelli's proofs of the reality of the vacuum, pioneer the calculus of probability, design and build the adding machine to aid his father's fiscal work, write witty polemics against the Jesuits, and plan the first horse-drawn omnibus as cheap transportation for the Parisian poor and a source of funding for charity hospitals, so the God of Abraham is more than the apparition; and Abraham, the intimate of God, is a figure less of simple faith than of radical departures. For it was Abraham who was called to leave the land and ways of his father's house (Gen. 12:1) and seek a new life and new understanding. Thus the Rabbis see in Abraham not the resigned and docile follower but the founder of a new and irreplaceable religious vision that would not have arisen without the questioning of a youthful iconoclast—as the Midrash, with characteristic vividness, pictures him. Philo sees in Abraham the self-taught philosopher, whose insight and character grew without instruction in a preexisting canon and led him to the good life and toward the highest goal of understanding.[2] And Maimonides, in keeping with the Rabbinic stories of Abraham's progressive disillusionment with all mere surrogates, sees Abraham as the prototype of the natural theologian, whose idea of God is cemented by the inner affinity of the human mind with God himself.

This is a book of natural or philosophical theology. Its arguments do not presuppose the veracity of Scripture or tradition but work from our common human understanding toward an apprehension, insofar as this is possible, of truths about God, his relation to nature in general, and his expectations of humanity in particular. Yet, unlike many works of philosophy, this book does not employ the dramatic fiction of writing as though nothing had been said before on its chosen topic. A philosopher can learn from the tradition that has long been the intellectual nerve and moral sinew of the people Abraham founded. None of us for the last four thousand years has needed to feel quite so alone as an Abraham when he made the first faltering steps toward apprehension and, indeed, communion with the one true God.

I cite the Jewish sources often here, and the sister traditions as well, frequently alongside the somewhat younger but formidable philosophical literature. But I do not believe at any point that I have argued from authority. If my themes are those that give meaning to Jewish commitment, I seek that meaning not by presuming such commitment and surveying the sources to shape its content—or lay out its options, cafeteria style—but by exploring the issues themselves. If my arguments are sound, they may lend credence to some of the ideas of the tradition that has enriched them. But equally often they contribute to a philosophical appreciation of the canon or an enlargement of our understanding of the philosophic options. Indeed, the synthesis of scriptural and Rabbinic themes with the kindred insights of the common human heritage, whether they seem hostile or sympathetic at first blush, can foster understanding as well as critical appropriation. For such cross-checking is a powerful means of revealing the potentialities of our ideas, the soundness of our reasoning, and the merit of our assumptions.

Despite its numerous descriptive statements, then, this is not a descriptive book. It is no more part of my intention to catalog the full array of notions mooted and images projected in Jewish sources than it is to survey and type the historic philosophical options. Either of those tasks is a worthy one, and both are widely practiced. But what I have attempted here is the more normative task of defining what seems reasonable to me and what I hope will seem reasonable to others, discerning, as the argument unfolds, the congruities and continuities of a corresponding reasonableness in the sources that can be clearly traced against their striking differences of idiom and imagery.

The subject of this book is the nexus between God and values. The idea of the divine, I will argue, is from the outset a value concept, reflective of our value notions, but for that very reason also capable of informing them. Yet, although I argue that all ideas of divinity are value notions, I do not think that God is a mere projective or subjective idea. For I find highly dubious the claim that all values are subjective. Among other flaws, it is self-refuting, for it sets up a standard of objective truth or reality against which to disparage value judgments, while expecting us not to notice that objectivity, reality, and truth are also values.

Some values, I believe, are real, and I find it hard to see how any values can be imputed—truths upheld, actions undertaken, or even entertained—without assuming that this is so. At least some value judgments must be true if any claims are to be made out. It is often said that there are no values without a valuer. This I find doubtful, since I think there would plainly be a value in being, even if there were no one to behold it—not a value *to* or *for* anyone but the intrinsic value and beauty of there being something rather than nothing, the goodness, in whatever kind or degree, of that something in itself and to itself.

But if that claim seems controversial, I find it much less so to claim that there is no value to a valuer unless there is something in which that value can inhere, something *of* which a valuation may be true or false, or sound or skewed, adequate, or narrow. Even if one only judges that a thing is bad or worthless, there must be some other thing, *to* which or *for* which it is bad or worthless, and *of* which, then, value is predicated, in order for it to provide a standard or be a judge. As Erazim Kohák puts it, "How can a relation between two intrinsically worthless entities give rise to value?"[3] If any value judgments are true, then, I would argue, there must be some real objects of value about which they are true.

Religion is the human response to extraordinary value, and monotheism is the religious mode that finds incoherence in the assignment of such value to disparate or competing beings but seeks the source of all values—moral, aesthetic, even ontic—in a single locus, the *Makom*, the Place, as the Rabbis often called God; the Good, in Plato's language, in terms of whose goodness all lesser and more specific goods are predicated, and from whose act all lesser goods derive.

What about evil? Does it have no source? A central insight of the monotheist tradition is the nullity of evil. This does not mean that evil is not a fact. It means that is not a power. The religious impulse is misdirected when it singles out for celebration or emulation anything less than the highest good; and that good will be found only through the purgation of all evil from our idea of the divine. This means that many of our fond or frightened notions of sheer might or implacability—even many of our notions of love, if they are vicious or meretricious—have no place in our idea of God.

But the purgation of our concept of divinity, although it demands a moral courage not unknown to Abraham and his successors in every generation, is not profoundly difficult intellectually, since such notions as vicious love or confusions, say, of exploitation or expropriation with justice—or brutality with discipline, creativity with arbitrariness, or clarity with aridity—are inherently unstable. They are sustained only by extraneous interests and readily dissolved by more adequate ideas wherever human thought is free to explore the inner dynamics and practical impacts of values and ideas. It is for this reason that I say that the idea of God is self-righting. The natural human drive for coherence and integration follows the inner dynamic of the very idea of value toward the purgation of evil from the idea of the divine; and the conception of God's absolute unity is part of the intellectual advance which the purification of that idea makes possible.

The heritage of Abraham is deeply suspicious of all lesser absolutes, whether in the form of a state, a party, a pantheon, or an image of man himself. There are, of course, pagan virtues. For a pagan ethos prizes many goods, just as it serves many gods. But it offers no principled way of excluding evil, or violence, or ex parte values, from sacralization. Thus paganism has long been a negative regulative idea for monotheists, much as, say, solipsism is in philosophical epistemology, orienting a critical response and guiding constructive work. The Rabbis liked to say that avoidance of idolatry was tantamount to the entire Torah,[4] and Maimonides, accordingly, plots a trajectory from Abraham's iconoclasm to the full-blown law of Moses:

> Abraham our father initiated the critique of these notions, in halting proofs and preaching, winning people over and drawing them to allegiance by his kindnesses to them—so that the master of all prophets might receive his prophecy and perfect the intent. (*Guide* III 29)

Maimonides draws this line from Abraham to Moses partly to rationalize the conquests of the warlike tribes of ancient Israel, whose history was bound up with a specific idea of the holy. But the line from Abraham to Moses—from the binding of Isaac to the giving of the Torah (*Guide* II 45.11)—has more than antiquarian significance. What began as one man's search, reflected in the orientation of his family and followers,[5] became, through the work of Moses, a nation's law and way of life, indeed, in the Rambam's words, "a guide to all men, from the earliest to the last" (*Guide* I 2).

Philo put the matter forcefully in describing Abraham as the original, of which the Mosaic laws were copies.[6] For the insights that formed the character of Abraham grew from and informed his apprehension of the unity and justice of God. Thus, in the biblical outlook, as Ze'ev Falk writes, "The confluence of divine and human virtues appears in the concept of walking in God's ways, which is a corollary to the concept of being created in the image of God. Abraham was chosen, 'in order that he might command his children and his household after him to keep God's way, to do righteousness and justice' (Genesis 18:19; cf. Exodus 33:13; Psalms 103:9)."[7]

The core prophetic insight of Abraham, radiating from the moment when he bound Isaac on the altar but did not sacrifice him, spread far beyond the people of Israel, albeit with many transformations. And it anchored the still evolving Rabbinic tradition of ethical monotheism, whose gradual penetrance of the ideas and ideals of the civilized world, Maimonides argues, makes credible the prophetic promises that one day all nations will pursue the essential obligations of charity and justice imposed by humanity's creaturehood to God, and will be led to an enduring peace not by warfare but by understanding.[8]

Yet despite the spread of monotheist institutions and ideas, values continue to be sacralized that thwart and flout such basic goals and givens as these. Sacred values are disfigured and deformed—from the killing fields of Rwanda, Cambodia and Bosnia to the sweatshops of China, the brothels of Thailand, the South African townships, the streets of Kigali and Mogadishu, and the crack houses, glory holes, and needle parks of the West. One cannot say that without monotheism there must be paganism, for the disjunction is not perfect: one might have no god at all. But rarely is that socially the case. Religion, it seems, abhors a spiritual vacuum. And if gods are expressions of values, monotheists are rightly chary of the values that leap in to fill the vacuum. For values not disciplined by an adequate moral vision hold no guarantee of the respect for persons, regard for nature, reverence for life, or deference to the human image that the traditions of monotheism have struggled, not always with success, to define and defend.

The argument of this book, as it unfolds, may show to some extent why this is so. But I can state here at the outset the intuitive basis of this important and orienting corollary to our understanding of the nexus between the idea of God and the idea of the good: without an overarching vision, an implicit or explicit appeal to transcendent and universal goodness, generosity has no intrinsic claim to superiority over cruelty, or justice over exploitation, care over destructiveness, or concern over negligence and neglect. For either member of any of these pairs is as much a value as the other; any can present itself or be presented in a positive light. And, when values are chosen for their intensity, or for being, say, "the object of any interest," rather than for their coherence or their affirmation of being and desert, there is nothing to exclude the prominence or dominance of such values as blind aggression, anger, anomie, or wantonness.

Monotheism, then, is not simply the belief that there is just one God; it is the quest for and allegiance to an idea of the divine that will prove adequate conceptually and morally. This means that sound morals are as requisite to theology as a chaste theology is to morals; and a sound monotheism is as intolerant of intolerance and fanaticism, even from those who are eager to stand forward as its most zealous devotees, as it is of violence and excess, when they are chosen as ends in themselves or projected onto the demands or needs of spurious deities. For the core moral insight of monotheism insists upon the spuriousness of any deity whose demands include the violative or the orgiastic. Indeed, just as the structural elaborations of the original monotheistic idea include a vision of heaven that is a construct of the monotheist's integrated conception of the good life and the good community, so the structural transformations of the monotheistic ideal include a vision of hell that is a projection of the sacralized violence that reached its moral extreme in the tofets of the ancient Middle East.

Maimonides speaks sympathetically but also disparagingly of the fragile and homiletic arguments that must first have characterized natural theology, arguments aided to definition and credibility in no immaterial way by acts of simple human kindness and generosity. The argumentation of the Rambam's day was far more impressive technically than the childlike intuitions that the Midrash links to the name of Abraham. But theological arguments are still delicate and vulnerable. The weakness of philosophical arguments in general and of arguments about God in particular, when it comes to convincing the unconvinced, is familiar enough to rank as a cliché. Recognition that the idea of God is a value concept helps explain the extraordinary resistance to conviction—quite beyond the familiar quotient of misology—characteristic of theological discussions, when such discussions are actually attempted.

Human beings, as individuals and as communities, invest their values in their ideas of the divine. So, for theists, theological commitments have an axiological primacy, even when they are not overtly assigned epistemological primacy. To question received or accepted views about the existence, character, or role of the divine is tantamount to questioning values themselves at their root, or at their notional summit—hence Aristotle's inclusion of such questions among the inquiries that receive a punishment rather than an answer (*Topics* I 11, 105a 5). But nontheists, too, have an investment in god-talk, or its avoidance and even exclusion. They fear, not without reason, that talk about God will lead inexorably to talk about what they should and should not, must and must not, do. And not just talk. So it is not surprising that moral and social revolutions are accompanied by religious and theological revolutions, and that the more radical revolutions of our times were accompanied by seemingly radical revolts against religion. Nor is the resilience of religious categories and religious discourse surprising. For even the revolution will have its saints and martyrs, its hagiography and festivals, iconography and rituals.

A society without gods is as much an illusion as a society without values not because of any overt communion of humanity with the divine principle, as the hoary Stoic (and Epicurean) elenchus *ex consensu gentium* might suggest but because our gods crystallize our values, and we humans cannot live without values and, indeed, do not live long without sacralizing some of them. Those who engage in god-talk and those who do not, then, might find it encouraging to recognize that their frustration with one another results not from speaking different, incommensurable languages but from assigning the same sense and syntax to different objects. For nontheists employ ideas of peace or love or death or truth or "change" with a dynamic tendency to float them above and set them in judgment over lesser values (or seriatim over each other), exactly as theists do when they speak of God. Not the languages, then, but the gods are different.

Anthropologically the question is not so much whether we humans shall have gods as what we shall deem worthy of divinity. But philosophically there are prior questions: What grounds have we for singling out anything at all for the special status of the sacred, or to warrant our penchant for uniting positive values and purging negative ones, or for thinking that God is one? Above all, once we have understood what God is thought to be, what grounds have we for thinking that God is real? In the pages that follow I attempt to answer these questions.

I think that to reject the category of the sacred is in effect to fall into a kind of indiscipline that oscillates between assigning no value to everything and assigning absolute value to anything—that the incoherence of a would-be nihilism, apart from undermining itself in its every act, has no way of protecting itself from the paganism and superstition it rightly fears. The intellectual purity and moral honesty that science requires and that any humanistic or existential ethic demands inevitably make tacit reference to some notion of an absolute, which remains abstract or implicit only at the risk of sterility or idolatry. Negative or even privative values cannot cohere, let alone provide an adequate anchor or compass in our daily, untransferable task of making moral choices. And free-floating values, given their head, too often become sensuous, then sensate, finally insensate, losing that head and turning blindly violent and destructive, claiming divinity for themselves long before their passions cool, to be succeeded by equally insensate guilt or by displaced, projective hatred, the product of still unreconciled or unresolved self-loathing and self-love. God's uniqueness and simplicity, then, are the reflex of an axiological synthesis that is rightly impatient of any ultimate less than the Absolute, and intolerant, in logical terms, of any Absolute less than Perfection itself.

What grounds have we to think that Perfection itself exists? It has been claimed that the very idea is incoherent, and this is a claim that I spend some time trying to refute. Indeed, I think that the idea of perfection, properly understood, cannot exclude existence. But such reflections do little good in a controversial context, since those who think the existence of God problematic obviously do not hold the requisite idea of perfection, or the relevant idea of God. So, although I seek to show that the ontological argument advanced by Anselm and Descartes is not fallacious in the way that Kant or Hume thought it was, I do not actually use that argument, except to help define the idea of God and elucidate a crucial point of conceptual contact between the Platonic tradition that surfaces in Anselm and Descartes, and the biblical tradition epitomized in the Mosaic theme of God's self-sufficiency, as trenchantly glossed by Maimonides. I do rely on a version of the cosmological argument developed by Avicenna at the juncture between scriptural cosmology and Aristotelian metaphysics. And, in specifying the difference the divine act makes, I draw heavily on the idea of being as value and on the biblical thesis that it is goodness, not just determinacy, that is the great theme of being.

Having discussed the logic of divinity and the existence of God, I turn to the moral demands made on us by the reality of Perfection. Recognizing that no mere facticity can entail any norm or obligation, I argue that Perfection elicits obligations from beings like ourselves by the fact of our aspiration. The nexus is not one of implication but one of invitation, powerfully conveyed by the biblical idea of divine commandments, *mitzvot.* Central among these is the command to emulate God's holiness, which we achieve by perfecting our humanity, morally, socially, and intellectually/spiritually. Thus the commandments of the Torah are rightly seen as specifications of the imperative to become Godlike. As Ben Azzai put it, all the *mitzvot* rest on the idea of humanity's creation in the image of God.[9] There is, I argue, no naturalistic fallacy, no loss of autonomy, and indeed no failure of specificity in such a conception of the divine law. The appeal that Law makes to us is in fact identical with the appeal morals makes to us, to pursue our perfection as human beings and unique individuals. Far from introducing arbitrariness, dogmatism, or authoritarianism into morals, God's commands set before us a standard of universality and objectivity—of truth and justice, to use the Torah's language—which we can both appropriate and elaborate, once we have grasped the nisus of the divine concern.

A survey of the biblical and Rabbinic normative tradition shows the propriety of this way of thematizing its laws, and leads me to examine the interplay of pluralism with monism in that thematization and to show the complementarity by which those rival approaches rise above their conventional dichotomization. The laws that most readily seem to escape the broadly moral analysis I propose are those that are described, reverentially or dismissively, as ritual or ceremonial laws. But an analysis of their themes and an adequate understanding of the category of ritual observances make it clear that these laws are symbolic expressions of and responses to the values that the Torah itself pursues. Far from being tangential, arbitrary, sheerly positive, or merely ornamental, their symbolisms are constitutive and orienting of the Torah's value system and the way of life it prescribes. They are no less relevant to its aims in orienting our lives toward the Holy than are theories in the construction of facts and in weaving together the fabric of a vision of the world. The biblical laws of diet and sex are a case in point, and their exegesis confirms the linkage of the canonical laws with the idea of God's perfection. The laws of Israel, I argue, can place those who follow them in touch with God in a way that is both practical and spiritual, intimate, intellectual, communal, and universal.

It is well known that the Hebrew Bible places God far above nature. It refuses to assign motives or prior circumstances to the act of creation; it prohibits plastic or graphic portrayals of the divine and insists that

> The nations are but a drop in a bucket,
> Reckoned as dust on a balance,

to him "who is enthroned above the vault of the earth,"

> So that its inhabitants seem as grasshoppers;
> Who spread out the skies like gauze.

—But remember how the passage ends: "Stretched them out like a tent to dwell in."[10] For the very verses that set God beyond the mists and motives of mythology make him the Creator of heaven and earth. The single line in which Isaiah (6:3) hears the angels' ecstatic paeans to God's transcendence, "Holy, Holy, Holy, Lord of hosts," ends with the unparadoxical, almost inferential, counterbalance: "The fill of all the earth is His glory," celebrating God's immanence. For what would be the beauty of transcendence that did not spill over into immanence and express itself in this world?

The very lines that hide God's face display his will. So Isaiah takes the same poetic pleasure in calling God "the Holy one of Israel" as Homer does in epithets like "rosy-fingered dawn." He delights in the idea that God's transcendence is made immanent by the presence of God's law among his people, as Moses suggests when he argues that the expectations of the Law are not remote or utopian:

> "For this commandment, which I command thee this day is not some wondrous thing beyond thy reach. It is not in heaven that thou shouldst say, 'Who will go up to heaven for us and get it for us, and cause us to hear it, that we may do it.' Nor is it across the sea, that thou shouldst say, 'Who will cross the sea for us and get it for us and cause us to hear it, that we may do it.' Rather, the thing is very close to thee, in your mouth and in your heart, that thou mayest do it." (Deut. 30:11–14)

This idea, that the Transcendent is made immanent by a way of life, finds its emblem in the Midrash informing us that where a human being's tefillin bear God's praises, God's tefillin, as it were, bear praises of his people Israel. The same meaning, I believe, is the sense of all the kabbalistic allusions to the interdependence of God and Israel—not that God is a figment of human wishes or imagination. For what would be the value of being honored by an imaginary companion, and how would that fulfill the promise that through the people of Israel will all the nations of the earth be blessed (Gen. 12:3)? Rather, the idea is that Israel's way of life and the conceptual clarity necessary to its sustenance are an ongoing commitment to a particular articulation of what God is and what God wills. The Ideal that is not drawn graphically is drawn morally and spiritually, in the pattern of our lives. This claim will be my major theme: that the way of life outlined by the Torah and the Prophets, the Sages, and philosophers of Israel provides a means of bridging the gap between immanence and transcendence, as first proposed when the very holiness that is divine transcendence is held out by God for human beings to emulate: "You shall be holy, for I the Lord thy God am holy" (Lev. 19:2), demanding of us nothing less than self-transcendence, and that by means of the *mitzvot* (Num. 15:40).

No claim is made in this book that the Torah's laws are the only possible way of life that could realize humanity's affinity to the divine. But the Mosaic, prophetic, and Rabbinic tradition is seen to be a dynamic and deeply humanistic articulation of that relationship, whose conceptual roots allow it to survive and adapt creatively to widely different circumstances, without losing its underlying moral purpose. Others who seek to share in that enterprise or to devise their own can be judged by humanity, in the end, like any other human beings, only by the moral fruits of their rival or complementary ideals. But the moral fruits of an idea are unlikely to be of a different species from its conceptual roots.

Turning back, then, to our own conceptual roots, it is with reflections on time, creation, and change that the book comes to a close, in a chapter meant to convey what I feel able to say about the role of God in history and the nexus between our own lives as individuals and members of a tradition, and God's life as the source of all that is good. Examining the idea of creation, I argue that this ancient and still vital conceptualization of God's relation to the world, through its celebration of newness, openness, and freedom, provides and preserves a platform for human creativity, sustained rather than smothered by the creativity of God.

Focusing on the work of Bergson and its critique by the process philosopher Charles Hartshorne, I argue that Bergsonian creativity chimes with the biblical idea of creation that is its ultimate source and fosters our idea of an unfolding cultural tradition, in which not only creation but revelation, too, as the Rabbis presumed, is an ongoing process. Rival and more fragmented ideas of time, I argue, are unsound metaphysically and vitiate the ideas of history and tradition, in both individual and civilizational terms. They also betray a curious interest in dethroning the timeless God of creation, perhaps predictably setting a puffed-up and all-too-revealing caricature of ourselves in God's place.

Symbols can orient us toward the Truth, and clearly it is the core idea of traditional Judaism to do just that. But mere orthopraxy does not suffice. Just as radical or banal evil can coexist with the loftiest sentiments, given sufficient bracketing and compartmentalization, so can almost any behavioral exercise or excess. What is needed, as Baḥya put it, is not lip service or even limb service alone but the service of the heart. For externals, even symbolic externals, acquire just the meanings that we give them. Those who divorce behavioral performance of the *mitzvot* from the normative themes and spiritual intensions of those *mitzvot*, as worked out in the intricate dialogue of the millennia-old tradition of monotheist praxis, are not serving the God of Abraham but some projection of their own. And when such projections take on the colorations of chauvinism and bigotry instead of the spiritual humanism that is the sole authentic and viable theme of monotheism, those who are deceived by their own revolving mirrors, to use Carl Sandburg's phrase, like any other idolators, risk substituting ugliness and brutality for the genuine object and goal of the universal spiritual quest.

This book is product of some twenty years' reflections on the subject it addresses, but it makes no pretense of comprehensiveness. It is not a systematic theology. It concerns only the nexus of God and values, and only grazes the surface of that subject. Thus, for example, in addressing creation, it focuses on what the idea of creation tells us about the contingency of the world and thus about the relationship of God and creation as values. It does not dwell upon the problems of theodicy, because I have discussed those to some extent in *On Justice*; and it does not discuss divine knowledge and governance beyond the tentative explorations of the last chapter. It does put forward a theory of ritual that I think will be of interest to students of human nature and society. But it does so in the interest of a larger exposition of the moral and intellectual function of rituals in human lives, offering a moral explanation, say, of the biblical laws against incest, and a moral rationale for the Torah's deployment of the ideas of purity and impurity in behalf of our pursuit of holiness. Similarly, when I consider the evidence for child sacrifice in antiquity, the claims of recent philosophers that God can be perceived, or of others that the very idea of God is incompatible with morals, or when I address romantic claims about the binding of Isaac—in all these cases, the aim here is to clarify the nexus between God and values, so as to allow the ancient project that interprets the idea of God and the idea of the Good in one another's terms to continue its work.

The first three chapters of this book originated in lectures I gave at Oxford as the first winner of the Baumgardt award of the American Philosophical Association. The lectures were published in 1981 under the title *Monotheism*. They are much expanded and modified here, replacing those early versions. The fourth chapter originated at the request of Irene Bloom of Columbia University and was presented at the Academy for Jewish Philosophy meetings, as was chapter 6. Both appeared in earlier versions in the academy's proceedings, under the able editorship of Daniel Frank of the University of Kentucky. Chapter 5 develops ideas that I first tried out in two essays published in the *Jewish Law Annual* and the *Journal of the American Oriental Society*, with Bernard Jackson, now of Kent in Canterbury, and Jeanette Wakin of Columbia as editors. The nucleus of chapter 7 was presented at the Jewish Law Association Jerusalem meeting and subsequently published in the conference proceedings. Part of chapter 8 was first drafted at the request of István Hargittai of Budapest and published in an early version in *Philosophy East and West*, under the editorship of Roger Ames. Another part began its life at an ecumenical conference on God and creation organized at Notre Dame and the University of Chicago by David Burrell and Bernard McGinn; an early version appeared, under their editorship, in the conference proceedings. I warmly thank these editors and friends for their insights and suggestions, which contributed in many ways to the thematic study published here.

Several friends have been intellectual companions, correspondents, critics, questioners, and gadflies during the making of this book. David Novak of the University of Virginia, Kenneth Seeskin of Northwestern University, Menachem Kellner of Haifa University, Steven Katz of Cornell University, Hava Tirosh-Rothschild of Indiana University, Josef Stern of the University of Chicago, Norbert Samuelson of Temple University, Martin Golding of Duke University, Seymour Feldman of Rutgers University, Alfred Ivry of New York University, Elliot Dorff of the University of Judaism, and other members of the Academy for Jewish Philosophy deserve special appreciation, both for their philosophical interchanges with me and for the work we have shared toward rebuilding Jewish philosophy as a discourse and a discipline. The same is true of Shlomo Biderman, Ben-Ami Scharfstein, and Marcelo Dascal of Tel Aviv; Zeev Falk and Shalom Rosenberg of Jerusalem. Others who contributed to my thinking while I was at work on this book include Mary Douglas, Alasdair MacIntyre, Clifford Geertz, Jack Bilmes, Calum Carmichael, William Craig, Jean Bethke Elshtain, George Fletcher, Herbert Fingarette, Richard Freund, Yehudah Gellman, Alan Grapard, Ephraim Urbach, Haim Cohn, Robert McLaren, Neil Gillman, Allan Arkush, Jonathan Westphal, Paul Seligman, Martha Husain, Al Baumgarten, Mike Saso, and Haym Soloveitchik. Several friends read the manuscript in whole or part: I want to express my thanks to Mark Murphy, John Woods, John Post, and Steve Odin for their suggestions. My particular thanks to Cynthia Read for her imagination, patience, and editorial care and grace.

The texts and studies that have bearing on my argument are cited in the notes, and those repeatedly referred to are listed in the bibliography, along with my own studies on related topics. But a few seminal works deserve special mention here: Urbach's *The Sages*, Shmuel Safrai's *Literature of the Sages*, Jacob Milgrom's commentaries on Leviticus, Louis Jacobs's and David Novak's numerous studies of the tradition, Moshe Greenberg's essays, and the studies of Zeev Falk on Jewish jurisprudence are, in my view, particularly important.

My wife, Dr. Madeleine Goodman, with whom I have often worked on other projects, spent much of the time that it took me to bring together the ideas of this book as an academic vice president of the University of Hawaii, providing its faculty with the same calm and good sense and a good measure of the love and understanding that she imparts to our home. As in my past books, I thank the people of Hawaii for the support they have given and continue to give to their university. This is my last book prepared as a professor of philosophy at the University of Hawaii, since Madeleine and I took up new positions at Vanderbilt in the fall of 1994, she as dean of arts and science, and I as professor of philosophy. We extend our aloha to all those who have been our friends over twenty-five years in the islands and our appreciation for the genuine warmth with which we have been welcomed in Tennessee.

Nashville, Tenn.
January 1995

L. E. G.

Contents

God of Abraham

1

The Logic of Monotheism

In common usage the name of God, like most philosophically interesting words, bears a variety of senses, some contradictory to others, some incoherent in themselves. But a Socratic process, threshing these usages against one another, can winnow out a coherent idea of divinity. Elementally, what is meant is something extraordinary, in which strong feelings and powerful energies are vested—powerful values. For energies here are values. Gods are the creators of nature or culture, the manifest or hidden causes, sources, essences, or identities of events. They are the authors of our traits, the springs of human motives and intentions, governing powers of the interests that direct the salient happenings in our lives.

In parts of China, now years after Mao's death, his memory has made a god of him. Rastafarians worship Haile Selassie, less for what he was than for a meaning now assigned to him. The followers of Reverend Moon venerate him, as the Buddha or Pythagoras, Jesus or Confucius have been venerated, for what seemed extraordinary about them—although the Buddha, at least, was rather actively uninterested in divinity and Confucius hardly claimed such dignities. In a Shinto shrine in Japan, Marilyn Monroe is worshiped. She figures, too, in the goddess cult of some acolytes of women's spirituality. Like Elvis Presley, she is deified partly for what she was, partly for the pathos of her death. Her cult canonizes and crystallizes deeply felt values—hopes, guilts, and fears. We too may ask, then, as Kipling did, "Is God in human image made no nearer than Kamakura?"[1]

Can a goddess commit suicide or die of a drug overdose? In matters of worship, it seems, coherence may count less than life or death or eros. Whiskey can be a god as well as wisdom. Evil is a god as well as kindness, as satanists sometimes admit. For the emotive power of thoughts or acts of violence is readily externalized, personified, given some dominion. When gin or scotch is offered to Pele, the goddess of the fire pit, or when human sacrifice was given her in the past, one value was poured into another: whiskey matters to Pele, because whiskey has power. Human lives are not negligible. That is why they were offered. Their value and the frisson of the violation of that value are funded into hers. For there is energy to be released not only in the preservation or celebration of a value but also in its violation.

Coherence and Divinity

The conflict of the gods in pagan myth, like that of heroes in the epic, does not diminish but trumpets their greatness. Yet that greatness is preserved when coherence asserts itself. Zeus steps forward as the god of justice, not of the thunderbolt and sky alone; he is the father of gods and men, just successor to darker powers. His erotic interests may seem ungoverned, but his rule is not brute fury. He protects households, hospitality, and oaths, partitions land, sea, and sky; his reign makes order.[2] Coherence, then, conspires with greatness to find unity in the divine.

Uniting opposites and fusing polarities, Heraclitus can call war the father of all and king of all, making some men free and others slaves: the thunderbolt still steers all things, but the truly wise and one god both does and does not answer to the name of Zeus. "God," Heraclitus says, "is day-night, winter-summer, war-peace, satiety-hunger—he changes as fire mixed with spices is named for the scent of each" (frgs. 53, 64, 32, 67). There is a unity behind diverse appearances, but it follows the thread of shifting interest from one arresting appearance to the next. When Thales says, "All things are filled with gods" (ap. Aristotle, *De Anima* I, 411a 7, 405a 19), he intends not the ordinariness of the gods but the extraordinariness of all things. Nothing is dead or inert. All things have life and power in them, like the lodestone.

Epicurus denied divine providence or influence—interference, he would say—in nature or human life. But his argument hinges on transcendence: "That which is blessed and immortal is undisturbed and causes no disturbance to another. It is not moved by anger or favor, for all such things are found only in the weak" (*KD* 1). Like any Stoic defender of providence, he argues from beatitude. Indifference and unconcern are simply corollaries of *ataraxia*, echoing what Achilles said long before, that the gods are free of care (*Iliad* 24:526). Similarly, when Plato argues that the gods are not venal judges, to be won with words or bribed with offerings, and rejects the human weaknesses of the mythic gods, replacing the deities of the poets with his own unbending Forms, it is to divine perfection that he appeals: it is unfitting to represent the gods as less than perfect beings. When he coins the term 'theology,' he defines it as a worthy account, the account worthy of a divine nature (*Republic* II 377–85; cf. 364–65).

The thrust of his critique of Greek myth is slighted when we import into our reading a present concern with artistic freedom, as though Plato's pressing interest were to regulate poetic expression, and as though the imagery he pinions and condemns were the "purely aesthetic" art of modern salons, and not the canon of values and ideals that animate a culture. Under Plato's smoke screen, it is easy to miss his demands for a conceptual revolution guided by the inner dynamic of the idea of the divine. For what Plato shapes, when he speaks of banishing the poets, is not a scheme of censorship but a plan of thought aimed at capturing the idea of justice in a mental model of the state. His objection to "the poets" touches their portrayal of the gods in the lineaments of human weakness, the notion that perfection makes the gods like humans, only more so. For, he reasons, we shall never be clear about justice while we fondly hope, as Cephalus does (*Republic* I 330d, 331b, d), that ritual attentiveness somehow buys us peace, a clear conscience, a good report, and welcome among the gods. We shall never know what justice is while we thoughtlessly assume that there are ways of "beguiling of gods by men," as some suppose who "produce a bushel of books of Musaeus and Orpheus . . . and make not only ordinary men but states believe that there really are remissions of sins and purifications for deeds of injustice, by means of sacrifice and pleasant sport for the living, and that there are also special rites for the defunct . . . that deliver us from evils in that other world, while terrible things await those who have neglected to sacrifice" (*Republic* II 364e). Plato's crocodile tears at the thought of banishing the poets mask his sterner purpose. He contrives to appear conservative or reactionary at the most revolutionary juncture in his thought, and modern readers are often taken in by the ruse. But Saadiah takes Plato's point when he argues that there is no penitence in the world to come, insisting on the moral finality of our choices.[3]

Even the most anthropomorphic myths assign the gods exalted natures, a stature or appearance beyond the human norm, an aura or nimbus, that makes divinity, if unconcealed, unmistakable. Fables, by contrast, may speak of gods in purely human terms. They voice secular impulses, an urge to treat all things as ordinary, to reject, or, like George Burns's *Oh God* films, set aside the extraordinariness of the divine. But to speak religiously of the divine is to speak of the extraordinary. Thus what religion quarrels with in magic is the pragmatic desire to make a utility of divinity, to turn religious awe into technology.

To the tribesman who finds a special presence in the well or spring, an awe or terror in the fever that afflicts his wife, a power in the stirring of lust or fear or laughter in himself, it is plain that the divine is something extraordinary. Agamemnon (*Iliad* 9.21) calls the panic and dispirit of his men an ill deception sent by Zeus. Both Helen and Priam ascribe their fate (6.357; 3.164) to the machinations of the gods, and when Hector puts on Achilles' armor, "Ares entered into him and his limbs were filled with courage and strength" (17.10). Homer preserves the immanence of the gods, even alongside their pictorial personifications, as when he describes the clash of Argive and Trojan forces:

> Ares drove these on, and the Achaians grey-eyed Athene,
> And terror drove them, and Fear, and Hate whose wrath is relentless
> she the sister and companion of murderous Ares,
> she who is only a little thing at first, but thereafter
> grows until she strides on the earth with her head striking heaven.
> She then hurled down bitterness equally between both sides
> as she walked through the onslaught making men's pain heavier.
> *Iliad* 4.439–45[4]

The terror of wild places, the power of rivers and cataracts, the silence of groves, even now give voice and form to gods. So does the vastness of the sky or ocean. Such experiences are labeled *mysterium tremendum*,[5] a term with some descriptive value, if it is not overlooked that the experiences may differ in kind and in the meanings assigned to them. Creative spirits have always noted such experiences; but, as the industrial age began, poets and painters preserved them as precious mementos, intimations of immortality, treasured all the more as natural wilderness retreated—its sensations enshrined, as if in reliquaries, pressed in the pages of gothic novels or impasted in the pigments of the Hudson River school. By the time we reach the paintings of George Inness or the narratives of Herman Melville or Henry James's *Turn of the Screw*, the unknown presence has a sharp ambiguity: Is it a spiritual or a clinical sign? The natural light has dimmed and mingled with the approaching city lights. Yet, even as the light is altered to an eerie urban glare, its meaning is not wholly lost in Bellows, Glackens, Hopper, even Wharton. The fear that mechanism might rob the world of ghosts or gods proves overanxious, as the spirits, vanished from the woods, dells, springs, and undersides of bridges, begin to creak and groan in industrial machinery and peer out from a desolated urban landscape. Androids, cyborgs, and automata soon chitter with medieval urgency in place of dryads and nymphs, and aliens become the powerful visitors from Elsewhere bearing wisdom, fateful gifts, and curses.

The new gods may be ugly or beneficent, lovely or malign. They may lie in wait in near-death experiences, at the far end of a fluorescent-lit hospital corridor, or behind the operating theater's surgical lamp, or may emerge from the gloaming in the distance on a country road or from a halogen-lighted autobahn. Mechanism does not banish the gods, it just renames them and alters their ancient images. The divine is still the extraordinary. Divinity remains a value concept.

Myth devours category distinctions typical in conceptual thinking. Notoriously, it collapses distinctions of self from other, subject from object, class (tribe, species, kind) from individual, cause from effect, things from names, or wholes from parts—not least in mythic expressions of the experience of the divine. Such nondisjunction of categorial distinctions is termed "compactness"; it is commonly ascribed to confusions, the inability of "the primitive mind" to differentiate what "primitive" culture has not differentiated formally or abstractly. Addressing the mythic mode, Eric Voegelin writes:

> We move in a charmed community where everything that meets us has force and will and feelings, where animals and plants can be men and gods, where men can be divine and gods are kings, where the feathery morning sky is the falcon Horus and the sun and moon are his eyes, where the underground sameness of being is a conductor for magic currents of good or evil force that will subterraneously reach the superficially unreachable partner, where things are the same and not the same, and can change into each other.[6]

The key word here is "can." For the crushing of categories is not uniform. And compactness does not merely "override the separateness of substances." It actively resists specific disjunctions of cause and effect, agent and patient, symbol and object, name and function. Yet it knows and uses, even combats, the very differences it is thought incompetent to recognize. So the categorial distinctions typically collapsed in myths are not outside the ken of mythmakers. Categorial clarity is very much at work in societies whose "overarching" worldviews might be framed in mythic schemes of striking compactness. By the same token, "primitive thinking" is alive and active in "advanced" societies, even among their most sophisticated thinkers. For the power of compactness rests not in ignorance but in the capacity of symbols to evoke their objects. The mythic poet and the astrophysicist who appeals to some version of the anthropic principle[7] have in common a deference to the impact of a symbol, often, the image of man. When myths merge cause with effect, or, as Freud or Marx did, individual with type, what we observe is fusion, but it need not be confusion.

If we avoid mistaking compactness for a symptom of a "mentality" or uniform stage of thought, we escape at least one way of stereotyping peoples and cultures and typecasting individuals. For we will not impose a unilinear lockstep on the internal diversity of a society or the protean flexibility of human consciousness. Such uniformity, if taken strictly enough, would render thought itself impossible, let alone conceptual development. For the notion of a purely mythic "stage" of thought proves incoherent when we focus on what is meant by thought. The error is in confining all thoughts within the boundaries of what is deemed canonical from an external standpoint that calls essential what it finds most exotic. The level of categorial oblivion posited in familiar accounts of compactness makes them, as I have argued, myths about myths, consciously suspending some of what we know, to heighten the impact of a representation, in this case, of the "primitive" or "archaic" other. As an alternative, I have proposed that myth is an idiom capable not only of coexisting with but of interpenetrating other, more objectifying modes.[8] Indeed, such interpenetration is vital, since myths do their work not by ignorance of categorial distinctions but by selective abstraction from them.

Yet the logic distinctive to myths, like that distinctive to dreams, is associative. The linkages of things are not stably syntactical or causal, as in our more detached descriptions of natural objects and events. Rather, the imagination, with conceptual constraints relaxed, springs from one arresting phenomenon to the next, its motives discovered in or projected upon the objects it confronts. Small wonder, then, that all things are filled with meanings and with gods. For, to the lively sensibility, no experience is devoid of the extraordinary. Thus, the aesthetics of Zen, and the Zen koan informing the inquirer that "the Dharma-Body of the Buddha is the hedge at the bottom of the garden"[9]—and the deeper analysis of the Upanishads:

> As bees make honey by collecting pollen from trees in different places and reduce the pollen to a unity; and as the different pollens can no longer tell the difference (or say), "I am the pollen of this tree, or I am the pollen of that tree," so too when all these creatures reach reality, they do not know that they have reached it. Whatever they are, whether lion, wolf, boar, worm, fly, gnat, or mosquito, they all become THAT (the ultimate reality). That which is the subtlest of the subtle, the whole world has as its self. That is reality. That is the self, and THAT art thou.[10]

Such remarks express the ubiquity of the Absolute, or, at a lesser pitch, the ubiquitous potential for encounter with the extraordinary.

Zen resists assigning these experiences to a transcendent source, seeking to focus on (or lose focus within) the immediate. It sites transcendence in the object, the extraordinary in the moment. It is in this sense at once the most pagan, the most secular, and the most aesthetic of religions—qualities that enhance its appeal in the West. Yet it is a religion, in virtue of its sense of the extraordinary, which it signals obliquely in its ethos and aesthetic of action and encounter. Only if it were indifferent to experience, not merely detached but bored, would Zen cease to be a religion.

Its resistance to integrating experience in clear hierarchies of value renders the values Zen does foreground unstable, ever liable to displacement by external pressures (industrial, political, pragmatic, militaristic) or interests arising internally, from the functional autonomy of ideas. These may be secular, desacralizing in thrust, or they may verge in the opposite direction, becoming fetishist, unless shaped and sustained by ritual or moral discipline. Such sifting and discipline become key functions of institutional Zen. It is untrue, of course, that Zen knows no hierarchies. The setting for Suzuki's koan is a monastery. When the acolyte, pressing his master, asks, if the Dharma-Body of the Buddha is the hedge at the bottom of the garden, "What is the man who realizes this truth?", the *roshi* answers: "A golden-haired lion." In other words: If everything is god or godhead, why should one aspire to enlightenment? To which the unhesitating reply is that there is god and god—as in the Indian story of the disciple who was told that he was God but was picked up and thrown in the ditch by the first elephant he tried to shoulder out of the road. On blaming his master for teaching him falsely, he was told that he *was* God, but so was the elephant.

The risk, when pure secularity strives to make itself a religion (or even a way of life), is that by placing all values on a par it will leave no room for the wonder and excitement at the core of any religious experience. To value all things equally is hard to differentiate from valuing none at all. Transcendence poses a parallel danger for theists. For, paradoxically, placing too great a gap between the world and God may rob the world of the very awe that first turned our glance toward the transcendent, leaving a wasteland of alienation, vanity, and anomie. Monotheism addresses this problem by striving to retain its primal vision of the world as an expression of God's creative energy. Thus the Sabbath is a recurrent symbol of the act of creation, and the Hebrew liturgy treats every raindrop as a miracle and a gift of grace.[11]

Religious responses, whether fixed in their diffuse settings or traced to a common source, reflect individual and cultural sensibilities. Even miracles, Naḥmanides writes, will not impress those who are not attuned to them: believers in sorcery will see mere magical manipulations.[12] One must know of a natural order before one can see meaning in apparent departures from it, and one must have a certain idea of divinity before one can identify specific acts as divine. Xenophanes argued, "No man knows or ever will know the truth about the gods . . . for even if one chanced to say the complete truth, one would not know it."[13] The argument is generalized in the Skeptics' claim that we can never know the truth, since even if we stumbled upon it we would never know it was the truth we had found. But in postmodern terms, the argument tells us that a framework for knowledge is needed if knowledge is to be recognized as such. It is not merely energy or splendor that gives us the AH! or the AHA! of religious experience but energy or splendor *perceived* as such, that is, *perceived as values.*

Thus value is inalienable in the idea of divinity. But the value ladenness of the idea renders the concept itself restless and sets up a dynamic that presses for its rectification. We see this not only in Plato's arguments that the gods are not venal, or Epicurus's inference that the blessed and immortal is not meddlesome, or the rival Stoic view that the divine must show responsibility and concern. It shows up in myths as well, in the displacement of baser and more homely gods by ever nobler and more transcendent gods. When Xenophanes smiles at the fact that Ethiopian deities are black, and Thracian gods red haired and blue eyed,[14] he is calling out the discrepancy between human bias and divine claims upon perfection. Thus he disclaims busybody gods who rush about the earth on assignations or other personal business: there is "one god, greatest among gods and men, in no way similar to mortals, in body or in thought." This highest god "always remains in one place, not moving at all; nor is it fitting for him to go to different places at different times, but without toil he shakes all things by the thought of his mind"; "all of him sees, all thinks, and all hears."[15] Xenophanes' gods are still physical and multiple. But the dynamic of the idea of divinity presses him in the direction of monotheism. The awful nod of Zeus becomes what that image seems to symbolize, a vitalizing control that shudders through nature from the power of thought. Divine thought and the perception that guides it are not centered in bodily organs but are as ubiquitous as the god's sway in nature. From here it is only a step to denial, in what is divine, of the limitations of particularity. This step is essayed on several fronts by Xenophanes' putative disciple and genuine heir, Parmenides.[16]

Parmenides founded metaphysics as the science of being on the thought of a single reality, unique, invariant, undifferentiated—an uncompromising generalization of Xenophanes' rejection of partiality. Reality either is or is not. This ultimate either-or overmatches our pallid version in the law of contradiction, which holds only that a state of affairs must either be or not be at a given time, in a given respect. Here there are no different senses of 'being', and no different times. What is just is and cannot not be. For to debar contradiction is to rule nonbeing impossible and unthinkable. And the same exclusion bars all plurality and change, since there is no variance without negation.[17] So powerful was the appeal of this idea that the Eleatic, Megaric, even Stoic followers of Parmenides still championed the law of contradiction, in militant opposition to what they saw as Aristotle's weakening of it—in his theories of potentiality and predication, change, matter, time, essence and accident—long after the original elenchus had been exposed.[18] For to the heirs of Parmenides the invariance of being was the absoluteness of the divine.

Clearly such monism is untenable. For even an illusion of plurality and change involves real plurality and real change. And Parmenides' monism is dialectically weak. For its radical dichotomy between truth and seeming[19] builds monism on the premise of a tacit dualism. Plato, unwilling to give up appearances or to make them absolute, compromised Parmenidean principle and found among sensory appearances a realm of half-truth, conceding that change involves equivocation.[20] Absolute clarity does not belong to this world of blur and flux, shifting appraisals and perspectives. Heraclitus was right about change, and the Sophists were right about truth, if we confine our view to the world of appearances and partial perspectives. Indeed, as Plato triumphantly reasons, Cratylus and Protagoras are interchangeable: Both make being and knowledge impossible (*Theaetetus* 152). But what follows is not skepticism or relativism. For we know that we have knowledge, above all about the good, as the life and death of Socrates bear witness. The reality that is constant, and so capable of being what it is, the unity that is one, and so capable of the selfsameness that Parmenides had seen as the hallmark of divinity, must be found in its fullness, not here but elsewhere. If all here is compromised and only semireal, then There, in the realm of the Ideas, is where the Ground and Source of even our partial reality and truth must be sought. If the world of changeable appearances falls short of unity and invariance, we must accept the division of reality from appearances and concede that Being penetrates the realm of becoming only partially. The invariant remains the real, and the One becomes the Good, the highest god, because it is the source of every value—truth, stability, unity, constancy, integrity, sameness, intelligibility, and beauty.

Aristotle did not concede, even in jest or irony or for the sake of argument, that nature is equivocal. But he did follow Plato in dividing the cosmos analytically, into those aspects that can be described unequivocally, in virtue of their forms or essences, and those particulars and per accidens relations (reflective of the ultimate Platonic "otherness" of matter, the unnameable substrate of the forms) which cannot be subjects of scientific inquiry.[21] Species are eternal; so are the heavens, the intelligences that move them, and those that move us. These things, though manifest, are divine; and Aristotle breaks with Plato not in denying the reality and eternity of the forms but in affirming their immediate presence in this world. Yet, whether immanent as in Aristotle or only imitated as in Plato, the divine remains the focal point of value, here understood as causal efficacy, epistemic and ontic primacy, transcendence of the play of time and chance.

Because divinity is a value notion, the refinement of moral ideas demands the refinement of theological ideas. Hence Hesiod's discomfort with the deities of the heroic age: he does not share the values celebrated in the Homeric epic.[22] Where Epicurus made his gods leisured and amiable people, Aristotle made his deity a self-sufficing, all-energizing intelligence. We fund our ideals into our gods. But this dynamic does not simply roll on ungoverned, leaving behind a trail of deities. Integration is demanded by the values themselves. For even perfection is imperfect until it is complete. It was a call to integration that moved the Eleatics. And long before them the gods of the sky and justice triumph over the tellurian or sylvan gods of terror or panic—because justice can rule, preside, make order, where bare divinity will only peer forth from its lurking places. Synthesis resolves the amorphous aura of the extraordinary, the magical energies of mana, the sensations and emotions of unschooled intuition, into coherent, even if somewhat capricious, personalities. But it goes further, playing off against one another the values it defines, molding not only gods but a pantheon, a society of deities whose diverse roles and relations mark the interactions among the values they represent.[23] And celebration of these values is not left to private impulse but reenacted socially, canonized in words, images, and stories, calendared in festivals, whose rhythmic balance mitigates the conflict and routinizes what now seems elusive in the experience as remembered, reconstituted, invented, or reinvented by the usages of ceremony.[24]

The values brought into focus in a pantheon gain definition through contrasts. So their interplay is naturally dramatic: the gods attain determinacy as persons, but the values they represent grow vivid when these are persons whose aims conflict. Reflected back upon the human condition, now magnified by their projection on the heavens, the contrasts become conflicts among epic heroes. Melodrama pits virtue against vice, but epic tries virtue against virtue—the cunning of Odysseus against the power of Ajax or the candid fury of Achilles. Every virtue is set against itself and all the rest. Thus the tragedies of Sophocles spring from the Homeric epic by pressing to the extreme the strengths the epic celebrates. The trial, or agon, of the tragedy tests the limits of each virtue; its resolution is recognition of those limits. The general meaning of this resolution (or, rather, failure of resolution!) is spoken by the Sophists: There is no good in absolute terms but only "good at . . .", "good for . . ."

What is good by the lights of Antigone's piety is not good in the eyes of Creon's statecraft. Even wisdom finds its limits—as Oedipus comes to illustrate and to know. Wholeness eludes the tragic hero, as it eluded the heroic gods.

So the matter might have rested, for some time in Greek thought, had not Socratic dialectic uncovered the interdependence of the virtues, seeing that courage cannot be stupid, piety dishonest, or love meretricious or unwise. The Socratic integration of the virtues showed that their conflict was more a device of theater than a fact of nature. It proposed a goodness that is not achieved at the expense of any other. Surely the cosmos had some principle of integration. Conflict, even among gods, could never explain its unity. If strife was indeed the father and king of all, there was still the logos behind all inconstancy and opposition, as Heraclitus himself acknowledged, a reasonableness both willing and unwilling to accept the name of Zeus. We must listen, Heraclitus urged, not to him but to that logos. Its gravamen, that "all things are one."[25]

Even earlier, Anaximander had found an equilibrium behind the flux of nature, the mark of a higher justice. Simplicius preserves his words a thousand years later: "The source of coming to be for the things that are is that into which destruction too occurs, 'by necessity; for they pay penalty and retribution to each other for their injustice, according to the assessment of time.'"[26] Pythagoras, too, had found harmony in opposition. But it was Socrates who proposed, partly by what he said, more tellingly by how he lived and died, that tragedy is not inevitable, that human goods can abet and moderate one another, under the governance of reason, to yield a life unmarred by inner conflict and a death that is not the breakdown of values too strongly taxed but a natural consummation, in its courage and serenity, of the same internal harmony that the life before it had revealed.

This integration is not universally accepted. Martha Nussbaum sees a deeper truth in the denial of its possibility that reaches its epitome in Greek tragedy.[27] Ibn Khaldūn and Thucydides before him, similarly find inadequacy in all human strength and goodness; in their different ways, each finds a higher truth in tragedy.[28] Generalizing what she sees as the shared insight of Aeschylus, Sophocles, and Euripides, Nussbaum argues that sincere pursuit of the ideals of the good life inevitably provokes irresolvable conflicts. She personalizes and naturalizes her point by taking as a model the conflict a young mother might face between parental and professional responsibilities. The ancient tragedians take up their tragic voice only when great figures press their greatness to extremes of hubris that challenge mortality. So an ancient audience would naturally deem them to be brought down by the weight of their own claims, and thus with a certain fatal if inhuman justice. Even modern audiences see inevitability in a tragic hero's fall, a result of overreaching. But Nussbaum finds tragedy and its roots even in the most ordinary choices. She rejects and seems to resent conciliation—the avenue so often pointed to by the tragedians themselves, most outspokenly through the voices of the chorus. Efforts to rank, prioritize, or compromise our commitments, she urges, are mere evasions, refusals to take life's dilemmas seriously. The very idea of a hierarchy of values for her smacks of insincerity or inauthenticity. Appeals to guidelines or criteria of choice are another evasion, pressing arbitrary preferences rather than facing up to the full responsibilities of our condition. One can learn from tragic outcomes, as Creon, through the death of

Antigone, learns that there is more to life than reasons of state. But ultimately, conflicts among genuine claims cannot be resolved.

The message Nussbaum draws from her reading of Greek tragedy, and of life, which she believes Greek tragedy captures irrefragably, is that a person is vulnerable to many events beyond individual control and needs to be supported and sustained by others, sympathetically. But behind this homely, social moral looms inevitable, irreconcilable, ultimately fatal conflict. Euripides' Hecuba may have thought that strength of character set her above the reach of fate, but her own response to the murder of her surviving son teaches her that even nobility is fragile. The queen turns a mere dog, blinding the murderer. Others, outside of fiction, whose character did enable them to face even a holocaust with unbowed integrity, are dismissed as mere beneficiaries of good fortune.

But all this seems profoundly wrong. Integration is not easy, but it is not evasion; and it is not good fortune but wisdom and courage that can enable human beings to confront catastrophe and ruin. In the daily crises and cruxes of human living, those who seek to order their commitments and to work out complementarities rather than stay fixated in conflicts are not evading but actively confronting the authenticities of life. To seek a highest good, as a vantage point from which to judge and choose and set priorities in our lives, rather than passively floundering, like Plato's democratic man, after every attractive end or value (*Republic* VIII 561), is not a philistine but a reflective strategy, more highly to be commended as philosophical than the theatrically satisfying but morally etiolated tragic sense of life. Bad faith can find a home as readily in disclaiming any answers as in formulaic nostrums that have not confronted the seriousness of what we must call not moral dilemmas but moral decisions.

The Stoics denied that we ever face the kind of crux that most interested the tragedians, in which virtue works its own undoing. One need never abandon integrity. For even to die, if necessary, is not tragic, since death is not ignoble. The only tragedy is betrayal of principle. This was not idle talk. Many Stoics faced their Neros and Caligulas, who tested their character and commitment far beyond the bounds of normalcy. The history of the holocaust has brought to light the story of Le Chambon, a French village that sheltered Jews throughout the war, under the threat and gaze of Nazi soldiers and Vichy rulers. Following the dictates of conscience and the teachings of their pastors, the villagers saved some five thousand souls, as many as the village population. They did not see moral ambiguities or dilemmas here and described their lives not as tragic but as blessed, since history gave them the chance to live (and sometimes die for) their faith rather than just call it to mind of a Sunday morning.

Plato's philosophical awakening came through his recognition that there is a resolution to the conflicts that epic and tragedy heighten for dramatic effect and that sophistry exacerbates, in the interest of advocacy as a profession. He saw that politics can conciliate interests rather than merely umpire their powers of force and fraud, and he welded the Socratic unity of the virtues to the Eleatic unity of Parmenides' visionary hexameters. The One became the Form of the Good, or God, the source of all being, underwriting Anaximander's justice and the logos of Heraclitus.

Discovery of this highest Unity, Plato tells us, springs from dialectic, the method Socrates practiced and, by his practice, taught. But it is not in dialectic itself that the discovery is made. For the experience is intuitive, outlined by the processes that presuppose it, but not reducible to any of their mental motions. Like Socrates' obeisance to the sun after a night of meditation, it consummates the integrative work of reason but is not a stage in the progress of that work.[29] As an intuition, and an intuition of Totality, it eludes discursive thinking and the language humanity has honed to sensory uses. But Plato points to it in the language of the mystery cults. For it intends the Divine as such, transcending time, multiplicity, change, and bias—transcending personality and all the partial goods and imperfect unities that in their own ways point toward perfect unity and truth.

Experientially Plato's beatific or ecstatic goal may be of a piece with the localized intuitions it integrates. But philosophically it stands above them. For all knowledge and moral wisdom, all scientific and aesthetic liveliness, are now seen as partial expressions of the totality of Goodness. Relative goods are real goods, since they partake of the Absolute Goodness of the One; but for that very reason, any of them can be brought to book. This, it seems to me, is the function of law in a society, and of reason in the individual. For we need not accept the cynical notion that a judge must be always and at the same time an advocate and can never rise above a parti pris. We cannot match the a priori denial of the possibility of integration with a corresponding a priori affirmation, since only time and experience can test our faith in the power of reason, by lateral and synthetic, nonlinear thinking, to discover or create complementarities of interest where sophistic thinking professes to see only conflict and emulousness. But we can say that human experience gives us ample grounds for hope, case by case, and issue by issue, that resolutions can be found to the conflicts that well up among us, and within us. The monotheistic idea of God is the emblem of that educated hope. For, as Plato saw, the Sophists' paradoxes of relativity readily dissolve with the recognition of the Absolute, in terms of which relativity is predicated. The moral conundrums of political struggle fade, as the varieties of goodness are acknowledged and recognized as manifold expressions of a single, unitary Ideal, toward which it is our task to advance, insofar as humanly possible (*Theaetetus*, 176).

God's Goodness, Integration, and the Binding of Isaac

Monotheism is achieved by the integration of the idea of divinity. The ancient Greek philosophers never complete that synthesis, for several reasons. The Platonists and Aristotelians, who made the most sustained efforts at fulfilling the vision of Parmenides, by resolving the relation of the many and the One, clearly left the task unfinished. All the more so did the Stoics, who also vied for the Eleatic legacy. For the fate of Plato's efforts hung on the power of his successors to relate the One to the Indefinite Dyad without metaphor or myth. Plato's nephew Speusippus can still be glimpsed, through Aristotle's tears of laughter, trying to work a solder to bind the Transcendent to the cosmos, by calling the soul a self-moving number, an ungraceful denouement for Plato's philosophy in the hands of his chosen heir.[30]

The Neoplatonists, attacking the same problem, leaned on Plato's concession that finitude is equivocal. So much did they make of the simultaneous identity and difference of their hypostases that the procession of the many from the One seemed in danger of collapse back into undifferentiation, if not incoherence. Aristotle's critique had left Plato's hypostatic Forms without a home. By housing them in the divine Mind, middle Platonists and Neoplatonists gave a function to Nous beyond sheer thought of its own perfection and answered Aristotle's challenge as to how the Forms could be causes. For the Ideas now were not just freestanding universals but archetypes constitutive of the reality of things, as their Aristotelian essences, and of the divine Mind, as the content of its thought. They were thus Goodness made determinate and Unity made accessible to participation and to knowledge. But the integrative benefit to be gained here was buried beneath the proliferating hypostases and godlets that sprang from the postulates of an a priori ontology in thinkers like Proclus, Iamblichus, and Syrianus, embattled pagans, for whom monotheism was anything but a core objective.

Peripatetics sought to avoid Platonizing equivocations—above all, the idea that nature enjoys only quasi reality. But the Peripatetic commitment to both immanence and transcendence preserves in nature the ambivalence that was the source of the Neoplatonic equivocations about the hypostatic world. Thus Peripatetics treated matter both as Platonic "otherness" and as a kind of undefinable and unknowable "thing," irreducible to the reality of the ideal and unaccountable in the unifying thematics of the immanent forms. Aristotelian accounts of motion, thought, and even potentiality founder tellingly on the ambiguity engendered by the conflicting motives of immanence and transcendence. And the immanence of divinity, conceived as immobility, made species and the stars ungenerated, invariant, and indestructible.[31]

As for the Stoics, their equivocations touched every part of the universe. God was both active and passive, natural and sovereign, overarching yet immanent, extended and pervasive, manifest, ubiquitous, and unseen. As Carneades put it, the Stoic God was infinite, omniscient, all-good, and imperishable, yet composite, corporeal, animate, rational, and virtuous—as though in need of ratiocination, movement, and improvement! If divination was revelation, Carneades asked, why was it so oblique and obscure? If reason is natural revelation, why is it so sparingly supplied? Stoic nature was fiery, intelligent, providential, determined, and determining. Stoic matter was finite, pulsing, seamless, moving, and alive, nonporous yet everywhere permeable. And Stoic nature was both matter and God. Time was played out in extenso yet eternally omnipresent, and somehow, like all multiplicity, ultimately unreal. Destiny was both fixed and participatory, determined yet, in the only sense that matters, open to human choices.

Monotheism alone will not resolve all these problems—at least not within the framework that creates them. Like Plato, it seeks unity in the divine but finds only the reflex of that unity in nature. Its goal, more modest than the sheer monism of Parmenides, is, for that reason, more attainable. God's transcendence allows the world its categories. The key to God's accommodation with multiplicity, change, contingency, and even chance is symbolized in the kabbalistic idea that God contains himself in the act of creation, not overwhelming creation but content to let it be. Kant sounds the same note when he calls freedom the condition of existence.[32]

Theologically, monotheism routs the powerful localism of pagan piety. That, I suspect, was a chief reason for Greek resistance to the monotheist idea. For the makers of Greek culture, Homer above all, fused the localism of tradition with a sense of immanence sacred even to the most universalist of Greek philosophers. Immanence, typically, was the substance of philosophic piety; pure transcendence was left to deniers like Epicurus, whose gods, on perpetual vacation, left the world ungoverned and humanity without moral and intellectual guidance. Aristotle in particular was at home with immanence. He stiffened and strengthened it with his intellectualist metaphysics and rationalistic science. Despite the seeming remoteness of the Prime Mover, Aristotle remained suspicious of too transcendent a Deity, as his relegation of creation to the realm of myth clearly shows.

Politically, the civil religion of the ancient Mediterranean city, another powerful localism, survived Cynic disparagement to become the more diffuse and portable Stoic fidelity. Indeed, civic religion acquired a special weight in the skeptical philosophy of a Cicero, who sharply divided what was credible philosophically from what could be expected of a Roman loyal to the state and faithful to the trust of his ancestors. Cotta, who speaks for Cicero's Academic skepticism in his philosophical dialogue, warms to this theme even in the midst of an immanentizing and naturalizing sorites that draws a continuum between gods, wood sprites, and natural phenomena:

> I am considerably influenced by . . . the plea . . . to remember that I am both a Cotta and a pontiff . . . that I ought to uphold the beliefs about the immortal gods which have come down to us from our ancestors. . . . I always shall uphold them and always have done so. . . . But on any question of religion I am guided by the high pontiffs . . . not by Zeno or Cleanthes or Chrysippus. . . . The religion of the Roman people comprises ritual, auspices, and . . . prophetic warnings. . . . You are a philosopher, and I ought to receive from you a proof of your religion, whereas I must believe the word of our ancestors even without proof.[33]

The rhetoric is capped by Cotta's remark: "I have learned more about the proper worship of the gods, according to pontifical law and the customs of our ancestors, from the poor little pots bequeathed to us by Numa . . . than from all the theories of the Stoics."[34]

Christians, Jews, and Muslims soon enough will mimic the Roman military and civil virtue of fidelity in their credos. But the appeal to faith as a communal obligation toward the pagan pantheon, however conceived, intensified as the Neoplatonists faced growing challenges from monotheism. Loyalty to the gods of hearth, polis, or imperium was at least as integral to *paideia* as was philosophy. It was very much alive in 410 when Augustine undertook to capture it for the City of God; and it flared balefully for the last time as a living focus of philosophic loyalty in the final abortive defiance of Justinian by the pagan philosophers of Athens, which ended in his closing of Plato's Academy, after nine centuries, in 529. Yet, despite the resistance of Greek philosophers, the syntheses that lead to monotheism were firm in the work of Plato, Aristotle, the Stoics and Neoplatonists, grounded in the insights of Socrates and the pre-Socratics. It was not mere propaganda when Eusebius called the entire philosophical canon a *praeparatio evangelica*, a harbinger of his own community's "good news."

The crucial step in integrating the idea of divinity is its purgation of terror. This harrowing of the pantheon is seen among the Greeks in the banishment of the Titans, the qualified submission to Zeus of Poseidon and Tartarus. It is the same purging that Aristotle makes the task of tragedy, taking the term from the mysteries. In a splendid reversal of fields, he transforms (or witnesses and announces the transformation of) the tragedy from a frenzied reenactment of Dionysiac terror to a mimetic art aimed at the Platonic conquest of that very frenzy. Pity and fear are not the real aims, as Plato had feared. Rather, these emotions are to be purged by reason's overcoming of our natural identification with the personae of the drama, through the objectification and externalization of the tragic flaw that becomes the cynosure of the action at the moment of discovery (*Poetics* 11, 1452a 30).

But conceptually the pantheon is purged not by the extrusion of base emotions from the human breast but by their expulsion from the idea of the divine. Aristotle marks the change by identifying as God that which is highest—most removed from privation, potentiality, and change, most self-sufficing, noblest, most active and least passive, able to move all things without engagement in motion—pure, self-thinking Intelligence. Plotinus goes further. The inner dynamic of the idea of God shows itself clearly when, crossing a boundary at which even Aristotle had balked, he calls God unbounded, infinite.[35] If being, in Platonic and Aristotelian terms, is definiteness, the God of Plotinus transcends even being. Divine unity, the source of reality in all things, thus transcends not only time, space, and matter, but thought itself.

The same conclusion, that the Absolute is the divine, was reached in the Hebrew tradition by a different route. The purgation of evil from divinity did not await the growth of formal dialectic but sprang from the prophetic moral consciousness and cosmic aesthetic. There was a dialectic. But it was concrete compared to the abstract Sophist wordplay that goaded Socrates into critical thought. Defending Sodom and Gomorrah, Abraham urges, "Will not the Judge of all the earth do justice?" God here is universal, not local or parochial; and the appeal—not a plea for mercy or refuge taking, as in Islam—invokes the moral logic of the idea of God. Zeus, too, was a God of justice, father of gods and men. But his eagle and his thunderbolt were something awful to his children. There was more than justice here. Similarly, Athena's gray eye was the emblem of a virgin's kindness but also of a virgin's wrath. It stood for wisdom and for war. None of the ancient gods was good to all and always. Apollo is learning and the lyre, but also plague. Answering Chryse's prayers when Agamemnon disdains the offer of a ransom for the priest's captured daughter, Apollo

> strode down along the pinnacles of Olympus, angered
> in his heart, carrying across his shoulders the bow and the hooded quiver; and
> the shafts clashed on the shoulders of the god walking
> angrily. He came as night comes down and knelt then
> apart and opposite the ships and let go an arrow. . . .
> First he went after the mules and the circling hounds, then let go
> a tearing arrow against the men themselves and struck them.
> The corpse fires burned everywhere and did not stop burning.
> Nine days up and down the host ranged the god's arrows . . .
> *Iliad* 1.44–53

Poseidon, similarly, appeared in the storm, earthquake, and tidal wave. Against such terrors one must learn the pleasure of the god and sate it. One who tests it knows no safety.

Thus in the sacrifice of Iphigenia Lucretius finds a paradigm of religious impieties—*tantum religio potuit suadere malorum* (*De Rerum Natura* I 80–101). The oxymoron wrests moral consciousness from the gods. But in Homer's universe, a value is delimited only when a god's acts are impugned; and that can be done only by another god—as when Poseidon presses his claims against Zeus. Power to question the divine itself, and thus refine its conception, presupposes a moral disengagement from prevailing norms, appropriation of morals by individual, critical consciousness. But in Genesis, God's will is known not by auguries or oracles but by the clear announcement of God's displeasure with lawlessness and injustice (Gen. 18:20–21). Abraham appeals to the very justice that moves God's wrath. The terror of first stating his demand must have been immense; but fear and confusion are calmed by moral courage arising in clear insight, an inference first voiced questioningly as a hypothesis, that caprice and tyranny have no true place in the divine:

> The men turned thence and walked on toward Sodom. But Abraham still stood before the Lord; and, drawing near, Abraham said, "Wilt thou indeed sweep away the innocent with the guilty? Perhaps there are fifty who are innocent within the city. Wilt thou then wipe out the place and not bear with it for the sake of the fifty who are righteous within it? Far be it from thee to do such a thing, to slay the righteous with the wicked, so that innocent and guilty fare alike. Far be it from thee! Will not the judge of all the earth do justice?" (Gen. 18:22–25)[36]

The moral divisions are clearly drawn. God knows the righteous and the wicked and knows that the righteous do not merit death for their righteousness. Conscience here grows confident enough to speak out for God as well as man. Justice is truth; even God cannot make it arbitrary. Abraham knows God's power to execute his sentence. But the source of that power is universal justice, the pivot of Abraham's plea.

The energies in which we humans meet what we take to be divine are not all terribly pleasant or nice. Central among them has been the kill, or the moment of truth just before it. The cave paintings of Altamira and Lascaux still witness the thrill of that moment, filled with power, hunger, longing, and danger, a natural locus of divinity and focus of celebration. The cult of animal sacrifice has roots in this moment, and the Hebrew verb for sacrifice is thus identical with the verb for slaughter. For to slay a beast, even domestically, bore much of the pathos of slaying quarry in the hunt. Even violation of a plant can be so freighted, as Vergil reveals when Aeneas tells how, soon after reaching Thrace, he sought to sacrifice to his mother Venus:

> . . . above a mound, a copse of dogwood
> and myrtle bushes bristle, thick with shoots.
> I try to tear a green branch from the soil
> to serve as leafy cover for our altars—
> But see an awful omen. . . .
> . . . For from that first tree's severed roots
> drops of black blood drip down. They stain the ground
> with gore. My body shudders, cold. My blood
> is frozen now with terror. I try again
> and tear the tenacious stem of a second shoot

that I may reach the deep, the secret root.
And from that second bark, black blood flows down.

Dismayed, I pray . . .
a moan rose from the bottom of the mound,
a lamentable voice returned to me:
"Why are you mangling me, Aeneas? Spare
my body. I am buried here. . . .
For I am Polydorus; here an iron
harvest of lances covered my pierced body . . . "
Aeneid 3.32–59[37]

The restless shade spreads into the dogwood, whose red bark bleeds with black blood, warning the heroes of his presence, so that they offer him fresh obsequies. Wounds inflicted even on a stand of grain have magic powers, rounding the cycle in which John Barleycorn and all his ilk are slain and reburied, to raise again the bearded heads whose death is life to farmers. The associative logic of myth fuses the two. Thus, with the Hebrews as with the Greeks, every meal was a ritual event, and rites might dedicate a victim to the altar or the table.[38]

The formal or ritualized meal is not the only relic of the hunt and its moment of truth. The preservation of hunting as a sport and the institution of bullfighting are others, along with the cult of sacrifice. Thus Artemis is not a minor deity,

flying after her arrows flown down some
tremendous valley-side. . . .
Chasing the mountain goats or ghosting deer . . .
taller by a head than nymphs can be
the goddess shows more stately,
all being beautiful . . .
Odyssey 6.103ff.[39]

Artemis, the Roman Diana, captures, crystallizes, personifies, and transcends the elemental moment in which she is discovered, and still sought. The terror of the goddess is the frisson of her discovery, which is death. For her arrows, like those of her twin, are the plague.

The autonomous horror of the kill, enshrined in a sacrificial cult, may lose the drama of its primal moment, but new life can be breathed into its sensate and emotive impact through symbols or acts of violation. We need not dig into the strata of the past to confirm the linkage between violence and the unschooled *tremendum* or to uncover the dynamic by which the sensate and the violative grow ever more demanding of excess. The linkages are visible (in controlled form) in ritual scarification, the games of the Aztecs and circuses of the Romans,[40] and closer to hand in the dogfights[41] and cockfights still staged on the outskirts of urban America; and nearer still, in our stadiums and on our television screens, in football games and hockey matches, prizefights, mock gladiator bouts, rock concerts, and rock videos. The linkage of blood with deity is salient in the efforts of some groups to revive or sustain cults of animal sacrifice. And the dynamic of excess is palpable in the reinvention of cults of violation by would-be satanists, and even drug smugglers, who reconstitute the dynamic of propitiation with scarcely a cosmology to sustain it, or a deity to receive the horror, beyond what the act itself may generate.

We know of ritual cannibalism not only from Mayan ruins. Carleton Gajdusek, who won the Nobel Prize for discovering the cause of kuru in a slow-acting virus borne by cannibal practices, photographed the cannibal butchery of departed loved ones among the New Guinea highlanders. I have seen his color slides. It may be comforting to deny the reality of such practices, to dismiss them as projections of evil on "the people just over the hill." But the practitioners do not see themselves as wicked. They are doing what they think proper or traditional. New Guineans were just as shocked to learn from Gajdusek of blood transfusions between unrelated persons as we may be to see the images of these tribal funerary customs. Ritual cannibalism and human sacrifice gain their impact, within the cultures that practice them, from the symbolic power of the violative, sought and prized in acts of propitiation or appropriation, celebration, purification, or consecration. Each rite has its own contextual meaning. But generically, power is found in acts of violation, and it is hard to sunder the idea of the divine from the images of death or violence.

Sacrificial cults, in the extreme, then, will ask for human sacrifices not despite but because of the enormity of the act. The evidence stands out in the history and prehistory of many peoples. Iphigenia's sacrifice may be filled with horror, but that is what makes it an act of necessity. The human sacrifices of old Hawaii, or the Zulu nation, were matters of accepted practice. And the enormity of the act led some ancient Semites to sacrifice not just enemies, stragglers, or slaves but their nearest and most precious, their own children, as we learn from the condemnations of the Prophets (Lev. 18:21, 20:2; Deut. 12:30–31, 18:10; Jer. 7:31, 19:4–6; Ezek. 16:20–21, 23:37; Ps. 106:37–38) and from the biblical narrative, which tells of the king of Moab (ninth century B.C.) offering up his firstborn son and heir on the ramparts of his besieged last city (2 Kings 3:27; cf. 16:3, 23:10). Not propaganda, this; for Moab's sacrifice was, to all appearances, accepted: "A great wrath came upon Israel, and they withdrew and returned to their own land." And Jeremiah's condemnations (early sixth century B.C.) lodge not with foreigners but with his own people, kings and commoners of the past and present, who have followed alien gods and built up the high places of the Valley of Ben Hinnom, outside the city, filling the place "with the blood of innocents," offered to Baal, "by burning their sons and daughters in the fire," an act abhorrent to God: "which I did not command or decree, nor came it into my mind" (Jer. 19:5).[42] Manassah's evils included the sacrifice of his own son (2 Kings 21:6), and Isaiah (57:5) condemns his hearers to their face, for slaughtering their children among the wadis and in the clefts of rocks.

The biblical ethos is forged in loathing for such acts. But the stories are not mere sparks from Israel's Kulturkampf with Canaan. Egyptian reliefs of the era of Ramses II (r. 1292–1225, the time of Moses) and Ramses III (r. 1198–1167) show besieged Phoenicians casting their children from the battlements. And the archaeological record expands beyond the biblical horizon, preserving physical evidence to confirm what the prophets report and condemn. For child sacrifice, as an institution, spread through the Phoenician diaspora to lands where alien influence did not so soon overwhelm it, amply attesting its persistence in the southern Mediterranean long after it had died out in the East.[43]

Archaeologists found the tofet of Carthage in 1922 and have studied those of eight other Phoenician cities. They learned the function of the sites only gradually, as the bones and inscriptions (over seven thousand stelae at Carthage) filled in the record of ancient texts.[44] The practice seems to have come to Carthage from the Middle East in the eighth pre-Christian century. It did not diminish with the growth of the city but increased, reaching peaks in times of crisis.[45] It continued in North Africa long after the Roman destruction of Carthage (146 B.C.), although forbidden by the conquerors. Tertullian (ca. 160–ca. 230), a native of Carthage, attests to its continuation in his day (*Apology* ix 2–4); Origen (ca. 185–ca. 254), in his time (*Contra Celsum* V 27). Porphyry (ca. 232–ca. 304), a Syrian, familiar with the practice, compares it with the human sacrifice still offered in his time at Rome. His Phoenician source for the nature of the practice, Sanchuniathon, is quoted in the translation of Philo of Byblos (ca. 100 C.E.).[46]

The sacrifices could be personal or public, occasional or calendrical. The victims, normally under four years of age, might be chosen by lot[47] or to fulfill a vow by their parents. All classes took part, not excluding doctors, teachers, civil and hieratic officers, scribes, and artisans. Indeed, the practice spread downward to the commoners over time. That is, it was fashionable. But fashion was not the motive. The intent attested in the inscriptions was to serve the god—latterly sometimes Tanit, but usually and originally Baal, identified in the stelae and texts of Roman times with Saturn or Cronus. The infants were dropped into the flames, according to Cleitarchus (third century B.C.), from a position in the arms of a bronze idol, possibly while still living, or perhaps after slaughter with a ritual knife. They were kissed and coddled to allay their fear, and music was used to mask parental grief.[48] For normatively the occasion was a joyous one, and a show of grief was unseemly at best. If a wealthy couple bought a child for sacrifice from some poor family, they might well refuse payment if the mother wept or cried out on seeing her infant slain.[49] But purchase of a surrogate rather than sacrifice of one's own flesh was deemed an abuse and could lead to demands for compensatory offerings. Thus two hundred noble children were sacrificed during Agathocles' siege of Carthage in 310 B.C., to atone for the use of secretly bought children in earlier sacrifices. Three hundred adults blamed for the abuses offered themselves to the god as well.[50] Animals were sometimes substituted for a human victim, but a premature or stillborn infant, or one who died soon after birth, was apparently deemed insufficient in fulfilling the vow of an expected child. So the questionable newborn, as the burial urns reveal, was accompanied by a somewhat older child. Italicus tells a story, thought to be fanciful, of Hannibal's angry response to a rival commander's demand that he sacrifice his firstborn and only child; but the choice of a favorite as a victim is much in keeping with the tenor of the well-authenticated evidence. Sanchuniathon, in particular, applies the phrase "best beloved" to those chosen for sacrifice.

Grief, although discouraged, was felt and expressed. The Phoenicians did not sacrifice their children because they were barbarous. Rather, they were barbarous in that they sacrificed their children. The motive was not cruelty but piety. This is what Phoenicians thought their gods desired and demanded. For horror was fused with divinity in their ritual structure. Violation of the deepest bonds of human caring merged with reverence of the most awesome deity.

Against this backdrop we can see that the story (Genesis 22) of God's command that Abraham sacrifice his long-awaited and beloved son would not have seemed to its first audience alien to ideals of piety. Child sacrifice was an institution in the land of Abraham's birth, well attested at the so-called Royal Tombs of Ur (cf. 2 Kings 17:31), paralleled and confirmed by the slaying of substitute kings.[51] The natural expectation, given the divine command, would be for Abraham to accept and obey, with terror.[52] But in Genesis the grisly and (in Lucretius's word) impious norm is reversed.[53] God commands Abraham to sacrifice his son. Yet an angel orders him to stay his hand. He does, and his test is over. God never intended Isaac to be slain.[54] "I know already that thou fearest God."[55] God knew eternally; he was not to learn from the trial. Its purpose, as Maimonides explains, was to show humanity (or Abraham!) the limit of human devotion. For some tests are demonstrations: they discover not new knowledge for the deviser of the trial but new understanding *to* observers and recipients of its report. Naḥmanides goes further: some ordeals bring forth virtues from their potentiality as dispositions to actuality as actions. Abraham's trial brought to fruition what he was capable of achieving, fulfilling his character and perfecting his righteousness.[56] Yet Isaac was not sacrificed.[57]

How did Abraham know what he must do, heed not God's apparent command but the angel who cried out to him, "Abraham, Abraham"? How could he know that what God had asked had never been intended? It is the reader, not Abraham, who is told from the outset that the ordeal was a test.[58] And Abraham could not fall back on "revelation"; revelation had told him two contradictory things. One voice had commanded the sacrifice; the other announced that he had passed the test without slaying Isaac. Which was to be heeded? It is here, with the knife poised in the air, as the painters and sculptors of the event have understood, not when Abraham stretches out his hand to take the knife, that the crisis comes. Should he listen to the angel who tells him to stay his hand, or obey the prior revelation: "Take now thy son, thy one and only, whom thou hast loved, Isaac, and get thee to the land of Moriah, and offer him up as a burnt offering on one of the mountains of which I will tell thee" (Gen. 22:2)? God had spoken entreatingly, Rashi writes, as to an intimate. Yet his command was as explicit as a legal writ. Spelling out its force, Rashi imagines a dialogue in which Abraham seeks to evade or diminish God's demand: "'Thy son.' 'I have two sons.' 'Thy one and only.'" (For, as Naḥmanides explains, "Isaac was the son of the mistress.") "'This one is his mother's one and only, and so is the other.' 'Whom thou lovest.' 'I love them both.' 'Isaac.'"

The angel is peremptory,[59] urgent in his repetition of Abraham's name, again intimate. As Rashi writes: "This is the language of love, when he repeats his name."[60] God is entreating Abraham. His own holiness—Israel's ethos as well as Isaac's life—hangs in the balance. But Abraham has no cushion of tradition to fall back on. He must decide alone and in the instant. Further prompting would be useless. But emblematically he chooses for all his heirs.[61] Looking up, he sees a ram caught in the thicket. He seizes it and offers it in place of the sacrifice he has determined not to give. He risks all on his trust, his knowledge that God is good, that the Judge of all the earth shall do justice. Then he awaits the outcome. The decision to offer Isaac had been deliberate. It was made after a night's sleep, rising early and walking three days' journey. As Naḥmanides comments (ad Gen. 22:2): "Had Abraham been commanded to do it immediately, where he was, the act would have been done in haste and confusion. But since it was done after walking for days, it was done with reflection and counsel. Thus the Rabbis in Genesis Rabbah (55.5). For Rabbi Akiba said, 'so that people might not say that God confounded and confused him and he did not know what to do.'" It was the decision not to offer Isaac that was impulsive. The barbaric offering had been subject to every thoughtful consideration.

Would Abraham be punished for refusing the sacrifice, or was he right to obey the second prompting? Confirmation comes swiftly. The binding had been sufficient, the slaying was not required. Indeed, the Rabbis comment, the ram had been prepared for this moment from the first days of creation[62]—thus Abraham's choice is part of what gives meaning to the very act of creation. He will not be punished but rewarded: "Out of the heavens a second time the angel of the Lord cried unto Abraham, 'By Myself have I sworn, saith the Lord, since thou hast done this thing and not withheld thy son, thy one and only, I shall surely bless thee, I shall surely multiply thy seed as the stars of the heavens and as the sand on the shore of the sea, and thy seed shall inherit the gates of their foes. And through thy seed shall all the nations of the earth be blessed, because thou hast hearkened to my voice" (Gen. 22:15–18). With boundless relief Abraham returns to his servants and completes his journey. Millennia later, Mendel of Kosov will write: "None but God can order us to take a life, but an angel suffices to demand that we save one—even if it contravenes a divine command."[63]

But what was "this thing" that Abraham had done? He had not slain his son. Yet he had hearkened to God's voice. How, if he did not burn Isaac? It was the angel's voice that was to be obeyed when it said, "Do not lay a hand on the boy; do not do anything to him" (Gen. 22:12).[64] The angel says that Abraham has not withheld his son, although he has not slaughtered him. Can one, then, give one's son without killing him? How has Abraham not withheld his son? Has he given him in other ways, perhaps before the demand for sacrifice, or while the two walked in silence together? For Isaac had questioned his father, "Here are the fire and the wood, but where is the lamb for the offering?" and Abraham said, "God will see to [*yir'eh*] the lamb for himself, my son. And the two walked on together." The Midrash glosses: "Isaac understood that he was going to the slaughter." Yet Abraham spared Isaac, and in that way gave him to God. His reward is not for blind obedience, then, but for (and through) moral insight. Thus the play on *yir'eh*, which gives the place its name: here God saw to his own sacrifice, and here he was seen in his true nature, "As it is said to this day, 'In the mount where the Lord reveals Himself'" (Gen. 22:14).

The reward of Abraham's steadfastness and trust in God's justice is the public discovery of an Absolute that brooks no evil. Thus the angel's promise, in God's name and with God's oath: Since you made no exception of your son to the command of goodness, and did not accept the ghastly but ready notion that the gravest enormity would be the greatest gift, for that reason you are blessed; and your successors, through the understanding that you communicate to them, will be a blessing to the peoples of the world, witnessing their own mastery even of their enemies—not by conquest but by the shared recognition that goodness is greater than violence and the only source of authentic power.

As with the Greeks, then, there was a trial, but its outcome was not tragedy but clarity. When Agamemnon slays his daughter, it is fate's decree. So are his betrayal and murder, and Orestes' vengeance, and the Furies' pursuit, until the train of retributions is exhausted in reconciliation. But here arbitrary violence and terror are debarred from the idea of God. The second revelation was the truth, and the first must be explained: "God tested Abraham." Faced with contradictory commands and left to his own conscience, he listened to the angel and spared his son. Only then did he learn that he had chosen rightly. The angel, of course, was immanent, like the one that prompted Judah's liaison with Tamar.[65] But so was the first prompting, the command to sacrifice Isaac. The real revelation lay in the resolution: Abraham had hearkened to God's voice and let God reveal something of his nature. For the God of heaven and earth does not violate the trust of parent and child. The claim of conscience sunders the blessing of Abraham from the curse of Atreus.

Abraham already knew God's alienness to evil. But he had not seen fully what this meant when he set out for Mount Moriah. As Rabbi Mordecai Leiner of Izbica (1802–1854) put it, "It does not say that the Lord [using the tetragrammaton] tested Abraham, but that Elohim [the Divine] tested him, meaning that the word came to him as through a glass darkly [as the *Zohar* puts it] . . . *Elohim*, referring to a power."[66] Doubt, as Yehuda Gellman writes, is at the heart of Abraham's trial. But so is the certitude of revelation, as Maimonides urges (*Guide* III 24), and the certainty of God's justice. It is Saadiah who shows us how these themes coalesce: For although he knew God's justice, "Abraham had to prepare himself for the worst, all the while depending on the fact that if God's intent was otherwise, 'God will show me.'"[67] The authority of the command to slay his son joins with the existential aloneness of Abraham, forced to choose and face the moral and practical consequences of his choice.[68] Abraham's trial tested his conviction not by probing the static intent of an immovable faith in an implacable unknown but by refining, strengthening, giving substance to his nascent conviction of God's goodness.

Faith here is not blind allegiance but conscious and increasingly confident loyalty to the inner logic of God, now confirmed by Abraham's trial and forged into a principle of character—for the logic itself did not need strengthening. Philo detects the vital nuance that divides the logical from the psychological and marks the moral precedence of the latter when, in his allegorical account, playing on Isaac's name, he argues that Abraham was ready to sacrifice his laughter, but God returned it to him, banishing from the ideal of piety the dour passions of terror and resignation: "The laughter here is not that which amusement arouses in the body but the wholesome emotion of the understanding, which is joy. This the Sage is said to sacrifice as his duty to God, thus showing in a figure that rejoicing is most closely linked with God alone. For mankind is subject to grief and fearsome evils, either present or anticipated. . . . But God's nature is without grief or fear, wholly free of passion of every kind, and alone partakes of perfect happiness and bliss." Drawing on the Stoic distinction of *eupatheiai*, or wholesome emotions, from the baser and debilitating passions that Spinoza will call passive emotions, Philo rejects the Stoic strategy of "not giving hostages to fortune" and the joylessness, lack of affect, or even cruelty that such a strategy can imbue. For what follows from the recognition, not merely logically but characterologically, of the fact that God alone has perfect joy is not the abjuring of joy, but its joyous appropriation: "The mind that has made this true acknowledgement, God, Who banished jealousy from His presence in his kindness and love for mankind, fitly rewards by returning the gift, insofar as the recipient's capacity allows. Indeed we may almost hear His voice saying: 'All joy and rejoicing I know well belongs to none but Me alone, the Father of all. Yet I do not grudge that this My possession should be used by such as are worthy.'"[69] The reappropriation of joy, the sparing of Isaac, the banishment of spite from God and anger from his cult are one and the same. God too, then, was tested at Mount Moriah.

Abraham survives his trial without tragedy through his trust that the judge of all the earth will do justice. The outcome is his confident invocation of the infinite and Universal God (*el ʿolam*; Gen. 22:33). The intellectual and moral dimensions of the virtue of faith fuse, as the purgation of the idea of God opens the way to the further purgation of will and heart. With brilliant economy, the Midrash says of Abraham, "He united the whole world for us" (Genesis Rabbah 39.3).

Modern readers may come to the biblical account of the Akedah or binding of Isaac fresh from Kierkegaard's famous meditation on the subject.[70] Kierkegaard read this text in the light of Kant's reflections. And Kant was guarding the moral construction of the idea of God against pious glorifications of unquestioning obedience. He wrote: "Even though something is represented as commanded by God, through a direct manifestation of Him, yet, if it flatly contradicts morality, it cannot, despite all appearances, be of God."[71] Moral autonomy here tests its strength by challenging all comers. But Kant's Enlightenment spirit also finds a certain delight in ragging scriptural stories, at least Old Testament ones, and damming the interpretive stream that allows their continuous reappropriation. So he adds: "for example, were a father ordered to kill his son who is, so far as he knows, perfectly innocent."[72] In effect, Kant reads Scripture against itself, calling morality to witness against the moral boundary stone which the Torah's ancient and compelling idiom sets at the very turning Kant wants to mark. His animus is clear when he applies his conclusion to a general diatribe against ecclesiastical authoritarianism, rejecting as unholy and incoherent the idea of a religious war and drawing a pale analogy between the binding of Isaac and the oppression of heretics by "an inquisitor who clings fast to the uniqueness of his statutory faith":

> That it is wrong to deprive a man of his life because of his religious faith is certain, unless (to allow for the most remote possibility) a Divine Will, made known in extraordinary fashion, has ordered it otherwise. But that God has ever uttered this terrible injunction can be asserted only on the basis of historical documents and is never apodictically certain. After all, the revelation has reached the inquisitor only through men and has been interpreted by men, and even did it appear to have come from God Himself (like the command delivered to Abraham to slaughter his own son like a sheep) it is at least possible that in this instance a mistake has prevailed. . . . This is the case with respect to all historical and visionary faith. . . ."[73]

Kant's aim here broadens to take in any faith founded in history and tradition: Morality is apodictic; historical faiths are mere contingent facts, subject to error and rival readings. The possibility of congruence or complementarity between moral imperatives and revealed or traditional religions is waved off in the heat of the struggle for conscience against the demands of church and state. So is the possibility that Kant eagerly grasped when he addressed the physics of Newton, that behind the empiric data lie laws and truths that transcend the mere facticity of the contingent.

But we stand in a historical situation rather different from Kant's. We must take our wisdom where we can find it, and the same revolutions that scattered such elements of wisdom as we can discover have also freed us to seek them and grasp them for ourselves. Neither church nor state, in the West at least, wields the measure of power over human conscience that Kant feared and fought. Morality, for its part, in whose autonomy he put such store, has shown itself at times to be a rather poor, weak thing, without the aid of culture, tradition, or scripture, to strengthen its resolve or counsel its intent. In our environment, morality does not so readily scorn allies. It may have learned somewhat of the insufficiency to its humane purposes of the bare idea of an independent and undirected conscience, the poverty of mere self-reliance, the thinness and chilliness of the unaided ideals of rationality and resolution. If Kant's brief, then, is preservation of moral purity from corruption by the political—including political impositions in the name of faith—his point remains sound, although many of the battles have been won, and although it is a cheap shot to invoke the Akedah as a pattern of religious persecution and cheaper still to equate historical faiths with political triumphalism or to identify a sense of uniqueness and commitment with intolerance and oppression. But if the point taken is that faith, scripture, and tradition are inevitably leagued against reason, morality, and conscience, the particularity of Kant's circumstances is betrayed in the generality of his reasoning, and his conclusion is contradicted by the very text he chooses as the butt of his polemic. For Genesis 22 speaks to the untenability of any idea of God not founded on the idea of the good.

Kant surely felt that he had laid to rest all chance of a theology at odds with morals, a ghost of the very paganism that Genesis combats. But long odds always draw some takers. Kierkegaard wrote *Fear and Trembling* while reeling from the loss of his beloved Regina not to death but by her engagement to another man. Walter Lowrie writes: "Certainly in *Fear and Trembling* there was no risk that anybody else might recognize Regina under the figure of Isaac. . . . The white light of truth is here so thoroughly refracted that even the reader who has such acquaintance with S.K.'s story as his contemporaries did not, may have need to be told that Abraham's sacrifice of Isaac is a symbol of S.K.'s sacrifice of the dearest thing he had on earth." So we descend from the moral austerities of Kant, who never had a Regina, to Kierkegaard's cosmic sense of loss: "The reader who is not acquainted with this story must be told that in order to liberate Regina from her attachment and to 'set her afloat' S.K. felt obliged to be cruel enough to make her believe he was a scoundrel who had merely been trifling with her affections."[74] How can Scripture possibly compete with opera!

But we need not reduce the impact of Kierkegaard's argument to the spurs that goaded it. For his target is not Regina in the guise of Isaac but Kant in the guise of Abraham. Thus the reference in the opening lines of *Fear and Trembling* to the philosophical doubt of "every *Privatdocent*, tutor and student, every crofter and cotter in philosophy."[75] For Kant earned his living as a *Privatdocent* for years before attaining a professorship in Königsburg. But Kierkegaard's persona was "nothing of a philosopher," "was not a thinker," and "felt no need of getting beyond faith"; he was "not a learned exegete" and knew no Hebrew.[76] Thus he thinks that God tempted

Abraham, and sees no test in the story, as one who reads Hebrew would; nor a demonstration, as a learned exegete like Maimonides does; still less an ordeal or challenge, as does Rashi's grandson, Rashbam (ca. 1085–ca. 1174), who calls Abraham's test a provocation by God.[77] For surely it is a challenge that fractures Abraham's notion that it would be piety to sacrifice his son.

Projectively, Kierkegaard pictures Abraham as shielding the horror of God's command behind a mask of cruelty: "'Stupid boy, dost thou then suppose that I am thy father? I am an idolater. Dost thou suppose that this is God's bidding? No, it is my desire.' . . . better for him to believe that I am a monster, rather than that he should lose faith in thee." And faith, Kierkegaard writes, "begins precisely where thinking leaves off."[78] "Faith," he adds, "is precisely this paradox, that the individual as the particular is higher than the universal"—where morality, as in Kant, represents the universal, and particularity represents sin.[79] "Abraham's relation to Isaac, ethically speaking, is quite simply expressed by saying that a father shall love his son more dearly than himself." A tragic hero remains stuck, as it were, "within the ethical," letting "one expression of the ethical find its *telos* in a higher expression of the ethical."[80] With Abraham, however, the situation was different.

> By his act he overstepped the ethical entirely and possessed a higher *telos* outside of it. . . . Abraham's whole action stands in no relation to the universal. . . . He did it for God's sake, because God required this proof of his faith; for his own sake he did it in order that he might furnish the proof. The unity of these two points of view is perfectly expressed by the word which has always been used to characterize this situation: it is a trial, a temptation. . . . in this case the temptation is itself the ethical. . . . How, then, did Abraham exist? He believed . . . the individual puts himself in an absolute relation to the absolute.[81]

But how can God be absolute if God is not good? And how can a human being conceive of an absolute except by way of the universal? Even the demand for human sacrifice, the all-too-concrete premise of Abraham's trial, springs from misplaced reasoning, the inference that the highest god would expect the greatest sacrifice. Kierkegaard makes the same inference when he speaks of the demands of the absolute. Indeed, he projects it onto Abraham, first in scripting the prelude to Isaac's binding, and again in reading into the trial a higher standard than the demands of goodness—as if to create an absolute beyond the absolute, a master that poetry or horror, paradox or particularity can reach, but fatherly love cannot. The issue, after all, is what we are to regard as absolute. If faith is indeed a virtue, we need to know, *faith in what?* How is an absolute approached, encountered, even sought? Is death the only absolute, so that slaughter is the only encounter and worship demands killing something; worship of the Highest, killing what is dearest?

Kant found what was moral in morality through the idea of a universal law. But that idea hardly entails that no moral claim can be particular. Kant knew that the moral law is empty if its commands against, say, theft or fraud do not issue the imperatives, "Do not steal this," "Do not cheat this man." The very case Kierkegaard has chosen refutes his confinement of morals to the universal. For the claim of father on son and son on father is particular. It is not just *a* father and *a* son, but *my* father, *my* son. That is why, despite their love of universals, the Greeks saw more horror in parricide than in murder—and why we see in parental abuse a darker crime than some mere scuffle on the playground. We do not ask parents to execute the sentence of the state on wayward or criminal offspring, or require spouse to testify against spouse in criminal proceedings, even in the cause of justice. Moral claims can be particular. And we can hardly expect any to be universal unless some are particular. For morals rise from the immediate to the universal; they do not descend from the abstract universal to the case at hand. But when Kierkegaard stands to defend the irrefragable demands of faith against the hubris of morality, it is Kant's morality of a universal moral law that he addresses. So he cloaks the moral demands of Isaac's uniqueness and Abraham's paternity, and even the claims of Isaac's posterity, under the guise of a universal imperative. Yet there would be no moral laws for Kant to speak about were there not such far more elemental and immediate claims as those of paternity, particularity, and posterity.

Kierkegaard, then, slights the biblical narrative by projecting onto it a conflict between a Protestant, indeed Lutheran, conception of faith and a rather pat or complacent post-Kantian sense of duty. Faith for Kierkegaard is the sole ultimate salvation; morality must recognize its merely human futility in confronting sin. It must acknowledge the inadequacy of repentance and yield to pure faith, whose ultimate test becomes the arbitrary demand to part company with morality—as though the content of faith or morality could be arbitrarily or independently selected or imposed. Thus the celebrated teleological suspension of the ethical, which Kierkegaard pastes over the biblical narrative. But where does Abraham agonize over sin, torment himself with the inadequacy of repentance, or know the anguish over faith that Kierkegaard assigns to him? Even the word 'faith' in the Hebrew Bible does not have the sense that Augustine forged by merging Plato's *pistis* with Cicero's *fides*. It means steadfastness, trust, and loyalty. It is more a moral than a cognitive term, and never a form of knowledge.[82] Still less is it a substitute for morals.[83] Justification by faith is as foreign to the Torah as cognition by faith, or the preoccupation with justification that seems to presume the inadequacy of life on earth and to expect its replacement with something better, could we but merit it. Blinded by his own inner struggle, Kierkegaard reads an academic Kantian morality into Abraham's mind and projects his own (rather pagan) notion of faith's conflict with that morality, at the very moment where the Torah seeks to awaken our consciousness to the indissoluble linkage of goodness to the idea of God.

If God is a particular, as Kierkegaard fervently urges, we must ask which particular he is. Clearly he is not death or dismemberment or any other horror. He stands above all attributions, as admirers of paradox and ineffability, who believe that God, in his uniqueness, transcends all definition, surely remember. What name, then, can we give him, other than one that expresses all that we know as perfection—as parents give a child a name that voices some part of their hopes for it, although hardly abandoning their attachment to this child in all its uniqueness. We do not abandon God's uniqueness or love him the less if we acknowledge that it is only through ideas, and their dialectic, that we encounter that uniqueness.

Perhaps we cannot give a name to God. But it is not unseemly to use the language of perfection, as the Torah does (Exod. 3:14) when it teaches that God's name is I AM THAT I AM, a phrase expressive of the absoluteness of pure being. Nor is it inappropriate, if we are called upon to emulate God's perfection, that human attributes are assigned to God. Thus Moses learns of God's mercy, love, and justice (Exod. 34:6). It is because we know God as an individual through such concepts that Scripture calls him a Father, or a Mother, or merciful, or faithful—but not impersonal or even infinite, since these are not characteristics which we can emulate. To picture or imagine God would negate his absoluteness. We can conceive him only as the consummation of all perfections. Here Plato joins hands with the prophets. For he argues that what is most perfect must be most real; and they, that what is most real must be most perfect.

I can encounter God with the aid of morality, then, or art, or the beauty of nature—but never despite them.[84] In violence or violation, or the romantically appealing notions of the arbitrary, actively uncaring, or chaotic, I encounter nothing divine but the mere reflex of human horror and alienation, dressed up in mystery and renamed a *tremendum*—as though Vergilian creeping flesh and bristling hair, or an existential sense of utter lostness, somehow manifested a power not only greater than our own (which is easy) but unique and worthy of worship. It is the goodness of God, integrating all affirmative values, that renders the God of Abraham universal. Had evil remained, conflict would be ineradicable—one deity or tribe of deities for one value or farrago of values and another deity or swarm of deities for another. Moral coherence would be lost and, with it, the very possibility of an idea of God.

What Abraham confirmed through the Akedah was that only the Perfect can be absolute. For only the absolute can be divine. It was this insight that the *mutakallimūn*, Muslim dialectical theologians, enshrined when they argued that there can be but one God, since rival deities would inevitably limit and ultimately destroy each other. The imagery was jejune, but the insight was sound.[85] Conflict no more comports with the logic of divinity than does limitation. A single universe and law of nature argue a single divine plan, as Aristotle held (*Metaphysics,* Lambda 10, 1076a). So does a single moral law, giving no ground for the appeal that what is a crime in one god's eyes might be a duty to another.[86]

To purge such conflicts, all values must be integrated, rendering God's commands genuinely irrefragable, not just stentorian. Only of a universal judge can universal justice be demanded. And only by the integration of all values—seeing through the presumed inevitability of tragedy—can such justice be conceived. If my gain inevitably involves your loss, universal justice is not a possibility. Human sacrifice and the rituals that share its logic symbolically play out such a no-win game.[87] If expression or fulfillment of one value inevitably suppresses or frustrates another, we reach the dynamic of tragedy and the Sophists' rationale of exploitation. But if we depend on one another for fulfillment, through community, there is a path to universal justice, and the law of that justice is God's law.

The very idea of universal justice, then, purges the divine of terror, slaughter and the plague, salacious and meretricious eroticism, and the iniquity of cunning. The shedding of such projections quickens with the division of the universe into opposing spheres—the pure and impure, sacred and profane, evil and good—polarities tinged with the colorations of judgment and justice. Universal justice, integrating all sound values, enthrones the God of monotheism as the sole divinity and dismisses the pagan gods as empty artifacts, things of nought (Jer. 10:14, 51:18), and evil itself, clinging to the name of being under the notion of the diabolical, is the last to be purged, when dualism finally yields to monotheism and acknowledges the insubstantiality of evil and the pure reality of the Good. But moral integration is not the only means of integrating the idea of divinity. The logic of perfection presses toward the same end. So does cosmology, discovering unity and integration in nature. Here the roots of naturalism and monotheism are intertwined, and a common discontent with what both will call superstition still recalls the residue of values that they share.

Pagan sensibilities, often pragmatic, are naturally projective, peopling nature with motives and intentions—favor, malice, concupiscence—that seem familiar and open to a bargain, calming an existence beset not just by hope and fear but by guilt and anxiety and their projective union in magical ideas of power and pollution. Groping toward objectivity, cosmology disengages from the genealogies and romances of the gods, lucid by its silence in the face of ignorance but coupling that silence with wonder and intense curiosity—a lust not merely for control but for understanding. The constancy of the celestial motions, the recurrent seasons, the consistency, from species to species and individual to individual, of the laws of life, all belie the occult actors of capricious intent—the masks that paganism fashions as interlocutors with the unknown. All argue the workings of a coherent system, with principles of its own, a pattern whose foundation is monadic yet beyond reduction to human purposes. This ground is the object of all scientific inquiry. But its transcendent Source, conceived as a summit of values that nature's energies, beauties, and sublimities only partially express, is the aim of monotheistic speculation as well, and the object of monotheistic worship.

Recognizing the inadequacy of all human projections, Genesis is silent as to the mechanics of creation and its motives. No implement or tool is mentioned, but also no envy, ambition, solitude, or solicitude. The person and character of God are undescribed; there is no talk of a scheme, a need to test or try men, judge or save them. Creation is the stark encounter of the Absolute with the contingent. Further description only weakens this telling asymmetry. Yet, through the idea of creation swells the awesome but reassuring sense of underlying unity and meaning. Values are integrated on the cosmic plane, and the synthesis parallels, reinforces, and draws strength from their moral integration.

It is from the structural parallel of the moral and cosmic syntheses that the biblical idea of God draws its sublimity. For it reveals the integration of moral values as a special case of the general integration of values. The God of justice is the Creator. Some scholars stereotype the cosmological "genius" as Greek and the moral as Hebrew—saying in effect that where Greeks philosophize, Hebrews legislate. This makes biblical cosmology the mere reflex of biblical morals and reads too much into the minds of the ancients our own impressions and valuations of their ultimate achievements. For what is Greek cosmology without the science that will grow from the first primitive overtures of Thales or Anaximander; and what is even biblical law, as the Rabbis so often remind us, without the Talmud, and the civilizational edifice that Mosaic moral culture nourishes and sustains? Besides, Socrates was a moralist, not a cosmologist, and Genesis frames a cosmology stunning in its metaphysical elegance, fused to moral concerns but not reducible to them. And that cosmology is no more to be divorced from the aesthetics of the sublime than from the morals and the politics of universal appreciation of the goodness of all creation.

I hesitate, then, to assign priority to the moral or the cosmic perspective. But there is no need. For all created things—all animals and plants, heavenly bodies, all features of nature, "the earth and all that is in it"—are values in the religious perspective. For the polytheist, all are potential foci of divine energy. For the monotheist, all are actual loci of God's expressive or creative act. Their integration requires only a purgation of evil and capriciousness from nature. Biblically this goal is achieved in cosmology, as in morals, through the idiom of judgment, by the projection of God himself as truthful judge, assaying all the works of his creation and seeing that they are good. God becomes, in one act of thought, the judge of all the earth and the creator of the heavens, since nothing escapes his dominion—the true Judge of all values, not their maker but their Source.

Moral values have an immediacy that even natural values lack. But Cornford went too far in reading social structures into the early Greek cosmologies.[88] For if compactness means anything it means that the social and the cosmic map one another. Thus the "temples" of the pagan heavens or the realms of the pagan earth, sea, and underworld do not merely mirror social moieties. For the social divisions themselves presume schemes of justice and are figured on divisions of responsibility among the gods—forms of cosmic integration. And, in the fuller unity of monotheism, God's absoluteness does not merely reflect the idea of universal (as opposed to tribal) rule but projects the ideal of universal justice, which bears, in turn, the sanction and imprimatur of divine authority.

Still there is the primacy of human experience to humanity. Mythical thought and magical practice do project values from nature upon humanity. But the more striking projection is in the opposite direction. A king or chief may be likened to the sun, a rock, a tree, or beast; but that only assigns him, in elevated degree or kind, properties he may naturally possess. More striking is the movement that finds human traits in the nonhuman world—as when the rock or wood or spring is endowed with life and intentions, or animal species acquire not only temperaments but personalities and social roles. The social and the ethical invest nature with a potential for integration far beyond what natural forces alone, or as items of fortune or misfortune, could possibly arouse. The discovery of pattern and beauty in the cosmos might come to any sensitive human being. But for Abraham it was a moral experience that "united the world" and lifted him, and us, from encounter with "the judge of all the earth" to invocation of "the God of the universe," *el ʿolam*.

Perhaps "moral experience" is too flat and abstract an expression. It was the questions Sarah would ask, the claims of Isaac, of all his progeny, and all who would reap blessings through them, that demanded rectification of Abraham's values, purgation and integration of his idea of the divine. Only if God is good can he be the universal creator and judge. And if he is good, no value escapes his dominion. Plato followed the same path. For it was on the Socratic unity of the virtues that he founded the unity of the Forms, the ontic unity recapitulating the moral and reaching the metaphysical by aid of the abstract terminology and argumentative schemata honed in Socratic dialectic over morals—their universality or particularity, subjectivity or objectivity. Only so could Plato ground a new cosmology and overcome the Sophists' false dichotomy of law and nature in the revolutionary idea of natural law. It was because Socrates, goading and goaded by the Sophists, had brought philosophy down from the heavens and into the agora that Plato could restore it to the heavens, no longer as a furtive utterer of gnomic conjectures but regnant in conceptual control of the deep and elusive unity that the *physikoi* had sought. Without the aid of formal metaphysics or formal dialectic, Israel had achieved a comparable integration, the moral ideas powerfully seconded by a wondrously tranquil cosmic aesthetic.

The idea of God, then, that emerges from moral experience and from contemplation of nature is that of a being of absolute Perfection. Preservation of this idea is the raison d'être of Israel's ethnic continuity. This Maimonides hints in taking as the motto of his essay on the logic of God, the opening chapters of the *Guide to the Perplexed*: "Open ye the gates, that the righteous nation that keepeth faith may enter" (Isa. 26:2), and in superscribing to the work as a whole Abraham's invocation: "In the name of the Lord, God of the universe" (Gen. 21:33).

Critical Theology

There are no experts on God. Absolute and transcendent perfection bars entry to our analytic intelligence. We know nothing of the Infinite but its direction—symbolically represented as upward but transcending all humanly delimited notions. The Hebrew epithet *yoshev bameromim*, he who dwelleth on high, no more names a spatial direction than it entails God's need for shelter. Thus the Mosaic iconoclasm, which led to charges of atheism against Jews in antiquity. The Roman soldiers who penetrated the Holy of holies swept the air with their spears, seeking the unseen God. Pagan popular imagination had filled the room with hideous abominations. A god was not real that could not be seen, touched, felt, smelt, even tasted or slept with. The Jews were atheists not just in their God's exclusivity but in his incorporeality and lack of the familiar determinations of objects. Even Spinoza's modern reassertion of God's infinitude and transcendence of objecthood was seized upon by his contemporaries, and by many since, as clear proof of his atheism; and the inclusionary theology by which Spinoza overcomes the hoary polarity of immanence and transcendence is thought incoherent because it does not agree that God cannot be There if he is here. The tendency persists to dismiss as "arid" or "unsuited to religious purposes" the insights of natural theology and rational mysticism, or any idea of God not bound to imaginative particularity and emotive demand. But what religious purposes could exceed intellectual love and ethical emulation, without ceasing to be religious? When religion becomes a therapeutic mantra, political talisman or economic wishing well, poetic toy or whipping boy, hex, curse, sexual icon, gambling fetish, permission giver, or seller of indulgences, it robs itself not only of clarity and coherence but of value as religion. Impure means and motives are as destructive here as they are in morals, undermining and giving the lie to the very intentions that orient the idea of holiness.

Any derogation from the Absolute is a derogation of the divine. He knows God best, the Rambam argues (*Guide* I 52), who can see most clearly his transcendence of the predicates used in our common language. So he knows God best who knows him least. Only when the Sanctum is empty of all things is it most truly the dwelling place of God. The disappointment of fideists and agnostics at this outcome of natural theology may express a still undissolved entanglement of their thoughts in projective hopes and anxieties—if not a disingenuous hope that others' minds are so entangled. But the God that *Sputnik* and *Soyuz* did not jolt in space is the same God who was too subtle to engage the Roman spears.

It is not because we cannot think conceptually that God eludes our grosser efforts to capture, bottle, or purvey him. We think conceptually enough in mathematics and the sciences, and in our daily lives. But perhaps we are unused to conceptual thought in the sphere of religion and have not often enough aroused the mind to ponder theology beyond Sunday school images or to study the Bible except as a collection of tales. Seeing the potential of imagery to mislead, Maimonides advised parents from the earliest age (in marked contrast to Plato, who for practical purposes was content that the belief of commoners should remain at the level of images) to inform their children that God is not a person or a thing (*Guide* I 35).

Hume, Bayle, Voltaire, and the diverse intellectual flotsam adrift in the eddies set up by the fall of such giants from naive faith were sure that the God of true religion is the God of simple faith. Failing to find that God, they knew that they (meaning religion) had failed absolutely. Their pose of melancholy loss is communicated to the Bertrand Russells and Walter Lippmanns of the twentieth century with some loss of learning, wit, and verve but no loss of the essential ingredient, an introspective (if not narcissistic) angst worthy of a modern day Rousseau. The Fitzgerald *Rubaiyat,* a fine expression of what Voegelin calls "the Victorian fashion of agnosticism" encapsulates perfectly the spiritual autobiography of such nostalgics:

> Myself when young did eagerly frequent
> Doctor and Saint and heard great Argument
> About it and about: but evermore
> Came out by the same door as in I went.[89]

The Sages replied long before: If you did not find, you did not seek. These grown men who weep for the lost God of their childhood seem to be mourning less for God than for their childhood, which indeed they never will recapture.

Voltaire describes a theologian as one who has devoted years to arcane languages and archaic civilizations, seeking God but knowing in the end no more, perhaps less, than when he began.[90] Ibn Ṭufayl's Absal, similarly, has frequented the credos of all men before he learns that God is met from the first in solitude. Thus the epigram al-Ghazālī offers a would-be disciple:

> Forget what you've heard and clutch what you see.
> At sunrise what use is Saturn to thee?[91]

Tradition can be an aid, but it may be a hindrance. Once the glass of naive faith is broken, as al-Ghazālī put it, it can never be pasted together or patched up. It must be either discarded or melted down and fused anew. Both the atheist and the thoughtful believer know that the God of naive faith is not to be found. They differ in their response—the atheist complaining that only the God of childhood or none will do, the natural theologian seeking a higher and hardier conception. Thus Plotinus argues that the One, being above definition, is above being in the sense that Aristotle gave the term, and that the prayer of the wise is silence. The Rabbis find the same idea in the Psalms (Midrash Tehillim 19.2 on Ps. 65:2), and Maimonides echoes their sense (*Guide* I 50, quoting Ps. 4:5). For Thoreau, even agnosticism is a triumphal motif, voicing the culmination of the mystic search: "Time is but the stream I go a-fishing in. . . . I know not the first letter of the alphabet."[92]

Childhood cannot be recaptured and we do not grow in human stature in the attempt. Now we are men, we must seek with the eyes of men. Personality cannot belong to God if God is absolute and personality is a confluence of biological exigencies, with a window on immortality. Life, consciousness, and power are metaphors that glimpse Perfection in splintered bits of mirror. Since God is simplex, their true sense must be synonymous with one another and with him. Since God is absolute they can name no experience as their source. Not that God lacks life or wisdom or power, but only that he transcends the finitude they suggest. The exigencies of a prophetic mission will force those who struggle to voice the idea of God to "speak of the Creator in terms of His creation," opening up to them a poetic license of their own, as Maimonides explained (*Guide* I 46). But to imagine that we properly describe God in these poetic terms is, as Rabbi Ḥaninah put it, like praising a king who had millions in gold for having silver (*Berakhot* 33b). For all these are notions from our experience.

The idea of divinity I have sketched does not limit God but only suggests his absoluteness. Attempts to preserve the traditional attributes and epithets, by contrast, do limit God, confining him within the bounds of human imagination. It will be clear, then, why the idea of God I have been suggesting cannot arise from linguistic analysis of the ordinary kind. For the usages of language are diverse, diffuse, and (understandably) often mutually contradictory, if not internally incoherent, reflecting or overstating the varied aspects of experience. Proverbs, as canons of folk experience, notoriously contradict one another. Folk wisdom is an intuitive grasp of which maxim to apply and when. But such savvy is no more help here than linguistic usage. For when folk wisdom speaks of the divine, the context, typically, is fixed by specific practical concerns. God becomes the unknown or those features of the unknown that are taken to control human destiny or fortunes. It is in this sort of notional and linguistic milieu that pagan religious sensibilities take root. But the dialectical refinement of those sensibilities leads, as I have shown, toward a critical idea of divinity. The pitting of value against value (which tact forbids in most social contexts) demands a higher integration and ultimate synthesis, achieved through the purgation of the negative.

Thus monotheism goes hand in hand with critical theology, a theology that examines the ideas it employs, and so continuously refines its concept of God, as the dynamic of the idea itself requires. By 'hand in hand' I do not mean coextensivity. Not all monotheists are philosophers, nor, certainly, are all philosophers monotheists. But every cultural setting that sustains monotheism will foster a critical philosophy of monotheism, explicit and conceptual or tacit, in the dialectic of values. The restless intellectual activity that is inseparable from the life of any culture repeatedly brings to articulate expression the demand for integration that is latent in laws, in art, in rituals, symbols, and institutions. Thus, in every culture where there is critical theology, monotheism will arise.

The evidence we have considered is not strictly ethnographic or doxographical, then. For to rely on such evidence is to cull from an ocean of material expressions that intend the divine, yielding, at best, a typology of notions, critical and uncritical. Even that would not be terribly revealing. For even in the most "primitive" societies individuals preserve the human capacity to think and speak at several levels and in diverse contexts, using categories that are to varying degrees ad hoc or of their own devising.[93]

Visiting with a traditional (not primitive!) Yemenite family in Israel some years ago, I was surprised to learn that the paterfamilias, a builder by trade, was building a bomb shelter in his then-new home. I asked if he believed his shelter would withstand an atomic shock. A Western contractor might answer, "That depends how near." My host responded with an iridescent[94] modern/ancient reply: "If that happens (God forbid!)—if they drop an atom bomb—the Holy One, blessed be he, will reach down and pluck it from the sky!" His knowledge of forces and stresses told him what his shelter could withstand. His tradition gave him a linguistic strategy to fall back on. Yet he knew that God is not a body. Such iridescence is too complex and shifting for analysis. So were the words of the same man's wife when she spoke of the loss of one of the youngest of her twelve sons in the Yom Kippur War, using the traditional formula, *Adonai Dayan Emet*—God is a truthful Judge. Her words seemed more a shield than a mirror of her intensions. Her meaning remained within her eyes and heart, unexpressed, and unalterably beyond analysis.

The texts I have drawn from the Torah, from Homer, Plato, Epicurus, Aristotle, Plotinus, Maimonides, Xenophanes, Spinoza, and others do not show that these philosophers agreed about divinity. Still less do they anatomize the idea of God in the dialogue of faith and doubt. In the iridescence of that dialogue, divinity may mean anything or nothing. Rather, these testimonies illustrate phases in the resolution of the idea of God, allowing the outlines of a process to be picked out, as from the well-stained nuclei of cells the phases of meiosis may be reconstructed, one cell in one phase, others in other phases. Here too, although there is a history, the illustrations do not reveal a process that happens only once. My paradigm cases tend to come from philosophers, for to work out conceptual dialectics is their profession. Together the philosophers who have labored toward refinement of the idea of divinity form a community of discourse. This is what Eusebius saw when he called all of Greek philosophy a *praeparatio evangelica*. A similar sense of community is voiced when Muslim and Jewish writers in Arabic call monotheist thinkers *ahlu ʾl-Ḥaqq*, adherents of the Truth, that is, God, who as the source and sum of all values is the source and sum of truth. But here community means a shared sense of goal and intent, not a common possession but a common enterprise.

Historically, Christianity was not pure monotheism but a compromise with pagan archetypes—even placing human sacrifice and the magic figure of the dying God once again at the heart of religious consciousness—although now applied to a moral and spiritual dilemma rather than to problems of pollution or fertility.[95] Hence Paul's resolve to know no philosophy but Christ, and him crucified (1 Cor. 2:2). When divinities are forged to answer pragmatic needs, both immanence and transcendence give way to the urgency of the pragmatic. But for monotheists God is not a tool, and the intellectual problems of the tradition are of no less urgency and immediacy than are the most pressing matters of praxis—nor, indeed, can the two realms be sundered.

The problems of God's transcendence are laid at the door of monotheism, with the claim that God has been sought too high—as when the ancient Israelites ordered Aaron, "Up! Make us a god that will walk before us" (Exod. 32:1)—one we can see, feel, and touch. Give us the divine in the immediacy of our experience—and keep it there. Aaron lacked the personal power to rebuke the mob and the words to expose the incoherence of their need for a manufactured god. But their own words obliquely spoke what he must have felt: "These are thy gods, O Israel, who brought thee up out of the land of Egypt" (Exod. 32:1–4). How could the people miss the ironic disparity between the transcendent power they had so recently experienced and still wished to possess, and the lump of fused gold about which they danced, cast from the amulets and charms of wives, daughters, and sons, and fashioned as a calf before their eyes? Aaron knew, if those who confronted him did not, that all their atavistic yearnings would never bring them back on the path by which they had come. Use, even urgency, would not sate them any longer, not once they had known the Universal, even glimmeringly. For what is claimed to be human (among *ḥulūlīs*), to have suffered and died (among Christians), to be nature (among Stoics) is the one and absolute Divinity, known already to be perfect and infinite, even by those who may hanker for pagan naïveté or romantically reject transcendence. Hence the nexus of paradox with mysticism, insofar as mysticism becomes a quest to contain the Absolute.

The ancient Stoics simply absorbed the contradiction, ignoring the militating of some features of their God idea against others. The *ḥulūlīs*, too, walked a tightrope of equivocations, endeavoring to speak of the Absolute in nonabsolute terms or vice versa, their incoherence obvious to their adversaries and veiled to their adherents only by the intensity of their enthusiasm. As for the Christians, it was possible politically to paper over equivocations with some measure of verbal conformity in councils and creeds. But, as Maimonides insists (*Guide* I 50), a creed is not its formulae but only the affirmation of what is understood. Thus the intuitive repugnance of Near Eastern Christians for the notion that God died on the cross or has three distinct natures expressed itself in the study of formal logic—particularly the *Categories*, whose central theme is the idea of substance and whose opening sentence exposes the fallacy of equivocation.

The logic of divinity, compromised but never denied by enthusiasts (or paradox would never yield its price), reasserts itself, by its own dynamic. Prophetic language points the direction of God's Reality but does not concretely signify his essence. Yet where usage may stray or potentially mislead, the dynamic of the idea of God restores the idea when its classic biblical *topoi* are probed. Indeed, there can be progress in our grasp of that idea (*Guide* I 59), insofar as it points toward transcendent perfection. Origen finds a kindred spirit in Philo. And the author of the *Divine Names* finds guidance in the reasonings of Plotinus and steals a march on the politicians of the councils by ascribing his work to an authority antedating and outranking theirs, Paul's Athenian convert, Dionysius the Areopagite.

God, Dionysius concludes, can only be what transcends all being and knowledge, the source of all true values. How can we reach so utterly transcendent a goal? The answer is found in the mystery of prayer. For in prayer we do not move God either physically or pathetically, since the Absolute has neither location nor emotion. Rather, we strive upward, toward perfection of our spiritual natures, as the Law exhorts us toward perfection of our moral natures,[96] in the hope that our striving and our progress, in thought and in deed, may in some way partake of the completeness of God's plan. But, whether through our efforts or those of others, the idea of God is self-righting, in the measure of the energy and intellectual penetration, and the freedom, of those who address its meaning and explore its potentialities for their thought and for their lives.

2

The Existence of God

By God we mean an absolute being, a being of infinite perfection. The synthesis that purges the idea of God of all projections of evil allows the goodness in all things to be understood in relation to God's goodness. All reality, conceived as a value, and all truth, conceived as the adequacy of things to their projects, can then be seen as God's work, expressing his will and idea. The idea of God readily conjures up folklore and mythic images, enriching, diluting, clarifying, or muddying its content. The core idea, I think, is not very far from what many myths and fables seek to convey. Thus the Midrash characteristically brackets its parables of God in an "as it were" (*ke-ve-yakhol*), focusing on a single point but barring implication to or from the contexts that familiar images might suggest—as if to say: "This sets no precedent." When visions stray from the idea of perfection, however, it is the work of imagination that must yield. For absolute perfection is the sole coherent outcome of the dialectical and moral honing of the idea of divinity. This, then, is the concept that philosophers must address, much as Abraham dismissed all deities that proved to be the mere work of human hands or were subject to diminution. Religiously, our matter must be more than a narrative or natural history of human fears and wishes.

Can We Talk About God?

Is there a being of infinite perfection? The question is natural. Children readily ask about ideas of divinity they encounter. How, after all, can they distinguish God from an imaginary friend, a figure of legend or fancy? Adult responses, whether meant affirmatively or negatively, can foster evasions or hypocrisy—cloaking, dismissing, or shifting the issue. But the question is legitimate and deserves an answer. The logical positivists, like their Pyrrhonist forebears and their many acknowledged and tacit heirs, held that no question is properly framed unless there are specifiable, unproblematic means of determining its answer. They confined such means to the realms of sense experience and mathematical-logical reasoning. Unless perception or deduction or the two in tandem can settle a question, it was taken to be no real question at all, and proposed answers were called meaningless. But an absolute being cannot be confronted as such perceptually, and deductive arguments reach certainty only by postulating their premises. So they can establish no matters of fact. Their conclusions only work out the consequences of what they assume. To positivists, therefore, it has seemed that any thoughts about God must be nonpropositional nonsense—beautiful, poetic nonsense, perhaps, useful in some contexts or dangerous in others, but nonsense nonetheless.

Let me dwell for a moment on the claim that God cannot be seen or sensed as God. For clearly God's existence is not like that of the prime number between the square of four and twice the square of three, sheerly a matter of deduction and convention. Existential deductions need existential posits, and logic, conceived as a closed formal system, makes no posits about the reality of anything—although it does, as a human activity, *presume* the existence of all sorts of things.

Our denial that God can be perceived as God seems to me central to monotheism. It lies at the heart of our rejection of all attempts to reduce God to an object of use. Biblically, such a denial is embedded at the core of God's epiphany, when he tells Moses: "Thou canst not see My face, for man shall not see Me and live" (Exod. 33:20). This is the obverse of the Self-affirmation: I AM THAT I AM. God will cause his goodness, that is, his acts, to pass before Moses. But even a prophet has no full view of God's infinitude. Moses confronts God conceptually, through the "pellucid lens" of a pure mind, as Maimonides puts it ("Eight Chapters," 7), but not perceptually, lest the very idea of absolute perfection be negated. For the sensory can be manipulated, even victimized. An object of sense is subject to appetites and passions, if it is a living being; to erosion and decay, if it is lifeless.

John Hick glosses "man shall not see My face and live" as "man shall not see My face *while living*." After death, he urges, we can enjoy the direct, perceptual proof of God's reality denied us in this life. Christian faith, he holds, is verifiable, eschatologically. He illustrates with a parable of two men "traveling together along a road".

> One of them believes that it leads to a Celestial City, the other that it leads nowhere; but since this is the only road there is, both must travel it. . . . They do not entertain different expectations about the coming details of the road, but only about its ultimate destination. And when they do turn the last corner it will be apparent that one of them has been right all the time and the other wrong. . . . Christian doctrine postulates an ultimate unambiguous state of existence *in patria* as well as our present ambiguous existence *in via*.[1]

The argument has a triumphalist, evangelical twang. But it is not as faithful to the idea of God as it should be to reach its destination. How can there be a last turning in a road that leads toward Infinity? Seeking to disentangle the epistemic claims of imagination from those of reason, Maimonides writes: "What we learn from mathematics is very much to the point. . . . it is demonstrated [by Apollonius of Perga, b. ca. 262 B.C.] in *Conic Sections* II (Theorem 13) that two lines between which there is a given distance at their point of origin may extend to infinity, the distance separating them constantly diminishing, without their ever meeting."[2]

How can a finite being transcend doubt while finite, and so conscious of itself as distinct from the objects of its awareness—or, as the Torah puts it, while alive? If, in some future state, of which the Pentateuch knows nothing, we gain certitude without loss of our individuality, how do we know that a being that makes us feel certain it is

God is rightly embraced as God? Perhaps the apparition is an imposture. If it purports to be God, surely it is an imposture. For how would a finite mind wholly know an infinite being, so as to leave no room for doubt? But if it claims only to represent God, yet convinces us of God's reality beyond it, how does such mediation differ from our present state, where the world's reality, beauty, and goodness argue for God's goodness and transcendence, but without effacing doubt?

Perhaps in glory we are relieved of our natural propensity to doubt. But loss of our critical capacities sounds more like the work of a mischievous imp or a psychoactive drug than of a benevolent Deity. And still subjective assurance is not knowledge. No matter how the critical itch is salved, the gap remains, while we live, between what we know and what we might wish to know. So it seems the Torah sums up our situation not only here but for any hereafter in which we retain conscious identity, when it says "man shall not see Me and live."

William Alston, calling numerous mystics to witness, argues that in an important sense God is perceived; human beings can directly apprehend God, comforting, strengthening, guiding, or sustaining them. Alston disavows a central interest in experiential proofs of God's existence. But he does hold, with Alvin Plantinga, that experiences of God's saving, forgiving, or imparting a message entail (or presuppose!) God's reality. So people can justifiably believe that God has been manifest to them or, as Alston prefers to phrase it, that they have perceived God.[3]

Surely, it would be curious if God is infinite yet incapable of being felt or seen. It always strikes one as a little odd that committed theists say that God is everywhere yet seem so often to place him elsewhere. But the perceptions Alston cites, however veracious they may seem subjectively, require interpretation.[4] The very directness that lays claim to epistemic primacy also opens any immediate experience to a variety of alternative accounts, as experienced mystics have always known. Even if I directly sense something *as* God, that does not entail that it *is* God. And how can a finite consciousness like mine experience God as God, if God is infinite Perfection? Echoing a classic argument of Aquinas's, Alston acknowledges that we cannot somehow engulf or literally "comprehend" God in his immensity.[5] If we humans do have immediate experience of God, then, it comes in glimpses that demand parsing and critical review, like any other intuitions—not only as to their origin but also as to their meaning. Abraham's experience is a paradigm case for us here: there is a validation of our ideas of God in the lives we lead. But it does not flash like the signal on a pinball machine. Experience is more than simple sensa or even a blinding flash. There are truths that far exceed the scope of our sensations. And if there are human intuitions that intend the Absolute as such—as I am sure there are—those intuitions are never unmediated by ideas.

Because they knew that God's infinity exceeded their grasp, the ancient Prophets, who were more than mystics, since they experienced God not merely as saving or forgiving, loving or sustaining, but as articulating a concrete message and a law of life, conveyed that message in words, often perceived as mediated by messengers or images. None knew better than they how intimately their receptivity played upon their circumstances, their moral and intellectual qualities and capacities. Yet the enormity of the intent placed their claims beyond perception—even where the message seemed most vivid and explicit. For how could any mere vision proclaim God's nature and desires or warrant a law of life? Far removed from the cheerful anthropomorphism of the Epicureans, monotheists cannot settle claims about God by appeal to sensory experience. They see that what is claimed goes far beyond what can be sensed. Does this mean it goes beyond the factual?

Broad-minded analysts know that language does many more things than declare facts. Interjections, questions, expletives, oaths, promises, curses, wishes, professions of love or hatred, commands, and prohibitions—all have places in the linguistic repertoire. Some adherents of religious traditions happily seize on such acknowledgments as a scientific imprimatur for religious discourse, as though a taxonomy were somehow a warrant of usage. But this is to confuse two rival senses of the idea of the canonical: classification may enshrine, but it does not legitimate. The Wittgensteinian welcome "This game too is played," may seem especially warm to theists after the chill reception of religious discourse by the positivists. But the welcome is halfhearted. It does not license religious discourse as a source or site of factual claims. What, then, is the real force of the admission that humans pray or swear or tell stories, if no reality is accorded the being to whom they pray, of whom the stories are told, or in whose name they swear?

Propositions that make truth claims still must have a truth value. For positivists and all who follow their account of factuality, a truth value, to be determinate, must be determinable by methods established in the usage of the natural sciences and mathematics. If God cannot pass muster by the same standards that gave us quantum physics and the H-bomb, affirmations of God's existence will still seem to positivists and their heirs to hold no factual significance. The commonplace reply that facts are not everything misses the mark and concedes too much too easily. For positivism never succeeded in validating the reality of any objects external to the mind. It did not vindicate the causal principles that are the chief achievements of the natural sciences. Nor can it sustain the seemingly more modest idea of the probable resemblance of the future to the past, or even the idea of nameable phenomena recurrent in diverse circumstances—gravity, say, or heterozygosity. The radical empiricism that positivism affords itself permits none of these. All require metaphysical assumptions of a sort that positivism excludes. And the verification criterion of meaning, which is the heart of logical positivism, is itself metaphysical, being neither a report of sense data nor a deduction from tautologies.

The bankruptcy of the positivist program shows us the necessity of returning to the more holistic ways of appraising experience, upon which the experimental method is founded and out of which arise the varieties of metaphysics whose diversities and ambiguities positivism hoped to scotch. Missing in positivist epistemology was any acknowledgment of the rational presuppositions of all thought, even those varieties of thought that positivists imagined to be wholly empirical.

The positivist dismissal of metaphysics rests on the assumption that two realms of utterances can be clearly distinguished: sentences testable perceptually and others that are demonstrable within some deductive system. Thus the dismissal of God's existence as unverifiable rests on the assumption of a realm of "common sense," that is, of sense perception and simple reasoning, where verification is possible. Otherwise, why single out any propositions invidiously as metaphysical? But the fabled land of common sense fades rapidly under critical scrutiny. Sense perception cannot establish the reality of any object independent of personal consciousness—neither bodies[6] nor other minds[7] nor even, if kept strictly to sensations, the substantial self. This is not just a matter of uncertainty or weak evidence. Without a metaphysics to link sensory phenomena to an extramental reality, there is no evidence whatever to count for or against the existence of anything beyond a single consciousness, let alone to warrant treating that consciousness entitatively. Its seeming memories and anticipations, with their apparent reference to the past or future, are indistinguishable from illusions. And probability is no viable substitute for certainty, since metaphysical assumptions are as necessary to probabilistic inferences from empirical data as they are to claims that certainties are learned from it.

Phenomenalists, especially since Hume's time, have busied themselves with redefining bodies, minds, causes, and other extramental entities as figments of consciousness (one cannot say mine, since solipsism is surpassed in pure phenomenalism, my self dissolving with all others on the Humean grounds that I do not perceive it in the way I seem to perceive sensory objects). But all this redefinition, designed at least nominally to save some favored class of objects and bring them into the light and dry, in a reconstructed version of the sciences, achieves nothing for external realities. They remain at large, unverified and (by these narrow means) unverifiable. No evidence counts for or against them. For no matter how high the subjective data are piled, like checks drawn on an empty account, they will never add up to a single fact about the world beyond the mind. The dismissal of inquiry about God's existence on the grounds of unverifiability, then, is specious. For the "commonsense" realm of perceptible things, with which beliefs about God are contrasted, is a fabrication for which, when verificationism is applied consistently, a phenomenal realm is substituted.

Some philosophers believe that phenomenalistic discourse is impossible to sustain, since language presupposes a community, or the reality of external things. This line of argument has a magical aura about it, as though the combination of wish and need could assure us that what we wish for is (lo and behold!) already ours. Presumptions, however, are not self-warranting. So our presuming a thing lays no solid groundwork for ontology. We cannot infer the reality of other minds or any other transcendental things from the presumptions of our language or our thought. For our thought might be mistaken, our language, misguided.[8] Phenomenalists from Sextus to Russell, Ayer and Philipp Frank show how a comprehensive transformation system can be devised to exchange statements that signify a transcendental correlate for others that do not. Ordinary language, in such a scheme, is regarded (once its inevitable confusions are dissolved) as a convenient system of idioms or useful fictions—causality, external objects, the entitative self—that are perfectly permissible, if the means of their unpacking into phenomenal components are kept ready at hand. Every transcendental judgment is prefixed, in effect, by a formal reservation: "as if," or "seemingly"—paralleled and parodied by the Beat generation's habit of prefacing all judgments by the word "like." Such devices can, in principle, purge the transcendental presumptions of language.

Yet the material terms and formal relations of the new language preserve a notional reference to entities no longer deemed real. Such linguistic souvenirs hint at the weakness of the phenomenal reduction. For where it is most complete and systematic it becomes dubious which is the fiction, our entitative assumptions or the notion that these have been replaced or rendered otiose. The problem is not with the power of translation rules to replace all entitative, causal, or otherwise transcendental statements with phenomenal counterparts but lies, rather, in the constant reliance on unreduced notions from the "precritical" levels of discourse. For the material terms and formal structures that give differentiated content to a phenomenal language are systematically parasitic on the "naive" language. Necessarily so, if the formal correspondence of analysans to analysandum is to be maintained (rather than the analysis degenerating into an unstructured and undifferentiated mass). So it becomes questionable whether anything has been eliminated at all of what was deemed epistemically problematic. The basic categories of experience—substance, quality, cause, things, mind—reassert their vitality and resist reduction.

Should phenomenalists make the further step of trying to differentiate normatively among appearances or opinions, customs, practices, or games, the reduction of problematic realities to unquestionable appearances becomes actively unhelpful. Here phenomenalists face a dilemma: to place all subjective givens on a par allows no distinction in principle, say, between scientific method, racial prejudice, and the rankest superstition. But the alternative is to reenter the realm of critical distinction making, where the idea of differentiating appearances from reality continues at work. Then all the problems of critical epistemology recur, explicitly or in surrogate debates about which sorts of appearances, practices, customs, and conventions can be taken seriously. For this reason I believe that phenomenalism cannot succeed in resolving the content of human knowledge to an unproblematic domain of appearances. Wholesale consignment of experience to the realm of the subjective solves the problem of transcending subjectivity only by conceding that subjectivity is not to be transcended; and in reducing objective to subjective claims it short-circuits the demand for critical distinctions among appearances, which was the heart of its original claim to epistemic rigor.[9]

Verificationism, then, offers no epistemic distinction between statements about God and other statements about the reality or character of extramental beings. Subjective judgments or internal states alone never warrant judgments about external reality. So the idea that talk about God is nonsense, for want of such clear perceptual standards as we use in verifying ordinary claims of fact, falls to the ground. Verificationism strictly applied allows no factual claims, unless they are reduced to sense data and robbed of all transcendental import. A strictly sensuous empiricism preserves statements of fact only as subjective appearances, that is, only at the cost of a Protagorean equation of truth with seeming. So long as the distinction between reality and appearance is preserved, there will be no distinction in point of sensory verification between assertions of God's existence and those of any other transcendental objects such as bodies, causes, others' selves, or our own.

Even allowing a phenomenalist reduction, however, sensory verification of quite ordinary judgments remains problematic. For now it consists in specifying the sensory phenomena for which a speciously objective judgment stands as surrogate. How, then, will verification verify? The naive judgment 'I see a cow' is naively verified by appropriate appearances. But, on a phenomenalist analysis, that judgment has no external reference but cites the same appearances. Its verification, then, amounts to repetition of what is now an identical judgment.

Pragmatism often seeks to remedy the situation with promissory notes, proferring additional subjective apprehensions in support of the initial ones that gave us the impression that we saw a cow. But when pragmatism drinks at the well of phenomenalism, it does not propose simply that these added apprehensions confirm the presence of a cow but that they, along with all the others that seem relevant, are all that we can or should *mean* by 'I see a cow.' The argument is rather like Berkeley's: if all we know of a cow is what can be sensed of it, then to be sensed is what it is to be a cow; if the cash value of the claim that we really see a cow is that we can feel as though we were milking it and drinking its milk, then such experiences are, or should be, what we mean by saying that a cow is what we see. This is substitution, not verification. It differs from other forms of phenomenalism only in a greater sensitivity to the affective side of confirmation, enriching the idea of verification with that of gratification.[10] But virtual reality machines are already subtle enough to make the untenability of this equation of subjective confirmation with objective existence demonstrable in practice, not just intuitively obvious—as it has been at least since the time of Descartes.

The same critique applies pointedly to operationalism. For it, too, is committed to a category error. To identify the meaning of a proposition with its means of verification is to equate propositions with procedures. As Dallas Willard writes of Schlick and Carnap:

> For all their talk about verification of sentences, one will search their writings in vain for any thorough account of *how* a sentence, being the physicalistic entity which it admittedly is, could be verified by the experiences of one or more individuals, or of what it would be for such a verification to occur. Blindness to the very scope and difficulty of the problems on this point is a sure sign of a *myth* in action: the "Myth of the Sentence," as one might call it. Reflection would at least force us to distinguish the sentence *token* (non-repeatable thing or event) from the *type*. . . . And then "the" sentence, as well as the experience thereof, must somehow be set into a clarified relationship to the relevant objects or facts, concrete or abstract, which the sentence is about. But there simply is no serious attempt to discuss these issues in writers such as Schlick or Carnap. It is not here a case of a mistaken view, but of there being no view at all.[11]

The point here hinges on the positivist reduction of sentences to objects that have no acknowledged status as signs or units of meaning. How can an object that intends nothing and is intended by no one be verified by anything?

Positivism, then, provides no adequate account of the verification of any judgment about the external world. This does not mean that the notion of a fact is discredited or that efforts to find critical grounding for proposed beliefs are misguided. It does mean that verification by reduction to sense data is an unworkable and ill-conceived project. Dismissal, then, of the question of God's existence on the grounds that proposed answers do not conform to the "usual" standards of verification through the senses fails. For no objective judgments are possible by the criteria that positivists traditionally proposed and that their heirs still cling to.

Turning to the analytic, it must be noted from the outset that the distinction of analytic or formal truths from factual or material ones is not absolute but contextual.[12] Any consistent set of postulates, whether or not they relate to nature or experience, may be posited as givens. Within the system they mark out, all valid deductions can be treated as analytic in the sense that their denial will generate a contradiction. Whether there can be a *purely* formal system, as mathematics is often thought to be, seems doubtful to me. In any system thought by human beings, such purity is clearly impossible, since all human thought is discursive and thus time-bound, inextricably bound up with at least some of the material conditions of our existence. Thus, in an important sense all our judgments are synthetic: all involve time and the movement of the mind from subject to predicate or, as in mathematics, from one term to another of a relation. Descartes's *Meditations* calls attention to this fact dramatically by reminding us that mathematical judgments are not exempt from error. Misapprehension and misdirection, taking up one term in place of another, systematic delusion, as well as the problem of undetectable deception by an omnipotent trickster illustrate the difficulties. At the heart of these problems lies lapse of memory. Slippage is possible wherever there is movement. Whenever thought moves, it may always mistake its object. Thus Descartes chose intuitions (self-consciousness, the idea of Perfection, geometric extension) rather than arguments as the elements of a reconstructed knowledge.[13] Plato voiced a parallel insight when he treated the roots of knowledge as rational intuitions and called natural science "a likely story" (*Timaeus* 29d).[14] As soon as knowledge entrusts itself to human understanding it becomes synthetic. For the mind must piece together, or, as Aristotle put it, "interweave," one notion with another. It may make sound or faulty combinations, but in so doing it is never immune to error.

Since there is no analysis without some prior synthesis, Kant could take as a paradigm case of his thesis that mathematical judgments are synthetic, Plato's '5 + 7 = 12', a proposition typically seen as analytic. Kant knew well enough that inferences in a closed system are formal rather than material. But he assayed such systems not by the connections they make once under way but by the materials they need to get started.[15] Mathematics must posit a kind of surrogate of matter, the discrete quantities of arithmetic or the continuous quantity of geometry, derived by abstraction, Kant thought, from the a priori conditions of inner and outer sense—time and space. The real existence of time and space is immaterial to arithmetic and geometry. But their natures are not. Space, in Euclidean geometry, for example, must be such that parallel lines never meet; the familiar number line allows no passage from 3 to 5 except by way of 4. The positing of such natures is not a demand of logic, as we learn from non-Euclidean geometries and quantum physics.[16] Rather, the relevant assumptions are free postulates from the realm of logically possible systems. And one need not, of course, posit quantities of any sort.

Relying on the subject-predicate format and Leibniz's account of analyticity, by which a proposition is analytic if the concept of its predicate is implicit in that of its subject, Kant argued that 12 goes beyond the givens: addition, 5, and 7. Givenness here is a mental event: if we strictly limit what we mean by the givens, '5', '+', '7', and '=' tell us nothing of 12. Imagining a somewhat self-caricaturing Leibnizian deductivist, Kant wrote:

> Suppose a philosopher be given the concept of a triangle and he be left to find out, in his own way, what relation the sum of its angles bears to a right angle. He has nothing but the concept of a figure enclosed by three straight lines, and possessing three angles. However long he meditates on this concept, he will never produce anything new. He can analyze and clarify the concept of a straight line or of an angle or of the number three, but he can never arrive at any property not already contained in these concepts.

Geometers readily demonstrate that the three angles equal two right angles, but the construction used in doing so is synthetic, not analytic: it yields new knowledge, in part because it brings new posits not supplied in the given, using a "chain of inferences guided throughout by intuition."[17] Indeed, the "new posits" needed include the parallels postulate, which the consistency of non-Euclidean geometries clearly reveals to be no demand of logic.

Ayer argued that Kant erred in offering a psychological rationale for the syntheticity of mathematical judgments, since their analyticity can be shown on logical grounds. For to deny '7 + 5 = 12' rapidly breeds contradictions[18]—but only if the idea of 12 is given. Ayer urges that "a proposition is analytic when its validity depends solely on the definitions of the symbols it contains." That stipulation seems unexceptionable if 'definition' is construed broadly, so as to include all the rules and principles that underwrite a formal system. But so broad a construal imports synthetic postulates; the deduction now is not founded solely and simply on the law of contradiction. If key concepts are unavailable, the professed analyticity evaporates.

In a universe where 7 and 5 have never been conjoined, 12 will be a new creation—the first dozen. The addends, we can say, in psychological terms, gave no hint of it. To the child who knows nothing of multiplication, the question whether this sum has factors or is prime is meaningless, as opaque as any question about the rainfall in New Guinea or the high-water mark of the Nile at Aswan. Contrary to Russell's hopes, arithmetic cannot be derived from sheer logic. The Peano Axioms (postulates, in fact) do allow its derivation from set theory, but they themselves are synthetic vis-à-vis logic. For logic per se says nothing of quantities or counting.

Consider a budget-model calculator, with just one decimal column for formulating and displaying sums. Its memory holds the digits 0 through 9, and it can generate numerals for their display. But neither memory nor display accommodates 10 or any higher number. The machine can add. But it has no 12; speaking psychologically, no notion of 12. Now enter 5, add 7. No 12 appears. The display may flash 9 or 0 or 1, or 2, or E for error, depending on the default mechanism, but there simply is no 12. The judgment '5 + 7 = 12' is synthetic in that conceptually 12 goes beyond just 5 + 7. This is obvious when we consider that 12 is also 6 + 6 and 72 ÷ 6, and so ad infinitum. 'Twelve' does not single out any one of these, without some counsel and direction—any more than it refers uniquely to the age of a particular child or singles out one sign of the zodiac as the twelfth. Why should we call 5 + 7 twelve, rather than the square root of 144, unless contextual cues are guiding us to the sort of answer that is looked for? Or are we to say that the concepts '144' and 'square root' are already presupposed in that of 12—and so for all the higher powers, so that to teach a child to count to 12 is to teach her all these powers and roots as well?

Terms like '6 + 6' or '72 ÷ 6' speak not a word of 12, except to an informed (and oriented) mind. When I think of 5 and 7 and adding, I may have no thought of 12, just as a small child has no notion of it. Why is that relevant? Not because a child is the test of innocence, but because the child will posit only what she knows or discovers. An adult may know that a circle's circumference has a fixed ratio to the diameter, yet not know whether π is greater or less than 3—still less how to calculate its value accurately. And not one of us knows its value exactly, even though the procedures for computing it are formal, not empirical, in every essential respect.

Thrasymachus warns us not to trust too much to childish illustrations. So let me make my point without citing budget-model calculators or the thoughts of children. In June 1993 Andrew Wiles announced a proof of Fermat's last theorem, first stated in 1630. Wiles's two-hundred-page proof took seven years of steady effort to devise, building on numerous prior efforts and continuing for another year and more of intensive labor after Wiles's first version of the proof was revealed. Until early 1995 it was not yet clear whether the proof was sound, but it was very clear that it was not strictly analytic: no mere analysis of '$x^n + y^n = z^n$' sufficed to show that the equation has no positive integer solutions where *n* exceeds 2. Whole new areas of the mathematics of elliptical curves had to be developed to afford the concepts in which Wiles could think through his argument. None of that theory was present in Fermat's seemingly simple claim that "it is impossible to separate a cube into two cubes, or a fourth power into two fourth powers or, in general, any power greater than the second into powers of like degree." If Fermat indeed saw arithmetic relationships that led him to think he could prove this "by a truly marvelous demonstration," which the margin of his copy of Diophantus's *Arithmetic* was "too narrow to contain," evidently those relations slipped away from him. And if they were too subtle for others to see in three and a half centuries of dedicated searching, they must have invoked properties that do not lie just beneath the surface.

Kenneth Ribet and Brian Hayes explain the basis of Wiles's argument:

> Suppose there is a counterexample to Fermat's last theorem, or in other words a pair of integers a^n and b^n whose sum is also a perfect *n*th power. Then there must exist a mathematical curve specified by an equation whose coefficients are determined by a^n and b^n. Call the elliptic curve *E*. One of us (Ribet) proved in 1986 that the curve *E* cannot have a certain property called modularity. What Wiles announced last June is that all elliptic curves in a class that includes *E* are modular. From this contradiction it follows that *E* cannot exist, and neither can the supposed counterexample to Fermat's last theorem.[19]

The reference to a contradiction shows what is analytic here. But what is synthetic is also clear. For only hindsight could reveal the relevance of conceptualizing the proposed countercase in terms of a specific category of curves. We see here, clearly, why there is no analysis without synthesis: there are no mere or sheer concepts but only the conception of A as ϕ, or ψ, and so forth. This Husserlian home truth about intensionality is sufficient to uncoil the pretensions of analytic philosophy about what might be called absolute analysis: if the knowledge we pursue is to be a form of thought, we will need some Fregean way of distinguishing sense from reference and some Peircean way of distinguishing type from token. For our judgments are never about A and B *tout court* but always about A taken or conceptualized as ϕ, and B as ψ. But distinctions of sense from reference or type from token are intensional. They presume some finite mind with specifiable interests and concerns. It is minds that synthesize one notion with another or distinguish one from another. One could never reach 12, or any other answer to a question, without some context of relations, intentions, and conventions by which a desired category of answer might be specified.

Thus Ayer himself falls back on psychological idioms when he speaks of synonymy and symbols. He even appeals to the notion of a perfect intelligence, in an effort to warrant the distinction between numbers (or concepts) as they are and as they are humanly thought of.[20] The reversion to psychology is natural—although a perfect mind does not think discursively. For synonymy is identity of meaning, symbols are bearers of meaning, and meanings exist only for minds. But the syntheticity of mathematical judgments need not be put solely in psychological terms. In a universe where '12' has no application, there is no sum of 7 and 5. Concretely, in the world of multiaxle trucks, four 18-wheelers do not a 72-wheeler make, no matter what the times tables say. This is not because no one has thought of such a truck, nor even because it cannot be built, but simply because the universe addressed contains no referent for the notion. We learn this not from the law of contradiction nor from any canon of discourse, save that of multiaxle truck talk, where '72-wheeler' denotes not a contradiction but a null set.

This week my neighborhood supermarket is selling twelve-packs of Diet Pepsi for $2.99 and cases of twenty-four for $6.99. Has some principle of arithmetic been violated? Are these prices irrational? I can report that there was no visible effect on other prices, as might be expected if mathematical judgments are tautologies and the violation of one generates incoherence everywhere. The price policy will seem irrational only to those who have no interest in clearing the market's aisles and storerooms of a glut of twelve-packs. So much for the notion that arithmetic, at least when applied to soda pop, is topic neutral.

All judgments, then, are synthetic, including those that we treat as analytic in specific contexts, invoking specific systems of postulates or frameworks of assumptions.[21] This is obvious from the form of judgment, which is complex and involves a linking of terms. In some way every predicate must go beyond its subject, if only to be predicated of it. Relational propositions require a synthesis of elements just as much as attributions do. Even identity statements offer more in the "predicate" or complement than is given in the idea of the subject. For the mental or linguistic act that affirms identity links one term with another, or even with itself again, but now repeated and so altered intensionally, given a new syntactical role, as it must be if it is to complement the subject and complete the judgment, rather than simply repeating itself or starting another sentence.

But if all judgments, as compounds or complexes, are synthetic (even those we call analytic, in that their subjects imply their predicates, given sufficient postulates, definitions, conventions, and exclusions), we must heed the medieval thesis that all combinations are contingent. This subject need not have been given, or this predicate applied. Even identities are contingent, as we learn from the reality of change, birth, evolution, and decay. Change can be an ally or an enemy of life, but it has never been a friend to logic, least of all the logic of fixed identity. Judgment is possible, as Kant saw, only through synthesis of the manifold of phenomena in time, which otherwise would annul the unity of consciousness, where terms are brought together. If synthetic always, judgment is fallible always. Thus Quine's thesis in "Two Dogmas of Empiricism": we have no basis for placing analytic sentences at an absolute remove from all the rest. For in some circumstances even the most sacrosanct and seemingly self-evident might be called into question, revised, or discarded.[22] The point I take from this—stating my own conclusions, not Quine's—is not that the laws of logic are at risk of overthrow but that what we may take for laws of logic can prove to need qualification, reformulation, or refinement. Quine treats only sentences, not propositions. So the truths aimed for by our essays at designing formal logics might remain above the fray—but only at the price of inarticulacy. The logic that can be spoken, we might say, is not the real logic. Indeed, the very claim to irrevisability contributes to the vulnerability of our attempts to frame logical rules. For if a proposition we have taken to be incorrigible proves inadequate, our response, predictably, is not to say that logic no longer holds but to seek some new formulation, more perspicuous or more limited, some rule or schema that will better hold the high ground assigned to logic, or some specific corner of it.

I emphasize the synthetic side of the judgments we find it convenient or appropriate to treat as analytic not because I want to blur the distinction between reason and experience. I think it is mistaken to draw radical empiricist morals from the argument of "Two Dogmas." What Quine argues there is not that logic is an empirical science but that the familiar analyses of analyticity are circular. The moral I draw is that inference is context-dependent. Logics are not self-contained fortresses of rigor but constitutive systems of norms about inference, designed to canonize specific types of reasoning. They gain purity and precision in one vicinity, typically at the price of imprecision or even paradox in another. Quine's own empiricist dogma, the half-hearted concession that logical statements are themselves corrigible, does not follow from the difficulties he raises about defining analyticity. Indeed, Quine still privileges certain sentences and puts them closer to the bone or midrib of inflexibility in his epistemic mesh, even after losing the test by which to segregate them. Thus he preserves the analytic-synthetic distinction, even as he disavows it.

My inclination is to say that the same sentence may be read analytically or synthetically in different contexts. The distinction is conventional—thus, intensional. But there is no need to discard analyticity. When the relevant assumptions are made and the relevant conventions invoked, some inferences spring more from the form than from the content of an argument. Thus some elements of our knowledge will be a priori, despite Quine's discomfort. But it is not my aim here to show that our knowledge contains a priori elements, or that these extend beyond the analytic. The first, I think, was shown by Plato and Leibniz; the second, by Hume and Kant, when they made clear that notions like causality, permanence, and necessity cannot be vindicated by empiric means alone, yet are indispensable to understanding. I stress the synthetic character of all judgments and the synthetic side of those we treat as analytic only to show the inadequacy of the reductive account of analyticity.

I doubt that any truths are known solely by reduction to tautologies or derived solely from the law of contradiction. If we want to show that *p* is true by revealing that not-*p* is a contradiction, to begin with we must know what we have in hand, that '*p*' affirms a genuine proposition, asserting a univocal state of affairs at a single moment. That is a good deal more than the law of contradiction tells us. Then, to reduce *p* to a tautology (or its contradictory to a contradiction), we strip away all distinctive reference and put *p* through a series of transformations, leaving quite a different proposition in the end—which is not to say that deduction is empty but that more goes into it than form alone reveals. The law of contradiction gives not the slightest hint to a young theorem starting out in life which way to turn. Being topic neutral, as it should be, it does not designate even a subject matter, let alone project a set of axioms or postulates. Yet it is from the various possible subject matters, the material relations of various classes and characters of things, that logical schematizations derive all their force. For how can we use the law of the excluded middle if we do not know which predicates are jointly exhaustive or mutually exclusive? And how can we invoke a premise to begin our reductio if we do not know what other propositions are relevant to the truth of *p*?

To proceed from a tautology or a set of tautologies to an axiom (if this can be done) involves a synthesis, typified by the postulation of quantities in mathematics. There is a further synthesis when we proceed from axioms to theorems. Even an identity statement, we have argued, is synthetic, since it avows a relation of identity and does not just stand pat with the given. The tautology 'A is A', viewed as a judgment (and not as an eternal object descended from the Aeon without somehow losing its timelessness) becomes a thought. But even if we grant that identities, tautologies in the strict sense, are indivisible truths, and forget their synthetic logical structure and psychological nature, the derivation of more complex judgments from them still requires the erection of an axiom system rich enough to permit judgments of greater complexity. With each step, equivalency to the given is left further behind. Any identification or predication has subjectivity and process among its elements. And, as the elaboration proceeds, the contingency introduced by the fact that the whole is a system of ideas, apprehended if not created by human intelligence, increases. So verification by reduction to identity is a chimera, for it omits the role of thought in creating and reflecting on a system of ideas. And the claim of analytically inclined philosophers that all of mathematics, taken as a paradigm of human reasoning, is a single vast tautology rests on inadequate analysis.

The deductive wing of the verificationist program is damaged further by Gödel's proof that in any consistent formal system powerful enough to allow the generation of a number theory there are formulas that are true, yet not demonstrable by deduction from its axioms.[23] Regardless how an axiom set is constituted, some (true) proposition, formulated in its terms, will inevitably remain undecidable by deductive recourse to those axioms.

Ayer seeks to deaden the impact of Gödel's findings by arguing that mathematical and logical systems need not reduce theorems to axioms but can treat all truths on a par.[24] But this blurs the distinction between theorems and axioms without profit. For it does not eliminate what Gödel showed: that there is a sense to 'truth' in at least some cases where reductive verification is impossible. Yet Ayer's unyielding grip on the claims that all a priori propositions are analytic and all analytic propositions tautologies relies for its very intelligibility on the reductive procedures that Gödel's proof renders less than universal. For what does it mean to say that all analytic statements are tautologies if it does not mean that in principle they reduce to tautologies? Yet that is what Gödel showed to be false.

Gödel's work does not cast mathematics to the ground in a heap, prove deduction impossible or the deductive method fruitless. It does not even mean that Gödel's formally undecidable propositions are absolutely undecidable. The propositions Gödel specified are *informally* decidable. But Gödel's proof does show the inadequacy of verification by reduction to axioms, upon which positivist ideas of analysis were founded. There is more going on in quite basic systems of arithmetic than logic alone can generate.

Because all judgments are synthetic, and because not all mathematical judgments are reducible to the axioms on which they are drawn (or demonstrable by discovering a contradiction in their denial), the second wing of the positivist idea of verification falls like the first. Strictly empirical verification is possible only if the facts to be verified are reduced to the very sensa that are to verify them, trivializing verification. Mathematical verification turns out to be possible in the sense the positivists required only if it is assumed that we have access to a realm where true theorems are equivalent to axioms; and axioms, to tautologies. The synthesis that makes an axiom system or a mathematical domain at all richer than a single tautology falls out of sight, and the material categories that might guide the free elaboration of the richer system are swept away—unless the formalist dogma is given up and rationality is allowed a role beyond mechanical computation. But even if reduction is made the mold and model of mathematical and logical reasoning, even if the syntheticity of identity is forgotten and the synthetic and creative work of mathematics is ignored, Gödel shows that the reduction of the a priori to the more obviously analytic is still not possible in every case.

The question, then, of whether God exists is no different from other questions in point of verification as positivistically understood. For none of our beliefs about the world are verifiable or refutable, confirmable or disconfirmable (since what has no bearing can neither add weight nor subtract it) by appeal to sensations alone. And no theorem of mathematics can be constructed without moving conceptually beyond what is given by its supposed elements or foundations. Since strictly sensuous verification is never an option for any empiric claim, and analysis can never enrich itself by spinning tautologies into the gold of discovery, there is no epistemic basis for singling out inquiries about God as preternaturally problematic. For the limitations lie in our understanding, not in the uniqueness of the Divine. It has not been shown that value judgments are intrinsically more problematic than judgments of fact, or that the inference to a first cause or highest being is more difficult in kind than the inference to other minds.

All the means we use in assaying our experience, then, remain as open to us in inquiring into the existence of God as they are with any other question. We may still comb the ideas of goodness, being, and necessity for what they can tell us about ultimate reality, and examine nature, history, and the moral order to see if life, or being at large, or the nature of right, or human freedom affords any insight into the reality of God. We can ask such questions without worry that their transcendental scope makes them epistemologically strange. For there is nothing stranger about the idea of perfection than about the idea of totality that we use in speaking of necessity or probability, and the inquiries that teach us that $f = ma$ or that gravity is "lawlike" carry us far beyond the bare empiric given. We return, then, to the existence of God.

Is God's Existence Impossible?

The very concept of God, as it emerges from the crucible of philosophical dialectic, suggests a being that cannot fail to exist. The idea of such necessary existence has been variously grasped or glimpsed for centuries. Hume showed clearly that no existence can be established wholly a priori. But by now it should seem doubtful whether any proof is ever wholly a priori. There does seem to be a sense in which God's existence is self-validating—not self-evident but clear to anyone who holds the idea of God in mind. For how can the All-inclusive lack reality? The argument is not that whatever is must be. For we know that many things need not exist. But Infinity must be real—not the abstract infinity of mathematics but the concrete Infinity of pure Goodness or Perfection. The Infinite does not negate itself. It does not withhold its own expression, and there is nothing beyond to debar its reality. I touched on this thought in chapter 1, when I mentioned Plato's view that what is most perfect must be real and the Torah's corresponding view that what is most real must be most perfect.

Clearly, a formal demonstration, if it preserves its purity, can only elucidate what has been presumed. But does that make the ontological argument unsound? Or is there sense to be gotten from the monotheistic I AM THAT I AM? Kant challenges the Mosaic idea by his reflections on the fact that the God of monotheism is no ordinary being. For, if God's perfection is infinite, only a proof that is at least in part a priori will do; no mere experience captures the Absolute as such. But can a proof that is in any measure a priori yield more than an ideal? What we must ask, then, is (1) Did the ontological argument seek to answer those who wonder whether or not God exists? and (2) Does experience give us no grounds to affirm the reality of the Infinite? I will answer that Hume shows that if we do not presume that God exists, no ontological argument can prove it. He does not find an inconsistency in the argument. If the idea of God entails existence, the inference from it of God's existence is as true as any truism. For just as no deduction yields conclusions stronger than its premises, none need yield conclusions less strong. What Kant shows, for his part, is not that God is a mere notion but that we encounter the God of monotheism by way of an idea.

1. It may seem odd for anyone to argue for God's existence from premises that assume it. But if the aim is not to show that God exists to those who did not know it (at least implicitly), no questions are begged. The two most famous statements of the ontological argument seem to intend something along those lines. Anselm describes his argument as a reflex of God's self-sufficiency: "I began to ask myself whether there might be found a single argument which would require no other for its proof than itself alone; and alone would suffice to demonstrate that God truly exists, and that there is a supreme good requiring nothing else, which all other beings require for their existence and well-being."[25] The point was not to prove God's existence to those who doubted it but to show that that existence follows from God's perfection.

Responding to Gaunilon of Marmoutier, the monk who took the part of the fool who "saith in his heart there is no God," Anselm appealed to shared spiritual experience. This was no mere ad hominem. Anselm hoped that meditation had opened up an understanding of God's perfection in a sense that could not exclude existence or allow it to be problematized.[26] He did not set his case before one who had no idea of God. Indeed, in first stating his argument he sought dialectical leverage in the fact that even the fool of the Psalms must have some idea of God, or he would not know what he was denying. The springboard of the argument was the attempt to inform the fool's idea, displacing the specious notion of a problematic being with that of a being than which none greater can be conceived.

Eadmer, Anselm's follower and biographer, described the purposes of the *Monologion* and *Proslogion* as follows:

> Putting aside all authority of Holy Scripture, he inquired and discovered by reason alone what God is; and he proved by invincible reasoning that God's nature is what true faith holds it to be, and moreover that it could not be other than it is. Then it came into his mind to try to prove by one single and short argument the things which are believed and preached about God—that He is eternal, unchangeable, omnipotent, omnipresent, incomprehensible, just, merciful, righteous, true, as well as Truth, Goodness, Justice and so on; and to show how all these qualities are united in Him.

Anxiety over the progress of the second work robbed Anselm of sleep and appetite and distracted him even from his prayers, as he pursued his elusive line of thought, until "suddenly, one night during Matins, the grace of God shone on his heart, the whole matter became clear to his mind, and a great joy and jubilation filled his inmost being."[27]

The *Proslogion*, with its startling new argument, as Robert Southern writes, "came out of that moment of 'joy and jubilation' at Matins probably in 1077. It is especially important to notice the reason for his joy. He had already, in his *Monologion*, succeeded in showing that God necessarily had all those qualities that are ascribed to Him in Christian doctrine. But he had not shown that all of them are necessarily united in the being of God. . . . This is what he aimed at in doing his *Proslogion*."[28] The goal was not to prove that God exists. This Anselm had already done at the start of the *Monologion*, arguing a posteriori, from God's role as Creator of all that is and Author of all that is good.[29] Thus, he frames the Ontological Argument, as David Novak stresses,[30] not as a proof but as a prayer: "May Thou who givest understanding to faith give me, so far as Thou knowest it to be profitable, to understand that Thou art as we believe. And indeed we believe that Thou art a being than which none greater can be conceived." Anselm assumes God's reality and addresses him but hopes now to show that God's perfection entails and unites all perfections, existence included. Similarly with Descartes.

Close readers of the *Meditations* may wonder why Descartes offers to prove God's existence twice. His argument in the Third Meditation is cosmological and largely a posteriori: the idea of perfection in his mind is an effect whose cause must be adequate, formally or eminently, to the idea it produces. The cause, then, must be Perfection itself. We can see the force of the argument from a pale analogy: if I meet someone who has an idea of a Buick, I may justifiably conclude that this person either has seen a Buick or is capable of inventing one.

In the context of still-unrelieved methodical doubt, Descartes's reflections, expressed as an argument that assumes causality and the precedence of perfection to privation, and of actual to notional existence, must be taken as an immediate intuition, leaving room for no deception. The intuition: that the idea of perfection is itself an expression of pure Perfection. Here too, then, there is an intellectual appeal to spiritual experience. A priori principles like the axiom that a cause must be adequate to its effect are supplemented a posteriori. Why, then, the second proof of God's existence, in the Fifth Meditation? The aim, I think, is not to prove God's existence again[31] but to establish its necessity. This, as Spinoza remarked, was of the highest moment.[32] For necessary existence implies unity and absolute simplicity, uniqueness, ineffability, and transcendence of all human notions—the core theses of negative theology. Descartes is characteristically oblique about his intentions, precisely because the idea introduced is ontic necessity. For the natural theology he founds on that idea is rather minimalist for the tastes of his contemporaries. But all that he is prepared to say of God follows from the idea of a necessary Being; and that, from the idea of absolute perfection. Thus the placement of the argument. It is not used to prove God exists. It takes that for granted. But it secures what Descartes thinks philosophy can establish about God's nature.

2. Neither Anselm nor Descartes, then, presents the ontological proof to show that God exists to those who doubt it. Both men use the argument to explore the idea of God and the concept of necessary existence. So the apriorism Hume rejects is found in neither. Yet the same defenses that protect Anselm and Descartes from Hume's charge of a petitio heighten the seriousness of Kant's charges. Kant, like Hume, objected to any claims to formal demonstration of a fact—understandably, given his project of teasing out the epistemic contributions of reason and the senses. Existence, he argues, must be known empirically, but necessity is an a priori category, found only in formal reasoning. So the idea of a necessary being is incoherent, no argument dependent on that idea is sound, and natural theology is ruined. For there is no viable concept of God other than as a being of absolute perfection, and that implies necessary existence.

Kant well understood the aims and assumptions of natural theology. His attack is all the subtler for that reason. It is not a modest reversion through skepticism to brute faith but a very Christian and scriptural reversion to morality as the basis of theology, once the idea of a necessary Being has been undermined. Christian, because Christianity always feared that the God of Abraham was too high for the children of Adam to reach; scriptural, because morality, along with cosmic wonder, is, as we have seen, an authentic foundation of biblical theology. So Kant knew where to aim. But is the idea of a necessary Being incoherent? J. N. Findlay drew that conclusion years ago in what he called an ontological disproof of God's existence.[33] By God, he wrote, is meant a being that cannot not exist. But all existential propositions are synthetic, all are contingent, so none are necessary. There can be, then, no necessary Being. Only analytic propositions can be necessary, and these can never assert existence. The argument, like Kant's, rests on Hume's dichotomy of matters of fact and relations of ideas. Relations of ideas can be dealt with only hypothetico-deductively and so can make no categorical claims about reality. Matters of fact must be judged by experience; they are not given as parts of some deductive system and so can involve no certainty of the mathematical sort—thus no necessity. A necessary Being, then, is a spurious hybrid. Existence must be contingent. To call God a necessary being makes him both necessary and nonnecessary, a square circle.

But how do we know that all being is contingent? Does experience show it? Experience varies. Our judgments are synthetic—thus their fallibility, as I have argued. But it is not reality that is fallible. Experience does not give us all of being—unless we arbitrarily equate being with seeming—and not just with seeming to anyone. For we have no idea what may seem to anyone, but only what seems to ourselves. Only in solipsism, then, are we assured that the contingency we experience is the truth about reality. And even then we have no assurance that contingency is necessary or persistent.

That things might conceivably have been other than they are is a fact about our thinking. It does not prove that all things are contingent absolutely. The possibility of science (and of any ordered system, like those of nature or of life) presumes some limitation on contingency. Further, contingency is as much a modality as necessity, and no more visible to the senses than necessity or probability. Even facticity is not a sensum. Hence the distinction between being and seeming. The claim that all existence is contingent, then, is a metaphysical projection. The offense is only compounded when it is said both that existence is inherently contingent and that modalities are never found in nature but only in judgments.[34]

The critique of necessary being rests on an analysis that confines necessity to propositions related by implication or exclusion to others that have been posited. With "matters of fact," considered as such, no such relations have been posited, so no necessity is found. Since no assumption bars positing a hypothetical state of affairs quite different from what actually obtains, it appears reasonable to treat all being as contingent. But the possibility of verbally denying any existential proposition without apparent contradiction does not prove that no state of affairs is necessary in itself, or made necessary by its causes. We simply do not know from that formal possibility whether all being is contingent or necessary, or some necessary and some contingent—or some, perhaps, necessary in some respects and contingent in others. In our formal systems of language and thought, we can be perfect nominalists about modalities and assume that necessity resides only where we place it or imply it. But such conventions say nothing about reality. If states of affairs can be contingent, so can they be necessary.

The presumption that contingency is the default position, so that we must regard the universe as contingent except insofar as we have constructed or construed its relations, seems to ignore the fact that contingency and facticity are as much or as little constructs of judgment as are necessity and impossibility. By an accident of history, claims of contingency seem epistemically less strong, less muscular, less revisionist of the untreated data or the unexamined things in themselves, than are claims of necessity or impossibility. Hume may be the culprit here. For when he argues (*Dialogues Concerning Natural Religion* VII) that the world might simply exist, or might have grown like a plant or been spun out, like a spider's silk, he suggests that to posit contingency is somehow less problematic, less costly epistemologically, than to posit necessity, or any grounding of contingency in necessity. But what is modally stronger need not be epistemically stronger. One can as readily jump the gun by assuming that a settled outcome is up in the air as in making the opposite presumption. Think of the gangster patsy in *The Sting*, who bets a fortune on a wager he has already lost.

Epistemic economy cautions against locating modalities in real states of affairs, primarily because we may not know the real modalities, and partly because most modalities are relational, since they reflect the structure of some etiology. The claim that only propositions or relations among them can be necessary or contingent plays on that caution. But caution cannot legislate to keep some facts or realities from being necessary, others from being contingent, quite apart from what we may say or think about them. Indeed, caution presupposes corrigibility and so presumes that modalities are real. An event may be necessary without our knowledge; we may not know the causes that make it so. What we take to be contingency might be illusory, a figment of our ignorance or a fiction of our knowledge. We simply do not know that necessity is not found in things. So what grounds have we for modeling reality on our modes of construing it? A realist can say that our modal categories seek to mirror the necessities and contingencies of nature. But what excuse has a modal nominalist for projecting a logicist bias—demanding that nature, like a closed formal system, hold no modalities but those we put there—and then privileging contingency?

The crux of Findlay's Humean argument was that all being is contingent, so that God, a noncontingent being, cannot exist. But the major premise is unknowable by strictly empirical standards and, if we reach beyond those standards, highly problematic and quite possibly untrue. So we do not know that the idea of a necessary being is incoherent. Findlay, characteristically, was fully alive to the limitations of his argument:

> I admit to the full that my argument *doesn't* hold for those who have no desire to say that God exists in some necessary and inescapable manner. . . . And my argument also *doesn't* hold for those who regard the Ontological Proof (or some other *a priori* proof) as a valid argument. Nor will it hold for those who are willing to say, with Rainer, that one might *come to* perceive the necessity of God's existence in some higher mystical state, nor for those who say, with Hughes and St. Thomas that God himself can perceive the 'necessity' of his own 'existence,' though both this 'existence' and this 'necessity' are something totally different from anything that we understand by these terms. I should indeed be naive if I thought I could trap the analogical eel in my dialectical net. But my argument holds for all those thinkers—who may properly be called 'modern' in no narrow or 'tendentious' sense—who accept Kant's view that there aren't any necessary facts of existence and who can also be persuaded to hold that a God who is 'worth his salt' must either exist necessarily (in the same sense of 'necessary') or not at all.[35]

Findlay rightly described as modern the post-Kantian view that there are no necessary facts. But neither he nor Hume nor Kant justified that view. In time, Findlay abandoned it. In an essay on what he calls "Absolute theory," he explains that Kant's rejection of necessary existence can apply only to the phenomenal world and makes all necessity "brute necessity"[36] —a stultifying conclusion.

Behind Findlay's Humean qualms lay a Kantian dilemma: God's perfection seems to place Him beyond the realm of particulars. Kant writes, "The *concept* of God and the conviction of his existence can be met with only in reason; they can come from reason alone, and not from inspiration or from any tidings, however great their authority."[37] If God is unique and therefore a particular, God is not subject to general ideas or theories and therefore not to proof. For only ideas come within range of the apodictic. The God that can be known as an individual, then, is not subject to argument. If God is absolute, Kant argues, his reality cannot be known as a matter of fact—pointedly not historically: "If God actually spoke to a human being, the latter could never *know* that it was God who spoke to him. It is absolutely impossible for a human being to grasp the infinite through the senses, so as to distinguish him from sensible beings and be *acquainted* with him."[38] Is God a universal, then, a being of reason? The crux of the dilemma is this: If God is an individual, God is not an absolute, and so is not the real God. But if God is an absolute, known only by proof, God becomes an ideal. And didn't the medieval nominalists or even Aristotle lay to rest Plato's notion that ideals exist?

The division is a telling one. But Kant's dilemma is an artifact of his enterprise of making the form of judgment (and its psychological preconditions) criterial in ontology. Kant knows that judgments can intend only sensory particulars because he has found or set the boundaries of all possible human cognition, limiting the a priori to its work of structuring experience as a system of general causal attributions. Perfection is removed to an ideal sphere that Kant will access for moral, but not cosmological, purposes.[39] But all this is arbitrary. Why is the Absolute any less a precondition of intellectual than of moral judgments? Surely we can intend the Absolute, by ritual, logical, poetic, or cosmological as well as moral signs. For a theme can be intended in an idea or sign that is not comprehended in the stimulant of that thought or sign, as Kant well knew. Plato, with his radical recognition that temporality compromises even logic, forcing us to choose between rigor and negation, was no less aware than Kant of the temporality of our consciousness. But he did not hesitate to show how language can point a direction that it cannot travel, that is, toward Eternity. And Maimonides, similarly, addressing the Rabbis' awe at the boldness of the Prophets, who dared to express in human terms what the act of creation marks as necessarily transcending all such terms, did not hesitate to show, by the deconstruction of all biblical characterizations of God, how all point beyond their specious referents toward a Perfection that they can intend but never touch. Yet Kant wrote: "No objects can be represented through the pure *concepts of the understanding* apart from the conditions of sensibility"—time and space. Does this mean that persons are unknown to us, since no sensory datum differentiates persons from machines? Or may we intend a person as a thou, beyond all possible sensations? Clearly we may, for we do.[40] And when we do, we see part of the meaning of the idea that humanity is created in the image and likeness of God.

Although challenging to theism, Kant's dilemma is precious to us for that challenge, since it tells us what God must be, if there is to be a God at all in the monotheist's sense. An absolutely perfect being will be both unique and transcendent. Combining all reality and goodness, God will omit nothing and be limited by nothing. Kant's challenge lies in the claim that any encounter with God must compromise God's absoluteness in the conditions of sensuality, whereas any rational awareness will make God a mental construct. The very demands of the idea of God seem to exclude God's reality, scissoring monotheism between a fictive universal and a sensuous particular, and exposing the contradiction—long latent in the conflicting demands we make, as philosophers and as worshipers—between celebration of God's perfection and acknowledgment of his immediacy.

Yet the noose is drawn too tightly around all our knowledge and practice if we must choose between sensuous particulars and nominal universals. When we understand a thing, it is always the animating idea that we grasp, not any inert or passive physicality, nor even the sheer sensuousness, which is apprehensible to us only through some filter of perception that invariably abstracts upon the vital thematics of a body's conatus—our own and that of the object. The sensuous is always apprehended as an idea, thus always drawn beyond the realm of sensuous particularity. But that idea is neither the identity of the thing (since it is ours, and limited by our interests and capabilities) nor other than the identity of the thing, since it is one of the manifold expressions of the thing's reality or conatus. So if we apprehend God in sensuously mediated ideas, that is no different from the way we apprehend anything else. And if we need to read ideas critically, to differentiate what they properly intend from what they merely seem to intend, we can, and must, do the same with our ideas of God.

Further, to cut off the intellectual from the real on the nominalist premise that the ideal can only be a universal, and the universal only a notion, is to misjudge both thought and reality by projecting the conditions of one onto the constitution of the other. All our ideas are thoughts. But that does not imply that thoughts are all that ideas can ever be. For how could we discover and confirm ideas in particulars if they were present only in the mind; how could they be present in the mind if they were not present in particulars, enabling them to be and to be known? Nor can we accept Plato's equation of the Ideal with the universal—which paves the way for the dismissal of the ideal as a mere abstraction. If we know God through an idea, there is no reason, then, to say that there is no reality which that idea intends.

The epistemic turn reaches a curious dead end when what began as an effort to overcome the skeptics' charge that reality is inaccessible and known to us only through the turbid and projective apparatus of our sensibilities ends, in Kant—or in pragmatism—with a plea of nolo contendere, announced obliquely in the project of reconstituting reality *as* projection. Kant's ambivalence here is as clear as James's: James will argue that if God is no more than a wish fulfillment, wishes have every right to be fulfilled. Kant, more gravely, held that if God is needed by morality, God must be posited, even if the idea of God can only be an incoherent ideal.

But is the ideal incoherent? Does the fact that we apprehend things intellectually only through general ideas prove those things themselves to be general ideas? Even the notion of a particular is no more than that, a notion. So are uniqueness, perfection, infinity, and absoluteness. But this does not entail that the unique or perfect, the infinite or absolute exists only notionally. Facing about toward the epistemic turn, we must distinguish the ontic from the epistemic question and differentiate what things are from how they are known, or we shall not avoid the hubris of imagining that the entire universe is our own creation—or the fall of finding ourselves unable to say that we know another human being, since we apprehend even individuals only through ideas.

To recognize that our apprehension of God through ideas does not make God a mere idea is not to dismiss the epistemic problem. It is just to say that if there is a problem about the reality of a perfect being, it is not settled by questions about our knowledge. But the real strength of the ontological argument is in showing that there is not a problem about God's being. If we think of God's existence as problematic, it is not God we are thinking of. Thus, when Deuteronomy (32:47) says of God's law, "It is not an empty thing," the Sages add, "—and if it is empty, that is on your account" (Y. *Peah* 1, *Ketubot* 8).

How we can know a being that is at once unique and universal, absolute and individual, remains to be addressed. But recognizing that our idea of God relies on abstract universals does not prove that God is not an individual. Indeed, as Maimonides shows (*Guide* I 61), all the Torah's ideas of God but one are projections of ordinary human notions. But that one, voiced in the Tetragrammaton, guides the sense of all the rest. For it intends God in his uniqueness as the Perfect. It is this idea that the ontological argument seeks to capture. It cannot prove that God exists to one who does not already grasp the idea of Perfection, who has not considered the idea of God in its full strength. A mystic might say that such a person has not met God, emphasizing God's particularity, even personality—knowledge as acquaintance rather than as understanding. But if God, as Perfection, is both unique and absolute, the conventional division between acquaintance and understanding dissolves. That is why Maimonides sees the Mosaic encounter with God in the understanding conveyed by the words I AM THAT I AM and finds in the Tetragrammaton a compact expression of God's Self-affirmation, confirming it in miniature, as if it were a cameo of the ontological argument.

As an argument, the phrase will have probative value to the elders of Israel. For they have pondered their ancient traditions about the divine and will recognize the necessity of God's existence as a corollary of his absoluteness. A mere cult name might hold sacral energy or nostalgia. But it would not signify the absolute goodness that Abraham's experience intends; and it would not have probative force. It would, as Maimonides argues, sound either alien or trite, depending on whether or not the Israelites had heard it before. But when God commands Moses, "Tell them that I AM has sent you," understanding and acquaintance fuse, and the thought that one controls God by knowing his name becomes a joke, as it would be a joke to say that one controls a man by knowing his name. When the name that Bible scholars like to treat as a totem invoking some tribal deity is seen as a compact token of absolute existence, encounter becomes knowledge, as when a man and woman love. Indeed, the same verb in the biblical idiom means knowing and making love, marking the union of encounter with understanding. For when Israel knows God, as when a man and woman know each other, the division between knowing how and knowing that grows shaky and scholastic, praxis merges with lucidity in joy and consummation. Thus the verse that tells us that God's law "is not an empty thing," and conveys Moses' last words to Israel, ends in a reasoning that would be crystal clear to Halevi,[41] dissolving Kant's dilemma about acquaintance and understanding by telling us how to know God, through his ways, in our daily lives, since we cannot see his face. It speaks of the law as a way of love and life, and so as a way of knowing: "For it is your life, and through this thing shall you prolong your days upon the soil which you are crossing the Jordan to inherit" (Deut. 32:47).

If we ask, then, how a unique and absolute being can be known, and agree with

Kant that sensation can never give a full or unambiguous answer, it does not follow, as the sole alternative, that there is some science of God, accessible, like astronomy or geometry, to academic consensus or experimental debate. Rather, the beginning of wisdom on this subject (and wisdom, rather than science is what we need here) is that God, as a unique and perfect Being, is known only gradually, whether by individuals or by peoples and civilizations, as lovers come to know one another through their life together. If there is an experimental method here, it is the method Gandhi spoke of when he called his life a series of experiments with truth. I think the Jewish experience is, in some measure, a history of such experimentation.

Part of what undermines Kant's dichotomy is an assumption that religious experience must be private, intense, instantaneous, or brief. This is to limit love to assignations and ignore the permanence of marriage, as though love were never a way of life. But an assignation cannot foster growth of understanding, and to read about an assignation is not to know love but to peek through the keyhole. Like Kantian morality, which locates virtue in Romantic or Protestant wise at some inner crisis point rather than in the whole life of a person, a community, or a culture, so Kantian religious phenomenology posits and rejects an evanescent encounter that reason cannot validate and sensation cannot authenticate—since it is fleeting, unrepeatable, inaccessible intersubjectively, unscrutinizable—at best, a subject of gossip. But encounters need not be private or momentary. They can be public and enduring.

Reproducibility is an aim in many rituals. And transformation of fleeting moments into some form of permanence is an intention in every kind of literature and art. Naḥmanides will argue, following Halevi's hints, that festivals and other rituals allow us to relive past encounters with the divine. The new encounters that result are not merely derivative; still less, imitative. They can be primary loci of engagement in their own right, enlarging and elaborating ancient experience, by its overlay upon our own. The capability of new experience to add value and significance to what calendared celebrations and other modes of disciplining time (and place) can salvage from the flood of history allows us to challenge the Kantian dichotomy of sensation and reflection, encounter and argument. For it shows that encounter can encompass argument and need not exclude ideas—that Israel's wrestling with the angel, that is, the idea of God, did not end in a single night or rest on the unaided strength of Jacob, any more than he left us to our own strength. Rather, that encounter continues, in many forms—in argument, exploring the potentials of a shared idea, and in experience and expression, which continue to unfold and develop that idea, intellectually and morally, aesthetically and spiritually.

The engagement of a culture or a civilization, in endeavors not just to recapture but to interpret and elaborate the significances of the Absolute, creates an enduring encounter, in which the evanescence and partiality of private experience are, in some measure, remedied. Thus the idea of the covenant, and its symbolization by marriage in the imagery of the prophets. In this relationship the potentialities of the idea of God are explored, not systematically but methodically, with all the resources that the cumulation of experience in diverse ages and contexts can supply.

When we speak of Israel's choosing God, we mean that the clarity needed in apprehending Perfection has been grasped, refined, enlarged, enhanced through time, in an ongoing experience whose theme is the Absolute—not just the idea of the

Absolute but the Absolute itself. The idea, as it emerges, is the product, but the experiments are not about themselves. They are about God and how we are to understand and know him. Thus our encounter with God is not just personal but communal and historical. Looking back through the layers of cosmological myth and sacrificial cult, moral law and civil code, prophetic admonition and Rabbinic imagination, we can see in the very diversity of idioms the same idea repeatedly voiced. The unifying theme is Perfection. This idea shapes and guides the whole experience, a paradigm of the historic encounter that Kant deemed impossible, since he understood encounter and immediacy—and even history—only in terms of sensuous particularity, and understanding only in terms of abstract ideas.[42]

An encounter with the Absolute can be historical, then, if it shapes the life of an individual or a culture. That life is what limns the theme not by analysis—still less by crude ostension—but by circling, seeking, defining what it seeks in the tenor of every normative act and gesture, as the motions of the planets might describe the sun, even if it were invisible, or as music is described in the dance. Kant thought that Judaism was not really a religion, since its earliest formulations of God's law related (so he claimed) only to external acts, did not appeal to moral conscience, and, even at their most ethically accessible, in the Ten Commandments, promised no reward beyond this life.[43] Multiple biases blinded him to the play of the idea of God as the regulative principle of Jewish life, much like the idea of organism in Aristotelian thought, or interaction in Newtonian physics. For Jewish life and law are as emblematic of the powers and problematics of God's encounter with humanity as the Kantian categories are of Newtonian science. Not that the *mitzvot* are Kantian categories.[44] But just as those categories intend Newtonian nature or Lockean common sense, the *mitzvot* intend the Absolute.

Does God Exist?

Simmering quietly almost throughout the history of Western philosophy is the question whether existence is properly expressed by a predicate: Is being a characteristic that things might have or lack? This issue is lashed to our ideas of God as an absolute being and existence as his gift. So we need to examine it carefully, beginning with Aristotle's work as the founder, in the West, of the systematic inquiry into the meaning of being as such.

Aristotle found the source of the faulty reasoning behind Parmenides' monism in a failure to distinguish different senses of the verb to be. Parmenides' exclusion of negation objected as strenuously to 'The sky is not green' as to the blanket denial of all being. Change and diversity as well as ultimate creation and destruction were deemed impossible, since all involve negation. Aristotle approved the rejection of absolute nonbeing, but he could not accept the denial of change and diversity, since it flies in the face of appearances. So he distinguished the permissible negation of 'He is not musical' or 'I am not what I was' (I've lost my tan) from the impermissible negation of being itself. 'Is,' he found, is used in a variety of ways: It has different meanings in 'It is one o'clock' and 'He is human.' Ten modes of predication seemed to cover its applications. A subject might be characterized as ϕ (a quality), or ψ (a quantity), or ξ (where 'ξ' names its species), and so through all ten categories. But any subject is designated univocally only under one category. And 'being' itself is not a category. In Scholastic terms, being is not an accident. The word has no separate sense of its own but works across the categories, referring in syntactically different ways to a single common notion, as, say, the word 'healthy' might be applied to a diet or an organism.

Perhaps Aristotle feared that if he gave 'being' a sense of its own, made it one of the categories, he would face an infinite regress about the being of being. Perhaps he liked his denial of any purely existential sense of 'to be' because it did not prejudge the meaning of 'being' but licensed all the categories in an open, pluralistic spirit, not trying to force so broad a notion into any narrow pigeonhole. Definiteness of any kind would be treated as the working sense of the term. But clearly one outcome of Aristotle's approach that was not at all unwelcome to him was to make the being of things in a way inalienable. A thing's substance, what makes it what it is, is, for Aristotle, an immanent version of one of Plato's forms, the essence of the Scholastics. Aristotle identifies it with the thing itself and equates it with the idea of the thing, as formulated in its definition, understood in scientific inquiry, and summed up in the name that designates any thing most perspicuously, that of its species. If we take away that essence, the thing will no longer be—not as what it was—as there is no animal, for example, without life. Distinguishing between essence and accident, it will now make sense to deny that a thing is ϕ or ψ without crossing the Parmenidean barrier against denying its existence altogether. Things, then, can change without losing their identities, and they can come to be and pass away, gaining or losing essential properties. But there still will be no absolute unreality, no absolute creation or destruction—not for Parmenides' specious reason, that all negation is incoherent, but for Aristotle's subtler reason, that 'is' means nothing except when it affirms the reality of a substance, or the pertinence to a substance of some trait, relation, or other categorial qualification. Matter, the underlying substrate of change, becomes ungenerated and indestructible, and a void remains impossible—not for any empiric reason but for the Eleatic reason that to posit a void or any absolute origination or destruction would return us, Aristotle reasons, to the paradox that Parmenides excluded, of affirming the reality of unreality. With the primary, substantial sense of being, then, the law of contradiction will apply with almost Eleatic starkness: A thing either is or it is not; that is, either is or is not a member of a certain species. Since existence is not an accident, things cannot be to different degrees, as if being were a quality. There is no way for anything to be more or less a man, say, or a dog, as one might be more or less musical or sunburned.

Platonic participation, however, did allow things to be what they are in the primary sense, to varying degrees. Forms were ϕ (where 'ϕ' names a perfection) to a higher (more eminent) degree than their particulars. And particulars live up to their forms to varying degrees—the real object of Plato's art of measurement. Here being is something a thing might have or lack, as suggested in Plato's thesis that being is imparted by the Forms. Aristotle himself was not immune to the approach. For he spoke of things' deriving their actuality from that which is most actual (*Metaphysics* 993b 22–26)—although careful to make clear he meant their actuality as (ϕ, ψ, ξ, etc.). When a being, especially a living being, achieves its potential, it is hard for

Aristotle not to say that it is realizing itself as an exemplar of its kind, and so becoming in a stronger sense what it is—becoming more real. True, for Aristotle an acorn or an embryo is no less 'oak' or 'man' than is an oak tree or a human adult. The reality of a thing is not located simply in the mature individual. The adult exists to produce the seed, just as the seed exists to produce the adult. So the telos and form are wholly realized in neither, but only in the full life cycle—thus, not in the individual but in the species. The being of a species is in its natural history or life, and a fuller or more active life more fully realizes the form or reality of the individual—a fact critical in Aristotle's ethics. As in Aristotle's affirmation that the Divine is pure actuality and in his epistemological reliance on the theory of Forms, then, we find here hardy survivals of Plato's thoughts about being, making it not just a matter of class membership but an aim actively sought, engaged in, or lived.

With our own knowledge of evolution and the open future, we must now extend this account. For every species is a project to itself, and its telos is not given from the outset, but emergent. So, for us, the dynamic sense of 'being' will be even stronger than it was for Aristotle. But, whether we know that species are emergent or assume the old essentialism, we see in nature that being cannot be a mere taxonomic assignment but must become an aim pursued. That is true for all species, above all for humans, who can know their own purposes and so must shape and choose the modalities of their realization.

Aristotle thinks that being, in the broadest sense, cannot fail, and that view is linked to his refusal to make being a category. But his views here, like Kant's on necessary being, stem not from analysis (as if analysis could settle such an issue) but from bias. Aristotle found deeply suspect any notion that the cosmos had an origin. Such accounts smacked of mythology, and for him philosophy began when Thales began to disentangle explanations of the world's nature from stories of its origin, by focusing on the material makeup of all things. Not only could no mere story (even a causal story) explain the cosmos, but it seemed rather irreverent to treat it as having begun. It was, after all, divine. Besides, it seemed irrational to seek some busy stage manager behind all causes. Such inquiries appeared not to anchor but to compete with the scientific aim of discovering the wisdom immanent in the irreducible variety of species. Part of this immanence was the permanence of the world and the immutable choric dance of the heavens and cycle of the generations in all living kinds, which gave visible and intelligible expression to the world's divinity. So the notion that being might have been imparted rather than inhering in things inalienably seemed not just primitive but sharply irreligious, unscientific, and antiphilosophical.

Yet Aristotle himself distinguished the question of what a thing is from the question of whether such a thing exists. He avoided treating all beings as contingent by confining the distinction to particulars. So Socrates was a contingent being, since Sophroniscus and Phaenarete might never have met, but spiders were not. They have existed and will exist eternally. Their existence, then, is necessary, for what will never occur is impossible. Evolution and extinction are impossible, for the same reason that no change has ever been observed in the motions of the heavens—the Parmenidean reason that reality must be real. Indeed, changelessness, for Aristotle, remains a chief mark of reality. For the working equation of being with determinacy means that whatever is real must be a "such"—a demand that Aristotle mistakenly interpreted to imply that whatever is real must have a fixed nature.

Even in antiquity Aristotle's categories were not universally accepted. Stoics and Neoplatonists argued vigorously on logical and linguistic grounds that existence *is* a category. They saw a common theme in all the many uses of the verb to be. For Neoplatonists this was the formal unity that shone through the material diversity of things. For Stoics it was the organic interaffectedness, *sympatheia* of all that is. Even Aristotelians sought integration. And if being was not a property, how could it measure the gradient we must climb?

Monotheism gave further import to the idea that being is a predicate. For myths often teach by a fictive abstraction from key features of the world. Genesis, with its consummate use of the mythic idiom, frames the whole cosmos as nonexistent, so as to raise the question what could have given it being. Here being is a characteristic that things might not have had. In the hands of the *mutakallimūn*, the biblical theme of contingency, adopted in the Qur'ān and linked to the dramatic imagery of apocalypse, was made the bulwark of a metaphysics set up to rival that of Aristotle. Where he had reasoned that reality must, in the last analysis, involve necessity, and saw the scientist's goal as discovery of why things must be as they are, the *mutakallimūn* reasoned that no finite thing need have been as it is, or need exist at all. All things depend, not just at the outset but always and in all ways, on the will and act of God.

Like Aristotle's derivation of the necessity of being from the seeming tautology that what is must be, the *kalām* metaphysics of radical contingency rested on flawed reasoning. It presumed that nothing more could or would be given in any act of creation than a single flash of being, unenduring, unextended, unconnected, spatially, temporally, causally, or logically. Thus the *kalām* tended to make nature, grace, human freedom, and moral right far more problematic than need be. God's children were sustained but seemingly had no allowance. Often, as in Ash'arism, persons were held accountable without ever being made responsible. Metaphysics was distended and logic itself contorted, all to celebrate God's utter power and the insignificance of creation—as though it had been forgotten that to disparage the gift is to demean the Giver. But what was incandescent in the metaphysics of the *kalām* was the one thing that Aristotle had most deeply buried: the act of creation. The account of being that elevated creation as scriptural cosmology showed it should be was the *kalām* metaphysics of contingency.

The Muslim philosopher Abū Alī Ibn Sīnā (Avicenna, 980–1037) forged a remarkable synthesis between that metaphysics and its Aristotelian antithesis. No *mutakallim*, Avicenna was not a professional theological litigator but a physician and astronomer, sometime jurist and minister of state. His powerful commitments to Aristotelian science spared him the *kalām* discomfort with the idea of natural necessity. The key to his synthesis was his recognition that things in nature might be both necessary and contingent—contingent in themselves but necessary in relation to their causes. This insight gives modalities a perspectival character without abandoning modal realism. For to look at a thing in itself is to isolate it from its causal context, setting aside our knowledge of its dependency on other things. Clearly such a perspective is a fiction, as Spinoza saw, since no natural object is ever wholly isolated from its causal milieu; none would exist without its causes and conditions. But if we mentally isolate a natural thing from its causal environment, we can see its radical contingency and thus highlight its dependence on its causes: nothing in the idea of such a thing, considered in itself, entails its reality; nothing in the idea of any natural kind implies how many (if any) exemplars exist. Yet if we think of the same object and posit the requisite causes and conditions, as if they were premises in an argument, its existence becomes necessary and cannot be excluded.

I say that Avicenna found a perspectival character in the idea of modality, since the modal aspect of a fact can be changed by changing one's assumptions about the relevant causes—positing them or suspending the assumption of their action. But Avicenna was not a modal nominalist. He saw that we can vary the modal treatment of all natural facts by varying our assumptions about their nature and causal connectedness. But, like the world as seen first from one eye and then from the other, these facts always have two sides to them. For all natural things are necessitated by their causes, yet none is necessary in itself. There is nothing in nature that cannot fail to exist.

Being, Avicenna argued, then, is an accident, an extra notion, over and above the essence of a natural thing. The *mutakallimūn* were right in holding that any finite thing can always be imagined not to exist. This is the truth that modern philosophers hold in mind when they call all existential propositions synthetic. Because finite particulars depend on their causes, we cannot deduce their existence from their essences; so we cannot treat existential propositions about them as analytic.[45]

A rationalist, Avicenna believed that all facts require an explanation and thus that all contingent facts must be explained in terms of factors extrinsic to themselves. For if a fact could be understood solely in terms of itself it would be necessary. Any contingent fact, then, leads us to a system and sequence of causes. This thought grounds Avicenna's argument for the existence of God *ex contingentia*, the argument from contingency or cosmological proof that Kant called "too well known to require detailed statement." The argument runs like this:

1. Something exists.

For I exist, this sense object exists—even if all is illusion, that illusion exists.

2. What does exist is either necessary or contingent.

That is, it either does or does not contain in itself the conditions of its own existence. But if it does, it is a necessary being. If it does not, it must have an external cause—of its being at all and its being as it is. This cause, too, is either necessary or contingent. But (Avicenna argued) there cannot be an infinite sequence of causes, or they would never reach the actual effect, which, *ex hypothesi*, they have. None of the links in the chain would have been real and had their effects, had not the prior links been made actual by real causes. So there must be a first cause; and this first link must contain in itself the conditions of its own existence. It must be self-sufficient, a necessary being. If so, it must be simple, ungenerated, indestructible, changeless, and absolutely perfect—that is, divine.[46]

How much of this argument can we appropriate? Crescas showed that even an infinite causal series would not be self-explanatory. Even such a system still demands a higher, self-sufficient cause.[47] Bearing in mind Saadiah's advice not to expect the Ultimate Cause to answer to the very descriptors of the things to be explained, we should not expect the cause of all events to be just another event, or the ground of all facts to be just another fact, as conditioned as the rest. Avicenna clearly saw this. For the sequence he proposed was not a temporal one like "A begat B, who begat C, and so forth," but a chain of ontic dependencies leading to higher and higher planes of actuality, related to one another as mind is to matter: What was Form or Intelligence on one level was matter to a higher Form on the next. But this hierarchy, he reasoned, could not go on ad infinitum if its effect was real. Any contingent reality, then, requires the act of a necessary (and so divine) being.

Avicenna's flights of disembodied intellects and even his rejection of an actual infinity are not, however, what concern us here. The heart of his argument is in the claim that the world and all things in it are contingent in themselves. The finite sequence of causes is just the mark of that contingency—the conditionedness of all things but God. Effects are made necessary by their causes, as we and all the other actors in nature give those effects reality. But the system as a whole, if all its members are both causes and effects, is contingent. There is no intrinsic necessity in it. What is sound in the idea that nature depends on God is not the spurious thought that God acts for us (so that our powers and all powers in nature are nugatory), nor the specious notion that God acts *as* us (so that we fancy ourselves now to be the Infinite, now to be lost in God's boundlessness), but the recognition that we and all natural beings owe our powers ultimately not to our own acts but to the Source of all goodness and strength. Such a view commands neither the quietism of moral paralysis nor the sometimes concomitant sense of invincibility found in some zealots, but gratitude and aspiration—celebration of God's goodness and generosity, and commitment to the good we can achieve and sustain. Of this I shall have more to say in chapter 3. But the matter at hand is the cosmological proof.

Kant's critique of it rests on his refutation of the ontological argument. For both, he says, invoke the idea of a necessary being.[48] Indeed they must. To show that God exists and not just that some higher life form is with us in the universe, we must come in the end to an absolute—a necessary being. Kant's worries about indeterminacy in the idea of such a being are, I think, misplaced. Our natural impulse to bring everything to terms, if given its head here, would only defeat itself, making the Infinite finite. Yet, to see determinate expressions of the Infinite, we have only to look around us, and within ourselves and one another: When Moses learned that man cannot see God's face, he was also shown God's ways.

Kant assumes that necessity is found only in logic. But what Avicenna was looking for and found lacking in nature was not logical necessity but self-sufficiency. That is still not found in nature. The idea of confining necessity to logic is simply unsound. As P. T. Geach explains, "to say that 'necessary' can only refer to logical necessity is equivalent to saying that whatever cannot be so, *logically* cannot be so—e.g. that since I cannot speak Russian, my speaking Russian is logically impossible."[49] There is nothing strange or logically exotic, then, in the view that God's necessity is not that of an analytic proposition but an ontic status that makes it absurd, given an adequate idea of God, to ask why God exists. Ontic necessity, as Shalom Rosenberg notes, has a variety of modern advocates, whose views parallel the thoughts of medieval writers like al-Fārābī and Avicenna who called God a Necessary Being.[50] Maimonides linked that phrase to the biblical idea of God when he glossed "The Lord sits at the flood" (Ps. 29:10) as a metaphor of God's ontic stability and Self-sufficiency (*Guide* I 11).

Kant says that the ontological argument is not just unsuited to controversy but radically unsound; it infects with incoherence any reasoning reliant on it. His critique, however, is highly problematic. For it conjoins two lines of reasoning, one of which assumes that 'being' is a predicate; the other, that it is not. The first is this: rephrasing the idea of necessary existence in the terms of post-Humean philosophy, a necessary being is one whose existence it is self-contradictory to deny; one could not consider such a being coherently without granting its existence. But that, Kant argues, is impossible. For "every reasonable person" must admit "that all existential propositions are synthetic"; and if 'God exists' were analytic, its affirmation would be "a miserable tautology."[51] Maimonides, by contrast, sees nothing miserable or trivial here but a limpid intuition encapsulated in the Tetragrammaton, compactly arguing the Self-sufficiency of Perfection. But he does not equate analysis with simply unwrapping a term. Like Anselm, he thinks that learning, tradition, and experience teach us the logic of perfection. The formal character of statements about God only reflects the Reality they intend.

Kant deems all existential propositions synthetic because it never seems self-contradictory to deny them. Change reveals the contingency of the objects of experience moment by moment. Here again we sight the asymmetry between necessity and contingency. For Kant tells us that "the unconditioned necessity of judgments is not the same as an absolute necessity of things." The former rests on posited relations; the later, on a delusion, projecting onto things in themselves the logical notion of necessity.[52] But with contingency it is Kant who speaks as if he were a modal realist.

To avoid making Kant's argument circular, the premise that all existential propositions are synthetic must be confined to finite beings. To include God would beg the question. Yet the contingency of all other beings is granted, indeed assumed, in Avicenna's argument. All existential propositions about *them* are synthetic. Conditions can always be conceived that would curtail their existence. This is not just a mental fact but a reflection of the dependence of things on their causes. To deny it is to reject not only science as an organized enterprise but all understanding of nature. Setting aside our knowledge of its causes, we can say of any natural thing that its essence does not entail its existence. But the Infinite cannot be curtailed, its existence excluded by something else. It is not dependent on the act of some other thing. God, as the medievals like to say, has no counterpart or correlative. What Kant must show, then, to give his objection force, is that an infinite being can be denied without self-contradiction. This seems dubious prima facie. Clearly, it cannot be inferred from our experience of finite things, nor from the linguistic policies that reflect that experience.

The claim that all existential propositions are synthetic rests on the distinction of essence from existence, *what* from *whether*, the same distinction that underwrites Avicenna's view that existence (for all finite things) is an accident. Thus Kant, like Gaunilon, argues that no matter what perfections thought may assign a thing, the question remains whether such a thing exists.[53] But Kant abandons the syntheticity of existential judgments when he writes: "'Being,' is obviously not a real predicate; that is, it is not a concept of something which could be added to the concept of a thing. It is merely the positing of a thing, or of certain determinations, as existing in themselves. Logically it is merely the copula of judgment."[54] The notion of existence in no way adds to the determinations of a thing, he urges. There is no difference whatever in conception between a hundred real thalers and a hundred possible or imaginary thalers.[55] Spinoza uses the same thought to prove that being is adventitious! He argues that neither the coming to be nor the persistence of anything in nature can be deduced from its essence, since the essence of all finite things in thought is no different before they exist than after.[56]

Clearly, 'being' does not behave like 'green' or 'blue'. But in denying it a content of its own, Kant undermines his claim that all existential propositions are synthetic. For what can this mean if not that to say of a thing that it exists is to tell more about it than is given in its idea? Kant seems alive to the difficulty. He does not attempt simply to reduce the verb to be to its "logical function" as a copula. When he says that 'existence' is not a real predicate, as he explains, he means that to say of a thing that it exists is simply to posit the thing. The maker of the judgment is the logical subject, the item becomes the complement, and 'exists' means 'I posit'.[57] The analysis forces existential judgments into a predicative mold, on the pattern of the Thai Prologue speaker in "The Little House of Uncle Thomas," in *The King and I*: "Ladies and Gentlemen, I beg to put before you . . ." Thus 'There is a city on the Hudson' becomes "Let us posit the characteristics of a city . . . " or "Given a city . . ." The influence of mathematical usage is clear, the anticipation of Quine is striking. The actual elimination of existential terms like 'is instantiated' or 'is located' is less than obvious, but overt existential import is clearly shifted from the object to the I.

The strength of the analysis is that it seems to have dissolved any substantive contribution of the verb to be—although Kant contradicts his claim that the idea of existence brings no determination to a judgment when he attempts (A600–601/B628–29) to derive the syntheticity of existential judgments from our need for sense experience. For that does assign a specific sense to the verb to be: namely, "warranted by sense experience." All the same, by sticking to his denial that existence is a real predicate, Kant can sum up with a flourish worthy of Gaunilon: "We can no more extend our stock of insight by mere ideas than a merchant can better his position by adding a few naughts to his cash account."[58] He does not say that the idea of existence adds nothing, only that it adds nothing substantive, nothing determinative. Like a zero, it makes an addition only when there is something to be added to. But the analogy is inverted. For existence is the quantity, not the cipher; predicates are what add meaning only when there is something they can apply to!

If existence were a determining notion, Kant reasons, the thing I posit would not be the one I deny or merely consider. This impressive argument rests on a fallacy. For to consider the nonexistence of any real thing we abstract from the assumptions that typically anchor its identity and rely on other marks to do that work. Here we do treat existence as an "accident"—just like any accident we abstract from when we consider that a thing might have "had" traits other than those it has. Strictly speaking, it is *not* the same thing that is regarded as existing and not existing, but two similar things that differ in that one of them is not assumed to exist. This exactly parallels the case with what we all confess to be (real) predicates. For (if genetics tells us anything about identity) it is not the same person I speak of when I ask you to assume that I might have been born female or Chinese. That contingency is perfectly intelligible: a person like me, with traits of personality or inner conscience like enough mine to permit an identification, might have had a different history, ab ovo. As long as our conversation allows us to agree on key traits to be kept constant, comparison of the virtual me with the original is possible; it does not matter which traits we notionally exclude or alter. The same holds for existence.[59] That is why we can talk about a possible hundred thalers or presume something to exist that does not.

Kant's case against existence as a real predicate was that any difference between the being deemed possible in one judgment and that deemed actual in another, would preclude the two judgments' intending the same entity. But in a real sense they do not. One of them at least cites an abstraction. If we organize our categories so that we can speak of the same subject now as existing, now as nonexistent, it is only by aid of the assumption Avicenna expressed by calling existence an added notion, beyond that of a thing's essence—treating existence as an accident. If we seek language to clarify the difference between the real and the imaginary, the term in which we do so becomes a real predicate.[60]

There's all the difference in the world between positing an imaginary or possible subject and positing a real one—or one thought to be real versus one assumed not to be. To mention just one difference: all real things have all the determinations that facticity demands. But fictive or hypothetical entities have only those that we assign them. So, if we change Kant's coins for banknotes and ask about the serial numbers on the hundred thalers he has in his right pocket and those on the hundred he only wished he had in his left, the question is answered in two different ways. Of course Kant posits that the imaginary bills have the same numbers as the real ones. By hypothesis, the bills are qualitatively identical, and Kant can posit whatever he likes. But the numbers on the real bills are there because they were printed at the mint; if we want to know them we must check the bills or trace their history. The numbers on the imaginary bills are there because we posited them; to find out what they are we must find out what we posited. They have no characteristics that we do not posit.

Certainly, we can posit wholesale and proclaim a fiction as detailed as reality—thus Kant's talk about "completely determining" a suppositious entity. But these determinations are merely penciled in.[61] If we do not assign a name or age or marital status or bank balance to the mintmaster who stamped the imaginary bills, those facets of their history never come into play. So it is not true that existence makes no difference in the character of things. At the very least, it determines whether a thing's properties are complete or skeletal. And that is just one striking difference that existence makes. We can name many more if we know what sort of virtual or real beings we are concerned with. Thus Gilson recalls an old story of Roland's horse: "A wonderful horse; he had all possible characteristics, all possible qualities. He was fast, he was strong, he did not eat, he did not drink. He had only one defect. He was dead."[62] If Pegasus was a mythical horse and Bucephalus a real one, Bucephalus ate real food; Pegasus lives on the virtual food supplied by fancy. Bucephalus grew tired after a race, but the wings of Pegasus offer no challenge to equine science—unless someone wants to engineer a Pegasus. As Kant himself noted, it made a real difference to his finances whether his hundred thalers was real or imaginary.

The word 'exists,' then, does not just set up some empty placeholder to await the predicates that alone impart reality. It can prepare us for a variety of thoughts about a subject, but it does determine and differentiate, albeit in a highly general way. Thus we know of the existent that it can have effects. Materialists use 'is' to affirm a physical reality; strict empiricists intend a sensuous validation. The two ontologies, although ancient allies, have a long history of tensions and conflicts, which the verb to be does not adjudicate. Its sense is open enough to allow even a materialist to understand Berkeley's claim that only minds and thoughts exist. But its openness is not vacuity. Only in fictions like those of mathematics is 'exists' applied to objects without reference to their relations of dependence or independence.

G. E. Moore notes two differences between 'is' and other grammatical predicates: (1) We say 'Some tame tigers do not growl' but do not say 'Some tame tigers do not exist'; and (2) 'This is a tame tiger and exists' is meaningless. I take exception to both these claims about our language. For I can certainly say of the cartoon child Calvin that his tame tiger Hobbes does not exist. And if someone thought that tame tigers exist only in fiction, I might, as a child innocent of all technical niceties, have taken that person to the circus and said of one of Clyde Beatty's tigers: 'This is a tame tiger, and it exists.' But Moore's two thoughts about usage lead him to suspect that 'This exists' is meaningless. He shies at that conclusion, since it would undermine the empiricist axiom that all existential propositions are synthetic, by making it impossible to say of anything "This might not have existed." So, seeking a sense for 'This exists', he ties existence to sense data; and sense data, via intensionality, to physical things.[63] But this unwinds all that has gone before. For, in various contexts, many concrete senses will give meaning to 'This exists'. One could even approach experience with an open mind and say of all sorts of things, "I may not know what existence is, but clearly *this* is real"—as Descartes said of consciousness. But once meaning is allowed to 'This might not have existed,' the notion that 'is' is not a real predicate dissolves.

Kant, we find, holds both views. In calling all existential propositions synthetic he distinguishes essence from existence and makes existence determinative. But in saying that existence adds nothing to the notion of a thing he effectually denies that existential propositions are synthetic. One might wish to rescue him by choosing for him one of his two conflicting strands of argument. We have seen good grounds for rejecting either. For the claim that all existential propositions are synthetic seeks to rule out a necessary being by making logic the only source of necessity and extrapolating the contingency of ordinary judgments from ephemera to God. And the claim that 'exists' is not a real predicate ignores the difference reality makes in any real subject. But Kant would be hard-pressed to choose between his two approaches. Nor does it help to present the two sequentially, to show that either cripples the ontological argument. For a Kantian cannot use either. The reason: despite Kant's conflicting assertions that "'Being' is obviously not a real predicate" and (on the same page) that every reasonable person must admit that all existential propositions are synthetic, the question whether existence is or is not a real predicate is just the sort that critical philosophy is supposed to exclude.

Kant's rival answers might well be added to the antinomies of pure reason, were it not clear that they spring from the same source as the first antinomy. For the view that all existential propositions are synthetic assumes the contingency of being, and the denial that existence is a predicate belongs to the Aristotelian metaphysics of necessity. For it takes existence to be inseparable from the concept of a thing—that is, a *real* thing. The new antinomy stems from considering beings now as possible, now as real—the same confusion that Kant found at the root of the original antinomy between creation and eternity.

In attempting to settle once and for all the highly metaphysical question of the validity of the ontological argument, then, Kant himself has fallen into a classic antinomy of pure reason, from which his critical philosophy, with its hostility toward speculative metaphysics, offers no escape. As soon as he sets foot on this slope, his skis slip in opposite directions. If all existential propositions are synthetic, 'is' does add something not contained in the subject; but Kant continues, dauntless: "By whatever and by however many predicates we may think a thing—even if we completely determine it—we do not make the least addition to the thing when we further declare that this thing is."[64] In attempting to adjudicate whether existence is a predicate, Kant has violated the boundaries he himself set to the work of pure reason. Given our human penchant for viewing things now as contingent, now as fixed and settled, he naturally invokes conflicting perspectives, deferring now to the mutability of things and our inability to know them a priori, now to their givenness and our power to treat them stipulatively, so that we can reason about them a priori, that is, with basic assumptions about their nature or reality taken for granted. Indeed, the scientist's causal standpoint (and Kant, like Aristotle and Avicenna, was a working scientist all his life) uses these rival perspectives in tandem. For it takes things to be necessary, in regarding them as established by their causes; but it treats them as contingent when it abstracts from those causes, even if only in the interest of insisting that without its causes the effect would not have occurred.

We find two contradictions, then, in Kant's refutation of the ontological argument: (1) His claim that all existential propositions are synthetic is inconsistent with his thesis that 'exists' is not a real predicate. (2) He slips into modal realism in insisting that all existential propositions are synthetic, as though the fact of mutability somehow gave him access to the *Ding an sich*. When a giant stumbles, can we do better? What can we say about existence and modality? We only compound Kant's error if we try to show that existence really is a real predicate. How could one know such a thing? What we need to show is that there are circumstances in which it is legitimate to treat 'is' as a predicate—as abstractable. But it is legitimate to abstract from the existence that all things have, and thus to make modality perspectival, not nominal. For the modal status of any judgment depends on the suppositions that support it—typically reflecting the causes and conditions we presume to operate, or abstracting from them. So there is no need to dismiss the idea of a necessary or a possible or contingent being; and no way to exclude such a being a priori.

All logical schemes are devised to meet conceptual requirements. The formal system does not originate such requirements but only signalizes them. We often think of subjects with a variety of predicates, some actual, some potential, like paper dolls that can be dressed in a variety of costumes. But we carry such play too far if we allow it to exclude talk about the possibility of notional beings or the contingency of real ones. Nor have we any grounds to equate existence with sensation or its sibling rival, materiality. We need not assume that what stays constant through change is always the "substrate" or the "matter." In sound, electricity, the reorchestration of a piece of music, what stays constant is the pattern; there is no enduring substrate. Indeed, Whitehead argues that such changes are the norm, and the Aristotelian kind, not just an exception but a mendacious fiction. So an open mind about existence is not just a commonplace of usage but probably good policy.

The mind is free, and so is language, to identify a subject by any trait we choose and to treat any other fact about it as a variable. That is what we do when we say of a given thing that it might or might not have existed or in asking others to put themselves in someone else's shoes. If it can be informative or useful to tell a man that he might have been born a woman, it is sheer stuffiness to say that existence cannot be a predicate. It is just as capable of use as a predicate as any property is; to deny that is to deny all thought of radical change, creation or destruction, evolution or extinction, spiritual rebirth or moral damnation. Which is to say that the denial that existence is a predicate masks in the language of logical analysis a metaphysical claim that is highly controversial and quite possibly mistaken.

We are free, then, to speak of being as necessary in one case and contingent in others and to block the a priori exclusion of our inference from contingency to a necessary being. Clearly, the ontological argument does not vault us from ideas to reality, and it leads nowhere without the idea of a perfect being. But our aim is not to use it to drag the unwilling to the reality of God but simply to show that the idea of such a being is not logically tainted. The only real trouble with that idea, I suspect, when all the special pleading is stripped away, is vertigo at the thought of Infinity, a yen to reduce all thoughts to finite, manageable terms—a motive counter to all that monotheism pursues in the idea of the divine.

The atoms of Democritus or Epicurus were necessary beings, since they were uncaused. As primal causes, they were unconditioned. Being indestructible, they existed under any circumstances. Was their nonexistence self-contradictory? Not in formal terms. But, for Epicurus, to deny absolute solidity (the atom) is to contradict sense experience, which, for him, is as absurd as self-contradiction; and Democritus gave his atoms the inalienable being that Parmenides had reserved to the primal unity. The survival of Eleatic logic is even plainer in Aristotle's eternal species. For him, ultimately, there would be a self-contradiction in claims that any species need not exist or have the nature it has. No ontological argument is in sight, not because Aristotle had no idea of necessary being but because he saw all basic realities—species, the cosmos, and its "principal parts," the heavens—as necessary beings. It seemed natural to him that the ancient search for *archai* would end with the discovery of essences. He could not say that the essence of things was existence. For that would leave the world undifferentiated. But he did analyze existence in terms of essence. He could not treat all existence as necessary, or reality would become immutable. But he did see what is actual as necessary—since facts cannot be changed. Particular events in the future remained contingent. But in species Aristotle found necessity:

the being of a thing, its essence, is necessary to it. To alter that is to destroy the particular; as long as this particular exists its essence remains unchanged in it, and that constancy is a logical necessity.

It was Avicenna, rendering an old insight philosophically articulate, under the influence of the *kalām*, and ultimately, of the powerful biblical idea of creation, who confined ontic necessity to God and argued that a necessary being is presupposed by the contingent. It was Anselm who saw in God's perfection the entailment of his reality. Kindred intuitions had been extant at least since Plato and Parmenides. But Anselm framed the argument. Its weakness lies not in any incoherence but in hopes that it might find controversial use. Its unsuitedness for polemics is pinioned in Aquinas's distinction between soundness and self-evidence. For Thomas agrees that God's perfection implies his necessary existence, but not everyone shares the requisite idea of God. Maimonides had shown that to reach that idea might demand lengthy exploration, special intuitions, or profound study of inspired traditions.[65] Anselm himself intimates as much, when he appeals to Gaunilon's religious meditations and experience. In a sense, the fullness of God's perfection is known only to God; so it is he alone who fully knows the argument's soundness.

The idea of God's perfection might be reached by reflection on the logic of piety, but it is not an idea that would be held by a naïf. The "fool" of the psalm (originally and in context, one whose acts seem oblivious to retribution) is, in the philosophical glosses, fixated in holding God's existence problematic. From that standpoint the ontological argument seems plain question begging. But given the idea of God as perfection and given license to treat being as an accident, a perfection, as Descartes purposefully puts it, the argument is sound. If being is a perfection and God's perfection is absolute, then God's being is necessary. That will be obscure only to those who persist in modeling God on imperfect beings. Kant fails to expose a formal fallacy in the argument, and since his refutation of the cosmological argument depends on the claimed incoherence of the idea of a necessary being, that too fails.

The classic contingency argument distills to this:

> There must be a reason for things' being as they are, either within or beyond them. But nothing conditioned can contain all that conditions it, or be its own cause. So there must be a transcendent cause of the determinations of being at large, including existence over nonexistence.

Leibniz highlighted the causal thinking behind such reasoning when he disengaged the principle of sufficient reason from the laws of logic. Spinoza had made it axiomatic.[66] To some rationalists like Averroës, causality seemed self-evident: if things have a determinate nature, he argued, something must determine it; otherwise they would be indeterminate and so would not exist. Leibniz was more circumspect, seeing that the causal principle is not an axiom of logic but a metaphysical assumption. Yet how could it be rejected?

It was Hume who taught Kant the alternative: for things need not be as they are. Avicenna, as a rationalist, had argued that since there is no contradiction in assuming that what is not is, there must be a transcendent cause (beyond the natures of all finite things) to make things as they are. Hume reversed the fields, arguing that since there is no contradiction in things' being other than as they are there is no transcendental reason (none beyond the nature of the mind) why they need be as they are. But the price to be paid is abandonment of the rationalist program of explanation. For explanation is a rationalist and realist enterprise. To explain is to answer or resolve a question, to alleviate a doubt. I can explain the moisture on my sill by assuming that it rained while I was out, that I left the window open, and that the wind was blowing. Given enough assumptions, what I see will follow from what I posit. Explanation differs from other ways of answering questions in that it fills not just the gap a question opens but the area around and behind that gap, relieving a doubt but also illuminating related questions—even helping us to see what our questions should be. So an explanation is more satisfying than a simple answer. It meets a more general curiosity. For the same reason it is costlier. Explanations are always metaphysical. They gain their powers of prediction and of satisfying the mind by making assumptions about the nature of the world and taking those assumptions beyond what is before us.

Explanation, I think, always involves mating our data, in ways that we find satisfying—aesthetically, formally—with ideas that we think we understand. Are the givens against which we measure what we hope to explain pure fabrications of the mind, imposed on the phenomena to create some semblance of order? Such antics would yield no explanation. The order we posit cannot exclude reference to reality; it rarely excludes reference to the extramental. For one does not explain things simply by invoking a categorial framework but only by ordering appearances in answer to what is taken to be the actual arrangement of things. Yet the categories used in explanation must be at least in part a priori, or there would be no discovery in matching data to pattern. Thus the role of formal values. Even analogy, which might seem wholly a posteriori when it compares one experience with another, needs the a priori category of likeness.[67] And, as Kant saw, all causal explanations have an a priori aspect, in that they invoke such concepts as necessity, uniformity, and permanence—none of which is an empiric given.

One does not explain the motions of a planet simply by a table of its sightings. We sketch an explanation when we see a pattern in those data—a circle (in a crude account), an ellipse (in a subtler one). We move closer to explanation when we can derive the pattern by a rule; closer still when the forces governing that rule are enumerated and related to one another and to other phenomena, as many as are relevant. I doubt if we can ever have a comprehensive explanation of a phenomenon. That may be an ideal which finite but increasing understanding can only approach. And no explanation of ours is ever fully conclusive, since there are always infinite alternative ways of accounting for the same appearances.[68] Yet there may be good grounds for preferring one explanation to another.

There are rival notions of explanation, but not all of them as readily accommodate the peculiar efficacy of explanation in its ordinary use. The notion that explanation merely marshals data ignores the satisfying fit of explanations to experience and slights elegance, symmetry, and other formal values. And 'marshaling' itself cannot be defined apart from formal and material—rationalist and realist—notions like economy, coherence, continuity, and comprehensiveness. If mental or ideal patterns are no more than that and do not represent realities, or if formal values are excluded, to block the a priori, data remain amorphous, and explanation loses its intellectual and predictive power.

The God of the cosmological argument is the final term of an explanatory program, and thus of quite a variety of streams of explanation that take their rise in the rationalist quest for understanding. Universal explanations, to do their work, need not (indeed cannot) deny or ignore the efficacy of proximate causes. But they do not take such causes as ultimates, because they do not find them to be self-explanatory. For every conditioned event there is always a prior cause, signaling the insufficiency of that which it conditions and urging us onward, beyond the merely conditioned, toward what can be explained only by its self-sufficiency, or absoluteness. This quest is not a new one. Retracing Abraham's steps toward the idea of God, the Midrash pictures him disgusted with the idols that were his father's stock in trade and recognizing that the sun, which sets, and the moon, which waxes and wanes, have not the adequacy required in Divinity.[69] Only what is beyond these, a Goodness that is the Source of all lesser perfections, is worthy of worship. Such a God will shed light and grace on all things, allowing us to recognize the world as God's work and charge. But only if God's act runs at the deepest levels of being, imparting perfection and delegating powers to created things, does God stand above the flood, as the unconditioned Cause and Creator.

Rationalism in its moderate form is the belief that some things are intelligible, that some aspects of reality answer to the understanding. In its strong form, it is the belief that all things are intelligible. Positivism also has two forms. The moderate form holds that some things are unintelligible; they simply *are*—as irreducible, unrelatable facts. The strong form holds that all facts are inexplicable. They do not connect to broader patterns and do not accommodate to categories otherwise identifiable as significant. Rather, the effort to find meanings in phenomena is idle play, like looking for figures in the clouds. Strong positivism regards phenomena not just as primary but as ultimate. A corresponding position in law stands with the positive dictum of the statute, not seeking a reason, utility, or goal.

Moderate forms of rationalism and positivism may seem mutually compatible, since neither makes a universal claim. Strict positivism is compatible with no form of rationalism, thus with no form of explanation. Unqualified rationalism is compatible with no form of positivism. But unqualified positivism is incoherent. It pronounces on existence and thus itself essays comprehensive explanation. Yet the pattern it assigns (although arresting in its totality) is the absence of all pattern, the impossibility of explanation. Unqualified positivism thus rests on a paradox. It seeks to render reality at large intelligible through the general pronouncement that it is unintelligible. An analogue is found, perhaps, in the art of Jackson Pollock, which creates order from an illusion of disorder. The shunning of (organic) form and (familiar) pattern and the partial surrender of the canvas to the play of chance create a seeming chaos, out of which coherent statements and even a subtly nuanced language emerge, expressive of varieties of disorder—much as the positivists (and existentialists) of Pollock's day use the language of unintelligibility to render experience intelligible through discussions of the nuanced varieties of nonsense and absurdity. But such orderly expressions of disorder cannot be absolute. They are parasitic on the varieties of order that they disown. Even the idea of the inexplicable assumes that explanation has some proper sphere, or the term would be opaque. Some Eastern philosophers urged that logic be used merely dialectically, to undermine all logical categories.

Here that would mean explaining away explanation itself, and that is impossible. So if any positivism is coherent it can only be a variety that is not comprehensive.

Strong rationalism might seem just as vulnerable, so that only a hybrid of moderate rationalism and moderate positivism can survive. For surely, it seems, not all things can be explained. If nature holds infinite facts, not all can be enumerated, let alone made sense of. And in a finite body of data, some items must be explained in terms of others, and some left unexplained, to avoid circularity, just as Euclid and the Dictionary must leave some terms undefined. But this reasoning is in error. For finite explanations can account for infinite data, as they do in scientific laws, and the limitations in our powers to explain and in our time for inquiry do not entail that anything is inexplicable in principle. As for the problem of primitives, first principles need not be unexplained. If self-explanatory, they leave no conceptual surds. Thus the quarrel between an unqualified rationalism, which sees all things as intelligible in principle, and that tempered rationalism which treats all things as intelligible, except first principles. For a rationalism qualified by positivism is a slipknot. It claims to explain some things by reference to others but presumes upon an understanding of those others, which ultimately it will not provide. Logically, this is kiting. It borrows on credit for which, in the end, there is no collateral. Qualified rationalism ends in positivism. So, at the last, nothing is explained.

What sort of explanatory principle would be self-explanatory? The quest for a first principle or *arche* of all things, pioneered by the Greek *physikoi* and continued in the search for an ultimate particle, a first moment of time, or a most general physical law, all seek an explanatory principle that will need no further explanation. Thus the Democritean atom, as pure being, neither came to be nor passed away but simply was (and is, and will be) without cause or further element. But can such atomism, or any quest for ultimate particles, or "theory of everything," relating the four basic types of force in nature, reach a principle that is self-explanatory? Or do attempts to make the outcomes of such inquiries the final word in our quest for understanding stunt that quest by giving us back a rationalism qualified and vitiated by positivism? For the atom, the element, the Universal Field Theory, if found, clearly does not explain itself. With any determinacy—of atoms, elements, quarks—we can always ask why these things are as they are. And if these particles or patterns are made ultimate, no answer is forthcoming. Conditioned "ultimates" cannot explain themselves without becoming self-sufficient. And how could any natural cause work so close to the root of nature without being conditioned in the interaction—becoming part of the system to be explained, rather than a final term of explanation?

Physics succeeds by focusing on specific variables that can be related tightly to one another in a single coherent and inclusive system. But it achieves its generality by abstracting from all sorts of values that do not lend themselves to measurement. Natural theology, too, must abstract if it is to find a universal explanatory principle. But as the focus of its abstraction it chooses not the measurable but the good. For it sees that the great theme of nature is not motion or extension or fields of force or radiation, or even determinacy, but goodness. Yet goodness must not be understood projectively, in terms of use or benefit to our specific, or personal, interests. The varieties of goodness are, as Aristotle said, as diverse as the varieties of being. No common thread unites them—except in the inner conatus that is the being of each thing. This, I take it, is the sense of the powerful sequence of questions God addresses to Job from the storm wind:

> Where were you when I laid the earth's foundations?
> . . . Who measured it with a line? . . .
> Who set its cornerstone
> When the morning stars sang together . . .
> Who closed the sea behind doors
> When it gushed forth from the womb
> When I clothed it in clouds
> Swaddled it in dense clouds
> When I made breakers my limit for it,
> And set up its bar and doors,
> And said, "Come so far and no further;
> Here your surging waves will stop"?
>
> Have you ever bidden the day to break,
> Assigned the dawn its place? . . .
> Hath the rain a father?
> Or who begot the dewdrops?
> From whose womb issues the ice? . . .
> Can you tie cords to the Pleiades
> Or loose the reins of Orion?
> . . . give an order to the clouds
> . . . send lightning on a mission
> and have it answer you, "I am ready"?
> Who put wisdom in the hidden parts?
> Gave understanding to the mind? . . .
>
> Can you hunt prey for the lion,
> And sate the hunger of the king of beasts? . . .
> Who provides for the raven
> When his young cry out to God for food? . . .
>
> Who sets the wild ass free?
> And looses the onager from bonds . . .
> He scoffs at the tumult of the city,
> And does not hear the driver's shouts,
> As he scours the hills for pasture,
> Searching for any green thing . . .
>
> Do you give the horse his strength
> And clothe his neck with a mane?
> Make him quiver like the locusts,
> His majestic snorting, terror,
> As he paws with force and charges into battle?
> He laughs at fear and does not break
> Or recoil from the sword . . .

Is it by your wisdom that the hawk is fledged
And spreads his wings for the south?
Does the eagle soar at your command,
Build his nest on high . . .
Lodge upon the fastness of a jutting rock,
And thence spy out his food . . .
His young gorging on blood?
Where the slain are, there is he.[70]

God does not browbeat Job but calls on him to see the varied kinds of goodness, in which all natural causes conspire, sometimes toward ends that please us, but always toward their own ends. What we need to explain all this is not some new law of gravity or some broader field theory, but a name for the Perfection toward which all things grope, the Source of the gifts—the strengths and energies—by which we strive. That name is God's, who moves things, as Aristotle saw, not by pushing them (and, in the Newtonian way, feeling them push back) but as the Goal and Aim beyond their motions, "the first and the last" (Isa. 44:6). The Rabbis touched this theme when they called God *ha-Makom*, the Place, the Ground of being. So did Paul when he sought to identify for the Athenians the unknown god whose altar he saw at Athens, by showing them that no mere artifact (or toy of human fable) could be the true divinity:

> God that made the world and all things in it, since he is Lord of heaven and earth, dwelleth not in shrines made with hands; nor is worshipped with men's hands, as though he needed any thing, since he giveth to all life, and breath, and all things; and hath made of one blood all nations of men, to dwell on all the face of the earth . . . that they should seek the Lord, if they might feel after him and find him, though he be not far from every one of us; for in him do we live and move and have our being. (Acts 17:24–28)

The kind of explanation that we seek in God is not of the sort that any conditioned thing could offer. To place any natural object in that role would be to revert to the kind of surrogacy for which Paul chided the Athenians. From the fact of their conditionedness we know all natural things to be contingent. But even if such things are allowed an intrinsic necessity to be just as they are, we are left with an unexplained positivity, since they still do not explain themselves. Rationalism remains incomplete. And so it must, unless the ultimate principle of explanation is absolute. This is the theistic option. It is not a necessity of logic, for we are speaking here of matters of fact, in regard to which our best notions are and must be mere hypotheses. The monotheistic hypothesis is that God, in the simple language that Scripture uses, made and sustains all things. For the causal principle should not be dropped arbitrarily but should be pressed and no residue of unresolved positivity retained. The outcome is that every explanatory principle must itself become explicable, and the Ultimate will be explicable not by analysis into parts or relation to causes ulterior to the ultimate but by reference to Itself, as a being that is self-explanatory, self-contained, perfect, and absolute—infinite, or divine.

There is no need, of course, for anything to be explained. But once explanation is allowed it cannot be said that there is no need for ultimate explanation. All explanations depend for their intelligibility on ultimate explanations. That is the reason for the sense of incompleteness in the partial explanations we typically receive: conventions of utility or tact block the path of inquiry that might have led onward toward ultimacy, and we are left with a kind of sterility or stultification, a dogma or a dictum marking the bourne beyond which we may not leave the common path and press into the deeper woods—as though talk of four forces, or tiny subparticles, or any entities assigned some sort of metric could possibly answer all the questions we have to ask of nature and experience.

It seems easy to propose that natural principles might be self-explanatory. But no likely candidate appears, and Spinoza offered good grounds for believing that there will be none: what is finite not only conditions but is conditioned by other finite things. And at this juncture what we seek to explain is the world at large. Findlay, long since having abandoned his ontological disproof, explains well why nature cannot simply speak for itself in its own terms:

> The world, considered by itself as an inclusive space-time system, and deeply pondered upon . . . has far too much unity, continuity, mutual accommodation, repetitive regularity, accessibility to knowledge and purpose and so forth, to achieve anything like the diremptive nullity of a Russellian class; yet it has also far too much looseness, uncoordinated collocation, undisciplined variety and harsh unamenability to knowledge and purpose to constitute anything like a self-explanatory, all-explanatory Absolute. . . . the world points uneluctably beyond itself: it not only is not, but also cannot be, all that there is.[71]

Monotheism is the belief, well grounded in our grasp of nature, that the divine is absolute and so not finite or contingent or conditioned. It is this concept, that the ultimate explanatory principle must be absolute, infinite and perfect, irreducible to the world's categories but explicable solely in Itself, that is expressed in the words "In the beginning God created heaven and earth."

3

Monotheism and Ethics

The idea of God allows us to integrate experience, promising to cap the work of reason in comprehensive understanding, consummating our quest for truth, beauty, and the good. Einstein's work is a model of this quest. The syntheses he sought were not mere essays in the direction of particulate simplicity. They sprang from a sincere faith that rationality in nature does not stop short at some surd, vacating all efforts at understanding, but portends a comprehensive intelligibility. Such faith is a special case of the religious trust in a still larger wisdom, of which our human ideas of value and perfection are only pale reflections. For monotheists today, as for the ancient Prophets, God is the reality that completes the pattern of our understanding—as the Primal Cause and Ultimate Good. Because God's reality is the apex of reasoning, the summit toward which all explorations point, the monotheist's affirmations of God's reality can bear no certainty. But we find their confirmations in every area of experience. In lesser notions of divinity, lesser gods, we find not the greater certitude of sensation or emotion but only incoherence—the intellectual incoherence whose expression is confusion, and the moral incoherence whose outcome is tragedy. We find a sounder certitude in the coherence afforded by God's universal relevance than in any sensory or emotive intuition.

The idea of God, like any idea, is necessarily a fiction, but it intends a reality no less than do our ideas of gravity or causality. Because God's reality is absolute, all the best we can say of him sounds like the children's stories that we dignify with the name of poetry. But when such poetry comes closest to the truth, we humans often try to bottle it in the reliquary of a canon, rendering insight as text and text as institution. Thus the words of Ecclesiastes (12:12), "Of the making of many books there is no end." Wisdom is sanctified as revelation when those visionaries whose insights seem most profound turn to a kind of counterpart of the poetic license of prayer: just as we take the liberty (or respond to the necessity) of addressing God at special moments and in special terms, so we find God addressing us in human language, the Infinite accommodating to human understanding and adjusting to the problematics of one age or culture, as if issuing from the dark or middle distance to meet our gaze. Here the idea of perfection takes concrete form in human minds, permits, indeed demands, a human voice to speak for it. When prophetic poetry is not mere automatism but a reflective, creative act, this reverse apostrophe is licensed by the recognition that all sound insight must spring from God's Self-revelation; for alongside the Absolute all acts of finite beings seem mere passivity.

God and Morals

But if God is absolute and infinitely transcendent, what possible message could he have for us, and what possible bearing could such a message have on how we choose to live our lives? (1) Can any mere existence have practical, moral relevance? How can any fact, even the reality of God, legislate values and issue imperatives? And, conversely, is there such a reality, or is the idea of God no more than a projection of our moral demands and spiritual longings? (2) If there are divine imperatives, how can they be specified? From a transcendental, universal Given, how can concrete and particular conclusions arise? And if such specification does not end in vacuity, does it not lead only to a fanaticism that tinges the quotidian with the lurid colors of misplaced absolutes? (3) Can any external standard impose obligations without destroying the autonomy crucial to moral agency? Does not a morality that takes refuge or even comfort in divine authority lose all claim to the title of morality? If so, the very idea of religion is vitiated. For what is religion if not a resting of human obligations on the authority of the sacred? Clearly, these questions must be answered. But not all philosophers have understood that the answers monotheism offers are not the same as those that naturally arise in other contexts.

1. The problem of facts and values has long seemed central to morals. Hume wrote of the strange transition he found when ethical writings move from talk of *is* to *ought*. How can merely existential premises yield prescriptive conclusions?

> In every system of morality which I have hitherto met with I have always remark'd that the author proceeds for some time in the ordinary way of reasoning and establishes the being of a God or makes observations concerning human affairs; when of a sudden I am surpriz'd to find that instead of the usual copulations of propositions *is*, and *is not*, I meet with no proposition that is not connected with an *ought*, or an *ought not*. This change is imperceptible; but is however of the last consequence. For as this *ought* or *ought not*, expresses some new relation or affirmation 'tis necessary that it shou'd be observ'd and explain'd; and at the same time that a reason should be given for what seems altogether inconceivable how this new relation can be a deduction from others which are entirely different from it.[1]

G. E. Moore used his Open Question Method to similar effect, to show that 'good' is not definable in naturalistic terms. The argument was subtle and powerful: whenever 'good' is equated with some natural property or item, the adequacy of the analysis remains open to question. That would be impossible if the analysis were sound. For analytic propositions are unquestionable; to question a thesis is to entertain its denial, and the analytic cannot be denied without absurdity.

Moore was at pains to apply his conclusions to the refutation of theistic subjectivism and all theologically grounded systems of ethical obligation: "To hold that from any proposition asserting 'Reality is of this nature' we can infer, or obtain confirmation for any proposition asserting 'This is good in itself' is to commit the naturalistic fallacy. And that a knowledge of what is real supplies reasons for holding certain things to be good in themselves is either implied or expressly asserted by all those who define the Supreme Good in metaphysical terms."[2] Antony Flew writes in similar spirit: "We cannot deduce any normative conclusion from premises which are all neutrally descriptive."[3]

Yet the monotheist's assertion of God's existence does not affirm a brute or "neutral" fact. Nor do ethical obligations flow from the reality of God by deductive or inductive inference. The monotheistic idea of God as absolute Perfection is rooted in the idea of the Good and regulated by that idea, even as our notions of goodness are refined and enlarged by monotheism. So here no open question will be found. To say of an act that it is right and that it is God's will become two different ways of saying the same thing. The paradox Moore expected in the querying of an analytic proposition now *does* emerge. For in monotheism goodness is constitutive in the idea of God. Theistic subjectivism, then, becomes a red herring, and the question whether right is right because God wills it, or God wills it because it is right, a pseudo-question. For in monotheism, normatively, God's will means what is right, and what is right is God's will.

Thus even the distinction between knowing and stipulating sinks into anthropomorphism: we humans must distinguish what we discover as fact from what we lay down as convention. But God does not conjecture about the right or need to reconcile surmise with commonplace, relying, as we do, on intersubjectivity as an index of objectivity or fairness. God needs no reality checks. For him, to know and to ordain are the same act. To assume that God might reject the right, then, is to substitute a less than perfect being for the God of Abraham. Thus Hume is disingenuous in saying that moralists may preface their moralizing by introducing "a God," as though the choice were an arbitrary matter. Had Hume encouraged his reader to dwell on diverse notions of the divine and the values they intend, the nexus of theology to ethics would not have seemed quite so arbitrary.

Does this imply that duties are *entailed* by God, made necessary by his existence—and obviated, perhaps, if God fails to exist—or that their assertion is somehow analytically equivalent to affirmation of God's reality? I think not. No statement and no fact *by itself* implies anything, as we have seen. There must be a context, and part of the context here is the need for subjects. Thus traditional monotheism sees creation as affording a milieu for human action and human choice. Obligations fall upon creatures. They do not belong to God; he is already perfect. It is because there is a gap between *is* and *ought* that we can speak of obligations. The gap is the division between facticity and Perfection. It is not denied but assumed in monotheistic ethics, poised in the dynamic focus of the Sistine ceiling, between the divine I AM and the human *ought*. No mere is *implies* an ought, or choice would be automatic and creation vain.[4]

Yet implication is not the only possible relation between God's perfection and human obligation, nor is it the fitting one. Obligations are not implied, except by other obligations, in the same sort of formal scheme that allows judgments to imply other judgments. Obligations are imposed—in the scintillating image of the Mosaic code, commanded. The very presence of Perfection issues a command which no imperfect being ignores. For even without sentience all beings pursue perfection. Thus the Psalmist's description of God's commands: "There is no speech, there are no words, their voice is unheard, yet their call goes out through all the earth" (Ps. 19:4–5). Biblically, creation itself takes place by commandments, just as Rabbinically it takes place for their sake.[5] God commands the light to shine, the firmament to form a sky, the waters to give place to land, the earth to put forth grass, the celestial lights to measure days, nights, and seasons, the air and water to teem with life, and all living beings to fructify. Everything in nature answers God's commands, acquiring order and goodness, projecting and pursuing perfection. Perfection imposes obligations not in itself but in a world where there are creatures whose ordered paths respond to God's imperatives—and subjects who grasp the idea of Goodness, after which all things strive, affectively or reflectively. God's goodness binds all to the good not by logic but by aspiration. It is in this sense that God and creation are counterparts.

Prophetic discourse marks the objectivity of moral norms by setting them down as commands from the mouth of God. So it is ironic to see moral objectivity played off against theism, as if no one's faith ever got beyond the pious sophistry of a Euthyphro. When the Torah underscores an obligation by calling it God's command, the stress is not on the rigidity that some associate with divine or human law, nor even on the commandment's provenance,[6] but on its absolute demand for fairness. Even in subjective perspective these obligations do not yield the bias or self-serving that Sophists might expect but inner appropriation of justice.[7] The Rabbis call it assumption of the yoke of the kingdom of heaven,[8] the onus of God's universal Imperium—a typically oblique challenge to the authority of Caesar. What we find here, then, is theistic deontology. The appeal to God is an appeal to the absolute, beyond all mere partiality: reality outbids facticity.

Thus monotheism sees no real distinction between 'ϕ is what ought to be done', 'ϕ is right', 'Ξ has an obligation to see that ϕ is done', 'Ξ has a right that ϕ be done', and 'ϕ is God's will'. Hebrew usage exhibits the interchangeability of these perspectives in its reliance on the idea of justice (*tzedakah*), where other schematizations of morals and law speak preferentially of right or duty. For 'justice' or some instance of it can be substituted for ϕ in any of the preceding schemata. As Plato saw, notions of duty, like notions of right, adopt a perspective that is too readily dismissed as an interested one; the idea of justice objectifies, placing us in the more universal stance of identifying no less with one party than with another. Thus biblical references to justice have the same objectifying force as biblical references to God as the author and authority of the Law.

But what motivates attacks on theistic ethics, I suspect, is often no animus against theistic subjectivism (which may be akin to the humanistic subjectivism of the critics, their own rationale writ large and competing for the same territory) but a dislike of specific religious dicta. The claim, in effect, is that false morals or bad conscience have been fathered upon divine authority or foisted upon Scripture. That case, I think, should be argued on its merits, point for point.

The broadest norm that the biblical commandments point to is the obligation to pursue perfection. Recognition of that obligation, concretely, at its most general or in some highly personal or socially embedded form, is an event or process in the human mind. It comes naturally in the biblical idiom to call it an act of God. But to discover God and to be discovered by him are the same event; monotheism makes no real distinction.

Since our highest values inform our idea of God, and have since the events encapsulated for us in Abraham's binding of Isaac, there is no question of a naturalistic fallacy in the monotheist's dictum that what is right is the will of God. But neither is there circularity. Just as the interdependence of reason and the senses does not make knowledge circular, since reason and perception are not singular propositions locked in mutual entailment, but ongoing processes, powers enriched and informed by one another's work,[9] so there is no circularity in the nexus of ethics to monotheism. For the dependence of values on God is ontic, not logical, and to make explicit the nature of that dependence is a perquisite of religion, not a prerequisite of ethics. The relation between God and the human good is one not of logical implication but of moral invocation. Just as grammar finds an understood subject for its imperatives, God's commands create his interlocutor. They are not the abstract entailments of some fact but the intimate or public appeal of an idea encountered by the mind or will, or, as the Torah puts it, uniting mind and will, by a heart.

We find no naturalistic fallacy in monotheistic ethics, then, because it relies on no reduction. God is no mere moral prop, since God is the Creator of the universe and Source of every good. But neither are morals reduced to the word of God. For our knowledge of what shall be counted as the word of God is and must be mediated by our highest conception of the good. This is so not only in dramatic confrontations of the type that Kierkegaard favors but also in the far more frequent cruxes at which we must interpret the traditions that articulate God's word in our moral lives individually, socially, and civilly.

Ethics is constitutive in framing our idea of God but does not exhaust its content, and theism is a source of moral resolve and sublimity of principle but far from being the sole source at which such values can be tapped. All human beings know a good deal about their obligations without turning to the idea of God. Morality can originate in personal grievance or social tact, sympathy or convention. We have a primary awareness of what the canons of perfection require of us—precognitively, since all beings, in their own ways, pursue their own good. So it is not necessary for the content of our obligations to be "derived" from knowledge of God's commands. By its modulation of the idea of the holy, religion may perfect morality (or pervert it) but is hardly necessary to its discovery. The logic that integrates our goals depends on monotheism, but the first glimmerings of those goals do not.

2. Antony Flew, long a gadfly with a special attachment to the church he knew best, offers this retort to Pascal's wager:

> Pascal's Roman Catholicism threatens with endless torture all those outside the true mystical body of Christ. But it is just as conceivable that there is a hidden God (Pascal's own "Deus absconditus"!) who will consign all and only Catholics to the fate they so easily approve for others. Since there is an unlimited range of pairs of possible transcendental religious systems, threatening as well as encouraging every conceivable way of life—including every variety of agnosticism and incredulity—with exactly the same inordinate rewards and punishments, such transcendentally backed threats cannot provide even a prudential reason for choosing one way of life rather than another.[10]

But Pascal knew that there are non-Catholic and non-Christian faiths. Like Anselm, he spent a good part of his life seeking grounds for the exclusion of Judaism. Our own options are broader than Flew's polarities. If our project or our problem is the specification of God's will, why should we omit the possibility of a universal, and so exclusive, theology that is *not* condemnatory? The Jewish sources assign a portion in the World to Come to the righteous of all nations (Tosefta Sanhedrin

13. 1–2). And Ben Zoma's remark, "Who is wise, he who learns from all men" (Avot 4.1), voices a doubt that wisdom will be found parochially.[11] Islamic salvation belongs only to Muslims, and (contrary to Mosaic majoritarianism—Exod. 23:2, Sanhedrin 3b, Bava Metzia 59b, Yevamot 40a) orthodox Islam presumes a timeless right answer to every juridical question. Yet Islam still promises a reward to jurists who err in good faith about some still unexplored question of law—and a twofold reward to those who decide it rightly. So independent judgment is not punished for an honest mistake.[12] Even Origen, who held the Christian view that there is but one path to salvation, reasoned that God's infinite mercy would exclude no one; everyone would finish the race and in the end Satan himself would be reconciled.[13] One Midrash goes far beyond Christian thoughts of the harrowing of hell, or Origen's winnowing of souls through cosmic history, to picture not just those of little or no faith but the wicked redeemed, not by sacrifice but by song: on Judgment Day, according to this characteristic aggadah, God will preside with King David at a great banquet for the righteous. At its close, God will pass the wine cup to Abraham, inviting him to lead the grace after meals. But Abraham will plead his unworthiness, so the cup will pass to Isaac, Jacob, Moses, Joshua. Finally David will accept the honor and sing a psalm so lovely that the hearty Amen from the pious in heaven and the wicked in hell will move God to send his angels to lead even these to paradise.[14]

Flew concludes too hastily that a transcendent God's demands must be obscure or arbitrary. For God's Face might be hidden while his will is not. If our question is, How can the Transcendent, known to us only as a lofty ideal, regulate the particularities of the here and now, sanctions are a mere distraction. One ancient homily pictures both the blessed and the damned seated in long rows opposite one another. Again a feast is laid, but both groups have their arms bound in splints and cannot put the delicacies into their mouths. The wretched suffer agonies, unable to enjoy the feast. But among the righteous each feeds his neighbor opposite, and all take joy both in the banquet and in the joy they give each other.

The little fable illustrates the dictum of the Sages that all is in the hands of heaven except the fear of heaven (Berakhot 33b). For here beatitude depends on freely adopted (but not so easily escaped) choices of attitude. Plato's image comes to mind, of the choice each soul makes of its own destiny (*Republic* X 617e). We see the triviality of eschatology and how easily we can make our own heaven or hell from the materials of this life, specifically, pleasure and pain. The same homily illuminates clearly how simple the nexus is between the God of monotheism and the principles of morality—much in the spirit of Micah (6:8, echoing Deut. 10:12): "It hath been told thee, O man, what is good and what the Lord expecteth of thee: only the practice of justice, the love of kindness, and modesty in walking with thy God." Note the pedagogical force of *doresh*, expecteth—not what God compels, still less what he entails, but what God morally expects of us, thus, what he teaches.

Transcendence does not render God's commandments arbitrary, subject to infinite conjectures. Even a pagan deity is more constant than that. For each pagan god catches the light of a particular value complex, celebrated or defined in its clash or contrast with other values. Only caprice, favor, venality, or anger interferes with such thematic clarity. The God who integrates all values brooks no such obscurity. Only goodness is There. As the Torah puts it: "A God of good faith and without iniquity, just and straight is He." And the text continues: "Is wrong His? No, His children's is the fault" (Deut. 32:4–5)—What is problematic lies not in God's transcendence but in the troubles we may have in comprehending the good. Even that is not as hard as it is sometimes made to seem.

Despite the well-known shibboleth of relativism, the core of human decency varies little from culture to culture, and its image wavers only in response to pressing needs or vested interests, the cant or demands of some class or caste. Most moral differences (polemics and apologetics apart) are differences of strategy, emphasis, or style, not of principle. True, a culture, like an individual, may grow demoralized in severe asperity, or through moral unpreparedness for wealth. There is cultural decadence, just as there is personal corruption. Cruelty, pain, and death, by a kind of natural psychic defense, can be confronted, *faute de mieux*, with gallows humor or even made positive values by the mind's deep unwillingness to accept evil as such. Plague or abject penury can make death a joke, just as decadence can make pain seem all that remains piquant in life. Yet the Ik, whose sufferings Colin Turnbull recorded, making such reflections smack of truism, have sued him for ethnic slander. They do not appropriate and will not acknowledge the norms he ascribed to them. In the Nazi death camps, it is said, values sometimes took strangely contorted forms. But even there the highest and most basic forms of human nobility and moral courage could reassert themselves. We are conditioned, not determined, by our surroundings.

Exotic lands are the traditional locus of radical variances in human moral standards. Exotic customs are frequently described in terms of what seems most exotic in them, and their alienness is accentuated by their embeddedness in social grammars and lexicons whose cues and intensions ego may not know. But whether the homily fills the hands of the righteous and the wicked with forks or chopsticks too long to reach their mouths, the meaning is the same.

Cannibals are a favorite recourse of those who seek some deep mystery in the demands of morals. Yet cannibals do not eat human flesh because they think it right to act savagely but because their culture has not purged itself of institutions built on the hope of finding divinity in the ritualized frisson of devouring brains or hearts or marrow bones. Custom inures and tradition can enshrine virtually any practice. But cannibals are not the only victims of the tyranny of usage. Any custom can become so much our own that clever thinkers will readily defend it. What matters is our capacity, both widespread and rare, to see the flaws in customs of our own. Without the cushion of snobbery or the veil of romance, the urbane are no gentler and the primitive no more innocent, en bloc, than humanity at large. But all human beings, except the very worst, are amenable to moral insight, communication, and instruction. Adolescent homosexuality was prominent in certain highland peoples of New Guinea, partly because marriage was wrongly feared as the cause of kuru, a deadly disease actually caused by a slow-acting brain virus spread by ritual cannibalism. When the isolated tribesmen found that others disliked or laughed at their practices, they rapidly abandoned them, even before learning the effective means of stopping kuru.[15]

When Albert Schweitzer first set up his medical station at Lambaréné, one of the tribal peoples he was treating was a cannibal group, the Pahouins. He noted their general aggressiveness and their tendency to lie and steal, clearly wondering whether and how his work and teaching might exert a moral influence on them. But it was he who proved the learner. When World War I broke out, recruits were taken from the area. Weeks later word came back that ten were dead. Now the cannibals were shocked: "'Ten men killed already in this war!' said an old Pahouin. 'Why, then, don't the tribes meet for a palaver? How can they pay for all these dead men?'"[16] The tally of human waste taken for granted in mechanized warfare and made possible by high levels of social integration was outlandish to the cannibals. They were not ignorant of human worth, any more than Schweitzer was, although some of their institutions gave it a nominal monetary price and others involved its ritual flouting. The culture that had borne Schweitzer, and to which he bore allegiance in many but not all ways, flouted it far more efficiently.

George Catlin, the American painter who traveled among the Indians of North America, documenting their culture and painting portraits of their leading personalities, observed the exposure of an aged tribesman, another favorite instance of those who seek a moral vagueness in the claim that moral standards differ widely from culture to culture:

> When we were about to leave the village of the Puncahs we found that they too were packing up all their goods. . . . My attention was directed to one of the most miserable and helpless-looking objects I have ever seen in my life: a very aged and emaciated man of the tribe, who was to be *exposed*.
>
> The tribe were going where hunger compelled them to go. The old man, who had once been a chief and a man of distinction in the tribe, was now too old to travel. He was reduced to mere skin and bones. He was to be left to starve, or meet with such death as might fall to his lot, and his bones to be picked by the wolves. . . .
>
> His eyes were dimmed. His venerable locks were whitened by a hundred years. His limbs were almost naked. He trembled as he sat by a small fire which his friends had left him, with a few sticks of wood within his reach and a buffalo's skin stretched upon some crotches over his head. It was to be his only dwelling, and his chances for life were reduced to a few half-picked bones laid within his reach, and a dish of water. He was without weapon of any kind to replenish his supply, or strength to move his body from its fatal locality.
>
> He had unluckily outlived the fates and accidents of wars to die alone at death's leisure. His friends and his children had all left him and were preparing to be on the march. He had told them to leave him: "I am old," he said, "and too feeble to march."
>
> "My children," said he, "our nation is poor, and it is necessary that you should all go to the country where you can get meat. My eyes are dimmed and my strength is no more. My days are nearly all numbered, and I am a burden to my children. I cannot go and I wish to die. Keep your hearts stout, and think not of me. I am no longer good for anything."
>
> They finished the ceremony of *exposing* him and took their final leave of him.[17]

The feelings expressed are those we would expect in any confrontation with unhappy choices. Necessity grounds the decision and the informal institution that supports it; individual character joins with ritual formulaic to salve the natural feelings of those who must travel on. What is depicted is not callousness but a culturally mediated confrontation with stark necessity. Catlin does not observe that Indians think it "perfectly fine and proper" to abandon their infirm along the road. On the contrary, they seem to feel much the same about it as anyone would and call on the resources of their culture not to exacerbate but to mitigate the harshness of the moment. Indeed, the very idea that any course of action might be widely accepted in a culture entails the active presence of moral standards and basic social tests of acceptability. Such standards might fail. They are not criterial of right or decency. But their general thrust produces little that is inhuman.

Catlin's general observations on the moral standards of the peoples among whom he traveled reflect the experience of many an ethnographer:

> I have roamed about visiting and associating with some three or four hundred thousand of these people under an almost infinite variety of circumstances. From their very many and decidedly voluntary acts of hospitality and kindness I feel bound to pronounce them by nature a kind and hospitable people. I have been welcomed in their country and treated to the best that they could give me without any charges made for my board. They have often escorted me through their enemies' country at some hazard to their own lives and aided me in passing mountains and rivers with my awkward baggage. Under all of these circumstances of exposure no Indian ever betrayed me, struck me a blow or stole from me a shilling's worth of my property.[18]

It is not obscure, then, what goodness requires of us, although circumstances may restrict our choices and culture may refine or debase them.

Flew's notion that God might require anything at all of us, that there is no telling just what behavior or way of life is God's will, burlesques the monotheistic idea, which finds no fault or flaw in God (Ps. 92:16). One hardly recognizes here the God who appeared to Moses, who is full of compassion and will brook no evil (Exod. 34:6–7). If the question is, 'How could the Infinite and Timeless prescribe laws for the finite and time-bound?' our only possible answer is 'How could God not?' The very idea of divinity is bound up with what is best and most perfect. Thus Amos (5:4–5, 14–15) speaks interchangeably of the quest for God and the quest for the good, and Hosea (4:1) equates loving-kindness, truth, and knowledge of God.[19]

Refinements in human ideas of God go hand in hand with moral progress. So when violence and evil are excluded as positive values they are purged from divinity;[20] they reemerge pari passu with the neopagan gods of evil. The conjunction only illustrates the dynamic of the idea of divinity considered in our first chapter: when the Stoics argue that God's will must be made known to man, they appeal to their ideals of duty and concern as fundamental moral goods. When the Epicureans urge that legislation is no interest of the gods, they too press their ideals—of tolerance and *ataraxia*, dismissing divine governance of man and nature as beneath the notice of the blessed and immortal. Even the Epicurean gods, in their sublime detachment, are held up for emulation, although normatively *ataraxia* alone should be the human aim. In every case, the divine is what is thought highest and best: just as the measure of our morals is found in our deities, so the pattern for our morals lies in our ideas of the divine. The core of monotheistic ethics is the identity of the love of goodness with the love of God.[21] There is no more ambiguity in what such a God requires of us than there is in our ideas of the good. Hence the centrality of Maimonides' claim that an adequate vision of God demands moral and not just intellectual virtues.[22]

It is sometimes claimed that linking divinity to morals harms morals when God is understood as absolute Perfection. Transcendence, it is argued, places God beyond moral relevance.[23] Monotheism is accordingly blamed for the "death of God," the seeming fading of God's moral relevance. The critics take transcendence to render emulation impossible: one cannot both take God to be transcendent—holy, in Isaiah's language—and fulfill the commandment of Leviticus (19:2), "Ye shall be holy, for I the Lord thy God am holy." Yet that, precisely, is what the Torah calls on us to do. It addresses our nature by giving holiness a moral and spiritual meaning germane to our humanity. For the Golden Rule, although essential to God's law, is but a corollary of the global call to self-transcendence that is God's chief commandment, the commandment to reach out toward God's own holiness.

Human holiness, however, begins with human nature; and the call to emulate God's holiness, then, contains no paradox, so long as we recall that what we seek is our perfection, not God's. God's transcendence would make divinity irrelevant only if we had no idea of the human good, if human self-transcendence were inconceivable and unknown.[24] But as things stand, the nexus of morality to divinity is the plainest conceptual shift we know, since it is from our highest values that our idea of divinity takes its rise. It would be a poor thinker indeed who could not rederive morality from the Ideal that has morality at its source. The emulation called forth by God's perfection—expressed biblically as pursuit of holiness and in Plato as the task of becoming as like to God as lies in human capacity (*Theaetetus* 176)—means pursuit of human perfection. The intellectual energies of the monotheist are thus extended not in seeking to prove that what God asks of us is moral decency and rectitude, reverence toward God and kindness toward man, but in delineating the dimensions of such obligations, a problem not of theology but of morals, law, and education.[25]

The Infinite, as such, is not specified. So the specification of moral rules out of the general demands of goodness and the application of such rules to particular circumstances introduces no finitude or particularity into God. What such laws receive from God is their imperative force, the demand evoked by the Highest in the will of all aspiring beings. To interpret these requirements is a human task, just as the very notion of a divine will is a human notion. The pure idea of God gives only the upward direction, toward the highest good. It does not chart a course. For even the idea of upwardness has meaning only with reference to the strivings of finite beings. Its moral force as a command addresses the strengths and needs of beings capable of conscious aspiration.

Yet God's infinite goodness comprehends the good of a cactus or a groundhog or an armadillo, and that good is channelized according to the specificities of their natures (cf. Gen. 8:19). In the same way there is a human good. We need not seek it in the far reaches of the cosmos (cf. Deut. 30:12–13) but can find its requirements within and among ourselves, in an adequate understanding of our own natures as individuals and of the demands made by our interdependence and our potential to enhance the human condition through mutual consideration, love, care, respect, and regard. Thus, as Maimonides explained, when the Sages explicated the biblical commandment "Ye shall be holy," they specified familiar human virtues: "They glossed: as He is gracious, so do you be gracious; as He is compassionate, so do you be compassionate."[26] It is because specifications of the divine imperative rest on the adequacy of our understanding of individual and shared human nature that the Rabbis did not hesitate to name concretely those aspects of God that man must emulate and to signify by their omission those which we are not called on to pursue: as he is merciful, so be ye merciful—but not "As he is impersonal, so be ye impersonal" or "As he is all-encompassing, so be ye all-encompassing." God's transcendence is transcendence in perfection. What we are called on to perfect in ourselves are the perfections in us, that is, the human virtues. Josephus aptly states the case when he describes how Moses structured the insights of Abraham and the traditions of his children into a way of life and a legislative system: "The reason why our lawgiver in his legislation far exceeded all other legislators in usefulness to all is that he did not make religion a part of virtue but had the insight to make the various virtues part of religion: justice, fortitude, self-control, and the mutual harmony in all things of the members of the community. All our actions and studies and words have a connection with piety towards God. For our lawgiver left none of these things indefinite or undetermined."[27]

Some theologians worry that divine transcendence sets up a sick variety of relativism in morals, the monotheistic idea functioning (like the Buddhist idea of emptiness, it is claimed) as a kind of touchstone against which excessive claims are tested: from the distance of Infinitude, all finite claims seem nugatory, and differences recede into triviality. All beings claim some share in the Absolute, but none can make good an absolute claim. With such thoughts in mind, Gordon Kaufman argued that religious absolutes provide excuses for outrages, since all merely human values pale beside them.[28] But this attempt to lay fanaticism and opportunism at the door of monotheism ignores the fact that absolute Perfection supports, sustains, and orders human values; it does not simply apologize for them, compete with, or dismiss them. Like Flew or Gaunilon's fool, Kaufman has slipped the word 'Absolute' from its only coherent meaning.

Taken dialectically, the argument can be answered dialectically. For if absolutes can corrupt by eclipsing lesser values, so can the complaint that there are no absolutes. The nihilism resident in such a plaint is inherently demoralizing. That, in part, is sometimes the intent. For nihilism, like relativism, can never be complete, and the transvaluers of values always have specific targets in mind. Their aim, historically, has never been the impossible one of defeating all ideas of the good. As Eugene Borowitz put it, paraphrasing a rueful remark from the Jewish "Lost Generation" of the 1920s and '30s: "We used to say we didn't believe in anything. But then we met some people who *really* didn't believe in anything." On one level, the issue is not what can be done in the name of the Absolute but what has been done. On another, the issue is not what can be done but what can be justified.

Any value, from the greatest to the least, can be the rationale of vice or atrocity—relativism serves as readily as the specious absolute that is its biographical forerunner or dialectical running dog. The question is not how we can get along without absolutes, in view of what has been done in their name. For we cannot. Rather, we must ask how we can define our absolutes so as to discredit the imposture of fathering human wickedness upon them and rationalizing human weakness in their name. The answer, plainly, is that we must formulate them wisely and hold to them thoughtfully. Only goodness can serve as a foundation, and the task of defining goodness is useful and necessary intellectual and practical work, extended over many lifetimes.

In defense of the religious idea, we can say that its explicit and only legitimate appeal is in behalf of goodness—not, as in relativism, against the notion that there is any such thing, and not, as in Kierkegaard, in behalf of the notion that there is something higher than the Good, because it is darker or deadlier. If the claim is that in a given situation there may be more than one optimal moral strategy, that seems self-evident. One does not need theistic or any other absolutes, such as nothingness or death, to recognize that fact. But if the notion is that in no situation is one moral strategy objectively superior to others, that claim is palpably false. The very credibility of diverse viewpoints rests on the recognition of objective merit in diverse claims. It is inconsistent to appeal to intersubjectivity and then deny that any choice can be rightly preferred to any other.

God's infinitude does not imply moral relativism any more than it implies nihilism or excludes pluralism. It legislates only an obligation toward perfection as we most adequately conceive it, not omitting the recognition that in human affairs, whether cognitive or moral, intersubjectivity is often our best touchstone of objectivity. The recession of all values before the Infinite is an illusion. For it is only to a finite viewer that distance diminishes an object and moral distance seems to entail a loss of moral significance. For the Infinite there is no loss of moral worth, no retreat of values into nullity or parity. Thus Plotinus, rejecting our moral myopia, described the Divine as a circle whose center is everywhere.[29] The Torah's intent is to foster our adoption of such a God's-eye view of the worth of every being. That is why the Golden Rule is a corollary of the commandment to emulate God's holiness.

3. What, then, of the Kantian and later Nietzschean issue of heteronomy? Its roots are Epicurean and run back deep into the soil of the Sophists' claims to humanism. For Kantian autonomy is a moral specification of Hellenistic and Hellenic *autarkeia*, and the Epicureans were among the first to make the charge that one who does not follow his own path (not that of duty or the gods!) perverts the course of morals. But Kant is commonly seen as discovering heteronomy, when he urges (on more Stoic lines) that a choice is moral only if it is genuinely our own; and thus, only if it follows no interest but expresses the free self-legislation of the rational will alone: all choices grounded in interests are heteronomous and so either nonmoral or immoral, depending on whether interest has usurped the role of principle or merely noted its irrelevance. Principle alone is of moment to morals.[30] Appeals to perfection are vacuous; those to divine perfection, worse: either parasitic on moral notions, or vicious, filling the place of moral judgments with notions "drawn from such characteristics as lust for glory and domination and bound up with frightful ideas of power and vengefulness."[31]

James Rachels tightens the screws somewhat, much as Findlay did with Kant's critique of the ontological argument. He proposes that there is no God, since a God must be worthy of worship, but worship entails absolute surrender of moral autonomy, which no moral agent can make.[32] The argument is not as telling as it seems. To begin with, it does not meet the issue head-on, by finding the alleged abdication of our moral judgment incompatible with God's perfection. Veering away from such theological critiques, Rachels finds a contradiction in the notion that worship can be a moral act, since no rightful authority can demand the surrender of conscience: "The first commitment of a moral agent is to do what in his own heart he thinks is right."[33] I wonder about that. For one's obligation is to do what is right, which is not always what one thinks is right. I also wonder about the mimicry of Kant, making God's nonexistence a moral postulate, where Kant makes his existence a moral postulate. Isn't it wishful thinking to make ethics dictate ontology? Leaning heavily on God's absoluteness, Rachels insists, "We cannot recognise any being *as God*, and at the same time set ourselves against him"—let alone dicker with him, as Abraham does over Sodom and Gomorrah.[34] Apparently, Rachels sees nothing odd in the idea of God's granting us moral judgment only to make us discard it.

If we stay with Rachels's rather stiff and truncated notion of divine absoluteness, and goodness does not enter the question at all—at least not in any humanly identifiable form—we must ask ourselves why such a God need defer in any way to our moral expectations—least of all by permitting humans to be moral decisors. The Ashʿarite tradition, which frames the mainstream orthodoxy of Sunni Islam, finds no impropriety in God's commanding us to do the impossible and then damning us for failing to do it. God, the Ashʿarites argue, not man, sets the standards, and there is no injustice to a chattel. If Rachels finds this uncomfortable, that is only because he places autonomy ahead of piety. But that begs precisely the question he has pressed.

Yet we need not go so far. Rachels assumes that moral autonomy is indivisible, an all-or-nothing affair, the fairest of human possessions, indeed the only one of moral note, not to be shared and never in need of aid. But perhaps worship does not entail surrender of moral autonomy at all, or not in any absolute or abject way. That, I have argued, and not the insignificance of human moral judgments, is what the binding of Isaac signifies. The whole Rabbinic enterprise, I think, is carried on in the same spirit, when it seeks to work out what we must take to be God's will by applying, within the ongoing dialectic of an integrated legal and moral system, our highest conceptions of the human good. Thus the Rabbinic insistence on care in the inspection of, say, a slaughtered fowl: God himself, the Rabbis insist, cares about the pennies a poor housewife might have wasted if an acceptable bird is deemed unfit to eat. Norbert Samuelson is on sound Rabbinic ground, then, when he recognizes the dialogical character of our relationship with God:[35] biblical norms not only acknowledge but demand that we interpret our ideas of God's will in the light of our moral insights.[36]

Some people, in the spirit of Kierkegaard, hold that there are higher goods than autonomy. Many take piety itself as a moral virtue and find merit in doing God's will. If so, the Enlightenment ideals of resolution and independence should at least be compared with their more self-effacing counterparts before we summarily dismiss religious ethics, as Kant does; or religion itself, as Rachels does—folding every kind of piety into the same authoritarian crust. Maimonides argues that, far from being infallible or even what is best in us, the moral judgment we commonly use places us on all fours with the beasts, since it generally follows subjective apprehensions of our interests. Unlike Kant, the Rambam has no quarrel with interests, but he is not content with subjective appraisals. It is reason, not our animal apprehensions of the good, that gives us an affinity to God (*Guide* I 2). Curiously, this position is not remote from Kant's, whose pietist background and moral purism led him to the view that our subjective moral judgments can never assure us of the purity of our own motives and so can never guarantee the justice of our cause. Like Maimonides, Kant finds in reason a higher ground of certitude, and, like Kant, Maimonides equates the dictates of moral reason in the minds of the pious with the word of God (*Guide* II 45.1; cf. II 35–39). Where, then, is the surrender?

It is the idea of human moral infallibility (a secularized offshoot of the idea of revelation) that sets up the specious competition between divine and human moral suasions. But the only plausible foundation for the claim that human moral judgments are infallible is some form of subjectivism, grounded in the spurious notion that I cannot do wrong if I follow the dictates of my conscience.[37] It was this notion that led Nietzsche to expand Kant's claim that autonomy is a necessary condition of morality into the far more problematic assumption that autonomy is sufficient to morality, laying the groundwork for the existentialist view that any choice of mine is right if it is authentically my own—my conscience, right or wrong—a view that ill consorts with the existentialist plaint that none of us has the wisdom to make choices for the universe, as morality asks us to do.

Clearly, if my moral notions are fallible or partial, if I can see that I might err and that what I take for moral reasoning might be bias in some appealing guise—as moral fallibilism would urge and as anyone has good reason to believe who has heard loaded pleas *in foro interno vel publico*—then I should be open to moral counsel where I can find it; I should heed communal and traditional laws and rules of all sorts, unless I have good reason to believe them wicked—a fortiori, laws and norms that come to me from God, as the commands that Rachels questions do, *ex hypothesi.* Of course I will retain my judgment. For who but I will decide whether to obey? Even the sheerest pietism cannot rob me of that role—or there is no virtue in acceptance. But the notion that I have nothing to learn from custom or tradition or the word of God itself, if I am privileged to receive it, is not humanism but hubris.

In addressing the problem of heteronomy, Emil Fackenheim takes up the ancient Stoic and modern Kantian and existentialist idea of moral appropriation: granted we do not invent God's law, he reasons, we do appropriate it, and in so doing choose it. So the pious do not abdicate the moral role.[38] The response is sound and good, as far as it goes. Sound, in seeing that neither autonomy nor surrender is absolute in normal human beings. Good, in showing that piety does not mean moral spinelessness. But still, it must be asked, on what grounds are believers to accept God's law, and how are they to know which law is God's? If a law is accepted on sheer authority, without question or grounding in justice, the moral objections return with a vengeance.

Yet who, apart from Søren Kierkegaard's highly problematic knights of faith—the phrase is redolent for me of Erich Auerbach's trenchant remarks about the medieval romancers' need to paper over the grisly work that was the real business of men like the now happily legendary Saint George[39]—what person of genuine piety would act or choose a way of life based on authority alone? Or are we really to believe, after all that Plato taught us, that piety is consistent with brutality or can thrive, unguided, alongside stolid thoughtlessness? Surely a person of pure and honest faith accepts obligations from authority only by assuming that authority to be well founded—in the legitimacy of a law, the sanctity of a relationship of family, community, friendship, mutuality, or fidelity—or by the inherent goodness of its author, as with God. We philosophers may seek to isolate by analysis the act of obedience from the values that inspire it. But no one obeys, just as no one acts, without some idea of the good. And if some acts of obedience are problematic, as they surely are, the fault lies in the habit of obedience or the notion of the good that guides it—the wrong law or the wrong god—not in the fact that some men sometimes rest their choices on systems of law or custom or sources of obligation they did not invent themselves. For we all do that when we pay our taxes. What else is representative government, custom, tradition, or any institution if not surrender, in some measure, of autonomy for reasons that we think, in some measure, justified?

It is here that we must confront issues of particularity that few philosophers between Ibn Khaldūn and MacIntyre have grasped and firmly held in mind. For what presents itself to us as the word of God, for moral purposes, is not the sheer epiphany of the Absolute, but the mediated ideal of humanity, as specified morally and prescribed culturally in laws and traditions, literary models, and systems of practice. True, we need not, indeed we cannot, accept or reject all that we receive en bloc, but we do receive and respond to integrated and concatenated systems of norms, not isolated precepts, which would have little meaning on their own. Part of the integration of such norms is their historical, ethnic, communal embeddedness, and part of their concatenation is their linkage to religious ideals and a heritage of shared experience, thought, and values, including ideas about the divine. The endeavor to settle great moral issues—abortion, capital punishment, homosexuality—outside the environs of some historical or ecumenical tradition has exacerbated those issues in our multicultural and often deracinated communities and transformed them from matters of moral and intellectual concern (or relatively homogeneous presumption) to battlegrounds of sophistic rhetoric, litigious struggle, political polemic, and worse. If such issues are to be addressed, rather than simply pacified in some brutish way, we will need not a stripping away of the traditions that articulate our moral insights, as secularists might suppose, but a dialogue among the human traditions that digs into their historic confrontations with the values that transcend historic particularity and discovers commitments we can share and syntheses and accommodations we can voice with moral conviction and credible authority.[40] It is in this spirit that I want to explore Jewish responses to the problem of heteronomy—not because they are privileged and still less because they are sui generis but because of what I think the best of them can contribute, in a comparative framework, to the dissolution of what I see as a confusion that casts its pall over practical as well as conceptual thinking.

A variety of Jewish thinkers have seized upon the issue of heteronomy. Some glory in it, finding in the idea that our obligations are commanded a refreshing sense of creatureliness that promises relief from the chill Enlightenment ideal of individual moral isolation, and a way of slamming shut the door that post-Protestant notions of personal conscience seem to leave open to the drafts of moral subjectivism.[41] Some have adopted varieties of legal positivism that graze the surface of incoherence. For what can it mean, for example, to claim that we are obligated to obey the commandments in God's (or any other) law, while denying that these are in any sense a moral code? It makes sense to try to disentangle moral obligations as conventionally understood in one tradition from those articulated in another. But how can a fundamental sense of 'ought', taken to be overriding, be distinguished from morality, rather than forming a part of it, offering to complement or counter other notions of right, and, by the same token, opening itself to their critiques?

As Sid Leiman notes, Jewish canonical and quasi-canonical sources speak with many voices on the subject of God's commandments.[42] Some of those voices are far from rationalistic, and few would accept reduction of God's commandments to the commonplaces of secular humanism that are sometimes equated with reason or morality by advocates and critics alike. A special interest in the particularity of God's commandments is natural, and it can become a mark of piety for such interests to focus on those duties that are not obvious corollaries of the Golden Rule. The deontologist's concern with acting from a sense obligation rather than for the sake of any goal seconds such particularism, and, for many Jewish thinkers, joins or interprets the motives of creatureliness, to focus moral interests on the sense of biddenness. Respect for the integrity of the Rabbinic system, with or without chauvinistic or apologetic overtones, or simple ethnic pride, links with these more spiritual interests in promoting Jewish legal positivism. For clearly Halakhah does not find sufficient detail in global maxims, or adequate foundations in external critiques—whether or not they call themselves moral.

This complex of motives finds an able advocate in Marvin Fox, who transmutes Maimonides' careful distinction of the commands of reason from those of interest into a halakhic positivism that risks sundering the Mosaic law and biblical theology from their moral moorings and leaving halakhic authorities without the moral guidance long constitutive in their creative work of interpreting and applying what they sincerely believe to be God's Law.[43] That sundering, a leitmotif in the work of Yeshayahu Leibowitz, is addressed in a balanced and tactful study by Aharon Lichtenstein. Lichtenstein warns that the purposes of Halakhah cannot be reduced to the ethical. Nor, we might add, can those of any legal system. Neither can they be obviated or overridden by the sheer claims of some alternative ethos. Yet the moral concerns of the halakhic system are undeniable:

> As for the outright rejection of the ethical moment, however, I cannot find such quasi-fideistic voluntarism consonant with the main thrust of the tradition. One might cite numerous primary texts by way of rebuttal, but a single verse in Jeremiah (9:23) should suffice: "But let him that glorieth glory in this, that he understandeth and knoweth Me, for I am the Lord who exercise mercy, justice and righteousness in the earth; for these I desire, saith the Lord." The ethical element is presented as the reason for seeking knowledge of God, or, at the very least—if we translate *ki ani* as "that I am" rather than "for I am"—as its content. In either case, the religious and the ethical are here inextricably interwoven; and what holds true of religious knowledge holds equally true of religious, that is, halakhic action. This fusion is central to the whole rabbinic tradition. From its perspective, the divorce of Halakhah from morality not only eviscerates but falsifies it."[44]

As a corollary, Lichtenstein adds: "However elastic the term *tradition* to some, it does have its limits, and antinomianism, which for our purposes includes the rejection of Torah law, lies beyond them. As a prescriptive category, the currently popular notion of *averah lishmah* (idealistic transgression) has no halakhic standing whatever."[45]

The limits here are moral, and their presence is of crucial import to Rachels's critique of religious ethics. For they show that at least one highly developed system of religious norms rejects the equation of piety with moral abdication. And they hint at what I think is a deeper truth: that no living system of norms can sustain itself in sheer, closed positivity. Rather, as a condition of ongoing life and normative power, such systems must be open to many sources of moral insight, whether from neighboring or rival traditions, internal critiques, or human intuitions of the demands imposed by the very idea of the divine. Thus, reading the passage "This day doth the

Lord thy God command thee *la'asot* (to make/do) these statutes and ordinances, and thou shalt keep and make/do them with all thy heart and with all thy soul" (Deut. 26:16), R. Yohanan, head of the Academy of Tiberias in the third century, took the words to mean that Israelites must regard God's commandments as though they personally had just received them at Sinai, and that when each Israelite performs those commandments with the appropriate intent (*kavvanah*) it will be as if he personally had made them for himself, and, in a sense, as if he had created himself. For the commandments give each of us a new soul; our acceptance of them makes us partners both in God's legislation and in God's act of creation.[46] Here we see, plainly expressed, the clear fusion of autonomy with acceptance of God's will that is the core of religious piety. As Spinoza wrote: "So far as religion is concerned, clearly the more a person loves God and the more wholeheartedly he serves Him, the more free he is and the more completely does he obey himself."[47]

The revealed imperative is, after all, not simply an external event. If ever it is to involve understanding and appropriation it must be an event within the human mind. Biblical images may present revelation dramatically as a public oathing ceremony: God standing on his lofty mountain, the people below; God thundering, the people swearing to accept his law—Moses as interlocutor. Yet, as with all biblical images, the crucial points lie in the departures from familiar scenes and icons. God does not simply stand, for God cannot be seen; Moses does not simply repeat, for certain things must be heard directly. And the people do not simply vow allegiance, despite the centrality of their consent—or because of it. For they learn that they stand in the place of all future Israelites. Can they consent for future generations? And what is it that Moses cannot tell them?

What they must hear for themselves is God's Self-proclamation I AM: laws can be voiced by Moses, but the underlying insight into the idea of God each hearer must fathom individually.[48] The same inner experience is carried forward in time. Now, as at the original epiphany, each contributor adds his tesserae to the mosaic of the Law and appropriates elements of its meaning in his life or her character. It is God, the Absolutely Good, who proclaims the general imperative to pursue the good and demands that we test the foundations and implications of any prescription. Culture and history may prepare us for certain norms, but moral awakening and the very sense of biddenness that centers any religious ethics must arise from within. Even the generation of Sinai cannot answer for their descendants but can only stand in their place. Tradition will aid latercomers, but they must see and hear and choose for themselves, using their own best lights to make out the concrete demands of Perfection. Where, then, is the heteronomy? God does not stand apart and impose morality as an alien demand. I AM comes first, and *Thou shalt* follows not by deductive entailment but by the dialectic of moral responsiveness. And *Thou shalt* fuses with *I will*, the inward appropriation that forms a moral identity. As Fackenheim explains, "The source and life of the revealed morality of Judaism" lies in the encounter of "a divine commanding Presence which never dissipates itself into irrelevance, and a human response which freely appropriates what it receives."[49]

A. I. Baumgarten astutely notes that the Torah itself presumes that it belongs to all, not just to the priests who may administer it. He finds the same theme in friendly sources like Philo and Josephus and unfriendly ones like Juvenal and Tacitus; in

Mekhilta he finds it stated in imagery redolent of the ideas of Renan: "The Torah was given in public, openly, in a free place. . . . Since it was given in the wilderness, publicly and openly . . . everyone wishing to accept it could come and accept it."[50] Asking whether a scholar may modestly decline the honor due his learning, one Rabbi urges that the Torah is not his, that he should feel free to waive *its* honor; to which the retort is made: "But in fact, the Torah is his" (*Kiddushin* 32ab).[51]

For the Rabbis such ownership meant autonomy not just in the minimal sense of freedom from heteronomy but in the stronger sense, of creative engagement, an idea they applied both to themselves as jurists and to every Israelite. For all Israelites were expected to study the Law, and knowledge here meant ownership. The people as well as the Sages were obligated not just to study but to enrich what they learned with their own insights.[52] Thus the central obligations of the Israelite everyman include faithful dealing, regular Torah study, procreation, hope of salvation, engagement in the dialectics of wisdom, and inference in study beyond the given (Shabbat 31a). All Israel is called upon, then, to be not only a nation of priests but a nation of philosophers and scholars. Addressing the issue of desuetude, the Rabbis comment trenchantly on the phrase "a statute of Israel, an ordinance of the God of Jacob" (Ps. 81:5): "Were it not a statute adopted by Israel, it would not have been an ordinance of the God of Jacob."[53] And Jeremiah expects inner knowledge of the Law to create not mere lawyerly expertise among the people (8:7–8) but a deep harmony in them with God and with one another (31:32; cf. 32:39–40). Here, and not in some specious notion of inventing one's own norms to serve one's narrow interests or immediate appetites, lies the true locus of autonomy in the Jewish normative tradition.

The normative response to God's commands is not a sense of chiddenness but love.[54] It is God and his beloved who meet at Sinai, now as in the distant past. Love is the normative motive for faithfulness (Deut. 11:1, 13; cf. Exod. 20:6). It is unconditional, wholehearted (Deut. 6:5), thus our own; but our own, too, in being practical, consummated. It is not the gaping love of a remote admirer or a skulking stalker. For its consummation is the praxis of the *mitzvot* (Deut. 10:12, 11:22, 19:9; Josh. 22:5), a life, not the furtive trysts of mystics, ecstasy seekers, and spiritual voyeurs. The gift of the commandments is the mark of God's love, and our steadfastness in them is the sign of our love's purity and stability. For real love is not contingent on the joys love brings: the *mitzvot* are not just prudential counsels, although it may be prudent to observe them. The imperative behind them is categorical, although they constitute a code, so that not every dictum is an absolute.

The image of a household and the chaste respect of those within it informs the precept of Antigonos of Socho when he figures our link to God not as a marriage but as service: "Be not like servants who serve the master for the sake of a bonus (*pras*), but like servants who serve the master not for the sake of a bonus, and let the awe of Heaven be upon you" (Avot 1.3). Antigonos does not say that there is no benefit in faithful adherence to the *mitzvot*, nor that we should ignore such benefits, but that these are not our proper motive. Here we escape the conditionality that is the real price of heteronomy. For the force of Kant's argument is that dependence on external interests vitiates the claims of any heteronomous maxim, by making it conditional. Antigonos is fully alive to this concern. The awe of heaven that he draws around our choices as their moral ground cloth is not fear of consequences but piety, the reverence that is another face of love, and without which love would be mere concupiscence, awe mere terror, and obedience mere toadying. Fackenheim writes: "While orthodox thinkers argued that the morality of Judaism is revealed but heteronomous, their liberal colleagues have often acted as though it were autonomous but not revealed. They would have prophets and rabbis speak with the Kantian voice of self-legislating reason."[55] The Scylla and Charybdis of legal positivism and moral hubris are well drawn here, but the worry that autonomy is anachronistically read into the canon is groundless. Antigonos of Socho is not a twentieth-century liberal but a third-century B.C. Rabbinic Sage who understands that loving God means taking his will as our own, grounding service in no conditions or expectations but in love. Even Kant excludes heteronomy no more vividly.

The Torah itself speaks of autonomy, not in Kant's language but in its own, when it calls on us to love God with all our heart, with all our soul, and with all our might (Deut. 6:5). What this means, as Maimonides explains, is that we serve God faithfully when we do what is right for its own sake. This honors God, by acknowledging the intrinsic goodness and wisdom of his commands. There is no such merit in service for pay (*sekhar*), or even a bonus (*pras*), as the Rambam accurately glosses Antigonos's term.[56] Only observance of the Law for its own sake is service out of love, and only so do we fulfill the *mitzvot* as given. Perhaps ironically, only such obedience confers the full benefits of righteousness: to do what is right for the sake of its benefits leaves the trompe l'oeil gap between expediency and right. Thus the admonition: "Justice, justice shalt thou pursue!" (Deut. 16:20). When justice alone seems to diverge from justice as a pragmatic goal, it is justice for its own sake, justice alone, that we must follow—intrinsic, not instrumental justice: justice when it serves apparent self-interest, and justice again when right and interest seem to diverge.

In those for whom love is the motive of obedience, it is plain how they are drawn toward the Perfect, and the question how love can be commanded dissolves. Here the commandment to love God, like all the others that rest on it, sets out as a norm the natural response of all aspiring beings toward Perfection. The will of the beloved is a command to the lover, who pursues what the beloved asks—no more by coercion than by entailment, but by unity of purpose. As Kant himself said, "All religion consists in this: that in all our duties we regard God as the lawgiver."[57] But the beloved must be worthy of our love. Thus, glossing "They shall say to me, 'What is His name?'" (Exod. 3:13), Maimonides explains that Moses phrased with courtly indirection his anticipation that the people of Israel would demand proof that there really is a universal God and that he spoke for him. Regarding this concern of Moses', Maimonides remarks, "Obviously this the proper answer to anyone who claims to be a prophet, until he offers proof."[58] Use of our critical intelligence is not excluded but mandated by our religious obligations.

What, then, of the idea that piety precludes criticism? Here Moses is the model: "On several occasions," as Ze'ev Falk points out, "Moses is described as having criticized the word of God, and instead of being punished, to have been followed by God."[59] Thus Moses was said to have criticized the idea that God should visit the sins of the fathers upon their offspring (Exod. 34:7; Num. 14:18), since the idea of corporate or communal accountability seemed at variance with individual moral responsibility (Deut. 24:16). God's response, according to the Midrash, was that Moses had become his teacher; hence his promise to record the ordinance of individual responsibilty in the name of Moses (2 Kings 14:6)[60] and similarly when Moses sought peace with the Amorites, although God had told him to make war on them (see Exod. 3:17, 33:2; Deut. 20:10).[61] But when Moses balked at God's command to make war on Midian, his judgment, it was said, was clouded by a sense of loyalty to the land where he had lived in exile: even a prophet's moral intuitions can be colored by subjectivity.[62]

Kant's call for autonomy expresses a revulsion with externalized ideas of duty, the rigid hypocrisies of those who make a church or creed, a code or law, into a surrogate for conscience. When he rejects hedonism as heteronomy, he turns the tables on the old Epicurean charge that a morality of duty is inherently immoral because it roots obligation in an external standard. The argument worked well against Stoics because it played upon their Cynic heritage of naturalism, candor, and directness. But it assumed that only pleasures can be proper (true or honest) motives of our own. The Stoics put virtue in that role, as the object of a higher, truer, more mature identity, sublimating lesser appetites and interests and constituting itself as an identity by the very values that it chose.[63] Kant follows in the Stoic path. But surely, if Stoics can treat duties as proper to the self while Epicureans treat them as external and regard only pleasures as true motives, religious sensibility, adopting God's will as its own and interpreting its own perfect expression as service to that will, can also constitute itself as a moral identity by that act, quashing the claim that religious duties are heteronomous. Indeed, Kant might have acknowledged the fact, had he not been distracted by religious pretensions that seemed to make the will of God a kind of mortmain, ossified in much the way that Kantian duty itself would one day seem to be in some of those who paid lip service to its formulae but in whom the Kantian moral pilot light may have gone out. Kant's brief was that duty, when properly appropriated, cannot be conceived as alien. The Torah means nothing different when it commands us to love God with all our hearts and to express that love by setting his commandments upon our hearts and before our eyes (Deut. 6:5–6). Kant, in turn, despite his romantic restiveness with externalized ideas of duty (the same authoritarian notions he is sometimes accused of truckling to), does not upset but fulfills the biblical idea of right when he defines religion as regarding all our duties as divine commands.[64]

Kant saw the will as the core of moral subjecthood and made its autonomy criterial to morality. But Epicurus found autonomy only in wholehearted enjoyment. Kant found bondage, heteronomy, in the pleasure principle. But Epicurus, equating real pleasure with peace of mind, the only estimable goal, made its pursuit our liberation. Lucretius celebrates the identification of the rational will with the pleasure principle when he plays on the words *voluptas* and *voluntas*. Religions now claim to find our true identity in the sense of creatureliness. That, from the Epicurean (or Nietzschean) standpoint, is their chief perversion and impiety. No transcendental ideal is freely chosen, Epicurus reasoned,[65] and even the ideal of duty fails as a moral foundation, by its alienness to our natural goals. Do we have some standard to reveal, in so embattled a context, what should count as the true self? Perhaps we do not need one.

If we think dynamically of the self, in Spinozistic terms, where the essence of a being is its striving (conatus) to preserve and perfect its own reality, the dichotomies between joy and duty, principle and interest rapidly fade.[66] The conatus, as the project of any being, grounds the aspiration toward perfection that is the universal receptivity to Divine imperatives. In conscious subjects, these imperatives are moral. For they involve the identity that persons choose, and, by choosing, create, obviating the need for anyone to define for us a priori what we are. Insofar as beings choose and grasp the project that becomes their own, existence clearly does precede essence, and the Epicurean is as much the creature and creator of his project as is Kant, or Antigonos. It is the conatus that hedonists fuse with the impetus to pleasure, by muddling pleasure with its natural aim, well-being. Nietzsche, similarly, takes part for whole when he speaks of a will to power. The conatus is the generic substrate of the will that Kant split into empirical and noumenal moieties, judged by the presumptive moral status of its maxims. But no such sundering of identity is necessary, only the clarity that existentialists (following Pascal, who in turn followed the Book of Job) call good faith, overcoming self-deception and attaining transparency in one's motives. Not that sincerity is a sufficient virtue, as deontologists are often tempted to believe. But, rather, any identity clear enough to own its acts and choices cannot be called heteronomous, even if its acts are evil and its choices ugly. For the notion that all wickedness is self-deception is just a form of wishful thinking, a sliver of the more wholesome Socratic rationalism of Plato, for whom wisdom always had an Object beyond itself and so could never be equated with mere self-complaisance.

Self-acceptance is never morally self-sufficient. So heteronomy can never be the only name for evil, and the wholesale condemnation that Kant aimed at all those who do not invent their moral standards for themselves misfires—just as it did when Epicureans aimed the same charge at the Stoics, for the seeming remoteness of their lofty ideals of duty. Among theists, as among nontheists, there will be hypocrites and timeservers, those who bend the will of God or the idea of right, or even the idea of pleasure, to their own perversity—and others whose integrity allows them to choose moral standards without forgoing the aid of their heritage and community. Such persons will live not just with a clear conscience (as if that were enough) but with recognizable, sometimes testable legitimacy—righteousness, to use the biblical term, *tzedakah*, a word that denotes justice, but with the connotative force of saintliness, and that suggests a plane of inner and interhuman peace[67] far exceeding what is praised and sought by Epicureans. If aspiration toward perfection is the generic identity of all beings, then clearly there is no heteronomy in the pursuit of perfection, nor in allegiance to the obligations we discover when God calls us to our own perfection and we find it in pursuit of God's commands.

Our three sets of questions, then, are answered: there is no transition from neutral fact to value, for God's existence is not a neutral but a value-laden fact. Still there is no implication from that fact of laws. For laws are concrete imperatives imposed upon, or called forth within, aspiring beings by the idea of absolute perfection. Such imperatives are specified in human terms for the human case. The process is not difficult, since our concept of divinity itself is rooted in our highest ideas of the good. But the process is cultural and historical, mediated by insights from all sorts of sources, expressive of social interactions as well as more personal inspirations. Morals inevitably test the authenticity of imperatives that claim divine authority, and such testing is a positive obligation in religious traditions that identify God with Truth. So the brickbat of heteronomy flies wide of the mark, especially if its target is monotheism. The locus of the general imperative toward perfection, which is the universal content of God's law, is the human psyche itself, specifically, that aspiring aspect of the moral personality which has at times, simplistically, been called the will or even been confused with some facet of itself, the appetite for gain or pleasure or power, but which forms the core identity of the moral subject. Taking hold from within, the divine imperative, problematic only in the measure of our adequacy in grasping its demands, is a true moral law. It entails no heteronomy, even though it is not simply our own invention.

How Monotheism Modulates Ethics

If religion is life with one eye or both on the sacred, monotheism is religion that traces the sacred to a single source. The values that diverse gods once spoke for are united; norms are integrated in a way of life. The biblical term for such a system of norms is *torah*, a guiding law. Etymologically the term connotes showing the way, projecting a path; it denotes a rule of practice.[68] The idea of a single God demands an integration of all values, just as the integration of values calls forth the idea of a single God. Morals are privileged in the resultant integration, since evil will not consist with systemic goodness. Benevolence becomes paramount. We can gauge the ethical impact of monotheism in three areas: (1) equity and equality, the dignity of personhood and definition of our responsibility to one another; (2) the concrete specification of our obligations; and (3) the assignment of positive value not only to various interests and concerns but to their integration.

1. The Torah's repeated admonition "One law shall there be for ye . . ." seeks more than uniformity. Its core motive is concern. Thus the writing and public reading of the Law (Deut. 24:7, 31:9–13) mandate universal awareness of its provisions and anchor its principles to that knowledge, and so to the interests of the governed—not just those present but all who come within its sway: "Ye shall have one law (*mishpat*) stranger and homeborn alike. For I am the Lord your God" (Lev. 24:22; cf. Exod. 12:49).[69] God's absoluteness provides a standard of objectivity, then, not just for the universal history of Genesis but for the relations of all nations, whose common descent is so salient a theme in Genesis. Bias and self-serving are rejected in favor of divine justice and grace (cf. Exod. 23:1–12; Lev. 19:34; Deut. 1:16–17). Strangers are the legal and moral equals of Israelites: "When a stranger sojourneth with you in your land, you shall not discriminate against him (*lo tonu ʾoto*). As the homeborn shall the stranger be who sojourneth with you. Thou shalt love him as thyself. For ye were strangers in the land of Egypt. I am the Lord your God" (Lev. 19:33; cf. Exod. 22:20, 23:9; Deut. 27:19).[70] The term "discriminate" is not out of place here. The Rabbis gloss the Hebrew as forbidding not just persecution and injustice but offensive speech and invidious attitudes. Nor is the reference to God otiose. It names the arbiter who holds the stranger dear. Specifying what God's majesty calls for, and summing up the Law, for the sake of which Israel was chosen, Moses tells his people:

> And now, Israel, what doth the Lord thy God ask of thee but to fear the Lord and walk in all his ways, to love him and serve the Lord thy God, wholeheartedly and with all thy soul, keeping the Lord's commandments and statutes, which I command thee this day for your own sake. Lo, unto the Lord thy God belong the heavens and the heavens beyond the heavens, the earth and all that is in it. To your fathers alone did He bind himself in love, preferring you, their seed, after them, among all peoples to this day. Circumcise, then, the foreskin of your heart and be not stiffnecked any longer. For the Lord your God is the God of gods and Lord of lords, the great, mighty, and awesome God, who regardeth not persons and taketh no bribe, but upholdeth justice for the orphan and the widow and loveth the stranger, giving him food and raiment. And you must love the stranger. For ye were strangers in the land of Egypt. The Lord thy God shalt thou reverence, him shalt thou serve, unto him shalt thou cleave, and in his name shalt thou swear. He is thy glory, and he is thy God. (Deut. 10:12–21)[71]

Paradigmatically, the stranger shares in the produce reserved for the poor.[72] Hermann Cohen writes: "The alien was to be protected, although he was not a member of one's family, clan, religious community or people; simply *because he was a human being.* In the alien, therefore, man discovered the idea of humanity."[73]

We were strangers, so we must treat strangers kindly. The inference belongs not to logic but to sympathy. Yet it grounds a law of constitutional scope, not a psychological claim. Sympathy might breed cruelty or contempt, as Spinoza showed.[74] Or it might be overruled by spite or vengeance, chauvinism or fear. But here it is transmuted to a categorical moral demand. Thus the reference to God. "Ye were strangers . . . " gives the sentimental motive, which only intentions can interpret; but "I am the Lord thy God" states the reason and guides the intention.

Consider what the Torah rejects:

> Lamech said unto his wives:
> Adah and Zillah, hear my voice;
> Ye wives of Lamech, hear what I say.
> For I have slain a man for wounding me
> And a boy for bruising me.
> For if the vengeance in behalf of Cain be sevenfold,
> Then seven and seventyfold shall be my vengeance.
> (Gen. 4:23–24)

In the rhetoric of machismo vengeance is the measure of a man's worth. Genesis, however, records the ancient boast not merely to display Lamech's hubris, but for the sharp contrast with its own ethos of his primitive assessment of worth as power to inflict harm. The Torah finds a society in which vengeance or the threat of vengeance, mitigated by blood payment, were long familiar as vehicles of justice. Its aim is to transform that ethos. Thus when we read "He that smiteth any man . . ." (Lev. 24:17–22; cf. Exod. 21:25), the issue has become proportionality, not talio. Accordingly, where a slave is concerned and monetary compensation might be pointless, freedom is the price of injury. In all other cases, status is irrelevant and compensation is proportioned to the injury, not the standing of the victim. Again with the special protection of the widow and the orphan (Exod. 22:24): their humanity, not their station, warrants kindness; helplessness deserves special concern—reversing Lamech's contempt for a mere boy.

In a culture where right is proportioned to power it might seem absurd to claim that the standing of an orphan, a widow, or a stranger before the law must be no less than that of the most powerful and prosperous. From the vantage point of the Absolute Source of all values, it can be no less. The God of monotheism universalizes mutuality, extending concern not only to the helpless or oppressed but to all persons. The Torah marks out the dignity of personhood even as it lays down the command to love one another as we love ourselves. No syllogism is needed, and none would be of value here. Rather, the Law spins human dignity out of sympathy, at the spindle of God's universality.

What exactly does it mean to treat another as a moral equal? Rarely does it mean self-immolation. The core idea is that one should not demand as a right for oneself what one does not treat as a right for others. What is forbidden is moral solipsism. But the Law does place as great a value on self as on other, as objectivity requires.[75] I am not *more* valued than others; there are circumstances where I may rightly be asked to risk my life or lay it down for theirs. Thus, as Louis Jacobs argues, Deborah, as a prophet, praises the tribes of Zebulon and Naphtali for taking up arms in their brothers' cause and blames Reuben and Dan, who sat out the conflict. Moses offers himself and his place in history as ransom for his people's sin. Tamar, Midrashically, would rather die than dishonor the name of Judah.[76] But while one may, or sometimes must, die for principle or for the common good, the Rabbis forbid taking another's life to save one's own. This conclusion they regard as *sevara*, intuitively obvious.[77] Rava argues: "Let him kill you rather than that you should commit murder. How do you know your blood is redder than his? Perhaps his blood is redder than yours" (*Pesaḥim* 25b, *Sanhedrin* 74a). The language is telling: if there are differences in the worth of persons, we cannot know them well enough to make them even relevant to the moral concerns of God's law. This cannot is the a priori cannot of morals.

It is sometimes thought that because liberality is voluntary it is not to be mandated. How, it is asked, can I be obligated to give more to others than I agree, and why would I, without force or fraud, agree to go beyond what reciprocity seems to me to call for. But the absolute primacy of ego, upon which such arguments are founded, is, for monotheism, an illusion of the same order as that of the fellow who worried that God helps total strangers. It may be claimed that egoism is a law of nature, which it is foolhardy to countermand. But there are many natural laws, and other-supporting actions and behaviors are also widespread among humans, mammals, birds, and insects. Edward Wilson has extensively documented the point.[78] Setting aside his anthropomorphism and the reduction of morals to mechanisms that is its apparent aim, we find widespread mutuality[79] and indeed self-sacrifice in nonhuman species, and there are good evolutionary models for its adaptiveness. Besides, ethics may demand more of us than nature does—or more than nature seems to demand when nature is viewed cynically.

The illusion that human mutuality demands only toleration is a wedge cleaving negative from positive liberties, speciously equating freedom with the absence of active external hindrance. But plainly positive and negative liberties are interdependent. The latter provide the milieu; the former, the means by which any freedom can be enjoyed. Committed liberals should be suspicious rather than welcoming to any insistence that we choose between the two. For a society in which negative liberties do not support positive ones is a selfish society; and one in which positive liberties are purchased at the price of negative ones is a tyranny.

The biblical command that we love one another as we love ourselves is not a negative rule of reciprocity, informing me only that I may harm no one, but a positive rule, demanding recognition of others' interests and calling on me to assist and respect them. I am to go out of my way to help others, not as a matter of charity which I am free to withhold, but as a matter of obligation. The Torah rejects that specious liberalism which makes liberality a matter of conscience, since too often the same thinking shifts mood and dismisses conscience as the softheadedness of small spirits. As Spinoza remarks (*Ethics* IV ad cap. 17), private sympathy is too narrow and private means are too slight to meet the requirements of human need—to which, of course, we must add that those needs can be met, by Spinoza's own model, not from some ever normal pot but only through human collaboration.

One could derive some responsibilities toward others from the prudential counsel that ego might one day stand in need of unpromised help. But the resulting maxims are no match for the Golden Rule. They turn charity and consideration into mere insurance. And the "hardheaded" could always opt for self-insurance. If prudence were the only ground for kindness, there would be no obligation to generosity. But generosity calls for aid that expects no return. What the Torah imposes is an obligation to aid others even when they are helpless. Thus again the reference to God: the obligation is categorical, not conditioned on my perception of my potential needs. What the Torah typifies by care for the helpless, who are in no position to requite their benefactor, has filial piety as its paradigm in Confucianism, since elders' gifts are past by the time they need the sustenance of offspring. In Aristotle the same responsibilities find their test in disinterested friendship, where benefits are conferred not to reciprocate favors, nor even for the sake of good fellowship, but simply in recognition of another's goodness. These cases are not sheer or abstract ideals. For, in Aristotle, friendship is not just the ideal relationship of virtuous men but also, in a broader, more diffuse but ubiquitous form, the cement of social relations in any healthy society. In Confucius, familial relations are the paradigm and element of all larger social bonds. And the Mosaic fellowship that calls for a love as strong as self-love is our regard for our fellow human beings.

The positive content of the biblical principle was well understood by the Sages, who made of it a distinctive juridical rule: *kofin ʿal middat Sedom*—"We enforce against the ethos of Sodom."[80] The reference is not to sexual practices but to the character Sodom showed by rejecting the rights of guests. That Lot's neighbors entertained loathsome intentions toward the strangers he had taken under his roof shows only the extremity to which their rapacity had led them. Patriarchally, the stranger (*ger*) was not a mere alien; as a guest, his interests were a trust as sacred as those of a family member. Thus, in the heat of moral bewilderment at his neighbors' violation of the sanctuary he offered, Lot even proffers his own household rather than breach his duty as a host. He goes too far, of course, but the welcome he had given was the strangers' due, a right, which he could not take back once tendered.

The Sodomite maxim is stated in Avot 5.10: "What's mine is mine; what's thine is thine." What, one might ask, is wrong with that? Is this rapacity or simply privacy? Doesn't *suum cuique* maximize the interests of all, by allowing each to look to his own and not interfere with others, neither abetting nor hindering except in what is due—aiding by means mutually agreed, hindering, with due process, where a penalty, civil or criminal, is needed to right some imbalance? Liberals from the times of Epicurus have presumed that the best social policy is laissez-faire. Lucretius even commends an attitude of detached amusement toward the troubles of our fellow humans:

> How sweet it is, when whirlwinds roil great ocean
> To watch, from land, the danger of another,
> Not that to see some other person suffer
> Brings great enjoyment, but the sweetness lies
> In watching evils you yourself are free from.
> How sweet again to see the clash of battle
> Across the plains, yourself immune to danger.
> *De Rerum Natura* II 1–7, trans. Rolfe Humphries

The poet is relishing detachment, not avowing inhumanity. Yet the detachment he commends is precisely what the Rabbis condemn:

> When trouble and sorrow become the portion of Israel, and the faint-hearted pull away from their people, two angels lay their hands upon the head of him who withdraws, saying, "This one shall not see the comfort of the community."
>
> When trouble comes on the community, it is not right for one to say, "I will go home; I will eat and drink, and things shall be peaceful for me." It is of this that Scripture says:
>
> [While Elam bore the quiver
> In troops of mounted men,
> and Kir bared the shield—
> And your choicest lowlands
> Were filled with chariots and horsemen . . .
> My Lord God of Hosts summoned on that day
> To weeping and lamenting,
> To tonsuring and girding with sackcloth.]
> Instead there was rejoicing and merriment,
> Killing of cattle and slaughtering of sheep,
> Eating of meat and drinking of wine:
> "Eat and drink, for tomorrow we die!"
> [Then the Lord of Hosts revealed Himself to my ears:
> "This iniquity shall never be forgiven you
> Until you die," saith my Lord God of Hosts.]
> (Isa. 22:6–14)[81]

To Epicureans, withdrawal is not only personally but socially the best policy toward the plight of our fellow humans—far superior to meddlesome attempts to improve their lot and lives, which soon grow into a wish to improve them and so to impose ourselves and our ways upon them. To say that such a stratagem ignores the possibility of crises that might confront the community is to say too little. For in a living community there is always a crisis for someone. Besides, Epicurean escapism is a response to crisis, not an alternative to it, and even as a habit for tranquil times it is not readily set aside when dangers are imminent. The idea of not imposing ourselves on others is a sound one, with applications from the missionary's hut and pyre to the soup kitchen and the welfare state.[82] But the flaw in the ideal of detachment is irresponsibility and unconcern, complacency rationalized as inner peace and disguised as tolerance. *Kofin ʿal middat Sedom* is an alternative. It means using the full power and subtlety of law to instill and implement an ethos of generosity. The maxim is a corollary of "Love thy fellow as thyself," which is, as Maimonides and Naḥmanides saw, the interpersonal application of the general *mitzvah* of *homoiosis theoi*, the obligation to become as like to God as humanly possible.

The presumption that we cannot aid without imposing is challenged by the biblical command to love our fellows *as* we love ourselves. For it means, as they love themselves and as we would wish to be loved—not meddlesomely but with aid we would appreciate if we were situated as they are. If experience is any teacher, our most generous act is not *cultiver notre jardin*, and human happiness is not maximized by benign neglect. The same invisible hand that fails to lead economies toward their full potential without thoughtful regulation and restraint exercises no hidden providence over the general quality of life merely because individuals mind their own business. On the contrary, I lose if my neighbor will not lend me a tool, and the loss is compounded when I, in turn, refuse him one of mine. Beyond the immediate losses, an ethos of impersonality breeds alienation and anomie, and these breed violence.

But I cannot share what I do not have. Both advocates and detractors of positive obligations tend to treat the notion as a kind of shorthand for socialism.[83] If socialism means state ownership of the means of production, I must agree with Hayek and other classic liberals that such ownership militates against fundamental civil and human rights.[84] Its ethos dislikes the pursuit of personal fulfillment and individual excellence that is both the end and the means of communal advancement. History has shown us graphically in this century how unwise it is to vest ownership and regulatory powers in the same hands. State or party control of capital not only fails to overcome the alienation of individuals from their labor, as promised, but cuts off the incentives, both economic and spiritual, that are the chief engines of social advance. Still worse, it blocks the checks and balances that can safeguard negative liberties, protect worker safety and public welfare, and steward the environment. Liberal societies, in practice, are those that do not entrust basic rights and responsibilities, economic interests, production, civil security, and defense all to the same hand. Rather, they differentiate ownership and management from government; they separate political representation from collective bargaining; they do not reserve eleemosynary and volunteer work to a single church, foundation, social movement, or benevolent society; they shield the press and broadcast media from any office of public information, and insulate the arts and education from their sources of financial support, whether public or private. Since economic freedoms are both a basis and a goal of the exercise of choice, liberal societies are those that allow demand to be the chief spur of production, promotion, and distribution decisions—not because anyone has discovered that demand is an infallible guide to the common good but because allowing demand to drive the market enlarges and enhances the market and does not substitute the judgment of planners or leaders for that of individuals as to their desires. For such substitution is inadequate, even given the best will in the world, and fraught with moral dangers when planners have agendas distinguishable from those of their constituents.

The marketplace is far from flawless as a social steering mechanism, a vehicle of social concern or a paragon of moral regard. Impersonal relations like those of trade do not assure the deserts of their participants. Indeed, as I have argued,[85] such relations are not foundational, despite their seeming elementality. They are not the framework on which morals, custom, and other cultural niceties merely embroider their refinements. On the contrary, the seemingly elemental formal relations of give-and-take, quid pro quo, tit for tat, rest on and presuppose more intimate, informal relations of trust, courtesy, fellow feeling and concern, moral recognition and demand. Far from maximizing benefits, the universalization of strict property notions (applied even to the human body and the most intimate human relations) creates a no-win game. Thus Rabbi Yoḥanan said: "Jerusalem was destroyed because its denizens judged in it according to the Torah." "What then?" the Sages asked, "Should they have followed the Law of the Magians?" Not at all, but they "judged strictly on the basis of the Law and did not expand beyond the strict sentence of the law [*lifnim mishurat ha-din*]."[86] The Torah, as a law of life, expects generosity. Its system breaks down without it. Correspondingly, the Torah presumes that generosity is possible and rational. There are goods to gain—peace, love, and justice among them—that it would be wise to seek, even at great cost. The prophetic vision is that no society survives without generosity. Every community depends on give-and-take, but the general inefficiency of all mechanisms—a fortiori, of human social exchanges—shows us why the Law prescribes rather more give than take.

Does the biblical demand for recognition of the subjecthood of others and placement of their deserts on a par with my own imply an altruism that exceeds and eclipses my obligations to myself? For others far outnumber me. Should I sacrifice my very being to the least pleasure of the world? The reasoning is specious. For I cannot serve others if I give up the power to do so, and the equal worth of all cannot exclude my obligation to myself. Rhetorically, the biblical rule appeals to my self-love; morally, to God's standpoint, where all subjecthoods are existentially equal. The elenchus that would submerge my interests beneath those of others neglects their responsibility toward themselves, toward me, and toward each other. I am not to be morally overwhelmed by failure on the part of others to do their share, but I am obligated to work toward a community and way of life that tends to ensure, to the extent feasible and reasonable, that we all do our share. This is simply the Kantian kingdom of ends.

If one may not assume a self-destructive burden, it seems unfair as well as counterproductive to alienate from anyone the major part of the product (or profit) of his energies in work. That follows from the positive worth of any subject, setting a quantitative limit that defines slavery or exploitation independently of the crucial qualitative indicator of consent. There are contexts, in the family, or in our freely undertaken humane or military, spiritual, or educational activities, or even in rather mundane service, where a person will give far more than can possibly be returned. Such actions arise out of love, friendship, devotion, or identification with one's beneficiaries or one's task. Even here we must ask not just whether such commitments are freely assumed and sustained but whether the giver is fulfilled or eroded by them.

Common need in a crisis may demand far more of us than would normally be asked. But in ordinary times we rightly reserve to the individual the freedom to privilege commitments to family, close friends, or personal ideals. It is neither arbitrary nor unfair for individuals to establish such primary commitments. Morally, they are the existential desert of the moral subject, a person's right of self-definition. But their utility is a corollary of the general inefficiency of all organized systems: energies can be expended in behalf of others only through some social system. The more intimate and the more reciprocal the bonds (and feedback loops) in that system, the more appropriately and effectively can energies be allocated. For this reason, no social system has been able to dislodge the family as a focus of human energies or to replace parents as the primary caregivers of the young. For the same reason, it is not selfish to focus certain efforts and activities at the level of the neighborhood rather than the city, or the nation rather than the world. Selfishness means neglect or minimization of the interests of the other; it is not the same as concentration of effort at a level where communication and interaction, interconnectedness and the bonds of mutual recognition render action most effective.

It is mendacious nonsense, then, to pretend that one can or should love the world at large with the same love that belongs to one's spouse or children, parents, closest friends or comrades. One's own receive a special love in virtue of the bonds of reciprocity, responsibility, and gratitude that prevent love's mere dissipation into the atmosphere of abstraction. No family or community is effective if its members are the same to one another as strangers, and one who truly feels and acts no differently toward those close to him than toward strangers has not elevated humanity but demeaned his intimates. The world community in which all men are brothers is one in which humanity at large regard one another as do the members of a well-integrated people or nation, not one in which literal and figurative brothers are treated alike. Otherwise the figure is robbed of its force. I must love others as myself in the sense of promoting their striving for perfection, acknowledging their subjecthood, and respecting their moral dignity, not in the sense of attaching to them the same personal regard I show to family members or even close associates, and still less in the sense of performing for them every office that I perform for myself. For that is not to respect but to negate their personhood, whose dignity would have no meaning without its boundaries and its privacy. Thus liberal systems preserve what totalitarian regimes attack, the freedom of individuals to form personalities, to identify widely or more narrowly with others on the basis of personal affinities, and to seek perfection by avenues left to individual discovery, appropriation, exploration, and enjoyment.

Yet the biblical command is not a merely formal principle of mutuality but a material principle of love—thus not an emptiness to be filled ad libitum by whatever one fancies. Sade, for example, proposed that no victim should be harmed with any torment that the abuser would not accept upon himself.[87] The love that God commands, by contrast, is not defined subjectively. It is measured rhetorically by reference to our subjecthood, but given direction by reference to God and by its implicit recognition of the aspiration of all self-conscious subjects toward perfection. As the Rabbis explain, it is our creation in God's image that teaches us not to apply the formal structure of the Golden Rule perversely, as if saying "just as our own dignity has suffered in the past, so should that of our fellow suffer occasionally."[88] Our obligation to others is concretely specifiable as an obligation to help rather than hinder, regardless of the inclination one may bear toward oneself, and regardless of the seeming appetite of some for self-destruction. For desires are not self-legitimating, and a command of self-love is presupposed in the command to love others. I must aid others toward what is perfection for them, regardless of my willingness to forgo their aid. Indeed, I am obliged not to forgo assistance, insofar as I require it, and insofar as it is assistance. And I must modulate my aid for others by a sensitivity to their aims and recognition of the delicate nexus between the good itself and the good as they conceive it.

2. There is a great watershed in ethics between Plato's view that we have no universal behavioral rule of morals and the biblical view that such rules can be, must be—and *have been*—spelled out for us. Plato defends his situationalism by instancing cases meant to show that new information can always reverse the tenor of what might otherwise seem the right moral stance.[89] Since human knowledge is finite, it follows that no universal rule concrete enough to specify a type of action can be right in every case. This does not mean that Plato holds laws to be impossible or moral judgment unattainable. For he takes both to be necessary to life but regards all human laws as very rough approximations of justice. Ideally, a mature and seasoned judgment will estimate each case afresh. Laws are just the surrogates of such judgment, an admission of its rarity. Thus Plato cannot condemn the murder of infants categorically. For there may be reasons of state or force majeure (not to mention the familiar case of deformity) that justify such a step. Plato deems it quite unproblematic to reason that if I knew that by killing this infant I was nipping in the bud the career of some Hitler and knew that I would not be imitated and that my act would not otherwise adversely affect vital social structures, reason would not only urge but command me to kill it. With this the monotheistic moral tradition takes the strongest issue, of which, again, the binding of Isaac can be emblematic. In justifying our blanket rejection of Plato's radical situationalism and its paradigm case, we like to say that we do not know what this infant will become. But that is only a rejection of the Platonic premise; and the a priori character of our insistence on our ignorance, once again, is a clear marker of the fact that moral, not cognitive, concerns are in play here. When we say that the babe is innocent and set aside as sick fantasies the sort of projective worries that find their place in films like *Rosemary's Baby*, we are voicing not superior knowledge of the unseen future but a set of moral presumptions, fictions in fact, like the presumed innocence of all persons until they prove guilty by their own acts. For Christians the doctrine of original sin is in tension with the global presumption of innocence. But that presumption grounds Christian ethics nonetheless. Thus Jesus' "Judge not that ye not be judged" (Matthew 7:1). Here we can rightly speak of Judaeo-Christian ethics. For Jews, innocence can be a fact. Yet we know empirically, statistically that the world might be a better place if certain infants were not born. And it is not impossible in principle that advances in the sciences might soon allow us an educated guess of just which babes to watch. Even with our present spotty knowl-

edge of behavioral genetics, proposals have not been lacking that we do just that. Some future state of knowledge might enable us to pinpoint fairly accurately just which infants it is best should never be raised. If Plato had such knowledge, his principles would, it seems, issue no blanket prohibition on our drawing up a "little list." That precisely is what our Law forbids—regardless of the social costs.

We believe, we say, in free will, an axiom implicit in any formulation of an imperative or command, as Kant pointed out emphatically and Maimonides before him.[90] Despite the seeming preponderance of evidence and the weight of causal influences, we presume that moral choice is possible: "All is determined, but choice is granted" (Avot 3.15). On the basis of this supposition, a moral postulate whether or not it is a law of nature, we tip the scales of judgment, presuming innocence, even overbalancing the weight of evidence, in behalf of a hope that we cannot always regard as well founded. Which is to say, our appeal to free will here is not the enunciation of a doctrine about the physics or the metaphysics of human action but a restatement of our moral commitment to personhood. We cannot, then, ground our rejection of preventive detention or cradle assassination on the idea of freedom, because freedom, in this case, is but another name for the dignity our moral principle seeks to protect. But we can identify that dignity, the sanctity of unsullied human deserts, the existential entitlement of every person to ownership of his actions, as the foundation of the deontic core of our legalism: our presumption in behalf of individual deserts, made systematic in the Mishnaic dictum "Judge every human with a bias in his favor [*lechaf zechut*]" (Avot 1.6), is no casual commitment, then, but a foundation of our idea of justice.[91] It is because of the deserts of persons *as* persons that we assume that if we must err in judgment it is better, more just by far, to exonerate the guilty than to inculpate the innocent. With the aid of this presumption that tempers justice with mercy, we actually do apply laws, in spite of human fallibility—hoping that when we err it will be on the side of mercy.

The dialectical force of the biblical command of reciprocity thus gives vivid expression to the moral warrant for our tipping the scales to some degree—in some ways absolutely, as the demands of privacy may dictate.[92] For such tilting is just what we would hope for if we were judged. But right, not sympathy, is the issue. If emotion held sway, a bad mood or a less than sunny disposition might just as well tilt the scales toward harshness; even the idea of freedom, as Spinoza clearly saw, can foster recriminations at least as readily as respect. How, then, do the pleas of sympathy translate into the claims of mercy? Viewing each human being from the standpoint of his own subjecthood, we move from our subjectivity to another's by reference to God's objectivity, where the fundamental deserts of personhood are preserved, and equal existentially. It is not principle that undergirds the ideas of personhood and desert, but personhood and desert that undergird the idea of principle. Morally, we must look at the world through God's eyes not in any mythic sense, of peering into the moral future, but by relying on God's fairness, which projects the worth of all beings, and that of persons in particular as subjects in their own right, not mere furniture in our pragmatic world: monotheism leaves no room for moral solipsism and demands of each of us a kind of moral ecstasis by which we overcome our moral myopia and, in the measure that we can, cease to view the universe in the animal perspective, that is, the perspective from which the worth of beings appears to recede toward a moral vanishing point that always has its origin at ego. The morals of monotheism take every person as a sacred subject; without the anchor that the moral objectivism distinctive to monotheism assigns to subjecthood, regard for persons would be little more than a pleasant fiction or tactful cant.

In the framework monotheism builds, the broad demands of perfection are articulated as concrete obligations. For commands must be specific; and the primary concern of a command ethics is not with the status of those it addresses—not even with their moral or spiritual status—but with their doings and their lives, as individuals and as cultures. Thus Jewish, Christian, and Muslim scriptures open into systems that interleave legal with moral concerns. They offer moral foundations for their legal requirements and press their prescriptions well beyond the realm of public law, to make demands of individuals and communities, expressing God's expectations not solely in some nebulous or general way but with reference to the full particularity of the human situation. Despite the detriments of formalism, the risks of legal positivism, the imposture of legal behaviorism as moral adequacy—and despite the sometimes reactive antinomianism of romantics, in their impatience with legalism and rigorism—this concreteness or specificity is a necessary and wholesome thing, if humanity is ever to envision the minimal demands of human decency, let alone attain the higher goal of human fulfillment.

Biblical ethics is an ethics of aspiration. Its central command is *imitatio Dei*. But it is not, like Aristotle's virtue ethics, largely an ethics of tendency. Nor is it, like Plato's social code in the *Republic*, an ethics of consequences that subordinates all principles to the common benefit. Rather, as a code of commandments, it is a law that identifies definite wrongs, acts that are heinous, regardless of their benefits, and others that are obligatory, despite their cost. Thus it knows of sins and crimes, not just of worthy or unworthy characters. It is a law, not just a set of "guidelines." But, by the same token, it is a code that demands a strict proceduralism regarding evidence and testimony, one whose elaboration will exclude self-incrimination (rather than merely permitting its refusal). It is a code, in other words, that acknowledges rights. For one counterpart of wrongs is rights.

3. The universal form of rules designed to apply in a variety of circumstances does not make them very effective as maxims of casuistry. The most universal norm, the pursuit of perfection, touches particularity in so many ways that it would lose normative force altogether unless diverse ways of life addressed it. No one of these is so compelling or comprehensive as to exclude all the rest. The choice among legitimate instantiations of the pursuit of perfection allows a wide freedom, grounded in taste, preference, and understanding. Rules, then, are necessarily underspecified. But, on another plane, they must be overspecified. For their very uniformity as rules and their engagement in the symbolic realm demand a specificity far beyond what the underlying moral imperatives alone can articulate. Later chapters of this book will consider some aspects of this overspecification. But I think it may be apparent here that even where specificity is pressed far beyond the broad requirements of global moral principles or values, moral imperatives still come into play. The choice of one symbol system over another, for example, will not be a wholly arbitrary matter but can be a moral issue subject to stringent imperatives. For monotheism will command a symbol system celebratory of generosity and light and will prohibit the celebration

of cruelty and violence as autonomous ends. A hint of this is contained in the Mishnah's striking inclusion of blasphemy among the crimes forbidden not merely to Israelites but to all the descendants of Noah, that is, to humanity at large. What do we make of this seeming extension of the Torah's universal moral concerns so deeply into the realm of human self-expression?

Consider the swastika, a symbol of strength and mystic cycles of recursion and rebirth in many ancient cultures, but latterly a symbol of the Nazi cult violence, which swept the world into the holocaust of the Second World War. The living memory of the events has already begun to dim and fade. The contemporary record suffers the inevitable erosions. Documents are purloined, destroyed, altered, or forged. Denials, trivializations, and distortions play political and iconographic tricks with the delicate threads of history and memory. Now the public must be trusted to read synthetic accounts of the vast and overwhelming events of our parents' generation, passively to watch their simulation or reconstruction on television or at the movies, to brave the sites of the Nazi ovens now grown cold, or pay to enter specialized museums, to learn the history of the National Socialist movement, whose announced policies and avowed passions consumed the flesh of six million Jews and dealt the people of Israel a blow from which we are not yet clear we can recover.

In liberal theory only actions may be restrained, and then only when they harm their victims. We distinguish between material and mental harm, and laws privilege the former. For, while verbal abuse and symbolic intimidation can at times inflict far more grievous damage, the moral nexus linking human beings is juridically deemed so tenuous and the range of the psychically offensive or noxious so diffuse that laws tend to look away from nonphysical forms of assault—like those of violent pornography—and place the burden on the injured to show how sights and symbols seared or scarred the mind.

Thought is free, and so, by extension, is expression. For thought is of little account if it cannot be loosed in words or images. Accordingly, the claim is made that symbols can commit no crime, regardless of their content or tenor, except in certain narrow contexts where words are conceded to amount to actions: fraud, threat, extortion, the contested realm of libel, and the disputed ground of overt inducements to panic and incitements to riot. Certainly no verbal or nonverbal expression of a political belief or affiliation, no matter how hateful, should, on this account, ever be regarded as legally impermissible. The assumption is that symbols are mere excrescences of the active life of a society and have no more effective role in shaping that life than a baby's babbling: in themselves they are unmeaning; they may lead to thought, but thought is inevitably creative, provided it is free. Yet surely we have learned, since the manifestos of liberal thought were penned, that dreams and cults and even the babbling of babes do shape reality and are not merely shaped by it.

What, then, we must ask, does a swastika mean? Its meaning was explicit years before the Nazi idea bore its most deadly fruit, glossed by the theorists and ideologues of the Nazi movement and by the demonic architect of that movement himself. It stands for a system of ideas and emotions the purport of which, inter alia, is that it was right to murder six million Jews and would still be right to murder the rest. It is the banner of the belief that violence is self-justifying.[93] It comes as close as expression can come to a transvaluation of values, taking good for evil and evil for good, as Milton's fictive Satan plotted in his wrath, but Hitler made the policy not just of a party but of a modern nation-state, its appanages, and its allies.

Liberalism, quaintly, does not condemn the transvaluation. Values, it claims, are the object of any interest. It sees no material basis for condemning any particular values as such, although it does deplore the actual immolation of the interest of some in behalf of what it must take to be that of others. Exactly what values, in particular, are paraded or, as in idolatry, celebrated here seems a matter of indifference. But to those who choose the highest good, it will be a matter of the greatest moment which values are flaunted and which are flouted. Judaism, in its founding axiom, does condemn the radical transvaluation and, understanding its symbolism, condemns it even as a mode of expression. Thus the condemnation of blasphemy.

The founding axiom of the Mosaic law is the reality of Perfection. The most immediate (and least understood) application of that axiom is the obligation not to take the name of God in vain. Popularly, this means that if I hit my thumbnail with a hammer I should say "Oh my!" or something about excretion or coitus rather than "goddammit!" This trivializes the commandment, although reverence for God's spoken name was meant as the margin (*seyag*) that sets off the actual obligation, as a hedge sets off a park. For to confine reverence to the name and ignore what that name signifies is surely to mistake the husk for the reality. In the Torah, where 'God' means absolute Perfection, and, operationally, means the Self-sufficiency that calls forth a striving toward Its goodness in all aspiring beings, to take the name of God in vain is to set it at nought or equate it with evil, to ignore or negate all imperatives voiced by the Reality of the Good, to fail to be morally alive to the call toward perfection—or actively to combat those imperatives, to reject the good and affirm evil, to advocate it for its own sake and abhor goodness. That is blasphemy.

Impious words might be uttered as a child might make a rude or obscene gesture without quite knowing what it means, or draw a swastika without a glimmer of the enormity for which it stands, perhaps in witless play with a vaguely apprehended taboo. That would not be blasphemy but innocence or ignorance, simple rudeness or bad taste. To blaspheme is to *use* the symbol, not just mention or quote it, or show it off for its ever-diminishing shock value, as paperback covers and movie posters sometimes do, exploitatively. Blasphemy uses the symbol with some awareness of the meaning it acquires in history—thus affirming evil at its most palpable, with seriousness and intent. That is what the Torah forbids, not just for Israelites but for humanity, along with the other Noahidic prohibitions against idolatry, sexual license, murder, rapine, devouring a member of a living animal, and the lone positive injunction, to institute a system of justice (Sanhedrin 56a). Humanity at large is not expected to pay lip service to Israel's God. For what is called for is not verbal deference to God's name, mindless of its meaning. Nor does the Torah envision the nations of the world as commanded to avoid making light of such a word. Rather, what is forbidden, by the moral law itself, is the negation of all that the idea of God stands for. It might seem that no rejection of goodness—of love, kindness, gentleness, generosity, fairness, and honesty—could be so sweeping. For who would wittingly negate all positive values, under the delusion that violence and cruelty, destructiveness, tyranny, and terror are better goods and grounds for rule than their opposites? But the memory of the Nazi holocaust still glares balefully enough to show how wrong such doubts would be.

Among the symbols that history has given meanings, there is an opposite to the swastika as a symbol of degradation and destruction. That symbol is not the Magen David, as might be imagined. For Naziism is opposed not to Judaism alone but to all humane values, of which the Prophets and Sages of Israel have been eloquent and urgent but by no means solitary spokesmen. The Magen David, the mystic hexagram of interlacing equilateral triangles oriented with bases and points toward heaven and earth, was explicated in the meditations of Franz Rosenzweig as emblematic of the interconnectedness of the transcendent with the here and now—of God with man and nature, through creation, revelation, and redemption.[94] It is symbolic, then, of Israel's special task or mission to mediate the sanctity of the Transcendent into earthbound existence ethically and spiritually, through the love of God, of man, and of nature.

But the rainbow is a more ancient and more global symbol, the biblical sign of a universal covenant, not with Israel alone but with humanity, the "children of Noah," and with nature at large (Gen. 8:21–22; 9:1–17). This covenant does not demand a mission borne through the generations by the individuals and institutions of an integrated national culture. Rather, the rainbow marks God's renunciation of global destruction. It is a symbol of God's promise to preserve the stable order of nature and of the corresponding human obligation to renounce wantonness and violence. This bow displaces the armorer's bow and marks an epoch in the human dissociation of violence from the divine. As the paradigm of nature's stability and of human harmony and hope, the rainbow signifies a universal covenant. No special ritual or explicit recognition of God's governance is demanded. God's acts are to be emulated and in a way fulfilled, through procreation, rejection of savagery, the preservation and cultivation of our human habitat. The charge, first given to Adam and renewed to the sons of Noah and their progeny, humanity at large, is to dwell in the world, to populate it, master it by accommodation and understanding, tend it as a garden, and perfect it—and, along with it, ourselves.

Are such symbols as the rainbow and the swastika, marks of integration and degradation, respectively, beyond the ken of law? I think a system of laws cannot survive that is unable to recognize or address evil at its most palpable and least disguised. If our laws cannot foster the symbols expressive of human harmony and creativity and discourage the celebration of evil for its own sake, but place all symbolisms on a par, they are in a parlous state as well as a bad one.

When Jonah, in the biblical fable, was summoned to prophesy against Nineveh, his mission was not to make Jews of the people of the great city but the more Noahidic task of calling them back to the common standards of moral decency, before lawlessness and violence engulfed them. Like our own, his task was largely educational—we must teach morals and the virtues to our children, not let the world forget what a Nazi is, what a swastika stands for, and, far more importantly, what values they oppose. Like most of us, Jonah was a latitudinarian, tolerant of excess in others. He was content to let the Ninevans stew in their own juices and had no wish to appear in the gates of that great city as a moralist—still less to expend his public credibility in dire and far-fetched prophecies of doom. But he overlooked God's covenant with nature. For in Nineveh, as in our own cities, there were tens of thousands of people who did not know their right hand from their left—and also, as God dryly comments, much cattle.

I have shown how moral rules are possible in monotheism, and how monotheism modulates our understanding of those rules. Diverse circumstances may modify the application of such rules—indeed, they must, if the rules serve in behalf of principles. But this does not mean that we can alter the requirements of our rules to suit our whim, or what we take to be our convenience. We adopt customs apt to our circumstances not only functionally in the narrow, utilitarian sense but symbolically, expressively. We can express a sense of continuity with the past—or a sense of alienness to it—through the manner in which we articulate our values and the style in which we address our commitments. But we can also assign old symbols new dimensions of meaning. Practice and expression are never at a standstill while we live. Yet they are never radically sundered, from one generation to the next, as long as we retain language, history, and the rearing of our children, telling them stories, and imparting values to them, by action and example. Customs fade, revive, or die. But the great principles remain, above the level of mores, as norms, ideals, and universal laws. Chief among these from the human standpoint is the worth of human subjects, as aspirants toward Perfection. This value is given normative force in the command "Love thy fellow as thyself." It is anchored not in convention but in human worth, as is expressed poetically in the words: "God created man in his own image, in the divine image created him—male and female, created he them" (Gen. 1:27).

4

The Doable Good: The Individual and the Community

Our last chapter examined some of the characteristics we might expect in prescriptions deserving to be thought of as God's, although we made no pretense of deducing such imperatives a priori but made constant reference to the Torah's articulation of the commands we are urged to hold constantly before our eyes. Now I want to reverse the fields and work somewhat more inductively, surveying the tradition to discover what it contains that we can think of as expressing God's will. This takes us out of the realm of theory and into the domain of what Aristotle called the doable good, where principles are concretized in practice.[1] Our work here is not simply descriptive. For the canon as we receive it accommodates the ideal of Perfection to a wide variety of circumstances and preserves the resultant crystallizations not merely archivally, as insects in the amber of time, but by subtly reworking them into the living fabric of normative practice.

In 1980 the Knesset of the state of Israel severed the last formal ties between Israeli and British law and instructed judges who found no grounds for a decision in statute, case law, or analogy to form their decisions "in the light of the principles of freedom, justice, equity and peace of Israel's heritage." A large body of British precedent and principle had been taken up as statute during the years 1922–1980, when British Mandatory law provided the requisite backdrop. In taking the historic step of severing the link to the colonial past and setting a more ancient heritage in its place, the Knesset was careful to specify that recourse to the traditional canon was for its humanity.[2] No parochial traditionalism was to be erected on the basis of this law. But the formal judicial process was reopened to a source of inspiration too long held at arm's length. The hope: to reenliven the universal human values of Jewish law. What are those values, and how can their timeless principles be disentangled from the particularities of specific epochs?

The question has been asked repeatedly in Jewish history, a fact that aids us in addressing it. For religions based on revealed scriptures characteristically regard their sacred texts not as fixed archaeological records but as timeless touchstones of inspiration, whose very ambiguities open up new and always relevant meanings. Fundamentalisms, whether minimalist or maximalist, movements of revival, renaissance, and reform, typify monotheistic cultures precisely because the mere positivity of a text or practice will never seem fully adequate to the deepest meanings and highest demands of the core documents. These, like any sacred symbols, will point beyond their historicity toward their Source, and new efforts will constantly be made to reopen their true intensions. Fictively these intensions are recovered from the past, but their practical locus is normative and in the present, constructed for this moment, no matter how atavistically their prescriptive force may be sought in recent or remote antiquity. Radical departures from the normative center of gravity, in pursuit of narrow themes will generate heresy, militancy, sects, or cults. Closely reasoned steps of argument and subtle shifts of emphasis, informed by sensitivity to the continuity and inner logic of broader themes, will yield evolution, enlarging and refining the potentials of the past. But whether inspired or misguided, such elaboration is always selective and interpretive.

Judaism conserves a rich variety of form and content in the historically variegated efforts to articulate its fundamental norms. But three basic idioms emerge—Mosaic, Prophetic, and Rabbinic. It is not my aim to analyze their differences sweepingly, as though the underlying values were exhausted once their syntax was parsed and the terms of reference in which they are couched accurately labeled—"Wisdom Literature," "Priestly Document," "Elohist Tract." Such analysis can be valuable, but as a means to an end, not an end in itself. When the end product is sheer fragmentation, snipping a text into tiny slips of paper or parchment whose scattered array belies thematic unities long evident to the authors and recipients of shared traditions, it may be useful to complement archaeological stratigraphy with something of the synchronic method of the biblical and Rabbinic authors themselves—not as a denial of historicity but as a means of trying to catch a glimpse of what lies beyond the excavation's rim.

For the Torah, as Maimonides explains (*Guide* I 2), is not a work of history or poetry (although it uses their techniques) but a book of laws. To be critically appropriated as a possession for all times, it cannot be read purely as an expression of one time, a repository of the language and limitations of its original audience, whose understanding it accommodates. It must be read as well as a contribution to an ever-living discussion, taken up in diverse terms in each generation, but always pursuing the same goals and resting its case on the same ultimate idea of what is absolute and, accordingly, what is compromisable. If we really believe that the Torah is inspired by the Eternal, and that it is a heritage (Exod. 15:17), we will not suppose that its normative message is spent in a single generation. My purpose here, then, is to look past the shifts of language and scene to uncover the perennial norms that give unity to the Jewish project of defining what the God of Abraham expects of us. Such a task is always and necessarily creative, inductive, active, and collaborative, rather than sheerly receptive, analytic, passive, or dogmatic. The aim is not to reach a point where we no longer sense whether we are reading Hebrew or Aramaic, Arabic or English, but to raise our own consciousness, through what we elicit from the old texts, to the level of their appropriable principles.

The theme we shall trace through its variegated expressions is the relationship of the individual to the community. For the normative traditions of Judaism, unlike many familiar views, do not see that relationship as the focal point of social struggle. In every period, the Jewish sources, like other traditional normative systems, reject the cliché of a zero-sum game between communal and individual interests. Rather than the competition that the Sophists envision, the Torah and the works that elaborate and explicate its themes set forth a complementarity of interests. Autonomy is not the antithesis but the aim of communal norms; individual fulfillment is both the means and the end of the Law's implementation. For this to be true, of course, such fulfillment cannot be defined arbitrarily, reductively, or subjectively. It must comprehend within itself the moral and the spiritual dimensions of our being.

The Mosaic Foundation

The people of Israel, who are the cultural bearers of the Jewish religion and law, an ethnicity forged by their linkage to that law, originate as a people in a crisis. Israel's experience as an identified minority, persecuted and enslaved in Egypt,[3] precipitates the Judaic idea of the individual and of individual dignity. The marks of that experience are visible in the norms of the Mosaic law and even in its cosmological, historical, and protohistorical preambles. Characteristically: "Thou shalt not pervert the justice due to the stranger, or to the orphan, nor take the widow's garment in pawn. Remember that a slave is what thou wert in Egypt, and the Lord thy God redeemed thee thence. That is why I command thee to do this" (Deut. 24:17–18).

The values that form Israel inform the West as well. They give normative content to Israel's identity but also underlie Christian claims to the testament of Israel, and Muslim claims to the parentage of Abraham and heritage of the Prophets. They underwrite modern secular revisions too, whether the debt is openly acknowledged or concealed by recasting and restructuring–in Locke, the Deists, Republicans, and Philosophes, Spinoza, Freud, Marx, Weber, Durkheim, Lévi-Strauss.[4] Even where specifics are sublimated or sublated, the original thematic remains crucial to the elaboration of the tradition.

What, then, is the legacy of Egypt? There is to be no permanent slavery among Israelites, except at the express demand of the slave.[5] The system of debt slavery that Joseph exploited in Egypt (Gen. 47:20) is abolished. Accordingly, there is no permanent alienation of land. What is sold is in effect a lease of no more than forty-nine years (Lev. 25:8–18, 23–25). So there is to be no permanently dispossessed class or caste. Priests and Levites may own no land but must depend on the dues reserved for them. They will not become a wealthy landed class like the priests of Egypt (Num. 18:20–24; cf. 34–35; Gen. 47:22).[6] No interest may be taken on loans to fellow Israelites (Deut. 23:20–21; Exod. 22:24), and their debts must be remitted in the seventh year, when the land enjoys its "sabbath" and lies fallow (Deut. 15:1–10; Lev. 25:1–7). After the seventh such sabbath, the land reverts to its ancestral owners (Lev. 25:8–55). So Israelites may always return to their familial estates. The cycle of debt slavery and dispossession, with its correlative amassing of lands in the priesthood, is permanently broken.[7] From the Book of Ruth we learn that the system did not function perfectly. But the ideas it enunciates became a permanent heritage.

The Torah holds forth its laws of land tenure, debt release, and redemption with a view to ending destitution (Deut. 15:4–5). Yet it allows for the persistence of need even as it pursues its elimination (Deut. 15:11). The appeal behind the provision of surplus "gleanings" and the produce of the corner of the field as the patrimony of the poor (Lev. 19:9–10, 23:22; Deut. 24:19–22) is the same as that underlying the prohibition of injustice to the stranger, forbidding retention of a day worker's wages overnight, taking a widow's clothing in pawn, or keeping a poor man's cloak beyond sundown (Exod. 22:25–27), or any person's millstone—the same as that which prohibits selling kidnapped brethren or entering a debtor's house to claim collateral: "Remember that you were a slave in the land of Egypt" (Deut. 24:6–7, 10–15, 17–22). Unlike Francis Galton or Garrett Hardin, the Torah does not seek the elimination of need by elimination of the needy. Galton, the founder of eugenics, hoped for a humane end to human misery through state aid to the advantaged and socioeconomic suppression of the destitute, to breed out the "inferior" and promote the "superior," gradually but inexorably. Hardin advocates a new ethic for "spaceship earth," triage of entire races and peoples, by withholding food aid from the starving to reduce their numbers and prevent their "swamping the lifeboat" or laying waste "the commons."[8]

The Torah, arising in a far less prosperous age, does not read the human condition as requiring or even permitting such desperate and self-defeating measures. It expresses confidence that life will flourish if creatures are fruitful and multiply and fill the earth (Gen. 1:28).[9] It seeks to ensure, through the active collaboration of all Israelites, that the poor not be allowed to die out and vanish from the land: to preserve their lives, restore them to their property, and see them established is a blessing for the nation (Deut. 15:7–11; cf. Lev. 25:35). Guiding the scheme is the precious value of human self-sufficiency—each man under his own vine or fig tree (1 Kings 4:25; 2 Kings 18:31; Zech. 3:10; cf. Prov. 27:18).[10] Thus, even when the remission of debts is overturned by a legal fiction, in the interest of commerce,[11] or when the growth of the idea of freedom leads to the abolition of slavery, the ideal of the economically autonomous individual remains, a fountain of concrete legal obligations: the poor can sue at law for their just maintenance,[12] and the highest charity is defined not as self-sacrifice or condescension but as imparting to another the means of self-sufficiency.[13]

Central among the Mosaic institutions that echo the Egyptian experience is the Sabbath. The petition for a break (the literal sense of *shabbat*) was the original demand Moses brought before Pharaoh (Exod. 5:1). The request was rejected: "Why, Moses and Aaron, do you sunder the people from their work? Go back to your toils" (Exod. 5:4). Pharaoh refuses to differentiate the slaves from their labors, just as he refuses to distinguish Moses and Aaron from the slaves. The Sabbath becomes a symbol of the existential autonomy of the individual, the irreducibility of person to task, and God himself is envisioned ceasing from his work (Gen. 2:2–3): even he is not confined to his task, and man, created in God's image, is freed by the Law, commanded to rest and thus to know himself apart from his uses. Even animals may not be worked on the Sabbath, lest servants be excluded from full enjoyment of the Sabbath rest (Deut. 5:14–15)—and lest we imagine that beasts are mere tools.

The Sabbath is called a sign (*ʾot*) of God's act of creation (Exod. 31:17). But it reenacts the cessation, not the work; and when the Torah says that God stopped and rested (*shavat va-yinnafash*—Exod. 31:17) the Midrashic poets can almost hear God's restful sigh, even now breathing into us the sacred soul (*nefesh*) imparted to humanity through rest, playfully taking the form of the verb (*yinnafash*) causally to suggest that God did not rest (Ps. 121:3–4) but gave rest and, with it, spirit. Israel's liberation is thus linked with God's creation. The Sabbath is a memorial of both (*zekher le-ma'aseh bereshit*; *zekher yitzi'at Mitzraim*). For God, too, does not act by constraint—not automatically. Freedom is the condition of existence, and creativity is the mark of freedom.

Again from the experience in Egypt, we have the commandment against looking down on the Egyptian (Deut. 23:8; cf. Isa. 19:25). The stated reason: that we were strangers in Egypt. The sufferings of our stay are not held against the nation, and the ethos of vindictiveness is inverted, giving the lie to Nietzsche's claim that the workshops of morals are fueled by the spirit of vengeance (*Genealogy of Morals* 1:7). For ethics here takes its rise dialectically in moral rejection of a merely reactive response, as the Torah expands and generalizes the commandment not to scorn the Egyptian: there are commandments not to hate one's brother in one's heart (Lev. 19:17), not to oppress a stranger (Exod. 23:9—"for you know the heart of a stranger"), to love the stranger (Deut. 10:19; Lev. 19:34), to love one's fellow as oneself (Lev. 19:18, 34). Even the idea of one law for the stranger and the homeborn alike (Lev. 18:26; cf. 16:29, 24:22; Num. 15:30) is a dialectical counterpart of the ethical response to Egypt. The process is still going on when Jesus admonishes: "Love thine enemies, bless them that curse thee, do good to them that hate you, and pray for them that despitefully use and persecute thee" (Matt. 5:44). The Torah does not issue that command, which might ring paradoxical when enemies could not be accorded a figurative or literal *clementia* from the heights of spiritual or temporal power. But it does command us to aid our enemy in righting and reloading his fallen ass (Exod. 23:4–5). For even enemies are human beings. And, as Maimonides explains, it is an object of the Law to cement the bonds that link us and to improve our character, through actions that will soften the pumice of irascibility in the soul. Spinoza follows and extends this reading when he offers a psychologistic model for the power of love in dissolving hatred, the answer to enmity that the Midrash calls heroic.[14]

A crucial corollary of the injunction to love the stranger and to love our fellows as ourselves is the idea of equality, a conception formative of the idea of law and of that of humanity. Human equality rests on and gives substance to the existential dignity which the law and the community exist to serve and promote—not in place of God's service but as the chief means by which God desires and intends to be served.[15] Before the giving of the Law, every man did what was right in his own eyes (Deut. 12:8, 13:19; cf. Judg. 17:6, 21:25). But in God's eyes, and so in the Law's eyes, all persons are of equal existential worth. Thus judges may not favor wealth and stature, or even poverty or merit (Exod. 23:2–3; Lev. 19:15). The proof-text: Exod. 23:6: "Thou shalt not pervert the judgment of thy poor in his cause." Maimonides glosses: "Even if he is poor in piety, do not pervert his judgment."[16]

The Torah freely reports that the idea of deciding cases by uniform rules came to Moses from a foreign source, his Midianite father-in-law, Jethro (Exod. 18). But uniformity alone is not equality. For persons might be treated uniformly according to their station. In Hammurabi's code the death penalty for theft was commuted to thirtyfold restitution if the theft was from a royal estate, tenfold if from a gentleman, fivefold if from a commoner. A blow is punished by sixty stripes of an oxhide scourge—if it was directed at a superior.[17] The idea that social dominance or prominence is profoundly irrelevant to the crucial issues of justice rests on the recognition that human deserts are at some level existential, and positive. That idea is alien to Hammurabi. Yet any broad uniformity militates in the direction of categorical deserts, and recognition of such deserts at some level is a moral necessity in any legal system: minimally, for example, there is a uniform desert of access to the laws.[18] The very idea of the rule of law presses for equal treatment of equal cases (Exod. 12:49; Lev. 24:22; Num. 15:16, 29). Thus the provisions for a permanent, public, written law (Exod. 24:7; Deut. 17:11; 27:3, 8; 31:11–12, 24–26) press toward constitutionality, as evident in God's command that each king of Israel closely study and follow the Law:

> When he sitteth on his royal throne, he shall write himself a copy of this Torah, from the book in the charge of the Levitical priests. And he shall keep it by him and read from it all the days of his life, so that he learn to revere the Lord his God by keeping all the provisions of this Law and performing all these statutes, and his heart not grow haughty toward his brethren, and that he not diverge to the left or the right from its command, so that his reign and that of his offspring in the midst of Israel may long endure. (Deut. 17:18–20)[19]

When fused with the idea of the inviolable worth or dignity of the individual as a creature of God, the invariance of rules becomes humanity's most powerful ethical and legislative tool. It meant, to begin with, that recompense for deaths or injuries must be proportioned only to the injury and not the stature or grandeur of the party offended against (Exod. 21:23–26; Lev. 24:17–22; Num. 35:29–34). The dignity of all human beings is alike for free or slave, man or woman, young or old.

It is the work of centuries, and a task by no means completed, to single out those dimensions of human dignity that are truly existential from the claims of ego or custom that are mere encrustations of our universal desire for dignity—at our own or others' expense. But an immediate requirement, when the equality of human dignities was first enunciated in a vengeance culture, was the distinction between murder, manslaughter, and accident. The Cities of Refuge are the Torah's response, protecting from blood vengeance homicides who are not premeditated murderers (Exod. 21:13, 18–19; Num. 35:9–29). Correspondingly, there is capital punishment (not vengeance) and a rejection of blood payment or corporate accountability for murder (Num. 35:31; Exod. 21:12, 14).

The Torah's insistence on individual accountability for offenses (Deut. 24:16) articulates the identity of the moral person and singles out the moral agent as the actor on whose choices and omissions, virtues and weaknesses, the fate of the community will depend (Lev. 26:3–33). Hammurabi's code rules that the *children* of a negligent builder shall die (230), that a creditor's son is killed if the distrained son of a debtor dies on his account (116), that an assailant's daughter dies if he causes the death by miscarriage of another man's daughter (209–14).[20] In the ancient codes, and not a few modern ones, property crimes can be capital. The Torah, as Moshe Greenberg explains, sharply divides crimes against persons from crimes against property: the latter are never capital. Thus adultery is a crime by a couple against God (Gen. 20:6, 39:8; Lev. 20:10), not simply by a wife against her husband. So there is "no question of permitting the husband to mitigate or cancel the punishment" (Lev. 20:10; Deut. 22:22–23), just as there is no royal pardon for murderers.[21] God himself oversees the uniformity of the Law, and God's character came clearly into the light when Abraham argued and haggled with him for the Cities of the Plain: better to spare the wicked majority than let the wicked and the righteous fare alike.

The procedural guarantees[22]—presumption of innocence, protection against self-incrimination, strict rules of evidence and testimony–that are the glory of Western law reflect the Torah's valuation of the individual. Thus the demand for two witnesses in a capital case—"no one shall die by the testimony of a single witness" (Num. 35:30; Deut. 19:15). Even habeas corpus and the right to a jury trial, which are not biblical institutions, take on the absoluteness and sanctity of biblical rights, which God himself should honor. Job, in the midst of his sufferings, can expect a trial.[23] And the visions of apocalypse called forth by thoughts of God's universal justice take on a juridical, procedurally safeguarded form, down to the inclusion of adversarial advocates for the prosecution and the defense. God himself formalizes his covenant with Israel by calling heaven and earth to witness (Deut. 4:26; cf. 31:28; 32:1, 40); no default will be determined on a single party's say-so. The earthly counterparts to these cosmic guarantees safeguard personal liberty, life—and property, to be sure—but, crucially, they protect human dignity, defined to engulf and transcend all of these.

The family, as biblically construed, is the matrix for the emergence of individuality (Gen. 2:24). Personal identity is preserved and nurtured by the protection of sexual privacy. It is not submerged in the identities of parents but matures and emerges sound and independent, capable of entering a mature relationship with another autonomous person and adequate to the construction of a new household. This cycle affords the Torah's rationale for the prohibition of incest,[24] and for all social institutions. As Albert Einstein wrote:

> The highest principles for our aspirations and judgments are given to us in the Jewish-Christian religious tradition. It is a very high goal which, with our weak powers, we can reach only very inadequately, but which gives a sure foundation to our aspirations and valuations. If one were to take that goal out of its religious form and look merely at its purely human side, one might state it perhaps thus: free and responsible development of the individual, so that he may place his powers freely and gladly in the service of all mankind. There is no room in this for the divinization of a nation, of a class, let alone of an individual. . . . It is only to the individual that a soul is given. And the high destiny of the individual is to serve rather than to rule, or to impose himself in any other way.[25]

The paradigmatic marriage is dyadic: a man leaves his father's and his mother's house and cleaves unto his wife. Despite the long tolerance of polygamy, the paradigm persists: the way of a man with a maid (Prov. 30:19), thy neighbor's wife (Exod. 20:14)–or Job's.[26] Marital exclusivity even models God's intimacy with Israel (Exod. 20:5, 34:14; Deut. 4:24, 5:9, 6:15; 1 Kings 19:10, 14; Joel 2:18; Zech. 1:14, 8:2). Ultimately, polygamy will be spat out—not simply in response to "cultural influences" (for one must always ask why one cultural pattern is appropriated and another rejected)—but by the powerful idea of monogamy itself. The same process can be seen in modern times among thoughtful leaders of Islam. For scriptural ideals can in time make intolerable what has long been tolerated, through their dialectic with social standards, cultural experiences, and intellectual judgments. Core values are reaffirmed, and what proves incompatible with them—anthropomorphism, slavery, polygamy—is ejected.

Biblical legislation, often explicated in the biblical narrative, does much to form the ideal of individuality as we know it. But in Mosaic and Patriarchal times the state is not the principal threat to personhood. The modern sovereign state, which both fosters and threatens individuality, the totalitarian state, which seeks to exploit and submerge the individual, even the omnicompetent welfare state, with all its techniques of empowerment and inducements to dependency, do not yet exist. The institutions that are created biblically are deemed ancillary, not antithetical, to individual interests, which in turn are not sharply set apart from communal goals. Traditional norms often presume the harmony of individual and group interests. Whether out of naïveté or wisdom, license is not mistaken for freedom and communal potentials for abuse are not seen as powers. The individual is not radically isolated from the social body to whose interests his own are linked.

The fundamental social commandment of the Mosaic corpus, "Love thy neighbor as thyself" (Lev. 19:18), typifies the Mosaic method of legislation and its goals in integrating the individual in the community. It both rests upon and fosters individuality. It addresses the individual and urges those whom it addresses to seek the good of others, by fostering fellowship and fellow feeling (*re'ut*, community)—a sense of common interests and shared concerns, making another's good one's own. That ideal is not left an isolated abstraction but interpreted in concrete actions that give it operational meaning—from the immediate ban on vengeance and grudges (vv. 17–18) to the prohibition of talebearing on the one hand and diffidence on the other (v. 16). Indeed, the commandments biblically linked with the Golden Rule form a tight nexus arising from the primal commandment to pattern ourselves on God's ways, and expressing itself, for example, in a delicately balanced pair of obligations to reprove our fellows when they do wrong, but not to shame them.[27]

The bond of the individual to the community is a familiar feature of ancient and traditional societies. Even a rather alienated figure like Socrates will not accept life beyond the polis that he knows, and where (however partially and unfairly) he is known (*Crito* 53D–54B; *Apology* 30–31). His alienation gives him the distance he needs to see and perhaps to state that fact, but not to alter it. Plato, who spent years away from Athens and was ready to assume a leading role in the life of some other polis, will address the question of justice only by dealing pari passu with the private politics of the soul and the public foundations of state legitimacy. Aristotle, a *metic* at Athens, finally forced to leave it on the death of Alexander, argues that a person who would live alone is either above or below humanity—a beast or a god; for man is by nature a creature of the polis (*zoon politikon*). But in each case, the linkage of person to polis serves the person and is justified by the worth of individual humanity, even (and especially) when individuals are called on to make sacrifices for the group.

Somewhat provincially, even chauvinistically, Aristotle argues that the fully human life, the humane life, is possible only for a free man in a (Greek) polis: slaves do not enjoy humanely fulfilled lives. Greek women rarely had the access to intellectual or public engagement that would have made them fully free. And non-Greeks seemed to Aristotle too submerged in stultifying autocracies, without the agora, palaestra, baths, theaters, schools, and walks that fostered the articulation of personhood in a public setting. It was in such institutions as these that Greek individuality came to be. Greek literature, science, mathematics, philosophy, and art are its testimonies, unique and irreplaceable. The Torah, with its own institutions of law, universal and objective history, and the unique, historically rooted monotheism articulated in biblical cosmology, mysticism, ritual, and morals, is a comparable and complementary gift, capable of synthesis with the best the Greeks can offer. Just as one story may absorb another as its subplot, Israel's ideas of universal history, objective truth, and justice subsume what they find valid in all cultures and spew out or transform what does not meet their overarching vision. It was not for nothing that God chose a stiff-necked nation inured to the practice of criticism. For, whether the fruits of Israelite criticism are intellectual or social, its roots are moral.[28]

Surveying the biblical canon, Maimonides, a philosopher imbued with the teaching of Aristotle as well as the wisdom of the Torah, finds that its institutions always seek the individual's perfection. He defines the generic purpose of laws not just Platonically, as the integration of disparate human interests, but also with a view to the value of individual differences, thus assigning laws the rather subtler project of integrating otherwise disparate characters: human laws seek only to regulate our material interactions—to adjudicate our conflicts, restrain aggression and overreaching, promote our material welfare and impartially allocate the goods and ills that the human condition lays before us. But a divine law pursues two higher goals: the improvement of our character (Plato's "education," Aristotle's moral development) and provision for our intellectual and spiritual fulfillment (Plato's vision of the sun, Aristotle's intellectual life).[29] These higher goals are approached by way of symbols, not merely by the familiar legal means of prescription and sanction. Paradigmatic actions draw us, through habit, to standards of reasonableness whose abstract description may be quite beyond us. But speech is not the aim here. What matters is our moral appropriation of dispositions toward thoughtful choice making. Once these are facets of our character, virtuous actions will be spontaneous and reliable. Thoughtful and appropriate choices will be, as Aristotle put it, second nature.[30]

Intellectual and spiritual perfection are not imposed but invited, through mythic symbolisms, the Torah's oblique discourse about God.[31] The problematics of that discourse, in which prophets boldly speak of the Creator in terms proper to his creation, awaken us to God's transcendence of all description and direct us toward the idea of God's absolute perfection, whose glory is his creation of each thing for its own sake–its perfection, an emblem of his goodness. No biblical injunction escapes these three headings: cooperation (civil and penal integration in pursuit of the common good), moral improvement (the establishment of kindness, generosity, and dignity in our ethos),[32] and intellectual perfection (the invitation to holiness, critical apprehension of God's transcendence, and the concomitant ability to interpret his Law to others, allowing them, too, to become morally autonomous and, insofar as humanly possible, intellectually self-sufficient.)[33]

Just as Aristotle grounded his understanding of politics on empirical study of some 158 constitutions, Maimonides did not draw his Mosaic jurisprudence from the air but founded it on his own catalogue of the Torah's 613 commandments, on his explication of the Mishnaic code, and on his codification of the halakhic corpus in the fourteen-volume *Mishneh Torah*.[34] No law was found whose purpose is subordination of the interests of the individual to the group. Although Maimonides did hold that the community is more important than the individual,[35] he grounded its importance biblically in the dignity and worth of its members. Laws, he acknowledged, in their generality, can disaccommodate individuals (*Guide* III 34). But even that is in the interest of those individuals, which animal shortsightedness (appetite and passion) might lead them to misperceive. For the individual is not always or necessarily the best judge of his own interests, and only lawlessness results when each person simply judges his own case.[36]

Maimonides did not expect each individual to work out his own destiny alone; he shared the Biblical idea that the destiny of individuals is wrapped up in that of their fellows, forebears, and descendants—that Abraham finds fulfillment not in his personal wealth, nor even solely in his personal discovery of God, but in the knowledge that through his descendants all the peoples of the world will be blessed; Moses finds fulfillment not in his personal fortunes, nor even in his personal experience of God, but in his responsibility for the people—seeking to know God's ways for the sake of learning how to govern (Exod. 33:13), wishing to God that every Israelite were a prophet (Num. 11:29), and praying to God (Exod. 32:32) to be blotted from his book if the people must be destroyed for their lapse. Moses will not accept life apart from the nation (and will accept no substitute nation) any more than Socrates will accept life apart from Athens.

The Prophetic Recension

In the writings from the times of the Judges, Kings, and Prophets of Israel the biblical ideals are reconstituted and the Mosaic ideal of individuality reformulated and reenlivened. Human individuality had been central to the Mosaic nisus. Yet no "definition" of the human person emerges in the Pentateuch. For the Mosaic idiom is not abstract but concrete. So, even when its work is reflective, no expression like *zoon politikon* will emerge. Besides, to speak of individuality is to speak of freedom; to define it is to limit freedom. The Torah bears enough prescriptive weight without setting boundaries to the normative personality. In later ages this was done, reading the roles of ascetic saints and Rabbinic sages into the lives of the Patriarchs or even of David, Boaz, Shem, and Eber. But the Mosaic Law, addressing all ages, defines no normative type but opens the space for human personhood to construct itself, trusting the same method of silence it used in allowing our minds to find the idea of God. For man is created in God's image, and God, too, is assigned no delimiting shape. Every title of perfection belongs to him, and all imperfections must be denied of him—even those implicit in our positive predications. The same, in moral terms, holds true for man: no vice must restrain him. The very word for sin is "stumble." No wrong is in our interest. Human fulfillment springs from righteousness, as God's rule is founded in righteousness (Prov. 10:2, 11:4–5, 19; 13:6, 14:34, 15:9, 16:12, 25:5). But no stereotypic role hobbles our steps. The character we are taught by practice and example finds its feet in any human context. For kindness, thoughtfulness, self-respect, purity, and holiness are always relevant. The intelligence that symbol and indirection invite us to develop at the growing core of our identity is an openness to understanding, cramped by no catechism but drawn toward God, who is infinite, and toward love and understanding of his creation, whose wonders, subtleties, and complexities are illimitable.[37]

The egoist is absent from the Mosaic canon except in passages of self-betrayal like Lamech's boast or Cain's "Am I my brother's keeper?" (Gen. 4:9). No heroic ego centers the Pentateuch, for the same reason that there is no portrait of the lineaments, ancestry, or deepest motives of the Creator: the Torah is not a saga but a law, filled out not with battle scenes or love triangles but with cosmology, history, ethical tableaux. God is absolute. Man is not, but his dignity, hence his freedom, is a kind of finite absolute. Like God, man is in a way inscrutable. But he too is an end in himself—so that all the prescriptions made to him can rest on two: the love of God and the love of self—the latter not a sin but an axiom, without which the commandment to love one's fellow as oneself becomes an empty formalism. Yet the Torah's love of self is not self-exaltation but a pursuit of self-perfection, including moral and spiritual self-perfection, as we express it. In the biblical idiom: "Circumcise, then, thy heart!" (Deut. 10:16, with Deut. 30:6; Lev. 26:41). Paganism is the ethos of Lamech made cult. The epic, we have suggested, celebrates human vices and virtues by making them reflections of divine counterparts—themselves projected from the vividness of the human drama. The epic hero is the human boaster projected to the heavens, with a bard's help, then reflected down again, now magnified to superhuman scale, and still bearing the aura of divinity. There will be heroism but no epic heroes in the Torah.

As the history progresses whose meanings the Torah defines, and as the people whose mission it elaborates move onto the stage of history, individuals do emerge: a David, whose lyric spirituality articulates a unique identity, a Jephtha whose desperate isolation bespeaks his hunger for social integration, an Amos or Hosea, voicing the interiority of prophetic experience. It might be imagined that notions of individuality and personality do not emerge from the communal matrix until, say, the Renaissance or the Enlightenment—with the new literary form of the familiar essay, one colleague says. But this is an illusion, spun from the romantic anthropology of the type canonized by Lévy-Bruhl and others who suppose that in traditional societies culture is somehow undifferentiated from nature, categories unreflective and undifferentiably compact—so that individuals *cannot* differentiate themselves from the mass, from one another, from the group and its norms, from natural objects and natural kinds fixed in the iconography of totem and taboo. Such anthropological views have long been discredited by the work of Lévi-Strauss, Mary Douglas, and Malinowski before them. The ideas persist through their romantic appeal and the projective uses made of their invidious characterizations of the "other," who is located elsewhere than we locate ourselves in the nature-culture polarity.[38]

As for the literary expression of personality—the essay, in which one personality addresses the less clearly delineated but still individuated persona of a single listener in intimate and less formal tones than those of the public harangue or treatise—it is not Montaigne's invention but emerges from the ancient epistolary art modeled in the letters of Seneca. It is well developed in the medieval Arabic *risālah*, which guards the intimacy of tone by preserving the epistolary fiction that a single close friend or confidant is addressed.[39] This is the form and tone of address adopted by the Ikhwān al-Ṣafā᾽ or Sincere Brethren of Basra, by Ibn Ṭufayl, and by Maimonides in the *Guide to the Perplexed.* But epistolary prose and essays are not the only avenues to the intimacy expressive of individuality. The same poet-warrior who danced naked before the ark of the Lord and created that spiritual intimacy by which *we* bless our Creator—David, the shepherd slingsman who sang his troubled king to sleep, who married that king's daughter and was loved by that king's son, even as he displaced him—is also the founding figure of an intimate genre, not of prose but of poetry. The genre of the Psalsm is not the work of a single pair of hands, any more than the Psalms themselves are. But it is the vehicle of a personality whose failings we know (with the aid of prophet critics close to the court) as intimately and deeply as we know the spiritual and material heights of his ambitions. It is no accident that David is the figure, despite his weaknesses, so often chosen as a namesake. For his personality does emerge as few do from antiquity. He steps forward as a hero and epitome of many of the Torah's humanistic values, although—and in part because—his individuality is never wholly predictable.

Sexuality is present everywhere in David's personality—in his beauty, his appeal to the maidens as a warrior, his flawed relations with Michal, his betrayal of Uriah, even in the last flickerings of bodily warmth in his deathbed—or its structural mirror image, the story of his Moabite ancestry told in the Book of Ruth. Biblical personhood finds its core in sexuality, the primal focus of adult individuality in us all. It is because we all have sexual aspirations, vulnerabilities, and deserts that the Torah legislates as it does, seeking not "to regulate every aspect of life" but to define and protect the libidinal core in which our individuality is invested. Even the modern (and ultimately incoherent) notion that some areas are too intimate for law to enter is a reflex of the privacy and dignity the Torah seeks to demarcate and defend.

Against rape the Mosaic canon addresses both a civil and a penal remedy. The offense is never a mere larceny against paternity. The heart of the crime is pinioned as the humbling of the victim—a degrading of her dignity. The Mosaic remedies clearly seek to mitigate the savageries of the ancient honor-shame culture we glimpse in the story of the rape of Dinah and the excess of her brothers' vengeance (Genesis 34). But the remedies proposed—death for the rape of a betrothed or married woman, or marriage without divorce for the (statutory) rape of a single woman (Deut. 22:22–28)—demand a civil society in which criminal penalties will be exacted and in which communal relations make marriage thinkable between a woman and her seducer.[40] The law here seeks only to enforce earnestness. The idea of premarital intimacy without courtship is no part of this model, and rape as a weapon rather than a concupiscent excess is not here addressed. Shechem's were the passions of an overardent suitor (Gen. 34:2–4, 6, 8–12). But the decline of civil standards brought excesses of a type only dimly presaged in Dinah's story (Judges 19–21).

With no central government to define and enforce due proportion, the atrocities of anarchy return, bringing back the exemplary vengeance condemned by Jacob in his sons (Gen. 34:30, 49:5–7) and the collective blood liability vigorously combated by the later Prophets (Ezek. 18:4). It was against the backdrop of such lawlessness that the prophet and judge Deborah emerged, responding to the needs that would create the Biblical monarchy. Her song gives voice to her people's sense of triumphant liberation from terrorized vassalage to a brigand state whose pillage had cleared the roads of travelers (Judg. 5:6). Deborah pictures the mother of the robber general Sisera at a latticed window awaiting his return, her well-protected ladies answering her doubts with images of the booty that has delayed the chariots: "a cunt, two cunts for every manhead." The women, whose fantasies egg on their sons' search for aggrandizement, picture the delicate finery of the female captives: embroidered cloth in many colors about every neck as spoil (Judg. 5:28–30). The day is not Sisera's, however, but Deborah's and Jael's. The song of triumph, fuller than Miriam's at the sea, is the work of an individual who proudly differentiates herself from the nation and its leaders, on their white asses: the precincts of Israel were vacant, the people could not draw water without the whirr of arrows—"until I arose, Deborah, until I arose, a mother in Israel." No words spoken for or about or against women since—not the long tradition of petulant misogyny or timid fastidiousness, nor even the sticky-sweet uxoritudes that seek to circumscribe a woman's "place" with platitudinous praise—could rob all women afterward of the sense of pride and vindicated right that accrues from Deborah's triumphant singing in the first person, not arrogant or spiteful but rejoicing in the restoration of civility: "And the land had peace for forty years" (Judg. 5:31).

The tradition of misogyny that grows from Hellenistic world-weariness and betrays itself in the obiter dicta of many later authorities is well entrenched in medieval Judaism. Woman in the abstract here often becomes the repository of projected ambivalences toward the emotions, the senses, and the body; and institutions are deflected from imparting dignity, to the assignment of disadvantaged or disparaging postures to women. Yet the accretion never wholly obscures the normative themes: Moses could learn from God himself that Zelophehad's daughters rightly claimed their father's inheritance (Num. 27:7; cf. 36:10), in keeping with the Law's concern for the survival of every Israelite house. The ruling did not establish the equal inheritance of daughters with sons in Rabbinic law. Rather, daughters and their descendants took second place to surviving sons and their descendants. But daughters came ahead of any other claimants, including fathers, brothers, sisters, grandfathers, and other kin of the deceased. And male heirs were obligated to support their unmarried sisters, even if it reduced the men to beggary. Commenting on the biblical provision, *Sifre* (133 to Num. 27:7) remarks, "Man prefers men to women, but the Creator shows equal regard for all." Drawing on this theme, Falk writes, "Just as the Torah uses human language to express divine ideas, it also uses the world of ideas of a patriarchal society to express universal truths. It therefore still requires feminist analysis and critique in order to create a more general and universal interpretation. The story concerning the daughters of Zelophehad, who brought about a correction of the law of inheritance, should be used as the model for this process, which is an ongoing responsibility of each generation and a special challenge of ours."[41]

Our ideas of equality may differ from those of Moses or the Rabbis. Such alterations are inevitable with the change of social and economic circumstances. Where we look for recognitions of autonomy, earlier sources may seek equality in the provision of maintenance. Not every age or situation makes possible the strong woman celebrated in Prov. 31, who invests in foreign trade and agricultural real estate while carrying on a flourishing textile and garment industry under her own roof. Such a woman is a fitting exemplar of the biblical ideal of economic self-sufficiency and is textually acknowledged as the fitting recipient not only of her children's praises but of the profits of her enterprise. Her activities are not found in every epoch and social circumstance. But what is constant is the ideal of dignity that emerges from her portrayal even more clearly than the tableaux of the economic enterprises on which her realization of that dignity depends. Thus Edith Hamilton writes:

> The Bible . . . looks at women as human beings, no better and no worse than men. . . . The Old Testament writers, writing of a general's great victory, Barak's over "Sisera with his chariots and his multitude," would set down how he cried out to a woman when she bade him go fight, "If thou wilt go with me, then will I go: but if thou wilt not go with me, then will I not go." And Deborah answered, "I will surely go with thee. [But the glory will not be thine; for the Lord will deliver Sisera into the hands of a woman]" (Judges 5:8–9). Bad women and faulty women are plainly dealt with. . . . "A continual dropping on a very rainy day and a contentious woman are alike" (Proverbs 27:15), but the criticisms are always reasonable and well founded. So too is the praise. After a long acquaintance with the remarkable ladies of the romancers and poets of other lands, it is refreshing to stand on firm ground with the author of the last chapter of *Proverbs*, whose mother, we are told, had taught him, and who had never an idea that woman was the lesser man or some bright angelic visitant.[42]

The Mosaic themes are not discarded by the Prophets but are taken up and reinterpreted: where Leviticus offered ritual means of purging unexpiated guilt, the prophets demand spiritual cleanliness and moral purity, eliciting more explicitly the underlying Mosaic premise that there is more to man than what lives and works and dies—not an afterlife, to be sure, but an aspect of our being not exhausted by our overt acts, a spiritual reality that lives and acts in prayer and intent, inwardly, not just as a presence in the Temple throng or fighting force. The idea is implicit in the Law—in the ritual concern with unaccounted blood (Deut. 21:7), in the institution of the Sabbath, even in the splendid dramatic irony of Cain's words to God, "Am I my brother's keeper?" But, as prophecy unfolds, the Mosaic theme of an unseen dimension becomes an open thesis—"man doth not live by bread alone, but by everything that issueth from the mouth of the Lord doth man live" (Deut. 8:3; cf. 1 Sam. 15:22–23). Now working on an explicit level, the theme is an organizing, structuring principle. The risk and worth of moral agency rise above price (Ps. 49:8).

The prophetic recasting of the Mosaic message modifies and simplifies but does not strike down any pillar of the Law. For all remain present and accessible in the Torah. But the core principles are underscored, the themes synthesized. Thus, Amos (2:8) reenlivens the outrage that first informed the ordinance against keeping garments in pledge (Exod. 22:25) and makes it emblematic of the full range of social neglect. Castigating luxury, he calls the Temple cult itself an obscenity, when it is tainted by the hypocrisy of those who would make of it a surrogate for moral purity (5:12–27; cf. Mal. 1:7–8).

"Hear God's word, ye Lords of Sodom"—so Isaiah addresses the elite of Judah and Jerusalem, fearless of the kings whose names preface his message, including Manassah, who will be his death.

> Give ear to the Torah of our God, you people of Gomorrah: "What need have I of your many sacrifices?" saith the Lord, "I am surfeited with burnt offerings of rams. . . . When you come before me, who sought this of you, to tramp through My courts? Bring Me no more false oblations. Incense is loathsome. . . . I shall not bear iniquity in assembly. . . . When you pray at length, I do not hear; your hands are full of blood. Wash and cleanse, shed the evil of your doings. . . . Seek justice, aid the oppressed, defend the fatherless and take the part of the widow. Come now, let us reason together," saith the Lord, "though your sins be red as scarlet, they shall be white as snow; though they be red as crimson they shall be like fleece . . ." (Isa. 1:11–18; cf. Amos 7:14–17).

A prophet, as R. H. Charles put it, paraphrasing Marcus Jastrow, is a "forthteller" not a "foreteller."[43] Muḥammad, who aspired to prophecy, well understood that a prophet was not merely a poet or a soothsayer; he deeply resented the notion that he was either (Qurʾān 52:29, 69:40–43). Rather, he was an admonisher, like those before him, bearing a message of accountability (Qurʾān 53:35–56). Saadiah analyzes religious scriptures in general in the same terms:[44] Prophets convey a moral message, and their warnings have the force not of mere predictions but of indictments. Surveying the indictments found in Amos, Micah, Isaiah, and Jeremiah, Richard Bergren finds that every charge cites specific "apodictic" commandments of the Torah, those in which God's categorical demands are voiced not as mere regulations of civil or religious life but as vital constituents in the very meaning of the covenant. All of the warnings of disaster address moral offenses or outright disloyalty—perversion of justice, acceptance of bribes, use of false weights and measures, usury, taking garments in pledge, usurping property, withholding wages, mistreating widows, orphans, and strangers, dishonoring parents. The Prophets indict lying, talebearing, perjury, theft, and the shedding of innocent blood. But the only charges in matters of cult are apostasy, sorcery, idolatry, and child sacrifice.[45] The crimes call for prophetic indictment and divine retribution, because they are secret—or so public that even the agencies that should control them are implicated in them.[46] The offenses threaten the very ethos that is the locus of God's covenant. They are the work of individuals, but they corrupt and imperil the nation, and the conscience of individuals must join with the responsibility of leaders to stem the tide.

When Micah (6:8) sums up the Torah's demands: "It hath been told thee, O man, what is good and what the Lord expecteth of thee—only this: the practice of justice, the love of kindness, and modesty in walking with thy God," the reduction is a synthesis, not a winnowing.[47] Thus we read: "Moses was given six hundred thirteen commandments. David summed these up in eleven (Psalm 15), Isaiah in six (33:16–17), Micah in three (6:8), Isaiah again in two (56:1), and finally Habakkuk founded them all in one principle, fidelity" (*Makkot* 23b–24a). Like the words of Hillel (*Shabbat* 31a), which it anticipates, Micah's summation could well bear the rider "The rest is commentary. Go forth and learn it." For the entire Torah can be construed as interpretive commentary, giving concrete definition to the ideals of justice, kindness, and humility. The Prophets, for their part, do not merely comment on the Mosaic norms. They voice the principles on which those norms and the accompanying narratives are commentary. They synthesize analytically, joining together the thematic threads to reweave the fabric: the individual who grapples with a Micah or Isaiah will not complacently presume that the world was made for his amusement or his family's prosperity. The acid cynicism of Ecclesiastes dissolves shallow worldliness, just as Israel's mordant irony at the exodus ("Weren't there any graves in Egypt?") dissolves all complacent afterworldliness.

Universal human brotherhood and the consent of the governed are corollaries (not foundations) of the biblical ideas of human existential equality and dignity before God. In Mosaic terms the relationship between God and creation is construed contractually, as a covenant entered freely: Israel has a covenant with God, publicly and unanimously accepted, acknowledging the misfortunes that will follow failure to keep its terms (Exod. 24:7; Deut. 27; 1 Kings 1:36; 1 Chron. 16:36; Neh. 5:13, 8:6). The consent of the governed is a consent to be governed. It means assumption of duties, communally, for all time, not individually or contingently but existentially. When Israelites accept God's laws—agree to keep the Sabbath as an eternal sign between themselves and God, to tell their children of the exodus from Egypt—they make a commitment not only to the preservation of their peoplehood but to the preservation of its meaning. They bring to bear the full force of culture and familial tradition to ensure that the core values that locate and lock that meaning in place will not be lost. The duties and dignities that the tradition embodies will be sacred to the community, which itself becomes an object of special concern because it bears these values and ideas. But the community as such will not become sacred. Even the idea of a king or ruler other than God, ultimately even the idea of a personal messiah, will become morally, and so intellectually, problematic. The individual must not "break away" from the community (Avot 2.4), but neither is he or she its creature. For the community exists to foster the growth of the individual, whose adequate development fosters the advancement of the community.

The Torah figures God's covenant with Israel as a marriage or a parent-child relationship, since these involve no mere exchange of goods but a giving of one's being. God, the Prophets say, reflecting on the vicissitudes of history, may chastise his people but will not forsake them. God calls it unthinkable to abandon his children or the wife he has espoused (Isa. 50:1; 54; Jer. 2:2, 31:20; Hos. esp. 11:1–11, 13:8; Ezek. 23). Or, with God in the maternal role,[48] God will give suck to her children at Jerusalem and not forsake them (Isa. 66:11–13; cf. 42:14, 49:15; Deut. 32:11; Job 38:28–29). Committing themselves to God and his Law for all their generations, the people recognize an existential bond with one another. Beyond any literal contract, this covenant touches our identities as individuals who share a common history, face a common danger and a common joy, and pursue a common destiny, as fellow Israelites, sharers in a transpersonal, intergenerational encounter with the one God.

Every nation's history, in its depth and complexity, progressively determines a unique path—in literature, art, law, plastic design. Unique, not fixed, for cultures change, grow, and differentiate, as individual decisions demarcate and explore the finer scale of our personal odysseys. Israel's historic commitment of its culture to interpreting the commands of the Transcendent forever sets the terms of reference of Jewish norms: truth and goodness here will always be inseparable. Since the values are universal, the principle, at this level of generality, may sound vacuous or commonplace. But even at so high a level of abstraction, subtle determinations have been made—truth, not relativity or emptiness; goodness, not power or cunning. Exclusivity is not the theme, for the values enunciated invite emulation. But, as history unfolds, the distinctiveness becomes pronounced.

In any culture commitments are made to symbolic modes that may seem arbitrary if viewed externally to their own logic. In Israel, these commitments are moral and intellectual. That is not unique. But perhaps what is distinctive is the moral reading given to the intellectual, and the intellectual, critical reading given to the moral: Israel shall have no other God, and, while the God of the Universe cannot be conceived to have no other people,[49] he will know no other people quite as he has known Israel, through the *mitzvot*, setting Israel apart as a nation of priests, a light and a blessing to the nations of the world. The blessing, that those who observe the lives of individual Israelites should be moved to say: blessed is the man whose God is that man's God.

In the Temple of Jerusalem, the Rabbis record, sacrifice was offered for the atonement of all nations' sins (*Sukkah* 55b). The Prophets in their way, too, pursue Abraham's idea of God's universality as Creator, Ruler, and universal Judge: all nations worship God, wittingly or unwittingly (Mal. 1:11; cf. Ps. 113:3–4). All will enjoy the universal peace that knowledge of the Lord will bring as it wells up over humanity "as water covers the sea" (Isa. 11:9), a counterpart of the ancient Flood provoked by human lawlessness, when water did not keep its place. None will be excluded from the prosperity and joy, when men beat their swords into ploughshares and spears into pruning hooks, nation ceases to wage war against nation, and they no longer study warfare.[50] The most powerful yearning for freedom and national rebirth renounces all desire for worldly domination: the nations whom hardship or custom has rendered wolfish or lionish in their ethos will lie peacefully with their more pastoral fellow peoples, once the ideas of the Law have in the fullest sense gone forth from Jerusalem. Israel shall be the little child that leads them, not by force or threat of violence but by example. Living by her laws, Israel will demonstrate the strength and wealth of human goodness, and other nations, whether peaceable or turbulent in their histories, will gladly build on her example.[51]

The prophet's is the moral voice of the social critic, visionary of the virtualities of defeat or triumph latent in every human choice, demystifier of God's intent. Boldness, as the rabbis tell us, is a sine qua non of prophecy,[52] and Maimonides argues that prophecy will not be restored to Israel until she has regained autonomy in her land. In exile and subjection, the spiritual and insightful, who have the philosophical and poetic gifts of prophets, lack the confidence to proclaim their visions—or even to see them clearly.[53] When a Moses confronts Pharaoh, or a Nathan, armed with no more than a parable, traps the passionate King David into passing sentence on his own act (2 Sam. 12), or an Elijah (1 Kings 18:18) answers an Ahab: "It is not I who have troubled Israel, but thou and thy father's house, by abandoning the commandments of the Lord"—intellectual courage transmutes alienation into action. Prophecy is not an eremitic wailing but a vivid analysis of the source and remedy of grievance, a historical and political as well as moral vision that refuses to sink into mere chronicling of national shames or royal glories. Here spiritual consciousness rises above mystic ascesis or sacerdotal sycophancy. As Amos says (3:8), voicing the compelling urgency that singles out a prophet: "The lion hath roared, who will not fear? The Lord God hath spoken, who can but prophesy?" The power of moral truth is never lost to the successors and heirs of the Prophets. It grounds the right to free thought and free expression (cf. Job 4:2, 7:11) and retains a broader base in the imperative to truth and the need to impart it. Maimonides describes this inner urgency in the language of emanation (*Guide* II 11, 12), but he reads emanation itself by reference to the highest form of charity, which makes the recipient self-sufficient, modeling God's creative act, like a teacher's imparting of insight. As Plotinus said, a candle is not extinguished when it lights another; when an idea is shared, the gift does not diminish the giver.

Perhaps we catch sight of what is most universal in the Prophets when we see (despite romantic notions of orality) that they were a literate band, not mere isolated eccentrics ranting in the city gates or at the thrones of kings. They taught and wrote, trained up disciples, and preserved the visions and words God had given them, as a heritage to endure beyond its moment. The desire to explain, to write books, to make others capable in thought, was itself an *imitatio Dei*. For God does not withhold but imparts truth, as he imparts being, to make his creatures, as it were, self-sufficient, allowing them to sustain their being, take charge of their lives, and pursue adequacy in their understanding—much as he is Self-sufficient in being, free in action, absolute in understanding, and rather proud of his own book.

The Work of the Rabbis

The Rabbis again recast and reconstruct, but still on the ancient Mosaic floor. The new idiom is studious, dialectical, respectful of sources, deferential to precedents, punctilious with distinctions. Superficially, the Rabbis seem to treat biblical precepts more as oracular springboards of homily and pegs of doctrine than as fixed legal dicta. Yet, beneath the apparent manhandling of language, they are profoundly sensitive to the moral and spiritual thematics as well as the jots and tittles of the text.[54] They save the vital biblical norms in an alien, hostile, even overwhelming milieu, in part by intellectualizing the life of Torah, shifting praxis into realms of symbolic virtuality, or into the realm of conscience.[55] The Temple cult is not practiced but studied; prayer replaces sacrifice as a vehicle of spiritual expression, and repentance replaces sacrifice as a medium of atonement.[56] Civil and criminal laws that once regulated a society now become intellectual delights. Talmudic *ḥaverim*, fellows of the Rabbinic collegiality, adopt the laws of Levitical purity, reenacting the old priestly role and laying claim to a spiritualized and intellectualized successorship to the Priests. As the laws of purity are extended to all Israel, every family table becomes a surrogate of the altar of the lost Temple in Jerusalem.[57]

The first task of the Sages who laid down the case law that grounds the Mishnah was to apply biblical legislation in concrete cases. In this sense these jurists (like American Supreme Court justices) were interpreters, not legislators. None of them was a Moses, or even a Hosea. Yet their concerns were profoundly practical. Safrai remarks of the Tannaim, the bearers of the traditions of practice codified in the Mishnah, that even their aggadah "is not like folklore, and does not contain spirits and fabulous creatures."[58] But as the discussions of Tannaitic decisions eddied and swirled to form the corpus that enlarges the Mishnaic code with the extensive and digressive commentary, the Gemara, much was swept into the discourse, of common sense, allegory, ritual fastidiousness, legend, logic, homily, rhetoric, hyperbole, superstition, wordplay, philosophy, anecdote, science, and lore. The engulfed material was of all degrees of relevance and all levels of sophistication. Narrowness and cosmopolitanism, cynicism and skepticism came together alongside their dialectical bedfellows, optimism, idealism, hope, credulity, and critical analysis.

Looking back on the priestly heritage, the Rabbis could sincerely mourn the loss of the Temple cult, with its clear-cut therapy of atonement "for all your sins," yet strike a melancholy ironic note, allowing for the case that the High Priest in the rites of atonement might well be an illiterate. Not the sons but the disciples of Aaron were the ideal.[59] The Temple cult and its world were gone. But the tragic loss was also an opening into which the Rabbis would build a way of life as far from the ways of the Priests as the Prophets were from the Patriarchs. All the while, the great moral and intellectual themes held steady, and, even as they innovated, the Rabbis could warrant new practice as "a reminiscence of the Sanctuary of Hillel's day."[60]

In the miniature history of Mishnah *Avot*, as Safrai points out, "The first saying, of the Men of the Great Assembly, sets down the requirement that the administration of justice be humanized"—this, he explains, is the meaning of "be cautious (*metunim*) in judgment," as the Rabbis' analysis, and ours, of the bias of biblical law clearly shows—"that a Sage raise many disciples, and that a 'fence' be made around the Tora."[61] The Torah itself mandates safeguarding the law (Deut. 4:2). But it is the Rabbis who achieve this, by reapplying—broadening and narrowing—the Torah's themes, gleaned from the hints of its language. Thus even the "fence," or *seyag*, often thought of as a margin of rigor, is in fact a margin of safety, guarding the humane values of the Law. For, as we have seen, one cannot expand the requirements of any law without fathoming and framing its intentions.

Safrai sees more yet, as he lists the formative maxims of the Rabbinic method: "The next saying states that the world is established on three pillars: Tora study, worship, and the doing of good deeds." The third voices the dictum of Antigonos urging service without view to a reward. "None of these views and conceptions are found in the Bible"—although they thematize its central concerns. All "are innovations of the Sages. Thus the programmatic opening of the tractate *Avot*, which states that it was from Moses and the Prophets that the Tora derives, in content testifies to the measure of creative innovation embodied in the oral Tora of the Sages."[62] As Novak remarks, "The Law itself requires judicial authority to be operative," but the very verse (Deut. 17:11) that ordained strict adherence to juridical rulings "was used by the Rabbis to justify rabbinic innovation, that is, the rabbinic creation of positive law." Just as Abraham had to take his stand, morally speaking, so did the Rabbis: "The covenant seems to call forth not only a human response" but "human initiative," even "the limitation of revelation to make room for this essentially human contribution to the covenant."[63] Indeed, the Rabbis modeled revelation itself not on a tug-of-war but on the more familiar dialectic of instruction, as a matter of cocreation. Thus, catching a hint of paradox in the words that cap the biblical account of Moses' receipt of the Decalogue, "when He finished speaking to him" (Exod. 31:18), they ask, "How could Moses have learned the whole of the Torah, whose measure is called 'greater than the earth' (Job 11:19)? Surely Moses was taught the principles"—and elaborated the rest on that basis.[64]

The very idea of an oral Torah was the vehicle of Rabbinic creativity and of the humanization that was its goal. As Safrai explains:

> Even where many details are given in the Written Tora, Oral Tora may not only explain and further specify, but also introduce substantial innovations. Deut 26:1–11 gives a detailed description of the commandment of first fruits or *bikkurim*, a subject which is further elaborated in the Mishnah tractate *Bikkurim*. In fact, however, there is much new material, such as detailed halakhot stating that *bikkurim* are not to be brought from fields which are under suspicion of having been stolen. . . . It is also stated that proselytes may bring but do not recite [the festive declaration] because of the formulation ". . . which God swore to our fathers to give to us" (Deut. 26:3). But one Tanna teaches: "A proselyte . . . may bring and declare. Why?—'And thou [Abraham] shalt be the father of a multitude of nations' (Gen. 17:5)."
>
> Although the roots of these sayings and halakhot can be pointed out in the Tora and the Prophets, it is evident that they imply a substantial further development. Indeed, in a historical perspective, it appears that Second Temple Judaism, and especially the Pharisees and their predecessors, did humanize the court system, attract a great number of students, make "fences" around the Tora, etc. Rather than just a commentary on the Written Tora, Oral Tora in this perspective represents a new creative development which sprang from deep religious sources. It represents the will to fulfil the commission imposed on man, spelled out in ritual or inter-human commandments in religious and ethical teachings.[65]

The fixity that was a bastion of stability and fairness in the written Law challenged the ingenuity of the jurists. The idea of a parallel oral law gave them the flexibility to create without seeming radically to innovate, and without departing from the framework of the written Torah. Thus the insistence that the oral law (as long as it was evolving) remain oral. This is not nostalgia for a preliterate age; the Mosaic Torah itself mandates that its Law be written. But orality gave room to creativity. As Rabbi Yannai put it:

> Had the Torah been given cut and dry, no one could stand on his feet. Why? "And the Lord said unto Moses . . ."—Said Moses unto Him: Lord of the universe, tell me, just how is the halakha? He said unto him "Turn aside after the majority" (Exodus 23:2); if the majority exonerate, the accused is exonerated, but if they convict, he is convicted. Therefore, the Tora must be studied both according to the forty-nine ways to declare impure and according to the forty-nine ways to declare pure.[66]

The Written Torah itself requires that judges exercise discretion. So they must study each issue and point of law dialectically. The Oral Torah is the stage on which they do so, and when it is written it becomes the record of their deliberations. As Falk remarks, "Study allows the sage not only to identify himself with the Torah, but to become a Master of the Torah, a title which should actually be reserved to God alone."[67]

Attuned to the idioms and institutions of a traditional society, Aristotle understood the position well. Facing Plato's ambivalence between the rule of law and that of men, he found a middle ground in custom and custodianship:

> Even if it be better for certain individuals to govern, they should be made only guardians and ministers of the law. For magistrates there must be [cf. Deut. 16:18]. . . . There may indeed be cases which the law seems unable to determine, but such cases a man could not determine either. Yet the law trains officers for just this purpose and appoints them to determine matters left undecided by it to the best of their judgment. Further, it permits them to make any amendment of the existing laws which experience suggests. So he who bids the law rule may be deemed to bid God and reason alone rule, but he who bids man rule adds an element of the beast; for desire is a wild beast, and passion perverts the minds of rulers, even when they are the best of men. (*Politics* III 16, 1287a 21–31)

Rabbinic creativity is never radical or arbitrary, nor even adversarial, although it is dialectical. The innovation it values does not uproot but brings to fruition the themes of the written Torah. But innovation it is. Thus, reflecting on their own creative role, the Rabbis remark that the laws of release from vows "hover in the air without support"; the detailed legislation of the Sabbath, the Festival Offerings, and sacrilege "are like mountains hanging by a hair, for Scripture here is sparse and the laws many" (Mishnah *Hagigah* 1.8). Juridical practice often established halakhah, and popular usage could void it. Thus the Sages' ban on gentile oil was overturned, since the ruling was not accepted in practice. The fanciful, often tenuous, Midrashic links of Halakhah to Scripture are frequently forged long after the legislative fact;[68] their verbal élan is emblematic of the equally subtle legislative creativity that they underwrite. Such creativity was both self-conscious and normative. Rabbi Joshua, revealingly, asks two disciples what innovation (*ḥiddush*) they have learned in the House of Study; when they demur with traditionalist cant, "We are your disciples and it is of your water that we drink," he admonishes them: "The House of Study cannot exist without innovation." The new idea they go on to report is a gloss of Rabbi Elazar ben Azariah's, which ends: "Just as a plant bears fruit and multiplies, so do the words of the Torah bear fruit and multiply."[69]

Some of what unfolds as a Rabbinic way of life and thought will prove stultifying, narrow, or superstitious. The sifting of sense from nonsense in the Rabbinic corpus is not yet completed. Indeed, it has barely begun. Yet for the critical and watchful, these veins yield gold. Commenting on a particularly astute affirmation by the Sages of divine transcendence, Maimonides remarks, "Would that all their words were like it!" (*Guide* I 59). The miasma of some Rabbinic passages renders all the more brilliant and beaconlike their core thematic insights. Many are pertinent to our theme: Rabbinic bookishness bespeaks an intellectualism that is no unworthy reflex of the spiritual purity and earnestness of the prophetic books and that blossoms as a reverence for the intrinsic value of learning; Torah for its own sake becomes its motto.[70] Study of Torah, of the Rabbinic apprehensions of God's Law, becomes a value tantamount to the entire prescriptive content of the Law itself.[71] Such study is an open-ended quest, but that fact creates no sense of the defeat that prior generations felt at the thought of unending exploration.[72]

The subject active in such study is the individual, abetted by a catena of study partners who link, mind-to-mind, with the lively community of fellow scholars in all lands and ages. The goal is individual understanding. Paradoxically, but perhaps predictably, the maturation of Talmudic study as a way of life led to a hardening and narrowing of independent explorations for those who worked within the set tradition. Yet it called forth, even demanded, the most independent explorations for those who ventured forth from it, in or even near its penumbra, to test its categories, claims and values in the larger world which was their proper sphere.

Practical fulfillment of the Torah is not discarded by the Rabbis, but it undergoes a sea change in their hands. The Tannaim (first century B.C. to second century C.E.) and Amoraim (second century and after) made it their task to concretize the biblical norms, define their boundaries, marshal them into system. Some brittleness in the new complex was perhaps inevitable. But limits were consciously set to the growth of rigorism and the overgrowth of legalism. The biblical commandments and the Rabbinic ordinances that interpreted them (e.g., the daily putting on of phylacteries for prayer, to fulfill the commandment to keep God's imperatives constantly before one's eyes and "bind them for a sign upon thy hand"—Deut. 11:18) were to be performed, as we have seen, not slavishly but "for the sake of heaven" (*Avot* 2.12; cf. 1.3, 2.4)—as intrinsic goods. Since the *mitzvot* were the will of God, their performance made them acts of worship and spiritual expression, quite apart from their proximate or specific functions. Thus each moment was to be infused with awareness of God's presence, imparting holiness to all creaturely acts, an aim not unworthy of the prophetic spirit or out of keeping with the Mosaic goal of making all Israel, as the bold metaphor had put it, a nation of priests. Even when exile and persecution had robbed the Torah of its full robustness as a political, military, economic, and social code, the surviving community, the providential remnant foreseen by the prophets (e.g., Zeph. 3:13), could still infuse communal and personal life with the mission of holiness (cf. *Avot* 2.19) and could keep it alive in practice—in marriage and family law, commercial dealings among Israelites, communal affairs, intellectual and devotional exercises, the dietary laws, Sabbath observances, and the calendar of festivals and fasts.

The ultimate subject, in all these dimensions of what came to be called Jewish life, was again the individual, articulated in the community and given a role and a goal by its norms, but still a freely choosing subject, whose life could be made an act of worship, by the inclination of the will. The perfection of individual life remained the aim. True, the notion that observance was an end in itself fed upon Rabbinic legalism to generate a kind of legal positivism.[73] But the same Rabbinic idea, of the intrinsic value of the *mitzvot* as God's commandments, allowed the moral, spiritual, and intellectual values that underlie the commandments to percolate through them to every aspect of life, throughout each workday, Sabbath, or festival, imparting the intensionalities of holiness to each act or gesture and forging a diction of piety that gave meaning even to what might seem the most trivial of human choices. Again the task of sifting legalism (and the obscurantism, authoritarianism, dogmatism, patriarchalism that were parasitic upon it) from authentic devotion (and its accompanying adventure of the mind and spirit) rested on the individual, the same who was the subject and the victim or beneficiary of the system at large. As Elijah, the Gaon of Wilna, remarked (the tradition in my family is that both of my mother's parents were descendants of his): Torah, like rain, nourishes both beneficial plants and noxious weeds (ad. Prov. 24:31, 25:4). Individual human choices, modulating the tasks of human living, determine whether beautiful or ugly characters emerge from engagement with the Law. For, as Spinoza shows (*Ethics* IV, prop. 4, cor.), the difference between piety or humanity and self-serving pride is wholly a matter of intention.

Both Bible and Talmud are the products of many hands and many centuries. If we include within the literature of Rabbinic discourse the Responsa, Codes, Midrashic elaborations of the legal (halakhic) and narrative (aggadic) phases of the tradition, we can see Rabbinic literature continuing down to the present day. The Torah, by contrast, speaks in so commanding a voice that only commentaries remain possible: imitations reek of parody, and even commentaries typically fall prey to their material, submerged in the authority of the text, gasping free of it in clever or irrelevant homilies, or embedded in it, free only to trace its themes and stories, expatiate on its words, elaborate on its laws, compare readings of its sense, dissociate or reassociate its strands and elements, or otherwise catch hold of its beauties or grow lost in its forests. Some of us today may strive to recast a way of life or thought congruent with the scriptural themes, but few rise to a synthetic grasp of Torah's values and ideas. The Talmud is a help in this regard. For it can open a window on the scriptural world—but only when Scripture itself is not submerged, reduced to the handmaid of Rabbinics.

Talmudic discourse, with its Aramaic jargon and technical shorthand, has its great strength in its dialectical character. Glossing God's "Let us make . . ." in Genesis (1:26), the Rabbis remark that even God commences nothing without consultation.[74] With rare exceptions (like the sustained forensic dialogue of the Book of Job, or the inner psychological dialogue of Ecclesiastes, or the dream dialogue of the Song of Songs) the biblical voice is not dialogic. Prophecy speaks with the authority of God himself. Rarely does it expect an answer. Rabbinically there is constant conversation and cross talk, voices raising and addressing problems about the Torah or one another's proposals and their implications—sometimes in a dialectic that extends across centuries. No corner of experience, science, or lore is irrelevant. That anything more than noise should be heard in this welter of voices is a tribute to the coherence of the Rabbinic problematic and the discipline of the redactors. The exposition is anything but thematic. Yet, to scholars intimate with the written and "oral" canon, a remark in any sector can instantly illuminate any other, with never a fear that the insight will be less than germane. It is dialogue in this community of discourse that hones Rabbinic thought and renders it self-critical, much as moral tact and cosmic wonder give the critical edge to prophetic discourse.

Reading carefully in the Torah, the Rabbis note that it is only after the creation of humanity that the world is described as "*very* good" (Gen. 1:31). Rabbinic humanism is the fairest fruit of the two thousand years of Rabbinic reflection on biblical themes. The full rigor of the legalism and proceduralism they derive from the Torah mitigates the severities and asperities of the Torah itself. Thus the laws of evidence and testimony are forged into a powerful obstacle to capital punishment: not only must two witnesses concur independently and in circumstantial detail before the presumption of innocence gives way in capital cases, but there must also have been explicit and immediate warning to the criminal for an offense to count as capital.[75] Self-incriminating testimony is not admissible. For, it is argued, a person may have a desire to die.[76] Duress is out of the question. Ancient survivals like the "bitter waters" are thickly hedged with restrictions (Numbers 5:12–29), rendering them legally moot and inoperative.[77] Simeon ben Shetaḥ (ca. 80–50 B.C.), a militant judicial activist of the days of Alexander Yannai, avowed,

> May I (never) see consolation[78] if I did not see one man chase another into a ruin; I ran after him, and saw a sword in his hand, the blood dripping, and the slain still twitching. I said: "Villain! Who killed this man? Either you or I, but what am I to do? Your blood is not given into my hands. For the Torah said: 'By testimony of two witnesses . . . shall he who is to die be put to death' (Deut. 17:6)." May He who knows men's thoughts undo the man who slew his comrade. (*Sanhedrin* 37b)[79]

Simeon had few compunctions about capital punishment,[80] but the Law made such punishment rare. In time, a court that issued one death sentence in seven years would be called a bloody Sanhedrin (Mishnah *Makkot* 1.10). Similarly, as Safrai remarks, "The laws of the 'rebellious son' which are laid down in Deut. 21:18–21 are so radically limited by Tannaic halakha, that Tannaic tradition itself drew the conclusion: 'The rebellious son never was and never shall be'" (*Sanhedrin* 71a).[81]

The humanism that fosters strong presumptions in favor of the accused pervades Rabbinic jurisprudence. Breaching any commandment—save those against idolatry, sexual license, and murder—is permitted, indeed required, to save a human life (*Sanhedrin* 74a). The proof-text: "You shall observe My institutions and My ordinances, which a man shall perform and live by. I am the Lord" (Lev. 18:5). The idea of a law of life is taken here in a strong sense, making preservation and enhancement of life cardinal principles of the Law:[82] One may break the Sabbath to save a human life or even to relieve pain.[83] Cattle must be milked on the Sabbath, to prevent "the suffering of living beings." A pregnant woman's cravings permit her to eat on the Day of Atonement—since they might be signals of vital needs. And ravenous hungers must be fed—if need be, even by breaking the dietary laws.[84]

Rabbinic humanism is typified in the Mishnaic agricultural laws: seeking definition of the corners of the field biblically to be left unharvested for the poor, the Rabbis discover that their size, like the measure of good deeds in general, has no upper limit (Mishnah *Peah* 1.1). They specify a minimum but leave the maximum open and praise a community that harvests with a rope (presumably to save labor) and so augments the portion of the poor. They also extend the laws of the corner to a wide variety of crops (*Peah* 1.4). Understanding the nisus of the law, they can act confidently to expand its coverage without concern that they might unwittingly undermine some unfathomable hidden purpose.

Taking it as an axiom that the Torah's laws exist to promote and enhance human lives, the Rabbis lay down rules to regulate wages, hours, commerce, prices, and profits (*Bava Batra* 8b)—their mandate, the spirit of the laws that forbid retaining a day worker's wages overnight or taking a millstone in pledge (Exod. 22:25–26; Deut. 24:6, 10–12). Similarly, they find a mandate in the Torah for free universal education.[85] Even the "natural law" of self preservation is bent to the demands of moral principle. To kill a would-be murderer is to prevent his sin, not merely "self-defense" (Mishnah *Sanhedrin* 8.6–7).[86] Only a presumption of deadly intent, not the protection of property, allows the use of deadly force against a burglar (Exod. 22:1), and one must not commit a murder even to save one's own life. If ordered to murder another or die, one must rather die, the Talmud ordains, resting on the presumption of existential equality we have noted: "Who knows that your blood is redder than his. Perhaps his blood is redder than yours" (*Pesaḥim* 25b, *Sanhedrin* 74a). Even to save a group one may not single out one member for death or defilement—"Better to let all be defiled than to betray a single soul of Israel."[87]

The Rabbis took seriously their task of interpreting the Law at its point of application. They freely used their authority, Sinaitic in their understanding, even to reverse the plain sense of biblical *mitzvot*, if it seemed to counter the Torah's larger thrust. They treated their boldest departures as self-evident, appealing to the canon at large to inform their inferences (*asmakhta*),[88] and proudly pictured Moses as unable to follow their technical debates. Even signs from heaven could not overrule their majority vote. For was it not written that the Torah is no longer in heaven but on earth? The responsibility to interpret it is ours, not God's.[89] Reading the biblical accounts of actions that seemed lawless by their standards, the Rabbis embroidered their own legalism and proceduralism over complete episodes. Their amazing synchronicity ironed flat entire epochs of history but opened the whole body of scripture as a living florilegium of exempla. From the biblical injunction against destroying fruit trees in time of siege (Deut. 20:19–20) they drew the categorical *mitzvah* they saw as the underlying premise: "Thou shalt not wantonly destroy" (*bal tashit*).[90] The method typifies their approach: The laws separating meat from dairy foods and utensils elaborate upon the repeated biblical injunction against seething a kid in its mother's milk;[91] the laws of slaughter (*sheḥittah*) again elaborate on biblical requirements, reaching an optimum, Maimonides argues, in balancing the concerns of humaneness and household economy.[92]

To elaborate a law one must grasp the values it seeks to serve. Otherwise, one could as easily forbid joining the *names* of milk and meat or the purchase of leather from improperly slaughtered animals. With an understanding of the relation of the dietary laws to the ideals of purity and peace, the Mosaic nisus grows clear, and modalities of elaboration can be debated. Hillel could confidently claim that in going to the baths he was fulfilling a *mitzvah*. His argument: if the Romans wash and scour the statues of their emperor set up in the theaters and circuses, and think this a worthy task and an honorable occupation, how much more should we, created in God's image, respect the human body and its form. But behind the midrashic argument stands the clear biblical thematic, here directly cited: "The pious man looks after himself" (Prov. 11:17).

Guiding the entire progress of Rabbinic elaboration is the delicately balanced assumption that perfection of human life is the Law's concern and that no human being lives a fulfilled life in isolation. Our condition is one of interdependence, and the very possibility of human dignity depends on mutual recognition, generosity of thought and action.[93]

If we draw together and sum up the values we encounter in the Mosaic, Prophetic, and Rabbinic norms about the individual and the community, we find economic autonomy as the root and fruit of freedom. Immense value is placed on creative thought and productive work.[94] But the individual is not reducible to social or economic functions. We are valued for what we are, not just for being "useful" or "productive" members of society. These two facts are linked: economic autonomy underwrites spiritual dignity and intellectual independence; these, in turn, are not simply ends in themselves. For the mind and heart belong to the ethical and intellectual subject. And it is the perfection of the human subject that the Law pursues. Supporting the dignity of that subject, we find a strict legalism and proceduralism, in the service not just of social order but of individual rights, conceived in terms of positive human deserts of well-being and of privacy. Personal interest here includes the moral, social, and spiritual dimensions of our identity. Distinctive institutions—laws, myths, and rituals—serve to enhance our moral development and to evoke spiritual discovery. Dialogue, criticism, and comparison strike off the rough edges of tradition, burnishing and polishing the values at the core. Crowning the system are the commitments of Rabbinic humanism. In the values it articulates and in subtly shifting the angle of a judge's seat from that of arbiter to that of arbitrator, this tradition still has much to offer the global culture in which it arises.

The life the Law was given to preserve and perfect is the life of the individual. The Rabbis underscore the value of that life when they write homiletically that to slay a single human being is like destroying the world; and to save a single life, like saving the world. The thought is not just of the progeny who might have descended from one couple, but of human uniqueness: ordinary mortal craftsmen, they argue, form things in a mold, and every casting is alike. But when the Holy One, blessed be he, creates human beings, no two are identical.[95] Each holds an irreplaceable world of possibilities; each is sacred. Shmuel Sambursky, the Israeli physicist and historian of cosmology, used to compare this Rabbinic teaching with the vexations of Greek philosophers over the idea of uniqueness: from Plato, who placed value, truth, being, and even unity at the plane of the universal, to Aristotle, who argued that there is no science of the individual and that what individuates particulars is accidental to their true being, down to the late Neoplatonists, who struggled with the notion of a universal yet personal "guardian spirit," and Averroës, who held that you and I are the same individual but for the matter that divides us, all of the thinkers who followed the gnomic counsel of Heraclitus, "Look to the common," were bemused by individuality and tended to equate uniqueness with idiosyncrasy and hence irrationality.

Following their biblically mediated intuitions, the Rabbis find uniqueness precious: each human being, like God, is unique. Each is like a species, exploring and pressing the boundaries of its nature, seeking to transcend its world of possibilities. The value of community is attendant on this prior value. Aristotle showed the value of the community by arguing that man by nature is a social animal. It is because of our social nature that our virtues and vices are culturally mediated and socially defined—affability, niggardliness, magnificence, magnanimity. The Torah, founding not only a system of law but a way of life, addresses the same fact, our social nature, in its own language, mythic where Aristotle is speculative, historic and particular where Aristotle is scientific and universal, intimate and normative where Aristotle is clinical and descriptive. It records (Gen. 2:18): "And the Lord God said, 'It is not good for the man to be alone.'"

5

Ethical Monism and Ethical Pluralism

Monotheism demands an integration of our ethical values and is itself sustained by that integration. But does it make us ethical monists, reducing all goods to a single aim? Or does it tolerate a plurality of aims in each of us and a diversity of styles in us all? Does it set up a competition between all our activities and some single highest good? Or does it foster an integration, in which activities retain their intrinsic value? In this chapter I want to consider two models of ethical integration—the pluralism of Saadiah and the ethical monism of Maimonides—and to argue that the apparent disparity between the two is overdrawn and the idea that they cannot be reconciled is illusory: the integration called for by monotheism does not immolate but preserves and presupposes the intrinsic worth of the activities that the good life integrates.

Saadiah's Ethical Pluralism

Maimonides avoided criticizing his great predecessor, Saadiah Gaon, by name. Systematic philosophy in Judaism owed its birth to Saadiah, and the Rambam was grateful for Saadiah's preserving the voluntarism of the Torah and injecting no fatalism into his reading of Scripture.[1] So he avoided mentioning Saadiah by name in the *Guide to the Perplexed*, for many of the key concepts of his philosophy are conscious rejections of positions Saadiah had defended. Maimonides rejects, for example, Saadiah's reliance on the notion of the *kavod nivra*, or "created glory," a supernatural manifestation of God. He prefers to treat all revelatory experience as an objective event within the mind, expressive of its natural affinity with God: Moses, who apprehended God directly, needed no medium but the "pellucid lens" of his own intelligence.[2] Maimonides emphatically rejects Saadiah's view that all creation was for man's sake.[3] He rejects Saadiah's claim that sufferings outweigh joys in this life, and thus rejects his notion of the moral necessity of recompense. For he recognizes this line of thinking as an outgrowth of the Epicurean reasoning of Muḥammad ibn Zakariyā' al-Rāzī. But, even as he uncovers the hedonistic underpinnings of the Epicurean dilemma, Maimonides builds on Saadiah's own rejection of hedonism and acknowledgment of the intrinsic worth of this life.[4] He rejects as unbiblical and untrue (*Guide* III 24) Saadiah's Rabbinic notion of "sufferings of love" (Berakhot 5a), unmerited tribulations imposed for the sake of future recompense (*ED* V 3). He criticizes Saadiah's argument for God's unity from the sufficiency of one God to explain the world,[5] calling it a *kalām* argument and implying that it lacks rigor. At times he ascribes ideas found in Saadiah obliquely to "certain of the *Mutakallimūn*,"[6] denying him the title of philosopher when he finds him on shaky ground conceptually.

How, then, will Maimonides respond to Saadiah's pluralism? For Saadiah rejects ethical monism. He writes:

> I find some people reckon, indeed they are certain, that it is man's duty to order his whole life by a single trait of character, preferring the love of one thing above all other objects of desire, and hating one thing above all else. Having looked into this view, I find it utterly mistaken, in several ways. To begin with, if the love of a single thing and preference of it to all others were what is best for us, the Creator would not have implanted in human nature the love of any other. Why He could have made us of a single element, or all of one piece. . . . Don't you see that even the most elementary actions cannot succeed with just one element? How then can the entire complex? For if a builder built a house of stones, or teak, or thatch, or nails alone, it would not do at all—as it would if he built it of all of these in combination. The same is true in cooking and food, in drink and dress, service, and all our other needs. Doesn't it open one's eyes to see that none of these specialized activities works with just one means, although all of them serve our comfort? How much less can the needs of our soul and character be met by a single object![7]

Saadiah's vivid analogy reveals the naturalism behind his pluralism. Like Aristotle, he sees life as a complex of activities. If the bodily functions, arts, and amenities all depend on complex acts, how much more does the concatenated whole of life itself? Or should we assume, Saadiah asks, Socratically, that the needs of the soul are simpler than those of the body?

I want to show in this section how Saadiah derives his ethical pluralism from his reading of the Torah and the human condition. The next section will show how Maimonides responds, integrating the distinct values of Saadiah's pluralism and subordinating them, "to a single goal." Then, in the final section of this chapter, I hope to show that the contrast between Maimonides' monism and Saadiah's pluralism should not be drawn too sharply. For the monotheistic philosophy that both Saadiah and Maimonides seek to articulate harmonizes their seemingly opposed approaches. The synthesis is of more than historical interest. For it can help dispel the notion that monotheism demands but one act of us. The integration of interests called for by the idea of a single Source and Focus of all values does not force a choice between scattershot pursuit of everything that attracts us and fixed focus on a single cosmic dot. The inclusive, rather than exclusive, understanding of the summum bonum will also reveal the complementarity of the contemplative and active ideals.

Saadiah was a rationalist in that he believed experience to be intelligible, but by temperament, method, and theory, he was also an empiricist. He took his knowledge from experience and his theology from inductive surveys of the biblical canon. His value theory rests on a dispassionate survey of the sources of human motivation exampled in Scripture and in life. He finds thirteen: (1) the ascetic impulse, (2) the appetites for food and drink, (3) the sexual drive, (4) passionate love, which is quite another thing, (5) the desire for wealth, (6) for progeny, (7) for development, agricultural or urban, (8) for longevity, (9) for power, (10) for vengeance, (11) for knowledge, (12) for piety and devotion, and (13) for rest. Any one of these alone, he argues, becomes a monomania and makes life one-sided and wanting.[8] Yet our proper aim, he urges, cannot lie outside this list. For these ends, or further specifications or generalizations of them, exhaust the repertoire of human motives. The good life must combine all these aims (*ED* X 1–3). But it does not give all equal weight (*ED* X 17); the Law prescribes the proper doses, quantitatively and qualitatively. But the key to the good life is mixture. For plurality is the hallmark of the human condition and of creation at large, the counterpart of God's unity (*ED* X Exordium). Those who try to reduce all goods to one only spoil the mix. The vanity denounced in Ecclesiastes is any attempt to render a single human goal the be-all and end-all of existence. Only the right balance of all human values escapes Solomon's condemnation of every isolated good![9]

Saadiah pursues his pluralistic theme when he responds to the Neoplatonic ideal of the beauty of simplicity by urging that it is a variety of colors that is cheering, a blend of tones that is harmonious.[10] Pure tones, he explains, are irritating, even physiologically, and (as Aristotle held) destructive if too intense; properly blended combinations can promote not just good cheer but (as Plato's *Republic* suggests) even justice. Linking the physiological data as he understands them with the theory of rhythms and musical modes, Saadiah presses on from sights to sounds and even scents. His earthy aesthetic reveals the motive of his seemingly odd appeal to our differentness from God's unity: our task is not to emulate that unity, for we are not simple but complex; our felicity is not a matter of resolving all to one. That is death and the silence of the grave. Rather, our senses find delight in complexity, and our souls find their perfection not in simplicity but in a kind of harmony, inwardly and with the world.

Saadiah considers his several goods in detail, criticizing each as inadequate to our well-being. His methodical enumeration takes the place of any systematic attempt at integration and parallels the rather linear exposition of his elder contemporary al-Rāzī,[11] but Saadiah's lively personality is visible in the contrast. Al-Rāzī, a physician, catalogues and anatomizes vices as pathologies of character; Saadiah discusses positive goods, the aims and ends of life, beginning with asceticism, perhaps because of the sweeping claims it made in his time.

He defines asceticism as rejection of all worldly values, negating all the other items on his list, with the possible exception of worship. But even worship, in the end, will probably be neglected by the pure ascetic, with his melancholy disposition. The rationale for an ascetic life, Saadiah notes, is the evanescence of all earthly goods, the vanity of human wishes. An asocial, unproductive, unexpectant life seems to promise the surest protection against grief, loss, anxiety, and the frustration of our hopes.[12] Saadiah does not query this reasoning, aware that it expresses a psychological rather than a logical dialectic, a hope of avoiding failure in the world's terms by abstaining from its contests. He ascribes the ideal of "total" abstention to a belief that even the sincerest efforts at wise living are doomed by man's innate nature: "Even if a person strives hard to gain wisdom in this life, he is overcome by folly. If he seeks purity, his own impurity overpowers him, if he seeks health, his constitution makes him ill, and if he tries to talk sense, his own tongue trips him up. As Job says (9:20), 'If I seek to justify myself my own mouth condemns me; even if I were perfectly innocent it would oppose me.'"[13]

Efros detects a Sufi flavor here, redolent of the literature of *Zuhd*, Islamic pietist asceticism; but Saadiah's ascetic also sounds rather Christian, perhaps monastic, his tragic view of life rooted in the idea of original sin: forces emergent from the depths of our own being suffice to bring us down, even before we contend with life and one another. Saadiah does not disdain the animadversion of depth psychology that he finds in Job's reflections on self-betrayal and slips of the tongue, but he does deny that to shun worldly success brings a success of its own. Abstinence is a good,[14] as is clear when we call it knowing our own limits. But a life of total abstention, single-mindedly pursued to an anchorite extreme fails by its one-sidedness. As Epicurus says, "There is a limit even to simplicity of living, and he who fails to heed it is as mistaken as the man who gives way to extravagance" (*Vatican Fragments* 63). The unworldly, Saadiah argues, are not even perfect ascetics. For they do prize their unworldliness. Yet anyone who singles out one good from all the rest is missing as much as they and is, in his own way, an ascetic as well: "Were I to collect all that I shall cite that is neglected by the devotees of each of these thirteen classes of activity, I would call the collection *The Book of Total Abstinence*."[15]

Pure asceticism, Saadiah argues, is a life-denying impulse. Given its head, it would halt all human life, undermine and ultimately destroy civilization. Symptoms that we today would associate with paranoia and depression result from the isolation and alienation of the anchorite, his inadequate diet and insufficient use of such amenities of civilization as fresh water. So the rejection of worldly goods cannot be accepted as a basis of the good life.[16]

Neither can food and drink, although they are necessary and, in an undeniable sense, good. For if these were our sole concerns, there would be nothing to rule out excess. To this extent at least, ascetics must be heeded. Not only can food be harmful, proving that it is not an unqualified good, but making the appetites ends in themselves only augments them, causing inevitable frustration to those who measure their happiness by appetitive gratification. For (as Plato explained) those who would live for pleasure seem to try to carry water in a sieve.[17] Reliance on appetite as a guide to life yields not just illness and frustration but moral vices. So the argument does not rest on prudential claims alone but appeals to shared ideas of human perfection: the gourmand defeats his own intentions but also palpably removes himself from the human fulfillment that, by hypothesis, he promised himself.

Few serious philosophers have advocated excess for its own sake. But the belief that the goods of appetite are the sole goods is an Epicurean axiom. Epicurus did believe that moderation optimizes pleasure, yet he wrote, "The body calls out to be freed from hunger, thirst, and cold. Secure from these and expecting to remain so one might vie with Zeus in happiness."[18] The reduction of happiness to physical comfort gives a target to Saadiah's charge. Epicurus knew that pleasures can be injurious but denied that this was any detriment to hedonism: "No pleasure in itself is bad, but the means by which some pleasures are produced bring with them troubles many times greater than the pleasure."[19] The remedy proposed is a sense of measure or proportion. But this sense is not itself a part of pleasure. So Saadiah's criticism stands: pleasures do not measure themselves, so no single pleasure or set of pleasures will constitute the good life.

Saadiah's distinction between coitus (*al-jimāʿ*) and love (*al-ʿishq*) has puzzled some readers. Wondering what distinguishes the latter from the former, Rosenblatt wrote, "Saadya seems to have in mind pederasty,"[20] since Saadiah calls the subject unpleasant to discuss ("repulsive to mention," in Rosenblatt's rendering). But *'ishq* is simply the love of the romantic canon. Saadiah found the topic unpleasant because he found the love conventions in vogue in his time highly artificial and distasteful.[21] The lexical distinction between love and sex was fixed by the empirical work of al-Aṣma'ī (d. 828), a pioneering Basra philologist who traveled among the Bedouins in quest of unspoiled Arabic usage. He asked a Bedouin woman what she understood by making love (*'ishq*). Her reply: billing and cooing, embracing and whispered endearments. "How do you understand it in the city?" Al-Aṣma'ī gave a more graphic description of lovemaking, at which the woman laughed: "Oh, that's not love; that's how to make a baby!"[22]

When Saadiah speaks of coitus he means just that.[23] That is not what he finds unpleasant to discuss. But *'ishq* is romance, and Saadiah's account of it echoes the quasi-medical descriptions that were literary conventions in his day: the palpitations of lovers' hearts, their mingled glances and mingled souls, the play of the zodiac with their destinies. The poetic conceits on such themes were hoary in Plato's time and were not, of course, confined to heterosexual relations. But homosexuality gains prominence in the canon of passion from a certain antinomian éclat, reflecting religious and social disapproval, and from the popular notion that the homoerotic is more purely erotic than heterosexual relations, where passion may be tempered by such mundane concerns as raising a family and sustaining a home. The argument persists even today among advocates of eros as a cardinal good that only bisexuality fully realizes human "sexual potential." Maimonides seems to have such thinking in mind when he argues not that the Torah restricts eros so as to curb deviant behaviors but that it regulates sexual activity to discourage the maxim that erotic gratification is an end sufficient in itself.[24]

The advocates of coitus, Saadiah writes, "maintain that it should be preferred to all other objects of desire in this world," because of its intense and unique pleasure and because it is "the means by which man, rational and sapient, comes to be." Besides, they argue, coitus allays melancholy and is the keystone of our sociability.[25] Saadiah does not dispute these claims; his openness is part of his dialectical method. But (much in the manner of the Pyrrhonists) he counterposes prima facie ills against prima facie benefits: sex hastens aging, is bad for the eyes, physically debilitating, exhausting, and defiling. Again the case does not rest solely on prudential grounds. Making one appetite our standard of value and canon of judgment inevitably results in lack of measure and so in excess and loss of control. Illegitimacy and the company of debauched and vicious persons are among the negatives. So palpable evils result from making coitus the summum bonum.[26]

Saadiah does not gainsay the *kalām*-like appeal he puts in the mouth of the exponent of sex: "If it were something reprehensible, God would have checked the impulse in His prophets and messengers, peace be upon them. But do you not see that one of them (Jacob) said, 'Give me my woman!' (Genesis 29:21); and another, without blushing, 'I went in to the prophetess' (Isaiah 8:3)."[27] There is no quarrel here with sexual gratification. The question is about its place. But if coitus is the sole or ultimate good, that question has no answer.

Eros similarly fails as the measure of life, since it too involves reason's loss of control and thus a loss of due order and balance (*ED* X 17–19). Saadiah is aware of the metaphysical claims made for eros; he knows even the myth of the divided self that Plato fathers on Aristophanes, and its quasi-Platonic rationale, in which various notions from the *Symposium* are fused to make love the cynosure of art, poetry, and thought.[28] But he has little use for the resulting claim that the erotic impulse is the root of all creative endeavor and the motive force of the universe, a view found in the oldest Greek cosmogonies, given classic form in the *Symposium*, and still current in Freudian theories of the sublimation of libido. Erotic mystics may treat human passion as a propaedeutic to its mystic counterpart.[29] But Saadiah finds such claims worthless and unseemly—as if God would promote lewd behavior and idle passion as avenues of religious discovery.[30] Saadiah does not dispute the traditional ascription of passion to the heart and eyes (although he does refute appeals to "destiny" and astral influences, arguing that if passions are fated by the stars there could be no unrequited love).[31] Rather, he invokes the biblical admonition to give our hearts to God (Deut. 6:5; Prov. 23:26) and not follow our own untutored hearts and eyes, "after which you go awhoring" (Num. 15:39). Here Saadiah is a *mutakallim*. But he is not without more cogent proofs.

Lucretius, in his diatribe against romantic love, pictures a would-be lover pining at the gates of his chosen object, almost like a modern-day stalker (*De Rerum Natura* IV 1183–87). Saadiah finds a parallel image in Jeremiah (3:2) and drives home a parallel point: "'Look up to the bare heights, and see: Where have they not lain with you? You waited for them at the roadside like a brigand'—turning day into night and rising at dawn—the secrecy, the deaths that are died each time one's shame is revealed."[32] The objection may seem circular. For a romantic might claim that it is not yet agreed that passion (for its own sake) is unseemly. But Saadiah's citation is seconded by his keen psychological sense. With passion, as with the other prima facie goods, there are prima facie ills to set off against the aims pursued: the trouble and the risks of a life of seductions, the possibility (about which Epicureans were always emphatic)[33] of disappointment once the goal is attained, the intellectual dishonesty that finds its paradigm in Richard Strauss's pretense that what Don Juan was really seeking was the perfect woman (all the real women were mere husks to be discarded in that quest). Disappointment seems inevitable when the intensity of passion is proportioned to the risks and difficulty of the quest. For these end when the stylized parody of courtship is over. And, as Saadiah remarks, the revulsion that follows disappointment is heightened by the intensity of the previous passion—whose real object, then, was not the beloved but the passion itself.

Even in turning the full force of his psychology of passion toward a critique of pure passion, Saadiah does not succumb to the temptation of calling passion evil. If romantic love is a prima facie good, then it is a good. Saadiah makes the same assumption as Plato regarding goods in general: all belong to a greater whole, a single common good. But where Plato links them all in a single hierarchy of value, under a single unifying Idea, Saadiah simply proposes their terrestrial combination. He does not reject any goods worthy of the name; he knows that the Torah values conjugal love as it values conjugal sexuality, and that Rabbinically this love is not a necessary evil but a divine commandment:[34] "As Scripture says, 'A lovely gazelle, a graceful doe, let her breasts sate thee at all times, and be thou ever ravished with her love' (Proverbs 5:19)."[35]

But to make eros the arbiter of life would make adultery an intrinsic good; seduction and seductiveness, ultimates. Here Saadiah senses a nihilism that makes him contemptuous of the claim that passion is the discipline of mystic love, a rationale that he dismisses as a mere seducer's line.[36] Passion has its place, between husband and wife, not only as a spur to life and the peopling of the world but also as a bond of fellowship between two human beings.[37] But clearly, and in keeping with the paradigm of Genesis and the Prophets, a second such attachment would violate the first and, as the series lengthens, vitiate all trust and intimacy.

The apologetic Saadiah finds for advocates of wealth is riddled with inconsistency. For every argument for the ultimacy of wealth pins its worth to that of some further goal—food, drink, sex, power. Yet the effort to secure wealth does show its value. Even scholarship needs patronage, represented by the scholars' place of meeting in the homes of the well-to-do. Saadiah grants that wealth is a blessing, to be used responsibly—worthwhile, so long as it is readily acquired. Extraordinary measures to secure it involve not just excessive trouble and risk but potential vices, showing that wealth is not an unqualified good. Saadiah does not explore the nexus between money and freedom: a liquid medium of exchange does aid individual freedom; so does access to a store of wealth. Money, then, has some use beyond its barter value. (Indeed, there are few human devices as effective in ensuring that one human being regards another's interest as his own.) Yet Saadiah's criticism retains its sting. The free choice of the consumer and the possessions that the wealth seeker hopes will enhance his life bring no guarantee of fulfillment and are marred by the fear of loss and the risk of compulsive acquisitiveness (*ED* X 8). So wealth alone cannot be the good for man.

Examining the idea that begetting children is the aim of life (a view akin to the sociobiologists' notion that the phenotype exists to replicate its genotype maximally), Saadiah is again evenhanded. There are dialectical arguments for and against the value of progeny, and Scripture can be quoted both pro and con. Saadiah does not take any of the arguments terribly seriously in themselves. Like the Skeptics, who sought epistemic liberty in the equipoise of arguments of various strengths (from cogent to dubious), he is content to show, by the very existence of countervailing arguments, that a given end is not an absolute and so not the summum bonum—since other aims are also sought. He does not overtly take the step Maimonides will take, of concluding with Plato that only the absolute can be the perfect guide of life.[38] He does value all prima facie goods instrumentally. But, unlike Maimonides, he does not set up a systematic hierarchy of means and ends. His openness and insistence that all values be taken seriously predisposes the ground for a pluralistic outcome and stymies the sort of absolute claims that are typically made both for and against reproduction as the aim of life.

If procreation cannot be a perfect and unqualified good, neither can it be an unqualified evil, despite the pains of parturition and the risks of sustaining one's offspring, fancifully hinted when the Book of Job (39:9) speaks of the falcon's chicks gorging on blood—as if it were her own. The very objections that extremists make to one another's views suffice to show that their positions must be qualified, and thus that procreation must be weighed alongside other values—qualitative alongside quantitative concerns. So procreation alone cannot be made the object of human life (*ED* X 9).

Development as a prima facie good is subject to the same sort of critique: if it were *the* good, questions about its value would be unintelligible. But there are utilitarian (prudential) and formal objections (since the desire for development, uncontrolled, undermines its own objectives), as well as intuitionistic objections (*ED* X 10). Environmental concerns were not unknown in Saadiah's age. The Ikhwān al-Ṣafā wrote a book-length fable seeking to define the proper relationship of humans and the other living creatures. A recurrent theme of this fictional gem is the concern that human settlements have spread beyond a single habitat and infringed on the domain of other living beings.[39] Saadiah's sensitivity to environmental issues reflects his openness to all recognizable value claims. The benefits he finds in construction and cultivation are subordinate to the larger aim of maintaining human life or confined to the subjective satisfaction of the builder and developer. Sensitivity to psychological dynamics leads Saadiah to note that such satisfactions have a counterpart in a great builder's sense of having failed to realize his design, and in the anxiety developers may feel over the completion and even appropriateness of their plans.

Saadiah knows that obsessiveness and perfectionism may blind the developer, spoiling his scheme or marring its execution. But he also knows the scruples developers may feel about the outcome of their work. And he does not leave the matter of appropriateness solely to the conscience of the developer: "If the development is agrarian, and the crop is not as a man proposes but rather as God disposes, there is constant anxiety about it. And if one uproots this growth and replaces it, the anxiety is redoubled." Perhaps there are certain crops that do not belong—that God does not intend, as Saadiah puts it theologically, emphasizing that the issue is objective rather than merely subjective. That is a judgment which a sheer commitment to development cannot guide, demonstrating that development is not the summum bonum, regardless of the place that governing powers may assign it.

Survival as the goal of life, like power for its own sake, is a rather nihilistic value. For it makes claims to which virtually any other value can be sacrificed but leaves little beyond a hollow shell of itself, if achieved apart from other goods. Saadiah offers a telling critique of sheer survival, as Maimonides does of its cousin, valetudinarianism:[40] "For once one reaches old age, all yearning falls away, and one comes to live only by compulsion, as Scripture says, 'Before the evil days come in which you say "I have no pleasure in them" (Ecclesiastes 12:1).'"[41] Granted, longevity allows us to achieve our goals not only materially but spiritually. (Thus Maimonides argues that medicine crucially aids us in securing the years that make possible fulfillment of life's aim.)[42] But, viewed as an end in itself, longevity lacks even this appeal, and against it must be pled the multiplication of life's cares—a weighty charge indeed, in view of Saadiah's belief that in this life troubles inevitably overbalance blessings. Just as the sexual urge is imparted to us to secure the survival of the race, a love of life is implanted in our nature to promote survival in the face of emotional defeat, not as a guide to the purpose of existence—as though mere existence could be its own justification or could provide its own argument or meaning. Again Saadiah plays off qualitative against quantitative values. But mere survival, abstracted from the qualitative aspects of experience, can make virtually no claim even to prima facie value—as offspring or development can.

Power naturally claims preeminence, since it can relegate all other values, indeed all things, to their proper places. But, like the other prima facie goods, its value, even in its encomia, is largely instrumental—in the service of joy, pleasure, wealth, the sense of authority and dominance. Saadiah might go further. For values like power, wealth, or prestige are readily plaited into a self-perpetuating circle of futilities ("vanities," in Kohelet's sense). Once made the object of an individual's or a group's existence, they can be pursued in endless but eternally nugatory cycles, since no member of the complex has intrinsic worth. It was with such thoughts in mind that Socrates (*Republic* 344–45) declared the unexamined life not worth living: it pursues values whose intrinsic worth has not been tested. The same reflections led Plato in search of ultimate values, which might validate the worth of instrumental goods and serve as standards to moderate and regulate their roles. And it was in recognition of the futility of a closed circle of subordinate aims that Aristotle sought a highest good, subordinate to none (*Nicomachaean Ethics* I 1). But Saadiah does not pursue this line of reasoning beyond the recognition that wisdom and the Torah will find the proper balance among the competing values (*ED* X 3–4).

Power is needed in establishing civil institutions and maintaining public security. But, taken alone, it is a source of arrogance, capriciousness, and foolhardiness, and a gateway to envy and rivalry. It is thus both dangerous and, intrinsically, at least as bad as it is good. So, in isolation, it fails both intuitionistically and prudentially.

Vengeance is a good in the satisfaction it may bring, but also civilly in a rather elemental way, as a primal motivation for establishing systems of justice, Saadiah concedes. But its drawbacks are well known. The thirst for vengeance is a melancholy, ruthless passion, inherently excessive, incapable by itself of discipline or control and thus inevitably destructive to those given over to it. Indeed, the peace of mind they promise themselves is an illusion, fostered by memories or anticipations of the joy of victory but belied by the restlessness of wasted days, scheming and hardening of the heart against conciliation. For vengeance is the enemy of peace, its contemplation destroys peace of mind, and its requital is certain—if not at mens' hands then at God's (*ED* X 13). But even as he views the thirst for vengeance as negatively as he can ethically, Saadiah ascribes it functionally to God—and in his cosmology, the retributive principle is the basis of creation (*ED* V–IX): no prima facie good is wholly evil.

Knowledge was the philosophical summum bonum par excellence. Aristotle made contemplation not only the highest human action but also the divine activity, on the grounds of its self-sufficiency, the perfect liberty of the mind, in which actor, action, and object unite in a single identity. The painters of the cosmic mural that we call the medieval Weltanschauung typically assumed that man achieves the pinnacle of his perfectibility when he stands in rapt contemplation of the One. In that consummate moment of mutual recognition between man and God medieval philosophers of all traditions found the purpose of creation, the summation of all that was good in it, the explanation of all that seemed insupportable, and the object for which all the energies of the cosmos had been set in motion. Yet, for Saadiah, other values are at stake even on a cosmic scale. Justice is one, setting the framework in which God's legislation itself will operate, as the heritage of Abraham would lead one to expect. Knowledge is a vital aim, but not sufficient to the good life.

Saadiah does not deny the pleasures or the benefits of the pursuit of wisdom—the satisfaction of curiosity about the world, "and to a great extent about the heavens." He grants the intrinsic value of intellectual inquiry as the distinctive grace of our species. But our existence depends on food, clothing, and shelter as well. These are not mere obstacles[43] or adjuncts to the pursuit of wisdom. They are necessities of life in the world. And that, Saadiah urges, is a value of its own.[44] Subordination of all activity to the search for understanding is rejected.

Aristotle's elitist claim that happiness demands exploiting others to perform one's menial tasks and secure one's mundane needs is singled out for particular castigation from the more democratic perspective of the Torah.[45] One who exploits others in this way (as Aristotle assumes one should with women and "natural slaves"—all who are not intellectually inclined) would simply be rejected by his fellows, Saadiah argues, and the value that might be gained from his advice (should he seek to put his understanding to practical use as Plato urges) would be lost. For, in the words Saadiah aptly quotes from Ecclesiastes (9:16), "The wisdom of the wretch is despised, and his words are not heard."[46]

The asceticism attendant on the pure pursuit of knowledge is, of course, a value distinct from understanding itself, and a negative one if countenanced to the unmeasured extent that unchecked thirst for knowledge seems to demand. A coarse, dull diet, Saadiah argues, will produce a coarse, dull nature, and even the quest for knowledge itself will be impaired, undone, like appetite, by its own excess. One is reminded of al-Rāzī's complaints against excessive hunger for understanding and his bitter boast that he had worn out his eyes with writing in a script as fine as an amulet maker's.[47] Exclusive concern with learning, Saadiah warns, only leads to neglect of the practical side of life, or the practical side of the Law, the supposed concern of the addicts of learning: there is an excess, then, even of the love of wisdom.

Even worship, which might seem to the religious sensibility the proper cynosure of human activity, is not deemed adequate by Saadiah. The angels, it is true, are said to praise God tirelessly, and their praises are thought joyous and pleasurable. In the Hereafter, as the Rabbis teach, time will be preserved only to set the rhythms of prayer. And, of course, God can never be sufficiently, let alone excessively, exalted. But humans have other needs—the sustenance of life, the begetting and rearing of children are precious in themselves (albeit not in isolation from all other goods) and are necessary even to the adequate consummation of human worship, which includes an obligation to raise up children. How else could that devotion be continued? Verbally Saadiah concurs with the pietist claim that perfect worship demands absolute reliance upon God. But he reminds would-be quietists that God himself gave us the means of securing our needs, through our own powers.[48]

In the abstract, worship might seem our sole concern, but what we abstract from, then, is the human condition. This is Saadiah's central thrust: that no one human good can succeed, even in its own terms, apart from the rest.[49] Saadiah's empiricism undergirds his worldliness, his demand that ethics treat of the human condition as we find it, relating to the values of human life as we know it—food, clothing, sex, love, development, retribution, even money—as well as higher values like wisdom and worship. There is no merit in an otherworldliness that seeks transcendence elsewhere, focusing our attention on some far-off state of pure contemplation or wrapt engrossment in the One, forgetting all else. This worldliness of Saadiah's is biblical: the Law is not far off, but here; its aim, to sanctify this life. But the outcome of Saadiah's openness to the world of experience and all the prima facie values it presents is a systematic pluralism in which no single good can be elevated to the exclusion of all the rest.

The final such good Saadiah considers is rest. Here again there was a heritage, both biblical and Aristotelian, to contend with. The Mosaic Sabbath is a divinely ordered moment in the cosmic plan, and the Sabbath grace after meals (following Mishnah *Tamid* ad fin) pictures the life eternal (*ḥayyei ʿolamim*) as a perfect Sabbath of rest. As for Aristotle, he regards leisure as the perquisite of the gentleman and prerequisite of the liberal life of contemplation and reasoned action, and conceives of God as an unmoved cause of motion.

Saadiah concedes that rest recreates both body and soul, but reminds any exponents of leisure as the goal of life that leisure exists only through labor and loses its value if it is not a counterpoise of work. Sloth destroys the benefits of other goods, especially those associated with the performance of our obligations. It can even render its victim incapable of seeing to his own bodily needs (so Saadiah interprets Prov. 21:25) and lead him to contribute to his own destruction—not (per hypothesi) from a self-destructive impulse but from the mistaken notion that leisure is the sole good. Obesity, tumescence, and circulatory ills are only a few of the clinical disorders that can arise from single-minded indolence.

Exclusive devotion to any one of the prima facie goods, Saadiah concludes, has been shown to be mistaken, since it necessarily neglects all the rest. The argument is plainly dialectical. Assuming the (relative) soundness of all the claims made for various prima facie goods leads inevitably to the refutation of any absolute claim in behalf of any one of them. The argument, to the extent that Saadiah provides one, is almost circular, since the initial concession, that all the prima facie claims have some (relative) merit, is very close to Saadiah's intended pluralistic conclusion. But the flaw is not as damaging as might be supposed to Saadiah's intent. Like Socrates, he is confident that he can win credence for at least some of his claims for and against each value he considers. The appeal is to experience, and Saadiah does not feel the need to argue categorically, as though his reader were an adversary who would seek systematically to undermine each claim he makes even at the expense of belying experience, relying on values that will subsequently be rejected, at least verbally, and ignoring one's own ethical intuitions. Besides, Saadiah's aim is normative and at least partly hortatory, not theoretical. His object is not a formal refutation of the supposed advocates of thirteen monomanias but the discouragement of any tendency to make too much of one prima facie good at the expense of others. The crucial point is that none of the isolated goods is sufficient of itself to the good life. None simply *is* happiness. Each requires the others, and none is reducible to another, although each is at least in part only instrumental.

A suitable mix of these goods is what is best, not mechanically or equally combined but in accordance with the dictates of "wisdom and the Law." The proper blend,

Saadiah urges, will be like a harmoniously compounded body, like a medicine, in fact, whose virtue is in the balance of its many ingredients. For often it is best in ethics, as in chemistry or engineering, for one tendency to check the action of another.[50] Aesthetically, harmony is achieved by a blending of scents, flavors, colors, tones, and rhythms, which call forth a natural response from body and soul that unmingled stimuli are powerless to produce (*ED* X 18). The best human life is similarly a blend of action and contemplation, sustenance, prosperity, worship, rest, sex, love, food, drink—even power or vengeance, when these are properly checked and modulated by other values that will impart to them a character in keeping with justice and the dictates of the Law (*ED* X 19). The same is true for other goods—repute, remembrance of the dead, righteous indignation, foresight—whatever commends itself to the intelligent person of pure intentions. The same is true for virtues as for goods: our proper concern is with balance, the roundedness of life, which must never be sacrificed to some narrow aim or crotchet.

Saadiah assigns rough priorities to his prima facie goods, following what he takes to be the Torah's preferences and the demands of life. But his rankings are rhetorical, not technical, and do not outline a clear hierarchy. He says, for example, that appetite should be heeded to the extent necessary for survival and the rearing of posterity; that desire may be gratified whenever its demands do not breach the bonds of the permissible. Wealth, procreation, and development may be pursued expansively, to the extent that God allows, provided one does not succumb to greed, rapacity, or lawlessness. The ascetic impulse should check these tendencies, but Saadiah does not tell us how or to what extent. Indeed he cannot, for his pluralism gives authority to no prima facie good over any other. We are to view this world as a vestibule to the next and to seek its goods not for their own sake but for the Hereafter. Yet repeatedly we hear that study and worship come after our material needs have been met,[51] in keeping with the Rabbinic reading of *derekh eretz* as a worldly occupation, without which learning is impossible (*Avot* 2.2, 6.6). Saadiah's pluralism affords no measure of the deference spiritual and contemplative values must pay to material needs, and cannot, if one value is no arbiter of the rest. The great exegete can only refer his reader to the Torah and to wisdom to guide us in apportioning our energies. It is left to Maimonides, by rejecting Saadiah's claims for the autonomy of all prima facie goods and systematically applying a hierarchy of means and ends, moderation, excess and deficiency, to create a coherent, hierarchical system among the prima facie goods of life, an integrated system that will adequately reflect the biblical ideal of an integrated life under the rule of a single Law.

The Maimonidean Integration

What stands out when we compare Maimonides' normative approach to Saadiah's is a shift from personal ethics to public law. Correspondingly, since laws are concerned with ways and means, the focus shifts from the choice of ends to the virtues that serve those ends. But, perhaps most strikingly, we find a monism that seems at first blush diametrically opposed to Saadiah's pluralism:

> A human being must place all the powers of the soul in the service of reason . . . and set a single goal constantly before his eyes: to come as close to God as humanly possible, by knowing Him and by making every act, motion, rest or word conducive to this end, so that none of one's actions is vain in that it fails to promote this goal—making it one's purpose, for example, in eating, drinking, sexual congress, sleeping, waking, moving, and resting, solely to preserve bodily health; and preserving one's health, to enable the soul to find its tools sound and fit, so that the soul may attain wisdom and acquire the moral and intellectual virtues and thus attain its goal.[52]

This sounds like just the sort of monism that Saadiah rebuffs. Yet even in calling on us to place all our powers and acts in the service of a single goal, Maimonides sets up no competition between the acts he lists and the single aim he proposes as their goal. The rich tapestry of human life is preserved; and the behaviors that are instrumentalized are subordinated, but not sacrificed, to the quest for God and godlikeness—not abandoned in the ascetic spirit but given meaning, in keeping with the method of the Torah.

The great difference between Maimonides and Saadiah here, then, parallels that between Aristotle and Plato. For where Plato sees a competition among rival goods, which reason must adjudicate, Aristotle trusts the idea of organism to arrange all the aims of a healthy life in the order most conducive to our highest aim, *eudaimonia*, in which contemplation is the noblest and freest but hardly the sole or all-sufficing activity. Maimonides, like Aristotle, sees the activities of life—waking and sleeping, eating, drinking, and making love—not as mere additive or partitive components of the good life but as organic constituents, means to an end, which life as a whole pursues, and which Maimonides, echoing Plato (*Theaetetus* 176), calls an approach to God. The quest is not a blinkered pursuit of mystic union, although its summit does promise contact or communion (*ittiṣāl*) with the divine.[53] Rather, it is an inclusive, active, and practical, as well as speculative and contemplative, realization of human perfection that makes us akin to God. The singleness of our goal and the unity of the good life represent an organic rather than an exclusive unity.[54]

The nexus between Saadiah's pluralism and the Rambam's ethical hierarchy lies in the idea of virtue, which modulates the idea of ethical checks and balances into a system of means, each of which has reference to all the rest, and all of which, accordingly, can be integrated into a coherent and harmonious way of life, for an individual or for a society. We can follow the shift from Saadiah's pluralism to the Maimonidean synthesis if we trace Maimonides' idea of virtue to its conceptual roots. Herbert Davidson remarks, "Maimonides nowise proves the principle that ethical virtues are intermediate characteristics. He merely postulates it. The problem of measurement, moreover, cries out. How can the distance between lechery and insensibility, between haughtiness and utter meekness, be measured in order to determine the precise mean."[55] But Maimonides need not prove that the virtues involve a mean, since that was done by Aristotle, and the germaneness of Aristotle's virtue ethics to the Torah's project was established effectively by Saadiah's deployment of Aristotle's model, a deployment implicit in Saadiah's measurement of the worth of each goal that he considers against the standard afforded by the others. The scale of measurement for each Aristotelian or Maimonidean virtue is marked by the goods and ills that concern all the rest. The calibration will appear suppositious only if we expect a foundationalist argument, in which no demonstrated theorem is made a basic premise. But Aristotle typically presumes all human knowledge except the case at hand—thus, all of ethical knowledge except the location of a specific mean. Saadiah and Maimonides both follow him in this.

Each of the polarized ends that Saadiah found wanting was lacking precisely in what was offered by the rest. Saadiah's plan of attack, then, was to check each good by the standard of the rest. That is just how Aristotle locates the mean that is the target of each moral virtue: we know, without circularity, when affability or thrift or candor has gone too far or not far enough by judging whether the actions our dispositions promote are beneficial or deleterious, noble or ignoble, in terms other than their own. The coward acts dishonorably; the rash, foolishly. Courage seeks a mean regarding risk or danger, but the scale we use to find that mean is calibrated by a variety of other goods and ills. That is why every virtue rests on reason, one's own or that embedded in the ethos one has adopted or grown up with. As in Plato, only reason can compare disparate goods, and reason does not complete its work until it has considered all pertinent claims. Thus virtue is no simple matter of measuring out a middle ground on a single unilinear scale. To find the mean, reason must consider one's social position and intent, the manner and consequences of each act, those with whom, to whom, and for whom it is done. So Aristotle glossed the traditional Greek doctrine of the mean in terms of dispositions toward appropriate choice. He explained those dispositions in terms of rationality and rationality itself, resolving Plato's metaphor of measurement, in terms of the varied objects or values to which reason must attend—thus backgrounding Plato's appeal to the pure form of the Good. Through this analysis, Aristotle preserves the Platonic unity of the virtues: one cannot be pious or courageous insofar as one is stupid or stubborn; or wise insofar as one is pusillanimous; or kind insofar as one is dishonest. Each virtue is tested by the rest, and, for that reason if no other, none can stand alone. The Torah, then, must integrate the virtues not merely by subtly or optimally blending rival goods but by guiding us to the integration of those goods and the virtues that pursue them in proper relations of subordination and superordination of means to ends in the hierarchy of human goods.

We have evidence of the functioning of a government, Maimonides writes,[56] when we see a frail money changer at his board, unintimidated by an oaf who begs for so much as a carob seed and is not only refused but driven off with verbal abuse. One who enjoys such protection might think that the state exists for no other purpose than to provide it. It is true, the Rambam argues, that fear of punishment restrains the oaf. But the money changer's viewpoint is too narrow. The government protects others too—including the beggar. And it serves higher ends than the protection of property. For it secures the conditions in which human life and property are possible at all and guides the uses to which they are put (*Guide* III 27). Knowing that a government affords protection tells us nothing, Maimonides insists, about what sort of government it is.[57] Further, if our task is one of governance, whether of ourselves or of one another, talk of the penal role of government, as if the sanctions of a law were its reasons, misses the point entirely. For it tells us nothing of how to legislate.

A system of law, the Rambam writes,[58] promotes human ends when it seeks to secure human welfare by creating conditions of public security, mutual trust, material welfare, and civil cooperation. Societies pursue these goals in the first instance by instituting civil and penal codes. Maimonides' Platonic rather than Thrasymachean or Sophistic view of the object of such codes is clear from his formulation of their rationale. He argues not from any primeval war of each against all but from human diversity: human natures and characters differ so widely—one man advancing against a lion while another cowers at a harsh word from his wife[59]—that only a common structure of law can unite them effectively, let alone foster the level of cooperation and trust that any worthy human enterprise demands.

In the service of cooperation and overcoming human strife and wrongdoing, the Law has resources beyond the sanctions of its civil and penal codes. It can create institutions, rituals, and symbols that will foster a pliant or irascible, thoughtful or stolid character. Still, a law that seeks to form human character only for the sake of improving our material condition, to make us "good citizens," in the sense the phrase is often given, does not rise above the mundane ends that, by Maimonides' (Farabian) analysis, mark a law as mortal in its inspiration. For human beings are not infallible about the nature of human happiness. A good law will not just advance human wishes but must also educate those wishes, improving not just the standard of living but the standards of the living (cf. Deut. 5:30, 6:2–3, 8:6–18).

Establishing civil security, regulating human interactions to promote the common weal, and restraining force and fraud are the minimal aims of a government. But even these are not defined, let alone achieved, without some thought of higher aims. For if force and fraud are to be restrained, we need to know by whom, against whom, and to what ends. What are the rightful deserts of the money changer and the beggar, and how are these recognized and reconciled, anchored and served, institutionally? Even in pursuing our most basic ends, we need standards that transcend them. But the Torah seeks a higher goal. It aims to perfect our moral and intellectual natures, and it is because its aim is divine that we know it is no mere product of human device (*Guide* II 40). Thus Maimonides glosses: "The Law of the Lord, which is perfect, perfects the soul" (Ps. 19:8).[60] Other systems of law, too, may seek humanity's perfection, but any such actual system, Maimonides is sure, will prove derivative, less comprehensive, or less fully developed in a continuous tradition of juridical elaboration.[61]

For Maimonides, as for Aristotle, the moral dispositions (*middot*), which are perfected as the virtues (*ma'alot*), are means to the good life. He subordinates them to the fulfillment of our intellectual capacities, since these situate the potential for divinization that is our highest goal. But neither sort of virtue has a purely instrumental function. One might argue that the two differ in nobility, by the Aristotelian standard that theory, speculation, contemplation—the pure acts of the intellect—are never mere means, whereas moral virtues, even when they are ends in themselves, serve us, both in our practical and our speculative quests. But the same is true of the intellectual virtues. For both practical wisdom (*phronesis*) and its speculative counterpart (*sophia*) have their fruits and uses. Reason is supreme not because it is never instrumental but because of its affinity to God.

The Torah pursues a hierarchy of goals: to provide its recipients with civil security and welfare, to aid them in perfecting their moral character, and to guide them in perfecting their minds. All of these are social goals and are sought by social means; the Law does not address the individual as an isolated being, and that is why it does not centrally concern itself with the rare or exceptional.[62] What it establishes is a way of life, not a personal or private religion. Even the highest of human intellectual acts, the beatific or revelatory experience that responds to God's epiphany,[63] although supremely private, is public in its significance. For the Torah's aim is not just the promotion of rare and isolated experiences but the creation of a holy nation,[64] a people who preserve and live by their shared idea of the Universal God.

The chief axiom of Jewish thinking, in Maimonides' view, is the Torah's divine authority. But this authority entails not the fixity of biblical laws in a mythic past but their living relevance in every age.[65] Thus Maimonides argues that the Karaites subvert the "prime axiom" by their disregard for Rabbinic precedent.[66] Karaite Biblicism and antitalmudic fundamentalism, he warns, make caprice the ultimate legislative arbiter, by disrupting the stream of Rabbinic dialectic. For what makes the Rabbis' immemorial quarrying of the canon for its precepts a responsible legislative method is the continuity given to their creative work by the shared recognition that the Torah is a law of life: whatever does not comport with its underlying goals in elevating human life and so falls short of the majesty of the divine Legislator will form no part of the Law's true import. This key assumption has been plainly visible to us in the idea of the oral Torah. A corollary is the view that the Law contains the principles of its own elaboration. As Maimonides put it in the opening sentence of the *Mishneh Torah*: "All the commandments were given with their explanations." By understanding the Law's purposes, the Rabbis were empowered and emboldened to broaden some of its provisions, restrict others, devise new principles, and annul yet others, all in the name of interpretation—making concrete and particular the abstract and universal, or making universal and thematic the concrete and paradigmatic.[67]

Maimonides' interpretive reach is clear in his Code. Like Moses (Exod. 18:22, 26), he upholds *stare decisis*. But in thematizing the moral dimensions of the Torah, he finds much to be done. He brings to his task formidable Aristotelian tools devised long after the age of Moses and honed long after the days of the Tannaim and Amoraim. He addresses the Torah's core interest in perfecting human character in the second section of the First Book of the *Yad*, which he calls *Sefer ha-Mada'*, the Book of Science. This book, he says, contains the "root principles of the Mosaic religion." But the moral principles are practical rather than speculative and seem to be included by virtue of the Rabbinic teaching that ethics is a prerequisite of Law (*Derekh eretz kadma le-Torah*), which Maimonides echoes and underscores in his doctrine that theological insight demands sound character.[68]

Yet the *Code*, unlike the *Guide to the Perplexed*, is a book not of theology but of law. Why, then, are moral precepts classed with the laws pertaining to the Torah's speculative axioms (*Hilkhot Yesodei ha-Torah*)? Hyamson suggests it is because they are rational principles for Maimonides.[69] This makes sense, as far as it goes. But Maimonides does not concede that any of the precepts of the Law are nonrational.[70] Indeed, he takes as the motto of his Code the verse "Then shall I be unabashed to scrutinize all Thy commandments" (Ps. 119:6): adequate understanding will reveal the rationality of each *mitzvah*. So the inclusion of moral laws in the Book of Knowledge cannot be explained simply by their "appeal to the understanding." Besides, the organizing principle of the *Yad* is normative: the doctrines of *Hilkhot Yesodei ha-Torah*, like the norms of *Hilkhot De'ot*,[71] serve in the perfection or reform of the soul, its 'treatment' in the Socratic term, used here—much as Baḥya, Socratically, treats philosophy normatively, as part of the moral obligation of the devout to purify their thoughts.[72]

What brings the practical concern with character and the practical concern with ideas together under the heading of science (*madaʿ*) is that both are accorded the same mode of elaboration. For just as general principles can be formed inductively from the study of particular cases, moral laws (even if formulated in terms of particularities) allow us to derive further duties from their themes. That precisely is what Maimonides does in *Sefer ha-Madaʿ*: He finds strictly ethical aims in just 11 of the 613 traditional *mitzvot*. But from these he builds a comprehensive ethics that regulates diet, hygiene, sexuality, and temperament. His method is Socratic: he collects particulars, forms a general inference, then deduces further particulars. Just as Aristotelian science trusts that sense can be found in nature, Maimonides' science of halakhic ethics goes beyond mere registry of the laws, to discover that the Torah vindicates a faith in the rationality of its principles. The basic commands:[73]

1. To pattern ourselves on God's ways (Deut. 13:5, 28:9)
2. To cleave to those who know him (glossing Deut. 10:20, with Prov. 13:20; see *Ketubot* 111b, *Pesaḥim* 49a)
3. To love our fellows (Lev. 19:18)
4. To love strangers (Deut. 10:19, with Deut. 10:18)[74]
5. Not to hate our fellows (Lev. 19:17)
6. To reprove wrongdoers (Lev. 19:17)
7. But not shame them (Lev. 19:17, with *Avot* 3.15)
8. Not to distress the unfortunate (Exod. 22:21)
9. Not to bear tales (Lev. 19:16)
10. Not to take vengeance (Lev. 19:18)
11. Not to bear a grudge (Lev. 19:18)

All of these commands are stated in general terms, but the first four are broader than the rest. Pursuit of the character they prescribe is the work of a lifetime; that life would then be a concrete interpretation of the ideal these *mitzvot* hold forth. Two of the four basic precepts are plainly cardinal. Thus Maimonides reduces the second and fourth to corollaries of the first and third, respectively. For the stranger (*ger*) is a fellow (*reʿah*), although there is a special commandment to love him.[75] And the commandment to cleave to those who know God is seen rabbinically as a means of cleaving to God.[76] Thus two cardinal ethical principles are culled from the Torah: to become like God and to love one's fellows. Hillel spoke of the second as the core of the Law, regarding all the rest as "interpretation," that is, concrete means of achieving it. He thus gave his theology its widely appreciated social and moral cast. But Maimonides, like Plato and following Ben Azzai (Sifra, Kedoshim 4.12, Y. *Nedarim* 41c), names homotheosis as the cardinal principle. In keeping with Rabbinic tradition, he interprets this in terms of the human virtues. Plato wrote: "We ought . . . to become like God as far as possible; and to become like him is to become holy, just, and wise" (*Theaetetus* 176b). Maimonides attaches to this norm the general ethical requirement to pursue the mean, which is understood to be the course of the wise (*ḥakham*; cf. the Greek *phronimos*). He also adds the supererogatory self-demand of the saintly (*ḥasid*) somewhat to exceed the mean, so as to shun the more dangerous or reprehensible extreme. He even brings aboard the characteristic pietist preference for the extreme in such areas as humility and patience, qualifying Aristotle's doctrine of the mean and re-evaluating the Stagirite's carefully calibrated means of "proper pride" and "righteous indignation."[77] But the object, consistently, is human perfection, through which our likeness to God is realized. Thus the Rambam departs from Hillel's famous exhortation not by rejecting love of our fellows as the root of interpersonal ethics but by anchoring that love in the broader and more basic principle of love of God,[78] in keeping with the Rabbinic gloss of the commandment to walk in God's ways: "As He is called gracious, so be thou gracious; as He is called compassionate, so be thou compassionate; as He is called holy, so be thou holy" (*Soṭah* 14a).[79]

Moral perfection is won through the habituation of moderation and the healing of unwholesome tastes, appetites, and dispositions under the guidance of the wise. Where Aristotle made the *phronimos* the standard and model of wise choices, Maimonides, in keeping with Aristotle's practice as a moral counselor, and his own as a physician, makes the wise advisers and therapists of the soul. The virtues of reticence and discretion, forthrightness and sincerity, candor and genuineness, truthfulness and honesty, all described in concrete, situational terms, are derived from the cardinal idea of homotheosis. So are seriousness, dignity and cheerfulness, cleanliness and physical vigor. For the wise, good food, a comfortable house, a happy married life are means to a higher end. Moderation of our appetites aids us to that end. Ascetic extremes are detrimental to it, just as sybaritic extremes are.[80] Thus, where Saadiah made the goods of appetite and passion ends in themselves but urged the irrationality of treating any one of them as all-sufficient, Maimonides treats them as means to an end and discovers the ground and principle of their moderation in their contributions to that end. For perfection of the intellectual virtues flows from intellectual activities, and these are grounded through our approach toward moral perfection. Where Aristotle had treated intellectual virtues as fundamentally a gift of the gods or fortune, Maimonides, perhaps influenced by the more democratic views of al-Rāzī, and surely by his Platonic reading of the aims of Scripture and the Torah's inclusionary enunciation of its own goal, sees every Israelite as sharing in the fruits of the intellectual life, either directly or through the Torah's system of symbols and beliefs. The biblical commandment of homotheosis (Lev. 11:44, 19:2) for Maimonides, then, fuses Aristotle's moral mean with Plato's ideal of divinization.

Reason is the guide, both morally and intellectually.[81] So the unity that links our activities does not obliterate or displace them but orders and regulates them in a human context: "Whether doing business or manual labor for a livelihood, one should set one's heart not just on earning money but on doing these things to secure the body's needs in food, drink, and shelter, support of a wife"—all with a view to knowing God, following in his ways, and raising progeny who will know him.[82] The ideal is not seclusion, nor even quite that of being in the world but not of it. Ibn Bājjah, although a *wazīr*, and perhaps for that very reason, idealizes a life of withdrawal and speaks of the philosopher as a "weed," alien to his surroundings. Ibn Ṭufayl, also a courtier—companion and philosophical confidant to the head of state—similarly idealizes an isolated life and treats all worldly engagements, even those in which we emulate God's concern for our fellow creatures and for the welfare of all of nature, as painful distractions from the pure contemplation of God. But Maimonides' singleness of purpose does not follow these Andalusian paradigms. Saadiah's pluralism, the Torah's worldliness, the Rabbis' practice of all manner of trades, and his own practice of medicine and love of the moral and intellectual independence that the ancient Rabbis sought, all chime with his robust good sense to banish even the pose of otherworldliness. Maimonides sees clearly that a law cannot lead an entire nation to turn its back on economic and social activity. He does not urge that worldly occupations and commitments be shunned or scorned, but rather that we make them means to our own highest end, thus giving a higher meaning to every wholesome act, even as he instrumentalizes it.

The Torah's moral precepts ground the philosophical—or, in Maimonides' term, scientific—elaboration of the Law. For the commandment to love one another gives concrete content to the call to self-perfection, forestalling any vacuous or escapist interpretation. The more specific *mitzvot* against vengeance and grudge bearing illustrate the Law's cultivation of moderate dispositions. Thus the Torah's history of Moses' flaw becomes an object lesson about irascibility and the delicate responsibilities of leaders as role models. The focus is moderation, from which many concrete ethical determinations will be derived. Thus, when the Torah invokes special protection for the unfortunate in the eighth of our eleven *mitzvot*, Maimonides sees a demand that depressed and humbled persons like widows and orphans be shown special gentleness and sensitivity. The moral dispositions cultivated by observance of the *mitzvot* will naturally call forth responses appropriate to all sorts of situations. But the unfortunate deserve special consideration; widows and orphans need invariant courtesy. It is not enough to love them as ourselves, for their property must be preserved even more carefully than one's own.[83]

The rest of the eleven *mitzvot* regard those whom we might treat with hostility or neglect. So, here too, habits of moderation are not enough. The biblical norm of a social bond among all Israelites specifies concrete obligations even toward malefactors. They are still *ḥaverim*, associates or comrades. Maimonides organizes the six commandments here into a tight, mutually modulating hierarchy: the command not to bear a grudge is a precautionary margin (*seyag*) against acts of vengeance and thus serves the Torah's purpose of securing Israel's tenure in her land.[84] Grudges, when nursed, foster irascibility and an ethos that confounds honor with pride and self-respect with vindictiveness. Grudges are, of course, mental rather than overt. So they are not subject to punishment. Nor, for that matter, does vengefulness necessarily involve an overt act. But, as Maimonides notes, vindictiveness is a highly vicious disposition, far closer than mere resentment to bloodshed and the breakdown of civil trust. So even the disposition toward vengeance and minor expressions of spite that cause no overt harm are forbidden. For the Law is concerned not just with aggression but with the perfection of character. And, as Maimonides argues with regard to covetousness (Exod. 20:14, 5:18), even desire can fester and so disrupt our character. Such obsessive emotions, and even dwelling on the thoughts that open the door to them, are harmful (and thus forbidden), quite apart from any overt acts they may engender.

What improves the social climate and strengthens the civilization the Law seeks to promote is an ethos that frowns on spite and expects a friendlier, more open response even to wrongdoing. Thus the admonition to help one's enemy reload the spilled burden of his ass becomes a paradigm of the disposition that is the Law's intent.[85] For legislation is small help against an ethos that is lawless or rude. Yet no virtue is mechanical. Automatic or mindless mimicry of love yields complaisance at wrongdoing. This is what the Torah forbids when it commands, "Thou shalt surely reprove thy fellow" (Lev. 19:17). Like the text, Maimonides connects this obligation with the admonition not to hate our fellow. For sullen hatred, like thoughtless love, bears in silence what it cannot forgive. But genuine regard extends to a concern for the character and acts of others. It is false tact to suppose that friendship, fellowship, or consideration demands our silence in the face of wrongdoing. On the contrary, if friends and comrades are entitled to material aid, all the more do they deserve good counsel. Thus reproof is not a counterweight to the golden rule but a gloss of what genuine fellowship requires of us, and a sound application of Aristotle's idea that the mean is reason's specification of what is appropriate, fitting, and indeed noble—here realized in an ethos of mutual responsibility. As Maimonides writes, "Anyone in a position to reprove wrongdoing who does not do so is complicit in the wrong." The Rabbis demand privacy in reproof, reserving public reprimands for the recalcitrant. The concern is not with avoiding offense to an offender but with shaming him onto the defensive, and so wasting the rebuke or rendering it counterproductive.[86]

If laws exist simply to restrain injury, we need only the minimal regulations whose sanctions suffice to forestall harm or promote desired behaviors. Justifications are irrelevant except rhetorically. But Plato (*Laws* 719–36) differentiates rational from positive laws by asking whether they answer the human question, *Why?* by a sanction or an explanation. Most laws, of course, have both aspects. But consider which is essential. In the common law tradition, for example, a law is invalid if it bears no sanction; but no justification need be stated. Biblical laws, by contrast, especially those involving no overt act, often have no overt or human sanction. But Maimonides' juridical work finds none without a rational purpose. For the aim here is adherence, not just compliance. In this sense the entire Torah is ethical, seeking not to browbeat or coerce Israel into behavioral conformity to the minimal conditions of civil order but to gain the people's loyalty. Hence the exhortations of Moses, and the telling formulation of the Law's authority in terms of a covenant (*berit*): steadfastness to the principles of the Law will effectuate its aims of civil reform and moral improvement far better than mere enforced behavior.

Since the Torah seeks allegiance grounded in the attachment of human purposes (the heart, in biblical parlance) to the Highest, the Torah itself and its exponents must address two related problems, one cognitive, the other, ultimately political. The first is the problem of communicating the idea of God to an entire people, making the idea that will orient all our actions not a stumbling block but a motive and a goal of emulation. The second is what our liberal heritage might lead us to call the problem of the enforcement of dogmas. But, more appositely, it is that of attaching human hearts to the idea of perfection. For the allegiance invoked is not credal but moral. What is sought is not belief in the Torah's principles but commitment to their Source, love of God. The covenant, as the Prophets insist, is a marriage contract, an existential bond. It seeks not lip service but devotion and creates not a church but a life.

Maimonides addresses the first problem through his analysis of prophetic discourse in the *Guide*, showing how the Torah can convey the idea of the Transcendent in language designed for use with ordinary objects and images. The key to that possibility is the fact that values found in ordinary experience do point beyond it, toward Perfection. This, we can see now, is the reason why the problems in discourse about anything—objects in nature, other persons, even mathematical ideas—echo our problems in talking about God. For everything we know is in its measure absolute, transcendent, a tiny mirror of the Infinite.

By allowing the Torah's talk of God systematically to deconstruct itself, Maimonides discovers that every biblical term applied to God points toward Perfection, by designating some specific perfection but excluding the limitations that any determinate human idea of a specific character would entail. Thus, behind the Torah's anthropomorphisms lies a negative theology of transcendence, and behind that, the idea of the Infinite and Absolute.[87]

How are credence and allegiance to be gained for the values on which the Law is founded? Since the Law does not act simply through sanctions, and since faith, in the Torah's language, means trust in the Good rather than affirmation of the magical or bizarre, the Law does not attempt to "enforce" beliefs. The cognitive question 'Why should I believe in God?' is biblically as unmeaning as the spurious moral question 'Why should I do what is right?' or the equally spurious epistemic question 'Why should I believe what is true?' These questions dissolve when one supplies an adequate understanding of goodness, truth, or God. And, indeed, Goodness, Truth, and God are identical.

Not surprisingly, then, there is no Jewish catechism, inquisition, or dogmatic credo. Maimonides' famous articles of belief are the exceptions that prove the rule. For they are offered to define rather than constrain belief, with a view to explaining how it is possible for nonphilosophers to gain immortality, if immortality requires intellectual attachment to the divine. Maimonides' answer is that the ideas and values that constitute such attachment can be conveyed culturally, through beliefs and images, which he, like Plato, takes to be a practical substitute for perfect knowledge. Indeed, these values and ideas must be so conveyed. For, as Plato complained, the genuine insights and intuitions that are the core of conceptual knowledge cannot be communicated except by indirection.

To know God is the central religious obligation.[88] But that knowledge, the Rambam holds, can be reached through reason. Only those who cannot follow the arguments of rational theology are to accept the corresponding beliefs on the basis of authority. And that authority here has no coercive machinery; it compels only by argument or imagery. Tradition is the vehicle of both, linking the two, and so uniting those who rely on pictorial and dramatic symbols with those who actively grasp pure concepts and creatively reason to make those concepts speak and sing. Indeed, the dreamer, informed by sound ideas, can become a philosopher, and the philosopher with imagination can become a poet, lawmaker, or cultural guide (*Guide* III 27–30).

The great division in Scripture for Maimonides, as for the ancient Rabbis, is not between law and morals but between norms and thoughts. Halakhah is the vehicle of the normative dimension of the Law; aggadah, of the cognitive. The two are linked not as fabric and embroidery but (to use the Torah's language) as hand and name: the norms act where the name is known and understood. The narrative provides the rationale for the norm. Aggadah, then, is the Torah's source of normative energy. Thus, in the first of the ten divinely revealed items (*dibberot*), the one that grounds the Law as a whole, "I am the Lord thy God . . .", the words are not in the imperative, but Maimonides numbers a *mitzvah*, since their gravamen bears an imperative force, the force we have recognized in the claim Perfection makes upon us. And although speech is not literally predicable of the Transcendent, Maimonides singles out this commandment in the Decalogue as revealed to Israel by God himself, along with its corollary, "Thou shalt have no other God before Me."[89] For, although no authority can command belief, adherence, or devotion, a reality, the Good, existentially confronted and experientially appropriated, can become constitutive in a personality and so in an ethos, and a supreme reality can orient a way of life for an individual or a civilization.

At this juncture between aggadah and halakhah and so between fact and value, in the idea of a God of absolute perfection, arise all the obligations of the Law; and all human endeavor and devotion are funded toward assimilation to the unique Source of all perfections. The exclusivity of focus demanded in that appropriation is as natural to it as it is in the human act of love, which is its counterpart and metaphor. But, in either ecstasy, love does not blot out but gives meaning to the balance of action and experience. All the laws of the Torah, civil and penal as well as ritual, serve no other purpose than to clarify and facilitate our response to God. But they do so not by vanishing nor by subsuming or displacing that response but by sustaining and giving it its concrete sense and instantiated application.

Toward the end of the *Guide to the Perplexed* (III 26–49) Maimonides classifies the objects of the Law under fourteen rubrics. While these do not correspond precisely to the fourteen volumes of the *Yad Ḥazakah*, they do cover its major subdivisions, reveal the principles of its organization, and show how the Rambam sees each major class of commandments as serving the three cardinal ends of ordering and reforming civil society, perfecting human character, and guiding the human intellect.

Hilkhot Yesodei ha-Torah concerns sound opinions, the beliefs that convey the essential elements of the true understanding that philosophers pursue in regard to God and nature and our relations toward both. Regulations regarding fasts and repentance fall under this heading, since moral reformation and spiritual purgation are prerequisites of theological insight and of the alchemy that transmutes sound opinions into critically testable philosophical ideas.

The wide-ranging regulations aimed at uprooting idolatrous practice or any acts reminiscent of it are subordinated to the aim of instituting sound views. For idolatrous practices enshrine unsound and unwholesome beliefs, just as monotheistic practices like the Sabbath foster sound, wholesome and sacred ones. By unwholesome and unsound views Maimonides means specifically that localization and particularization of value, power, energy—divinity—which contradict God's universality and absoluteness (*Guide* III 29–30). So confident is he that divinity is manifest in the natural order that, in keeping with a homily of the Sages, he can regard abandonment of idolatry as tantamount to fulfillment of the Law. For what differentiates monotheism essentially from paganism is the idea that the divine is simplex and universal. Atheism here is seen as something of a sham. The real question is not whether anything or nothing shall be celebrated and emulated as divine but whether our celebration and emulation should be integrated in a comprehensive way of life, or diffuse itself in pursuit of disparate or conflicting values and goals. Here the pluralism that rejects integration bares its teeth. Concrete surrogates of the divine, the Torah's graven images, all too readily become barriers to God's service—even when the intent was to make them stepping stones. As Maimonides writes, "Sometimes idols are taken to be broken but are preserved and become a snare" (*Guide* III 37). For disparate values, once made gods, in the nature of the case show little reverence for their rivals and soon enough, it seems, demand violence as the mark of their absoluteness. Thus the claim that all the laws of the Torah are implicit in the rejection of idolatry—and its counterpart, that the rejection of idolatry is implicit in all its laws.

The moral laws, as we have seen, seek the perfection of our character. That goal is instrumental, both as a foundation of social order and as a prerequisite to intellectual perfection (*Guide* III 38). But beyond these two uses, the perfection of character is an intrinsic good, one way of realizing our likeness to the Creator ("Eight Chapters," 4, 5).

The most elemental commandments pursue social welfare through the reform or perfection (*tikkun*) of society. This again is a good in itself, but also a prerequisite for the perfection of humanity. For, as Maimonides explains,[90] no one can contemplate the mysteries and wonders of existence if hungry or in terror of his life. The Torah's ideal of reform rests on the biblical idea of deserts, which makes one's fellows second selves—friends, by Aristotle's definition—by treating them as such, and thus by paying special regard to the interests of the weak and helpless. Because the deserts of our fellow human beings are to be seen from God's standpoint, that is, in terms of their own interests, the social principles of the Law need not appeal to ego's perceived self-interest, and the existential deserts of one person are normatively interchangeable with those of another, as the imperative "Love thy fellow as thyself" requires.

The commandments that deal with torts are checks against negligence and aggression (*Guide* III 40). Their intent, then, is partly moral but more largely regulatory, to minimize wrongdoing or trespass and maximize the commonweal.

Penal laws pursue both general and specific deterrence (cf. *Guide* III 35.6). Their basis is reciprocity (*Guide* III 41). If harm is done only to property, punishments may be mitigated. But with great crimes and injustices, mercy cannot warrant setting aside the sentence of justice. For mercy must apply to society at large, not to the condemned alone. True, we are forbidden to return runaway slaves (Deut. 23:16–17). That commandment benefits not just the slaves but their benefactor and enhances the social ethos, teaching us compassion for the least fortunate. But the felon forfeits such consideration. To be tender to him is to be cruel to "all other creatures," his potential victims (*Guide* III 39 ad fin). Punishment follows actions; so it is not for those who are compelled, as is clear in the case of forcible rape (Deut. 22:26). There is no guilt by contagion. But Maimonides quietly drops Saadiah's retributive theory,[91] since it would introduce a value independent of self-perfection into his axiology and project human notions of retribution onto the pure idea of God.

The commandments that deal with property serve to regulate commerce and other modes of cooperation (*Guide* III 42). They are necessary to the continuance of civil society but they also anchor civil life to the principle of mutual assistance. I have an affirmative obligation to aid others, an obligation rendered concrete in such biblical institutions as interest-free loans and gratuitous trusteeships.

The observances instituted for the various times and seasons serve, as we have seen in the case of the Sabbath, not only a moral (recreative and purgative) function but also an expressive, celebratory function vital to the maintenance of the central communal notions (*ārā'*) that give the Law its motive force. Concurring in an Aristotelian theme that al-Ghazālī rejects when he finds it in the Persian ethicist Miskawayh, Maimonides grants that festival celebrations enhance the sociability and sense of fellowship that are essential to the health of a community.[92]

A special class of *mitzvot* seeks to focus our devotion upon God (*Guide* III 44). These concern prayer, blessings and such acts as acquiring a Torah scroll, affixing a mezuzah, or laying tefillin. Worship in the strict sense was the Temple cult. But these acts give canonical expression to the biblically prescribed love of God, channeling that love into specific pathways.[93] Thus the twice-daily recitation of the Shema, with its proclamation of God's unity, reflects on the covenant and on the command to make God the focal point of our love and not to go awhoring after the desires of our hearts and eyes but express our love through the fulfillment of all the precepts of God's Law (Deut. 6:5–9; Num. 15:37–41).

Three classes of *mitzvot* regulate the Temple, its sacrifices, and its ritual purity (*Guide* III 45, 46, 47). Maimonides explains the biblical cult of sacrifice as an accommodation to an antique way of thought: in ancient times, when sacrifice was the language of worship, it would have been too jarring and dislocating to expect Israel not only to accept the new Mosaic ideas of God but also radically to change their idea of the mode and aims of worship. So sacrifice, and even the idea of propitiation were retained. But the sacrificial cult was refined, regulated as to time, place, and manner, modulated to remove all hint or reminiscence of pagan practice. The Israelites were led "by way of the Red Sea Wilderness" (Exod. 13:17–18)—taken the long way round—to wean them from their primitive religious notions (*Guide* III 32). The proliferation of sacrificial laws, then, serves to restrict rather than enhance the role of sacrifices in Israelite worship and to bar any practice connected with pagan cult (*Guide* III 28–30). But these are no idle matters: where pagans had offered sons and daughters to their gods, the Torah substitutes a dove or a handful of flour (*Guide* III 47, citing Deut. 12:31). The terror of pagan piety is erased by the ethical law and the idea of a single God, in whom all true values are united. Israel's sacrificial worship was a stage in emergence of that idea. But Maimonides is emphatic in his historical posture: he sharply distinguishes the laws of Levitical purity connected with the Temple service from those regulating our ordinary diet.[94] He includes rebuilding the Temple on its site among the marks of the messianic ruler of Israel but does not list the sacrificial cult among the institutions the messiah will restore—adding a striking fillip to his suggestive remark that the Messiah will reform (*takken*) the breaches of the Law[95]—that is, perfect it, make good its lacunae, and repair the flaws in its observance.

The final classes of *mitzvot*, regulating diet and sexual behavior, are seen by Maimonides as part of the moral discipline of the Law.[96] We shall discuss these two rubrics in chapter 7. Suffice it here to say that when we do so we must put aside the incoherent and long-discredited idea of taboos. For it is characteristic of the Torah's methods to set universal, moral themes where particularistic totems might have been expected, as is clear in the sense it gives to the ideas of sanctity (*kedushah*) and purity (*tehorah*): the Torah moralizes the symbolism that mediates our relation to God just as it moralizes the idea of divinity itself.

A Synthesis of Maimonidean Monism and Saadian Pluralism

The task of reconciling or prioritizing conflicting or competing values or ends is, as Plato recognized in the *Republic,* essentially political; in fact, it is the essence of the political process. We may view this process in terms of funding priorities and take a majority vote and compromise of interests among elected representatives as sufficient to establish a just distribution of resources and hence a proper ordering of priorities. But Maimonides follows Plato in assuming that the task of assigning priorities is properly the work of reason and that it must deal with far more than material resources. If we chart only monetary expenditures, we risk not only missing the right answer but even missing the right question. For, as Maimonides sees, we define ourselves by the goals we choose.

At first glance Saadiah may seem to assume that any conflict of values should be resolved simply by their interplay or intermixture—thus, democratically, in Plato's sense, by the mere jostling of rival appetites and interests, whether in the mind or in the state. But, in fact, he denies that the melding of values is to be achieved mechanically or by their random mixture. He counts on the Torah and wisdom to show us the proper priorities. Maimonides, too, relies on the Torah to establish the rule of wisdom in human life. The subtle difference between the two is that Maimonides sees the object of the Torah as an organically integrated system of optima. He thus makes the Torah a guide to reason without making it a substitute for reason: knowing that the Torah aims for an optimum, whether a mean, a maximum, or a minimum, and understanding the principles on which that integration is to be achieved, allows us to interpret the Torah's ordinances in the light of its objective and its favored system of means.

Saadiah's pluralism, similarly, pursues not a farrago of disputing goods but an integration of those goods. For he has tested all thirteen of the aims he isolates not simply by their own standards but by one another's. But, unlike Maimonides, he does not make full use of the powerful Aristotelian theory of the virtues. Nor does he systematically exploit the organic model of means and ends that was so constant a theme in Aristotle's thought, reflecting his biological training and practice, and so appealing to Maimonides, who, like Aristotle's father and the Stagirite's ancestors on both sides, was a physician—as Maimonides' talk of the bodily organs as the soul's instruments or tools vividly reminds us. But, although Saadiah does not describe the integration he seeks in organic terms, integration there is, described as a harmony or blend. And, although the diversity of life's activities, active and contemplative, is reduced to unity in Maimonides, the unity is not that of simplicity, but that of an integrated whole. Similarly, in making contemplation the highest and most self-sufficient human activity, Aristotle does not forget that contemplation of nature is no distraction but a constituent of our lifelong contemplation of God. And in calling rationality our noblest and most distinctive gift, he does not forget that rationality humanizes our lives not just by bringing us to the summit of pure thought but also by guiding our practical activities, as individuals and as societies.

Maimonides, like Plato, conceives of reason as integrating the values over which it presides; like both Plato and Aristotle, he understands that task in personal and social terms. Thus he sees the ladder of Jacob's vision as a symbol of the complementarity of the active and contemplative phases of human life:

> "And lo, the Lord stood upon it" (Genesis 28:13)—stably abiding at the summit of that ladder, one end of which is in the heavens and the other on earth. This is the course that anyone must follow who would rise to apprehension of the One who surmounts that ladder. For He abides eternally at its summit—to speak in keeping, obviously, with the imagery of the text. The *angels of God* here are the prophets, of whom it is said, "And He sent an angel" (Numbers 20:16), "And an angel of the Lord came up from Gilgal to Bochim" (Judges 2:1). What wisdom, when it says that they were "ascending and descending" (Genesis 28:13), ascent before descent! After ascending and reaching a certain rung on the ladder, comes their descent with whatever they have learned of God's Word, to govern and teach the people on earth, as suggested by the image of descent.[97]

Like al-Fārābī and Avicenna, Maimonides believes that reason comes to us from on high. Whether we are prophets or ordinary human beings, we win our understanding from the same Source, the divine Logos, or reason principle.[98] This understanding can be communicated, obliquely, through words but often more effectively by practice and example, which weave its message into an ethos. Like Plato, al-Fārābī, and Ibn Ṭufayl, Maimonides knows that all communication is mediated by symbols—myths and rituals, as well as texts and words. And, like them, he knows that such symbol systems are the subtlest and most sensitive of our social institutions.

6

Monotheism and Ritual

Ritual has a wider influence on our lives than many a functionalist is inclined to admit—or even allow. Yet those who most disparage its role are often quickest to condemn the woman whose nylons have crooked seams, the man who wears mismatched socks or comes to work without a tie—or the student without a brightly colored beanie topped by a red plastic propeller, if de rigueur this year, say, at the freshman banquet. Much of what passes as a conflict between ritual and freedom, or even between ritual and reason, is in fact a conflict among rival ritual claims, and one question we must ask about the norms by which people live, or would like to live, or would like others to live, is why and how rituals dare make any claim at all.

Students of Jewish thought are often taught that Saadiah Gaon, following a Rabbinic distinction between commandments that would have been unknown without revelation and those we should have been obliged to invent had they not been revealed, distinguished rational from positive (or revealed) commandments. The Rabbinic distinction was built on a presumed scriptural distinction between ordinances (*mishpatim*) and statutes (*ḥukkim*). It became a focal point of discussion because it seemed to suggest that *mishpatim* are known, even deducible by unaided reason, while *ḥukkim* cannot be anticipated or even understood by reason alone. Saadiah, it is said, distinguished obligations that are a matter of prudence from those that are ceremonial in nature and thus not obligations of reason but simply matters of obedience to God.[1]

Some have celebrated Saadiah's rationalism on this ground, and others have deplored it. But I want to begin my reflections on ritual obligations from the recognition that Saadiah did not make the distinction commonly ascribed to him but held a subtler, simpler, and more sensible view. Where Saadiah's chief detractors may see incoherence and ambiguity, I see a solid foundation for our own thinking about the relations of law, reason, and ritual, a foundation that preserves the best of the Rabbinic teachings on the subject and is enlarged and enhanced in the philosophy of law and ritual that Maimonides develops out of Saadiah's approach. After elucidating what I see as the insights of the tradition that Saadiah and Maimonides faithfully represent, I want to argue, in the spirit of that tradition, that all laws have a ritual aspect, and that all sound laws are rational. Once these points about the nature of law are established, I think it will be clear why Saadiah did not draw the sharp dichotomy so commonly ascribed to him: the simple reason is that it is false.

Rational versus Ritual Commandments?

This is what Saadiah said in introducing the topic of the commandments:

> What I must premise at the outset of this Third treatise is what we recognized at the end of the First as to God's reason for creating: that, being eternal and alone, he acted purely out of benevolence and grace. The same point as to his beneficence in creating is found in scripture—as the Bible says, "God is good to all; his mercies are on all his works (Psalms 145:9).
>
> His bounty toward creation began with the bestowal of being, giving existence, which creatures did not yet have, as he says of the most distinguished of them, "All that are called by my name, whom I created for my glory" (Isaiah 43:7). But he gave them more: the means of attaining perfect happiness and bliss, as it says: "Thou makest known to me the path of life. The full of joy is thy presence; at thy right hand, blessedness eternal" (Psalms 16:11). This means the commands and prohibitions he gave them.
>
> The first thing that would occur to reason to ask on reflecting on these words is this: "God had it in his power to give us perfect blessedness and everlasting bliss without issuing any commands or prohibitions. Wouldn't that be a better way of showing us grace, since it would spare us the burden of those commands?"
>
> To clear up this point, let me say, on the contrary, it was better and more generous for God to give us the means of attaining eternal blessedness for ourselves, by fulfilling his commandments. For reason deems one who earns a good by working for it to gain many times over what one does who simply receives it without effort, as a favor. Reason sees no comparison between the two.
>
> This being so, our Creator preferred us to the richer portion, so that our profit from its requital would be many times greater than the profit of one who expended no effort. As it says (Isaiah 40:10), "Lo, the Lord God cometh with power, and his arm will rule for him. Lo, his reward is with him, and his recompense before him." (*ED*. III Exordium)

Saadiah does not see the commandments as a penance, a fruitless discipline, or arbitrary exercise, but as an enhancement of the human condition even beyond mere (!) eternal bliss, since an earned benefit is better than an unearned one. God's justice allows enhancement of the reward of the deserving. So responsibility is no arbitrary burden but a challenge, and the world is the better for being a place in which rewards can and must be earned. This is the sense Saadiah gives his important thesis that the world was created for the sake of justice: the world is the arena in which man in general and Israel in particular can earn a transcendental reward, so that God can manifest his justice in fact and in act, and not merely possess it as an attribute.

It is this metaphysic of morals that frames Saadiah's thoughts on the purposes of the commandments (*ED* III 1):

> Reason calls for a response to one who does us a kindness, either by returning the favor if the giver needs such reciprocity, or by rendering thanks if the giver has no such need. Since this is a universal requirement of reason, it would be unthinkable for the Creator to ignore it in his own case. Rather it was imperative that he command his creatures to serve him and thank him for their creation.
>
> Reason also demands of the wise that they not permit themselves to be insulted

or abused. So it was imperative as well that God restrain his creatures from such behavior.

Reason again requires that creatures be kept from trespassing against each other in all sorts of ways. So it was necessary as well for a Wise God to prohibit this too.

And reason permits the wise to find useful employment for those who can do work and to reward them accordingly, specifically to enhance their welfare. For this benefits the worker and in no way harms the employer.

But if we sum up all four of these headings, the ensemble would comprehend all the laws our Lord commanded us:

He required of us that we know and serve him and devote ourselves to him with sincere intention, as it says: "And thou, Solomon my son, know the God of thy father and serve him with a perfect heart and a willing soul, for all hearts doth the Lord search and every inclination of thought doth he comprehend" (1 Chronicles 28:9).[2]

Further, he forbade us to address him with any ugly disrespect. Not that it would harm him, but simply because it is out of keeping with wisdom to tolerate this. Thus, for example, it says: "If any man shall curse his God, he shall bear his sin" (Leviticus 24:15).

And He did not permit us to infringe upon or wrong one another, as it says: "Ye shall not steal or defraud or lie to one another" (Leviticus 19:11).[3]

But Saadiah does not proceed directly to the fourth class. Instead, he generalizes his thesis about the first three, placing them all in a single category and linking all acts of worship and piety under the first rubric, all forms of polytheism and impiety under the second, and all human acts of goodness, justice, truthfulness, fairness, and generosity under the third. All of the *mitzvot* serve the goods already mentioned: they express gratitude toward God, eschew the disrespect of impiety or obscenity, or seek to avert our wronging one another. For Mosaic justice subsumes our positive obligations toward one another under the prohibition of injustice, since depriving another of his due is injustice, and our fellow human beings deserve aid, support, and love, not just a suspension of overt aggression.[4] Beyond our duties to one another and to God, there are no further obligations. But God does have a fourth reason for giving commandments, and it is this that grounds Saadiah's famous distinction:

> Implanted in our minds is an innate approbation of each of the three foregoing classes of obligations (or disapprobation of the corresponding forbidden acts), as Wisdom, which is reason, says: "Truth doth my palate love, and wickedness is loathsome to my lips" (Proverbs 8:7). But the second great division is of those things that reason does not regard as good or evil intrinsically, which our Lord added to the tally of our commandments and prohibitions so as to augment our reward and the happiness we attain through them, as it says, "The Lord delighted for his righteousness' sake to make the Torah great and glorious" (Isaiah 42:21). What is commanded in this category becomes good, and what is prohibited becomes evil, by being commanded, since it serves as a way of worshipping God. It is thereby assimilated in a derivative way to the first category.[5]

Rosenblatt, in translating this passage, seems embarrassed at the thought of what is neutral in itself becoming good when commanded by God. Perhaps he equates this idea with the theistic subjectivism that Saadiah emphatically rejects.[6] He renders:

"What is commanded of this group of acts is, consequently [to be considered as] good, and what is prohibited as reprehensible; because the fulfillment of the former and the avoidance of the latter implies submissiveness to God. From this standpoint they might be attached secondarily to the first [general] division [of the laws of the Torah]."[7] But Saadiah does not say that intrinsically neutral acts come to be *considered* good or evil when commanded by God but that they *become* good or evil. He also explains why: these neutral acts acquire significance as acts of worship. In what follows I think it will become clear that no theistic subjectivism (or other form of relativism) is implied in the idea that divine commands, or other ways of situating actions in a context, can transform intrinsically neutral acts into significant and therefore morally freighted acts.

If we ask now how Saadiah distinguishes rational from nonrational commandments, the answer is that he does not. All the *mitzvot* are rational; none differs from the rest in rightness or prescriptivity. Saadiah distinguishes the commandments he calls rational not by their rationality but by their intrinsic rightness, which we have the innate ability to recognize. "Like men shall ye die" (Ps. 82:7), Saadiah argues, means *like ordinary men*, as in Jer. 32:20, "both on Israel and on men," that is, the generality. There is no implication that Israelites are not human.[8] Similarly, calling some commandments rational does not imply that the rest are not (Saadiah has some hard things to say about the linguistic expertise of those who read Hebrew that way), but only that those singled out are rational par excellence, since their rationality is transparent. Other commandments deal with actions we do not recognize as intrinsically good or evil. Considered strictly in themselves, they may be neutral. But the Law makes them significant. We deem them matters of discretion only from an artificially abstract, decontextualized perspective, as bringing a napkin to the table might be a neutral act but might have a moral significance, large or small, positive or negative, when done in response to a request.

Purely symbolic observances can serve a good, by giving us useful employment and allowing us to earn the reward of our labors. But once an act is made a proper act of worship, its intrinsic neutrality is underwritten by the value it serves. Any act that is morally neutral in the abstract can acquire a moral significance in context, through its bearing on our relationships with one another, with nature, or with God. We cannot evaluate any piece of behavior without knowing its social and symbolic significance. This does not mean that actions have moral weight only by convention. But an act isolated from its moral environment is not an act at all but an abstraction. Beyond this general corollary of ours to Saadiah's point, Saadiah wants to argue that the actions he concedes to be neutral in themselves, at least at first blush, before the tribunal of untutored reason, may have some intrinsic moral significance. So he adds, regarding his second broad category: "Moreover, on closer consideration, one must recognize that these have some slight benefits and partial explanations from the standpoint of reason, just as the first category has major benefits and momentous significance from the standpoint of reason." This refers to the actions taken narrowly, without regard to their adoption as means of worship. Such means, in the nature of the case, are symbolic; and a symbol, by definition, has a (partly) arbitrary relation to its object: bowing is not submission but an expression of submission. Clasping our hands in prayer (as Jews did in ancient times) is not humility but an expression of humility.

No symbol works *as* a symbol, that is, expressively, unless it is distinct from what it expresses or represents. Still, Saadiah reasons, the acts that gain moral significance by being made acts of worship need not be wholly neutral in themselves. A red rose symbolizes love, though not through any intrinsic connection of redness with love. Yet there is a structural relation between the intensity of red and the intensity of love; the color suggests blood and blood is linked with life and death, and these again with love. The acts and objects that will serve as symbols in the worship of God are never wholly neutral. Purity, as we shall see in chapter 7, is made a symbol in that worship, and spiritual purity is never wholly arbitrary in the symbols it chooses, never wholly unconnected to bodily and moral purity, even at its most spiritual.

Reason has ready access to the categories implanted in it. It knows the value and the point of serving God and sees the import of the acts and omissions that earn our ultimate reward, the conduct that ensures the justice or injustice of our comportment toward one another. When it comes to the special employment God has for us—the work of art that is to be our lives—reason finds itself on foreign soil; we catch only a syllable or two of meaning in the language of that land. But is that language insignificant? Certainly not in Saadiah's view. To hold that God will augment our reward for performing useless or pointless actions would contradict the heart of Saadiah's rationalism and destroy his central thesis that the purpose of creation is the expression of God's justice.

If human reason comprehends no more than a smattering of the wisdom in the special commandments by which Israel will distinguish herself, that is no sign that those commandments lack wisdom. Saadiah repeats throughout his writings that such commandments seek a higher good and express a higher reason than human reason knows. In fact, he develops a theory of how such commandments help us toward the happiness and perfection that is their reward. And he should. For if these commandments did not enhance our being, and their sense or savor rested solely on the notion that they allow acknowledgment of our loyalty and devotion to God, the question would remain, Why did God choose to be worshiped in this fashion rather than some other? Some theistic positivists would think that question unanswerable, even meaningless. But Saadiah cannot agree, as long as he contends that God's actions are wise and insists that creation is not, as he puts it, just a bad joke, that the burdens God imposes are not just busywork.[9]

Consider Saadiah's anatomy of Scripture: all scriptures (evidently including the Qur'ān, whose language Saadiah sometimes echoes),[10] are tripartite, embodying law, sanction, and historical episodes that link the two:

> All the books, however numerous, of the prophets and sages of every nation, are made up of three elements. First in precedence is command and prohibition. That is one rubric. Second, reward and punishment, the fruits of obedience and disobedience. And third, the reports of those who lived virtuously in the land and so fared well and those who lived corruptly and so were ruined. For no reformation (*istiṣlāḥ*) is complete without these three components.[11]

Saadiah's analysis echoes Plato's account of laws, fusing the Platonic "preamble" with scriptural narrative and the Platonic sanction, characteristic of positive law, with the prophetic understanding of God's requital of obedience and disobedience—

through our actions, in keeping with Muʿtazilite thinking and the Rabbinic idea that destiny underscores human choices by promoting the penchant through which they are made.[12] Saadiah's object, in context, is to demonstrate how essential tradition is to the project of biblical legislation. Without tradition we would lack the clear connection between legislative norms and success or failure that enables us to call the life of sincere devotion to the precepts of the law virtuous, wholesome, or good. Without examples of the worldly working of the law we would not have the clear nexus of obedience, assent, and appropriation that enables us to recognize violation of the Law's principles as vice and to see its inherent or consequential destructiveness. Nothing here is arbitrary. It is not the case, as in Ash'arite teaching, that God might have commanded just the opposite of what he ordained, or condemned what he commanded. We know God's goodness and can vouch for the authenticity of the revealed text precisely because we can recognize the legitimacy and goodness of its commandments. Saadiah illustrates with a medical example. A good physician does not just tell us to do this or not do that, but to do this and not do that, because following this advice will cure or prevent a headache, as it did for so-and-so.[13]

Why, then, did God give commandments to the virtuous, who do not seem to need legislative medicine? Saadiah finds four reasons: first, to inform them of his will. Good intentions are not enough. If one wants to serve God, one needs to know how. In general terms, as we have seen, we fulfill our divine mandate by perfecting our humanity. But that end does not specify its own means. As Saadiah writes:

> Reason ordains thanksgiving to God for His bounties but does not specify its form, its formulations, times and manner. So reason itself needed messengers to give this expression definition and to give it the name of prayer, to assign it specific times and formulae, its own distinctive postures and the specific direction one is to face. Similarly, reason rejects fornication but tells us nothing specific about how a woman is to be espoused exclusively to one man—whether merely orally, or by a simple monetary exchange, or by her consent and that of her parents alone, or whether there must be two witnesses, or ten, or all the people of the town, or by wearing her husband's insignia—or his brand. So the prophets bring us dowries, wedding contracts, dual witnesses. Again, reason rejects thievery but tells us nothing about how people are to acquire property so as to make it their own. Do goods belong only to the maker, can they be acquired through trade or inheritance, or appropriated from what belongs to no one in particular, as in hunting and fishing? Does a sale occur when a price is paid, or only on possession, or simply on a verbal commitment? . . . Again, with regard to crime and punishment. Reason deems that every crime has its proper sanction but does not specify what it should be—whether a reprimand is enough, or castigation should accompany it, or flogging as well, and if so, how many stripes . . . or whether only capital punishment will suffice. Does every criminal who commits a given crime deserve the same punishment, or should some be treated differently from others?[14]

Since reason alone cannot specify its own demands, then, prophecy is needed "not only for the positive religious commandments, to make them known, but also for the rational commandments, since people cannot fulfill them in practice without emissaries to show them how" (*ED* III 3). Beyond this, God gives commandments to the virtuous to ensure them their full reward. Alluding to the talmudic motif (*Kiddushin*

31a) of the superiority of acting from obedience over acting out of inclination,[15] Saadiah argues that an act performed without a command, spontaneously, merely, say, because one is good-natured, would merit no reward. Responding to an Ash'arite argument, he even argues (in proper Mu'tazilite style) that a God who rewarded unprescribed acts might equally punish un*pro*scribed acts; but God's justice allows no punishment without a prohibition. Finally, citing Ezekiel 3:21, Saadiah argues that the virtuous need laws as reminders, to keep them on guard against any weakening of character or moral backsliding.[16]

What God commands is identified, throughout, with virtue; what he prohibits, with vice. What might have seemed neutral in itself becomes obligatory when commanded by God not merely (as in Ash'arism) *because* it is commanded but because of its role in expressing thanks. We might suppose that Saadiah's saying that certain actions become right or wrong as divinely assigned work or as insults to God's majesty allows him to regard at least some of these actions as arbitrary, confirming the dichotomy between rational commandments and those that have "slight" if any rational basis. But such a view would ill consort with Saadiah's emphatic rejection of theistic subjectivism, and he rejects it explicitly in his treatment of the causal impact of the commandments.

What Saadiah says is that obedience or disobedience leaves its imprint on the soul, purifying or corrupting us and making us not only more or less deserving but also more or less susceptible to requital. The theory is rooted in the Mu'tazilite riposte to Ash'arite theory, but Saadiah finds it well attested in Scripture:

> Our Lord made it known to us that obedience on the part of His servants, when preponderant, is called virtue; and disobedience, when preponderant, vice. . . . These acts leave their imprint on the soul, rendering it pure or sullied, as it says in the case of sin, "he shall bear his iniquity" (Leviticus 5:1), "he shall bear his sin" (Leviticus 24:15), "and they set on their soul their iniquity" (Hosea 4:8), "its iniquity shall be upon that soul" (Numbers 15:31). Even though these things may be hidden from human beings, or not plain to them, they are patent to Him, as it says: "I the Lord search the heart and try the kidneys" (Jeremiah 17:10).[17]

God's justice rewards or punishes us not for random behaviors but by *and through* our virtues and vices.[18] The Torah does not inform us tautologously that one who disobeys God is guilty of disobedience. Nor does it simply tell us that disobedience is wrong—as though one who contemplated disobeying God would be moved by another commandment to obey the commandments, or by the knowledge that such rebelliousness is unwanted. Rather, it tells us that wrongdoers bear the consequences of their acts, not on their heads but in their souls. Their guilt and the merit of those who keep the commandments redound to their injury or benefit, through the dynamic of their actions, making them weaker and less free or better and stronger persons, as well as affecting them consequentially, through God's requital of good and evil acts:

> Since the soul does not act in isolation, sheerly by its own constitution, it needs something coupled with it to accompany it, through which it can act in its own interest. For it is only through actions that it will reach lasting blessedness and perfect happiness, in accordance with what I explained in the Fifth Treatise, that obedience augments the luminosity of the substance of the soul, and disobedience

> muddies it, as Scripture plainly states: "Light is sown for the righteous," etc. (Psalms 97:11; cf. Proverbs 13:9).[19]

Far from an extrinsic justice, God acts directly on the substance of the soul and through its very nature. Reward here, as in the Torah, is very compact with the life of the *mitzvot*.[20] The same substance that sustains the soul and renders it capable of action bears the consequences of its actions, their fruits, as Saadiah calls them—not external responses but expressions of the inner dynamic of choice itself. The same divine light sheds joy and blessedness on the righteous but torment and agony on those who flout God's commandments of righteousness.[21] So what God commands, then, is not only useful work but the work of soul building.

We can see that Saadiah regards none of the *mitzvot* as arbitrary but takes all of them to exemplify rational principles from his rejection of the free, allegorical mode of exegesis that the Arabs called *ta'wīl*. He offers colorful and extended illustrations to show that, given its head, such a method can prove anything: the ban on leaven at Passover might mean that harlotry is forbidden, the prohibition of kindling on the Sabbath might mean that armies may not be brought into the field.[22] To head off such capriciousness, Saadiah devised rigorous hermeneutical rules, which he scrupulously obeyed himself, founded on the canons of reason, science, language, and tradition.[23] Without some such discipline, exegesis becomes arbitrary and turns to woolgathering.

Saadiah's method (and any workable hermeneutics) requires a thematic exploration of the canon it addresses. This Saadiah has done when he groups the *mitzvot* under the goods they serve. Without such a linkage, guided by our moral understanding and aided by the traditions that bring such understanding to focus, we would have no way of knowing when to take Scripture literally, how to extend or confine its dicta. To acknowledge the discipline in Saadiah's hermeneutics is not to spread a blanket endorsement over his every exegetical aperçu, but it is to recognize with him and with the Rabbinic tradition for which he speaks that if any of the *mitzvot* are treated as brute positive demands, we are in that measure deprived of access to an understanding of what it is that they demand.

Following in the footsteps of Abraham, Saadiah excludes any idea of God that does not equate his will with the good. He is a chief advocate of this core idea of monotheism, voiced with gemlike concision in the Psalms (97:2): "Righteousness and justice are the groundwork of His throne." At Job 34:17–19 he renders "How can one who hateth justice prevail in his own affairs? Or wilt thou overrule Him who is great in justice? Is 'scoundrel' to be said unto the king or 'unfair' to the openhanded, who favoreth not princes and sustaineth not lavishness in the presence of the poor, since they are all His work?" Glossing, Saadiah finds seven arguments here, "refuting the notion of divine injustice." Three, which he calls basic, take aim at the Epicurean dilemma, arguing that God is not weak, venal, or unknowing. But the four that he calls subsidiary ground God's sovereignty in his justice:

> First, *Doth one who hateth justice prevail?* (v. 17). This means that when a man is unjust and hates just rule, his own affairs are not well ordered or successful, as it says, "A man is not established by iniquity" (Proverbs 12:3). But He, whose concerns run in perpetual order and stability, is on a plane which precludes His being unjust. Second, *Or wilt thou condemn Him who is great in justice?* (v. 17). This

> means that the doings of the Creator cannot be impugned and His judgment overruled by some denier. For it is absurd to impugn the Truth Itself. Third is his saying, *Is 'scoundrel' to be said unto the king?* (v. 18). Here Elihu makes clear that the king deserves to rule only for his justice. So it is absurd that He be a rightful king and yet be vicious. Such a thing could occur only among humans, through a struggle for power. Fourth, *'unfair' to the openhanded?* For munificence means bestowing more than is deserved. One does not call a giver lavish if he retains anything that ought rightfully to have been given. Munificence begins where fairness leaves off. Hence, since it is established that His bounty surpasses the lesser level, it goes without saying that He is fair.[24]

Someone who confuses power with force or holds the incoherent notion of arbitrary authority might imagine a god who simply commands what he pleases, without regard to right or justice. Such a God might reward behaviors arbitrarily assigned for that purpose. But Saadiah rejects such notions of power and of God. God's power has authority because it is founded on justice. God's rewards are for work that is valuable, even if we do not immediately see the full measure of its value.

Is Saadiah's View Coherent?

In a paper first published in the early 1970s, Marvin Fox argues against the very idea of rational commandments: "Whatever interpretation may be put upon those talmudic passages which seem to support the claim that some commandments are rooted in reason, it is clear that Saadiah is the first major Jewish writer to refer to certain commandments specifically as *sikhliyyot*. . . . there is no philosophically acceptable sense in which Saadia can be said to have shown that there are rational commandments."[25] Where Saadiah deems all of the *mitzvot* rational, although we may not immediately see the sense of some, Fox holds that none are and that it was wrongheaded of Saadiah to try to show that any are rational.

Fox rests his case on what he calls an incoherency in Saadiah's idea of rationality: "When we pay close attention to the variety of ways in which Saadiah uses the various terms for 'reason' and 'rationality' in his book, we see that no simple explanation of these terms will suffice. In fact, it may not be possible at all to emerge with a completely satisfactory explanation, precisely because Saadia appears to say a variety of things that are not internally consistent."[26] Fox hedges by excluding from his purview the Rabbinic discussions that anchored Saadiah's idea of rationality and the *kalām* discussions that framed the issue in his day. He rationalizes this refusal to contextualize as an effort to address Saadiah on his own terms: "Whatever the origins of his doctrines and whatever purposes they may have been intended to serve, we must still try to see and understand them in their own context. Saadia's readers are not required by him to know the entire intellectual history of the concepts and arguments that he develops."[27] This disclaimer from a historian of ideas, coupled with demands for a "completely satisfactory," "simple explanation," seems to load the dice for failure.

But, in fact, in his commentary on Job, Saadiah does offer readers unfamiliar with the backgrounding history of speculation on what he calls a perennial issue a straightforward and indeed simple standard of what counts as rationality: he says that those who are tested with sufferings but maintain their integrity and allegiance to God, as Job did, will discover, when they win the recompense to which their extra measure of devotion entitles them, that the enhanced blessings they receive were well worth their suffering. For readers who may not be conversant with the pertinent Rabbinic and *kalām* discussions, Saadiah makes graphically clear what is at stake:

> Recompense for tribulations with which He has afflicted us and which we have borne with fortitude . . . can be called a reward. For the tribulations are not on account of some past sin on the servant's part. They are spontaneously initiated by God. Their purpose, therefore, lies in the future, as the prophet makes clear: "Fortunate is the man Thou chastenest, O Lord, and whom Thou teachest in Thy law" (Psalms 94:12). The Allwise knows that when we are visited with sufferings they are abhorrent to our natures and harrowing to us in our struggle to surmount them. So he records all to our account in His books. If we were to read these ledgers, we would find all we have suffered made good, and we would be confirmed in our acceptance of His decree.[28]

Saadiah here makes perfectly clear his standard of rationality in human choices: it is our objective interest. It is the apparent disparity between God's justice and the suffering of innocents, he argues, that leads many who ponder the human condition, as Job did before his enlightenment, and as the Ash'arite theologians did in Saadiah's time, to conclude not that God is unjust but that his expectations are arbitrary.[29] But God does not conform creation to our desires: "Wisdom is not identical with what creatures yearn for, nor is the right course of action that which human beings are pleased with. . . . The proper object of concern is not whether the decrees of the Allwise gladden His creatures or grieve them. For what is agreeable to them is not the standard of His wisdom. Rather His wisdom is the standard for them."[30] But God does maximize our interests, as we would see if we had full knowledge of the case—and *shall* see when that knowledge is laid open to us. Even martyrdom, if its recompense is borne in mind, "is actually better than continued life in the world. Of this it says, 'For Thy favor is better than life' (Ps. 63:4)." It is for this reason that Saadiah can equate reason or rationality with wisdom.

Fox attempts to drive Saadiah into an equivocation or inconsistency by noting that he sometimes takes rationality in a formal sense, as in denying the rationality of the claim that fire is cold or neglecting the requirements of syllogistic entailment. But none of the commandments of the Torah "is rational by this standard," that is, none of them states an analytic truth.[31] Readers who have a genuine interest in the *material* sense that Saadiah gives to the idea of reason will find its core spelled out brilliantly and faithfully in Spinoza: "Since reason demands nothing contrary to nature, it demands that everyone love himself, seek his own advantage, what is really useful to him, want what will really lead man to a greater perfection, and absolutely, that everyone should strive to preserve his own being as far as he can. This, indeed, is as necessarily true as that the whole is greater than its part."[32] Spinoza insists that our personal well-being depends on that of others and cannot be achieved to their detriment or by any sacrifice of virtuous principle.[33] For many exponents of rational choice presumptively equate rationality with the narrow interests of the atomic ego.

Saadiah would no more accept that than he would equate objective interests with their subjective apprehension.

Spinoza's warrant for claiming that reason bids us pursue our own interest with as solid a demand as it makes upon our credence when it asks us to affirm that the whole is greater than its part is that the essence of each existent is its striving to preserve its own being. For a being to exist is for it actively to affirm its essence, to strive to preserve and promote its distinctive existence, affirm its own character. To fail to do so is to deny or reject itself. Now some can debate, or pretend to debate, whether beings *ought* to preserve or express their own character. But no one can deny that no obligation is more basic. Thus the fundamental incoherence of self-negation, in pressing for one's own annihilation. It is here that we see the sense in which self-interest is an imperative of reason, not that, say, suicide is impossible or unintelligible but that it involves a primary contradiction of what is affirmed by the intension of any action. It is not *formally* inconsistent to deny our own being in this sense, but it is ontically so. For the being that seeks to negate itself simultaneously affirms itself. It seeks protection, surcease, peace, in the very act by which it blots out its own claims to affirmation and existence. Less dramatically, we find a parallel negation, ontic self-denial, in morbid shyness, agoraphobia, fear of success, and kindred pathologies, including various addictions and compulsions, where self-preserving impulses are deflected or deceived into self-thwarting or self-crippling, perhaps by the internalization of ambient or depersonalized hostilities encountered in a competitive or indifferent social milieu.

Philosophers who deny that self-affirmation is the dynamic essence of any being can still see the sense of Saadiah's argument. For even if our own active existence is not seen to involve self-affirmation, one can grasp what Saadiah means by rationality if one simply posits one's own interests as a desideratum and takes rationality here to mean "conducive to one's (objective) interest." To understand Saadiah's treatment of reason fully, we have only to generalize Spinoza's thesis, as he does, in social terms, when he makes piety the unselfish desire for others of what one desires for oneself. Given Saadiah's moral realism, and abandoning the Cartesian primacy of the subjective, we can see why he regards, say, acceptance of the truth as a demand of reason. For reason calls on us to recognize *any* objective value and thus demands acknowledgment of the truth and expects gratitude for favors and just requital of human choices. Reason here is not equated with tautology.

Fox chides Saadiah for making reason a source of knowledge, teaching us, say, to approve of truth and reject falsehood. The criticism is that such preferences are not analytic: "There is no analysis that one can produce of the statement 'Truth is good and falsehood bad,' that can show it to be necessarily true, given Saadia's own definition of necessary truth."[34] Now this is an odd procedure, to fault a philosopher for using a word in a variety of senses and then to fault him again for not making one of those senses trivially reducible to another. When Fox uses the idea of analyticity (despite a nod in the direction of Quine's discomfort with it) to find "no element of rational necessity" in the predilection for truth that Saadiah ascribes to rationality, one can only wonder who exactly is equivocating.

Fox goes on to quote Nietzsche's "shattering question" about why we should prefer truth to falsehood. He suggests that anyone who is "offended" by the suggestion that "reason" might just as well have chosen falsehood is merely expressing arbitrary prejudices, since "There is nothing internally contradictory about the assertion that truth is bad and falsehood good." Saadiah "offers us no ground" for treating a preference for the truth as on a par with the law of contradiction.[35] But if we recall Aristotle's thoughts in the *Metaphysics* (IV 4) about the law of contradiction, we can see its affinity to our preference for truth. For both are too basic to be proved without a question-begging dependence on thoughts that will in turn depend on them. So both must be treated as truths of reason, in the important sense that nothing can be used to prove them; yet we cannot do without them, unless we are to avoid all claims—on the specious premise that everything must be proved. But even that presupposes the pertinence of making truth claims and has no value if the quest for truth is abandoned. Aristotle gave as good a dialectical argument as there is in support of the law of contradiction when he showed how those who might like to scrap it reduce themselves to silence. The same argument serves equally for truth: one can indeed be quite uninterested in truth, but one certainly cannot *say so*—least of all while professing to discredit specific philosophical views.

Turning to the *mitzvot*, Fox surveys Saadiah's applications of the concept of rationality and writes that here "the difficulties increase dramatically." He finds in Saadiah "a variety of cases in which he asserts that something is required by reason, but none of them is a case that on examination meets the standards of rational necessity he himself has set."[36] In other words, Fox presses his equivocation. It might behoove us, in the interest of charity—or science—to watch Saadiah when he takes the idea of reason beyond the analytic. But Fox's charity runs out after he writes in a parenthetical preterition, "It is needless to add that we do not want to subject a tenth-century philosopher to criticisms concerning analyticity or essentiality that are familiar to contemporary philosophers." Since the rule of charity is a hermeneutical and heuristic principle and not just a matter of compassion, those who fail to extend it are themselves the losers. Saadiah can no longer profit from our indulgence. But if we can learn from philosophers who are not Quine, we might also learn from philosophers who are not Carnap.

Observing that Saadiah assigns to reason the principle that earned benefits exceed those that come solely by grace or favor, Fox writes, "Saadiah labels as a rational judgment that which cannot qualify as such by any known standard, unless he uses the term 'rational' very loosely to mean something like 'reasonable' in the sense of 'based on widespread experience.'" But how many "known standards" of rationality did Fox try before reaching this global conclusion? Consider what we know about Saadiah: he took creation to be an absolute act of grace, representing infinite generosity because it answered to no prior desert.[37] Why could he not regard the reward reserved to the righteous in the hereafter, which he took to be vouched for by God's justice,[38] as even greater, since it involves eternal bliss, whereas creation, which expresses infinite bounty, gives us only a finite existence whose sufferings, by Saadiah's account, are never overbalanced by joys?[39]

Saadiah does not deduce infinite requitals from the disproportion of earned to unearned deserts. For that would show us only that the requitals of the hereafter exceed those familiar here, not that they are infinite. Rather, his premise is that there are specific actions and passions, acts of kindness, sufferings of innocence, and crimes as well, whose moral significance far exceeds the limits of retributions in this world. Paradigmatically, martyrdom and multiple murder hold transcendent moral significance. Such acts and sufferings, he argues, given God's justice, can only be requited in the infinite hereafter. Saadiah's key premise here comes from his moral intuitions and plainly extends far beyond the reach of common sense or "widespread experience." His comparisons of finitude and infinitude may sound somewhat mechanical and arithmetic, but the problem is not in Saadiah's idea of rationality but in our human reliance on arithmetic imagery to express moral and spiritual truths. Glossing Isa. 55:9 ("High as the heavens are above the earth, so high are My ways above your ways and My thoughts above your thoughts"), Saadiah writes: "The Allwise says that His ways, in goodness and generosity, are higher and loftier than the beneficence and grace bestowed by creatures, as the heavens are above the earth—not to suggest and end at that limit. On the contrary, He symbolizes His generosity by reference to the heavens only because our senses can reach no higher."[40]

In holding that merit rises higher than favor alone could bring us, Saadiah is moved in part by the idea of the authenticity of existence. He argues strenuously that life is not a joke, a tasteless hoax at man's expense, a cheap, empty, or pointless charade. His argument hinges on his claims about man's reward and the earnestness of the human situation, and it is such thoughts, I believe, that lead him to insist that life must be lived through and cannot be morally short-circuited, since only here, in our temporal existence, with all its vulnerabilities, do we choose and so exercise our own, existential character as living persons.[41] Saadiah is moved as well, perhaps, by related thoughts, that Christians or Muslims rely excessively on grace and too little on the human moral appropriation of responsibility that the Rabbis called assumption of the yoke of the kingdom of heaven. But the basis of his claim for the *infinite* superiority of earned deserts to sheer favors is the recognition (which he best represents by the scriptural image of the light sown for the righteous) that the Torah and its *mitzvot* open a window on transcendence for us. Even the act of creation, a pure expression of God's grace, did not fully do that but only made actual the subject and the arena of testing from which that higher reach can be attempted: God not only created us but also gave us the Torah (cf. Mishnah *Avot* 3.18), which is something more, as Fox surely would acknowledge.

Fox goes on to criticize Saadiah for saying that capital punishment, among other penalties, is a demand of reason. This seems to him to mean that Saadiah is (equivocating by) taking reason in a conventional sense as something fallible and corrigible. For Fox assumes that capital punishment is notoriously problematic, since in our own times it is controversial and since he finds Saadiah arguing for it by analogy: just as we sacrifice a limb to save the body, so reason dictates that we sacrifice one member to save a whole society from corruption—"analogical argument is the basic form of all probability claims, but it certainly cannot lead to conclusions that a rational man must affirm as necessarily true."[42] But analogical arguments can lead to conclusions that any rational person must accept as true, *if that person accepts the aptness of the analogy*. Further, arguments from analogy are often effective as a teaching device, because they reveal a formal structure without reliance on too purely abstract a repertoire of concepts. The crucial point, however, is not that Saadiah had a right to use analogy in bringing to the surface what he took to be the rationality of the Torah's use of capital punishment, but that we must distinguish our own sense of controversy about such issues from Saadiah's sense that, once understood, they would be transparent. Saadiah might differ with some moderns about what reason requires here without using an untenable or inconsistent idea of reason itself. But his argument hinges on what he takes to be objective interests in the individual or the body politic, not on formal claims about consistency and inconsistency: Saadiah does not think that disagreement about capital punishment will survive clear understanding of it. If one knows that life is more precious than limb, as Saadiah thought any rational person would,[43] and if one knows that to execute, say, a murderer for the crime of murder is in no relevant way different from sacrificing a limb to preserve a life, then one does know *by reason* that capital punishment is justified. To disagree one would have to dispute the aptness of the analogy. Formally, the reasoning is impeccable, although Saadiah does rely on reason for material appraisals of the value of life and limb, just as he did to recognize higher values, when he spoke of God's recompense as better than survival in the world. All analogical reasoning is based on likeness; its weakness in generating formal schemata reflects the possibility of disagreement about what likenesses are pertinent. But disagreements over apt or inept comparisons do not vitiate the soundness of an argument based on an apt comparison.

Fox criticizes Saadiah for holding that requital of benefits, rejection of insult and abuse, and restraint of wrongdoing (or injury, in the rendering Fox prefers) are dictates of reason, when these are plainly not "logically necessary or required by a correct metaphysical understanding of the essences of things, since their contraries are not self-contradictory."[44] But Saadiah takes reason to be alive to these axioms of his because he does not share the radical empiricist assumption that reason can have no material content and does not regard the being of things as making no legitimate claims. In his thinking, reason can be attuned to theses about value because reason is, at bottom, an intuitive recognition of specific values or goods, the idea vividly exemplified in Saadiah's thesis about our immediate attachment to the truth.[45]

Perhaps Fox is so thoroughly imbued with the spirit of radical empiricism or naturalism that he finds the very idea of a material or valuative content for reason foreign to his thinking. But to impose an alien view on a philosopher is not to find a flaw in that thinker's coherence, nor is it to "try to see and understand" his views "in their own context." It is merely to equivocate; as the schoolmen put it, to quibble over terms. The question whether rational judgments can have a material content is not settled by the bias of radical empiricists. The arguments of Leibniz, Kant, and Plato about the role of the a priori in our scientific thought and everyday experience remain unanswered. Philosophers still dispute whether logical or mathematical theorems deal with objective facts and whether such claims can be made without rational intuitions, or even ontological commitments. Saadiah plainly thought that reason has a material and valuative content. If Fox has arguments to refute this view and silence the Platonic legacy, he has not included them in his dismissive remarks about Saadiah. And if his arguments succeed, he then must face the question, What can it mean for a theist to speak of the *mitzvot* as acquiring (absolute, transrational?) authority from their being commanded by God? If God is absolute, can he be known except by reason, material reason, of just the kind that Fox disavows? Fox may say that he knows God by faith or that he does not know God at all. I'm not sure what it means to speak of faith as if it were a way of knowing—making it, in effect, both the warrant and the content of a claim to truth, and making it impossible in principle, as Saadiah seeks to do, to discriminate critically among divergent claims upon our credence. I find it easier to understand what Saadiah meant by calling reason a way of knowing. But that Saadiah had an answer to questions about what reason knows and that it was not the answer of a radical empiricist or a stark naturalist[46] does not make it incoherent.

Fox links Saadiah's views on rational knowledge of truths about values with theories of moral sentiment and intuition. He argues that intuitionism would make moral standards "completely contingent," a position that Saadiah "regards as absurd." But the claim that we have moral knowledge is not coextensive with those theories of moral sentiment that regard our moral notions as mere opinions or feelings and in no way commits Saadiah to subjectivism. Nor, of course, are all moral intuitionists subjectivists or relativists. The most prominent form of moral intuitionism in Saadiah's time, as in the twentieth century, was realist and objectivist.[47]

After attempting to reduce Saadiah to sentimentalist or subjective intuitionism on no stronger warrant than his appeal to a notion of moral knowledge, Fox attempts to reduce him to utilitarianism, because he offers justifications or explanations of various laws in terms of the benefits they afford. Does not Saadiah support the prohibition of murder and fornication by arguing that murder is destructive of human life and that fornication puts us on a par with the beasts, letting no man know his own father so as to honor him or receive his legacy? "What we have here," Fox announces, "is only a hypothetical imperative, whose necessity is simply rooted in the rule of reason that one who chooses an end is bound by reason to choose the means that are requisite for its realization. There is no necessity whatsoever in these ends, and hence they do not bind us categorically. A utilitarian view of rational morality is no stronger or more binding than the ends it recommends. Whoever finds these ends attractive will be constrained to choose these commandments as means, but no man *qua* rational must necessarily find these ends binding on him."[48]

But knowing that the end does not always justify the means—especially if they are means that taint the end they serve—does not commit one to abandoning the pursuit of ends by means. Besides, one can certainly believe that murder is wrong intrinsically and still argue that it is wrong consequentially as well. An appeal to harms and benefits is helpful in talking morals with those who may not be sympathetic toward one's ideas about intrinsic rights or wrongs. Such an appeal to consequences *is* dialectical. That is how it opens grounds for discourse and potential for conviction of those who do not share all of Saadiah's premises. But it does not commit him to reducing the commandments to their alleged "functions" or cashing out moral rules as prudential maxims. On the contrary, as we saw in chapter 5, Saadiah argues at length that no one isolated good suffices for the good life and that choice of any one good in preference to the rest leads to an obsessive, destructive, radically incomplete existence, which only the Torah's inspired arbitership among competing goods can adequately overcome. By making the Torah the arbiter among values, Saadiah assigns it the same role Plato gave reason in the *Republic* and wise legislation in the *Laws*. His position is compatible with a broad eudaimonism but radically incompatible with utilitarianism or any other reductive teleology, since it finds no common denominator among the diverse goods that compete for our attention and indeed rejects the very possibility of such a single common coin.

One might suppose that Saadiah's ethics differs from utilitarianism only in its pluralism and so remains a reductive naturalism. But when he treats our disparate ends as incommensurable and refers their disputes to a transcendent standard, he has lifted ethics out of any reductive naturalism. The higher standards God teaches in the Torah are the same as those to which Saadiah argues that God-given reason grants us partial access. But even these higher aims need not reduce the value of the *mitzvot* to that of the ends they serve. For these specific means may be of the essence: How do we respect human dignity without laws against murder, adultery, rape, and incest? How do we honor God or show him gratitude without the means that God, in Saadiah's view, specified through prophecy as proper and appropriate?

Fox goes on to accuse Saadiah of reducing wisdom to the Greek idea of *techne* and omitting all reference to the speculative. The charge is, of course, untrue: even in the two pages Fox cites from the Rosenblatt translation[49] Saadiah leans on "the speculative method," and lists astronomy and cosmology along with the practical sciences among humankind's distinctions. But Saadiah's theme, in mentioning these sciences and the arts that spring from them, including the art of government, is not reduction of reason to *techne* but demonstration of human dignity in terms broad enough to convince even those who deem the achievements of speculative reason problematic. Saadiah takes his cue here from the sort of discussions that we find reflected in the writings of his younger contemporaries the Ikhwān al-Safā', where human superiority rests not on our vaunted skills, intelligence, or cultural achievements but on our being subject to divinely imposed obligations and responsibilities.[50] Rather than contrast the achievements of human practical and speculative intelligence with the special dignity of such obligations, as the Ikhwān do, Saadiah sees in human reason marks of the appropriateness of revelation: human attainments make it only fitting that humanity alone is "subject to commandments and prohibitions, reward and punishment." The theme is an ancient one, a mainstay of the humanist tradition, revived in the Renaissance and Enlightenment by thinkers from Pico to Fichte, Mendelssohn, and Kant under the rubrics of the dignity and vocation of man. Saadiah's treatment, notably, rests human dignity not on technical achievements but on moral insight and responsibility. He argues, much as Kant and Mendelssohn will, from the access Fox discounts, of reason to higher values. Kant, who is the source of Fox's expectation that morals should reach beyond the prudential, will single out practical reason as an exception to the empiricist bent of his tale of the understanding, giving morals a rational grounding through the ideas of freedom, dignity, the moral law, and the pure ideal of reason. But, as readers of Kant know, there are no categorical imperatives unless reason can progress beyond analysis.

Turning to the revealed commandments, Fox writes as if it were inconsistent of Saadiah to ascribe them to God, and again inconsistent for him to find any practical value in them. But Saadiah's position is simply the Rabbinic one that our insight into what is valuable is limited and that God's grace shows us more about what we must do than unaided human reason would discern. Fox ridicules Saadiah's rationales for the laws about incest, as though the purported inadequacy of his account somehow proved the folly of reason. But scientists do not abandon the presumption of nature's intelligibility merely because they have found, repeatedly, that specific models prove inadequate or incomplete. Anthropologists and social theorists have sought for centuries to comprehend the aim or end or wisdom behind the all but universal prohibition of incest.[51] Their disagreements and divergences of expression do not invalidate the inquiry. And the purported failure of Saadiah's Rabbinically inspired efforts (*Yevamot* 37b) to account for the Torah's incest laws in terms of such familiar values as rejection of dissoluteness or development of a workable mating system does not undermine his larger thesis that there is wisdom in such laws beyond what humans might have planned.

In a recent book Fox argues that we may *appreciate* the rationality of the commandments once we know them, but we could never have anticipated them, that is, derived them a priori.[52] But even in science, when rationalists claim that the workings of the world are reasonable or intelligible they rarely mean that we could have anticipated the laws of nature a priori, and I doubt if any believe that we could have anticipated these laws without awareness of their terms or the concrete evidence behind them.[53] If today's wide-ranging social theories are so far from shared understanding of as basic a norm as the incest prohibition, it seems reasonable to agree that a world legislative assembly could hardly have drafted such a prohibition out of the whole cloth. But that is just Saadiah's point in arguing that the rational basis of some laws may elude us and that specification of their modalities is not obvious from their general concerns.

Fox accuses Saadiah of inconsistency for holding that God revealed to us through prophecy the manner in which we should worship him, and for seeming to imply that in such cases—perhaps in *all* cases—we see aspects of the rational basis of the Law only after it is revealed. This Fox pillories as an "appeal to the authority of revelation"[54]–as though Saadiah's allegiance to reason somehow excluded revelation. But the dichotomy between reason and revelation is Fox's, not Saadiah's. When Saadiah affirms that we know the Law in its fullness through revelation but accept prophecy itself not simply on the basis of miracles but by recognizing the veracity of its teaching (*ED* III 8), Fox senses inconsistency once again. Yet this is just the biblical obligation to reject false prophets (Deut. 13), which depends, as Saadiah sees, on our critical capacities: a self-proclaimed prophet who commands us to commit adultery, he argues (and today, at least, the case is not purely hypothetical), should be rejected as decisively as if he had commanded us to accept falsehood and reject truth.

Pressing further his claims as to the arbitrariness of human reason, Fox takes Saadiah's words to mean "approval of lying" and "disapproval of truth," but the sense is better captured in our idiom of calling black white and white black. Maimonides, we recall,[55] says that Moses hesitated at the burning bush because he expected the Israelites to question his vocation, and *rightly so* (*Guide* I 63). The Torah itself (Deut. 18:22) makes truth the final test of prophecy and urges us not to stand in awe of a prophet whose words are false. *Sifre* (178) sees here a positive obligation to speak out against imposture. Since veracity is the ultimate criterion (*Sanhedrin* 89a) and prophets are moral teachers, Saadiah relies on our God-given reason for an acid test: immoral teachings prove imposture. We can see here the obverse of the Rabbinic claim to prophetic authority.[56] For, while the Rabbis did not share the Prophets' visions and disavowed miracles and oracles as anchors of their authority, they took in a strong sense the admonition of Deuteronomy (18:15) "unto him shall ye harken" and reasoned that they would not lack the mantle of prophecy if they used their reason to expand the Law, within the parameters laid out by prophetic inspiration (*Shabbat* 135a, *Bava Batra* 110b). Wisdom, then, remains the hallmark of divine authority.[57] If we abdicate our critical intelligence, we will not be closer to God's absolute will but simply morally adrift.

As Saadiah explains, still echoing Deuteronomy (13:2–4), signs and wonders can vindicate a claim to prophecy only if it meets the test of reason: "If Reuben and Simon come before a judge, and Reuben claims, say, that Simon owes him a thousand dirhems, the judge will ask for evidence; if it holds up, the money is due. But if he claims something absurd, as it were, 'He owes me the Tigris river,' his claim is null and void, since no one has title to the Tigris, and the judge may not call for evidence on the matter."[58] Maimonides, accordingly, interprets the admonition not to listen to a prophet who commands idolatry (Deut. 13:4) as meaning that one should neither argue nor seek signs from him (*Code* I iv 5.7). For the idea that anything less than the Absolute is worthy of worship is repugnant to reason and cannot be shored up by argument or evidence. Not that dialectic is abandoned. But, as Aristotle saw, rejection of truth itself makes discussion impossible. For Maimonides that means rejection of God's absoluteness.[59] For Saadiah it means rejection of basic moral principles.

At the core of the faith of Abraham, as I have argued throughout this book, God and the good are inextricably intertwined. It is not an analytic truth (until our posits make it such) that no one owns the Tigris, that God is not a stock or stone, that permission of adultery and incest is alien to his law. Yet Saadiah, who was a judge, knows that one cannot try a case without discerning rational from irrational claims—or understand the Torah without bringing to the task a basic human grasp of right and wrong, true and false, black and white—an understanding open to learning and growth but not so open as to take any law to be as sound as any other, any claim to be defensible, or any hunk of metal to be the God of Abraham.

Fox's strictures on Saadiah's idea of the complementarity of reason and revelation rest on a fallacy all too frequent in Jewish studies. A sharp dichotomy is set up, and any thinker who bridges it is charged with inconsistency or confusion. Beyond this, we note a methodological problem. Wherever Fox professes himself mystified by Saadiah's meaning, he has stuck closely to the passage at hand. A hermeneutical counsel that Saadiah offers and obeys might yield a more sympathetic understanding: seek elsewhere in the canon glossed. That is the method behind the artful homilies of the Rabbis, and Saadiah elevates it to a science. But Fox's object, it seems, was not sympathetic understanding but expression of pique, aimed ultimately not at Saadiah but at the phantom of reason.

Why and how did reason become an enemy rather than an ally or a tool? The familiar answer from our Jewish legal positivists[60] is that commandments that have reasons are too readily reduced to their purported aims and then dismissed with the claim that the same ends can be achieved by other means.[61] I am rather dubious of the premise that the aims of the commandments are so readily reached by other means, although in some cases that may be so. But, since the fear is so often voiced, one should say that we do not bolster the *mitzvot* or their standing in the life of Israel by treating them as arbitrary dictates. If the choice of the life they prescribe is arbitrary, and so as sound as any other, so is the decision to reject them. Many members of the American immigrant generation were given no more grounds than the authority of tradition for cleaving to the *mitzvot*, and many of them and their offspring rapidly found other lifestyles and traditions that were at least as appealing. Only the claims of rationality—problematic as they sometimes seem in beings of limited wisdom, and always to be distinguished from any mere caricature of reason—can warrant preferring one way of life to another. If that choice is not always as obvious as Saadiah hopes, neither is it ever quite as arbitrary as Fox fears. Thinkers who feel in themselves an allegiance to the life proposed by the Torah are well advised to seek and voice the sense in which wisdom can be found in it, in human terms that they can communicate to their children or spouses, just as those who wonder whether there is wisdom in the life of the Torah are well advised to study the closely concatenated chain of tradition in which a version of such wisdom is elaborated—not always in terms immediately reducible to the most current fashions but for that very reason all the more informative and enlightening.

The Rationality of the Commandments According to the Rabbis

The ritual laws of the Torah represent a challenge to the rationalist philosopher—not an anomaly but a matter worthy and deserving of reflection and explanation. Although no one genuinely committed to the project of reason believes that an explanation replaces what it explains, I would like to offer an explanation here not of the Torah's ritual laws but of the relationship of the rational to the ritual as categories that the Torah and other systems of law deploy. But first I want to look back at the Rabbinic discussions that Fox excludes from his discussion of Saadiah and then at the manner in which Maimonides refined and elaborated Saadiah's thinking on this subject.

The classic proof-text for the distinction of rational from ritual commandments is a talmudic remark apropos Lev. 18:4: "My ordinances shall ye perform, and My statutes shall ye keep and follow; I am the Lord your God." Guided by the exegetical presumption that there is no redundancy in the Law, the Sages seek distinct nuances in the terms *mishpatai* and *ḥukkotai*, "My ordinances" and "My statutes": *Mishpatai* were "things which, had they not been written, it would be a religious duty to write them"; *ḥukkotai*, "items which Satan and the nations of the world malign" (*Yoma* 67b). Rationalists rejoice in this passage, because its rhetoric suggests that some commandments are so vital that it would have been imperative to institute them, even if it meant altering the Torah! But Jewish legal positivists, apprehensive that a penchant for naturalism might alight here, argue rightly that the passage in no way implies that human reason, working unaided, could have deduced the substance of the commandments. Fox points to another talmudic text that quotes R. Yoḥanan as saying: "If the Torah had not been given, we might have learned modesty from the cat, not to rob from the ant, chastity from the dove, solicitude toward our wives from the cock" (*Eruvin* 100b). Noting the parallel with the admonitions of Proverbs (6:6–8, 30:25–31) that we can learn from the behavior of animals, Fox adds:

> Neither the biblical nor the talmudic statements suppose that man would by himself have known what is good. Rather, having been taught by the divine commandments to know good and evil, man can now look with admiration at certain animals which instinctively live in accordance with some of these divine patterns. By choosing to imitate these animals, natural man can make his life somewhat more decent and tolerable than it would be otherwise. By such imitation alone he could never arrive at ideas of obligation or commandment, certainly not at a theory of natural moral law. . . . If there were no antecedent standard, how would man have known which animals to imitate? How would he have been able to decide that the chastity of the dove rather than the sexual habits of the rabbit were the appropriate model?[62]

All this is sound, and one could go further. For *Yoma* 67b offers the laws against idolatry, incest, bloodshed, robbery, and blasphemy as model *ordinances*. Three of the five are ritual commandments by conventional standards. The model *statutes* prohibit eating pork or wearing fabrics of mixed linen and wool (*shaatnez*; Deut. 22:11, specifying the "mixed gender" of Lev. 19:19) and institute release from levirate marriage (*ḥalitzah*), the purifications of "leprosy" (*metzorah*), and the rites of the scapegoat (Lev. 16:7–10). But levirate marriage has a social purpose clearly stated in the Torah: that the name of a childless brother not be blotted out in Israel (Deut. 25:5–10). The purpose of release is also explicit: some surviving brothers will be unable or unwilling to marry the widow.[63] Obviously one cannot deduce the concrete requirements of a law a priori. But that is as true of laws against bloodshed and theft as of dietary or marriage laws.

Every law needs specificity and demands some reliable grasp of its aims and coverage. Readers of the English Bible who imagine that one of the Ten Commandments reads "Thou shalt not kill!" often have worries about war or even animal life that are ungrounded in the Decalogue. Knowing that the Hebrew text forbids murder, not "killing," eases some of the confusion. Knowing how to discriminate murder from manslaughter (Num. 35:16–25) clears up more. But to apply any law, we need access to the values it intends, delimits, and assigns pragmatic significances.

In the task of interpretation and the legislative work that inevitably accompanies it, we are hampered enough by the ambiguities and the complexities of human situations that we need all the help we can get. To set tradition and reason, the authority of revelation and the counsel of understanding, at odds with one another is poor strategy. A priori formalism could never deduce the objects, let alone the contents, of any law. But neither could sheer fiats ever be specific enough to give prescriptive guidance to an insistent mechanical literalism. As Saadiah makes crystal clear, even with "bloodshed" and "robbery" we need context and tradition to demarcate what is proscribed. No sheerly positive text can do this. Even revelation, no matter how explicit, gives no guidance unless we know how to evaluate its aims.

When Fox says we would not know whether to take our moral lessons from the bonding of doves or the promiscuity of rabbits, what makes his argument sound is its appeal to values: mere behavior provides no moral instruction, let alone any idea of obligation. But neither can sheer fiat. We must know what issues deserve concern, and we need some means of weighing their relative importance. Part of the task of any legal code is to make that clear—just as the rules of a game are incomplete until we know the object of the game and how to tell when we have won or lost, or are playing worse or better. Saadiah is helpful here, since his idea of reason and the aims it can find in the Law are not narrow and reductive but broad and open to what the Torah itself will teach—not just in prescriptions but in precepts, principles that define areas of normative concern. Having illustrated rational laws by the prohibitions against homicide, fornication, theft, and lying, he writes: "I observe that some people suppose that these four classes of depravity are not objectionable at all. They deem objectionable only what is painful or worrisome to them; for them the good is confined to what is pleasant and restful to them. . . . But to slay an enemy is pleasure to the slayer but pain to the victim, and seizing another's property or spouse is pleasure to the taker but pain to the loser. So on this view the same act will be both wise and foolish at once."[64] The seeming rationality of an Epicurean egoistic hedonism[65] is made hopelessly incoherent by the narrowness of its moral horizons.

Not just the egoism but the narrowness is at fault. Saadiah can warrant what he takes to be a biblical abomination for lying by arguing that lies distort reality and bring conflict and ugliness into the soul.[66] The appeal to conflict echoes Plato's idea of justice as integration and anticipates Kant's (ultimately Socratic) claim that lying embeds a contradiction between the aims of communication and those of deception. But the reference to ugliness also suggests that lying is an insult to creation. The argument is ingenious, perhaps informed by the midrashic charge that when Job cursed his day he "defaced God's coinage"—that is, in wishing himself dead, he insulted God's image, which he bore: since all creation bears God's stamp, any lie is an ugly affront to God.[67] Saadiah offers similar rationales for each commandment he discusses in this context, not all as ingenious as this one but none, in the nature of the case, simply utilitarian.

I cite this discussion not to commend or condemn the particulars of Saadiah's *ta'amei ha-mitzvot*, nor to pile up further arguments against the notion that his rationalism makes him a utilitarian. Rather, I want to point out that Saadiah can explain why (and when!) lying is wrong, where a strict utilitarian cannot. He does not approach the Torah with an a priori notion of the goods a law might serve but lets the text inform and enlarge his idea of the good. This is the inductive method he learned from the practice of the Arab grammarians and Hebrew philologists, who guided his higher education.[68] It is a method far more open to a presumptively revealed text than any reading that assumes we know exactly what the categories are that the text must address. Yet it does not require setting aside everything *or anything* we know before turning to the text. Indeed, such know-nothingism, besides being self-deceiving, is crippling to an exegetical encounter. Saadiah's hermeneutics, rather, depends on putting all that we know into dialogue with what we read. But he does not begin to read only after concluding that the work of reason is finished.

What the Sages highlight when they speak of what it would be obligatory to add to the Torah, had it been left out, are not laws that could have been drafted a priori as distinguished from laws that our wildest dreams could never have anticipated. For no laws can be deduced a priori, and many can be drafted arbitrarily, without the least color of inspiration—to express sheer positive authority, particularity, or a sense of belonging, like a secret handshake. No one can say that the objects of the laws against incest are clear a priori. Yet neither are the laws of *ḥalitzah* so arcane that no human mind could have anticipated their purposes.

But if the distinction between *ḥukkim* and *mishpatim* is not a matter of a priori deduction versus arbitrary fiat, still less are the Sages distinguishing laws that serve some utility from those that have none. Rather, at issue are laws whose aims are so central to what is right, and to the objects of the Torah, that it could not be conceived as God's law without them. From these we must distinguish laws whose purposes are remote enough from the central foci of human moral concern or the manifest objects of the Torah that hostile critics (the adversary or *saṭan*[69]) or persons alien to the Torah's methods (the nations) might not see the good in them and might subject them to obloquy or ridicule. The biblical prohibitions of blasphemy, idolatry, and incest are all ritual commandments in that they seek to regulate our use of symbolism by assigning cosmic significances to elemental human actions and relations. But that makes them central thematically to the Torah; its normative scheme would be inconceivable without them. The laws of levirate marriage and *ḥalitzah* serve purposes, too. They belong to the weave of biblical legislation. But to outside observers or unsympathetic critics their purposes seem (or can be made to seem) arcane or obscure; their means, arbitrary and irrational. The point is not that no purposes are in play but that the Law itself must define, delineate, and modulate them. Those who regard the familiar as intelligible and the unfamiliar as absurd will naturally have trouble with such laws, until acculturated to the language they speak and the frame of reference they evoke. Then the risk is that they will be unable to criticize or modulate them further.

The locus classicus for Jewish legal positivism is a remark of Rav's (ca. 175–247) quoted in Genesis Rabbah (44.1): "What does it matter to the Holy One blessed be He whether one kills a beast by slitting its throat or chopping off its head? The point is to refine man." Positivists seize upon the passage to show that the commandments are arbitrary fiats. But that claim twists the language and ignores the background of the remark, violating both text and context. Textually Rav is quoted a propos the sense of "refine" in 2 Sam. 22:31, where God's words and the Torah are what refine us. Contextually, as Urbach showed, Rav's words echo Rabbi Akiba's (ca. 45–135) response to the Roman Rufus Turnus, who asked "Why is not the infant born circumcised?" Akiba's reply: "Because the Holy One, blessed be He, gave Israel the commandments only to refine us." Rav generalizes and so thematizes the point:[70] the biblical term *tzerufah*, refinement, means not an arbitrary but an improving discipline.

The image is drawn from the assaying of silver and other precious metals, where each trial or proof removes more dross and yields a purer and more precious sample. Naḥmanides explains: "The commandments were given 'to purify men'—to make them like refined silver. For one who refines silver does not act arbitrarily or capriciously, but to remove any impurity. So the *mitzvot* serve to eliminate from our hearts all evil belief, to alert us to the truth and remind us of it continually. . . . The benefit accrues not to God . . . but to us—to inure us in compassion . . . form a soul that is purified and refined, so making us wise and alive to the truth."[71] The imagery was pointedly apposite, since Jews suffered for their loyalty to the commandments: God's discipline made the sufferers all the more precious.[72] To see here not an assay but an arbitrary imposition would only twist the knife and ignore the problematic that elicits the argument—which is, we note, an argument from analogy. The problem posed arises from God's transcendence: "What does it matter to the Holy One blessed be He . . ." The assumption is that it does matter, for the commandments *were* given. There must have been some good reason. The most general reason: to perfect the recipients, who are made better by the life of the *mitzvot* than by the bare fact of creation.[73]

Can a law refine us by demanding sheer deference to authority? Perhaps that would be a virtue in Plato's "auxiliaries," who need no judgment of their own to act, since they are mere fictive men, abstract emblems of Plato's functional analysis of human ends. But not in red-blooded human beings and still less in a people chosen to become a kingdom of priests and a holy nation. Every symbol contains something of the arbitrary, if only to differentiate it from its object and to signal that it is a symbol and not unmeaning behavior. But symbols address intelligence and invite efforts at understanding. We understand, as we learn, by recreating significances, not simply recording them. So we shall never find allegiance, as opposed to mimicry, in mere behavior. And behavior alone never amounts to morals.

Admirers of authority sometimes forget that the idea is generic, not specific; much depends on what kind of authority one questions or respects. Discipline, similarly, is a means to an end, not an end in itself. One must always ask: Discipline for what, or against what? The Rabbis say "against lapses and in behalf of holiness." Thus Rabbi Eliezer ben Jacob said, "Whoever has tefillin on his head and arm, fringes on his garment, a mezuzah at his door, is secure against lapse, as it is said, 'A threefold cord is not soon broken' (Eccles. 4:12)" (*Menaḥot* 43b). And *Mekhilta de-Rabbi Ishmael* glosses the text calling the Sabbath, "a holiness to you," as teaching that the Sabbath enhances Israel's holiness. The early Amora Rabbi Hama ben Ḥanina elicits the thesis that the *ḥukkim* were given to refine our character from a fanciful etymology: "They are graven (*ḥakukim*) on the inclination."[74]

Urbach finds two streams of Rabbinic thought as to the sense or savor of the *mitzvot*: they were given to enhance our reward, or they were given to refine us.[75] Saadiah conjoins these streams, arguing that observance enhances our reward *and* our being, lightening and brightening the soul. His synthesis springs from the recognition that our reward is not an extrinsic response to arbitrary acts but the very purification that observance effects. This idea is no radical invention of Saadiah's. It is the nisus of the Torah itself, discerned through his inductive surveys of the commandments and their biblical rationales, and summed up in the Torah's promise that the commandments will make us holy and godlike. Thus the Rabbinic contention that the reward of one mitzvah is the power to fulfill another, that "one mitzvah draws another in its train" (*Avot* 4.2). The commandments can be compact with their rewards because they are not random behaviors but constituents in the good life.[76] If God's commands were arbitrary, the power to fulfill more of them would be at best a token reward. But Saadiah can say that the mitzvot strengthen the soul in the Aristotelian sense of fostering its virtues and in the Platonic sense of purifying and clarifying its substance, enhancing its capabilities (and its deserts) for eternal bliss.

Maimonides' Development of Saadiah's Position

Maimonides, we have seen, is often critical of Saadiah, not usually by name—just as Saadiah himself avoids naming the Midrashic source he castigates for assuming that angels once consorted with mortal women.[77] In introducing his commentary to *Avot*, the Rambam criticizes "Certain of our modern scholars who were infected with the illness of the *Mutakallimūn*" for calling 'rational' those commandments that the ancient Sages said it would have been an obligation to write, had they not been included in the Torah. Those Sages, Maimonides insists, preferred the word *mitzvot* to distinguish this category from God's statutes, *ḥukkotai* (Lev. 18:4), which the Satan and the nations of the world assail. The criticism, it has long been noted, is directed to Saadiah. But the critique is semantic: Maimonides objects to calling some commandments rational because it suggests that the rest are not, a view, as we have seen, that Saadiah never held.

Saadiah's actual distinction is not rejected. Maimonides uses it even as he criticizes Saadiah's misleading terminology. Reverting to *Yoma* 67b, he contrasts the laws of the red heifer and the scapegoat with those against homicide, robbery, larceny, fraud, and bodily injury, to dissolve an aporia between a Peripatetic preference for virtue over self-restraint and the Rabbinic promise that rewards are proportioned to the temptation overcome (cf. *Avot* 5.26). The Aristotelian view, he argues, applies to recognized vices; the Rabbinic view, to the positive laws (*shimi'im*, echoing Saadiah's term). It is here that a sense of creatureliness and duty has its proper place, he argues, citing a Rabbinic dictum: "One should not say, 'I do not desire to eat milk and meat together' or 'I do not care to wear clothes of mixed wool and linen,' or 'I find no attraction in a consanguineous union'; rather one should say, 'I do want it, but my Father in heaven has forbidden it'" (*Sifra* to Lev. 20:26). But when it comes to acknowledged virtues and vices, "There is no doubt that a soul which longs and clamors for any of these is deficient." So, "Both views"—that is, Rabbinic deontology and Aristotelian virtue ethics—"are correct, and there is no contradiction between them."[78] The distinction, then: "Those commandments whose utility is plain to the masses are called ordinances (*mishpatim*); those whose benefits are unclear to the masses are called statutes (*ḥukkim*)."[79] The definition is Saadiah's.

Specifically addressing legal positivism, Maimonides writes:

> Some people think it dreadful to give grounds for any of the laws. They would like it best if no intelligible sense were found in any injunction or prohibition. What drives them to this position is a malaise they find in themselves but cannot articulate or adequately express. They suppose that if these laws afford any benefit in this existence of ours or were legislated for the sake of this or that purpose, they might as well have originated from the insights and opinions of any intelligent being. But if they are a thing with no intelligible significance and lead to no benefit whatever, they must surely come from God—since none would be the outcome of any human thought process. For these feeble intellects, it is as if man were higher than his Creator. For it is man who speaks and acts purposefully, while the deity does not but simply orders us to do things of no benefit to us and forbids us to do things of no harm to us. Exalted be He, and exalted further still above such notions! In reality, just the opposite is the case, as we have shown (*Guide* III 25, 27, 28) and as

> is made clear by the words, "As a good for us each day, to keep us in life as we are today" (Deut. 6:24), and "who shall hear all these statutes and say, 'Surely this great people is a wise and discerning nation'" (Deut. 4:6). It states explicitly that even the statutes (*ḥukkim*), all of them, will manifest to all nations the wisdom and discernment in which they are conceived. If the laws have no knowable, rational ground, afford no benefit and forestall no harm, then why is it said of one who professes or performs them that he is wise and discerning and so manifestly worthy that the nations will think it remarkable? Rather, as we said, each of the 613 commandments most certainly does serve either to instill a sound belief or remove an unsound one or impart a rule of equity or eliminate inequity, inculcate good character traits or guard against those that are vicious. (*Guide* III 31)

Even at his most critical, then, Maimonides builds on Saadiah's work and strengthens his claims. He expands on Saadiah's approach to the rationality of the commandments by developing three distinctions present in Saadiah only in embryo: (1) between the general purpose of a law and its specific means, (2) between acts and virtues, and (3) between God's ultimate, inscrutable purposes and his proximate aims for humanity, which we can know and which we do find served in the Torah.

1. Where Saadiah argues that human reason captures only a smattering of the rational aims of the ritual commandments, Maimonides follows Saadiah's qualitative rather than his quantitative differentiation. He relies on the same Aristotelian distinction between means and ends that he used to find organic unity in the Torah, taking his cue from Saadiah's challenge to the Karaites about the need for specificity in legislation. It is this Aristotelian, organic approach that allows Maimonides to group the commandments systematically by their now familiar aims: establishing secure and prosperous relations among men, improving human character, and fostering the insight that is our highest goal. The Torah, Maimonides argues, achieves its three great aims consummately and is thus unrivaled as a system of law. All other schemes are either derivative or degenerate forms of the Mosaic approach, if indeed they go beyond the merely human aims of civil security and basic economic cooperation. The three aims support one another: the civil foundations, as in Aristotle, are essential to the humanity of human life. Moral development promotes civility and is a prerequisite of insight. Spiritual growth requires special skills and efforts but is the goal toward which all our activities should aim, regardless of their intrinsic worth, and it too fosters human betterment. One who wants to question whether these goals are indeed recommended by reason may need a richer conception of reason, as well as of the *mitzvot*.[80]

In grouping the *mitzvot* teleologically, Maimonides develops Saadiah's idea that the broad aims of legislation underdetermine its content. When ends are construed broadly, the means will naturally appear arbitrary, in any legal system. The problem is compounded when the aims are very broad and the means very specific, or when the aims are at all obscure to us, shrouded in mystery, or in history, and the means seem radically *over*determined relative to those aims—as is typical with ritual obligations. So, accepting Saadiah's premise that worship is due to God, Maimonides agrees that this broad theme does not determine the form or even the mode of worship. Thus his account of how Israel's spiritual infancy was coddled, as an embryo is cossetted in the womb, or a newborn mammal is nursed before it is ready for solid food.[81] But what this means is that the pagan practices of the surrounding nations became determinative in the institutions of God's Law for Israel.

The general purposes of the Law, the Rambam argues, are transparent. But when it comes to particularities—why these specific means are addressed to this generic aim—human reason rapidly swims out of its depth. Even so, a kind of anthropology, studying pagan literature and customs, can help fill in the gaps between broad themes and specific practices.[82] What we grasp about the ritual laws, then, is not simply "a little" but their general aims. What we lack and what it would be a fool's errand to seek, the Rambam writes, is comprehensive understanding of their means.[83]

2. Saadiah tends to fuse actions with the corresponding virtues, and virtues with their consequential and constitutive rewards. The trend is not unusual, and it can have its benefits. Thus Saadiah's talk of virtue and vice as matters of preponderance in actions rather than dispositions adds an interesting (if simplifying) nuance to virtue theory. But Maimonides sharply (and rightly) distinguishes actions from virtues even as he presses the biblical idea of the compactness of virtues with their rewards. In a key passage (*Guide* III 53), for example, he differentiates the virtue of justice, which enhances our character, from the mere practice of justice in conformity to the Law. The distinction intended, as I have shown,[84] is not between supererogatory and minimal demands but between the dispositions of character that underlie our choices and the actions that effectuate them. Either term may be considered instrumental: right actions facilitate right choices by forming good habits; virtues promote right actions, since a virtue is, by definition, a disposition toward appropriate action. The commandments nurture certain kinds of choices, both for the life those choices foster for the individual and the community, and for the ethos they will produce, again individually and communally. Neither virtuous actions nor the virtues themselves are valued solely for their intrinsic worth. Both contribute to the good life materially, morally, and intellectually.[85]

By sharply distinguishing actions from virtues Maimonides can make much clearer than Saadiah does what sort of benefits ritual laws may provide. For our question is not why reason would commend holiness, as though God might just as well have ordered us to become an *unholy* people and a nation of mountebanks, catamites, bullies, or buffoons, instead of a nation of priests. Rather, the issue is *how* specific prescriptions can make us a nation of priests and a holy people. By introducing well polished technical concepts of ethos, virtue, and moral disposition, from the Aristotelian conceptual tool chest, in place of Saadiah's poetic, Platonizing remarks about the substance of the soul and how it is clarified and brightened or sullied and darkened, Maimonides can harness his moral psychology and ethology to his anthropology. Adding the idea of symbols and symbolism, as he does in assaying what practices the Torah regards as reminiscent of pagan worship, he can show generically how rituals can affect our character. He can also exploit al-Fārābī's Platonic account of imagination to suggest how specific sorts of mythic, poetic, and ritual symbols can be intellectually fruitful and spiritually suggestive.

3. Maimonides is much less convinced than Saadiah that we can gauge God's purposes. If God is perfect, he has no needs; if he is absolute, one action of his is as much to his purpose as another, and no creature exists solely for another's sake. One cannot believe, Maimonides argues, that the heavens exist to serve mankind; we must

overcome the hubris of deeming ourselves God's noblest creations, for whom (as in Saadiah's world) all else was created (*Guide* I 2, III 13). Yet man is as much an object of God's plan as any other creature. If there are things on which our lives depend (since we are finite beings, but higher than the plants and animals we find on earth), they do exist for our sakes as well as for their own. To say that God acts without purpose is to make his actions futile, idle, or vain. To say that he might have achieved his plan without the means he used is to impugn his wisdom; nothing is otiose. The complex nexus of causes that is nature allows its denizens to achieve their goals in the manners appropriate to their natures—at their own speeds, as it were.[86] That is the beauty and grace of the act of creation.

Saadiah touches on this theme when he calls the imparting of natures a critical phase of creation.[87] But again Maimonides richly develops it, giving a meaning to our persistent use of the idea of purposes in a world whose ultimate purpose is beyond our ken: God hid his face from Moses, the most perfect of all prophets; a fortiori will he conceal his inner Self from humanity at large. But human life does not require us to know the absoluteness of God's Wisdom as *he* knows it. What Moses saw was "God's back," his wisdom and goodness in nature and their lessons for the governance of human lives. Such insights guide not only the scientific but the legislative enterprise: to be holy and become like God, we must know what perfects us as human beings (*Guide* I 53–54).

That is why the human image can be a powerful source of guidance in interpreting and elaborating ritual laws. Not that human perfection is so unproblematic or uncontroversial that we need only turn to it like an icon for ready reference. On the contrary, our penchant for projecting spurious goals and specious values on the image of a perfected humanity must constantly be disciplined. Our image of humanity needs to be enriched and enlightened by every rational, critical, experiential, intuitive, and traditional resource we can find, to crosscheck our readings and counteract vain or unwholesome ambitions. But we are not without a compass if we know that the governing aim of our laws is the perfection of our natures. We can regulate and modulate our practices by that knowledge, as Maimonides does when he cautions against excessive asceticism and extends Saadiah's medical conceit by exposing the vulgar fallacy of supposing that if a little medicine is good for us a lot will be all the better,[88] and as Saadiah did when he argued to the same effect (*ED* X 4), relying not on analogy but on psychology, to show that the life of the anchorite is melancholic, bitter, unfriendly, and ultimately self-indulgent and unholy. Our ideal of humanity will be crucial.[89] For no matter how powerful and sophisticated a car one drives, one cannot steer it unless one knows where one is going.

Toward a Philosophy of Ritual

Having cleared some of the rubble from the ground and discerned the outlines of the mighty structures that once stood on this site, I want to say a word now about ritual and law. My claim, announced at the outset, is that all laws have a ritual aspect and that all sound laws are rational. Let me explain first what I mean by ritual, for I think it is obvious from what has been said up to now that I will take a law to be rational if it faithfully serves some human good. By ritual I understand symbolically freighted action that bears part of its significance in the modalities of its performance and, as a matter of primary intention, uses those modalities themselves symbolically, to express attitudes toward the values that the act symbolically intends.

Since human beings are symbol-making, symbol-finding, symbol-reading creatures, and since much of our symbolism is self-conscious or mannered, and most of it value-freighted, the realm of ritual will be large on this account. I do not think it will be all-encompassing. Much of our behavior is not action in the classic sense, since it does not pursue a consciously chosen purpose. Much of our activity is not symbolic, or, if taken as symbolic, does not bear its symbolism as a matter of primary intention. When we signify, we are always in some measure aware of what we mean to signify and of the fact that we are signifying something. But in ritual, self-consciousness goes further; the reflexivity is of a higher order. We are not just using actions to signify a value but are expressing a stance, posture, or attitude toward that value, by the very manner in which we act.

I'd like to say a word now about the effort to define a notion like ritual. This will consist of three appeals in behalf of logic and semantics. To begin with, (1) a definition of 'ritual' should be based on the recognition that ritual is a genus, not a species. There are different sorts of rituals. We should not equate the realm of ritual with that of religion. Not every ritual act is religious, and not every religious act is a ritual. (If I refrain from lying out of love of God, that is a religious act but not necessarily a ritual.) We should not define 'ritual' so as to make the phrase 'religious ritual' redundant or 'secular ritual' meaningless. (2) We should not resort to persuasive definitions.[90] Ritual should not be *defined* so as to render impossible the judgment that someone's participation in a ritual is improper or insincere. Ritual may be an achievement word, like 'poetry' and 'art' or 'culture'; but it is a mistake breeding only incoherence to define 'ritual' so as to include only rituals one favors or admires, rendering 'good ritual' or 'effective ritual' or 'successful ritual' redundant and 'bad ritual,' 'unsuccessful ritual,' or even 'empty ritual' sheer contradictions—*or sheer tautologies!* We should not define the extension of the class such that we must understand what rituals are by no other notion than the one in which we express what we hope rituals can be, wish they were, or fear they may become. If there is to be good poetry and bad poetry, then the criteria by which poetry is identified cannot be the same as those by which poetry is judged, and the sense of 'poetry' in which we say "The Chrysler building is sheer poetry" must be different from that in which we say that doggerel is bad poetry. People who say that rituals are "confirming" or "integrating," that they bring people together, are not only being too general; they are also being too wishful, forgetting that rituals can rend people and groups asunder, that the Nuremberg rallies were also rituals. (3) Finally, we must avoid the vice of false abstraction or typifying a salient case—generalizing in pseudo-abstract terms about a broad class of things by addressing just one experience, type of event, or object that means a lot to us. Without attention to countercases, philosophy will never go beyond stereotyping and rather unreflective autobiography.

The criteria of ritual are not met in all intentionally symbolic acts, but much of human behavior is ritual in nature. Taking a walk or having a conversation can be rituals on my account, although just walking or just speaking generally are not. Baseball surely has a ritual aspect. So does cricket. The ritual aspects become clearest if we compare the two, not so much by their differences athletically or in the rules of play as by the modalities of performance and participation—the dress and demeanor of the players, the use and abuse, presence or absence of backchat and catcalls from the stands. Most symbolically significant actions carry overtones expressive of who or what we are or think we are, or would like others to think we are. Consider the ways that different people dress or dance, speak, or write a letter or a note. Most social activities carry an expressive load through familiar modalities of manner that address the values intended in those acts.

By this standard, reciting a poem or displaying a painting is in some respects a ritual act. That is why we can so readily discriminate between recitations and other forms of verbal behavior, or between displaying a painting and just hanging it out to dry or shelving it in a storeroom, acts which generally do not have symbolic aims as a matter of primary intention. Poets often recite their poems in a particular tone or timbre, slowly or with particular sonority, volume, emphasis, or inflection. The fashion in recent years in English is to use a rather flat, prosy tone. But that too carries a message, just as the poem does. The rhythms, rhymes, assonances, and alliterations that may lend their art to poetic compositions serve to set *these* words apart as objects of special interest, calling attention not just to the senses of the words but also to the special function they are called upon to play in this composition or recitation, the value assigned to the poem as a poem, quite beyond the aim of simply communicating or communicating simply. Paintings, similarly, are framed, literally or situationally, by their placement, for example. So are sculptures, stories, and theater pieces, in their own ways. To make an utterance or expression into an artwork is to ritualize it, that is, to assign a significance to the act of expression itself by its very manner.

Etymologically, rituals are actions said to be done in a certain manner (thus, "properly," *ritu*). Often there is an element of repetition or stylization. I do not take these marks as definitional, because I think they are secondary to the heart of ritual intent, and because I think the coverage they give us of the class of ritual acts is somewhat crude: many things are done in a certain manner. There is a proper way of building a house, making a bed, or fixing a leak. Yet these need not be rituals. There can be a manner in, say, scanning the horizon or calling hogs, without these actions being rituals. But when actions are done in a certain manner *in order* to express an attitude toward some value, I take them to have a ritual aspect. When these expressive dimensions of the action are underscored by mannerism, style, repetition, or other modalities in the mode of action itself, the ritual aspect becomes more prominent or explicit.

Rituals often become institutions. They are *made* institutions, because human beings have social interests in the values they intend and in fostering specific attitudes toward those values. But we should not confuse rituals with institutions. Not every institution is a ritual: the IRS is not. And not every ritual is an institution. Some are performed only once, as when David danced before the ark of the Lord. The prophet who tells the story may admire David's spontaneity, but liturgically it is the disapproving Michal who wins the day: David's songs become an institution; his dance does not. Even some prayers are uttered only once. What would become of sincerity without spontaneity, or of spontaneity itself if *all* rituals involved repetition, tradition, or the normative intentions of the group?

One cannot say that counting cars, bird-watching, or fishing is a ritual. But they may be in certain circumstances—as fly fishing is in *A River Runs Through It.* One cannot say, I stress, that all rituals are religious. Birthday parties, swim meets, letter writing are rituals but usually not religious in any central way. The Japanese tea ceremony and the old Chinese custom of gazing at the moon with friends are rituals, but not generally religious rituals. Prayer is a religious ritual, but "celebration" is religious only sometimes. Repetition is a modality capable of quite a range of expressive nuance, so it is widely used in rituals. It marks the rhythms of time and the seasons, not only of the year but of the moment, and of life, voicing analogies and recurrences that are not to pass unmarked, lending intensity along with the reassurance of regularity. But repetition is not of the essence in ritual. One might pray only once in one's life, and then in a form of one's own devising. Manner is essential, but it functions as a marker of expressive intent. Had Hannah prayed with less spontaneous immediacy Eli would not have taken her for a drunken woman.

Is kissing a ritual? It is when it is done to express an attitude vis-à-vis some value. The symbolism need not be portentous or profound. People kiss hello, good-bye, goodnight, or thank you. The values involved have to do with meeting, parting, generosity, or kindness. The attitudes expressed might be gladness, sadness, greeting, or gratitude. The corresponding emotions might be heartfelt, shallow, perfunctory, or insincere. It is possible to be false in nonverbal as in verbal expression, since what is outwardly expressed does not always match the inner intention. Our expressive range is potentially as broad as the spectra of our attitudes themselves. And those, in turn, are differentiated by their objects as well as by the postures we adopt toward them. Kissing is a ritual when it is part of a symbolically significant sequence of overtures and responses, as in courtship, but not when (or insofar as) it is done solely to gratify our osculatory impulses. In such a case people say, "I didn't mean anything by it" or "It didn't mean a thing." Sometimes a kiss doesn't mean what it is taken to mean. Symbols can be misappropriated, given or taken incorrectly or in bad faith.

A conversation is a ritual. Its conventions and expectations create a subtext to what is more overtly said. Normally there are pauses for replies, for example, and some common focus of interest—not just a welter of words or barrage of utterances at cross purposes or without reference or relevance to each other. The values intended in the manner of a conversation might include the dignity or desert of each party to be heard, the seriousness or casualness of what is discussed, the friendship, fellowship, or collegiality of the participants. Attitudes toward such values are expressed through signs of attentiveness, boredom, disagreement, respect, responsiveness, concern or unconcern, impatience or fascination, among many other possibilities. A sidelong glance at the clock can be more telling than anything said out loud. Generally there are ways of marking when a conversation is entered, who the participants are and are not, and when the conversation is ending or over. The conventions may be subtle or tacit, the regularities informal rather than rigid, but they are as necessary as linguistic comprehension. For without such cues and signs, much of the symbolic work, unspoken but transacted between the lines, would remain unaccomplished. The formalism (however informally signified) is not what makes the conversation a ritual. It is a condition of communication, a sign of tacit interactions that are given expression symbolically. It is the attitudinal intensionality behind that symbolism that grounds the visible formalism and is the real basis of the ritual character of a conversation.

Rituals have intensions (with an *s*, not a *t*), that is, they make reference beyond themselves. All symbols intend objects—things, acts, values, or ideas. But rituals universally express attitudes as well. A word may intend a thing; a sentence will intend a state of affairs. Some rituals, like some sentences, are performative. They accomplish the very acts they symbolically address. A wedding does that; so does a prison sentence, or the act of picketing. But even when a ritual is performative, it always intends more than it pronounces. Ken Seeskin asks whether a ritual act can have intrinsic value. The simple answer is yes, both in the act and in its ritual modalities. But the value depends on the act and on the nature of its modalities, not on the fact that this act is a ritual. If a priest blesses the parish animals, that may be wise or foolish, expressive of goodwill or of cynical calculations about the locus and focus of the religious interests of his own flock. If a Klansman burns a cross on an interracial couple's lawn, he is expressing attitudes toward what he may call miscegenation. The act, like any other, must be judged on its merits or lack of merits. Ritual is its genre and vehicle, its medium. To ask if rituals have intrinsic worth seems to me like asking if books are any good, or if paintings are worth much. Some are, of course. But I wouldn't commit too much to any of these sight unseen.

Rituals vary in illocutionary force and carry as wide a range of connotative senses and intensionalities as language acts do. A marriage ceremony, unlike the simple words "I now pronounce you man and wife," and the act of passing sentence, unlike the mere words "I sentence you to twenty years in the state penitentiary," necessarily intend an attitude toward the act, the parties, and others as well. The wedding ceremony (and the festivities surrounding it) may express joy or honor. Or, if the ceremony is performed perfunctorily, its subtext may lean in quite another direction. But there is always an attitude expressed toward certain values, and the means of its expression is in the modalities of the performance.

As a ritual (which it normally is in our society), sentencing typically expresses the dignity of the law and authority of the court, the gravity of the offense, the displeasure of society, the guilt of the offender. A judge may assert some of these values verbally, but the symbolism of sentencing, as a ritual, is distinct from such explanations. It is the manner that does the expressing here, and what it expresses is not the values at stake but an attitude toward them. Normally, in our court system, the party to be sentenced is expected to be present, to hear the sentence, and stand while hearing it. The symbolism affirms the court's legitimate jurisdiction, expresses society's demand for accountability, avows the offender's responsibility for wrongful actions or omissions, acknowledges to the public, who are represented among those present, the dignity of the offender as a moral agent expected to accept such responsibility. But the ritual symbolizes the attitudes deemed normative toward these values. Since crucial norms are at stake, the manner that bears this second-order message is highly regulated by convention: even though the law does not require the judge to speak in a grave voice when passing sentence, judges generally know that this is what to do. There are also prescriptive rules about the matter: judges are elevated, wear robes, enter the courtroom after others are seated, and are met on entering by the rising of those present. In jurisdictions of British heritage, judges wear a wig.

Yet the norms about a ritual, conceived as an institution, whether overt or tacit, do not determine the minds of the participants. Nor do conventions, despite their prominence wherever there is symbolism, determine the thinking or even the usage of those who may employ them. One can use conventional symbols with unconventional or unexpected intent, as when the trappings of a courtroom are used for purposes of satire or ridicule in a play or movie. The Talmud (*Yevamot* 104a) remarks of a certain Rabbi that he performed *ḥalitzah*, ritual release from levirate marriage, "with a slipper [rather than a shoe], alone [not in the public square], and at night [not in broad daylight]." But rather than simply declare the act void, the Rabbis marveled at its boldness.[91] Just as a poet who sounds the usages of a language can play with meanings and intensions, so can a ritualist who knows the limits and potentials of the language of ritual. This is true not just for iconoclasts but for traditionalists. I remember being asked by an elderly Yemenite patriarch in Rehovot whether I didn't think it unseemly to intersperse long strings of *mi-sheberakh*s between the *'aliyot* of the Sabbath Torah reading—how did we handle such things in Honolulu? My host found the practice of his congregation undignified and was sure I would agree. He decided (partly by observing the worship of his fellow congregants through what he assumed were my eyes) to initiate a change, and later proudly told me he had done so, modeling the new practice on what I told him was our custom.

Because rituals intend values and express attitudes toward them, rituals can be burlesqued, profaned, or vitiated. Objects of value, after all, have an existence outside the attitudes one may adopt toward them. Various groups and human society at large have interests in such objects and in the usages, symbolisms, and attitudes addressed toward them. Part of the care invested in the proper performance of rituals that are institutions expresses social concerns that the values intended not be misconstrued; part shows a concern that the attitudes expressed be the fitting ones. Just as words can be used to assert lies or affirm errors, ritual symbols and the attitudes they express can be mishandled. A judge who cannot separate gravity from abusiveness, a justice of the peace whose demeanor suggests that marriage is a farce, or a captain who gives orders in a tone that leaves his troops in doubt whether he expects or intends to be obeyed fails in the ritual dimensions of his task. His manner is inappropriate, ambiguous, conveys the wrong message. There are norms about rituals because it can be a matter of moment that the right message be conveyed.

Religions use rituals to express attitudes toward spiritual values in various ways and for various reasons, among them, the oblique acknowledgment of the holy. For the transcendence of the holy does not allow it to be signified directly. Even when it is taken to be immanent or immediately present, the holy is never on the surface; even when discovered in the casual or equated with the banal, it is never equated with the casual or the banal *as such*.

All expression, of course, is symbolic. Even when I point directly at your cap, my fingertip is not your cap. It indicates your cap. For what has a fingertip to do with a cap? Context, convention, and intention are needed even in so simple an act of signifying as this. Words have only the most tenuous linkages to what we hope to signify by them. Words are significant sounds, or graphic representations of such sounds, but rarely is the object represented a sound. Even onomatopoeic words are conventionalized, somewhat self-consciously, to make it clear that they are *representing* a sound, not just making one. When words represent things (always, I would argue, by way of a concept or idea, unless they are proper names), they are linked to what they represent by conventions that are largely arbitrary. There is no intrinsic connection of word to object that would allow one to predict, without knowing the usages of a language, what objects a given word will represent, or vice versa. It is because of the flexibility and friability of the nexus between symbols and their objects that exotic rituals so often appear bizarre to those unfamiliar with their usages.

Ordinary language and symbols regularly signify objects that are transcendental, that is, separate or separable from the mind. Religious language and symbolism intend objects and values taken to be transcendent, that is, beyond the ordinary or empiric.[92] The attitudes that religious rituals express are extraordinary as well: reverence, awe, sometimes terror. When they express gratitude, it is not typically of the kind found in a bread-and-butter note. The excesses often associated with religious ritual reflect the enormity of the objects and values intended: when Shiʿites flagellate and slash themselves in a procession, or the devotees of Attis castrated themselves, when the Christian *penitentes* nail themselves to crosses, or ancient pagans offered their children as a sacrifice, these ritual acts intend or intended a holiness of such enormity that no ordinary sacrifice would suffice, no mere fast or vigil was commensurate, no ordinary enthusiasm would reach, no mere discipline could express the passion of Ḥasan and Ḥusayn, the frenzy of Attis, the suffering of Christ, the terror of the unseen god.

Symbols are not deducible from the objects or values they intend. But, as with the red rose, there is a *structural* correspondence: great things are represented by great things, pure by pure, impure by impure; extraordinary awe by extraordinary manifestations of the ordinary signs of awe. All the potentials for structural mapping are present, even the perversity of transvaluation, representing the pure by the impure, and impassivity by violence and violation. So rituals, like theology, need discipline and dispassion. Religious rituals map but also excite or cool the passions.[93] Modulations of ritual can express, but also guide and channel theology, cool and soothe the fevered brow of metaphysics—as when ethics affirmed itself and, in the enormity of human sacrifice, exposed the radical inauthenticity of the teleological suspension of the ethical. For ethics tempered metaphysics, whose vehicle was ritual, in the awesome change of thought epitomized in the unbinding of Isaac.

Religious rituals, like other rituals, serve functions beyond the symbolic. Prayer may be a way of communicating with God, of cementing a community, of causing rainfall and blessing the crops, or the animals brought together on the church steps. Marriage is a way of uniting couples and formalizing the bond between them. Sports events are certainly a way of making money, and so are faith healing sessions, whether or not they are a way of curing illnesses. Taken at face value, the liturgy of *Kabbalat Shabbat* is a way of reconciling God with his exiled Shekhinah, assuring them a conjugal visit on the Sabbath. But, beyond the real or notional pragmatic impact of a ritual as a performative act, it still, and always, intends values, and in the modalities of its performance expresses attitudes toward those values. The same pragmatic act without that symbolism and expressive stance would not be a ritual.

We can read a book sitting and holding it in our laps, or we can read from a Torah scroll, written on specially prepared parchment by a trained scribe with special ink and in a special hand, reading only when the scroll is spread out on a table after being carefully removed from an ark devoted to housing just such scrolls. The reading can be silent or spoken, or it can be cantillated in musically ornamented phrasings that parse each sentence and give artful emphasis to key words. No intimate knowledge is needed for any human outsider (since all societies have rituals) to discern that this reading is a ritual. Nor is it hard to make out, as the scroll is lifted on high, displayed, bound up, rolled, wrapped in lavish clothing, and carried through the room, that the scroll is being honored. Now why would a scroll be honored? What we celebrate in triumphal procession, singing verses from the Psalms in marchlike cadences, is the values, norms, and precepts recorded within. We symbolize what we do not state directly. Any reading relies on symbols. But if the message of this reading is the content of the text, the manner of the reading is symbolic, too, of the glory and transcendent value—the holiness of that text.

Not every symbolism is so plain. Systems of symbols are complex, multifarious, open-ended, as diverse and multifaceted as language, which brings symbolism to its most explicit. Symbols are anchored in convention but reach into the heavens like some parasail of creativity, through poetry and other originative modes of expression and thought. Religious rituals are often communal and share a base of common intentions or historic associations. But, like the usages of language, the public symbolisms of ritual depend ultimately on custom; and customs shift and diverge from epoch to epoch, community to community, individual to individual, and moment to moment.[94] Ritual reaches a high form in prayer, where poetry and language make the symbolism overt and in some measure transparent, even self-explanatory. But here, too, meaning is never fixed and absolute. Where there is a text there is a subtext; and where there is symbolism arise occasion and opportunity for appropriation, misappropriation, evolution, growth, and loss.

If ritual is not mere form and repetition, neither is its authenticity confined to the unrecorded and ineffable experience of ages past or locales exotic and remote. It is not merely an encrustation, fossilization, ossification of what was otherwise unique, living, original, inimitable, individual, and spontaneous. For it is also, as Mary Douglas argues, the structuring mode that gives content, direction, categorial interpretation, to otherwise inchoate experience.[95] Seeking the ancient roots of Hebrew prayer, Moshe Greenberg shows that such prayer is both structured and individual. It finds its voice and form in the common stock of human language, the language of petition, thanksgiving, confession, acknowledgment, praise, and blessing. Its roots are not adequately discerned by those who dichotomize it "into spontaneous, free invention on the one hand, and preformulated, prescribed prayers on the other." Neither form is "degenerate" or original. Each is in-arched into the other, strengthening the prayer itself, shaping its language, bearing aloft its themes and sustaining the direction of their flight.[96]

Opposing the dismissal of ritual as mere rote and combating the romantic notion that only the unique and spontaneous are authentic, Mary Douglas writes of the efforts of sophisticated theologians to dissolve the prescriptive hold upon "the Bog Irish" of the traditional Catholic abstinence from meat on Fridays:

> The Catholic hierarchy in England today are under pressure to underestimate the expressive function of ritual. Catholics are exhorted to invent individual acts of almsgiving as a more meaningful celebration of Friday. But why Friday? Why celebrate at all? Why not be good and generous all the time? As soon as symbolic action is denied value in its own right, the flood gates of confusion are opened. Symbols are the only means of communication. They are the only means of expressing value; the main instruments of thought, the only regulators of experience. For any communication to take place, the symbols must be structured. For communication about religion to take place, the structure of the symbols must be able to express something relevant to the social order. If a people takes a symbol that originally meant one thing, and twists it to mean something else, and energetically holds on to that subverted symbol, its meanings for their personal life must be very profound. Who would dare to despise the cult of Friday abstinence who has not himself endured the life of the Irish labourer in London? Friday abstinence must be interpreted under the same rubric as Jewish abstinence from pork . . . pork avoidance and Friday abstinence gain significance as symbols of allegiance simply by their lack of meaning for other cultures. . . . [Against the backdrop of Hellenistic persecution], eating pork came to be abhorred as an act of betrayal as well as of defilement."[97]

The authentic meaning of a ritual is not its meaning at its point of origin. That may be interesting, but it becomes important in religions only because they seek continually to capture the transcendent, and often seek to recapture it from the past, when its appearance has been recollected or projected there. Rather, the authentic meaning of a ritual is the meaning given it by its practitioners, severally or collectively. Thus the momentousness of their responsibility: *their* intentions are the meaning of their ritual acts. If they misappropriate a symbol, alienate it from the sacred and assign it to the realm, say, of competitive emulation, social bonding, ethnic pride, or personal prejudice, the ritual takes the significance they give it. For it is their act. This does not mean, however, that they can make it what they want: the actors are still acting expressively, and to do so they must use a repertoire of symbols which (like the symbols of language) cannot fail to have a range of socially familiar and accepted senses, connotations, and associations. Whatever an individual intends in an action will be the intension of that act, whether or not that corresponds to the ancient or socially legitimated object of the act. But by that very token, the act may fail of its normative aims, fall short of, or surpass the traditional intent.

That there are facts about rituals does not imply that there are no values about them, that there cannot be a right and wrong in ritual beyond the relative and technical question of whether behaviors have been executed as prescribed. Like any symbolic system, systems of rituals establish constitutive norms, norms laid down and significant within the system. But because rituals intend values beyond themselves and express attitudes toward those values, rituals can be appropriate or inappropriate in the symbols they invoke, just as language can be rightly or wrongly, truthfully, erroneously, or mendaciously applied.

In the Iatmul society of New Guinea a mother's brother (*wau*) traditionally responded to a serious offense against a third party by his sister's son (*laua*) with the ritual of *naven*:

> The *wau* dresses in a tattered and filthy version of the costume worn by widows, and hobbles about the village, exposing his genitals, pretending pregnancy, and gen-

> erally making a spectacle of himself. The show delights everyone except the *laua* and his close kin, and the *laua*, especially, responds to the performance with expressive signs of shame. The *wau* finally brings this portion of the proceedings to a conclusion by running the cleft of his buttocks down the shin of his *laua*, to the mortification of the latter. A ceremonial exchange of goods then takes place, the *wau* offering a dead chicken to the *laua* for a spear and strings of shells. Feasting follows, and often a delayed exchange of pigs and other valuables between *waus*, *lauas* and members of their clans.[98]

These actions appear bizarre and disgusting to most outsiders and perhaps to the participants too, since this act of abasement seems clearly to draw upon the emotive force of its symbolism. External accounts of such behavior might easily get stuck in fascination with its exoticism or might hastily reach relativistic conclusions about the practices that "we" and "they" consider acceptable or unacceptable. But we should not ignore the functional value of the ceremony in a society where violence is frequent, formal rules are widely seen as made to be broken, and symbols, especially those of status, are prominent—a society, then, not radically unlike our own.

What matters, if our interest is in norms, is that in any society where grave offense or injury has been given, amends *are* appropriate, and part of amends is a symbolic expression of shame or regret. Cultures differ in the symbolisms they assign to diverse intensions, in the intensity deemed appropriate in diverse circumstances, in the extent to which shame or responsibility is transferred or shared, or its expression is objectified or internalized, stylized or underscored. They differ, too, in the precise occasions where they treat formal and informal amends as adequate, appropriate, or obligatory. But they do not differ in regarding amends that are in part symbolic as a fitting sequel to an offense, any more than they differ in regarding expressions of gratitude as an appropriate response to generosity.

Rituals have their own distinctive ailments—scrupulosity, for example, where the niceties of performance become obsessive. Many such problems can be traced to the structure of symbolism itself. Because symbols intend an object, they are naturally associated with that referent and easily made its surrogate. Magic is one such surrogacy, substituting symbols for facts and acts, assigning them power over things, with no greater warrant than the presumptive sanctity of the symbols. It is natural for the gestures and the items by which holiness is intended to be invested with a borrowed holiness, especially since the manner in which those gestures are performed and those objects handled is itself freighted with attitudinal symbolism. So there are ritual objects, objects that acquire significance in a ritual context. To mishandle such objects is to mishandle symbols. For it is as symbols that these objects acquire a determinate, contextual significance.

Thus, despite the rarefied usage of certain rather bohemian or romantic Zen practitioners and Sufis, one cannot readily express reverence irreverently—as many a folk mass reveals. I once spoke in a synagogue where the rabbi wanted to teach his confirmands the joy of religious spontaneity by having each young person make a Torah reading *yad*, or pointer. But many, ultimately most of the students, taking the line of least resistance, brought increasingly crude items for this task (or homework chore, as it was seen). By late spring all were bringing twigs bound up with string or rubber bands. The message conveyed was quite contrary to what the rabbi had hoped, or what the traditional intensionality of using a *yad* might have suggested. Originality had evaporated, but casualness remained, along with some residual reference to nature and spontaneity. In the response to such crude experiments with "creativity," ritual acts and objects might well be vested with a borrowed sanctity, protective of the symbolism that is their more normative aim.

Yet it is critical to remember that such sanctity is borrowed, and not to forget from where it was borrowed. When a symbol stands between us and its object, it intends that object, but its very position risks making it a surrogate. That is one key difficulty we Jews have with idolatry. Thus the Torah's dramatic irony when Aaron fashions a golden calf for the people out of their own jewelry, and they proclaim: "This is thy God, O Israel, which brought thee up out of the land of Egypt!" (Exod. 32:4). Symbols can be an avenue or an obstacle, and rituals, when made an end in themselves, can block the very pathways they might have opened. Our modern-day religious positivists are an object lesson in that regard, and before following them into a dogma of the pure positivity of the *mitzvot*, one might learn from the extreme case of the ritual positivists of the Mimamsa Hindu school, long studied by my friend Shlomo Biderman. The Mimamsa reached the point of claiming that ritual correctness in accordance with the sacred texts demands such concentration that any thought of the divine would distract the mind and vitiate the ritual. The solution was not greater *kavvanah*, to use our own term, but banishing all thoughts of God. True piety was found only in the atheist officiant. Such Orwellian extremes violate and reverse the very values a ritual might have served and afford a perfect reductio ad absurdum of the religious positivism that is now far more typical among orthodox Jewish intellectuals than any such notion as fundamentalism.

Ben-Ami Scharfstein, another friend, who is Biderman's colleague at Tel Aviv, asks me, in correspondence, if the Mimamsa practice or theory is not a countercase to my claim that all rituals express attitudes toward values symbolically intended. For the Mimamsa prize ritual for its own sake, not for what it might intend: "To them, there is no symbolic action involved. Maybe the closest Western analogue is the Kantian notion of the moral act as self-justifying." But clearly the Mimamsa highly value the ritual act. The rituals of a (doctrinaire) adherent of Mimamsa are distinctive not in failing to express an attitude toward intended values but in focusing that value in the ritual performance itself. The risk is not of incoherence but of idolatry.

Ritual and Law

But enough about ritual for the moment. Let us speak about laws. Laws are prescriptions and proscriptions deemed vital enough that we accept their imposition on ourselves, because we expect to see them imposed upon each other. Since these norms are often important enough to bear sanctions, there is a premium on making them minimal in key respects. Few laws try to reguiate thought; for thoughts are hard to regulate, and we are not so eager to see each other's thoughts regulated as willingly to submit to regulation of our own. All laws pursue some good, since no one would accept regulation without some reason. All sound laws honestly serve some genuine good and on balance tend to promote its achievement. That is what makes them rational. Just laws, I think, must serve a good that can be met without too severely compromising other goods. That is what makes legislation so delicate and dialectical a process. But our present task is not to legislate but to discern the basis of legislation, the service of some prima facie good.

Ritual enters the picture because the goods laws serve invariably underdetermine legislation. The legislator seeks to specify the "doable good" or, more often (given the minimalist bias of even the most invasive schemes of law) the *un*doable evil—wrong, *nefas*. But the concerns that guide sound legislation are always generalities—values like the sanctity of life or security of property, the dignity of art or clarity of boundaries. What a legislator must *set down* are specifities; and what a judge must evaluate are particularities. To protect the sanctity of life, we must legislate against murder; to distinguish wickedness from negligence, we must set apart murder from manslaughter, and distinguish both from accident. So intentions enter into law, and since intentions are invisible, we need objectifying tests—an entryway for convention—if principle is ever to guide the norms of practice.

If we want to protect property, we must decide at what level, define what property is, classify the kinds we hope to protect, and determine by what means. We must set criteria of ownership and specify what entitlements ownership does and does not confer. In the United States, for example, most salaried workers would be guilty of a crime if they tried to keep all of their wages; public figures have little control over the noncommercial use of their likeness but can restrict commercial use of their name, likeness, or creative expressions. In ancient Israel, wayfarers could take produce from a stranger's field or vineyard without guilt of criminal trespass, but not more than they could pluck without a sickle or carry in their hands without a vessel (Deut. 23:25–26). Acts punishable by law on the little island of Oahu, where I lived for twenty-five years, were not crimes biblically—not because morals are relative, nor because some cultures deem theft perfectly acceptable, but because laws must construct such ideas as property and theft, as Saadiah explains, if they are to give formal expression to the desire to protect any property and preserve the related values of life, personal security, prosperity, dignity, order, and fellowship.

Every society must determine what sort of sanctions its laws require. Will the sanctions that guard property be as grave as those that protect persons? Shall major and violent thefts be treated the same as petty larcenies? Where do we draw the lines? Here again conventions become active. They order and differentiate, and in so doing send a message about who is in charge and why, about what a society stands for and what it will not stand for. The gap between principle and praxis is mediated by legislative fiats that draw symbolic boundaries to guide action into approved pathways and away from proscribed margins. It is here that we begin to see the necessity of a ritual dimension to any law—a dimension that grows pronounced in the Rabbinic approach to law.

Laws are not symbolic in the first intention. Symbolism is not what they are about. But all laws have symbolic significances, and all express attitudes toward the values they intend. No punishment can undo a murder or rape, restore what has been violated in a mugging or robbery, or even a burglary. Indeed, that is never the intent. Penal laws may seek deterrence or reform, but they also, always, intend a message, express a norm, in uniquely coded symbols reserved for those occasions when vital social standards clearly have been overstepped. Whether or not a punishment effectively deters some future crime, it expresses a societal attitude about specific values. Punishments do not restore a balance or repay a debt. But ritually they undo a wrong, demarcate and underscore a convention. They exact but also limit retribution, allowing restoration of the offender's presumptive deserts. Despite the biblical *measure for measure*, legal sanctions and their limits are always underdetermined by the legislative aims they serve. But the hierarchy of punishments must order the severity of offenses, ritually treating each as commensurate with a tangible impairment of privilege—as though symbolism or even suffering could measure a wrong.[99] So punishments are always rituals, and to the extent that laws involve punishments, or any sanctions, laws are rituals as well.

To be a ritual is not part of the definition of a law. But all laws are rituals nonetheless. Because laws are underdetermined by the general purposes they serve, all laws have a degree of slack, demanding specified equivalencies and boundary conditions, objectification of such intangibles as intention, privacy, personality, interest, and concern. These determinations are not sheerly arbitrary. But the specifics that spell them out are, in the nature of the case, marginal to the chief pragmatic interests of a law. They would be irrelevant, but for the fact that without them there would be no law.

Since laws always address values, the manner in which slack is taken up speaks of those values, creating a ritual. Rituals specify much more detail than is predictable from a minimal, functionalist account of the behaviors they invest. Yet that overspecification itself is functional, symbolically, as a matter of primary intention. Because laws set up a system of virtualities delineating societal expectations in sensitive terrain, their ritual function is essential, not tangential or incidental. When Maimonides says that the general ends a law serves do not specify its means, we can think of the rule of the road: there is no intrinsic right or wrong side for driving; reason finds little to choose between one side and the other. But reason can speak decisively (although not analytically) to the need for automobiles to keep to one side in any integrated traffic system.

All laws use means radically underdetermined by the aims or goods those laws pursue. Convention fills the vacuum, and with it come symbolism and subtexts. Surely not in trivial realms like rules of the road, one might object. But symbolism is most active in what may seem the most trivial realms. The symbolic associations and ritual assignments of the left and right hands are well known, but one who doubts that individuals, communities, and societies say much about themselves by the way they drive and keep or fail to keep, enforce or fail to enforce the rules of the road does not do much driving, or has not done much "comparative driving" in diverse constituencies and jurisdictions. Woody Allen once said in a film that the only cultural amenity of Los Angeles was that California makes it legal to turn right on a red light. But even this convention reflects an ethos: only where pedestrians' right-of-way is respected is it safe (where traffic keeps to the right) to legalize a right turn on a red light. Ritual is the descant that makes a law more than mere prescription, transforming it to an institution that can express and evoke an ethos—vocalizing its notes, if you will, to make a law a song.

Herbert Fingarette argues that laws seek to control the will and so must use force and suffering to humble recalcitrance.[100] He brands as "ceremonial" laws that lack a penal sanction. But I think this dichotomy is too sharply drawn. Ritual laws often bear grave penalties, and many civil laws rest mainly on persuasion, incentive, social pressure, conscience, or ethos. The legislative role, Fingarette argues, is inconsistent with divine mercy. Song, he says, is law's antithesis.[101] But in Jewish thought the giving of the Law *is* an act of mercy and grace, and the Torah describes itself not in terms of sanctions but vividly in terms of song (Deut. 31; cf. Ps. 119:54), fusing poetry with precept, aggadah with halakhah. Fingarette finds this anomalous: "The *concept* of law excludes song, and so to the extent there is 'song' the rule of law is undermined or ignored. Sure one may 'temper' justice with charity, but it's still the case that justice is not charity, charity not justice; they are different and incompatible concepts."[102] But we begin to grasp the Mosaic idea when we see that in Hebrew, justice and charity bear the same name, *tzedakah*. Justice demands mercy, and charity is *suum cuique*.[103] As to the compatibility of law with song, surely any hybrid proves its vitality by its survival and fecundity.

Jurists in the tradition of Bentham, Austin, Hart, and Kelsen, as though on grounds of logic, draw the boundaries of the concept of law so as to exclude the marriage of law and song. What moves them is the fear of vast and uncontrollable vagueness. But the Rabbis, too, are aware of that problem. Thus their juridical work of concretizing, restraining and expanding, adjusting and shaping, to sculpt the demands of justice conceived as charity. Poetry is of the essence in their legislative work. For they achieve specificity, typically, by way of ritual, where the Torah itself characteristically constructs its *rationales* by way of myth. And so they must, for the Law they serve, as we have seen, has moral and spiritual as well as civil or social aims. As Bernard Jackson writes, "The Decalogue prohibits 'coveting.' . . . the Decalogue was not intended for human enforcement."[104] It is hardly, for that reason, a mere ceremonial law. Indeed, it was to distinguish the still operative Decalogue from the presumptively obsolete balance of the Torah that Christian polemical exegetes advanced the idea of ceremonial law.[105] And the presence and persistence of moral categories in the Decalogue and of the Decalogue in the Law are emblematic of our central thesis here, that no law finds in the general themes of its legitimation the operational specificity that any law requires. All laws contain an arbitrary aspect that is the ground and matter upon which the valuative attitudes of the law are figured.

Consider the presumption of innocence and its *reversal* in the case of the biblical *rodef*, or pursuer. As Edna Ullmann-Margalit writes, "Presumptions operate as corrective devices which regulate in advance the direction of error, where errors are believed to be inevitable. A presumption, on this view, reflects a social decision as to which sort of error is least acceptable on grounds of moral values and social attitudes and goals."[106] Presumptions, by setting a tilt or bias in the law, make a statement, express and institute an attitude toward specific values. Whenever we make rules we make presumptions[107] and thereby express and establish attitudes about the fundamental choices and determinations a law must make.

The law itself seeks justice, but in the very manner in which we enforce and interpret, refine and relax the law we voice attitudes about the values that we take to constitute justice and to coexist or compete with it. The presumption of innocence is not a way of maximizing material justice. Nor is it a way of maximizing formal justice or uniformity. For its impact will vary from case to case. Rather, it is a ritual that sets a boundary of inviolability around the deserts of personhood when those deserts are most gravely challenged by the threat of criminal sanctions. Similarly, the priority of persons to property, so central a theme in biblical and talmudic law;[108] the presumption of death in the English common law of missing persons, or the resistance to that presumption in the Rabbinic law of the *agunah*; the biblical insistence on a formal bill of divorcement (lest the biblical odium for adultery become a means of oppressing undivorced cast-off wives)—all these are rituals that enshrine specific values and priorities. All draw boundaries, establish categories, and express attitudes toward the values the laws intend.

Conventions are never purely arbitrary. They have their own agendas. In secular laws this might be as simple as the affirmation of authority, national or local solidarity. But consider the Torah. A subtext in all Jewish ritual, perhaps in all social ritual, identifies the *we*. Thus we say "our God and God of our fathers," "our God, King of the universe," in so many ritual blessings. The focus is on God and the bounties, beauties, and marvels he provides—not least the commandments, our paramount blessings, as the *ayāt*, or verses (literally, portents), of the Qur'an are the paramount miracles of Islam. It would be a misdirection to call group cohesion the core aim of ritual, merely because it forms a lowest common denominator among many ritual practices. That common thread or theme stands out because the rituals salient to study are typically social institutions. But rituals are not always social in setting and do not always seek unity. They do always express specific attitudes toward specific values. We can never capture the intent in the elevation of the Host if we simply keep our eyes on the congregation, when all their eyes are focused on the Host, and their minds are rising on tiptoe to reach with it and beyond it.

If rituals do unite a community, it is not by bare affirmation but by reference to and deference toward that community's bonds of identity in history or destiny, shared risk or need, joy in simple goods, or the presence of the sacred. Shared values and the objects or experiences they invest are what give definition, social energy, normative authority, material content, and direction to any communal identity, making a group not just *a* group, *a* people or community, but *this* group, *this* nation, with this culture, these values, this history, this land, this mode of government, and these ideals. Such foci of definition are centrally presented in the Torah, addressed in all three of Saadiah's scriptural modes: history, destiny, and norm—integrating the ritual and moral *mitzvot* that bind history to destiny and give a meaning and a mission to the identity of Israel.

The Torah's entire contents, as given and as elaborated, are ascribed to God as Legislator but also as justifying Source and Aim. God is the fountain of the goodness that the Law invokes, prescribes, and serves. So the constant message behind every symbolism here will be God's goodness and the human values of kindness, holiness, truth, justice, and mercy which emulate that goodness. As in any law, obligations and their attendant symbolisms are specified by conventions. These are not arbitrary, but they are radically underdetermined by their larger aims and higher themes. Knowing those themes in a general or abstract way would never allow deduction of these means to their fulfillment. Yet all laws serve purposes, pragmatic and expressive, and the two are inextricably intertwined, rendering the pragmatic expressive and the expressive pragmatic.

In some laws symbolism is the chief aim. These are ritual laws in the strong sense. It is a convention in America, with its heritage of secularizing legislation and Enlightenment abstraction, politely to ignore them, or more strenuously to deny their presence or propriety. This itself is a ritual: ritual is associated with religious faith and worship. And faith, in the civil credo, is a matter of internal conscience; worship, of personal aesthetics. Neither is a proper topic of legislation. But in a time when worship could include human sacrifice, ritual law was central to the legislative project. What we must recognize now is that such a time is by no means locked safely in the past. Superstitions of the New Age or the old are more than quaint curiosities, and the idea that faith means not just a credo or a catechism but the right to withhold surgery, blood, or antibiotics from a dying child, the obligation to die and poison one's children with cyanide-laced Kool-Aid, or the need of one sister to gouge out another's eyes "to exorcise a demon" is no mere relic of the past. The law does and still must intervene; its calming influence, even in regulating the extremes of symbolism, is no mere matter of inertia or the mortmain of tradition; and the law that is written on the assumption that such concerns are dead letters presumes too much and invites the quicksilver of history to refute its presumption.

The birth of Christianity and its vast campaign to spread monotheism to the peoples of the world led to a dismissal of Jewish "ceremonial" law. What had been the banner of monotheism was now a tattered rag, buffeted in the wind by being sharply set against the still vital force of what were taken to be the Bible's entirely separate moral precepts. Even social and moral laws that were not largely ceremonial in aim were furled and bracketed. Ritualism had been the charge of the biblical Prophets against ancient Israel, and of the Rabbis against the Sadducees. Now the same charge was turned against the work of the Rabbis and the Prophets themselves. As Mary Douglas writes, "The belittlement of ritual is nothing new. . . . Paul's thunderings against the judaisers have been basic texts of the Reformation: 'For Jesus Christ neither circumcision availeth anything, nor uncircumcision: but a new creature' (Galatians 6:15); 'Let no man therefore judge you in meat or in drink or in respect of a festival day or of the new moon or of the Sabbaths, which are a shadow of things to come' (Colossians 2:16–17)."[109] Paul's rhetoric reverses the Rabbinic image of the Sabbath as a foretaste of the World-to-Come, emptying the symbol of its meaning by insisting on the inadequacy of the lesser to represent the greater, and ignoring what Douglas, inspired by Lienhardt's work with the Dinka,[110] rightly sees as the true efficacy of symbols: granted they cannot replace what they represent, they can structure our very reality by their representations of it, and of the values it portends.

Ironically but predictably, the charge of ritualism became a cannon of schism and reform within the church: "The Papists, in the eyes of Calvin, had gone after the shadow, after superstition and empty ritual."[111] And when secularity and humanism, appalled at the religious wars that marked the birth of modern culture (which seemed to render medieval intolerance only more efficient, national, and systematic) took up the mantle of Christianity as the new arbiters of humane values, modernity did not abandon but only generalized the Christian polemic against archaic Hebraisms, even as it laid claim to all that was thought purest and most precious in the Bible. The outcome was the notion that the Torah (a fortiori the Talmud) overregulates human life. Generalizing that theme and losing touch with the intensionalities of the old symbols bred polemical denial of the practical relevance of all symbolic norms.

In the West at least (and here I must exclude the Islamic countries, Japan, and the newly reviving religious ethnicities emergent from the ruins of the former Soviet empire), perhaps we have now gained sufficient distance from the fanatical demand that ceremonial symbolisms be enforced with whip and sword that we can look back on the idea of ritual laws in general and Jewish religious symbolisms in particular not simply with romantic nostalgia (which is common and cheap enough) but with a certain respect. We can understand and reappropriate their celebrative and other attitudinal functions. And we can begin to see that laws that work primarily in the symbolic sphere are crucial in setting the tone, modulating the ethos, orienting the aspirations that will chalk up our worth—not merely our success but the very terms in which our failure or success deserves to be judged.

The Enlightenment heritage can be narrowing, and romantic iconoclasm, itself a secularization, soi-disant universalization, of ancient Christian polemical universalism, can be parochial. We have something to learn from the Confucian sympathy toward ritual (*li*) as a chief means of cultivating human character.[112] As Plato and Confucius saw, properly attuned ritual can, like music, foster that virtue which the Chinese call *jen*, or human heartedness, and which in Hebrew is called *ḥesed*, loving-kindness, piety, or humanity. Here we can see the wisdom in Saadiah's thought that acts which might be neutral or empty "in themselves" can be morally significant in context, and of Maimonides' clear differentiation of the principles that justify a norm from the means they deploy. These two insights, Saadiah's, with his characteristic sensitivity to the subtle interactions of psyche with society, and Maimonides', with his Aristotelian sense of the organic (rather than deductive) nexus of means to ends, go a long way toward explaining how rituals can become normative, even obligatory.

Our findings here are not confined to those norms whose chief aims are symbolic; they apply to all laws. The arbitrary dimensions we always see in law but notice most where laws chafe are often features of law as a symbol system. Humanistic rules of evidence and the Rabbinic prohibition of self-incrimination are not derivable from the pragmatics of legislative efficiency. They enshrine and protect specific values: the sanctity of personhood, dignity, and desert. They define and delineate the values they intend. And those values would not fully emerge if laws and institutions did not give them positive, prescriptive, and detailed social articulation. Arising from the law's expressive aspect, these protections, material though their impact is, belong to the ritual side of law: we bar tainted evidence not to promote justice but to mark the limits we set on the value of evidence. Such restrictions may well seem irrational to those who are alien to the spirit, or intentions, of our laws.

Much of what is at stake in laws against rape is a symbolic issue, a matter not of assessing material or psychological damages but of maintaining symbolic boundaries. The same can be said of incest. Laws against incest, as we shall argue in our next chapter, are not vestigial taboos, as Utilitarian schemes might be tempted to represent them. They are constitutive protections of the integrity of human identity. Thus their authority does not cease at the presumptive boundaries of damage to the psyche, any more than my freedom to swing my fist extends literally to the tip of your nose. Such boundaries are needed wherever bonds of close kinship are found; and of the essence is not the varying definition of close kinship, but that what is defended and defined are the boundaries of personhood. The society that fails to protect them has not just sacrificed the interests of some of its members but opened its own veins.

Facing the old canard, then, that once we know the aims of laws we can achieve the same ends by other means and so dispense with the *mitzvot*, we can now respond clearly that to achieve the end without the means is not quite so easy as it sounds. If rituals are symbols and serve simply to express a message, the complaint would run, can't we just *say it*, speak the message, without resort to this or that particular mode of expression? My answer is threefold: (1) The symbols we use are not so readily changed without systemic changes in the acts they help to constitute, define, or modulate—marrying, divorcing, punishing, or rewarding. To "punish" privately or in secret, or hastily, without trial and deliberation, is not to punish. It fails to achieve the social function of punishment. (2) Symbols can bear intrinsic, consequential, or associative value in their very modalities. There is treasure in their poetry and in the catena of tradition they draw with them. Their rich and manifold subtexts embody insights that go far beyond the bare pragmatic import of the actions they instill with meanings. To act "naturally" and "without ritual or symbolism" would be like trying to speak without connotations. Such speech would be the most artificial of all; its subtext, if rendered into words, would be angry, alienated, nihilistic. For denial of affect is not transcendence of affect. There is no expression without sign and symbol, and no signifying without valuation and the subtle or not so subtle discontinuity between what is subjectively intended and what is socially apprehended. To abolish that gap would erase the difference between minds and things, that is, abolish privacy and personhood. (3) Perhaps most crucially, because rituals are a vehicle of our values, they become a means not only of their expression but also of their criticism and evolution. Symbolism sets a table, as it were, at which the dynamics of values can be explored, tested, compared, and worked out. Religions and cultures, then, need rituals for the same reasons that mathematicians need diagrams, poets need words, or painters need canvas. Granted, a picture can be painted on paper instead of canvas. But no painter would pretend it was the same painting, that crayons allow the same expressive work as oils, tempera, or watercolors, or that the ends intended in a painting can be achieved by a picture painted solely in the mind.

Kierkegaard's Climacus in the *Concluding Unscientific Postscript*[113] conducts a thought experiment to gauge the impact of religion on men's lives. He imagines that the pastor has preached a sermon on the theme "A man can do nothing of himself, but with God he can do everything." All the people nod their heads and seem to understand and appreciate the message. But on Monday Climacus sends a spy to the Copenhagen Deer Park, who finds the same people getting along quite well without God, pursuing their various interests and pleasures. They seem to have no notion of the "everything" they can do "with" God. Should they have? Should the parson's words have transformed them? Should their attentiveness have given them supernatural powers, or robbed them of their natural ones? Or is there another, spiritual sense of self-transformation? Clearly, Jewish ritual observance is a way of living with

God. It gives ordinary actions—eating, sleeping, dressing, doing business—symbolic meanings and through the modalities of their performance expresses attitudes toward the Holy. It does not remove us from the realm of nature, any more than it can set us above moral responsibility. But by investing our actions with an intention toward the Holy it puts us into relation with the Transcendent.

Halevi makes the same point when the Jew in his dialogue says that he has never been far from the presence of God and does not need the thought or imminence of death to place his actions in the light of the Transcendent. To explain, the rabbi tells of a traveler, an intimate of the king, who is chided by his fellow courtiers for not seeking royal protection when embarking on a dangerous journey. "Madmen!" he replies. "Isn't one who relied on him in time of safety more entitled to expect his aid in time of danger, even without voicing his request. . . . All my doings have been at his command and instruction, while you have honored him according to your own estimate and conjecture—yet he fails you not. How then will he abandon me on my journey, since I did not speak out as you did but trusted to his justice."[114] The thought is that of the Psalms (91:1): To one who lives in his presence, God is no mere *mysterium tremendum*, dreaded only in crises. Thus Joseph Karo, in the *Shulkhan Arukh*, the authoritative code of Jewish ritual, takes as his theme the motto *Shiviti ha-Shem kenegdi tamid* (Ps. 16:8)—every action becomes an expression of devotion. With this idea the table is indeed set for the refinement of individual character and communal culture.

But rituals lose the value they gain as expressions of devotion and recognitions of God's holiness if robbed of their symbolic significance or assigned some rival meaning. We can give a dimension of sanctity to every ordinary action—a fortiori to actions that directly address the Holy, where the task of ritual is to focus, define, and regulate our intent. The Torah aims to modulate our lives, making the whole life of Israel a symbol of God's holiness. Thus it commands us to become a nation of priests and a holy people, to seal God's covenant in our flesh, to strap God's words as a sign upon our hands and set them as a guide before our eyes, to write them on our doorposts and our gates, to teach them to our children, speak of them at home and when we go out, when we lie down and rise up. As the life of Israel becomes a symbol of God's holiness, Israel itself is made holy and godlike—but only if the meanings are retained and the symbols not made ends in themselves. For a symbol emptied of its meaning becomes flaccid and useless and is all too easily replaced with some other symbol or filled with some alien meaning that is of no aid in the building of character and understanding but may indeed be detrimental. Thus in all religions we find those who preserve the outward signs of piety with no visible benefit to character or understanding. The symbols are uncoupled from their normative sense and have lost the coherence of system and the efficacy of signs.

Let me sum up. By a ritual I understand a symbolic action that has values among the objects of its intension and that expresses attitudes toward those values through the modalities of its performance. I have shown that rituals can be rational actions, in spite of the apparent irrationality that results from their particularity. When rituals are made law, that particularity may chafe. But all laws have a ritual aspect, since their broad moral purposes underdetermine the precise prescriptions needed to regulate concrete actions. All laws draw conventional but pragmatically crucial boundaries—between intentional or unintentional acts, important and unimportant affronts or infractions, between persons and property, persons and other persons. All laws necessarily assign an "official" pragmatic significance to the various categories they identify and discriminate; they could not otherwise function as laws. In all systems of law the specifications that institute or implement the underlying values carry a symbolic load. Thus laws establish and perpetuate significances and express attitudes toward the values they define, by the very manner in which they are promulgated, enforced, interpreted, modified, obeyed, or disobeyed. So all laws are ritual institutions; all have a ritual aspect. But what are called ritual or ceremonial laws are those in which the ritual aspect is prominent or dominant; the symbolic expression of normative attitudes toward specific values, a paramount concern. To legislate in such areas (as all societies do, when the area seems important enough, whether they acknowledge that fact or not)[115] is a legitimate and vital social function, if only because certain crucial values cannot be given social form without such expression. The general values of peace, purity, joy, love, and truth that emerge as themes of the Torah's legislative intent are such values. Not that we would know nothing of these broad ideas if the Torah did not commend or command them, but that such values demand specification in praxis, lest they decline into vacuity, or indeed never emerge into concrete effectuation as goals and norms and indeed, sometimes, restrictions on our otherwise protean behavior.

Tolerance forbids imposing social symbolisms. That is an important partial truth. For thought and expression deserve to remain free.[116] But the shyer other half of the same truth is that tolerance, the privacy of thought, freedom of consciousness, and inwardness of allegiance are sustainable only by the maintenance of the invisible boundaries of personhood, which only rituals can demarcate and therefore only rituals can defend.

Marvin Fox argued that Saadiah Gaon was unable to propound a coherent idea of rational law. But we have seen that Saadiah, ably seconded by Maimonides, does have such an idea and does not ever (as some may believe) discriminate a class of ritual laws that is *not* rational. Yet my purpose has been broader than the defense of Saadiah and Maimonides, who seem to breast the centuries despite occasional unsympathetic responses to their ideas. Fox finds Saadiah calling self-contradictions irrational and so attempts to hold him to a purely formal notion of rationality. I think I have shown pretty exhaustively that such a reading can be imposed only by ignoring most of what Saadiah said about rationality. We can hold a practice rational if (and to the extent that) it serves some human good. And just as we need not accept a purely formal notion of rationality, we need not accept the correspondingly sterile instrumentalist notion. Aristotle saw that there would be a paradox in calling a person wise in a practical sense (*phronimos*) in whom reason functioned only instrumentally. Plato, similarly, saw in Thrasymachus a man who was sophisticated about means but a baby when it came to examining ends. In the same way, guided by a confluence of philosophical, religious, and moral traditions, Saadiah saw clearly the paradox and futility of knowing the means to our ends without knowing how to find and sustain sound ends for our lives. In choosing and defining those ends, we rightly rely on human reason and the guidance it receives from culture, tradition, and its own insight into God's perfection.

One of the things we can learn from Saadiah is not to define the human good so narrowly as to exclude expressions of thanks to God for our existence and the bounties by which our lives are ornamented and blessed. One of the things we can learn from Maimonides is that while the exact manner in which we express such thanks is radically underdetermined by the broad theme of gratitude, it is not for that reason morally neutral or arbitrary. Expressive actions and modes of action have significances in history, in our lives as individuals, and in the array of human cultures. They are linked into systems that give them contextual meanings, and bound up with a host of values that we cannot rightfully ignore. Human actions are never found in isolation and can be evaluated "in themselves" only by abstraction.

Some philosophers imagine that an act or expression, belief or strategy cannot be rational unless those who contemplate it are prepared to specify the grounds on which it alone and no other action should be performed. This, I think, is excessive. There are many worthwhile human aims, and many appropriate and effective ways of pursuing them. The idea that there is just one rational aim is constrictive and misleading, unless that aim itself is construed very broadly, as we saw in chapter 5. And for any worthy aim there may well be a variety of alternative means of achieving or pursuing it. This does not imply that none of these will be any better or more appropriate than any others, or that we have no grounds for choosing among rival ends or means, just as we choose among rival theories.

It is easy to confuse rationality with utility in a rather narrow sense, and so to ignore the critical import of the symbolic and expressive dimensions of human action and experience. In a kind of functionalist atomism, many people imagine that we can isolate an action from the context that gives it significance, and abandon, alter, or reverse it without larger impact on the social and natural milieu. Enlightenment and romantic ideologies make us too ready to imagine ourselves as isolated, asocial, ahistorical, and acultural beings—moral titans, in effect—and to overlook the intermeshing of our acts and choices with those of everyone and everything around us. The functionalist atomism so symptomatic of the sexual revolution, the individualistic attitude toward divorce, even needs-based, consumerist ideas of religion are cases in point, built on the idea that my preferences can tailor-make my lifestyle, or my God. But what I wanted to focus on here is the old fallacy that Plato exposes at the root of the perversity of the tyrannical mind, who supposes that he cannot prove that he is really in charge unless his actions are truly outrageous. One outcome of such infirm logic is an encouragement of the human appetite for the supernatural, overlooking God's universal governance in nature to seek invasions, disruptions, violent and spectacular light show. The same illogic is at work in morals: for God merely to expect of us what is reasonable and in our interest does not seem imposing enough an assertion of authority. There must be something outré, immoral, violative (at least counterintuitive, like the sacred monkeys in *Brideshead Revisited*) if not human sacrifice, ritual incest, antinomian excess, or Dionysiac frenzy—as if the demands of human decency and dignity, generosity and pursuit of perfection, love of nature and understanding, were not responsibility enough, not a project worthy of God's command. To find a purpose for a ritual, to see it as action made poetry, expressive and definitive of values, seems somehow insufficient—as though we ennobled God by ascribing to his will commands that have no reasons, and made ritual acts purer and more pristine by voiding them of content as devotions, celebrations, acts of thanksgiving, or charity—individual or communal expressions of our aspirations and the direction in which those aspirations bear us. If an act is not bizarre, we seem to be saying, superstitiously, if it is not arbitrary and pointless, how do we know it came from God?

We recall Maimonides' splendid answer to that question, as well as his critical comment that religious positivism places the creature above the Creator: we know that a norm comes from God if it leads toward our perfection as human beings. Not toward service of our "needs"—not even our need to revel in the irrational, but toward fulfillment of our identities, as individuals, as members of a culture and a community, and of the human race. We become like God, the Torah teaches, by becoming holy. We become holy by perfecting what is most godlike in ourselves—our minds and spirits, and the character that sustains the mind and spirit, as the body sustains the actions on which character depends. Our appetite for mystery will find ample cause for wonder in plumbing the meaning of human fulfillment, the nature of our embodiment, and the wellsprings and limits of human freedom, creativity, and kindness. But the quest in search of these will not prize mystery for its own sake, and the understanding that it seeks is not in principle unattainable, although there will be no single, simple, one-word answer as its outcome.

For every person who does not take ritual laws too seriously there are three or four more in every culture who take them much too seriously. Ironically, the two attitudes often coexist. For it is much easier to disparage the rituals of others than even to notice our own. Humanity needs a critical reexamination and reappropriation of ritual norms, in search of those that serve the human good, even if only indirectly and, as Maimonides puts it, by numerous intermediate steps. But the hunger for authenticity that bespeaks that need will not be sated or nourished by a quest for uniformity. We hardly need to revert to the religious wars of Swift's Big- and Little-Endians. But neither should we presume that ceremonies are always a sheerly personal matter. A society that tolerates polygamy (as America has begun to do) has sacrificed real interests, violated real boundaries, and will, if the Torah contains any truth at all, pay a real price. A society that values tolerance so highly that it will sacrifice a million lives to AIDS rather than restrict sexual acts, even to the extent of monitoring AIDS-infected prostitutes, has paid and continues to pay a price in human tragedy. And when the AIDS vaccine is finally found and those whose lifestyles claim numerous sexual partners revert to the behaviors that the AIDS epidemic, with its tragic toll of infected partners, bystanders, and infants, has only partially restrained, the reversion will be an invitation to the next opportunistic infection. Ritual makes a difference here. It can make a larger difference. For, properly modulated, ritual is a matter of tact, privacy, and boundaries, implicit symbolisms, spoken and unspoken commitments to life, to truth, to the highest Good, to personhood—dignities preserved, not violated. Culture can outpace the ceaseless mutation and evolution of viruses, but only by constant thought and thoughtfulness.

7

The Biblical Laws of Diet and Sex

There is no general agreement about the aim of laws that seek to regulate our diet and sexuality. Perhaps diverse goals are sought. For systems of law vary in object and impact;[1] and perhaps correspondingly, there are conflicting theories about what laws should do—utilitarian and functionalist, positivist and formalist, theistic, naturalistic, and conventionalist. But in considering the Torah's rules regarding what Israelites shall eat and how they shall express themselves erotically, we can profitably set aside prior notions of the proper sphere of law and try to see the intent of the laws from their own standpoint. We begin to do so when we recognize that these laws, calling on Israelites to share both the loathings and the affections of their God (Deut. 7:25, 14:3, 17:1, 24:4), aim to frame an ethos. They are educational, then, in Plato's sense.[2] If so, they can be understood with reference to the ideal of life they project and judged by their effectiveness in guiding us toward that ideal.

Nourishment, with all that is needed to procure it, and sexual gratification, with all that seems necessary to express it, are basic human needs. But, as myth and other expressive modes show, intensity of experience fosters and so can be expressed by a muddling or fusing of categories, whether of time, space, identity, causation—or here, the distinctive terms of diet and sexuality themselves. Both have a vegetative phase, of cultivation and nourishment, courtship and reproduction, but also an animal phase, of appropriation, which harbors a potential for violence, direct or expressive. Foci of such potential are the moment of the kill in hunting or husbandry, the cut in harvesting, the rending of flesh consumed, the possibility of rape and the orgiastic, as extensions in extremis of the pathos of the erotic. Any moment can be a theater of violence. But elemental appetites, heightened by exigency, frustration, teasing, excess, or abuse, are especially vulnerable. It is here that cultures seek to modulate not just intensity itself but its preconditions, outcomes, and significances. The structural symmetries of diet and sex afford a powerful resource in this regard. For mandates in one realm offer vivid surrogates that can map the other.

Purity and Impurity: A System of Meanings

Signs of such mapping are found in the polarity the Torah draws between the pure (*ṭahor*) and the impure (*ṭame*). "Rituals of purity and impurity," Mary Douglas writes, "create unity in experience. . . . By their means, symbolic patterns are worked out and publicly displayed . . . disparate elements are related and disparate experience is given meaning."[3] The observation is fruitful because it is generic. What specific unities and patterns do these rituals create? Can we read the meanings and values inductively, as Plato does when he observes the armed dances, training camps, and unyielding music of Crete and concludes that the island's laws are designed for war?[4] With this question in mind I ask, What things are called *ṭahor* and *ṭame* in the Torah? Pursuing the Maimonidean method of ordering the senses of such terms according to their empirical proximity or transcendental remoteness (*Guide* I 1–50; cf. II 45), I find seven basic senses:

1. Homogeneous or unadulterated versus adulterated
2. Hygienically clean versus unclean
3. Suitable versus unsuitable as food
4. Suitable versus unsuitable conjugally
5. Suitable versus unsuitable for sacrificial use
6. Morally acceptable or elevated versus morally unacceptable or debased
7. Spiritually elevated or edified, verging toward the Transcendent (*kadosh*) versus spiritually impure, debased, degraded, depraved

In none of their Pentateuchal occurrences do *ṭahor* and *ṭame* bear just one sense; every occurrence gives them connotations that lap at the boundaries of one or several others. Ritual suitability, for example, is influenced and limited by physical purity or impurity, by perfection and imperfection, and by moral considerations. Thus the commandment "Thou shalt not bring the hire of a whore or the price of a dog to the House of the Lord for any vow, for both are loathsome to the Lord thy God" (Deut. 23:18) figures moral impurity onto physical uncleanness: immoral practices yield tainted funds. The language is used associatively—a natural metaphor. For even apes, when given signs, express disapprobation by the sign for "dirty." If we gloss "the price of a dog" as the hire of a catamite, the condemnation is redoubled by the imagery embedded in the language.

The Prophets are keenly sensitive to the polyvalence of the idea of purity. Isaiah (1:16), calling for moral reform, writes: "Wash yourself, make yourself clean, put away the evil of your doings." The psalmist answers his own question, "Who shall ascend the mount of the Lord?" with a lucid metaphor: "He that hath clean hands and a pure heart" (Ps. 24:3–4). But while these meanings are not isolated, they are distinct, forming a system in which the more empiric map, mirror, and point to the higher senses. So the ritual law teaches as it exercises semiotic control.

The value toward which the system points and to which it gives pragmatic definition is the holiness ordained in the thematic command "Ye shall be holy, for I the Lord thy God am holy (Lev. 19:2; cf. 20:7, 26). The entire system of purity is presented as a solution to the problem of defining holiness, that is, transcendence, in proximate terms. Thus, guided by Lev. 18–20, Maimonides places the laws of diet and sex under the rubric of Holiness in his *Code*.

Closest to what might seem a purely physical sense of *ṭahor* in the Pentateuch is that in which it is prescribed that the gold of the Tabernacle candlesticks must be pure (Exod. 25:11, 17, 24, 29, 31, 36, 38, 39; 30:3; 37:22, 23). The reference is to refined metal, but the overtones are in senses 5 and 7. For the candlesticks are for ritual use, dedicated to the sole God, who is absolute. They are symbols, then. The purity of their gold is a metaphor, obvious but striking. Thus the candlestick itself is called pure (Exod. 31:8, 39:37, Lev. 24:4), given a metaphoric character: it is pure by the purity of its matter and the sanctity of its use.

Ṭahor shows an empiric use again in Exodus 24:10. What is described is a color, or the absence of color, "clear (or pure) as the heart of heaven." But the object is God's epiphany. Visible purity stands as surrogate for an Absolute that bears no visible mark (Exod. 20:4–5). The highest and most empiric senses meet. Nowhere in the Pentateuch is *ṭahor* or *ṭame* given a value-neutral sense. Not that the terms name some magic energy or aura of capricious ambiguity, to be pent or harnessed. On the contrary, precise ritual and moral significances are assigned to empirically identified hygienic states. Where magic seeks to constrain the unknowable, Leviticus has precluded magic.[5]

We all respond to a scab, a running sore, a corpse, infected fabric. How are such feelings to be addressed? By avoidance, or braving our feelings, out of kindness or machismo, as when Saint Catherine drank a bowl of pus? We cannot, as Mary Douglas shows, explain rules about "dirt" simply by appeal to innate disgust or horror, nor (simply) by reference to hygienic suspicions.[6] The reason, I think, is not just the protean variability of human responses to (and definitions of) "dirt" but the inherent ambivalence of distaste: psyche and culture can dramatically transpose attraction and aversion. This is the real alchemy behind the fabular alchemy of magic, pinioned when Spinoza defines cruelty as the desire to do evil to one whom we pity[7]—a seeming paradox explicable by the natural desire for distance from an object of pity. Similarly, one might feel that one has conquered purulence by swallowing one's loathing. The heart of the ambiguity is captured in the Hebrew root denoting both craving and disgust—*t'v*.[8] Those who imagine that Leviticus regulates too nicely (or not nicely enough) too fine a realm of intimate detail do not reckon with the ambiguity of purulence and its opposites and kin. No society can leave these areas unregulated, by law, custom, or that blend of custom and creativity that we call taste. Does one kiss the corpse, bury it, or hang it in the closet? At issue is not what Leviticus regulates but how, to what effect, with what intent?

Biblical hygiene is not about neatness but about contagion—with symbolic moral and spiritual associations and dietary and sexual overtones and implications. The unwholesome is identified and treated—by isolation, incubation, bathing, destruction. Once terminated, the treatment is punctuated ritually and hygienically, to render unambiguous a newly established status. Rule-bound procedures mark the term of impurity. Uniting the rules is a clear determination to present a response that is neither unfocused nor ad hoc. Thus priests identify, isolate, diagnose, and pronounce clean or unclean suspected cases of biblical "leprosy." The isolation is physical; the diagnosis, empirical (Lev. 13:2–39). So are the distinctions between benign and pernicious baldness (vv. 40–43), or between virulent (*mam'eret*) and nonvirulent infection (vv. 47–50). The stated concern is with contagion; the test (spreading, change of color) shows that contagion is a spatiotemporal process. Virulent infection in a fabric is eradicated by fire; laundering is enough for the less pernicious sort; in intermediate types of case, only the affected portion is discarded. The interest in conserving woven goods yields phased responses that vividly reveal the Law's nisus: there is no horrified rejection of a garment—or its owner. Pernicious infections can be isolated, confirmed, and eradicated. They cannot vault time gaps, pass through walls, or survive fire. Incantations are irrelevant. Innocuous conditions do not become dangerous by their resemblance to pernicious ones, nor by confusion in names. Even moral status makes no difference—as it would in the dream logic of myth. The case of Miriam (Numbers 12) is the exception that proves the rule: she grew white with leprosy for criticizing Moses' marriage to a black woman. But neither the cause nor the cure in this case finds parallel in the laws of leprosy. Biblical virulence is physical, as shown by the "leper's" warning cry (Lev. 13:45–46). And victims are not permanent pariahs; once healed, they are clean (Lev. 14:4). For the condition is natural, not magical; the isolation, hygienic. The Law, then, seeks to confine leprosy not just epidemiologically but semiotically, to *define* its uncleanness *as* physical, and our responses as hygienic.

Because it sets a boundary to concerns with purity and impurity this is ritual legislation. It assigns symbolic significances to empirical occasions and ordains specific attitudes toward the values intended. The idea of purity brings these laws within the symbol system, even apart from the higher concern with holiness. But in ancient Israel the regulations governing symbolic expressions of attitudes toward central values are entrusted to the priests, whose descent links them symbolically to Israel's past, quite apart from any clinical qualifications or diagnostic skills they may acquire. Here the office is not a perquisite, like the priestly portions of sacrificial animals. Nor have priests any magical powers by which to discharge their responsibility. Indeed no magic is allowed for in quarantining and diagnosis.[9] Liturgically, the priests are not holy people but "the people of Thy holiness," *ʿAm kedoshekha*, charged with maintaining the boundary-marking symbols by which Israel responds to the holy. Contagious diseases, their diagnosis and confinement, and confinement of the responses to them, belong to them precisely because the priests of Israel are not sorcerers or shamans. Their role deprives these occasions of magical significance, confines their import to the hygienic. For the same reason, blessing the people is entrusted to the priests (Num. 6:22–27). It is they who conserve the terms in which the very idea of blessedness is articulated: "So shall they put my name . . ."—not otherwise, not by another name or another hand. Israel has no *morbus sacrus*. But "leprosy" might have become such, had the dynamic of values been left simply to run its course or channeled contrary to the sense the Torah legislates. Thus the priestly office is to maintain the values of the Torah that link purity with the holy and block the magical inversion of purity and purulence. For the superstitious awe of disease might have been crippling spiritually as well as epidemiologically.

With running "issue," again a ritual significance is cast on a hygienic base, and again we see a concern not just with impurity and contagion but with the horror of impurity and contagion. Thus the ordinances are addressed to Aaron along with Moses, signifying a matter for the priests. Again contagion is by contact, not by glance, name, or affinity; and the effect has temporal bounds. There is a sacrifice for the *ṭame*. But, like every *ḥaṭat*, that offering works symbolically, removing not guilt or pollution themselves but the sense of guilt or pollution: sacrifice is no more a means of literal cleansing than it is an alternative to the restitution of misappropriated property. Cleansing here is by washing, not by penitence, self-abasement, or ritual defilement.

A flow of semen or menses is assimilated to the same model. But now what is contained is not contagion but the emotive response alone. Even permitted intercourse conveys "impurity," but this is cleansed by bathing and awaiting the evening (Lev. 15:16), terminating any sense of sexual impurity. For, as Ibn Ezra and Abravanel explain, it is not semen but death that conveys impurity: living sperm begin to die as soon as they leave the body. If puritanism, sexual diffidence, or scrupulosity gains no firm hold here, it is because the Law does not fret over our sexual nature but cleanses hygienically while it tacitly answers any sense of impurity with the purifying sensations of the bath and the symbolic boundary of evening.

With corpses, more is at stake than hygiene. Any dead body is ritually defiling, but human bodies bear the human image and so require special treatment (Num. 19:11–22). The corpse of a possible murder victim raises larger questions (Deut. 21:1–9), which find their ritual solution in the *ʿeglah ʿarufah*, whose symbolic message is made explicit: "Suffer not innocent blood to abide in the midst of Thy people Israel" (Deut. 21:8). But the symbolism is fittingly complemented in a pragmatic vein, by making the priests and town authorities acknowledge responsibility for crimes within their jurisdiction. When they say ceremonially that they knew nothing of the bloodshed whose evidence they have found, they avow their civil responsibility. Pragmatically, the Torah's gaze falls on the moral and social issues; symbolically, on deference to the human image.

The idea of hygienic impurity broadens to include environmental pollution, which in turn becomes a metaphor for moral outrages like the early ransoming of homicides (Num. 35:31–34): A victim's blood defiles the land not magically but morally. For the defilement is removed not by ceremony but by punishment. But symbolic outrages, too, can pollute the land; paradigmatically, the exposure of executed criminals' bodies overnight (Deut. 21:22–23). Night again forms a barrier, a fixed symbolic term beyond which punishment becomes outrage, and, as with a day worker's wage, a moral issue. The criminal is dead; there is no direct question of his interests. But, as in pornography and mutilation, desecration of the human image is itself a moral issue.

Incest, Violation, and Personhood

The biblical laws of diet and sex find their context in the laws of purity and impurity. These are the terms that provide their algebra, each sense interpreting the rest. Sexual offenses are moral and symbolic outrages that pollute the land. The practices of Israel's predecessors caused it to "vomit them forth," as if it had been forced to swallow some unwholesome or disgusting thing (Lev. 18:24–28, 20:22). But it is the practices that are called disgusting; the land was not made permanently unfit for human habitation but unfit for those who practiced such loathsome doings (*toʿevot*). It was cleansed when it was cleansed of their abominations. The expropriation, then, is modeled as a natural as well as a moral process. For vomiting has causes, not grounds: the rejected mores are not merely ungenerous or offensive; they are insupportable by nature, abominable not just in human eyes but before God. Here moral and ritual concerns interlace. God punished the practitioners, for and through their impurity. Their decadence made them incapable of tenure in the land. They were dispossessed in favor of Israel, whom it would behoove to heed the grounds of that disinheritance.

The sexual practices of the Canaanites violated standards which they ought to have known and respected. Are there grounds for that claim? I do not think we have reached bedrock in finding explanations for ritual restrictions even in a horror at cannibalism or incest. For to escape circularity we must discover what is wrong with such all but universally abhorred acts. The real or false naïveté that often passes for moral inquiry in our society imparts more than academic interest to that question.

The Rabbis group the laws forbidding sexual congress with kin under the rubric of *gilui ʿarayot*, a phrase derived from the repeated biblical admonition not to expose the nakedness of any of one's own flesh (*kol sh'er besaro*). Conventionally this is read as a mere euphemism: one is prohibited cohabitation (another euphemism) with near kin, as listed in the lines that follow (Lev. 18:6–18); there shall be no coitus with them. But plainly more is said than that. For the Torah is not embarrassed for words to name coitus. Has the text anticipated the Rabbinic mode of making a margin (*seyag*) about the law, so that incest is forbidden and, in the same spirit, exposure as well? That, too, is too simple. What we see is not a law with its gloss but language that bares the law's intent: incest defined as a violation of privacy.

The prohibition is presented not as "the ultimate taboo," if 'taboo' means an unaccountable restriction, but as a moral law protecting the dignity of close kin. Thus each potential victim has a nakedness, *his* nakedness, *her* nakedness, or, with relations by marriage, the nakedness of a blood relation (e.g., 18:16). Exposing that nakedness has moral consequences: The mere potential for shame demands these restrictions (18:18). Thus the force of the word "expose." The victim (of what is still sometimes called a "victimless crime") is morally laid bare: "If a man take his sister, the daughter of his mother or his father [even a half sister; the relation is specified to render vivid the nexus of with parental dignity, which heads the hierarchy of protected dignities] and see her nakedness and she see his, that is a disgrace,[10] and they shall be barred from the sight of their people, for he has exposed his sister's nakedness and must bear the onus" (Lev. 20:17). Ibn Ezra glosses the special responsibility of the brother as based on the assumption that he was the seducer or sexual aggressor; David Hoffmann (1843–1921)[11] argues that the brother bears a special guilt, since he ought to have protected his sister. Critically for us, the Torah sees incest as violative even when it is consensual.

Inevitably the Torah will place incest in a moral light. It is wrong not just because God condemns it but because of the dignity it violates. That dignity might seem no more than a name that reifies the prohibition, the rationale for an immemorial taboo. But, on the contrary, although the prohibition helps define the privacy of personhood, there would be no prohibition if there were nothing to protect. The widespread abhorrence of incest in all human cultures is evidence that its prohibition is no mere ornament of nicety, at or just beyond the margins of social utility, but a foundation stone of social structure. Just as cooked food marks the boundary between nature and culture,[12] so the incest prohibition marks the boundary between the individual and the family. Its terms frame the dignity of personhood.

It is sometimes too little appreciated that consanguineous matings carry serious genetic hazards, especially when permitted or encouraged over multiple generations.

Inbreeding heightens homozygosity in a population, reducing heterozygote advantage, that is, the protection afforded by undamaged replicate genes in the diploid human genome, as no careful observer could fail to note.[13] But strictly genetic explanations of the incest prohibition do not account for its centrality in human social systems, or for its casual or ritual violation. Nor do they adequately explain the power of the normative repugnance for incest—even when the partners have no reproductive potential—or account for the varied kinship systems that expand the prohibition, say by banning erotic contact with nonblood relations like stepmothers.

The Freudian account of incest is tangled in circularity. It assumes "the Father" to be outraged by the incest (actual or intended) of "the Son" with "the Mother." But why should he be? Why would possessiveness reach the pitch of outrage unless already tinged with ideas of dignity, honor, individuality—the very notions that Freud seeks to explain by his myth of the Oedipal origins of identity and guilt. Again, the constraints that civilization calls for and what the Torah ascribes to God's commands are made to seem arbitrary and factitious. An alternative picture emerges if we credit the cultures of the world with some appreciation of what they are about, and allow the biblical legislator some capacity to articulate, in the language of purity and impurity, what the incest prohibition intends.

Incest is violation, a moral breach, not just a breach of unaccountable social forms. Encroachment by a father, mother, sibling, son, or daughter on the sexuality of another, often a minor and dependent, is an invasion fraught with psychic risk and morally freighted by its denial of the boundaries of privacy, inchoate in a child or adolescent, and fragile in any of us. Like rape, incest violates personhood, in which sexuality is a vital constituent—even when there is no overt violence, threat, or coercion, even in the rare case where it may be countenanced by the victim. For it is personhood, not the will alone, that the biblical laws and general norms of humanity seek here to protect.

Genesis 2:24—"Therefore shall a man leave his father and his mother and cleave unto his wife, and they shall become one flesh"—models the Torah's central norm for relations between the sexes. The cherishing and loyalty conveyed by the image of "cleaving" rests socially, psychologically, ontologically, on the moral independence of the man the law addresses, and of the woman, who is his counterpart.[14] Without the existential self-definition of the human person as an autonomous individual there is no moral freedom for the founding and sustaining of families, and the moral identity that might serve as the nucleus of an integrated personality capable of mature relationships is compromised. To give credit to the cultures of the world and to the biblical legislator is to allow that incest restrictions enshrine a recognition of this elemental fact. All cultures grasp it on an intuitive level. The biblical legislator articulates it as a moral fact, grounding a system of prohibitions, which, like all sound legislation, has a positive ideal of human life behind it.

There is no quarrel here with the forming of communal identities. That is what man and wife are supposed to do—to become one flesh, as Genesis expresses it poetically, using the same term for the new identity as that which marks blood kinship (Lev. 18:6). But how can man and wife cleave to one another to become one flesh if they may not differentiate their identities—centrally, their sexual identities—from the familial matrix? Personal identities are formed in this matrix and emerge, in part, through the respect accorded them. So there are many ways of thwarting or deflecting their emergence, many ways of violating personhood without ever striking a physical blow, and even without neglecting to secure compliance, passive or active. Sexual ways are central among them, not exclusively but importantly, because of the centrality of sexual identity and gender roles in the formation, expression, and maintenance of an adult identity.[15] Thus incest, Biblically, is not coercive violation of another's will by overpowering that person's body, but psychic violation of another's personhood, through a domination that engrosses or expropriates that person's sexuality. It violates the ethereal boundary between social and personal identities that the family exists to foster, a boundary that individualistic—atomistic and mechanistic—moral theories, in their naive conception of the limits and defenses of the self, often have no conceptual apparatus to define, let alone protect. It is the vulnerability of our sexuality that the Torah intends in speaking of exposure.

Nakedness here is not a thing but a situation—not a euphemism for an organ or an act but a state of defenselessness (see Gen. 42:9; Ezek. 16:7), quite a different idea from that of nudity.[16] It involves shame or humiliation, not intrinsically but by convention (Gen. 3:11), that is, by symbolism in a social context. For nakedness expresses helplessness. Clothing confers and expresses dignity. Stripping removes it (cf. Isa. 20:2–3; Job 22:6). When Ham saw his father's nakedness, his compromised state, drunk and disheveled, genitals exposed, his glance, followed by relating the incident rather than modestly covering the exposure, would provoke a father's curse. There need be no search for any "dark and horrid crime" on Ham's part. There is no question of sexual violation of old Noah in any modern sense. At stake, as the story presents it, was simple human dignity, the same as that protected by the biblical laws, described in identical terms.

But Ham is no mere object lesson. He is the father of Canaan (Gen. 9:18, 22), on whom the curse of his lewdness rests (v. 25); and he is the ancestor of the Egyptians (Gen. 10:6). Canaan and Egypt were the termini of Israel's wanderings between exodus and nation building, mediated by the giving of the Law at Sinai. The customs of Canaan and Egypt form moral termini that situate the ethos of Israel and thematize that law: "I the Lord am your God. You shall not copy the doings of the land of Egypt, where you have dwelt. Nor shall you copy the doings of the land of Canaan, to which I am bringing you. You shall not follow their norms [*u-beḥukkotehem lo telekhu*]. You shall practice My norms and faithfully observe My laws (Lev. 18:2–4)." We are not left in the dark about which norms are meant. For God's laws, which immediately follow the admonition that these are the laws of life (Lev. 18:5), are those of *gilui ʿarayot*, the prohibitions of adultery, Moloch worship, homosexuality, and bestiality. The implication is that the rejected norms are contrary to the laws of life but were salient among the practices of the Canaanites and Egyptians. All of them violate the sexual dignity that the Torah ascribes to each human being, the dignity that Ham, their ancestor, violated thoughtlessly, archetypally, in view of the story's now visible barb.

Did the Canaanites and Egyptians practice the abominations fathered upon their remotest ancestor? Biblical polemic might not be the fairest source of evidence, although we cannot ignore the historical relevance of the Torah's moral critique. We do know independently that the Egyptians and the peoples of Canaan followed practices that are biblically termed abominations. But our concern here is not with those customs per se but with how the biblical legislator thought of them. Egyptian religious culture, as biblically perceived, focused on death and the afterlife,[17] a preoccupation toward which the biblical celebration of life stands in outspoken contrast. Canaanite culture, as projected biblically, was orgiastic, that is, it tinged sexual energies with violence.

In a ritual intensification of the magic power of royal birth, the Egyptians, like the ancient Hawaiians, apparently instituted royal incest,[18] not as a casual or aberrant social phenomenon but as a symbolic expression of sacred values. Yet Egypt's highest values, even beyond deified royalty, were those that looked toward death and past it to the afterlife. The solemn and deadly symbolism of Egyptian afterworldliness was graved on the minds of Israelites as a celebration of death that seemed to embalm the living world in a sealed tomb and mortgage the whole fertile land of the Nile in mortmain to its hereditary priesthood. Thus the bite of one of the ancient Jewish jokes that we have already had occasion to mention: "Weren't there any graves in Egypt . . . ?" (Exod. 14:11); and thus, as we have seen, the landlessness of the priests of Israel, the banning of the permanent alienation of land, and the maintenance of Israel's priests and Levites as a dependent rather than privileged class.[19] Egyptian culture, viewed not through the excited glow of archaeological discovery and decipherment but through the living memory of bondage, anchors one of the extremes that will orient the biblical ethos. The Mosaic law of life reads the ancient incest prohibition not as an arbitrary restriction, whose incomprehensibility might render it subject to systematic transformations—now solemnly preserved, now solemnly violated for the frisson of release that its capacitance as a norm might allow—but as a moral principle, intelligible at once in the language of shame and dignity and so always restorable by reasoning and consideration, beyond the pull of the magic of ambivalence.

Blood and Symbolic Violence

We know far less of the customs of Canaan than of Egypt. But we have seen the evidence of human sacrifice, and we also know of temple prostitution. Clearly, these were salient for the biblical legislator. Violence and violation are the norms we glimpse through the occasional chinks that biblical condemnation opens in a more general wall of disapproving silence. How thoroughly ingrained or isolated the values surrounding violence may have been in Canaanite culture, or how sublimated into symbolic celebrations evocative of its frissons, diffusing and perpetuating the offending ethos, are questions not readily answered. It would be hard enough to answer such questions even about the polarities of violence and gentleness so prominent in the still-living culture of Europe and the Americas today. But clearly the celebration of violence that the Torah singles out as Canaanite was doubly offensive biblically. For it compounded violation of personhood with the idea of the holy. Blood as a symbol of life and its violation was a cynosure of the rites the Torah ascribes to the Canaanites, and blood thereby acquires a special significance in the Mosaic system that steadies itself by its alienness to those rites. When Canaanites "passed their seed to Moloch" (Lev. 18:21, 20:1–5), they committed an atrocity justly compared with incest, violating the personhood of their children, as our oldest gloss reveals (Deut. 18:9–10; cf. 2 Kings 23:10, with 21:6; Jer. 7:31). It is moral outrage that fixes the language of the biblical prohibition: the victim is not merely someone's son or daughter but *your* offspring; someone has consented that this be done and indeed arranged for it.

The power of a sacrifice lies in the power of the bond it breaks. As with Iphigenia, it is not just *a* death, a captive or straggler, but the death of one whose god-fierce claims are violated, releasing emotive energy, making the sacrifice attractive, heady, even to a god. This is the violence the Torah condemns, even at the price of the promised immediacy of the divine. No god worthy of worship would accept such offerings. Even the ritual self-violation of scarification, which evokes the frisson not of the kill but of the sacrificial cut, or the fortitude to overcome it, is forbidden to the priests of Israel. They serve not in violence and violation but with symbols of peace—the bullock, lamb and dove, grain, wine, cakes, and oil. The Levitical cultic repertoire points to the tranquillity of the moral life as clearly as the music and dances of Plato's pacific mode evoke resolution and freedom (*Republic* III 399; *Laws* VII 814e).

Sexual links can be forged without harm to personhood—but only with consent, commitment, and perfect trust. Hence the laws against rape and seduction, and those that mandate marital exclusivity. Adultery, like incest, violates privacy—much as comparisons between sisters would expose the nakedness the Torah protects, or as parental privacy is breached by coupling with a parent's spouse, a daughter-in-law, or a mother and daughter (Lev. 20:11, 12, 14). As the sexuality of a family member is inviolate, so is the trust of a spouse. The perfect steadfastness that completes that trust cannot be shared. This we can understand ethically—that adultery is betrayal—whether or not our moral apologists are quite ready to agree.[20]

We can likewise make explicit the Torah's axiom that to violate one's own personhood is as criminal as to betray that of another. So we can follow the symmetries in the Mosaic penalties for adultery and fornication and trace a common moral thread in the bans on scarification, self-mutilation, bestiality, homosexuality. The Torah sees even a violation of the human image as a real violation of human dignity. In combating cults of cruelty it protects, defends, and defines its own ethos and its ideal of personhood and of God. God here is the God of Abraham, the God of justice. Thus Jacob's sons lapse into a prepatriarchal mode when they use circumcision as a ploy to wreak a bloody vengeance on Dinah's rapist and his people, for "defiling" their sister (Gen. 34:5, 13, 27). We can find a hygienic point of contact with that thought, since a sexual assailant may convey infection. But even here the idea is moralized. The crime was in the intent: "He humbled her." What is primitive in the brothers' response is that they take the offense as a pretext for blood vengeance out of all proportion to the crime. Their response is not moral but expressionistic. The defilement has become a miasma over their honor and repute. The Mosaic Law is more critical about imponderables. Humbling is a wrong, especially when the victim is at a disadvantage, as in the Law of the Fair Captive (Deut. 21:10–14; cf. Lev. 19:20). But the idea that rape pollutes the victim in a way that would render her unfit for marriage is rejected. And because the crime is moral it does not incriminate the victim (Deut.

22:25–27). The asymmetry of victim and rapist, like the symmetry of adultery and fornication, shows that magical pollution has been displaced by moral offense. Thus the references to crimes that "defile the land."

When the Torah forbids a husband to remarry a former wife who has since married someone else, the remarriage is called defiling to the land in terms that are explicitly moral (*lo' taḥtī' et ha-aretz*; Deut. 24:1–4). For the woman is not "impure" or "unclean" to anyone but her former husband. It is the act that is impure. The woman is free to remarry; that is the functional meaning of her bill of divorcement. But the man who divorced her "cannot" (*lo yukhal*) remarry her once she has been another man's wife: "it is an abomination [*to'evah*] before God," a source of sin to the very land, because this practice or institution (sc. temporary marriage) violates the sanctity of wedlock, by breaching intimacy, making the woman's sexuality a semipublic object—not necessarily a commodity, as Hertz suggests, although that potential, too, is present,[21] but an object that reduces personhood to functionality. The offense is moral; it degrades the ethos, concretely represented by the land, which bears a burden of sin, elsewhere called pollution.

What, then, of the ban on menstrual coitus? Here many moderns bridle and turn the Torah's ethical categories against its text, suggesting that to legislate in this realm invades familial privacy, marital intimacy, and sexual dignity, if not personal freedom—as though these laws were of the bureaucratic sort, overseen by regulatory agencies rather than the conscience and consciousness they seek to inform. Countless denunciations accuse the Torah of regarding menstruous women (superstitiously) as impure, even accursed.[22] But in context we find no basis for such claims. For the Torah explains its prohibition not by reference to impurity[23] but by reference to exposure, specifically, exposure of the source of blood. The heart of the concern, perhaps, is that the mingling of blood with eros may overlay images of violence upon our sexuality. For the Torah is concerned with the images linked with the sacred. Thus, its command that God be symbolized not by any image but by the act of creation and that, in turn, not by a thing but by a day and its actions and cessations.[24]

There is little to support our reading, except that it seems to be the explanation given by the text. But if correct it provides a key to the association of impurity with menstruation quite beyond the ritual and hygienic notions of uncleanness. The prohibition against "approach to uncover nakedness" that mentions impurity assigns that impurity to the period, not the woman. "The time of her uncleanness" (Lev. 18:19) means the time when it is impure so to approach her. For the violation of this command is one of the wrongs that is said to have polluted the land—"rendered it impure" (Lev. 18:24–30). When repeated (Lev. 20:18), the prohibition mentions no impurity but refers to the woman's "infirmity" (*davah*),[25] the standard biblical term for menstruation.[26] But the overlay of blood upon the erotic, central as it is among the semiotic foci against which the Torah legislates, is itself but the paradigm of an impure and rejected ethos. The pollution was that of the Canaanites; they had defiled themselves, culturally, by their practices. I cannot think of a more graphic anatomy of an ethos: the nation was corrupt because of its institutions (*ḥukkot*; Lev. 20:23); its orgiastic rituals patterned violence upon sexuality. It is erasure of that pattern that the Mosaic symbolism seeks.

Religion and Ethos

Religion, as we have seen, is often thought of as a matter of opinions and so sharply set apart from the practical. But biblical religion is a congeries of symbolically freighted acts together constituting a way of life. These symbolic freightings color each life they touch with theme and meaning. So they are hardly incidental to life's purpose. Biblically, to regard commerce, diet, or lovemaking as nonsignificant and seek to confine ultimate meaning to just one realm labeled "spirituality" is to deaden every aspect of life and falsify the spiritual. For spirituality grows and flourishes only when expressed in character, actions, social patterns, and interactions—in courting, marrying, making love, taking prisoners, lending, borrowing, and, of course, worshiping and eating. To seal off any part of life is to render it inauthentic or insincere. Thus, as the Torah discovers, only ethics can achieve so thoroughgoing an integration as ethics requires, ethics not of just any sort but focused by the love of God as the Absolute Perfection, who calls forth, or commands, our aspiration toward perfection ("Ye shall be holy . . .") and our love of humanity ("Love thy fellow as thyself")—two *mitzvot* that cannot remain mere generalities but must be spun out into a system of practical and symbolic applications.

The Torah assumes an earnestness like its own in all Israel. Thus the scriptural use of an irony of intention, expressing outcomes as if they had been purposes. This dramatic irony, so widespread in the Prophets, is rooted in the consequentialism and eudaimonism of Deuteronomy and the entire Pentateuch. What it means here is that the Torah takes symbols seriously, its own and those it combats. For the lives of individuals and nations are patterned by symbols—Egypt's, by slavery, hierarchy, the Egyptian way of death; Canaan's, by the frisson of blood and the orgiastic. The Torah seeks to shape the life of Israel by guiding Israel's symbol system, crystallizing the alternatives, and expecting the wholesome moral intuitions that it teaches and fosters to provide the necessary and appropriate response of commitment and aspiration. It does not enter the Mosaic way of thinking to imagine that a nation might reach such a stage of alienation as to live by one set of symbols and worship by another.

If the biblical concern with regulating diet and sex seemed strange to Enlightenment Deists and Protestant divines who thought of religion as a matter of faith, modern liberals reared on secularism find it even more so. Why should any behavior be regulated that does not palpably harm some victim other than its author? Are not diet and sex areas of personal conscience rather than social consequence? If hygiene can be technically managed and erotic gratification seems eminently separable from reproduction, or even emotion, why should ancient taboos against homosexuality or bestiality or incest, or the hoary dietary restraints of the Torah have any sphere of application, let alone imperative force? Adherence to such laws becomes (at best) a purely personal matter or ethnic "eyepatch." The mythology of functional atomism renders almost invisible the nexus of ethical concerns that underlies these laws. Yet orgiastic practices are far from vanished in our world. Indeed, they have proliferated, and with the weakening of secularized creeds and codes and the heightening of the sensate, we can already perceive within their frissons the still lurking, if subjective, pagan gods. It is against these that the Torah itself sets its protective margin (*seyag*), to check the play of cruelty with no less a barrier than the ritual of food and the erotic.

The paradigm here is in the laws forbidding menstrual coitus and prohibiting the seething of a kid in its mother's milk. These are not the Torah's minimal demands. Those are found in the seven *mitzvot* classed as given to the "sons of Noah," humanity at large—paradigmatically, the laws against adultery and incest and against the consumption of flesh rent from a living body. It is easy to understand (and takes ingenuity to deny) that adultery is a moral offense against one's own and at least two others' personhood—quite apart from any reproductive, hygienic, or social consequences. And consuming a limb torn from a living animal is clearly an act of barbarism that would have little point without some notion of capturing the life of the victim by its violation, or some comparable expressive intent, as when men bite off the heads of rattlesnakes or push the envelope of machismo or Bushido by eating fugu, the highly poisonous fish consumed as an act of daring by a certain class of Japanese gourmands. Restraint of such extremes is something we may think we can take for granted. But biblical legislation is more explicit than many another scheme of laws in spelling out its expectations and in taking them beyond the minimal. The Torah does not take such matters for granted for the same reason that it avoids much abstract vocabulary. The reason: that it is a Law for all times, not just for one.

Life, we have noted, is full of ritual expectations. When we walk into a room we do not usually slink along the walls. But the Torah rests nothing on that and so shows no interest in the question. Incest is quite another matter. Here the Torah sees moral significance. But, unlike adultery or theft, here ritual articulation is needed to set forth the very principles and not just the particularities. All law, as we have seen, is ritual. But some laws constitute the principles they serve—in a sense, create them, by framing the core of their concern in the boundaries they lay out. Incest laws do not create the concerns they address from the whole cloth, any more than property laws create the concern for property. But by defining a concern institutionally, a law frames it as a cultural issue: the Torah takes up what might seem the arbitrary question of who reveals whose nakedness, and makes it a moral issue, so as to foster and protect personhood within the family. By so doing it makes room for a certain kind and degree of human individuality and shapes a certain kind of family. The personality the Torah seeks to protect or define, or allow room for self-defining, is only a virtuality without such a law. The same, in a sense, is true of property. But ritual comes closer to the core in defining incest than in defining theft. For men at least imagine that they know what theft is and why it is wrong, without recourse to ritual. But no one could speak of incest in moral terms without reference to personhood or some similar value, which the laws of incest themselves help to constitute.

Far more than incest prohibitions, the Torah's law against seething a kid in its mother's milk (Exod. 23:19, 29:31, 34:26, Deut. 14:21) is a constitutive rule: the core concern is framed by the legislation itself. Yet here, too, there is a principle behind the ban. It aims at the frisson of cruelty—thus specifying the maternal relation, evoking the elemental bond whose violation might yield emotive energy. Just as paternal exposure typifies what the incest laws proscribe, here maternal violation typifies cruelty and so defines a moral concern. The Rabbis elaborate not conceptually but ritually, forbidding all mingling of milk with meat, or mixing of dairy and meat utensils. They chart their course by the frisson of seething: no blood upon milk, no milk upon flesh. But the ritual is emblematic not just of the gross prohibitions of incest, cannibalism, or human sacrifice but of broad themes of the Mosaic ethos, framed as a radical alternative to the horrid ethos that would countenance such extremes: the ritual separation sustains its significance not by a historic connection with revulsion toward Canaanite practices but because it typifies the Torah's response to the frisson of the violative.

Clearly, the prohibition against consuming blood (Deut. 15:23; Gen. 9:4; cf. Lev. 17) addresses the same concern. It takes aim at any illusion that we grow in power through violation of living energy. Biblically, "The life is in the blood." But the beast is dead before any civilized human would consume it. And blood conveys no magic to be sought or feared. It is simply spilled upon the ground. Here ritual speaks not to sacralize but to desacralize. The sexual fat (*ḥelev*) and the sciatic nerve acquire no magic aura from their historic and sexual associations (Gen. 32:25, 32). They are denied any mana to confer. The illusion of power in violation is the only fallacy the Torah seeks to block: humans do not share in the "sweet savor" offered before God, and Israelite priests never seek the transference of the Pythian prophetess, never become the oracles or muddle their identities with the All. Sympathetic magic stands poles apart from their charge. And the rites of the Mosaic sanctuary purify its altar not from demonic visitations but from the far more ethereal moral taint of contamination wrought upon it by the sins of Israel.[27] If we read the ancient cultic ritual in the language of its time and mark its meanings by its departures from the familiar, we find even here transmutation of the magical into the moral.

The Torah's emphatic repudiations of all pagan themes and symbols (Exod. 20:3–4, 22:17, 23:24, 34:15–17; Josh. 24:16–23; Judg. 2:3; Lev. 19:31; Deut. 18:9–14) guide us to the subtext of the Mosaic symbol system that militates so powerfully against magic. The Law abhors necromancy[28] but is open to prophecy (Num. 11:29; cf. Deut. 18:15–22). Its sacrificial ritual is extreme only in the chastity of its symbolism, which reduces the frisson of violation to a kind of minimum, giving grounds to Maimonides' sense that the whole elaborate cult of the Sanctuary aims to restrict sacrificial worship, take it out of private hands, limit its venue and occasions, and wean Israel away from the obdurate idea of propitiation (*Guide* III 32). Thus, when the sacrificial cult loses its moral hold—a process well under way even before the loss of the second Temple—the cult is so regulated by the sacralizing nostalgia of the Rabbis that the Talmud becomes its reliquary and loss of its details makes its restoration a practical impossibility. But the dietary prohibition of blood and fat transcends the cultic context. These are laws free of temporal or geographic constraints (Lev. 3:16; and Sifra ad loc.), since they intend primal ethical themes.

We do not hear much of the arbitrariness of the arbitrary dimensions of the laws of modern nations, perhaps because no divine authorship is claimed for our civil, penal, or traffic codes. But to understand the Torah we must see that here divine authority connotes what moderns mean by rationality: that the laws serve effectively in pursuit of sound goals. Why, then, do we inquire so assiduously into the roots of the restriction against seething a kid in its mother's milk, as though we might find the meaning of a living ritual in deep antiquity? We certainly do not ask as often or probe as deeply into the historic grounds for the choice of red and green as the colors that halt and permit the flow of traffic, as if we could understand the traffic code and its "true purposes" if we knew the "reason" for this coding. Visitors from Alpha Centauri, studying our traffic systems, would need to know, of course, what every color meant. If they studied wisely they might uncover a higher-order rule, explicit in no code, that rights to proceed, and hierarchies of precedence thereto, are important earthling values in industrial societies. But this would scarcely tell them why. Elaborate investigations of red or green wavelengths and their historic associations might uncover hints but would do little to confirm the hypothesis that safety is a paramount concern in all these rules of precedence. If it were proposed, in support of that hypothesis, that red is the color of fire and, in folklore, a color bulls abhor, the speculative theorist might be laughed at or asked why traffic should not proceed on red and halt on green. Yet broad themes are grasped readily enough, inductively, with help from the redundancy of their expression in the dicta and structures of a law. When reasons are sought for particularities underdetermined by the broadest thematic goals, inquiry will naturally lead away from the guiding values of the law, toward tangential interests—historical, anthropological, linguistic. But our core aim in interpretation, whether elaborative and legislative or pragmatic and judicial, is to know not why words are spelled as they are but what they mean. Here the relevant meaning is that the Torah projects an aesthetic and emotive repertoire in which seething a kid in its mother's milk is a paradigm of cruelty.

The Law might have issued a blanket admonition, "Thou shalt not be cruel." But cruelty is a rather abstract notion, susceptible of diverse, even conflicting glosses, as to intent, degree, mitigating circumstances, scope, and the like. The vacuous pseudo-commandment "Thou shalt not be cruel," or its still more vacuous affirmative counterpart "Thou shalt be nice," tells nothing about how, let alone why, to whom, to what extent. "Thou shalt not seethe a kid in its mother's milk" tells a great deal, even if one knows nothing of any Canaanite customs to which it may allude, against which it may rebel, at the least of which it may have drawn a line. It forbids not just the wanton causing of anguish but even the extraction of some thrill or sense of power from the evocation of anguish. This gives the Rabbis the clue they need to expand the law, creating a sphere of positive obligations and a realm of ritual expressions that unfold humane sensibilities at a level of virtuality and allow them to strike the ground of praxis and engage pragmatic issues informed and refined. The device is comparable to the effects of music and gymnastic in Plato's scheme, to sports in American ritual and mythology, or to vegetarianism in the postindustrial counterculture—but without the nutritional costs of vegetarianism or the moral costs of an athletic ethos of aggression and emulousness, when these are projected as the themes behind a nation's way of life in all its geographic, economic, and historic circumstances.

The Torah, of course, modulates the values it deploys, finely adjusting the symbolic message. For tradition can control the proliferation of ritual themes, preventing any one category from taking over like a semiotic cancer or shifting into its own negation. This control, which is nothing but the continuous reaffirmation and redefinition of the underlying thematic, is crucial to the ongoing life and flourishing of any culture. As Aristotle wrote, in a passage we have already cited in part, "Customary laws have more weight and relate to more matters than written laws, and a man may be a safer ruler than the written law, but not safer than the customary law" (*Politics* III 16, 1287b 4–6). In historical perspective, this issue of moral safety and the specific problem of moral inversion grow even more critical. For it is one thing to make a theme, say, of purity—in various of its senses a common preoccupation of many traditional legal systems. It is quite another to keep the idea constant, to define the limits of its sway, and to attach a chaste and disciplined version of that concept firmly to the idea of the Holy, as the purification procedures of the Torah do.

Prohibited Species

A variety of animal kinds are biblically prohibited as food to Israelites. An animal's flesh is permissible only if (1) it walks on land on four feet with cloven hooves and chews its cud, or (2) it swims in the water and has both fins and scales, or (3) it flies in the air and is not a bird of prey or carrion bird. No crawling creatures are permitted, but certain locusts are allowed. Mary Douglas sees a normative essentialism here: only a *proper* bird, beast, or fish is fit for food; others seem, as it were, deformed.[29] Paradigm beasts are the bullock, sheep, and goat; paradigm birds, doves and quail; paradigm fish, bony fishes, which even modern biologists call true fish. But the Torah knows that every species is true to type and applies its phrase *le-mineihu*, "after its kinds," to clean and unclean alike (Gen. 1:12, 21, 25; 6:20; 7:14; 11:16, 22, 29; Deut. 14:15). How else could the Torah and its audience have used species names and descriptions? One can hardly describe the anatomy and ethology of any "kind" without assuming that species breed true. An actual sport or maimed specimen is clearly distinguished and barred from use as food (Mishnah *Ḥullin* 3) or sacrifice (Lev. 22:20; cf. Num. 17:2), even if from a permitted kind. Dietary "uncleanness" is not deformity, and frogs are unclean as food.[30] But whole kinds are barred, as types, even if perfect, on grounds of uncleanness (Lev. 11:4; cf. v. 8). What does this mean?

The Torah classes all living flesh as clean or unclean for dietary purposes, a remarkable and distinctive taxonomic project. "Totems" are not at issue.[31] For the Law does not bar or assign certain kinds to certain tribes but prohibits and permits the same to all—a mark of moral concern. Unclean animals (sense 3) are ritually defiling when dead, and thought of as hygienically unclean (sense 2). They are unsuitable for sacrificial use (sense 5). But Israelites are not forbidden to handle or exploit them; indeed, the species are subject to the firstborn levy dedicated to the Temple, paid in cash because of their unfitness as offerings (Num. 18:15). Nothing is said against riding horses or camels, wearing buttons of shell or belts of crocodile hide—although the Law is enlarged with respect to pigs.[32] Skins of the *taḥash*, variously identified as the dugong, dolphin, or badger, form the covering God orders for his Tabernacle (Exod. 25:5; 26:14; 35:7, 23). None of these is allowed as food for Israelites. The Aggadah does romance the *taḥash* somewhat, but it does not become sacred. Indeed, the hide is used to sole sandals (Ezek. 16:10). Similarly, the dyes used in the Tabernacle fabrics come from the "scarlet worm" (*tola'at shani*; Exod. 25:4, 28:6, Lev. 14:4, Num. 4:8), murex gastropods (*tekhelet*, *argamon*; Deut. 5:7, 16), and similar sources. Their entire kind are impermissible as food; the dyes are precious, but neither sacred nor defiling. The senses of the idea of purity are communicating but not blurred.

Species unfit for food are not unfit to dwell on earth. Noah was commanded to save pairs from the Flood—not seven pairs, as with the clean animals; but offerings were to be taken from those (Gen. 7:2, 8:20). Nor are the "unclean" unfit as food for all, but only for Israelites: unclean *for you.* The unclean birds, fish, and insects are "detestable" (*sheketz*) to you (Lev. 11:12, 13, 20, 23). As with sexual defilement, to eat these creatures is disgusting (*to'evah*; Deut. 14:3) and defiling not just ritually (Lev. 11:31, 40) but morally (v. 43)—*for Israel.* For the dietary scheme is a means of expressing and so attaining holiness (v. 44), and to violate God's command to seek holiness is a moral lapse (vv. 45–47). At stake here is not a horror at the hyrax because he is "deformed." For God saw all creation, that it was good. Besides, cows, giraffes, even some antelope and goats may look odd to the unaccustomed eye, yet they are permissible.

The Torah does not say that a horse or a camel is anomalous or that a shark or kite, eagle, mouse, or coney are not proper birds, beasts, or fish. Rather, it declares them unclean, loathsome, and disgusting. The terms, redolent with meaning from their other uses, are made explanations of the food exclusions. God created no improper kind. But to eat some creatures is loathsome. To treat this as sheer theocratic fiat does not tell us why *these* species are singled out. There is certainly no claim that they are especially dear to Jehovah. On the contrary, the pig is the arch-unclean beast. Everyone knows its filthy habits, and the ancients may have known it as a vector of disease. But the Torah never specifies disease as the reason for its prohibition, and pork remains unfit food for Israelites even if the swine are daily bathed and their flesh seared to kill their parasites. The uncleanness, then, reaches beyond sense 2.

Clearly, it matters that the Israelites in Sinai were alarmed by devastating plagues, ascribed not simply to the wrath of God but conjointly to the foods they ate and the sexual unions they entered (Num. 11, 25). God promises Israel, "If ye truly heed the voice of the Lord thy God and do what is right in His eyes, give ear to His commandments and keep His laws, all of the diseases which I laid upon Egypt, I shall not lay upon you; rather will I be your healer" (Exod. 15:26; cf. Deut. 7:15, 28:60). But no specific point is made of the liability of mussels, oysters, lobsters, and clams to toxicity or spoilage. Something more is at stake, not unrelated but not reducible to hygiene. To eat a creature is to eat what it eats and, associatively, *as* it eats. For with symbols, associations are of the essence. Predators and scavengers tear at flesh, living or dead. And what is torn is forbidden—along with the predators at the head of the food chain and the scavengers at its base. Thus: "Ye shall be people of holiness to Me, and meat that is torn by beasts in the field ye shall not eat but shall cast to the dogs" (Exod. 22:3)—for what is torn (*ṭerefah*; cf. Gen. 37:33; Num. 23:24; Lev. 17:15) is carrion.

Clearly, a Law that makes purity a vehicle of holiness for all Israel (Lev. 11:43–47) will forbid Israelites to eat what is loathsome. But why would anyone be tempted to eat what seems or should seem disgusting and unclean? And how can a law tell us what to find distasteful? Here habits are decisive. For it is not the form but the nature of a beast, as biblically conceived, that bars it from Israel's table: if the ethos is the object, ethology must be our subject. Mice and insects do carry diseases; snakes and some desert lizards are venomous. But mushrooms, after all, are not forbidden. The serpent goes on its belly and eats the dust (Gen. 3:14); that is reason enough to make it unfit food. Unclean habits render a species symbolically unclean, quite apart from the issues of hygiene. Israelites do not eat predators for the same reason that they do not hunt. They do not eat swine because, in the pig, the habits of predator and scavenger intersect, as they do in dogs[33]—more so, perhaps, since pigs will turn upon and devour their own kind.

If predators are paradigms of savagery, scavengers are paradigms of death and putrefaction. The mouse is the biblical exemplar, loathed for its stealth and indiscriminate diet (Lev. 11:29, Isa. 66:17). Mice and other vermin create and live from filth and decay. The categories are not arbitrary: predators are to the orgiastic ethos of Canaan as scavengers are to the graveyards and granaries of Egypt—the mice and cats of the temple courtyard, dogs, scarabs, monkeys, and crocodiles.[34] The concern is not with magically acquiring their natures. Rather, these kinds are proscribed in part because of what they are and represent; in part, to forbid our becoming commensal with them.

Who would eat a tiger, osprey, vulture, kite, or dog? Necessity might provide an explanation in some cases. But Halakhah renders even pork permissible in time of necessity (*Yoma* 82a; cf. 83b). Holiness, as biblically conceived, is one of those necessary luxuries of a culture, like justice, freedom, mercy, or gentleness of language, a refinement of life rather than an exigency, an amenity, necessary not as food or shelter are necessary but as the baths and theaters, agoras and palaestras are necessary to the civility of civil life in Aristotle's polis. Holiness is made possible with foods (as with sabbaths, *shemittah*, gleaning, and free loans) by allowing certain things not to be maximally exploited. The clear presumption is that fit food is ample (cf. Deut. 8:10, 14:2–3) without consumption of the enjoined kinds. But some might find attraction in the idea of eating loathsome species with lust or gusto (*ta'avah*; cf. Num. 11:34), for the thrill of eating a predator, squelching disgust for a scavenger, swallowing vermin. That frisson—sharing emotively in the violence, verminous pestilence, squamous sweetness of the victim, transposing revulsion into appetite—is what the Torah, as a moral law, seeks to purge, a frisson that paganism might elevate from *horribilis* to *mysterium tremendum*.[35]

The test case is the locust, for locusts supplement the diet of desert peoples, and their habits do not make them notable as objects of disgust or vectors of disease, although their appearance has never been welcome to agrarians. Here there has been a divergence of tastes (with divergence of habitats) between two Jewish cultural traditions: among Ashkenazi Jews, the desert need for locusts became a curiosity of history, and the fiction arose that the taxonomic differentia of permitted insects has been lost. But among Oriental Jews locusts remained permissible. A good friend vividly remembers building bonfires in years when locusts flew (they were not said to "swarm"), to attract the creatures. The children popped the tasty insects into their mouths without a shred of doubt that piety allowed the snack. What was not held loathsome was not seen as impermissible then, or in Mosaic times—although generally the taxonomic boundaries were drawn wide, excluding as food any species whose biblical genus was loathsome.

Each nation must define its ethos. Food laws are as sound a means as any—more effective, perhaps, than most. We English speakers tend to avoid and even restrict the eating of dogs, cats, horses, and most vermin. In the Torah, dietary regulation goes hand in hand with sexual regulation, working, like any law, at the interface of the symbolic and the moral. Modern legal systems, liberal or otherwise, are often more concerned with the exchange of goods and information or ideas than with food or the erotic as such. But no nation is without food restrictions, and never are such restrictions unconnected to character. Likewise with sexual restrictions, whether tacit or explicit, rigid or casual. Absence or denial of such standards is itself rooted in an ethos—if not the tyrannous ethos of machismo, then the tatterdemalion ethos of Plato's democratic man, who loves liberty but is vulnerable to corruption, especially by ungoverned appetites. It is in the endeavor to regulate appetite without tyrannizing over the mind, body, or spirit that the Torah seeks to define sexual as well as gustatory tastes. Using the language of purity and holiness, impurity and abomination, it fashions an analogy between the two spheres.

Since flesh must not be torn, a system of slaughter is devised to erase the frisson of catching at a slaughtered beast's flesh. Maimed and deformed beasts are not eaten, setting images of violence at a further remove. The species permitted are docile. What makes them fit for the altar makes them fit for the table. There must be no thrashing struggle in their death, as when a boar or lion is stuck with a spear or brought down by dogs—no hint of violence transposed from appetite to taste, to celebratory occasion, no delectation of slime or swarming, spread from the table to the culture. The emotions of the table are those of pleasant fellowship, projected in the biblical tableaux of convivial enjoyment of the produce of the land (Deut. 7:12–13, 6:10–11). The images of the bed, like those of the board, are those of peace: a bridegroom's duty, before any other service, is to rejoice his bride (Deut. 24:5).

The ethos here is tuned between the sharp and the flat. The aim is not a sensuous or sensate culture, yet there is no denial of the senses or the appetites. The mean is not indistinct. Like the right note, it is located by its tone: "See how good and pleasant it is for brethren to dwell together" (Ps. 133:1). Asceticism, taken to extremes, yields alienation and a form of madness, as Saadiah saw. But a sensuous culture treats sensuous gratifications as though they were absolutes, and a sensate culture seeks ever more intense sensations, transforming all material culture into a toy for titillating and finally tormenting acquired sensibilities. Once these become arbiters of value, as they will in time in a commercial and industrial society, even religion is bent to the same end. For religion can never be more than the reflection of our highest aspirations.

Circumcision as a Paradigm of the Torah's Method

The rejection of sensuality as the foundation of Israel's culture, its displacement by ethical consideration and spiritual growth, anchored in the ideal of the holy, is nowhere plainer than in the law of circumcision. There are hygienic foundations, historic roots, and symbolic associations. But, as with the dietary laws, these do not communicate the law's distinctive aim in situ. Maimonides' placement of circumcision among the sexual laws, reading it as an expression of the Torah's rejection of sexuality as the arbiter of morals, is far more helpful, and this quiet antipriapism explains the Rambam's codifying circumcision with the *mitzvot* that express our love of God.[36] For circumcision timelessly displays the Torah's priorities. Claims that it curtails or enhances erotic gratification or control may evince anxieties about castration, but they are unfounded physiologically. The circumcised and uncircumcised seem equally to enjoy erotic sensations and lead equally fulfilled erotic lives.[37] But any evidence that circumcision is hygienic (and there is firm evidence today)[38] reveals that conservatism against bodily modifications yields to hygienic (hence ethical) concern. Deference to the ethical suffices to transpose circumcision (and it alone) from the category of mutilations to that of "preparations," making uncircumcision, categorially, a defect (Exod. 6:12; *Tanḥuma*, Tazri'a 5). Appropriately, circumcision is shifted from puberty, as in other cultures, to the eighth day of life (Gen. 17:10–13, 25–26). For the covenant of Abraham is not a preparation for puberty but a spiritual symbol of the primacy of the moral, and thus, of the nature and strength of Israel's commitment to the Holy.[39] Note the progression: by giving deference to the hygienic, the law becomes moral; by giving primacy to the moral, it becomes spiritual.

It is because circumcision visibly expresses the precedence of the ethical—not in the abstract but by a concrete symbol—that it is (by metonymy) called "the covenant" par excellence, the outward sign of Abraham's moral bond with God, "sealed in our flesh."[40] But symbols never rest, so even the outward sign acquires a moral sense: we are told to circumcise our hearts (Deut. 10:16), opening the soul, humbling the spirit, and devoting it to God's will—whose paradigms are the commands to protect orphans, strangers, and widows (vv. 18–19; cf. Deut. 6:5). Thus we return to the moral and spiritual idea of purity, from which circumcision draws its biblical meaning.

The brunt of our argument has been ethical. We find an ethical theme that runs through the biblical legislation about diet and sex, expressed in the language of purity and impurity and the stronger terms orienting that polarity, holiness and abomination (or loathesomeness). The Torah's aim in these ritual laws, as in the rest, is the perfecting of our humanity by purifying our motives and relations. Its goal is to make Israel a holy nation, whose symbols and usages express and foster regard for humanity in self and others, respect for life and personhood—and, correspondingly, the purging of dark passions and sordid, life-denying appetites. We are never fully aware of our motives, Kant argued.[41] Freud offered ample corroboration. But the moral problem generated by our lack of perfect self-knowledge is not insurmountable. The Torah addresses its effort to reform human morality not only to the conscience but also to the unself-conscious seat of moral attitudes and intentions which it locates in the heart, and which it commands us to circumcise. It frames not only moral injunctions but customs designed to attune our lives, our dreams, even the motives unspoken in an embrace or the intentions that accompany the taste of our food, to the idea of the Holy.

It would be convenient to suppose that the spiritual and moral senses of the Torah's idea of purity evolve historically from the more physical, hygienic, or empiric senses. But there is no textual instance of a univocal occurrence of the relevant terms, and to hypothecate such senses militates against the central object of the text in their deployment. For the intention, clearly, is to suffuse the empirical and pragmatic with holiness, by way of the moral, spiritual, and symbolic freighting of the idea of purity. Even the sense 1 occurrences of 'purity' are connotative in the ritual (and hence spiritual) dimensions. And even the ritual senses bear moral and spiritual overtones, purifying not only the service but the idea of God, strengthening and gaining strength from the subtle weld of monotheism, which joins the idea of divinity not just with that of absoluteness or transcendence but also with that of goodness.

No loftier spiritual expression can be found than Isaiah's ecstasy, "Holy, holy, holy—the Lord of hosts: The fill of all the earth is His glory" (Isa. 6:3). The idea of holiness here points toward infinite transcendence but not mere beyondness or absoluteness (pictured as power in the phrase "Lord of hosts"). Rather, the intent is transcendent goodness, perfection, which the worshiper ritually reaches after, rising on tiptoe at each utterance of "holy."[42] But if God is goodness and not a mere beyondness, his act is in the world. Indeed, it is the world. In the prophet's brilliant epiphany, glory shines not through nature from beyond it but *as* nature.

In Isaiah, as in Heraclitus, then, the way up is the way down. Jacob's ladder both rises and descends.[43] For the Torah's core idea is God's epiphany on earth—in the divine act of creation and in the human fulfillment of his will, through laws and institutions. Isaiah (40:26) reaches spiritually to the stars, and beyond, to their Maker. But Moses, who guides Isaiah's gaze, draws down an ethos from that beyond, anchored in the imperative: "Ye shall be holy, for I the Lord your God am holy." The distinctiveness of the Mosaic law is not in claiming or proclaiming God's authority but in rendering that authority articulate as law. The point is not the epiphany, not that Moses saw God or prophesied, but that he conversed with God as we human beings do with one another (Num. 14:14; cf. Deut. 5:4), taking the inchoate matter of transcendence—conventionally mute, ineffable, inarticulate—and forging from it an integrated law that uniquely figures the ethical upon the spiritual and both upon the physical, each informing the other and framing the symbols that will interpret and expand the idea of the Absolute thus captured—and so preserve it not in a relic but in a way of life. Not least of the cross-linkages securing the moral fabric of that way of life, spun out from the moment of prophetic inspiration, in which God leans down to answer our groping toward him, is that which discovers that the pollution that made the Land untenable by its prior settlers is not a magical miasma but a moral malaise. It is this discovery that weaves respect for persons and life itself onto the loom of the multipronged idea of purity.

8

Time, Creation, and the Mirror of Narcissus

Mounting evidence supports the idea that the world is of finite age. Sir John Eccles writes of "Einstein's derivation in 1915 of an expanding universe from his geometric account of gravitation, the General Theory of Relativity":

> To him at that time with his belief in a stationary everlasting universe, the idea of an expanding universe was highly distasteful, so he introduced a cosmological term into his equations to counteract the derivation of expansion. Then in 1912 the red shifts observed by Hubble in the spectrograms of galaxies produced empirical evidence for the expanding universe. Forthwith Einstein rejected his cosmological term, calling it "the biggest blunder of my life," and accepting the distasteful expanding universe.
>
> The clear formulation of the expanding universe from an initial great cataclysm was first made by Lemaître in the early 1930's and in 1940 Gamow refined this proposal, and applied the emotive term "Big Bang" to the cataclysm. However the initial estimates by Hubble for the rate of expansion were too high. They gave a date for the Big Bang of only 2 billion years ago, which was in conflict with other estimates for the age of the Universe. Hence there was then good reason for the alternative hypothesis proposed by Gold, Bondi and Hoyle, the steady-state hypothesis: the Universe had always existed; there was no origin in a Big Bang; the observed expansion was exactly compensated by the continuous creation of atomic particles; these particles in time aggregated to form new nebulae. Hence the composition of space was approximately steady, and it was isotropic, despite the continuous recession of already formed nebulae from each other. In terms of Natural Theology it would appear that, in their efforts to escape from a supernatural creation in the Big Bang by a Transcendent God, they had unwittingly proposed continual creation by an Immanent God!
>
> However, redetermination of the recession rate of nebulae now gives a much earlier dating for the Big Bang, about 19 billion years according to the present best estimates. We shall see that, because of the continuous slowing of the expansion rate by gravitational pull, this figure has to be reduced to 10–12 billion years, which is in good agreement with dates that can be derived for the origin by several methods. Furthermore the evidence for the Big Bang has now become most convincing by the discovery of the predicted faint "echo" of the Big Bang, as an all-pervasive microwave radiation with a frequency corresponding [to] the average temperature of cosmic space, 3.0 degrees K.[1]

Only a few years ago the "big bang" and "steady state" theories seemed near-equal rivals. Both theories involve ideas of creation. The steady state requires continuous origination of new matter. The big bang opens the possibility of a moment of creation, not of a finished cosmos but of an evolving universe, emergent in phases, rather more as suggested in the biblical account of a phased creation. Neither theory leaves room for Aristotle's eternal cosmic rhythm, preserved without essential change through infinite ages. That model has faded since Galileo's day, and evolutionary views increasingly command the evidence. Defenders of special creation have been on the defensive since the mechanics of biological evolution began to be understood; they forge alibis against the evidence and treat the fossil record as a special test of faith.[2] But creationist cosmologists have become almost triumphalist. Fred Hoyle, the chief advocate of the old steady state view, some years ago retreated to an ingenious account of the extraterrestrial origins of life, which, as Spinoza might have said, proved only its author's brilliance. Religiously inclined cosmologists find astronomy vindicating biblical theism.[3] *Science News* tells of physicists ready to dismiss the ancient axiom *ex nihilo nihil fit*: if matter and antimatter combine to annihilate one another, could not nothing become something, if "separated" into matter and antimatter? The magazine's cover pictures William Blake's sinewy God the Father measuring, with celestial dividers, the cosmic *tohu ve-vohu*, between Alpha and Omega, while about his bearded head the rotund words echo in the void: "OH I GOT PLENTY O' NOTHIN', AN' NOTHIN'S PLENTY FOR ME."[4]

The big bang, of course, does not imply that God created the universe. Logic allows that the cosmos might have come to be by itself, or from some lesser cause. And the evidence may allow an eternal cycle of origins and destructions. Some of the ancient Rabbis used to wonder (Genesis Rabbah 9.2) if this world was created only after several prior trials were discarded. But the homiletic riposte was always open: perhaps ours is one of the failed essays. Some physicists argue that the force of the original explosion will one day be spent and gravity will start a gradual but accelerating contraction, climaxing in a cosmic implosion, then, perhaps, another explosion. If the world oscillates between implosion and explosion, the big bang is not the unique event, the absolute beginning. But it may have been. Absolute origination is one explanation of what we see. And origination can be explained by creation.

Peering into the explosive past from the safe distance of the present, as we now can do, with telescopes like the one now in space that bears Hubble's name, we still will not see all that we may wish to know about creation. We must remember Saadiah's advice: when we set out to find the cause of nature we are not seeking yet another natural phenomenon but something that transcends time, change, and perception, and so can explain natural events rather than simply needing explanation along with them.[5] That is why Aristotle reasoned that the cause of all motion must itself be unmoved, and why Plato saw that the Ground of all becoming must transcend temporality and particularity, the distinctive marks of natural existence. Our thirst for sensory evidence should not trap us into taking our principle of explanation back to the level it was invoked to explain. Sensuous divinities and what Voegelin called "historicized" images of creation[6] are symptomatic of a drive to reduction that equates reality with what we or our machines can palpate or manipulate. It was not this that the biblical writers and ancient philosophers and sages hoped to awaken to us or in us. What I want to consider in this last chapter are the values intended by the idea of creation, as a unique event in the distant past, but also as an ongoing expression of God's active presence.

When a medieval creationist like al-Ghazālī argued that all processes, being temporal, are originated, he and his readers readily inferred origination from change.[7] They accepted Plato's sharp division of being from becoming. What was eternal was unchanging and so nontemporal. Temporal events were bounded by a beginning and an end. We cannot so readily appropriate al-Ghazālī's argument. Few of us have followed Plato quite as far on the "second voyage." Yet we have better reason than Philoponus had to believe that the world had a beginning, and we cannot isolate ourselves in a historicist cocoon from the powerful argument lodged in a rhetorical question asked by many medieval philosophers: How can anything create itself? We have learned from Hume to say that if things did begin, they might have begun of themselves—for no reason at all, or no reason beyond their own natures. But we saw in chapter 2 how much we give up when we think this way—ultimately, the idea that anything can be explained.

The watershed between us and our forebears is not that we have found an unconditioned world but that we more freely posit origination without creation, blinkering from ourselves the consequence, that in so doing we have obviated explanation. The *forming* of a world does not need a demiurge. So sensualist or neomythic theologians now project the same images as are common in naturalistic fable—the same molten lava as primal element, the same swirling mists and gases, cast as God's spirit brooding on the waters. But absolute creation is not to be imaged or imagined. Could we witness the events of the beginning, whose light and radiant energy are only now reaching us from deep space, after traveling for ten billion years or more, we would not discern creation perceptually from the mere eruption of being out of nothingness, or out of something very small. Our view of genesis would differ in no religiously relevant way from our present view of the world. For this too—all that we see, not just the molten basalt and the steam of Kilauea but the desk before me, the window I look through, the trees beyond—all has an origin as much flung from the primordial event as the light of the most distant stars.

Our forebears who conceived the idea of creation or accepted or defended it when they read of it in Scripture had no ringside seat at genesis. What did they mean by creation? Did they jump the gun, buy the story before they grasped its premises or fathomed its conclusion? Or have *we* settled for an incomplete account? For reason, as Saadiah argues, affords our only access to the idea. Images of creation—the cosmogonic vignettes of a Cecil B. DeMille movie or a *Nova* telecast—are curiously shorn of the values the idea once proudly bore, values that made it in some ways easier for the ancients to call the world created than it has become for us. Biblically, the story of creation takes the form not of science but of myth, an account kept alive by the values it projects. To grasp what is at stake in the ancient idea, we can reawaken some of those values. They show startling vitality. I will group them under the headings of contingency, design, and newness. After touching on these, I want to turn to their coherence with some related values often thought to compete with the idea of creation, and some that are genuinely at odds with it.

Contingency

Generalizing still more ancient myths of origin, the Torah advances a comprehensive version of the cosmological argument. God's reality, transcendent and thus undescribed, is found through the reality of nature. All of this—heaven and earth, light and shadow, sun, moon, and stars, all that grows or creeps, walks, flies, swims, prowls, or laughs—need not have been. The Torah knows that God is good because creation is an act of grace (*ḥesed*; see Ps. 89:3). God made the world good and judged it good (Gen. 1:18, 31). The goodness of being is a theme not out of place in the cosmogonic prelude to God's Law; it is an axiom of that Law. For it is in support of being that the Torah legislates. As the Law draws to a close, the same axiom is restated: God calls heaven and earth to witness to the perfection of his work, now not only in the realm of nature but in the Law itself (Deut. 32:1–4; cf. Ps. 19).

In Avicennan terms, only God is self-sufficient. The world and all things in it are dependent: necessary by reference to their causes but contingent in themselves. Their essence does not entail their existence; their idea does not assure its instantiation; nothing about each thing and kind requires its reality, and the whole of nature need not have been. For Avicenna the world's contingency seemed compatible with its eternity, as the ageless product of eternal emanation. But to other monotheists it seemed clear not only that a conditioned world was contingent but also that a contingent world had begun. As al-Ghazālī argued, protective of the Qur'ān's creationism, Neoplatonists could give no meaning to God's creativity if they did not believe the world to be originated. What sense was there in speaking of an Author (*Ṣānīʿ*) if the universe could not fail to exist and the cause made no real difference to the reality or character of its effect? Eternalism, al-Ghazālī argued, made the philosophers unwilling or unwitting atheists (*TF* III, IV, X). Maimonides judged more gently. Committed to the idea that the Torah teaches by symbol and indirection (*Guide* III 27), he would not dogmatically impugn the faith of Aristotelian philosophers. Of course they were theists. But the nexus they preserved between God and nature was perilously attenuated. What theists seek is God's goodness as the source of goodness in the world.[8] But how do we ascribe goodness in the world to the act of God, if that goodness was always there? Surely, Maimonides argued, God's authorship makes more sense if it chooses among alternative possibilities. Temporal creation, as distinguished from eternal emanation, leaves room for that possibility. Besides, if emanation is necessitation from divine simplicity, the world's differentiation becomes needlessly problematic, and change of any kind begins to seem impossible. So creation seemed preferable theologically and more probable epistemically than God's eternal authorship (*Guide* II 19–22).

For Aristotelians and those who came under the powerful spell of their philosophy, the very idea of creation seemed to undermine itself, by presupposing the cosmic principles it promised to explain. For how could any change not presuppose matter, from which to begin, and potentiality abiding in matter, to make the alteration possible, and time, eternally measured by the ceaseless motions of bodies, to mark the progress of the change? The world might be formed, some allowed;[9] it was not created. But, as Saadiah pointed out, *formatio mundi* is no less a denial of absolute creation than is Aristotle's eternal cosmos (*ED* I 2–3). And it was no more satisfactory to Aristotelians than de novo creation.

The key Aristotelian claim was that a beginning of change is itself a change and so needs time in which to occur; thus, Peripatetics argued, creation cannot be posited without supposing eternal time, and with it, motion, matter, and materially grounded potentiality. Maimonides' refutation was swift and incisive: it was suppositious, he argued, for Aristotelians to project their ideas of matter, time, potentiality, and change, notions gleaned from the settled order of nature, onto a radically evolving world—let alone onto the moment of origin. A perfect man who had no idea of his beginnings would deny that humans could emerge from the womb: surely respiration, nutrition, locomotion, and excretion are impossible in that environment; how could life be sustained there? Such a priorism, however, is deceiving. Natural necessities, and even time itself, emerge with the emergence of the natural order. The necessities of nature are not logical necessities. The entire natural order is just one of the possibilities God might have chosen.[10] We cannot know its principles, or even its categories, a priori. God knows the world as the inventor knows a clock, prior to its making, even prior to its design. But human knowledge is typically a posteriori: we take the clock apart to learn how it works (*Guide* III 21).

The brunt of the objection is against a metaphysics that, pace its advocates, seems to allow no scope to virtuality. Freedom, as a value ascribed in different senses to God, humanity, and nature, is part of the metaphysical freighting of the idea of creation. Creation points to the openness of the future and the possibility of discovery. Thus, despite his Ash'arism, al-Ghazālī is even more outspoken than Maimonides in linking empiricism with creation. For empiricism underwrites his mysticism as well as his critique of essentialist accounts of causality.[11] The intellectualist philosophy, he argues, might lead one to deny that something no larger than a grain can devour an entire town and then itself. Yet fire has that nature. Philosophers ascribe the effects of opium to its coldness and say that earth and water are the cold elements. Yet pounds of earth and water have not the effect of a single dram of opium. Just as the blind know nothing of color, so those who lack practical experience know nothing of the complexities of nature, the reach of God's power, or the strengths and liabilities of the human soul.[12]

The alliance of empiricism and creationism is no accident.[13] Since the world is not an eternal, self-sufficing substance, nor the passive product of fate, extruded from the entrails of the gods, pressed between the rollers of the seasons and ground out between the upper and nether millstones of heaven and earth, it does not trivially bear its explanation on its face. Nature's character, biblically, is not a product of inevitability but an expression of the living God. It reflects God's grace not as fatality but as the image of his own freedom and creativity. Thus both Maimonides and Saadiah treat the causal dispositions of things and the human power of choice as gifts of God. Freedom and contingency are the first elements of a perennial idea of creation.

Avicenna, too, recognized these values in the idea of creation. He saw emanation not as an alternative but as an interpretation of creation. The eternity of the cosmos was not a mark of its inherent necessity but an expression of God's essential and immutable creativity. Critics of eternalism like Maimonides and al-Ghazālī did not, for their part, reject emanation. They adopted it but sought to strip it of its eternalist connotations, and Avicenna's work made clear the feasibility of that approach. For contingency was the linchpin of his analysis of being, and creationists like al-Ghazālī and Maimonides did not reject that analysis but only held contingency to be preserved most effectively by the red-blooded notion that the world's dependence upon God is manifest in its finite age. It was because emanationists shared the values of contingency and freedom that creationists could argue effectively with them dialectically. And Ibn Ṭufayl, seeking to reconcile Avicenna with al-Ghazālī, urges that creationism and eternalism are equivalent theologically.[14] Maimonides makes a similar claim when he derives the chief doctrines of rational theology from the premises of the Neoplatonic Aristotelians (*Guide* II, introduction). He parts company with these philosophers when he treats their eternalism as a postulate and in fact unwarranted, rather than a self-evident axiom or demonstrated conclusion. But he is careful to show that neither creation nor eternity can be demonstrated apodictically. For any such proof would make creation (or emanation) a matter of necessity and rob God of the volition that Maimonides saw was central to the idea of creation.

Responding to the Aristotelian notion that the world's possibility needed an eternal substrate, al-Ghazālī went out of his way to subjectivize modal notions: "The possibility of which they speak comes down to a matter of subjective judgment: Whatever the mind can consider as existent, finding no obstacle to the making of that judgment, we call possible; but if we find such an obstacle, we call it impossible. If we cannot deem it non-existent, we call it necessary. All of these are subjective determinations with no necessary external reference."[15] Al-Ghazālī's claims, paralleling some of Kant's, raise serious questions for the theistic enterprise, and for the cosmological argument in particular: Given the limitations of our judgments and the parochialism of anchoring absolute possibility and necessity in matter, can we make any judgment at all as to the contingency of nature?

As Maimonides' examples of the fetus and the clock, and al-Ghazālī's of the dram of opium and the "grain" of fire, suggest, one realm or sea of evidence lies in the enterprise of science itself: if all things are necessary categorically, then the necessity of logic is coextensive with that of nature, all real possibilities are actual, and the sciences in principle could be deductive. If all necessities are subjective, on the other hand, then science is impossible. But if science is possible and any part of inquiry is necessarily inductive, so that we cannot infer how things must be because things, in interaction with one another, have dynamic control over their own destinies, then there is contingency in the world, things are not fixed eternally in the necessities of their natures but might have been—might yet be—otherwise. In that case we can read the necessities of nature, even those that we schematize in logical terms, as hypothetical rather than categorical necessities—contingent in themselves, in Avicenna's language, although necessary with reference to their causes.

Induction is our necessary method in the sciences.[16] But does this requirement stem from the nature of things or strictly from the predispositions and limitations of our understanding? Does it reflect the openness of the future or the structure of our minds? I find the realist explanation more credible, since it places being first and makes knowledge dependent on the way things are. Our minds *are* capable of non-inductive thinking about nature; they are just not capable of assuring the accuracy of their premises without recourse to experience. The lesson of empiricism, I would argue, is relearned and the theses of empiricism given new meaning with each new scientific discovery. I count the process of discovery itself as an argument of cumulatively mounting force in support of the realist account of the necessity of induction and, thus, in support of the reality of an open universe. This is to understand the gift of freedom in a particularly strong sense.

Others, deferring to nuances of experience that seem salient to them and incompatible with real contingency, may draw different conclusions. But our failure to find deductive certainties in experience confirms the world's contingency and so supports the idea of creation in one of the key dimensions of meaning that al-Ghazālī and Maimonides gave the term. By enlivening us to the nexus between empiricism and creationism, they show not the inevitability of creationism but the kind of price one might have to pay in apriorism if one abandons the creationist mode of explanatory discourse. From the ancient biblical idea of creation, then, we learn that goodness in the world argues for a divine Creator. From the medieval discussions we learn that empiricism reflects the contingency of the world's existence and character, and thus obliquely argues for creation once again.

Design

Along with the ideas of value and contingency expressed in the idea of creation is the idea of purposiveness. The worth of the world is bound up with its purpose and the ability of creatures to fulfill that purpose. The idea of design emerges naturally enough from the thought of creation, since accounts of creation are modeled on myths of craftsmanship: the features of nature, like the works of culture, are products of divine intentions. Viewed in this light, whether in a hopeful spirit of appreciation or with an anxious eye toward propitiation, nature is scaled to human wishes: the cosmos becomes our abode (Isa. 45:18); the heavens, a tent over our heads (Isa. 40:22); the seas, highways for our transport (Ps. 104:26; Prov. 30:19; Qur'ān 2:164, 10:22, 14:32, 16:14, 17:66, 22:65, 43:12, 45:12); the meadows, fields for our crops. Warfare and disease become instruments of chastisement; death and its sequel, vehicles of judgment. Saadiah still thinks this way when he argues that this world was created as an abode of trial, to determine whether we will do God's will:[17] all things were made for man, and man that he might worship God.[18] Voltaire might archly draw a line between easily agreeing that the eye was made for seeing and doubting that the nose was made as a perch for a pince-nez. But the Stoics were typically earnest when they urged that a thing as noble as a soul was given to a pig only to keep its meat fresh.[19]

Teleology careens dangerously toward anthropocentrism. The trouble may go beyond our human tendency to reduce all purposes to our own. The very category of purpose is perhaps inextricably projective. Thus Spinoza's overt rejection of teleology rests on recognizing that classic design arguments typically rely on a *reductio ad ignorantiam*; Hume's rejection of such arguments flows from a recognition that the modern versions depend on stretched analogies between nature and a machine. Both men find suspect the projection of human purposes onto nature at large, Spinoza saying that our ability or inability to find order in a system reflects the limitations of our intellect; Hume, that notions of the world as a machine are at best projections of our limited experience.[20] Later, more scientistic thinkers argue less subtly, urging that the world is not a system but a chaos or (taking a contrary tack!) that machines might construct, govern, or even reproduce themselves.

A careful analysis of the idea of creation is as instructive here as in the case of contingency. Foster sagely contrasts creation with artisanship, the ordering and forming of nature and its parts by a Demiurge or craftsman god. The key to the contrast is a difference between crafts and fine, that is, creative, arts: a craftsman works with a preconceived purpose, to a predrawn plan, accommodating to the limitations of the available materials. But in creative arts the purpose emerges only as the work is done, the plan itself is a product of the creative act, and the materials (ideally) are not arbitrarily afforded and externally limiting but organically appropriate vehicles, called for, not just obeyed, necessitated by determinations inherent in the work.[21]

Plato's Demiurge "consults" the eternal pattern of the Forms, as a craftsman consults a blueprint, paradigm, or jig—or as a culture hero consults the needs of his presumptive, or presumptuous, beneficiaries; he works with existing, often recalcitrant, materials. But a creator God, like a creative artist, chooses his materials as well as their form or order. Radically so, in the case of the God of Abraham, since he is their maker. A craftsman god must submit his will to his understanding; any failure to do so is a failing in the world. But in a Creator, the end itself, in Foster's words, is a product of the activity; thus a will is expressed that is not reducible to any prior purpose, our own or that of any external plan or destiny. Here again we catch some of the savor of Maimonides' insistence on a volitional aspect in God's determination of nature—of existence over nonexistence and of all the particularizations of nature, law, history, and the powers of human character. And we feel some of the force of his remark that God's knowledge, unlike that of the human being who wants to follow the workings of a clock, is inventive and productive, not merely mimetic. Even when Maimonides marvels that Plato, like the talmudic Sages, uses the word "consults" to describe God's work,[22] he brings something more to the image than is contained in Plato's vision of a Demiurge who consults the Forms. For the consultation that the Rabbis mention is deliberative; its outcome is itself a product of the creative work. And, to be fair to Plato, we must add that the pattern consulted by his Demiurge is a living being, suggesting the dynamism, if not the creativity, of the model and the liveliness of its representation in nature.

Maimonides linked the volitional in God with matter[23] and thus with the absoluteness of creation. The idea of a pattern or design was not unwelcome to monotheists, so long as that plan did not become an independent hypostasis. Philo, paradigmatically, saw the rational principle of creation as an attribute of God, his wisdom, made manifest as a word, the Logos.[24] The Talmud's trenchant commentary on that approach is the famous remark of Mishnah *Sanhedrin* (4.5), which we noted near the end of chapter 4, that a mortal craftsman's mold or type turns out each exemplar exactly like the last; but when the Holy One, blessed be he, makes human beings, no two emerge identical from the mold.[25]

Nature, too, is a unique original. Its plan is immanent, not externally imposed. Thus, as Maimonides argues, it is absurd to seek a single purpose in it. It is not an artifact like a machine or tool. When Scripture says that God created all things for his glory, it means that (like a creative artist) he created all things for their own sakes—to fulfill their own natures and to manifest perfection in their own distinctive ways, through their God-given strengths. It is in this sense that "the heavens declare the glory of God";[26] in this sense, that it is possible for us to fulfill the injunction to make all our actions for the sake of heaven.[27] "God saw that it was good" is surely neither an ex post facto discovery nor an arbitrary stipulation. Rather, we stand, as it were, looking over the Artist's shoulder, sharing his satisfaction at the adequacy of the execution of his plan.

Here again, then, two criteria emerge that help us to judge that the world has a Creator, without our being eyewitnesses to the event. The two arise in our practice of science, but less as findings than as critical underpinnings, vindicated more by the success of the enterprise than by any isolated datum. They are the intelligibility and the autonomy of nature. The fact that nature can be understood, that rational explanations are possible, that causal regularities warrant inductive intuitions, shows the appositeness of the idea of creation.[28] As for the autonomy of nature, by this I mean that things exist for their own sakes—that beings project ends; and human beings, purposes, which they can, at times, fulfill. Neither of these ideas *entails* that there is a Creator. But each is a datum allowing explanation.

The resident teleology of autonomous agency is what Spinoza did not exclude but acknowledged as the very essence of things, under the name conatus. In his *Short Treatise*, he called it providence.[29] For we need not impose our own purposes to recognize the art and the miracle of creativity in the fact that beings of all kinds can project and pursue values of their own. Such purposes are not precluded but presupposed in the work of Darwin and his successors. Intelligibility, too, is corroborative of divine creativity, as Einstein intimated when he said that the most incomprehensible thing about the universe is that it is comprehensible. The idea of creation offers a line of explanation of that comprehensibility: nature is an act of God; its intelligibility is an expression of God's wisdom, to which we have access, as broad or narrow as our own understanding will allow.

The ancient philosophers and the classic exponents of design did not mean something radically different from this. It was part of what Plato meant by the metaphor of a craftsman working to a plan that was in fact a living idea. And the metaphor was preserved by Aristotle, even when he rejected the image of a world that was literally a product of divine work:

> Of perishable plants and animals we have abundant information, living as we do in their midst, and ample data may be collected concerning all their various kinds, if only we are willing to take sufficient pains. . . . The scanty conceptions we can reach of celestial things give us, from their excellence, more pleasure than all our knowledge of the world in which we live; just as a half glimpse of persons whom we love is more delightful than an accurate view of other things, whatever their number and dimensions. But in certitude and completeness our knowledge of terrestrial things has the advantage, and their greater nearness and affinity to us balances somewhat the loftier interest of the heavenly things that are the objects of the higher philosophy. . . . if some have no graces to charm the sense, yet nature, which fashioned them, gives amazing pleasure in their study to all who can trace links of causation, and are inclined to philosophy.

> Indeed it would be strange if representations of them were attractive because they disclose the mimetic skill of the painter or sculptor and the originals were not more interesting, to all at least who have eyes to discern the causes. So we must not recoil with childish aversion from the examination of the humbler animals. Every realm of nature is marvelous. And, as Heraclitus, when the strangers who came to visit him found him warming himself at the furnace in the kitchen and hesitated to go in, is reported to have bidden them not to be afraid to enter, since even in that kitchen gods were present, so we should venture on the study of every kind of animal without distaste; for each and all will reveal to us something natural and something beautiful. The absence of chance and conduciveness of everything to an end are to be found in nature's works in the highest degree, and the end for which those works are put together and produced is a form of the beautiful.[30]

Medieval analysis refines the idea of creation and renders it more precious and more precise, following up on Plato's image of the cosmos as an organism, not a machine. A mature and modern creationism sees God's purpose and plan as constituted within and through the work rather than outside and prior to it. Matter is integral in what the creative act provides. For what is created is not an implement but a creature. The gift of existence includes each creature's chance to be in some measure an end in itself, a thing of intrinsic worth, thus testifying to the Creator's glory.

Here again, then, we find indices for evaluating the claim that the world is not merely originated or eternally necessitated but created by a transcendent God: intelligibility in nature—the possibility of science, explanation, understanding—militates in favor. It does not prove the world created. For there are rival accounts of our understanding. But it tends to confirm creation. The more our grasp of nature grows, the more extensively confirmed are those models that view the world as a manifestation of divine intelligence.[31] Similarly, all autonomous value—not just the values of intelligibility, but the beauty, goodness, and sheer exuberance of nature—can be read as an expression of divine creativity. The discovery of such values inherent in things can, of course, be taken to support a kind of radical pluralism, egoism, even anarchism. But where the natural world is seen as an ordered system, such projections are excluded by cosmology and rebuked (as romantic projections should be) by the moral self-discipline of the inquirer.

Clearly a stronger claim is made here than the mere compatibility of creation with the world's order, beauty, and freedom. For the claim is made that accounts of our understanding that dispense with divine intelligence offer a weak explanation that does not do justice to the human phenomenon. And, similarly, our claim is that accounts of the beauty and order of nature in general that dispense with divine generosity do not do justice to nature itself. Our evidence, perforce, is finite and experiential. But, to the extent that the values resident in the idea of creation more effectively conciliate and save the data, those data support creation as against rival accounts. The exuberance of being specifies the meaning of creation, showing us in God's act not an imposition but an imparting of freedom and power, the relative independence by which all natural things establish themselves in their milieux and express in their own ways the pure and universal, otherwise unspecified grace and glory of God.

Newness

According to ancient tradition, God created miracles in the twilight of the sixth day.[32] But creation belongs to the morning. The Torah relates no genealogy of the gods, no theomachy before the world's origin—partly out of monotheistic chasteness but partly to convey the sense of freshness and beginning. The opening word of the Torah is *Bereshit*, "in the beginning." The story that will unfold begins at its logical and ontological beginning. There was no prior history. Even the celebrated ban, "Whoever reflects on four things, it were a mercy had he never come into the world: what is above, what is beneath, what is before and what is after" (*Ḥagigah* 2.1), does not outlaw metaphysics, which is, after all, practiced and modeled, invited and encouraged by the Torah. Rather, what it seems to disparage is any quest for a cause of the Cause of causes, the motives of the All-Good, the genealogy of God. Genesis is a story of absolute origination. Its chaste imagery suits the naturalistic clarity and metaphysical economy of the account. Stage designers still seek that mise-en-scène when they hang a pure blue-gray scrim as a backdrop to balletic scenes and allow a wisp of mist to suggest God's spirit brooding on the waters. But architects catch the mood more clearly in a sheer, brilliantly lit, clean surface.

When Arabic philosophers contrast genesis with an eternal cosmos they use the words *ḥadīth*, new, and *qadīm*, ancient. The created world is not old but young, of measured age, beyond which stands God alone, eternal, timeless. When occasionalists sought to prove creation a necessity, from the logic of finite being, the outcome was an affirmation of continual new creation. Emanation, too, was continuous creation, the newness generalized to a constant renewal of becoming. But voluntaristic versions preserve the idea of its newness more vividly, complementing and interpreting contingency and design: the world is an invention. It did not have to be; its structure and particularity are not mere entailments of God's goodness or unity; they serve no need of his but express his glory, as a work of art (in lesser measure) serves no utilitarian functions but expresses and embodies an idea, and exists (in some ways) for its own sake.

The ancient meaning of the newness of creation, then, is freedom once again, God's freedom as Creator, and each creature's echoing freedom to be. For Genesis is a universal story. Everyman is born in the forming of Adam and the infusion of God's breath of life into our otherwise inert earth. Thus the newness of creation abides beyond the first creative act. Nature renews itself in each moment, and the seasons mark not passing or cyclicity but birth and new growth out of decay.

Again the ancient idea of newness acquires a new meaning in later hands. But now the pioneers of the change are modern rather than medieval. New force is given to the idea of newness by the discovery of evolution and, more specifically, by the idea of emergence. For being itself is active and dynamic. Creatures *use* the powers and freedoms they find within themselves. They grow, persist, reproduce, striving to preserve and promote their own being, express, perfect, and develop their natures. Their essences are not fixed but evolving, not merely self-actualizing but emergent, susceptible of a redefining in which they themselves are actors.[33] It is in this sense (not the passive sense of the *kalām*) that creation is continuous and ongoing, renewed at each moment. Thus the daily Hebrew liturgy argues playfully that God "in His goodness reneweth each day, continually, the act of creation, as it is said, 'To Him who maketh great lights, for His favor is eternal.'"[34]

If God's act is eternal, his work will be present at all times. Intelligibility is most evident cosmologically in the past, in the determinate order of nature; grace, in the openness of the future; creativity, in the present, in the efficacy of freedom, where determination meets the openness of possibility and marks it indelibly with its unique character and stamp. Again we see the creativity of the artist and not the artisan. For evolution does not work to a blueprint; its design is fully real only in the execution, and static not even then. Stars emerge from dust, elements from stars, compounds and living beings from elements. No feature of a higher order is present in its constituents, or even describable in their terms: chemical properties are not deducible from the laws of physics or even describable in their terms. Similarly with biological properties and the principles of chemistry, or with psychological traits, powers, and capacities in relation to biology: the principles of the prior order afford the environment; the "matter," in Neoplatonic terms. But at each new level of integration new capabilities, new powers of expression and self-direction, new degrees of freedom emerge. This is what we must understand by the need for a prime mover, the incapacity of inanimate matter to enspirit and envigorate itself. Physics does not "determine" chemistry any more than the notes of a key in music "determine" an étude of Chopin; it sets the stage, as chemistry does for biology, and biology for psychology, preparing the ground, as it were, for the emergence of consciousness, intelligence, a soul.

The laws of physics set parameters for chemistry, and those of chemistry for biology. This is what reductionists have in mind when they say that physical laws determine chemistry or that biology is determined by chemistry in turn, the higher-order properties accounted for by reference to a Democritean mystique of complexity. But what is this complexity? Subtle atomic interactions generate properties that are not describable in merely atomic terms and whose outcomes are not predictable from the atomic givens. I am not speaking here about indeterminacy, as though the blind statistical distribution of electrons somehow made a haven for fugitive human freedom, rescuing rational volition from blind necessity by subjecting it to blind chance. On the contrary, I am speaking of the emergence from a world of atoms and electrons of beings that are not adequately described in the language of atoms and electrons, beings that project ends and existentiate themselves through the values they define for themselves, acting in their environment and controlling, in some measure, the very matter they are made of and the forces that give it shape. Chemistry emerges from physics synthetically, as geometry might be said to emerge from arithmetic, and similarly, biology from chemistry. The principles needed to derive one from the other can be known only by one who already comprehends both. Here, where knowledge must deal with realities, not just with the stipulations of mathematics, such comprehension, ultimately, would be infinite.

In the electric, magnetic, and other properties of subatomic particles, to be sure, the basis was laid for chemistry, and thus for biology as well. But it is only in the interaction of the subtly varied constituents of nature that such potentialities are fulfilled. The complexity that emerges is not (as the medievals imagined) the additive product of nuanced variation in the mingling of the givens but their constructive product, in which the dynamics of the more primordial forces are mastered by new orders of being, capable of increasingly self-integrative expression and self-directive activity. Complexity is not the explanation but the outcome of this dynamism. The explanation is the restless urge toward transcendence present in all things, the active and dynamic conatus that is the essence of each being. Selves are the emergent product of the evolutionary dynamism that flourishes in our universe and whose efflorescence is manifest not only in our own being but in the commandeering of chemical forces by the biological, and in the birth of stars.

Mechanists will say that evolution is no more than the survival of the stabler or more durable among the random products of chance combination. But this is to put the cart before the horse. For values like stability or durability, and the subtler values of reproduction, or the adaptability represented by an evolutionary strategy like sexual reproduction, have no meaning apart from the interests that the emergent beings project and constitute as aims. In Aristotelian terms, chance is the intersection of causal trains among events not regularly related by the natures of their constituents; it is called fortune or "luck," when the outcome recognizably affects the interests of the participants. Chance in this sense abounds in nature—so much so that the randomness of interactions is a chief source of natural order. Of course it is of the essence that interactions contain a large random component, insofar as they relate things not intrinsically or even regularly related. But it is also of the essence that interactions are opportunistic. Beings tend to express their identities upon and through one another. In so doing they enhance their environment, from their own standpoint, exploit the orderliness of randomness itself to generate stabler, higher-order, and more information-rich complexes, compounds, and communities, which are capable of still greater enhancement and enrichment. In this sense randomness in nature is not helter-skelter, and opportunity is a natural product of the self-actualizing character of things and the rich potential of their surroundings. It is the dynamism of individual things that pessimists (projectively) neglect when they argue somberly that all energy flows to disorder. They regard it as somehow accidental that beings can generate order even out of the flow to entropy.

Newness in its ancient application means freedom from history and determination, the fresh and unencumbered start that belongs to the universe at large and, in lesser measure, to every creature in it. In more modern terms, newness is evolution and emergence, in which the past is not the sole determinant of the future but present actors are determinants as well, and the powers imparted to creatures make them in some measure self-transcending, capable of rising above the limitations of their primal natures, self-creative in some degree, imaging the artistic creativity of God. Just as we have visible evidence of the world's roundness when we look to the horizon, so we experience its newness when we recognize its unencumberedness, in the fact of evolution or the possibility of human creativity. The world, we find, is still abuilding.

We can know the world to be created, then, by discovering its newness, not only in signs of its finite age but in marks of another newness that are freighted with significance for us and that enrich our idea of God's act—when we see the extent to which the world is unencumbered and recognize the ability of its creatures to be true to form not by remaining true to form but by creating themselves, individually, intellectually, generationally, historically, and by species, genera, phyla, and kingdoms.

God's creativity here is far more immediate than the distant and therefore ancient stars. Its evidences are no less to be found at the objective of a microscope than in the eyepiece of a telescope. They are, in the Qur'anic (50:16) phrase, nearer to us than our jugular vein.

Our analysis of the idea of creation gives us many things to look for that will count as evidence of God's creation. It has closed off no area of our knowledge or understanding from such explorations. And it has given us some fairly decisive considerations, which rival theses might account for otherwise or attempt to discount or dismiss, but which together make a case for creation while adding richness to its meaning: a universe in which understanding is possible but science is necessarily empirical, in which there are freedom and evolution and in which beings exist for their own sakes and according to their own emergent nisus, in which worth is intrinsic and not merely instrumental—a universe that is open rather than closed, that has an open future, not blockaded by an infinite or overreaching past—is the sort of universe that a transcendent God might be conceived to have created as an expression of his glory. That is the sort of universe, I believe, in which we live.

Time and Creativity

To understand the continuing relevance of the idea of creation and its linkage to the idea of creativity, I want now to examine the concept of time. For the claim has been made that creation, paradoxically, renders creativity either impossible or irrelevant, since it means (so we are told) either that God determined all things for all times or that God abandoned what he created. I want to show that both these views are false and that creativity, as our historical analysis suggests, is not at all incompatible with creation, from which it springs. But in showing this I will need to discuss a fundamental disagreement about the nature of time, a disagreement expressed in some philosophers' disappointment with the legacy they received from Henri Bergson.

"If Bergson believed anything," Charles Hartshorne writes, "it was the asymmetry of time, the openness of the future and determinateness of the past."[35] But Bergson, Hartshorne argues, too readily forgot that the denial of determinism, so central to his philosophy, rests on the denial of the symmetry of time. Determinism, Hartshorne urges, following Peirce and Bergson himself, takes an essentially symmetrical view of time. That is why, on Laplace's model, one can as readily retrodict the past as predict the future, given an adequate knowledge of the present state of the world and its unchanging laws. The core of Bergson's message was that the determinism that negates human freedom and closes the open future arises in a false analogy between time and space: space is an affair of mutual exclusion of elements, "whereas time is an affair of mutual inclusion." By preserving a certain symmetry in both space and time, Hartshorne argues, Bergson compromises the ultimate asymmetry of time and falls into "the most glaring confusion in *Time and Free Will*."

Is there a kind of symmetry in time? Bergson thought there was. He described it in terms of the mutual inclusion of temporal moments. What are the consequences of denying that claim? I want to argue that Bergson's idea of the mutual interpenetration of temporal moments allows expansion of the idea of the specious present from a brief span of subjective immediacy to the full duration needed in nature for the unfolding of an event. This expanded view of duration will accommodate actions sustained over long periods, including extended collaborations by members of a community or a culture over history. Time, I will argue, can be asymmetrical in one respect and symmetrical in another: the interpenetration of temporal moments is not a denial of the unalterable differentness of the future from the past. Rather, it is an affirmation of continuity.

But my motive here goes beyond affirmation of that simple fact. The idea that there is a certain symmetry among the moments of time proves critical in relating traditional ideas of creation to Bergson's own emphasis on creativity. The attempt simply to discard creation for more recently favored notions of process, by contrast, endangers many of the insights and values, both scientific and moral, that Bergson sought to preserve within his broad conceptions of creativity, duration, and the asymmetry of time. Following the thrust of some of the more stridently eternalist recent readings of the outcome of a debate that has continued since Western speculation about cosmology began, we find a starkly scientistic outlook that seems to be inseparable from the endeavor to cut off the future from its past, whether in human or in cosmic terms. Toward the end of this final chapter I want to examine the rhetoric and the consequences of this outlook, after first offering some counterarguments to its claims.

Surely it is true that time is profoundly asymmetrical. The unlikeness of the future to the past is critical to its being future. Even if Nietzsche, Epicurus, and the Stoics are right about eternal recurrence, an idea that was tempting to no less a philosopher than Plotinus,[36] still recycled events are not the same as what they repeat, or there would be no meaning to the claim that the same events recurred: there must be at least the fact that *this* Socrates, Xanthippe, and Meletus are repetitions of *those*. But is time symmetrical in some respects, or is it simply a confusion for Bergson to speak of interpenetration, the *mutual* openness of temporal moments to one another?

In *Matter and Memory* Bergson discovers the same interpenetration in space that he had earlier found in time and used to break down the linearity of events. Zeno's paradoxes rest on the assumption that time and events are either a Euclidean continuum or a Pythagorean pointillistic series. But, in fact, Bergson argued, the moments of time are neither the dimensionless knife edge that temporal analysis invokes as a virtual limit nor the static freeze-frames of a misplaced spatial analysis. On the contrary, each particular moment of change involves an onwardness—what Plato called 'becoming', and Bergson 'duration'—which no merely geometric model can capture and which static abstractions only deaden, in fictive denial of the fact of change, as anatomical sections cut from the living tissue with microtomes arrest and thereby negate the processes of life they are meant to reveal.[37]

Time itself is denied by the analysis that seeks to compose it in the Augustinian way, of a vanished past, an unborn future, and an infinitely diminishing present.[38] The present, Bergson saw, cannot be instantaneous or atomic. It must have duration—both asymmetrical, melting into the future even as it emerges from the past, and blurry-edged, not bounded sharply by dimensionless points, since the dimensionless point is a mere fiction of geometry. The same is true of space: it is impossible to compose what will have magnitude out of what has none.

Bergson's real quarrel, then, was not with space but with overreliance on a fiction most familiar from its use in the analysis of space: the fiction of separateness, of discrete and frozen temporal moments, in this case, that are at once fully determinate (thus fixed) in their character, yet somehow (paradoxically) determinative—each of the character of the rest and holding, without omission, all that ever was or will be in all the rest. Bergson first expressed what was misleading in this fiction by saying that time is not like space, but he came to see that space itself is not like space in the sense that the economies and abstractions of geometry would have it. The Cartesian project of geometrizing nature is as much an underrepresentation of matter as it is of time.

To render time atomic is to render change impossible and, as Hume saw clearly, to arrest causality—thus Hume's sly insistence that time is a succession of infinitesimal instants:[39] the static, durationless instants of Humean time prejudge the question of causality in favor of a kind of logical atomism. But suppose (like true empiricists) we had begun from the *fact* of change. Or suppose we were to understand change not in terms of succession but in terms of the conditionedness of one moment or event by another. Then causality would be a given,[40] and the simple sensa of extreme empiricism would be recognized for what they are, elaborate constructs, achievements of perceptual and cognitive synthesis and selection.

Only if the moments of time themselves have real duration is change conceivable,[41] and only in such duration is there the theater of action for causality, which will not merely *determine* the future out of the givenness of the past but also allow actors to differentiate the future from that givenness—allow genuine change, and indeed evolution, emergence of what is *conditioned* by the past (to use Spinoza's word) but never precontained in it, or locked in place by what is already over and done with. When Leibniz held that the past was great with the future, and the future laden with the past,[42] he knew better than to imagine sheer preformation: it was because mere geometric figures could not explain the forces of cohesion or mutual exclusion among bodies that Leibniz remedied the Cartesian reduction of bodies to extension, by proposing *intensive* qualities that would allow the emergence of events not yet *present* in their causes.[43] Similarly Bergson, admiring the cosmogony of Lemaître, settled on the fact that the primitive datum of energy/mass from which the world emerges cannot contain or determine all that it will engender. As Lemaître wrote, "Clearly the initial quantum could not conceal in itself the whole course of evolution; but according to the principle of indeterminacy, that is not necessary. Our world is now understood to be a world where something really happens; the whole story of the world need not have been written down in the first quantum like a song on a phonograph record."[44]

Bergson's early arguments about time relied on the phenomenology of felt duration. His descriptions were of consciousness, and his paradigm case of duration was our awareness of a melody. Bergson's father was a musician, and the son knew well that our hearing of a melody cannot be composed of durationless instants if we are ever to hear it *as* a melody, hear its notes in relation to one another, as parts in a whole, or even as rhythmic or tonal contrasts.[45] The same, we must say, of the rich complexity of an orchestral chord; the same, we now know, of our perception of colors: they are perceived relationally, against a contextual background, and the comparative process is, of course, a temporal act.[46] Our ability to mix (or even see!) a hitherto unknown shade of blue, which was such a mystery for Humean epistemology, is no mystery at all when we recognize that there are no atomic sensa but that even the "simplest" patches of color are complexly constructed syntheses of very complex events.[47] Thus a psychological dissolving of the conundrums of dogmatic empiricism was a by-product of Bergson's biological, indeed evolutionary, epistemology, which saw perception as an act not only of synthesis but of abstraction, filtration, and exclusion.[48]

Because of its pioneering reliance on phenomenology, Bergson's theory of time set up a sharp contrast between public or cosmic time and subjective time. It relied heavily on James's idea of the specious present, the moment that is immediate for consciousness, and it seriously attempted to measure that present, marking it off against public time—despite the affirmation that spans of time are not strictly superposable. Values were assigned between a maximum of 12 seconds, the longest span that James believed consciousness could hold together as a single now, and a minimum of .002 seconds, the briefest event that seemed accessible to sense perception.[49] Committed followers of Bergson still take seriously this confounding of psychological temporality with real duration. But Bergson himself came to see that public time, cosmic time, the time of natural events, must be structured in the same way as phenomenal time: the dissolving of sugar in his coffee was a sequence of natural events isometric with his own impatient expectation of its outcome.

Strictly speaking, Bergson's reference to subjective experience here was quite unnecessary. Natural time no more requires anchoring in phenomenal time than phenomenal time requires natural time to authorize it. If the present is the locus of events, it will last as long as those events require. This will be denied only by those who bear a metaphysical animus against the notion that events occur. Thus Bergson's central thesis about time is as true of physical as of psychological events, and Kantian or post-Kantian phenomenology is not needed to validate it. Time in nature, as in consciousness, has the character of duration, and its asymmetry is not a matter of perception or intuition but a fact of nature: in nature, as in thought, time is not a series of atomic instants, whether dimensionless or instantly evanescent, but the inexorable onwardness of change itself, the inevitable qualitative differentness of the future from the past, and the inevitable referentiality of the present to the future and the past. That reference is made by the events themselves, and must be if they are to have unity as events. Objective moments, then, interpenetrate as much as subjective ones do; and the flow or stream of consciousness that loomed so large for Proust, or Joyce, or Virginia Woolf, is just a special case of the nature of time at large. For what Bergson first saw in terms of memory and anticipation is equally true without the mediation of consciousness, for causes and effects, preconditions and aftermaths.[50]

The specious present, then, is misnamed not only on Čapek's ground that there is nothing false or illusory or even secondary about it[51] but also on the ground that there is nothing essentially subjective about it: the thick temporal present necessary to the occurrence of any event is the time the event requires to unfold.[52] By that standard, the present (like an Aristotelian place) is of any size, or many sizes, from a duration much shorter than consciousness can capture to one that spans the centuries. In the writing of a book or the birth of a volcano, the event is a whole not because of any imagined discreteness from other events but because of the organic connectedness of its parts, the conditioning of what comes later by what went before, and the dependence of the outcome as a whole upon what happens now. The present is not over until all that can give determinacy to the whole has occurred. Then and only then the present lapses into past, the imperfect becomes perfect; the indeterminate, determinate. Thus the events of a war or of history in general, the subtle collaboration across the centuries between an Edward Fitzgerald and the many poets whose quatrains were gathered under the name of Omar Khayyam,[53] the composition of a Bible or a Talmud through an intricate dialogue or continuing discourse across the generations, and the collusion or falling out of authors and their readers, translators, and interpreters, or of painters with those who view or scorn their works, all reveal that the idea of a single definitive present (let alone a rapidly passing one) is a sham. There are many presents of varying durations and with no more perfect discreteness than events themselves possess.

Time is thick because events are nested within one another, much as places are. And Bergson's pedagogical explanation that time is unlike space because in time there is no simultaneity of mutually excluding parts is only a first approximation. For, as Čapek makes clear, where Bergson and his many critics were never perfectly clear, the real impact of relativity on Bergson's philosophy is to exclude the notion of instantaneous, universe-wide simultaneity. If so, the effect of Bergsonism on relativity is not at all to wreck or seek to derail but to complete Einstein's project of discovering the ultimate temporality of space itself.[54] Bergson's philosophy achieves this end not by the Kantian expedient of arguing that space can be apprehended only in a temporal tour by consciousness through its parts and regions but by the more properly Bergsonian recognition that the parts of space make reference to one another and can do so only through the medium of differentiated time. What follows is the recognition, despite all Eleatic wishes, that time cannot be excluded from the most fleeting snapshot of the universe—or rather, we should say, from the universe itself.

The intuitive, naturalistic core of Bergson's insight about time rests in the fact that time is not truly one-dimensional. *Space* allows an event to occupy a durational present, beginning *here* in one respect before it has begun otherwise elsewhere. Here and now, without reference to Einsteinian relativity, in a single inertial frame and with middle-sized objects that may or may not be observed, we find the thickness of duration, the cross talk of referentiality—the linear dimension, or *longeur*, of an event, but also, in the multifacetedness of the same event, its *largeur*, which in turn involves the temporality of space, the need for time in which the parts of an event or act come together as a whole occurrence.

Bergson's brief was the overcoming of determinism. A false analogy between time and space, he argued, led mechanists to suppose that time was a continuum of atomic instants, each one of which was ultimately static and each one of which uniquely determined and was determined by any of the rest. The result was the denial, in effect, of the fundamental psychological, biological, indeed physical asymmetry of duration and the collapsing of time into a series of strata or slices whose relations of mutual implication made them in principle undistinguishable from one another—thus eliminating time altogether. To dissolve time in such a fashion was a desideratum, perhaps, for Megarian or Stoic would-be monists of the stamp of Diodorus Cronus.

But if achieved it would prove a disaster for those scientific or scientistic determinists whose tight grip upon the twentieth century Bergson sought to relax.

Bergson's strategy was to argue that time is not a discontinuous continuum of discrete moments; the *now*s that represent the present are not isolated and dimensionless instants but interpenetrating and persistent spans that afford a platform to action and so to freedom. Where mechanism collapses the present and thus time itself, since time is nothing if there is no present, Bergson reclaims time, by the very expedient Proust would adopt from Bergson's teaching, recapturing the past, through the recognition that consciousness and ultimately everything present makes itself what it is through retention of the past: "There is no consciousness without memory, no continuation of a state without the addition, to the present feeling, of the memory of past moments. That is what duration consists of."[55] Phenomenology or analogy, and ultimately the pure analysis of the anatomy of natural events, broadens the claim to a fact not merely about consciousness but about the character of the cosmos: Time is "the indivisible and indestructible continuity of a melody where the past enters into the present and forms with it an undivided whole which remains undivided and even indivisible in spite of what is added at every instant *or rather thanks to what is added*."[56]

The strength of Bergson's account is that it leaves room—he would say *time*—for the emergence of the future. Because it allows actors to differentiate the future from the past, it allows for creativity, a creativity that is emergent—neither locked within the past nor radically severed from it. But this is not enough for Hartshorne. Objecting to any form of symmetry between past and future, he denounces mutual inclusion as vociferously as mutual exclusion. There is, he insists, nothing mutual in the case: "Nowhere does Bergson make clear that symmetry, rather than dependence or its negative, is the mark of space and asymmetry, of time." Hartshorne's target is Bergson's sense of continuity, indeed community, between the future and the past. Potentiality, he insists, is mere virtuality, no determinant at all, since it is nothing actual. This Bergson saw but failed to follow up on: "It is absurd, as Bergson sees, to imagine exact duplicates of actual particulars and baptize them as antecedent possibilities (or group them as denisons [*sic*] of possible worlds). . . . Possibilities are always more or less general. Becoming is *creation of particularity*, not its rebaptizing as 'actual,' whatever that could add if particularity were already there."[57] There is a major point here, of much relevance to the ontological argument, as we have seen: a possible dollar is not the same sort of thing in the least as the actual dollar that might replace it. Indeed, it is not a thing at all but a notion, an abstract generality, dependent on the suspension of some but not all of the assumptions we normally make about the world. But Hartshorne overstates the implications of this idea.[58] It does not imply that the past has no purchase on the present or that virtualities lie wholly in the future, untouched and untouching present action. To make that assumption would be to reatomize time, to overcome the atomization of mutual implication only to fall into a new atomization of radical isolation and absolute indeterminism. Surely the future does not create itself. Agents act in the present, against the background of conditions they inherit from the past.

Whitehead adopted and assiduously adapted Bergson's idea of duration.[59] But he both departed from Bergson and in a way enshrined what Bergson had taught, by the special emphasis he gave to what he called "perpetual perishing." He once claimed to have tried to do for perishing what Aristotle had done for becoming. The very fixity of the past, he argued, makes it an inextricable element of the future, grounding the sense we sometimes have "that what we are is of infinite importance."[60] It is this special perishing, a notion forecast in Plato and central in Philoponus (for similar Christian reasons to those that move Whitehead—or the cinemateurs of *Places in the Heart*) that Hartshorne wants faithfully to preserve when he castigates Bergson for neglecting time's asymmetry: "Bergson shows no sign of realizing that a definite plurality of unit cases of becoming . . . can be combined with emphatic acceptance of the unity of present with past. It is only the unity of past with present that must be rejected. Where in my childhood was there any unity with my present state? I might have died long ago. Retrospective unity does not entail prospective unity."[61] Hartshorne, it seems, does not agree that the child is father of the man. But he can hardly fail to admit that the choices I make now contribute to what I will be. They are registered in my character, and have been ever since I was a child. If this be false, there is no such task as education, and no such event as a life.[62]

The radical asymmetry of time that Bergson missed, Hartshorne argues, is that while the past does influence the present the present cannot affect the past: "Nothing we do will ever change the career of Shakespeare between his birth and his death."[63] This seeming truism is meant to be as damaging to Bergson's conceptualization of time as Hartshorne's telling comment about possible worlds is to philosophers who imagine that possibilities live somewhere else than this world, as constituents of (actual) possible worlds. Granted, efficient causes cannot touch the past. But much that we call past is not past at all in the sense of this precise asymmetry. True, "possibles" are not ready-formed particulars lurking in the wings and lacking only some key of entry to actuality. But that does not mean that there is no mutuality between past and future. When the past is active, in memory, or in causality, it is not as past but as present actuality that it acts. By playing a role in the formation of the future, even if only as a springboard or dialectical antithesis, it becomes part of the present and is distinctively affected not in the sense that the facticity of what is truly past is altered retroactively but in the sense that the significance of what is past, whether for consciousness or for nature, is made other than what it was.

Past events, as causes or as matter for creativity, do not remain what they were, and indeed are not over, not in the sense conveyed in natural languages by use of the perfect tense, over and done with, *Carthago fuit, Carthago ruit*. The continuing presentness of what is in some senses and for some purposes past is the very meaning of duration, and duration, as we have seen, can be much longer than Bergson supposed. What we call a past event is in some of its aspects far more lasting than the event that in other contexts we might call by the same name. There are some places, and not in any mystic or subjective, or legalistic sense, where World War II has not yet ended. Indeed, in some respects, there is nowhere in the world where it is over fully; we still belong, as Yehuda Bauer rightly argues, to the generation, to the same historic present, of those who perpetrated and underwent the Holocaust. The war continues to exercise its effects. And its outcome (thus, its impact as a whole), for that very reason, continues to be influenced and changed by the responses of living subjects now.

To deny the purchase of the past upon the present and of the present on the whole it forms with the past is to deny causality, just as clearly as it is a denial of freedom to deny the power of the present to break away from the past. As Kant saw vividly, moral freedom has no meaning without causality. For only through causality can the will effectuate its designs. The echoes of the past die, blurred and averaged into forgetfulness by the din or dissonance of new and other old events. How little we know now of Elam or Ebla—how little we know of Amalek, despite the Torah's admonition to remember. Indeed, that injunction is accompanied with the command to blot out the name of Amalek. It is true, as Bergson saw, that the ability to forget is the counterpart and condition of the ability to remember. But consciousness is not nature; the presentness of memory is not the living presence of the past (which might lie all unconscious in the genes), and the unalterability of what is past is not the same as its persistence, but its complement, the aspect no longer accessible to praxis. Who can deny, on learning of the suicide of Primo Levi or the schizophrenia of some child of the camps, that Hitler, long after his demise, is still exacting casualties, or that the Holocaust left no intact survivors? Who can deny that in retaining obloquy for Hitler or respect for Cicero we affect the consummation of their designs?

Our actions affect the fulfillment of the hopes of our forebears in many crucial ways. Insofar as we constitute a community with other beings, past, present, or future, our actions affect the achievement of their projects. It is certainly of consequence to the career of Shakespeare or Horace or Thucydides whether his work continues to be read; to anyone who has made efforts or sacrifices for posterity, it is of moment whether those efforts fall on barren ground or are taken up and carried forward. It is for this reason that it is relevant to latercomers to determine which, if any, of those projects deserve to be taken up, how, if at all, they are to be carried forward, and in what respects. The living present may involve participants in a single action that endures over centuries. In cultural or communal terms individuals who are centuries apart may share in a single action, or a system of actions that constitute a history, an economy, a progress or progression of culture or civilization. The wise or ignorant choices, happy or unhappy turnings of later actors, are as consequential to the success or failure of their predecessors' efforts as the latter are to the former.[64] Such mutuality or community in a project only inchoately given in its earlier stages does not, of course, amount to strict or comprehensive symmetry of the future with the past. Time, like many another sequence, is symmetrical in some respects and asymmetrical in others. But the level at which there is in fact a mutuality, say between those now living and their forebears, does show in just what sense the present time, like the present place in Aristotle, is a relative notion capable of indefinite expansion: it is the expansion characteristic of the ever-enlargeable idea of the *we*, and not merely the subjective we but the equally expansible objective *it*.

The cross-referentiality of the moments of time and their nestedness in one another, within systems of presentness defined only by the relevance of their components to a given event, action, or concern, does damage a Whiteheadian dogma of centrality to Hartshorne, the dogma of the consequent nature of God. For it means that the past is not merely antecedent to the future, but is its prologue, laying out conditions and parameters that *can* influence and in their measure determine the future, as well as setting the stage for creativity and the emergence of what is genuinely novel.[65] God is more than an album for the storage of past occasions, and God is anything but hampered by limited potency in the way that Whiteheadians of Hartshorne's school like to claim. We see divine efficacy as much in the determination of the future by the past as in the emergence of the new. Both aspects authentically represent God's creativity, and the miracle of that creativity is nowhere more evident than in the coalescence of actuality out of virtuality at every present moment. This is what we mean when we say that God is present not only in all places but at all times. Divine agency is apprehensible under different aspects in the acts of finite beings: both in the certitude of proximate causality and in the creativity of emergence.[66] Not that time is symmetrical in some all-engulfing sense. The moment has the determinacy of actuality only insofar as it is past, and the future can influence the past only in a retrospective way—only to the extent, in fact, that the future is not yet future but is seized in the same present with the past, as a virtuality to be appropriated and (here Hartshorne is quite right) given definition in the very act of being given actuality.

In referring to the present in which agents act, take up the past, and define the future (whose limitations are indeed the parameters assigned it by the past), I am referring to moments whose discreteness from one another is purely notional. But that, of course, does not imply the unreality or illusoriness of the time in which we live and act. Time is neither a razor edge whose end is simultaneous with its beginning nor an atomic fragment of consciousness that does not linger even long enough to be noted as a now. Rather, since the present is the platform or worktable of events, its duration is as long as their occurrence requires. A given event, as identified by one set of criteria, might be completed long before the ending of the larger sequence in which it forms a part, and from which it draws significance when identified by other criteria. In the deathless words of Yogi Berra, "It isn't over 'til it's over."

As long as an event goes on—even if it takes years or centuries, like the fighting of some wars, or the building of cathedrals or civilizations, or revolutions in human relations or consciousness—every moment remains intimately connected to the rest, and the actions undertaken now play their role in determining the ultimate meaning or impact of the whole. Hartshorne's attempt to find an absolute asymmetry behind the level of symmetry that Bergson saw thus vitiates a part of the truth that Bergson sought to explain. It reinstates the false linearity that Bergson sought to show us how to escape and sunders the connectedness of duration, all for the sake of a rather trivial point about the doneness of what is done and some rather dubious theological claims that amount to a preference for *natura naturata* over *natura naturans*.

Creation and Symmetry

Surely there is one sense in which temporal moments are symmetrical: the moments (or virtual moments) before the world began, if it began, are undistinguishable. It was on that basis that Parmenides, Aristotle, Proclus, Averroës, and Spinoza sustained the eternity of the world: empty moments have neither anteriority nor posteriority, but all collapse into nullity; they do not exist. The argument is causal at the root: if all events need an objective determinant, genesis would never come about; no potential moment was better or fitter than the rest as the first moment of creation. Creationists from Philoponus to al-Kindī, to Ibn Gabirol, al-Ghazālī, Maimonides, and

Leibniz saw in voluntarism the only escape from such fixity:[67] the world was indeed created, but will, not reason or necessity, *made* the difference, where none was found, among the prospective temporal moments, making one the first. The determinant was subjective, not objective: God chose to create and chose the moment and the manner.

The rejection of radical creation, as we know, has been a thesis of philosophers almost from the beginning. Anaximander (ap. Aristotle, *De Caelo* II 13, 295b 10) derived the earth's stability from symmetry: "It stays still because of its equilibrium. For it befits what is seated at the center and equally disposed toward the extremes not to be borne a whit more up or down or to the side—and it is impossible for it to move in opposite directions at once—so it stays fixed by necessity." And it was probably Anaximander himself who adapted this argument to time as well. For, just as he sought to sketch the figure of the earth and sea in his map and to chart the rhythm of the seasons with his gnomon, he enshrined the symmetry that gives stability to change in his idea of the justice of time, which obviates an absolute creation, by overseeing the coming to be of all things out of the Indefinite and their passing away into their proximate sources "according to the assessment of time." Thus, in Aristotle's words: "In order for generation not to fail it is not necessary for perceptible body to be infinite actually, since it is possible for the destruction of one thing to be the generation of the other, while the sum of things remains limited" (*Physics* III 8, 208a 8).

Parmenides argued explicitly from the likeness of each moment to the next that being has no origin: "For what creation will you seek for it. . . . And what need would have driven it on to grow, starting from nothing, at a later time rather than an earlier?" (ap. Simplicius, *Phys.* 145, 1). He even alludes to Anaximander's Justice, as what "holds reality fast," not just spatially but temporally, so that it cannot come to be or perish but remains forever fully actual, since "it must either fully be or not be." Parmenides' argument from the equivalence of all moments is taken up by Aristotle and elaborated by Proclus, Simplicius, and the Muslim Aristotelians in their polemics against absolute creation. Passing from the Jewish Averroists to Spinoza, the idea of an immutable order loses its aura of divinity only in the mechanism of the nineteenth century, where it lodges in the metaphysical certitude of the conservation of matter. But the aura is never wholly lost, from the time that Anaximander claimed the *apeiron* to be immortal and divine as well as inexhaustible. For, in modern as in Hellenistic times, the counterpart of mechanism is nature mysticism, diffusing the aura of eternity in the afflatus of romantic poets and transcendentalist painters and essayists. Dispersed and secularized, etiolated in the aesthetic of the sublime, but still outspoken in spiritualism and pantheism,[68] it persists in steady state cosmology, although battered by entropy and evolution and all but finally exploded by the big bang.

Hartshorne praises eternalism in Bergson as "the well argued rejection in *Creative Evolution* of the idea that 'there might have been nothing at all.'" He writes, "Hume's belief that all existential statements are contingent is incorrect; since 'something exists' is necessarily true. 'Nothing,' the zero, the naught, has only a relative meaning; absolutized, it becomes nonsense. 'Nothing at all' either expresses an incoherent thought or implies some qualification, such as 'nothing to the present purpose.' I have only admiration for Bergson's reasoning here."[69] But this is sheer dogmatism, the reflex of Kant's or Aristotle's, or Moore's about the need for 'being' to have some specialized sense. The only way we have of knowing that something exists is phenomenal: It is true, as Descartes observed, that I cannot escape the givens of my consciousness, but it does not follow, as Descartes well understood, that my mind is a necessary being. I cannot think my own nonexistence; but that does not make it impossible. The existence that is necessary can only be of what is absolute, and monotheists are rightly chary about assigning absolute existence to just anything—as they are of assigning absolute weight to just any value. Hartshorne is rather casual about this. Just as he is ready to say that some being, any being, is necessary, he is correspondingly ready to downgrade divine transcendence: "The highest conceivable form of reality, deity, is only the highest conceivable form of becoming or duration. . . . Berdyaev is the clearest of all [about this]. . . . For he hints at a divine kind of time."[70]

But was Bergson an eternalist? His disciple Jacques Chevalier claimed him as a creationist, much as he and others were eager to claim him as a Catholic. The facts are a bit more complex: Bergson played down the idea of an initial moment of creation because the great theme of his philosophy was the ongoing creativity of the divine. But his voluntarism, his finitism, his commitment to the idea of entropy, as developed, for example, in the work of Émile Meyerson, his rejection of the discrete, atomic matter and infinite, absolute space of the mechanistic science of his day ally him squarely with creationists, albeit in a sense modified by his own predilections and biases.[71] The atomist tradition from Democritus and Epicurus to al-Rāzī, Gassendi, and the modern materialists made space absolute and time in effect reversible, with the constant random play of the changeless, Democritean, ultimately Parmenidean, particles. It was against this vision of nature that Bergson's life's work in philosophy set its face. Entropy seemed to him to argue unequivocally for the irreversibility of time, as the world's determinations argued for its continuing origination.[72]

Bergson objected to Kant's first antinomy, between eternity and creation, on the grounds that both horns of its dilemma treat the universe as a completed whole. He rejected the idea of time with nothing in it. But he did not imagine (as Hartshorne does) that if the world came to be it must have been preceded by illimitable eons of eventless time. Against the idea of absolute time, either full or empty, from eternity, he took up the classic creationist view that time itself is among the features of the world that first appears with creation. This was the position of Philo, Augustine, Philoponus, al-Ghazālī, Maimonides, and others, who accepted the Aristotelian teaching of the relativity of time but found in it a response to the Aristotelian eternalist elenchus that held it absurd to number moments in which nothing yet had moved or changed or even begun to be.[73] In Bergson's case, as Čapek makes clear,[74] the same position flows naturally from the deep harmony of his view of time with Einsteinian relativity: time has no meaning apart from events. But Hartshorne fails to see that time relativism does not commit one to eternalism but takes a well-trodden route through a creationism that regards time itself as created—or, in Bergson's case, we might say, emergent. Granted, as Aristotle saw, that there can be nothing gradual about the origin of time—the becoming of becoming, still, Eliot Deutsch's idea that time is what actions make of it[75] well expresses the nuance Bergson sketched in the idea of the becoming of time.

Ironically, Hartshorne's discomfort with creation compromises Bergson's thesis of the asymmetry of time. For that asymmetry is just what is at stake in the idea of creation: only God is necessary and self-explanatory; the world is contingent, temporal, perhaps ephemeral. Each individual and each event is unique, never to be repeated. When a Christian theist like Philoponus made the perishing of things a central thesis of his cosmology, he did so *in behalf* of creation, not as a counterpart or alternative to it. And the same dialectic is found in the vivid contrast of God's eternity with the world's temporality and contingency imaged in the powerful Qur'anic phrase: "All things perish except His face."[76] As we have seen, the idea is formalized and universalized in *kalām* theology and forged into a systematic metaphysics by Avicenna, following the lead of Plato's *Timaeus*: what is temporal is evanescent and contingent; what is immutable and (in Plotinus's term) impassive is ultimately creative, whether continuously, as in the model of emanation, or in the discrete but unremitting fulgurations of Leibniz, the continual re-creations of the *kalām*—or the act of Genesis that created heaven and earth, the sea and all that is in them. The monotheistic idea of perishing is the counterpart, ultimately, not of Aristotelian becoming but of biblical creation.

A crucial argument of creationists like al-Ghazālī and Maimonides was that the eternalist thesis rests on a determinism so strict as to debar change altogether and stymie emanation at the Source.[77] Aristotle had paid deference to Parmenidean logic while maintaining the reality of time and change in his distinctive model of alteration. He preserved Parmenides' thesis that a thing must be what it is and made it the cornerstone of First Philosophy. Change was a conjunction of unchanging form with unchanging matter. The Eleatic objection to a thing's becoming what it was not was answered by distinguishing essence from accident, form from matter, actuality from potentiality: things become actually what they already are potentially. The potentials reside in matter. Matter remains constant, and the changeable object remains unchanged in the only sense that really counts in logic—it preserves its essence, unless denatured, that is, destroyed, as by death. The corollaries, that all change requires a substrate, whose nature limits the scope of alteration, and that no change is absolute or radical, were welcome and scientific-seeming. But there was a price to pay: since neither essences nor matter were altered or destroyed, not only absolute creation and destruction but even the evolution and extinction of species were impossible, a priori. Sports of nature were by definition insignificant, a child's coloring outside the eternal boundaries of species. The key that Mendel would find, but that Epicurus would forecast (see Lucretius, *De Rerum Natura* V, 837–77), unlocking the dynamic of biology to human understanding, was thrown away because of its resemblance to hoary myths of cosmic origin and the vulgar awe of common man, who thought the extraordinary or monstrous significant just because it was beyond the common.

The Aristotelian scheme, then, was both heuristic and limiting: it opened vast fields for observation, classification, and inductive hypothesis. But it held quantitative differences rather unimportant, viewing all but gross differences of scale as nonessential, inflaming Aristotle's impatience with Plato's zeal for mathematics into a general bias against the significance of measurement. Similarly, normative Aristotelianism deemed "unnatural" events uninteresting. So for centuries it silently blocked the path to controlled experimentation, by which investigators (using Bacon's model of Elizabethan torture) would one day take nature to the limit to make her yield up her secrets. It devalued efficient causes in favor of formal and material ones, further tilting explanation toward the conceptual and qualitative and away from the mechanical and precisely measured, and elevating Aristotle's equation of cosmogony with myth into an axiom that accounts of origins are somehow not a form of explanation—making history not a real science, and treating the order seen in biology or astronomy as a design without a past.

Creationism, less intellectualist, but more empiricist in bent, proved fruitful here, giving birth to the ideas of evolution,[78] universal history,[79] the contingency of matter. It saw nature, including human nature, in terms of possibilities, where essentialism looked to regularities. Each view fostered a variety of science, and both were deeply religious—the Aristotelian finding marks of divine wisdom in the invariance of natural patterns, the creationist finding hallmarks of God's grace in the emergence of novelty in nature, human life, and history. Neither view was so narrowly framed as to be incapable of responding to the other; so both, in a way, were and remain resistant to refutation. But Bergson's bent toward what could be validated in experience[80] tugged him insistently away from the unique event and toward the ongoing process.

Hartshorne, however, takes him to task even for this—for ignoring Karl Popper's concern "that if no conceivable experience could falsify an existential assertion, it is not empirical in the usual sense."[81] The criticism is not that Bergson committed himself to views that are unfalsifiable but that he gave preference to the view that he deemed best confirmed by the evidence: Bergson has betrayed metaphysics by appealing to experience. "He seems not to see Popper's point . . ."—as though Popper's *Conjectures and Refutations* (London, 1963) lay open before him! But why should Bergson's metaphysics observe Hartshorne's stipulations—especially if they bring it up against Popper's legitimate concern that unfalsifiable claims say nothing about the world?[82] How odd to invoke Popper, of all philosophers, to show both that metaphysical claims are nonempirical and that is what they *should* be!

Čapek argues, much in the spirit of Bergson, that creationism is not crucially verifiable, since all the evidence that seems to converge on a first moment of time can be taken as pointing not to an absolute origin but to the most recent in a series of big bangs. The most Čapek will say is that the evidence is compatible with absolute origination and that, in turn, with theistic explanations. We can go a step further, as we have seen. For the evidence can be read as suggestive of creation: creation is a possible hypothesis, but it may prove the most acceptable. For the evidence may render the existence of anything in nature prior to the big bang diminishingly credible, and the observed character of nature may, as we have suggested, support a creationist hypothesis. Here Bergson's emphasis on continuing creation is vitally relevant not as an alternative to the unique event but as an avenue of access to the character of divine creativity.

Classical process theology is not so accommodating. It dismisses creation, where exponents of creation welcome creativity. Robert Neville thus trenchantly condemns the Whiteheadian sundering of God from creativity for slipping into a kind of positivism:

> The basic ontological problem is to account for the unity of many and one through creativity. . . . Whitehead's response . . . would have to be that . . . there is no decision responsible for the basic togetherness of one and many in creativity. . . . Creativity must simply be accepted as something given. The issue here is whether the irrationality of the category of the ultimate must be accepted. . . . If Whitehead accepts the irrationality of the category of the ultimate, he accepts an irrationality in one place yet does not accept it in an analogous one; he might as well say that events happen with pure spontaneity and no causation. We rightly boggle at this. It is a betrayal of rational faith.[83]

This is just the issue posed by Spinoza's insistence on the distinction between the self-caused and the uncaused. Neville, challenging Hartshorne, finds a lasting significance in the idea of creation: "The important category at the ontological level has to do with creation *ex nihilo*, not with creativity," he writes; "at the cosmological level something like Plato's irreducible contrast between *being* and *becoming* exhibits more intensity for experience than the swallowing of being in becoming or vice versa."[84] For Plato's contrast finds a balance rather than seeking a reduction. Neville, in that spirit, proposes a synthesis of creation with creativity when he writes: "God is the creator of every determinate thing, each in its own occasion of spontaneous appearance. In contrast to God's ontological creativity, cosmological creativity is the descriptive fact that the spontaneity in occasions brings unity out of multiplicity."[85]

Paul Weiss puts the matter less technically: "To create is to make something be, to give it an existence. If Socrates' existence does not belong to him, if it is not truly and fully and indelibly his, then surely he was never created."[86] Weiss here takes aim at Thomism, but I see a powerful affinity between Maimonides' position and Neville's partly Thomistic response to Whitehead and Hartshorne. For Maimonides and Thomas would concur that freedom is the sine qua non of creation. If we generalize that point, we see the act of creation continued in the creativity of each being. Finding creativity in all emergence and not regarding that creativity as the blind outcome of mechanics, we do not take its immanence as the mark of self-sufficiency but as the hallmark of pervasive grace. So the idea of divine creation remains fruitful for us in all our inquiries. We link Bergson's creativity to Maimonidean creationism; specifically, to Maimonides' affirmation, following the hints of Saadiah, the Rabbis, and Scripture, that nature, in both its rational and its arbitrary-seeming aspects, is the vehicle in which God's character is made manifest[87]—in more familiar terms, that nature is an epiphany.

Granted, absolute creation will never be verified or falsified conclusively. The same is true of any categorical claim of fact, including all the claims of science, since any hypothesis can be modified to account for seemingly conflicting evidence. The real question is how much damage must be done to the fabric of our knowledge, how much evidence must be explained away or swept under the carpet to preserve a single, increasingly isolated notion? The most we can say of any transcendental claim is that it is confirmed or disconfirmed by the evidence, harmonious or inharmonious with the consilience of experience. In these terms we can say that the findings of cosmology and physics tend to confirm the world's origination and to disconfirm its eternal, steady state existence—whatever construction is put upon those facts.

Popper's suspicions of irrefutable claims are sound. Such claims are too well hedged to amount to a commitment. But it was creationists who brought concern with falsifiability to metaphysics—when al-Ghazālī and then Maimonides argued that the God of emanation seemed to make no detectable difference in the world.[88] The same criticism can be returned (with a few hundred years' interest) to today's process theologians: creationists can cite evidence for the world's finite age. In classical philosophy, from Plato to Philoponus to the high Middle Ages, such evidence was construed to include evidence that the world or matter might be destroyed. Thus Philoponus used entropy, as well as he could understand it, and the apparent changes observable in celestial bodies, to show that the world system might run down, that the stars were not "simple substances" and therefore not immutable.[89] Rather, the whole cosmos was corrosible, corruptible, destructible, ergo contingent, transitory, not the sort of thing that could endure forever or of its own accord—therefore, created. Today the account is easier. The red shift and the apparent "echoes" of the original cosmic boom support the thesis of the world's origination. One family of explanations infers the world's birth from the fullness of God's grace, an absolute creation. What such reasoning has in common with the older tradition and with Bergson is commitment to the empirical consequences of its theses. We say that the evidence supports creation, but the evidence might have been otherwise. We know what sort of evidence would count against origination.

This Hartshorne finds offensive. He defines metaphysics "as the attempt to deal rationally with noncontingent, nonempirical truths about existence," and takes Bergson to task because "he seems to think that metaphysics is empirical."[90] But how are we to deal rationally with truths about existence if we cut ourselves off from our experience? Hartshorne urges that "only introspective observation" can give us metaphysical insights[91]—as though introspection were somehow independent of experience. Clearly, he is right that necessary truths will never be apprehended by "vision or touch" unaided. But any theorist must exceed those limits. To make of metaphysics something more than a general account of being and then to posit introspection as our self-sufficing guide is to invent both the subject and the faculty ad hoc, and to sunder them from any sort of knowledge that might aid them, or to which their reflections might be relevant. Our experience may be limited, but we will not get knowledge without it, and Bergson, I believe, was quite right to treat metaphysics as an empirical inquiry, albeit not a collation of sense data, any more than any branch of theory is that.

Hartshorne complains that to make metaphysics empirical is to make God just another contingent being in need of explanation. But that is a plain confusion. That our knowledge is contingent (and corrigible) does not make its object such. Finite experience often leads us (as in morals, or in causal explanations, or even in our talk of conscious subjects or persistent objects) to project beyond the immediate givens of sensation. No thought police bar the way. There will be problems in any such projection, and we can expect disagreements about rival outcomes, as well as the more systematic difficulties raised by skeptics, who apply in one context the standards of criticism they borrow from another, hoping that the implicit validation of the borrowed standards will not be noticed before they are returned, to be objected to in turn. But the possibility of diverse interpretations of the evidence, and even of systematic, or seriatim, objections against all sorts of inference and interpretation, does not leave us without standards of appraisal. Clearly some philosophers make more coherent sense of experience than others do. But, if a truth is indeed noncontingent, it will be exemplified in experience without exception or contradiction, and any philosopher who does not wear blinkers will take cognizance of it in some form, at some point. Dispensing with experience will not strengthen such discussions but weaken them. Indeed, it will deprive metaphysics of its matter, the objects and values it is to interpret and explain. And reliance on introspection alone, if that were possible, would only heighten the troubles we already have in communicating with one another and checking the validity of our insights.

Hartshorne argues that pure potentiality is no real thing, and that pure nothingness is inconceivable. But creationists do not argue that the world came from nothingness but from God. What they mean by ex nihilo is that God's ultimate creative act was conditioned by no prior limitation but only by the limitations inherent in finitude itself and in the determinate character of the things to be created.[92] Leibniz expressed it well in the idea of compossibility. It is true, as Hartshorne argues, that in itself possibility is a mere abstraction, resting for us on the negation of something actual. But it does not follow that we cannot abstract completely from all the conditionality and givenness of things and conceive the entire universe as contingent. This, precisely, is what Genesis calls on us to do: none of this need have existed. The world is not a necessary being, does not contain within itself the conditions of its own existence. If a necessary being is to be sought, as the ground of all that is contingent, it must be sought as the counterpart of the contingent. If philosophy begins in wonder, there is no good reason why it should not at times begin with wonder about why anything exists at all.[93]

Jacob Agus shows us vividly where we land if we follow in the direction Hartshorne approves. He does this by translating the metaphysical propositions of a Bergsonian eternalism back into the language of ritual and myth, from which they are sprung and out of which Bergson seeks escape into the cool Parisian air. Agus writes:

> Bergson wavers between the concepts of life and spirit . . . a blind, cosmic life-force which is unconcerned with individuals, purposeless and ruthless . . . and . . . the *élan vital* . . . conceived after the analogy of the human spirit . . . revealed in the progressive refinement of man's ethical conscience and in the esthetic organon. . . . The tension between the representation of God as Life or as Spirit reflects the dichotomy between Judaism and ancient paganism. The premonotheistic pagans celebrated the rhythms of life in their cults. There were vegetation gods, dying and coming back to life. . . . None of the gods represented an ethical absolute. . . . In Judaism, God . . . is Thought and Justice, Love and Sublimity. . . . It is in the hearts and minds of human beings that He is best revealed. God is not subject to the rhythms of life. The ancient agricultural festivals were given fresh meaning in the Torah. . . . The rhythms of sacred history were substituted for those of nature.[94]

The idea of creation captures both the moral and the metaphysical absoluteness of God, as ultimate Cause and Judge, God of history and the moral law as well as God of nature and its laws. It is in recognizing the same one answer to the moral and the cosmological quest for ultimates that monotheism overcomes the partiality of pagan religiosity and integrates both life and the cosmos.

Despite Bergson's evangelical rhetoric about God as love, Agus argues, the élan vital, even when manifested in the spirit of man, does not adequately represent divine holiness, wisdom, reason, justice, or power. Rather, it reduces God to the energies of nature (and culture!), no longer merely cyclically envisioned but still pulsating with vernal and destructive force, still celebrated as much in the orgiastic rites of spring and autumnal sacrifice, death, and rebirth as in chaste prayers and pacific meditations or ardent but conscientious visions of the working out of justice in history, the moral liberation of human life from tragedy.[95] Monotheism, where it finds one world, seeks one God and pursues one good—the same law and existential deserts for all. But paganism celebrates all energies, whether creative or destructive, and neopaganism arrogates to itself the power to create the energies it serves, typically by a psychologistic act of will, but more rarely, yet more saliently, by acts of violence or violation, material, social, or symbolic. Energies here are exalted not for their merit or coherence with one another in thought or in a life but for the intensity of their frissons.

Fortunately, we need not follow Bergson down the path Hartshorne seems so warmly to approve. Teilhard de Chardin, for one, as Agus notes, takes the spiritual turning in Bergson's philosophy. Indeed, Teilhard's vision of the Omega Point[96] returns Philo's favor of conceiving the Logos as God's immanent wisdom. For it shows how creation and creativity are linked in the project of nature and human perfection, as intimated in the Hebrew liturgy, where the Sabbath, time's symbol of eternity, is "last in the making, but first in the design."[97]

The idea of creativity does not undermine but rather endorses the idea of creation, by its reference to the values of moral and cosmogonic power. Thus Bergson himself did not follow the élan vital into neopagan vitalism but described God, in *Creative Evolution*, as a kind of "supra-consciousness," a phrase Teilhard echoes. In *The Two Sources of Morality and Religion*, Bergson spoke of God as the Creator of creators.[98] It is not immanence that jars with monotheism in Bergson's thinking, or it would hardly do for Agus to counterbalance the élan vital with the spirit in the heart of man.[99] The trouble, rather, is the reduction—of God to life, or "passage," power, Thought or thing—of Thou to *this*. As Job (26:14) expressed it, after surveying the awesome majesty of God's rule over nature, "These are but the fringes of His doings, and how little a snatch of hearsay do we have of Him."

Toward the end of his life, Bergson wrote about the special role of mystics in articulating the moral and social meaning of God's love—taking the Hebrew Prophets as paradigms of his intent. He also told of his admiration for Catholicism. His chief reason for rejecting conversion to that faith was equally telling: the rise of Hitler left him unwilling to sever his Jewish roots when his people were facing persecution and would soon be facing death for their links to one another and their common past. In 1937 he wrote: "My reflections have led me closer and closer to Catholicism, in which I see the complete fulfillment of Judaism. I would have become a convert, had I not seen in preparation for years a formidable wave of Antisemitism, which is to break upon the world. I wanted to remain among those who tomorrow will be persecuted."[100] When the Pétain regime agreed to collaborate with Hitler, Bergson returned all his French medals and awards: "He stood in line to register as a Jew and wore his six-pointed star with pride until the day of his death."[101] In the climate of the day, these simple, existential acts of moral courage speak as loudly and almost as clearly as an intellectual articulation of the values, reasonings, and commitments borne by the idea of creation.

The Mirror of Narcissus

George Wald, a Nobelist in biology for his work on the biochemistry of rhodopsin, the photoelectric pigment of the eye, had a famous classroom lecture on nature or the world, which he developed into a kind of performance piece, presented to the scientists at Los Alamos and in many other communities. At least on one occasion he linked it with the name of Bergson.[102] When I was an undergraduate in his prize-winning biology lab course for nonscientists, the lecture was known around Harvard, with Wald's encouragement, as "From the Electron to Hamlet." Taken in reverse, it might have seemed to argue a reductionist sort of thesis, about man as a few cents' worth of chemicals, or the like. But as he gave it, it was a humanistic credo on the construction of complexity out of simplicity, a Lucretian exercise in the issuance of life and splendor from the merest subatomic lego-units, with never a nod in the direction of emergent evolution, let alone orthogenesis, élan vital, or Aristotle's priority of the actual to the potential. In later versions, however, heard by literally thousands of symposiasts and readily obtained in careful transcripts of the taped voice of the speaker—lecturing familiarly, always without notes, never quite repeating the same words—all that changed. The materials stayed much the same as in the 1960s, with some new arguments and illustrations; the order of exposition was identical. But the theme now was the need for consciousness within, behind, beneath the cosmos. More than one listener asked Wald if he had changed his tune because he was growing older, but he just smiled and said that he hoped he was growing wiser.

The argument was that "we live in a life-breeding universe," that matter, as Wald once put it in a thought he shared with Einstein, "won in the fight" with antimatter, and so did, say, *L*-amino acids win out over *D*-amino acids, although both of these symmetrical kinds might have seemed at the start to have an equal chance. Had the universe begun with exactly equal parts of matter and antimatter, all would have been annihilated in the big bang. "But . . . there was a little mistake in the equality, of one part in one billion. And when all the mutual annihilation had finished, one part in one billion remained, and that's the matter of the universe."[103] Again, if electrons and nucleons were not so far apart in mass, the proton would not remain undisturbed by the behavior of electrons and there would be no solid matter, no crystals or complex stable compounds. Similarly (pace R. A. Lyttleton and Herman Bondi), if there were a difference in the charges of a proton and electron, of $2 \times 10^{-18}e$, where e is the actual charge of either, "that almost infinitesimal difference in charge would be enough to overwhelm all the forces of gravitation that bring matter together in our universe. So we would have no galaxies, no stars, no planets. . . ."[104]

Climbing the "scale of states of organization of matter," Wald argued that only carbon, hydrogen, oxygen, and nitrogen have the "absolutely unique properties . . . on which the existence of life depends,"[105] and that without water's strange property of expanding when it freezes, ice would sink and grow ever thicker on the bottoms of all bodies of water, accumulating intolerably and making life there impossible. Further, a star much larger than our sun "would probably never have a planet bearing life," since its mass denies it enough time on the "Main Sequence" for life to evolve.[106] In general, "we find ourselves in a very curious universe. It possesses exactly those properties that breed life," and that fact, Wald argues, in the great tradition of natural theology that stretches from Genesis to Paley, but with suitable hesitation, ellipsis, periphrasis, preterition, and apology, is best explained by consciousness. Of consciousness itself Wald says, "It *has* no location. It will *never* be located"—much as Socrates hinted when asked how he wanted to be buried: "Any way you like, if you can catch me!" (*Phaedo* 115C).

Addressing the idea of the ineluctability of consciousness Wald went on:

> When this idea struck me, I was elated. I enjoyed it immensely. But I was also embarrassed. I thought, "My God, Wald, senility is hitting you in a big way." The idea violated all my scientific feelings. But it took only a few weeks to realize that that kind of idea is not just centuries old but millennia old in Eastern philosophies. . . . consciousness or mind is not, as I had believed and most biologists tend to believe, a late product in the evolution of life on this planet. . . . On the contrary, it was there all the time. The reason this is a life-breeding universe is that the pervasive existence of mind guided it in that direction for a reason.[107]

The warrant, then, for connecting these thoughts with Bergson's lies in a distinctively modern gloss on the idea that the symmetry of time brings God into contact or communion with himself: evolution/creation is working out a plan that links mind in the universe with mind in us.

None of this is unfamiliar to philosophers, theologians, historians of ideas. The thought that thought is responsible for nature is, as Wald suggests, perennial—in the Vedas[108] but also in Western philosophies and religions. There are problems aplenty in the claim, from matters of verification and interpretation, to the provenance of the notion—is this just an idea we have suggested to ourselves or preserved for some use quite alien to its explicit content? I want to focus on just one use of this trend of thought: for it matters very much if we begin or end our search for God by looking in the mirror. That move has become almost a standard topos in the literature of scientific confessions. But even before its current vogue, Teilhard warned in the same breath against the 'I' that "closes the door on all the rest and succeeds in setting himself up at the antipodes of the All" and its dialectical counterpart that treats personality as "a prison from which we must try to escape," into the impersonal, the universal, or the collective.[109]

A statement much like Wald's was made on the same platform by the biophysicist Harold Morowitz, then of Yale, who speaks of a "new covenant" emerging gradually, "from the experiences of individuals who seek to understand the world."[110] Morowitz is a bit more blunt than Wald: he types the new covenant as pantheism and contrasts its revelations with the moral and spiritual revelations of the ancient God that was encountered as a person. He speaks warmly of Bergson and Spinoza, and glowingly of Richard Lovelock's Gaia hypothesis as a religious opening: "The new pantheism" he writes, "reasons from science to a cosmic intelligence that is not unrelated to our existence."[111] What volumes are spoken by that academic litotes—not unrelated to our existence! "What we are discussing is the ascendancy of God, the waning of God, and the rebirth of god. The subject matter is so awesome that any attempts in this direction seem tinged with hubris. But if these matters are vital to human existence and human happiness, then we must proceed."[112]

This is not the place to wrestle with the curious greased logic of Gaia-ism, or Morowitz's response to it.[113] "The bottom line," as Morowitz draws it, "is that our understanding of molecular biology, ecology, geophysics, meteorology, and hydrology now makes it clear that the detailed working of all the features of our planet is necessary for continuing life. This lends great force to the argument from design and urges us one step further. The precise workings of all the different components to make possible intelligent life on earth suggest that the plan of the universe somehow had us in mind."[114] If the argument is vital to human happiness, then, on Jamesian grounds, let Wald's hesitancy and humility, let hubris itself, be damned.

Such protestations as those of Wald or Morowitz might seem welcome to theists, especially when they bear the authority of scientism, confessing that it came to scoff but stayed to pray. John Eccles, a Nobel neurophysiologist, is proud, in his Gifford Lectures, to cite the arguments of J. A. Wheeler that unless the universe were of a critical size there would be literally not world enough and time for intelligent life to evolve: "For example, the mass for 10^{11} galaxies with a total of 10^{22} stars, gives the time scale from Big Bang to Big Crunch of 59 billion years. If we economize and have the Big Bang producing the mass for one galaxy of 10^{11} stars, which is still an immense universe, the time from Big Bang to Big Crunch is reduced to 1 year!"[115] Again the inference is to design and plan, intention, and ultimately (in Eccles's version), grace. But the fly in the ointment when Wheeler elaborates the argument is its peculiarly subjectivist cast:

> No search has ever disclosed any ultimate underpinning, either of physics or mathematics, that shows the slightest prospect of providing the rationale for the many-storied tower of physical law. One therefore suspects it is wrong to think that as one penetrates deeper and deeper into the structure of physics he will find it terminating at some n^{th} level. One fears it is also wrong to think of the structure going on and on, layer after layer, *ad infinitum*. One finds himself in desperation asking if the structure, rather than terminating in some smallest object or in some most basic field, or going on and on, does not lead back in the end to the observer himself, in some kind of closed circle of interdependencies.[116]

Wheeler fittingly wonders whether the search for ultimate causes, what Aristotle called first principles, is really a matter of finding ever-smaller particles and subparticles that display no special readiness to yield an answering simplicity—and no readiness at all to provide explanatory ultimacy in any other sense. But then, instead of saying that the search for explanations must expand itself to a search for other sorts of ultimates than those of spatial composition, must embrace the search for ultimate values, a "why?" and "wherefore?" as well as an "out of what?" he almost startlingly turns inward not to a critical examination of the conditions of our inquiry (as in Kant or Freud) but to the self as the ground of being, not pausing to ask whether the human mind, the all-judging observer, has the capacity for the role it is addressing.

Like the born-again athlete who gives testimony in the service of muscular Christianity, the enlightened scientist is welcomed in all simplicity and innocence. Eccles writes:

> Wheeler (1977) defines two contrasting views on the genesis of the Universe: "... Life is accidental and incidental to the machinery of the Universe.... Or ... is the directly opposite view closer to the truth?—that the universe, through some mysterious coupling of future with past, *required the future observer to empower the past genesis?* Nothing is more astonishing about quantum mechanics than its allowing one to consider seriously on quite other grounds the same view that the universe would be nothing without observership."[117]

The dichotomy is, of course, a false one: that either the universe is an accident or it is somehow devised for or by our minds. This Maimonides calls the height of hubris, to take things nobler than ourselves—the celestial bodies—and treat them as existent solely for our sakes.[118] If we balk at the idea that the stars are nobler than ourselves, since we no longer view them as alive, and probably not as delegates of God's power that pay fealty to their sovereign Lord, we should recall that for us the stars are worlds, and some of the apparent stars, galaxies, that is, worlds of worlds—for even Saadiah says the Milky Way might be an ascending mist, or an enduring portion of fire, but it might be an aggregate of small stars.[119] Eccles wants to link the future to the past, but he seems to find the meaning of the future and the power of the past in human observership.

Here the eternalism that Hartshorne prizes and elevates in Bergson's thought and the sundering of the present from the past by which Hartshorne breaks the cord that ties his philosophy to Bergson's begin to show their character and potential. For just as that eternalism threatens Bergson's broader creationism, the sundering of past from present puts at risk the very values of freedom, contingency, empiricism, and the open future in whose behalf—or on the basis of which—Bergson's theses of natural creativity and human freedom were argued. Hartshorne's eternalism was meant to compromise divine transcendence and push Bergson toward immanence. But when the human quest for explanations doubles back upon itself, we glimpse the outcome of an immanence disconnected from any ultimate Source or Goal. Blinding God, reducing supraconsciousness to subconscious memory, and the groping of evolution to a rudderless themelessness called creative only out of courtesy or nostalgia was just the first step. A nameless mechanism stands in the wings. Hartshorne may think he hears a joyous meaning in the songs of birds,[120] but the deeper harmonies and rhythms of the cosmos, once his break with Bergson is complete, will no longer sound as melody, since their relationality, the inner intentionality of one moment toward another, has been broken. The next step is the emergence of the self-selected surrogate for the Unmoved Mover and the Highest Aim and Good, the eager understudy for the role of God. The nameless mechanism has assigned itself a name.

The anthropic principle invoked by Wheeler and many others, in behalf of a kind of humanism, compounds the fracture that process eternalism began. Where ancient creationism sought the end product of creation in the first intention of divine thought, this modern version misappropriates the Bergsonian symmetry of time, blocking it before it can reach the absoluteness of divine purpose, making human thought not just the aim but the condition and ultimate origin of nature. What process philosophy contributes here, vividly in Hartshorne's thinking, is demotion of God to the role of "fellow learner," and a compensatory elevation of man to fill God's shoes. Seeking a heritage for this view, its advocates call it Socinian, in a sense that Leibniz defines lucidly as the tendency "to conceive of God (on the pretext of upholding his liberty) . . . as a man who takes decisions according to the circumstances."[121] By conceiving God "on human lines," as Leibniz put it,[122] the new, process Socinians render divinity no more than a developing condition, a modality perhaps, of the world's flux.

Freeman Dyson's Gifford Lectures of 1985 typify the approach. Dyson invokes the anthropic principle to find in "meta-science" a meaning and purpose for existence that science itself, as he construes it, seems to debar: "Laws of nature can be explained if it can be established that they must be as they are in order to allow theoretical physicists to speculate about them."[123] Dyson links his "taste" for the anthropic principle, which "seems to imply an anthropocentric view of the cosmos," with a conception of the divine which he labels Socinian and attributes to the influence of Hartshorne:

> If I remember correctly what Hartshorne said, the main tenet of the Socinian heresy is that God is neither omniscient nor omnipotent. He learns and grows as the universe unfolds. I do not pretend to understand the theological subtleties to which this doctrine leads if one analyzes it in detail. I merely find it congenial, and consistent with scientific common sense. I do not make any clear distinction between mind and God. God is what mind becomes when it has passed beyond the scale of our comprehension. God may be considered to be either a world-soul or a collection of world-souls. We are the chief inlets of God on this planet at the present stage of his development. We may later grow with him as he grows, or we may be left behind. As Bernal said, "That may be an end or a beginning, but from here it is out of sight."[124]

There is more to Hartshorne than this, but what Dyson takes from him and finds vital in his thought is the chance to place God not within thought but within reach. Quoting from Dante, but subtly shifting the poet's sense, Dyson ends his final lecture:

> Can you not see that we are the worms, each one
> Born to become the angelic butterfly
> That flies defenseless to the Judgment Throne.

Among process theologians, the idea of taking God off his pedestal often has a marked Christian or even Jewish emotive appeal, since it opens up devotional, mystical Christian, or Kabbalistic themes of divine suffering. But the unfolding of these themes, especially among the scientistic, proves anything but Judeo-Christian. The image of the butterfly is lovely, disarming hearers who might have thought that physicists never speak of butterflies, let alone quote Dante. But some ambiguity remains: Does the soul take flight to stand before the judgment throne, as Dante imagined, or to sit upon it? And behind the image of the butterfly stands the suffering and dying god. For the humanization of God is never unaccompanied, in these versions, by the divinization of man—not just to fill the vacuum left by God's dethroning, for to meet that purpose *any* surrogate would do. Rather, the blurring of subjective boundaries and objective distinctions between humanity and divinity is the goal. Thus Dyson's modest, almost Aristotelian, "I do not make any clear distinction between mind and God. . . . We are the chief inlets of God on this planet."

Religion is corrupted not only by stringency but also by a corresponding or complementary willingness to play the permission giver, pardoner, seller of indulgences, preacher of complacency in the name of self-acceptance or self-esteem. But here theology goes further, licensing the venerable and dangerous idea that man is God. Curiously enough, the seemingly abstract and innocuous metaphysical issue about the symmetry of time becomes a key to that turnabout.

Bergson's mutually interpenetrating, overlapping moments allow us to conceive the entirety of time as taken up in a single, comprehensive whole, the totality of history, evolution, the emergence of stars and galaxies. In such a whole, God's eternal design and the unfolding project of creation are not alien to one another, and time indeed becomes the moving image of eternity. God is not a product or a process but the transcendent Source and Aim of all, the perfect Good toward which all actions grope and by which all are guided, the Perfection portended in all striving. Creation is not cut off from creativity but is its condition, and creativity is creation's ever-present means.

Bergson's idea of duration allows the omnitemporality of all events, linking the whole history of creation into a single present moment, with meaning and direction to be found in every part within the whole. But, as Errol Harris remarks, with his usual astuteness, this is not a permission of which Bergson avails himself. Bergson's "steady refusal to see the process of evolution as a whole," which is "only a facet of his constant opposition to mechanism and determination in which *tout est donné*," leaves the future open, as intended, but by the same token gives no wholeness to the flow of time.[125] That outcome was not necessary. Pace Hartshorne, the future can be open without severance from the past. Even the subsumption of past and future into a single vast event would not deprive the actors in it of their agency or freedom, since they are actors, not puppets in that history. But Bergson clearly feared the loss of agency, and this fear shaped and overshaped his philosophy.

His failure to link the alpha of creation to the omega of evolution opens the door to the process reduction of God. The new Socinianism seizes the opening and discards Teilhard's Bergsonian linkage of alpha to omega through duration. It rejects creation with the old canard that if the world is of finite age, God has been idle or unemployed lo these billions of years.[126] Instead of a divine purpose to guide and govern, as a beacon of Goodness answered by the good in all things, the cosmos is now piloted by a blind spontaneity that seems to have our name embroidered on its cap. Time is now the absolute, and God, just another timeserver. Man becomes the maker of values—creator and judge of the universe.

The pride of Neoplatonists was the thought that the long arcing line of creative emanation led down to us and—through the miracle of human consciousness, back to its source in the Divine. But here the world is spun forth from our own minds, and the return is to ourselves. The inability to trace time to a source beyond itself is symptomatic of the shift in roles. The suffering God becomes the bearer no longer just of human sins but now of human guilt, anxiety, and fear. The father God is kept on too, at times, to hear the plaints of Job, since these will not be shouldered by the new man in the head office. But wherever vitality, creativity, emergence, youth, spring, life, or sustenance is found, the New Boss will be the one to take the credit.

For hubris there is always one more step, and that step is taken, not atypically, by Bernhard Rensch, an astute but problematic evolutionary biologist.[127] Rensch is not as innocent of Kant or Freud as the scientists who seek to ground an amorphous idealism of pantheistic tinge on the vaunted influence of the observer in quantum physics. He sees that the subjectivism of the anthropic principle licenses not merely man's discovery that the world was made for or by him but also man's power to reinvent himself as God. Like Wald, Rensch finds much that is attractive in Eastern philosophy. Like others of that penchant, he may not fully know the discipline that such philosophies demand of their adherents. Perhaps he expects the idealism he finds in Eastern thought (once decontextualized and so deracinated) to prove tractable to his projects of transvaluation and self-empowerment.

Speaking for the power he will reckon as divine, Rensch's pantheistic drift seems somehow to render God not transpersonal but inhuman—dehumanized, yet all too human:

> We are quite rightly brought up to think modestly of ourselves. . . . But when we study man's phylogeny, it must also seem to us extraordinary that this species, *Homo sapiens*, with his "godlike intellect," as Charles Darwin called it, has emerged as the crown and culmination of the whole process of evolution. . . . Not only has this strange *Homo sapiens* come to an understanding of himself and the universal laws; he has developed further godlike qualities, creating his own new and complicated environment, changing almost the whole face of the earth. . . .

The Faustian role brings responsibilities not for unintellectual toilers or even for "a large proportion of so-called intellectuals," but for "those engaged in creative intellectual work," planning for the future, developing institutions. They must become gods or demigods, the masters of human destiny: "Men have often referred to themselves as gods, or demigods. Rulers among the Egyptians, Romans, Chinese, Japanese and Incas have done so. . . ." Evolution is completed, and "its apparently most developed of creatures" are ready to take charge.[128] By a consummately Orwellian irony, freedom and creativity, the very values in which Bergson found a point of contact between man and God, will be the banners we shall follow back to the closed society that Bergson rightly named, prophesied against, feared, and faced with all his courage. The gods we are to worship, who will hand down our laws, shall be ourselves—or our own images, blown up to the gigantic proportions of idolatry, as in the final scene of *The Wizard of Oz*, by the puffing behind and within them of our own wind. As Rensch writes:

> Medical skill continues to improve, eating habits are more sensible, homes are healthier, better lighted, better ventilated. . . . The increasing tempo of scientific development will often lead to states of conflict. . . . This will lead to a spiritualization of the meaning and symbolic content of rites and customs. . . . In modernized Islamic countries there is a strong movement to have done with many ancient customs; women have ceased to wear the veil and are now emancipated, and polygamy is abolished. Many communist countries have broken with religious tradition, and modern China has gone through a rapid transformation of many customs. Examples like these show what can and what will happen in other countries. Ethical and moral ideas that do not conflict with scientific facts are the only ones that will survive. . . . The tendency to theosophy . . . will possibly increase. . . . A panentheism like that of medieval mystics may link religion with philosophical views. In our age of space research and increasing biological and psychological analysis of life, many people will find it more and more difficult to imagine Heaven and Hell, angels and

> devils—and it will become impossible to imagine a god who thinks like human beings, for such thinking is absolutely bound to certain physiological processes in a complicated central nervous system. Hence, many humans will abandon religion altogether, or be content with Spinoza's '*deus sive mundus* [*sic*]' or Goethe's 'God-Nature,' the Hinduist Brahman, or the Buddhist Nirvana. All these processes will probably take many centuries. Religious customs, the worship of a superhuman being to whom one may pray in straitened circumstances, will be an urge, in spite of rationalistic counter-arguments. But the whole of mankind will finally be forced to realize that it will have to master its fate by itself.

This messianic litany of unilinear progress has already, in the few years since it was written, proved tendentious, more wishful than prophetic, more conflicted than coherent in its prescriptions; more stereotypic than incisive in its analysis of cross-currents and alternatives to its vision.

We have already reflected in chapter 1 about what God is. But, in the light of what is now being made of the élan vital, a word is in order about what God is not: God is not we, or even some subgroup, caste, or class of the we. The symmetry that links the future with the past does not transform creatures into their own creators, although we do in our own ways create, and in a sense create ourselves, not radically but more or less adequately. The asymmetry that divides the future from the past does not cut it off completely and is not a barrier to meaning, causes, reasons, powers, values, and potentials. It is not a barrier to God, to judgment or accountability, sundering past from future morally. Inevitably, in view of entropy and the fragility of what is complex and delicacy of what is subtly balanced, we show more skill in radical destruction than in radical creation. We know we are not gods when we see the bias, ignorance, and intolerance of the very projects in which the name is claimed for us, or smell the odor of the camps still lingering on the clothing of those who step up to claim the title of Creator. We have, as the existentialists were fond of saying, some measure of the freedom and responsibility of gods, but much less of the authority, and very little of the power. There will always be something more divine in knowing how and when to die and suffer than in knowing how and why to conquer and to kill. But even suffering and death will not make us gods. As Rabbi Ḥama ben Ḥanina remarked pointedly, "Man was made mortal because the Holy One foresaw that some . . . would proclaim themselves gods" (Genesis Rabbah 9.5).

Like Rensch and Morowitz, Václav Havel is touched by thoughts of the intricate web of life, clearly also by the earth ethic, perhaps too by a more ancient land mystique. But Havel also knows what we are not. Speaking of the not-yet-alienated life-world that he calls our natural world, he writes:

> In this world, categories like justice, honour, treason, friendship, infidelity, courage or empathy have a wholly tangible content, relating to actual persons and actual life. . . . The natural world, in virtue of its very being, bears within it the presupposition of the Absolute which grounds, delimits, animates and directs it, and without which it would be unthinkable. This Absolute is something which we can only quietly respect; any attempt to spurn it, master it or replace it with something else appears . . . as an expression of *hubris* for which humans must pay a heavy price, as did Don Juan and Faust.
>
> To me, personally, the smokestack soiling the heavens is not just a regrettable

> lapse of technology. . . . It is a symbol of an epoch which denies the binding importance of personal experience . . . crashes through the bounds of the natural world, which it can only understand as a prison of prejudices . . . an unfortunate leftover from our backward ancestors, a fantasy of their childish immaturity. With that, of course, it abolishes as mere fiction even the innermost foundation of our natural world: it kills God and takes His place on the vacant throne, so that henceforth it might be science which, as sole legitimate guardian, holds the order of being in its hand. . . . The fault is not one of science as such but of the arrogance of humankind in the age of science. Humans simply are not God, and playing God has cruel consequences. . . . We have rejected our responsibility as 'subjective illusion' and in its place installed what is now proving to be the most dangerous illusion of all: the fiction of objectivity stripped of all that is concretely human, of a rational understanding of the cosmos, and of an abstract schema of a putative 'historical necessity' . . . and technologically achievable 'universal welfare,' demanding no more than experimental institutes to invent it while industrial and bureaucratic factories turn it into reality. The fact that millions of people will be sacrificed to this illusion in scientifically directed concentration camps is not something that concerns our 'modern person' unless by chance he or she lands behind barbed wire and is thrown back drastically upon his or her natural world. . . .

Writing in the last days of Soviet power, Havel readily sets his problematic into the same specious present as the days of the German death camps and locates his own country and the West in the same life-world:

> The chimney 'soiling the heavens' is not just a technologically corrigible design error, or a tax paid for a better tomorrow, but a symbol of a civilization which has renounced the Absolute, which ignores the natural world and disdains its imperatives. So, too, the totalitarian systems warn of something far more serious than Western rationalism is willing to admit. They are, most of all, a convex mirror . . . of its own deep tendencies . . . not merely dangerous neighbours, and, even less, some kind of an *avant garde* of world progress. Alas, just the opposite. . . . Perhaps somewhere there may be some generals who think that it would be best to dispatch such systems from the face of the earth and then all would be well. But that is no different from a plain girl trying to get rid of her plainness by smashing the mirror which reminds her of it.[129]

Another specious remedy, if we don't like what the mirror shows us, rather than smash it, is to bend and distend it to make its surface more convex, blow up our image larger, so that at least in some moods we forget that our own image is all that the shiny surface shows. As the anthropic principle reveals clearly, we humans like to see our own image. We readily make nature our mirror and then try to reach beneath its surface, enamored of what we see and eager to get closer, forgetting that Narcissus drowned in that illusion. The Narcissus in us vainly wants to be the author, judge, and ruler of the universe. It paints itself as such in a form of subjective idealism and moral solipsism that rests on forgetting that an author's power is vitiated if his work is just a wish. The world itself remains, the natural world, creation, its image only blurred by the ripples or stains we leave on the waters; its realities and requirements, untouched. The self, human nature, with its foibles and its graces, also remains. The image we saw was not ourselves but just an image, painted not by our minds but by the light. When it rises up to meet us, what we touch is not the self but the water. The self (as all real mystics know) is not caught but lost by self-absorption. It is recovered only when we "objectify"—look away from our own image and toward nature and other persons.[130]

The move to metaphysics is the move from reductive, partitive questions that seek ultimacy in ever-finer levels of analysis, at a cost of ever-more-remote abstraction from the wholeness and thickness of life, what Havel calls our natural world, and toward larger questions, where ultimacy is understood in more comprehensive terms. There is nothing wrong with the partitive type of question, but, as even Thales saw, the milling of reality to ever-finer stuff is not the only kind of quest, and success at that is no guarantee of skill in answering or even adequately framing questions of another kind. Metaphysics demands a kind of discipline and chastity of mind that the arrogance of scientism does not provide, although the humility of science might. Following the suggestive remarks of Maimonides, Spinoza explains that there is an aspect of God or nature that we understand in terms of intelligence, because we have intelligence, and an aspect that we understand in terms of matter, because we have that too. But, he argues, there are infinite other aspects—as there must be, in view of the exuberance of being—which we can never know, because we have nothing in common with them.[131]

What is engaging in Wald's or Wheeler's Bergsonian meditations is the endeavor of a naturalist to seek explanations for the coherence, even commodiousness, of nature. Here science and religion come together—the questions of Aristotle and those of Job. The intricate, intimate, inner connectedness of things is somehow the stuff of the relations that respond to our *why*s. But it is childish sophistry to pretend that such anatomies are revealed by the announcement that the stuff of those relations is there because we put it there. Plotinus had a far grander and more cosmic idea of mind than Bernhard Rensch or Freeman Dyson does, but he saw clearly that the highest God cannot be mind, because, as he insisted, even against Aristotle, mind is not the very best of things.[132]

Notes

Abbreviations

APQ	*American Philosophical Quarterly*
ARN	*Avot de Rabbi Nathan*
CUA	Catholic University of America
ED	Saadiah Gaon, *K. al-Mukhtār fī 'l-Āmānāt wa 'l-I'tiqādāt*
EI_2	*Encyclopedia of Islam*, 2d ed.
HPQ	*History of Philosophy Quarterly*
HUC	Hebrew Union College
IJMES	*International Journal of Middle Eastern Studies*
JAAR	*Journal of the American Academy of Religion*
JAOS	*Journal of the American Oriental Society*
JBL	*Journal of Biblical Literature*
JHI	*Journal of the History of Ideas*
JHP	*Journal of the History of Philosophy*
JJS	*Jewish Social Studies*
JP	*The Journal of Philosophy*
JPS	Jewish Publication Society
JQR	*Jewish Quarterly Review*
JTS	Jewish Theological Seminary of America
KD	*Epicurus*, Kyriae Doxai
LCL	Loeb Classical Library
LLA	Library of Liberal Arts
LSU	Louisiana State University
MGWJ	*Monatschrift für Geschichte und Wissenschaft des Judenthums*
PAAJR	*Proceedings of the American Academy for Jewish Research*
PQ	*Philosophical Quarterly*
REJ	*Revue des Études Juives*
SPCK	Society for the Promotion of Christian Knowledge
SUNY	State University of New York
TF	al-Ghazālī, *Tahāfut al-Falāsifa*
TT	Ibn Rushd, *Tahāfut al-Tahāfut*
Y	Jerusalem Talmud
YJS	Yale Judaica Series

Preface

1. The Memorial of 1654 quotes Exod. 3:6; Pascal apparently kept it with him throughout his life.

2. Philo (b. ca. 20 B.C.), *De Abrahamo*, I i, LCL 6.7.

3. "A Dialogue on Value," *Journal of Speculative Philosophy* 5 (1991): 11.

4. *Mekhilta* ad Exod. 12:6, ed. Lauterbach, 1.36.

5. Maimonides (*Guide* I 63) contrasts the public role of Moses as a lawgiver with the private role of the Patriarchs as the founders of a family that would become a people. But he notes the public side of Abraham's role as a natural theologian in glossing Gen. 12:5 "and the souls he had gotten in Harran," that is, his followers.

6. *De Abrahamo*, I i, LCL 6.5.

7. Ze'ev Falk, *Religious Law and Ethics*, 25, also quoting Deut. 8:6; cf. David S. Shapiro, "The Doctrine of the Image of God and *Imitatio Dei*," in *Contemporary Jewish Ethics*, ed. Kellner, 127-51.

8. *Code* XIV, Laws of Kings and Wars, xi–xii, uncensored text; cf. my *On Justice*, chap. 5.

9. *Sifra* to Lev. 19:18; see Alexander Altmann, "*Homo Imago Dei* in Jewish and Christian Theology," *Journal of Religion* 48 (1968): 235-59.

10. Isa. 40:15, 22, JPS translation.

Chapter 1

1. Kipling's 1892 poem "The Buddha at Kamakura" was an attack on religious chauvinism, inspired by a reference to "the Japanese idol" at Kamakura. It ends:

> But when the morning prayer is prayed
> Think, ere ye pass to strife and trade,
> Is God in human image made
> No nearer than Kamakura?

2. See F. M. Cornford, *From Religion to Philosophy* (1912; reprint, New York: Harper, 1965), 31–35.

3. *ED* IX 4, ed. Kafih, 269, trans. Rosenblatt, 334.

4. Trans. Richmond Lattimore (Chicago: University of Chicago Press, 1959). Cf. Athena, as a meteor at *Iliad* 4.75–86; Ares, as a retreating cloud mass, 5.864–70; cf. 19.86, 137; and see E. R. Dodds, *The Greeks and the Irrational*, 3ff., 39–42.

5. Rudolf Otto, *The Idea of the Holy* (1923; reprint, London: Oxford University Press, 1969).

6. Eric Voegelin, *Order and History:* vol. 1. *Israel and Revelation*, 3.

7. See chapter 8.

8. See my "Mythic Discourse"; and G. E. R. Lloyd, *Demystifying Mentalities* (Cambridge: Cambridge University Press, 1990).

9. See Aldous Huxley, *The Doors of Perception* (London: Chatto and Windus, 1954), 12–13; and R. C. Zaehner's response, *Mysticism, Sacred and Profane* (Oxford: Oxford University Press, 1961), 5, 20–22.

10. *Chāndogya Upanishad* 6.9, "the *locus classicus*" of *Advaita Vedānta*; cf. 6.10; quoted in Zaehner, *Mysticism, Sacred and Profane*, 139.

11. See the *Nishmat*: "For even one of the thousand thousand millions and myriads of myriads of favors which Thou has wrought with us and with our fathers." Birnbaum follows talmudic hints in glossing the countless millions of favors here as drops of rain. *Ha-Siddur ha-Shalem*, 331–32.

12. Naḥmanides, on Gen. 14:10, ed. Chavel, 1.85–86, trans. 1.186–87; cf. David Novak, *The Theology of Nahmanides Systematically Presented*, 42.

13. Xenophanes ap. Sextus, *Adv. Math.* VII 49.

14. Xenophanes rebuked Homer and Hesiod for their accounts of the gods; Diogenes Laertius, *Lives of the Philosophers* IX 18: "The Ethiopians call their gods snub-nosed and black, the Thracians say that theirs have blue eyes and red hair"; "Why if cattle and horses or lions had hands, and could draw and do the things that men can, horses would draw the gods like horses, and cattle like cattle; they would make their bodies like their own," Clement, *Stromateis* VII 22, 1, V 109, 3; trans. after Kirk, Raven, and Schofield, items 168–69.

15. Xenophanes, Fragments 23–26, ap. Clement, *Stromateis* V 109.1; Simplicius *in Phys.* 23.11, 23.20; Sextus, *Adv. Math.* IX 144.

16. See Diogenes Laertius, IX 21–23. Of the Eleatics, Aristotle writes, "Xenophanes was the first of these to posit a unity—for Parmenides is said to have been his disciple . . . with his eye on the whole heaven, he says that the One is god" (*Metaphysics* A 5, 986b 21).

17. See Proclus, *in Tim.* I 345; Simplicius *in Phys.* 117.4; Plato, *Sophist* 237a; Kirk, Raven, and Schofield, 242–53.

18. See Sextus, *Adv. Phys.* II 48, 85, 120; *Adv. Gram.* 311; Cicero, *De Divinatione* I lvi, 127, where the Stoic urges: "The passage of time is like the unwinding of a rope: it creates nothing new but only unfolds each event in its order." Change would be innovation and is thus impossible: a thing is what it is and can be no other. Diodorus Cronus rejects motion on the grounds that each thing is where it is, revealing the link of Parmenides' logical invariance to the geometric paradoxes of his pupil Zeno: How can the arrow have a definite position at every moment from firing to landing and yet be in motion? For having a definite position is the very definition of being at rest.

19. See Sextus, *Adv. Math.* VII 111; Simplicius, *in De Caelo* 557.25.

20. See *Sophist* 241 D, 254–60; Paul Seligman, *Being and Not-Being: An Introduction to Plato's* Sophist (The Hague: Nijhoff, 1974), 44–63.

21. Cf. Plato, *Sophist* 257 B–C; Seligman, *Being and Not Being*, 81; Aristotle, ap. Alexander of Aphrodisias, in Daniel Frank, *The Arguments "From the Sciences" in Aristotle's* Peri Ideon (New York: Peter Lang, 1984).

22. Cf. Dodds, *The Greeks and the Irrational*, 28–34.

23. Cf. Cornford, *From Religion to Philosophy*, esp. 13ff.

24. Cf. Arthur D. Nock, *Conversion* (1933; reprint, Oxford: Oxford University Press, 1965), 12; André-Jean Festugière, *Personal Religion Among the Greeks* (Berkeley: University of California Press, 1960), 2, 20–21, 51, 105, 118.

25. Heraclitus, Fragments 1, 50, 53, 61, 80 ap. Sextus *Adv. Math.* VII 132; Hippolytus *Ref.* IX 9.1; 9.4; 10.5.

26. Anaximander ap. Simplicius, *in Phys.* 24, 17; after Kirk, Raven, and Schofield, 117–18.

27. Martha Nussbaum, *The Fragility of Goodness* (Cambridge: Cambridge University Press, 1991); and her interview with Bill Moyers. Nussbaum exempts the *Oedipus* cycle from her general treatment of tragedy, arguing that at times the fallen hero is more a passive victim than an active agent whose very strengths are his own undoing: "We may feel satisfied that the agent has not actually *acted* badly—either because he or she has not *acted* at all, or because (as in the case of Oedipus) the thing he intentionally *did* was not the same as the bad thing that he inadvertently brought about" (25); cf. 282–83. But this misses the thrust of Sophocles' tragedy: Oedipus's offense springs from and typifies the human desire to master fate by the use of will and reason. His incest and parricide are not his crime but his punishment, reflecting the futility of his life's challenge to the power of fate. His self-blinding is not his punishment but his expiation, acknowledging the inadequacy of a merely human wisdom

that is purblind to the real meaning of the riddle of the Sphinx: what goes first on four legs, then on two, then on three, is man. What obscures the riddle for humanity, whom Oedipus is meant to typify, is denial, failure to acknowledge mortality. It was in teaching the poverty of all human powers that tragedy laid claim to its ancient religious role, celebrating the power of the gods, even if irrational, and humbling our hubris. Platonism reversed the fields when it taught as a Socratic discovery the radical inversion of the Delphic maxim, making KNOW THYSELF point not to mortality but to divinity in each of us.

28. See my "Ibn Khaldūn and Thucydides."

29. See *Republic* VI–VII, 503–10ff.

30. Aristotle, *De Anima* I 4, 408b 30–35: "Of all the opinions we have enumerated, by far the most unreasonable is that which declares the soul to be a self-moving number." Speusippus hoped to use the intermediacy of numbers between the Ideas and particulars to weld the many to the One; cf. *Metaphysics* XIII 2, 6–9.

31. For the tensions in Aristotle, see Van Den Bergh's appendix to *TT* 2.215.

32. Immanuel Kant, *Lectures on Ethics*, 252. For divine self-contraction, *tzimtzum*, see Gershom Scholem, "Schöpfung aus Nichts und Sebstverschränkung Gottes," *Eranos Jahrbuch* 25 (1956): 90ff.; cf. David Novak, "Self-Contraction of the Godhead in Kabbalistic Theology," in *Neoplatonism and Jewish Thought*, 299–318. In its earliest uses *tzimtzum* explains the specificity of the commands of the Infinite: "Had he come to them in his full strength, they would not have been able to endure." Exodus Rabbah 34.1. For the general theme of accommodation, see S. Benin, *The Footprints of God* (Albany: SUNY Press, 1993).

33. *De Natura Deorum* I xxii 61; III ii 5–6, LCL 289–91.

34. *De Natura Deorum* III xvii 43, LCL 327; cf. *De Divinatione* II xxxiii 70, LCL 450.

35. See A. H. Armstrong, *The Architecture of the Intelligible Universe in the Philosophy of Plotinus* (Amsterdam: Hakkert, 1967), 1–28.

36. The traditional rendering, "Far be it from Thee," preserves the jussive force and courtly tone of the Hebrew. But Abraham's *ḥallilah lekha* seems stronger than the English, entailing a profanation, even an obscenity, as Novak suggests (*Jewish Social Ethics*, 53): For God to punish the innocent with the guilty would be a profanation of his name, an outrage against his nature. In some of their repetitions I preserve the traditional "righteous" and "wicked." The reference is to the innocent and guilty, but both terms have a stronger force.

37. Trans. Allen Mandelbaum (Berkeley: University of California Press, 1971).

38. See Porphyry, *De Abstinentia* II 1–11; Mishnah Avot 3.4: "Rabbi Simeon says: If three have eaten at one table and not spoken words of Torah over it, it is as if they had eaten slaughtered victims of the dead, as it is said, *All tables are filled with vomit and filth without the All-inclusive* (Isaiah 28:8). But if three have eaten at one table and spoken over it words of Torah, it is as if they ate at the table of the All-inclusive, as it is written, *It was said to me: 'This is the table that is before God'* (Ezekiel 41:22)." The midrashic argument hinges on the contrast of the two proof-texts. For if one table is the Lord's, clearly *that* is not defiled. So Isaiah must mean tables at which God's presence (*Shechinah*) is not invoked; for he has just said (28:5) "the Lord of Hosts will be a crown of beauty and a diadem of glory to the remnant of his people." So Simeon glosses *beli makom*, familiarly rendered, "and there is no [clean] place" as "without the All-inclusive," giving *makom* its Rabbinic sense as an epithet of God, the Ground of being. R. Simeon assumes, with R. Ḥananya ben Teradyon (*Avot* 3:3), that discussion of Torah invokes the *Shechinah*. In default of such invocation, it is presumed negated—hence, *all* tables (cf. 1 Sam. 14:31–35). Not that pagan gods lurk to snatch table scraps of unsanctified conversation unless the *Shechinah* is invoked to dispel them, but that meals intended to be secular in effect celebrate what does not merit veneration—"sacrificial victims of the dead"—the mute values and inchoate energies deified in pagan cult. Every meal

is a sacrament. Failure to dedicate it to God gives it by default to lifeless corpses. There is no secular meal, then, but only consecration or desecration of the All-inclusive.

39. Trans. Robert Fitzgerald (Garden City: Doubleday, 1961).

40. Primally, Lévi-Strauss argues, every victory in sport is a kill: "As all the North American mythology confirms, to win a game is symbolically to 'kill' one's opponent; this is depicted as really happening in innumerable myths." *The Savage Mind*, 32.

41. *New York Times*, August 22, 29, September 3, 10, 16, 17, 30, October 1, 2, 3, 5, 8, December 12, 1974, March 28, 1995.

42. Cf. Tanḥuma, ed. Buber, Va-yera 50, p. 109.

43. Curtius Rufus, *History of Alexander* IV 3.23; the Tyrians, besieged by Alexander, treat the practice as outmoded—although the proposal is made.

44. See L. E. Stager, "The Rite of Child Sacrifice at Carthage," in *New Light on Ancient Carthage*, ed. J. Pedley (Ann Arbor: University of Michigan Press, 1980), 1–11; Lloyd R. Bailey, "Gehenna: The Topography of Hell," *Biblical Archaeologist* 49 (1986): 187; and the fine survey of the evidence in Susanna Shelby Brown, *Late Carthaginian Child Sacrifice and Sacrificial Monuments in Their Mediterranean Context* (Sheffield, Eng.: JSOT Press, 1991).

45. Ennius, *Annales* VII, ed. E. M. Steuart (Cambridge: Cambridge University Press, 1925), 31 corresponding to fragment 4; Pompeius Trogus ap. Justin XVIII 6.11–12; cf. XIX 1.10; and ap. Orosius, *Historiae Adversum Paganos* IV 6.4–5.

46. Porphyry, *De Abstinentia* II 56; Eusebius, *Praeparatio Evangelica* I 9.40; cf. Justin Martyr, *Apology* II 12.5; Cicero, *De Re Publica* III ix 15.

47. Silius Italicus, *Punica* IV 765–822.

48. Minucius Felix, *Octavius* XXX 3; Cleitarchus, ap. Schol. in *Rep.* 337A.

49. Plutarch, *De Superstitione* 171.

50. Diodorus Siculus, *Library of History* XX 14; Lactantius, *Divine Institutions* I 21.

51. See Henri Frankfort, *Kingship and the Gods* (Chicago: University of Chicago Press, 1948), 264; E. A. Speiser, *Anchor Bible Genesis* (Garden City, N.Y.: Doubleday, 1979; 1964), 165.

52. Cf. Martin Bergmann, *In the Shadow of Moloch: The Sacrifice of Children and Its Impact on Western Religions* (New York: Columbia University Press, 1992).

53. Speiser writes: "If the author had intended to expose a barbaric custom, he would have gone about it in a different way." But to make historic events emblems of biblical norms is *the* method of Genesis; see chapters 4, 6, and 7 and Calum Carmichael, *Women, Law, and the Genesis Traditions*. Here the norms forecast are those of *pidyon ha-ben*, redemption of the firstborn; Exod. 13:2, 22:29 with 13:15, cf. 34:19. Hannah never imagines that she has promised more to God than her son's lifelong service, as she states: "I will dedicate him to the Lord all the days of his life, and no razor shall ever touch his head" (1 Sam. 1:11). She can be confident, in Jeremiah's words, that no thought to the contrary ever entered God's mind, because hers is the God of Abraham.

54. Thus Ta'anit 4a, glossing Jer. 19:5: "'Nor came it into my mind' refers to Isaac the son of Abraham."

55. Note the perfect tense of 'know'. As for *ʿaṭṭah*, Mandelkern finds both *nunc* and *iam* as senses. I take it in Gen. 22:12 as in 43:10, where the JPS aptly renders Judah's protest: "We could have been there and back twice if we had not dawdled"—that is, twice already, or by now, *iam*.

56. Ramban, *Commentary on the Torah*, Gen. 22:1, trans. Chavel, 1.275.

57. Drawn by the Christian ideal of vicarious atonement and moved by Jewish suffering, the allegorist Ephraim of Bonn, writing during the First Crusade, elaborated the Midrashic fancy that Isaac *was* sacrificed, a notion rejected by sound exegetes as early as Ibn Ezra (ad Gen. 21:19). Moderns of romantic bent have made this myth their own, following the lead of

Shalom Spiegel, who published Rabbi Ephraim's poem in his *Me-Aggadot ha-Akedah*, translated as *The Last Trial* and reprinted in Judah Goldin, *The Sacrifice of Isaac: Studies in the Development of a Literary Tradition* (1950; reprint, New York: Schocken, 1967). Its evocation of the holocaust gives this reading near canonical authority among some of our contemporaries. Bruce Zuckerman writes, "In the *Akedah* there is a primary theme that tells of a son almost sacrificed but who was saved by a merciful God at the last moment. But beneath this theme another older theme plays an harmonic inversion that tells not only of the son's death but also of his subsequent resurrection" *Job the Silent*, chap. 2, "The *Akedah* Model" (New York: Oxford University Press, 1991). But resurrection is foreign to Genesis—not because the Torah knows of no afterlife but because excising such pagan topoi is central to its aims. Even more foreign is the idea of redemptive violence. For the revision, see J. Levenson, *Death and Resurrection of the Beloved Son* (New Haven: Yale University Press, 1993).

58. Nahum Sarna explains: "This information is provided to the reader, not divulged to Abraham, in order to remove any possible misunderstanding that God requires human sacrifice as such. . . . the reader knows that the son will not be slaughtered" (*The JPS Commentary: Genesis*, 151).

59. As Sarna notes, urgency is expressed in the angel's crying out from heaven, rather than waiting to manifest itself on earth; *JPS Commentary: Genesis*, 153, citing Gen. 21:17.

60. See Exodus Rabbah 2.12, cf. Genesis Rabbah 46.2; Exod. 3:4; 1 Sam. 3:10.

61. See Gen. 17:7–9, 19. Thus Deut. 30:19: "choose life"; and see Deut. 12:29–31: "When the Lord your God has hewn down before you the nations you are about to invade, to disinherit them, and you have taken possession and settled in their land, beware of being lured into their ways, after they are ruined. Do not seek out their gods, asking, 'How did these nations worship their gods, and I will do the same.' You shall not do the same for the Lord your God, since they did for their gods all that is loathsome and hateful to the Lord, even burning their sons and daughters in fire to their gods." As Maimonides explains (*Guide* I 36), the Torah expresses repugnance to the moral logic of the very idea of God as divine abhorrence. The Prophets clearly grasp the message. Human sacrifice becomes a reductio ad absurdum (Mic. 6:7). Hosea (13:2) spells out its fatal logic: "They that sacrifice men kiss calves."

62. See Rashi, ad Gen. 22:13.

63. In Martin Buber, *Tales of the Hasidim* (New York: Schocken, 1947–1948), 2.96.

64. Rashi sees in the angel's choice of the word *me'umah*, anything, a hint of *mūm*, a wound—insightfully, for scarification is a surrogate of sacrifice, and scarred victims, like defective officiants, are barred in Israel's sacrifices (Lev. 21:17–18). Such signs of mutilation violate the wholeness and purity that will point to God's goodness and perfection; see chapter 7.

65. See Gen. 38:15–16; Maimonides, *Guide* II 6, ed. Munk 2.16–18.

66. *Mei ha-Shiloaḥ* (Jerusalem, 1976), 1. 16; with 2.12. See M. Faierstein, *All Is in the Hands of Heaven: The Teachings of R. Mordecai Joseph Leiner of Izbica* (New York: Yeshiva University Press, 1989).

67. Saadiah, *Commentary on the Torah* (Jerusalem: Mosad ha-Rav Kook, 1963), 401.

68. See Jerome Gellman, *Fear, Trembling and the Fire* (Lanham, Md.: University Press of America, 1994), 37–43. To act without clarity, as Gellman notes, is, for the Izbicer, a sign of love of God. But Abraham acted not utterly without clarity but in imperfect clarity, and his act and choice enhanced the clarity of all who would come later.

69. Philo, *De Abrahamo* xxxvi 201–4; trans. after Colson LCL 6.99–101. For *eupatheiai*, see David Winston, "Philo's Conception of the Divine Nature," in L. E. Goodman, ed., *Neoplatonism and Jewish Thought*, 21–42. For the pragmatic priority of the psychological to the logical, see Aristotle, *Topics* I 2, 101a 37–101b 3.

70. Søren Kierkegaard, *Fear and Trembling*, trans. Walter Lowrie (1941; reprint, Princeton, N.J.: Princeton University Press, 1969); cf. Milton Steinberg, *Anatomy of Faith* (New York: Harcourt Brace, 1960); G. Outka, "Religious and Moral Duty: Notes on *Fear and Trembling*," in *Religion and Morality*, ed. G. Outka and J. P. Reeder, (Garden City, N.Y.: Doubleday, 1973).

71. *Religion Within the Limits of Reason Alone*, trans. Greene and Hudson 81–82.

72. *Religion Within the Limits of Reason Alone*, 82.

73. *Religion Within the Limits of Reason Alone*, 174–75.

74. Walter Lowrie, translator's introduction to *Fear and Trembling*, 10.

75. Kierkegaard, *Fear and Trembling*, 22.

76. Kierkegaard, *Fear and Trembling*, 22, 26.

77. *Rabbi Samuel Ben Meir's Commentary on Genesis*, trans., Martin Lockshin (Lewiston, N.Y.: Mellen, 1989), 95–97. Rashbam's proof-texts: Exod. 17:7, Ps. 26:2, Job 4:2. Alerted by parallels in *Midrash Samuel*, ad 1 Sam. 6:1, he writes: "[*N*]*issah* is equivalent to *contraria* in the vernacular"—as in the chivalric lists, or the gladiatorial images of Stoic morals; cf. the JPS: "God put Abraham to the test."

78. Kierkegaard, *Fear and Trembling*, 64.

79. Kierkegaard, *Fear and Trembling*, 65–66.

80. Kierkegaard, *Fear and Trembling*, 69.

81. Kierkegaard, *Fear and Trembling*, 70.

82. See Plato, *Republic* 534A; Heb. 11:1, Rom. 3:28–30. In his Barcelona Disputation of 1263, Naḥmanides sums up the Jewish view: "I stood up and said, 'It is clear that a person does not have faith in what he does not know'" (*Kitvei Ramban*, no. 107, ed. Chavel, 1.320); cf. Maimonides, *Guide* I 50: "Belief is not what is said but what is thought when a thing is affirmed to be as it is thought to be."

83. "Every virtue," Maimonides explains, "is called justice (or righteousness, *tzedakah*)"; *Guide* III 53. So when Gen. 15:6 reports that Abraham trusted (*he'emin*) God's promise, and this trust was accounted to him as righteousness—the sense is that his steadfastness was deemed a virtue, not a surrogate for virtue, and still less, an alternative means of justification. For a Christian rejection of the surrogacy of faith for works, see James 2:14.

84. Cf. Kenneth Seeskin, *Jewish Philosophy in a Secular Age* (Albany: SUNY Press, 1990), 119; Marvin Fox, "Kierkegaard and Rabbinic Judaism," *Judaism* 2 (1953): 160–69.

85. Cf. Spinoza, *Ethics* I, props. 1–8.

86. Cf. Plato, *Euthyphro* 7b–8b.

87. As Lévi-Strauss explains, the Aztec games sought a symbolic equilibrium between the living and the dead; *The Savage Mind*, 32.

88. *From Religion to Philosophy*, chap. 2, an essay deeply tinged with the thought of Lévy-Bruhl, Durkheim, Frazer, and Jane Harrison's *Themis* (Cambridge, 1912).

89. *Rubaiyat* 27, 1889. Voegelin's remark is from *Order and History I: Israel and Revelation*, xii.

90. *Philosophical Dictionary,* trans. Peter Gay (New York: Harcourt Brace, 1962), 480.

91. *Mizān al-'Amal*, ad fin., ed. Dunya (Cairo: Dār al-Ma'ārif, 1963), 409.

92. Henry David Thoreau, *Walden*, 1854 (New York: Random House, 1950), 88.

93. See Paul Radin, *Primitive Man as Philosopher* (1927; reprint, New York: Dover, 1956); and my "Context," and "Mythic Discourse."

94. I owe 'iridescence' to a lecture by J. N. Findlay, New York, March 1976.

95. See Anselm's *Cur Deus Homo?*; cf. the Christian recasting of the *akedah*, Heb. 11:17–19.

96. *The Divine Names* III 3, trans. C. E. Rolt (1920; reprint, London: SPCK, 1975), 81–82, 86.

Chapter 2

1. John Hick, "Theology and Verification," in *The Existence of God*, ed. John Hick, (New York: Macmillan, 1964), 260–61.

2. *Guide* I 73.10; cf. "Eight Chapters," 5.

3. William Alston, *Perceiving God: The Epistemology of Religious Experience* (Ithaca, N.Y.: Cornell University Press, 1991).

4. Alston calls the perceptions that concern him "essentially independent of any conceptualization" (*Perceiving God*, 37). But how can that be squared with his claim that mystics perceive God, "*as* so-and-so . . . as *goodness* and *power* . . . as a *plenitude*." Isn't a concept, most basically, the notion *in terms of which* a thing is intended?

5. Alston, *Perceiving God*, 60: "I don't have to perceive the whole of X in order to perceive it." Cf. Aquinas, *Summa Theologica* I Q. 12, art. 7:

> What is comprehended is perfectly known. . . . But no created intellect can attain to that perfect mode of the knowledge of the divine of which it is intrinsically capable. . . . For a created intellect knows the divine essence more or less perfectly in proportion as it receives a greater or lesser light of glory. . . . God is called incomprehensible not because anything of Him is not seen, but because He is not seen as perfectly as He is capable of being seen. . . . Hence Augustine, in his definition of comprehension says: "a whole is comprehended when it is seen in such a way that nothing of it is hidden from the seer, or when its boundaries can be completely viewed or traced". . . . He who sees God's essence sees in Him that He exists infinitely, and is infinitely knowable. But this infinite mode does not extend to enable the knower to know infinitely. Analogously, a person can have a probable opinion that a proposition is demonstrable, although he himself does not know it as demonstrated." (Trans. after Anton Pegis, in *The Basic Writings of Saint Thomas Aquinas* [New York: Random House, 1945], 1.101–3; cf. Nicolas Malebranch, *Entretiens sur la Métaphysique* [1688], II 5–8, trans. Willis Doney [New York: Abaris, 1980], 47–51.)

6. In Kant's refutation of idealism, only an ad hoc metaphysical postulate allows the inference that subjective temporality implies anything beyond itself. Moore's proposed alternative, relying on perception, presupposes what it seeks to prove and declines sharply into dogmatism. See *Critique of Pure Reason*, B274–79, Kemp Smith, 244–47; G. E. Moore, "Proof of an External World," (1939) and "A Defence of Common Sense," (1925), in *Philosophical Papers* (New York: Collier, 1962), 32–59, 126–48.

7. Alvin Plantinga shows that "belief in other minds and belief in God are in the same epistemological boat." See his *God and Other Minds: A Study of the Rational Justification of Belief in God* (Ithaca: Cornell University Press, 2d ed., 1990, xvi, chaps. 8–10).

8. Wittgenstein's celebrated Private Language argument builds on the linguistic presupposition of a social community. But if we do not know that there are other minds, the underpinnings of our discourse are part of what must be established.

9. See my article "The Trouble with Phenomenalism."

10. William James says of Memorial Hall at Harvard:

> If I can lead you to the hall, and tell you of its history and present uses; if in its presence I feel my idea, however imperfect it may have been, to have led hither and to be now *terminated*; if the associates of the image and of the felt hall run parallel, so that each term of the one context corresponds serially, as I walk, with an answering term of the other; why then my soul was prophetic, and my idea must be, and by common consent would be called cognizant of reality. That percept was what I *meant*, for into it my idea has passed by conjunctive experiences of sameness and fulfilled intention. Nowhere is there jar, but every later moment continues and corroborates an earlier one. ("The Relation Between Knower and Known," in *The Meaning of Truth* [1909; reprint, Cambridge, Mass.: Harvard University Press, 1975]).

11. Dallas Willard, *Logic and the Objectivity of Knowledge: A Study in Husserl's Early Philosophy* (Athens: Ohio University Press, 1984), 208.

12. See my "Context."

13. Ironically, Descartes is often taken to task both for believing that mathematical truths hold by God's fiat and for thinking them objective rather than conventional—as though a realist like Descartes should have thought the existence of just three natural dimensions any more or less than a fact of nature ordained by God.

14. Cf. Anne Freire Ashbaugh, *Plato's Theory of Explanation: A Study of the Cosmological Account in the Timaeus* (Albany: SUNY Press, 1988).

15. See Lewis White Beck, "Can Kant's Synthetic Judgments Be Made Analytic?" *Kant-Studien* 47 (1956); reprinted in *Kant: A Collection of Critical Essays*, ed. Robert Paul Wolff (Notre Dame, Ind.: Notre Dame University Press, 1968), 3–22, citing *Prolegomena* art. 2 C 1, *Critique of Pure Reason* B14, and Schultz's reply to Eberhard in *Rezension von Eberhard's Magazin*, 408–9.

16. Kant's campaign to show that only Euclidean space permits "experience" might suggest that he had no inkling of a non-Euclidean geometry. But it was because logic could not exclude that possibility that he worked so strenuously to privilege Euclidean geometry pragmatically; *Critique of Pure Reason* B17, A47/B65, A163/B204; cf. Norman Kemp Smith, *Commentary*, 117–20.

17. *Critique of Pure Reason*, A716–17/B744–45.

18. A. J. Ayer, *Language, Truth and Logic* (1946; reprint, New York: Dover, 1952), 78.

19. *American Scientist* (March–April 1994): 147.

20. Ayer, *Language, Truth and Logic*, 86.

21. Ayer argues on a single page (*Language, Truth and Logic*, 81) that there are diverse "logics" and that "every logical proposition is valid in its own right. Its validity does not depend on its being incorporated in a system."

22. Willard V. O. Quine, *From a Logical Point of View*, 20–46.

23. Kurt Gödel, "Über formal unentscheidbare Sätze der *Principia Mathematica* und verwandter Systeme I," *Monatscheft für Mathematik und Physik* 38 (1931): 173–98; trans. John van Heijenoort in *From Frege to Gödel: Source Book on Mathematical Logic 1879–1931* (Cambridge, Mass.: Harvard University Press, 1966).

24. Ayer, *Language, Truth and Logic*, 81–82.

25. *Proslogium*, preface, trans. S. N. Deane in *Saint Anselm: Basic Writings* (1903; reprint, La Salle: Open Court, 1968), 1.

26. Reply to Gaunilon 1; see A. B. Wolter's translation in J. F. Wippel and A. B. Wolter, eds., *Medieval Philosophy* (New York: Macmillan, 1969), 163. For Anselm's idea of meditation, see R. W. Southern, *Saint Anselm: A Portrait in a Landscape* (Cambridge: Cambridge University Press, 1990), 91–123; Gregory Schufreider, *Confessions of a Rational Mystic: Anselm's Early Writings* (West Lafayette, Ind.: Purdue University Press, 1994).

27. Eadmer, *Vita Anselmi* I xix, quoted in Southern, *Saint Anselm*, 117.

28. Southern, *Saint Anselm*, 117.

29. *Monologion* I, trans. Deane, 38–40.

30. David Novak, "Are Philosophical Proofs of the Existence of God Theologically Meaningful?" *Conservative Judaism* (November–December 1980): 12–22, 15.

31. The heading reads "and again of God, that he exists"—not that God's existence will be proved again but that more remains to be said of it.

32. Spinoza, *Principles of Descartes' Philosophy*, I prop. 5, Scholium; prop. 11.

33. First published in *Mind* (1949), Findlay's "Can God's Existence be Disproved?" was reprinted in *New Essays in Philosophical Theology*, ed. A. Flew and A. MacIntyre (New York: Macmillan, 1964), 47–56, 71–75.

34. Findlay, on a single page ("Can God's Existence be Disproved?" 54), commends the "modern view" that "necessity in propositions merely reflects our use of words" and makes being inherently contingent—when he rejects as hopelessly old-fashioned the attempt to "trace contingent things back to some necessarily existent source" rather than "merely connect the *possible* instances of various characteristics with each other." To complicate the issue, Findlay allows that the latter endeavor may yield what many see as a kind of nontautological necessity. The concession seems to countenance in science what the main argument rejects in theology. More importantly, the treatment tellingly privileges possibility and contingency, as though they were somehow less metaphysical (and more real) than necessity.

35. Findlay, "Can God's Existence be Disproved?" 73.

36. J. N. Findlay, "Why Christians Should Be Platonists," in *Neoplatonism and Christian Thought*, ed. D. O'Meara (Norfolk: International Society for Neoplatonic Studies, 1982), 223–31, quoted here, 224–25.

37. "What Is Orientation in Thinking?" in *The Critique of Practical Reason and Other Writings in Moral Philosophy*, trans. Lewis White Beck (New York: Garland, 1976), 301.

38. *The Conflict of the Faculties*, trans. Mary Gregor (New York: Abaris, 1979), 63.

39. As Kemp Smith points out, Kant reflects warmly on the theism of his Leibnizian-Wolffian predecessors in The Ideal of Pure Reason, but in the Amphiboly has already rejected its underpinnings: the priority of affirmation to negation, the dismissal of evil as deficiency, the compatibility of all (real) predicates or perfections, and the union of all perfections in God. Kant writes: "The principle that realities (as pure assertions) never logically contradict each other . . . has not the least meaning either in regard to nature or in regard to any thing-in-itself" (A273–74/B329–30). We have seen in chapter 1 how concrete the meaning of that idea can be. But Kant insists that the offending principles lead to God's reality only by way of a natural illusion. He adds: "If, in following up this idea of ours, we proceed to hypostatise it . . . we should be overstepping the limits of its purpose and validity. . . . we have no right to do this, nor even to assume the possibility of such an hypothesis" (*Critique of Pure Reason*, A580/B608; cf. Kemp Smith, *Commentary*, 522–25). Even in lectures that seem to temper the tempest to the shorn lamb, Kant writes: "What interest does reason have in this knowledge? Not a speculative but a practical one" (*Lectures on Philosophical Theology* [ca. 1783–1784], trans. A. W. Wood and G. M. Clark [Ithaca, N.Y.: Cornell University Press, 1978], 24).

40. Here again Kant passed the issue to morals, making personhood and freedom sheerly moral ideas and reducing the substantial self to a posit of immortality. But some questions about human agency and thus about subjecthood do not reduce to the Enlightenment preoccupation with an afterlife. Besides, if human dignity rests on personhood, personhood should be an ontic status, not simply a moral postulate—lest dignity and its ground become identical and the claim that persons deserve respect dissolve into a tautology.

41. See my "Judah Halevi," in *History of Jewish Philosophy*, ed. Daniel Frank and Oliver Leaman (London: Routledge, 1995).

42. The churches and the Islamic *umma* also lay claim to this legacy, which is all to the good if the claims are not meant triumphally, as though Israel's mission were superseded. But the proof, for any claimant, is in deeds, not words. As Jesus said, "By their fruits shall ye know them. Do men gather grapes of thorns or figs of thistles?" (Matt. 7:16; cf. Genesis Rabbah 16.3).

43. Kant, *Religion Within the Limits of Reason Alone*, trans. Greene and Hudson, 116–17.

44. Joseph Soloveitchik's "*Ish ha-Halakhah*," *Talpiot* 1 (1944): 651–735, trans. Lawrence Kaplan in *Halakhic Man* (Philadelphia: JPS, 1983), is sensibly deflated by Rachel Shihor, "On the Problem of Halacha's Status in Judaism: A Study of the Attitude of Rabbi J. D. Halevi Soloveitchik," *Forum* 30–31 (1978): 146–54. Categories, we must remember, are not willfully chosen.

45. Avicenna's metaphysics founds the formal distinction of essence from existence. Étienne Gilson, *History of Christian Philosophy in the Middle Ages* (New York: Random House, 1955), 186, finds an apparent anticipation in the *Fuṣūs al-Ḥikam* ascribed to al-Fārābī (ed. Friedrich Dieterici; Leiden: Brill, 1890). But Shlomo Pines showed that text to depend on Avicenna's *Risalat ul-Firdaws*; *Revue des Études Islamiques* 19 (1951): 121–24. Fārābī did lay the groundwork for Avicenna's distinction, by pressing the distinction between hypothetical and categorical necessity. So, too, did Plato's distinction of Forms from their instantiations. But the essence/existence distinction gains its full meaning only through the conflict between Aristotelian and *kalām* metaphysics. See my *Avicenna*, chap. 2.

46. See A. J. Arberry, ed., *Avicenna on Theology* (London: Murray, 1952), 25–27; George Hourani, "Ibn Sīnā on Necessary and Possible Existence," *Philosophical Forum* 4 (1972): 74–86; William L. Craig, *The Cosmological Argument from Plato to Leibniz* (London: Macmillan, 1980).

47. Ḥasdai ibn Crescas, *Or Adonai* (1410) I 3, in H. A. Wolfson, *Crescas' Critique of Aristotle* (Cambridge, Mass.: Harvard University Press, 1929), 221–29; 479–97; cf. Spinoza, Ep. 12. Crescas addresses al-Tabrīzī (fl. thirteenth century); M. Mohaghegh, ed., *Tabrīzī's Commentary on the Twenty Five Premises from the* Guide of the Perplexed (Tehran: McGill University Institute of Islamic Studies, 1981); cf. Herbert Davidson, *Proofs for Eternity, Creation and the Existence of God in Medieval Islamic and Jewish Philosophy* (Oxford: Oxford University Press, 1987), 388–405.

48. *Critique of Pure Reason*, A604–8/B632–36. Kant's immediate target is Alexander Baumgarten's Leibnizian reasoning in *Metaphysica* (Halle, 1779). Hume's, in *Dialogues Concerning Natural Religion*, is Samuel Clarke's *Demonstration of the Being and Attributes of God* (London, 1705); see Edward J. Khamara, "Hume vs Clarke on the Cosmological Argument," *PQ* 42 (1992): 34–55.

49. P. T. Geach, "Aquinas," in *Three Philosophers*, ed. P. T. Geach and G. E. M Anscombe (Oxford: Blackwell, 1963), 114–16.

50. Shalom Rosenberg, "On the Modal Version of the Ontological Argument," *Logique et Analyze* 24 (1981): 129–33; R. L. Franklin, "Necessary Being," *Autralasian Journal of Philosophy* 35 (1957): 97–110; Alvin Plantinga, "Necessary Being," in his *Faith and Philosophy* (Grand Rapids, Mich.: Eerdmans, 1964); R. M. Adams, "Has It Been Proved That All Real Existence Is Contingent?" *APQ* 8 (1971): 284–91.

51. *Critique of Pure Reason* A598/B626.

52. *Critique of Pure Reason*, A593/B621.

53. *Critique of Pure Reason*, A601–2/B629–30.

54. *Critique of Pure Reason*, A599/B627.

55. *Critique of Pure Reason*, A598/B626.

56. *Tractatus Politicus* II 2, ed. A. G. Wernham (Oxford: Oxford University Press, 1958), 266–67; cf. *Ethics* I, prop. 8, schol. 2, ed. C. Gebhardt 2.50–51.

57. See S. Morris Engel, "Kant's 'Refutation' of the Ontological Argument" (1964) in *Kant: A Collection of Critical Essays*, ed. R. P. Wolff (Notre Dame, Ind.: University of Notre Dame Press, 1968), 189–208; quoted here 196–99.

58. *Critique of Pure Reason*, A602/B630.

59. Cf. Jerome Shaffer, "Existence, Predication and the Ontological Argument," *Mind* 1 (1962): 307–25, esp. 318–23; R. M. Adams, "Theories of Actuality," *Nous* 8 (1974): 211–31; Kenneth Seeskin, "Is Existence a Perfection?—A Case Study in the Philosophy of Leibniz," *Idealistic Studies* 8 (1978): 124–35.

60. Cf. Alvin Plantinga, "Kant's Objection to the Ontological Argument," *JP* 63 (1966): 537–48.

61. The properties of any real thing are infinite, although managed for most practical

purposes by our addressing only a few at a time—treating realia notionally as though they were fictions. To deny that things have infinite properties, one would have to exclude all relational properties. But that would have the curious effect of excluding almost all the properties we ever name or think.

62. Étienne Gilson, *The Spirit of Thomism* (New York: Harper and Row, 1966), 64.

63. G. E. Moore, "Is Existence a Predicate?" in *Philosophical Papers*, 114–25.

64. *Critique of Pure Reason*, A600/B628.

65. *Summa Theologica*, question 2, art. I; Maimonides, *Guide* I 1–64.

66. Spinoza, *Ethics* I, Axiom 2.

67. It was by recognizing that likeness is an a priori idea that Plato could refute radical empiricism. For we presume the idea of similarity, or the basis of that idea, in any of the primitive comparisons presumed by empiricist accounts of concept formation.

68. New data can alter the relative credibility of rival explanations. But damaged hypotheses can be unendingly refurbished, with lemmas that never become categorically impossible. Karl Popper saw that if a hypothesis cannot be verified conclusively by induction, neither can its probability be established inductively, since a false hypothesis may be unendingly confirmed. But Popper thought a single countercase could disconfirm a proper hypothesis. This overlooks the possibility of deceptive phenomena. That reality is observable or answerable to experiment is itself a metaphysical hypothesis. So the notion that disconfirmation is epistemically asymmetrical with confirmation seems to be mistaken. And even refutation of one (say, unreconstructed) hypothesis does not diminish the alternatives, since infinitude is not reduced to finitude by finite diminutions. I think it would be foolish as well as false to deny that we ever have good reasons for preferring one hypothesis to another. But the fact remains that empiric data alone (if there are such things), can never, unaided by values and metaphysical premises (inferences that go beyond the empiric givens) reduce the variety of alternative hypotheses below infinity—at least not as long as refurbished hypotheses are allowed.

69. Apocalypse of Abraham 1–7; Genesis Rabbah 38.13.

70. Job 38–39, trans. after the JPS version, with some help from Saadiah.

71. J. N. Findlay, *Ascent to the Absolute* (London: Allen and Unwin, 1970), 205.

Chapter 3

1. *Treatise,* bk. III, pt. 1, sec. 1, ed. Selby-Bigge, 455–70; quotation on page 469.

2. G. E. Moore, *Principia Ethica* IV 67 (1922; reprint, Cambridge: Cambridge University Press, 1960), 114; cf. II.

3. Antony Flew, *God and Philosophy* (London: Hutchinson, 1966), 5.16, 1.15–18.

4. The late A. C. Graham sought a morality in the simple maxim "Face facts." But, as he saw, more is involved in facing facts, if this maxim is to have normative force, than merely acknowledging them. One must accept or confront them; the variety of possible responses shows amply that facts alone do not set our proper mode of address: "'Face facts' does not tell me what to do about the facts to be faced. . . . Certainly I cannot deduce which goals to pursue from the facts to be faced." As Graham argues, one's idea of facts as well as what it means to face them must be enriched before one can find normative force in the maxim, even cognitively; *Reason and Spontaneity* (London: Curzon, 1985), 2–3.

5. Genesis Rabbah 1.1.

6. The Midrash understands the Torah perfectly when it reasons that God would rather the people abandon him and keep his commandments than abandon the *mitzvot* and preserve the thought of him—for the light of the Torah would inevitably bring them back to God; Lamentations Rabbah, second introduction, citing Jer. 9:11.

7. Maimonides (*Guide* III 53 on Deut. 24:13) glosses "This will be justice for you . . ." as signifying that justice benefits the doer, by improving his character—just as in the Socratic calculus injustice harms the doer. Contrast the lawyerly idealization of adversarial juridical relations.

8. As Ze'ev Falk writes, "[T]hese yokes are not imposed from above, rather they need express assent on the part of every individual, twice a day" (*Religious Law and Ethics*, 116; cf. Ephraim Urbach, *The Sages*, 1.400–419).

9. See my "Six Dogmas of Relativism."

10. Flew, *God and Philosophy* 9.15.

11. Cf. *Avot* 4.3, *Ta'anit* 7a, Genesis Rabbah 28.9; but see 13.6.

12. See EI_2 3.1026b s.v. *idjtihād*, and 4.1101a s.v. *khata'*; cf. Avot 4.16, the motto from R. Judah bar Ilai; Maimonides ad Avot 1.3, on Zadok and Boethus and the weighty responsibility of Antigonos of Socho.

13. Origen, *De Principiis* (ca. 215–230) II x 3, ed. Paul Koetschau (1913), trans. G. W. Butterworth (1936; reprint, New York: Harper and Row, 1966), 146; Rufinus suppressed the passage in his Latin version; see the rest of chap. x, and III vi 9; cf. Rosh Hashanah 16b–17a.

14. Adolf Jellinek, ed., *Bet ha-Midrash* (Leipzig, 1853–1877), 5.46; Louis Ginzberg, *Legends of the Jews*, 4.115–16.

15. See Carleton Gajdusek, *Abstracts of the American Pediatric Society*, 74th Annual Meeting, Seattle, June 16–18, 1964; M. J. Goodman and L. E. Goodman, *Sex Differences in the Human Life Cycle*, 274–75.

16. Albert Schweitzer, *On the Edge of the Primeval Forest* (1922; reprint, London: Black, 1956), 102; cf. 104.

17. George Catlin, *Letters and Notes on the Manners, Customs and Condition of the North American Indians* (London, 1841), ed. M. M. Mooney (New York: Clarkson Potter, 1975), 236–37.

18. Catlin, *Letters and Notes*, 91.

19. See Falk, 82; Hans W. Wolff, *Amos geistige Heimat* (Neukirchen-Vluyn: Neukirchener Verlag des Erziehungsvereins, 1964).

20. Cf. Dodds, *The Greeks and the Irrational*, chap. 2.

21. Glossing Hillel's epitomizing of the entire Torah in the Silver Rule (Shabbat 31a), Rashi suggests that unless Hillel meant only the interpersonal Torah, "thy neighbor" should mean God. But the Kabbalist Isaiah Horowitz (ca. 1555–ca. 1630) in *Shenei Luḥot ha-Berit* (Jerusalem, 1963) fuses the humanistic *peshat* with the theocentric *derash*. As Louis Jacobs explains, "Both loves—of the neighbor and of God—are really one since God is One and all is from Him. The love of the neighbor is part of the love of the God who created the neighbor. By loving one's neighbor one fulfills God's purpose. . . . Since there is a divine spark in the soul of man, who is created in God's image, the love of one's fellow is quite literally the love of God" ("The Relationship Between Religion and Ethics in Jewish Thought," in *Contemporary Jewish Ethics*, ed. Menachem Kellner, 55).

22. Maimonides, "Eight Chapters," 7; cf. *Guide* II 36.

23. See John Stuart Mill, *An Examination of Sir William Hamilton's Philosophy* (1867), 119–29, in *Mill's Theism*, ed. Richard Taylor (Indianapolis: Bobbs Merrill, 1957), 89–96.

24. See my "Determinism and Freedom in Spinoza, Maimonides and Aristotle."

25. We can see here how it is a pseudo-question to ask, "Why should I do what is right?" For every creature's condition calls it toward perfection. Our task is to articulate the demands of perfection and keep to the course it sets for us.

26. *Guide* I 54, citing Sifre to Deut. 10:12; Sota 14a, glossing Deut. 13:5; Shabbat 133b; Leviticus Rabbah 24; cf. *Guide* III 54; "Eight Chapters," 5, 7.

27. Josephus, *Contra Apion* (ca. 96 C.E.), LCL 2.170–71.

28. Lecture by Gordon Kaufman, University of Hawaii, May 23, 1977.

29. See Plotinus, *Enneads* VI 5.4; cf. I 7.1, V 1.11, VI 9.8.

30. For further reflections on Kant's moral purism, see *On Justice*, chap. 3.

31. Kant, *Groundwork*, trans. Paton, 98–100, 108–12.

32. James Rachels, "God and Human Attitudes," *Religious Studies* 7 (1971): 325–37. The parallel with the early Findlay is drawn by Philip Quinn in *Divine Commands and Moral Requirements* (Oxford: Oxford University Press, 1978), 1. Rachels opens with Kant's words: "Kneeling down or grovelling on the ground, even to express your reverence for heavenly things, is contrary to human dignity." Yet Kant volunteers that when he meets a good man his heart bows. As for groveling, the canonical Jewish genuflection of the *Amidah*, at the words "Blessed art Thou, O Lord," marks the word "Blessed"; but one returns to an upright posture before reaching the word "Lord," in keeping with the dictum "The Lord raiseth up those that are bowed down" (Berakhot 12ab citing Ps. 146:8). The true God's majesty is liberative, not oppressive, precisely because of God's moral grandeur and corresponding moral intimacy with the bowed down.

33. Rachels, "God and Human Attitudes," 335.

34. Rachels, "God and Human Attitudes," 332. Rachels supplements the text: "Even as he bargains with God, Abraham realizes that there is something radically inappropriate about it," appealing to what Maimonides would call courtly language: "He says, 'Behold now, I have taken upon me to speak unto the Lord, which am but dust and ashes. . . . O let not the Lord be angry . . .' (Genesis 18:27, 30) [ellipses are Rachels's]. The fact is that Abraham could not, consistently with his role as God's subject, set his own judgment and will against God's. The author of Genesis was certainly right about this." So Abraham's moral courage is dissolved, along with whatever meaning Genesis holds up before us by singling out this act, one of the few events in Abraham's life that it records, setting Abraham on a plane with Job and hardly as a paragon of obsequiousness.

35. Norbert Samuelson, "Revealed Morality and Modern Thought," (1970), reprinted in Kellner, 84–99, esp. 95.

36. As Ze'ev Falk writes, "A reconciliation between autonomy and theonomy could indeed be found, if the theonomic system would refer its believers not only to the divine will but to their own responsibility . . . ask the person to make independent decisions and thereby follow the divine will. . . . This concept could be found in any system of theonomy, *a fortiori* in that of rabbinical thought, which delegated authority of legal interpretation to human beings, even against Scripture itself" see *Religious Law and Ethics*, 114; cf. pp. 115, 131–32.

37. Rachels rejects any simple form of subjectivism on the grounds that it precludes moral discourse; see his *Elements of Moral Philosophy* (Philadelphia: Temple University Press, 1986), 25–38. In "Subjectivism," in Peter Singer's *Companion to Ethics* (Oxford: Blackwell, 1991), he finds it "encouraging" that a properly nuanced and qualified subjectivism, analogous to an ideal observer theory, comes close to joining hands with several varieties of prescriptivism (440). Yet he makes no similar gesture of rapprochement with theistic ethics, stating the theistic position as a dogmatic insistence on *defining* the good as the will of God, allowing no room for the dialectic by which moral and religious discourse have historically informed one another.

38. Emil Fackenheim, *Encounters Between Judaism and Modern Philosophy*, 33–77.

39. "From the very beginning, at the height of its cultural florescence, this ruling class adopted an ethos and an ideal which concealed its real function" see Erich Auerbach, *Mimesis* (1942–1945), trans. Willard Trask (Princeton, N.J.: Princeton University Press, 1973) 138. I hope that Auerbach's remark about such butchers, borne out of a sensibility that Cervantes did so much to inform and given heightened intensity by Auerbach's witness against SS thuggery, has not lost its power by being made the basis of an industry of stereotypic reductions of the noetic enterprise as *uniformly* engaged in the same concealment.

40. Such efforts are exampled in David Novak's *Jewish Social Ethics*.

41. See Hermann Cohen, "Das Problem der jüdischen Sittenlehre: Eine Kritik von Lazarus' Ethik des Judenthums," *MGWJ* 43 (1899): 385–400, 433–49; *Jüdische Schrifen* (Berlin, 1924), 3.1–35.

42. See Sid Z. Leiman, "Critique of Louis Jacobs," *Religious Studies Review* 2 (1976), reprinted in Kellner, 58–60.

43. See Marvin Fox, "Maimonides and Aquinas on Natural Law," in *Interpreting Maimonides*, 124–51. Fox writes: "Finding no rational ground for moral distinctions, Maimonides avoids the dangers of social chaos by turning to the Hebrew Bible and the rabbinic tradition. Here he finds all that human beings need to learn in order to live in such a way that they can move from the lower perfection of a decent bodily existence to the ultimate perfection of true metaphysical knowledge" (149). Fox here follows Leo Strauss's destructive distillation of the *Guide to the Perplexed* but allows the inherent ambiguities of legal positivism to turn that reading from its skeptical to its authoritarian aspect. The question of whether the tradition is necessary as well as sufficient to the good life is ignored. For Fox does not make clear why one should not just chant "Hare Krishna!" instead of studying and practicing the laws of the Torah. Further, the two metaethical views Fox imputes to Maimonides, the denial that there are objective moral truths and the affirmation that human beings can pursue perfection, are inconsistent with one another. But Maimonides, in fact, makes no such denial. He proposes a shift from the subjective standards commonly designated in terms of good and evil to objective values, which he describes as a quest for perfection.

44. Aharon Lichtenstein, "Does Jewish Tradition Recognize an Ethic Independent of Halakhah?" in *Modern Jewish Ethics*, ed. M. Fox, 62–88; quotation on page 67. Falk complements this observation with numerous examples of the legalization of properly moral themes in Halakhah, and the corresponding moralization of Halakhic legal themes; see *Religious Law and Ethics*, 98–103.

45. Lichtenstein, "Does Jewish Tradition Recognize an Ethic Independent of Halakhah?" 67–68; for *'averah lishmah*, transgression for its own sake, see Gershom Scholem, *The Messianic Idea in Judaism and Other Essays on Jewish Spirituality* (New York: Schocken, 1971), 78–141.

46. *Tanḥuma*, ed., Buber, Tavo 3 (23b); *Tanḥuma* Tavo 1 (119a); see Safrai, 108.

47. *Tractatus Politicus* II 22, ed. A. G. Wernham, 280–81. The rendering here is my own.

48. See *Makkot* 23b; cf. Maimonides, *Book of the Commandments*, Positive Commandments, 1; Negative Commandments, 1.

49. In Kellner, 72. Fackenheim continues: "Puzzlement and wonder arise for the Jewish philosopher because—if he is to believe the testimony of both Jewish life and Jewish thought—what Kant thought impossible is real." Creative and critical response combine in making appropriation both autonomous and receptive.

50. A. I. Baumgarten, "The Torah as a Public Document in Judaism," *Studies in Religion* 14 (1985): 17–24, citing Deut. 24:8; *Mekhilta*, ed. Lauterbach, 2.198.

51. See Louis Jacobs, *Religion and the Individual*, 40–41.

52. Safrai, 104–5; Sifre Deuteronomy 48, ed. Buber, p. 112, Yalkut Shimoni, Tavo 938.

53. Y. *Rosh Hashanah* 1.3, 57b. For the Rabbis' exercise of legislative creativity, see chap. 4, n. 67.

54. See Mishnah *Sota* 5.5; cf. *Sifre* Deuteronomy 32, ed. Finkelstein, 54.

55. Fackenheim in Kellner, 71.

56. Maimonides, *Commentary to Mishnah Avot*, 1.3, trans. David, 3.

57. *Religion Within the Limits of Reason Alone*, trans. Greene and Hudson, 95.

58. *Guide* I 63.

59. Falk, *Religious Law and Ethics*, 120–21.

60. Numbers Rabbah 19.33, 55b.

61. Deuteronomy Rabbah 5.13.

62. Numbers Rabbah 22.4, 60c, and *Tanhuma* ed. Buber, ad loc.

63. See Cicero, *De Finibus* III vi 21, LCL 239.

64. *Metaphysics of Morals*, trans., Mary Gregor, 233–35; cf. *Religion Within the Limits of Reason Alone*, 170ff.

65. Besides fear of the gods and the hereafter, Epicurus specifies fame, unlimited survival, excess, luxury, abstract or objective justice, and immortality as delusory aims; *KD* 7, 14, 19, 33. Immortality is a will-o'-the-wisp; honor, a great good—to those who do the honoring, if they honor the wise. Friendship and laughter are the goods Epicurus loves—partly because they are not readily made idols. Even simplicity, he argues, can be overdone—if made an ideal. The greatest fruit of self-sufficiency is freedom; see *Vatican Fragments* 14, 32, 63, 78. To ascribe to the gods concern with human doings, is, for an Epicurean, the height of impiety. Not only does it derogate from the blessedness of the divine, but it seeks the good where nature did not set it. As Lucretius writes:

> Unhappy race of men, to grant the gods
> Such feats, and add bitter vindictiveness.
> What sighs and groans they gave themselves, what wounds
> For us today, what tears for our descendants!
> Is this devotion—putting on a veil . . .
> Turning in the direction of a stone,
> Running to all the altars, falling flat,
> Prone on the ground, holding out hands to pray,
> Sprinkling the altars with the blood of beasts,
> Swine, sheep, and ox, entwining vow with vow?
> Ah, no. In true devotion lies the power
> To look at all things with a peaceful mind.
> *De Rerum Natura* V 1193–1205, trans. Rolfe Humphries

Cf. the Oxyrhynchian Papyrus, in A.-J. Festugière, *Epicurus and His Gods* (1955), trans. C. W. Chilton (New York: Russell and Russell, 1969), 64.

66. See my *On Justice*, chap. 3; and for the location of the self, 203.

67. See Prov. 3:18: peace and pleasure conjoin in the life of the Law; cf. Gittin 59b: peace is the goal of all the *mitzvot*.

68. See, e.g., Lev. 6:2, 6:7, 6:18, 7:1, 11:46, 12:7, 13:59, 14:2, 15:32, Num. 5:29, 6:13.

69. The new JPS renders: "one standard"; Exodus paraphrases: "one Torah."

70. The command not to mistreat the stranger is repeated thirty-six times; *Bava Metzia* 59b; Maimonides, *Book of the Commandments*, introduction, Rule 9, trans. Chavel, 2.400.

71. Cf. Joseph Albo (d. 1444), *Sefer ha-Ikkarim*, III 25, ed. and trans. Isaac Husik, as *The Book of Principles* (Philadelphia: JPS, 1930), 3.243.

72. See Deut. 14:23 and Hertz ad Lev. 19:34, p. 504; Menahem Herman, *Tithe as Gift* (Toronto: Mellen, 1992).

73. Hermann Cohen, *Religion of Reason Out of the Sources of Judaism*, 127.

74. Spinoza, *Ethica*, III, Definitions of the Emotions 38, ed. Gebhardt, 2.201.

75. See Ahad Ha-am, *Essays, Letters, Memoirs*, trans. Leon Simon (Oxford: East West Library, 1946), 128ff.

76. Louis Jacobs, *Jewish Values* (London: Valentine, Mitchell, 1960), in Kellner, 177, citing Judges 5, Exod. 32:32, Gen. 38:25; cf. Sanhedrin 75a.

77. The Mishnah, *Terumot* 8.12, applies the same reasoning to honor.

78. Edward Wilson, *Sociobiology* (Cambridge, Mass.: Harvard University Press, 1975).

79. See Douglas Boucher, ed., *The Biology of Mutualism* (London: Croom Helm, 1985).

80. *Berakhot* 29b; *Eruvin* 49a, *Ketubot* 103a, *Bava Batra* 12b, 59a, 168a; see also Shmuel Shilo, *Israel Law Review* 15 (1980): 49–78.

81. Ta'anit 11a, the free translation quoted is from H. Polano, *The Talmud: Selections* (London: Warne, 1978), 271; I fill out the Isaiah passage from the splendid version in the JPS *Prophets* (Philadelphia: Jewish Publication Society, 1978).

82. Cf. Robert Allinson, "The Golden Rule in Confucianism and Christianity," *Asian Philosophy* 2 (1992): 173–85.

83. See Jakob Petuchowski, "The Limits of Self-Sacrifice," in Fox, *Modern Jewish Ethics*, 103–18.

84. See Frederick Hayek, *The Road to Serfdom* (Chicago: University of Chicago Press, 1944).

85. See my *On Justice*, chap. 1.

86. *Bava Metzia* 30b. See Shmuel Shilo, "Lifnim Mishurat Hadin," *Israel Law Review* 13 (1978): 359–90; cf. Elliot Dorff, "The Interaction of Jewish Law with Morality," *Judaism* 26 (1977): 456–59; Falk, 98. Generosity here becomes a legal norm: parties are called upon to claim less than their maximal entitlements. The Rabbis resort to moral suasion or social pressure in the interest of equity, lest the Law become a thicket of overlapping statutory requirements. As Dorff notes, "Rav held that conduct beyond the strict requirements of the law was actionable because it was, in fact, the law." Rav's proof-text was Prov. 2:20, "That you may walk in the way of good men and keep the path of the righteous." *Lifnim mi-shurat hadin* means supererogation. The concrete demands of that broad principle cannot be made statutory without generating an infinite regress. Yet, even to know the direction in which the Torah expects us to exceed its statutory demands one needs to know its aims.

87. Marquis de Sade, "Dialogue Between a Priest and a Dying Man" (written in prison, 1763), in *Oeuvres Complètes*, ed. Annie Le Brun and J.-J. Pauvert (Paris: Pauvert, 1986), 1.501–12. "Toute la morale humaine est renfermée dans ce seul mot: *rendre les autres aussi heureux que l'on désire de l'être soi-même* et ne leur jamais faire plus de mal que nous n'en voudrions recevoir. Voilà, mon ami, voilà les seuls principes que nous devions suivre, et il n'y a besoin ni de religion, ni de dieu pour goûter et admettre ceux-là: il n'est besoin que d'un bon coeur" (512). "All human morality is locked up in this one maxim: *to make others as happy as one would wish to be oneself* and never to do them more harm than one would be willing to undergo. There, my friend, these are the only principles we need to follow, and it takes no religion or god to acknowledge and enjoy them, just a good heart" (Sade's emphasis). Cf. Margaret Crosland's translation in *The Passionate Philosopher* (London: Peter Owen, 1991), 29. Questions of harm arise because Sade's hedonism rejects Epicurean calm, equating the most intense pleasures with pains and injuries and finding unlimited prospects of enjoyment in the compounding of physical violations with affronts to honor and violations of personhood, spirit, and the social safeguards of dignity. When reciprocity is the only principle, reciprocity itself is sapped. Even if Sade breaks his implicit promise, he can laugh that nothing was said of good faith. As for the good heart, who is to judge, once dignity is abased, what a good heart might demand in opening up the "other" to undreamed possibilities of experience, corruption, and degradation, which only begin with the willful debauching of the priest of Sade's dialogue.

88. Genesis Rabbah 24.7.

89. Typically, in *Republic* I 331C.

90. Kant, *Groundwork* chap. 2, trans. Paton, 80; Maimonides, "Eight Chapters," 8.

91. Cf. Mishnah, *Sanhedrin* 4.1.

92. Privacy here includes the right to define one's own project, to be free of torture and

mind control, self-incrimination, and a wide variety of other invasions and violations. It does not include a right to state-financed abortions on demand.

93. See Uriel Tal, "Violence and the Jew in Nazi Ideology," in Baron, Wise and Goodman, *Violence and Defense in the Jewish Experience*, 205–23.

94. Franz Rosenzweig, *The Star of Redemption*.

Chapter 4

1. *Nicomachaean Ethics* I 7, 1097a 20–23; cf. 1096b 33–34.

2. *Sefer Ha-Ḥukkim* (The Statutes of Israel), 1980, 163, officially translated as *Laws of the State of Israel* (*L.S.I.*). The 1980 principle was founded on Israel's Declaration of Independence, 1948 (1 *L.S.I.* 3): "The State of Israel . . . will foster the development of the country for the benefit of all its inhabitants; it will be based on freedom, justice and peace as envisaged by the prophets of Israel." The Supreme Court of Israel ruled that the declaration did not have constitutional or legal force but did express "the vision of the people and its credo" and contain "the guiding principles for the interpretation of statutes" (Zeev *v*. Acting District Officer of Tel Aviv, *H.C.* 10/48, in *Selected Judgments of the Supreme Court of Israel* 68, and Shtreit *v*. the Chief Rabbi of Israel, *H.C.* 301/63, 18 *P.D.* 11/598).

3. "And there they became a nation . . .": Deut. 26:5; Passover *Hagaddah*.

4. See C. L. Becker, *The Heavenly City of the Eighteenth-Century Philosophers* (1932; New Haven, Conn.: Yale University Press, 1968); J. M. Cuddihy, *The Ordeal of Civility* (New York: Oxford University Press, 1974); Peter Gay, *Freud, Jews and Other Germans* (New York: Oxford University Press, 1978); Eugene Kamenka, *The Ethical Foundations of Marxism*, 2d. ed. (London: Routledge, 1972).

5. Exod. 21:1–6; Deut. 15:12–18. Some modern commentators think that the law banning return of fugitive slaves (Deut. 23:16) could never have been enforced, since its effect would have been to abolish involuntary servitude. That, I believe, was the intent.

6. "In contrast to temples in other cultures, the Jerusalem Temple did not possess land. . . . a man would be disgraced for selling the 'field of possession,' even as a man would be glorified for redeeming his meadow and thus reclaiming it. . . . The great influence of this ruling can be seen from the fact that for generations after the destruction of the Temple most of the land in Palestine remained in the possession of small farmers. Even the *colonatus* laws of the later Roman administration were only introduced in Palestine towards the end of the fourth century, considerably later than was normal in the Roman Empire" (Safrai, 132).

7. See Neal Soss, "Old Testament Law and Economic Society," *JHI* 34 (1973): 323–44; cf. Henry George's appreciation of Moses.

8. See Francis Galton, *Hereditary Genius* (1896; reprint, London: Macmillan, 1925), 33–40, 343–45; Garrett Hardin, "Living on a Lifeboat," *Bioscience* 24 (1974): 561–68.

9. Cf. Isa. 45:18; Mishnah *Yevamot* 6.6, *Gittin* 4.5: procreation is a good and central to God's purpose in creating the universe.

10. For the Rabbinic ideal of economic self-sufficiency, see *Avot de Rabbi Nathan* 31.1, ed., A. Cohen, *Minor Tractates of the Talmud* (London: Soncino, 1984), 29a.

11. Hillel established the device known as the *prosbul* (lit. "for the Court"), fictively transmuting private debts into public obligations to mitigate the effects of biblical remission (*shemittah*) by preserving credit even in the face of the Sabbatical year. His authority was Deut. 15:9; see Mishnah *Shevi'it* 10.3, trans. Danby, 51. See Falk's discussion of the evolution of the norm, from a moral suasion to a formal institution in *Religious Law and Ethics*, 101–2.

12. Deut. 15:7-8; *Sifre* Re'eh 116, ad loc., ed. S. Zuckerman and S. Luria (Wilna: Fine and Rosenkrantz, 1866); Deut. 27:19; Isa. 10:1, 3:14–15, 1:16–17; Prov. 3:27; Ben Sirah 4:3,

34:21, ed. E. J. Goodspeed (1938; reprint, Chicago: University of Chicago Press, 1965); Josephus, *Antiquities* xx 9.7, LCL 9.505; *Against Apion* ii 27. "A community that has no synagogue and no shelter for the poor must first provide for the poor" (Judah ben Samuel he-Hasid [d. 1217], *Sefer Hasidim*, ed. J. Wistinetzki [Frankfurt: Wahrmann, 1924], 374–75; cf. *Tosefta* Peah 4.9: refusal to give charity is tantamount to idolatry. *Shabbat* 104a: charity must "run after the poor," not passively await them. For the institutions that realize these ideals, see J. Bergmann, *Ha-Tzedakah be-Yisrael* (Jerusalem: Sifre Tarshish, 1944; repr., 1975).

13. Maimonides, *Code* VII 2, Gifts to the Poor 10.7, trans. Isaac Klein (New Haven, Conn.: Yale University Press, 1979), 91: "The highest rank, which is unsurpassed, is that of one who upholds the hand of an Israelite reduced to poverty by giving him a grant or loan, entering into partnership with him, or finding him work, to strengthen his hand, so that he need not beg. Of this Scripture says, 'Thou shalt sustain him; as a client and a resident shall he live with thee' (Leviticus 25:35)." I translate according to Maimonides' sense and Saadiah's understanding of the *ger* as a client, which the Rambam here adopts. Cf. Isaac Napaha ad Isa. 58:8 ff. in Bava Batra 9b; Louis Jacobs, *Religion and the Individual*, 25–27.

14. Spinoza, *Ethics* III, prop. 43; IV prop. 46; cf. Prov. 24:17, 25:21; *ARN* 23.1.

15. Deut. 4:1; 5:30; 8:1; 16:20; 30:6, 16, 19; Lev. 18:5; *Avot* 4.24.

16. Maimonides, *Code* XIV, I Sanhedrin 20.4–5, trans., A. M. Hershman (1949; reprint, New Haven, Conn.: Yale University Press, 1967), 60–61. Sarna glosses "thy poor" as "Those who depend on you for justice" (*JPS Torah Commentary: Exodus*).

17. See G. R. Driver and John C. Miles, trans. *The Babylonian Laws* (Oxford: Clarendon Press, 1955), 1.17, 2.500.

18. Cicero abused legality in claiming that Catiline's conspiracy denied him access to the machinery of justice.

19. I translate in accordance with the traditional reading adopted in the codes. The JPS parses verse 18 to make the Levitical priests the actual scribes, but the constitutional theme is unaffected.

20. Driver and Miles, trans., *The Babylonian Laws*, 2.83, 47, 79.

21. Moshe Greenberg, "Some Postulates of Biblical Criminal Law."

22. The concept is biblical. In the *JPS Torah Commentary: Numbers*, Jacob Milgrom explains that the word *mishpat* in the seemingly odd phrase *ḥukkat mishpat* (Num. 35:29) means procedure. Thus: "Such shall be your law of procedure"—your judicial or procedural rule, the law that regulates the administration of justice.

23. See Job 10:2, 15; 13:15, 18; 14:17; cf. Shevu'ot 31a; and see my commentary on Saadiah's *Book of Theodicy*, introduction, 35 n. 8.

24. See chapter 7.

25. Albert Einstein, Sept. 15, 1933, *Out of My Later Years* (New York: Philosophical Library, 1950), 23; cf. Henri Bergson, *Two Sources of Morality and Religion*, trans. R. A. Audra and C. Brereton, 95. See Midrash *Tanḥuma* Nitzavim, 25a; Philo, *De Decalogo* X 36–43, LCL 7:23–29; with *De Confus. Ling.*, XXXVII 183–98, 4.111–19; Louis Brandeis, *The Jewish Problem and How to Solve It* (New York: Zionist Essays Publication Committee, 1915), 5; Yehiel Michael of Zlotchov ap. Martin Buber, *The Way of Man According to the Teachings of Hasidism* (London: Routledge, 1950), 17; Zusya in M. Buber, *Tales of the Hasidim*, trans. Olga Marx (New York: Schocken, 1947–1948) 1.251; Buber's *Between Man and Man*, trans. R. G. Smith (New York: Macmillan, 1947), 200.

26. For Job's monogamy, see Ginzberg, *Legends of the Jews*, trans. Szold, 2.241.

27. See chapter 5, n. 86. Maimonides, "Eight Chapters," 4; cf. *Code* I, The Book of Knowledge, II Ethical Laws 6.8, ed. Hyamson, 55b.

28. Cf. H. A. Alexander, "The Critical Temper in Judaism," separatum (Los Angeles: University of Judaism, 1985).

29. *Guide* III 26–28, II 40, ed. Munk, 3.57–62, 2.85–87.

30. *Nicomachaean Ethics* II; cf. Plato, *Laws* 719E–720; *Guide* III 33, ed. Munk 3.73–74.

31. *Guide* III 28, ed. Munk, 3.60b–62; cf. Ibn Ṭufayl, *Ḥayy Ibn Yaqẓān*, trans. Goodman, 156, 161–65.

32. *Guide* III 35, ed. Munk, 3.75–77.

33. *Guide* II 6, 12, 36–38, III 17.5, 18, ed. Munk 2.16–18, 24b–26b, 77b–83b, 3.34b, 37b–39.

34. Maimonides, *Book of the Commandments*, trans. Chavel. The Mishnah Commentary, written in Arabic, is the *Kitab al-Siraj* or *Perush ha-Mishnah*, trans. Fred Rosner (New York: Feldheim, 1975). The Code is the *Mishneh Torah*, called the *Yad Ḥazakah*; the YJS English translation is nearing completion.

35. *Guide* III 12, ed. Munk, 3.18–22.

36. Maimonides, *Guide* III 34, II 40, III 26–28, 32, I 2, ed. Munk, 3.74b–75, 2.85–87, 3.57–62, 3.69–73, 1.13–14b.

37. Cf. David Bohm, *Causality and Chance in Modern Physics* (London: Routledge, 1957), 130–46.

38. See my "Mythic Discourse" and chapter 1, 6–7.

39. For the origins of the *risālah* form, see my essay "The Greek Impact on Arabic Literature," 476.

40. I speak of statutory rape, since the verb *yifateh* entails seduction. But Dinah was not seduced but "humbled" by Shechem (*va-ye'aneha*—Gen. 34:2).

41. Falk, *Religious Law and Ethics*, 54; cf. 119.

42. Edith Hamilton, *Spokesmen for God: The Great Teachers of the Old Testament* (New York: Norton, 1949), 99–100.

43. M. Jastrow, "*Rō'eh* and *Ḥozeh* in the Old Testament," *JBL* 28 (1909): 42–56, here citing p. 56: a prophet's "main purpose is to speak out in the name of a Deity, to speak forth rather than foretell"; R. H. Charles, *A Critical and Exegetical Commentary on the Book of Daniel* (Oxford: Oxford University Press, 1929). As Harry Orlinsky writes, "It is sad that scholars continue to refuse to distinguish between the diviner-seer (foreteller) and the prophet (forthteller), i.e., between the likes of an Eli, Samuel, the unnamed 'men of God,' Nathan, Ahijah, and Elisha (from the eleventh to the ninth centuries)—all of whom were diviners and attached to shrines or to diviner guilds or orders, and constitute a phenomenon common to the ancient Near East—and those like Hosea, Amos, Isaiah, and Micah, who make their appearance after about 800 B.C.E. and are a uniquely Israelite phenomenon" (in Baron, Wise, and Goodman, *Violence and Defense*, 57; cf. Orlinsky's *Essays in Biblical Culture*, 39–65).

44. Saadiah, *ED* III 6, ed. Kafih, 130; trans. Rosenblatt, 155; see chapter 6.

45. Richard Bergren, *The Prophets and the Law* (Cincinnati: HUC, 1974), esp. 182–83; cf. Numbers Rabbah 11.7. Zedekiah's rescinded emancipation proclamation on the lifting of Nebuchadnezzar's siege (Jer. 34) provokes a "prophetic judgment speech," although the offense seems to violate a non-"apodictic" law, the Sabbatical release of slaves (Deut. 15:12–15). But the real offense, Bergren argues (68–79), was against a covenant with God, since besieged Jerusalem had sworn to free the slaves. This cuts matters very fine. For Jeremiah stresses that real penitence was demanded—concretely, restoration of the Torah's remission of slavery. The people had broken their bond, but in doing so had reverted to ignoring God's law.

46. Falk (*Religious Law and Ethics*, 71) lists "the duty to restore lost objects (Deuteronomy 22:1–3), the exemption of the mill from seizure in distress (Deuteronomy 24:6), the duty to restore a pledge at dawn (Deuteronomy 24:10–11), as well as the provisions in favor of employees (Deuteronomy 24:14–15) and of disadvantaged persons (Deuteronomy 24:17–22)" as paradigm cases of moral rules. He adds that the prohibition of false weights and measures (Deut. 25:13–16) appeals to conscience rather than to public sanctions.

47. Cf. 2 Sam. 15; Hos. 6:3; Jer. 22:16, 31:34.

48. See Phyllis Trible, "Depatriarchalizing Biblical Interpretation," *JAAR*, 41 (1973): 30–48, reprinted in *The Jewish Woman: New Perspectives*, ed. Elizabeth Koltun (New York: Schocken, 1976), 217-41: "Israel repudiated the idea of sexuality in God . . . the nature of God in Israel defies sexism"; cf. Trible's *God and the Rhetoric of Sexuality* (Philadelphia: Fortress Press, 1978); Virginia Ramey Mollenkott, *The Divine Feminine: The Biblical Imagery of God as Female* (New York: Crossroad, 1984).

49. See Amos 9:7; Israel is not alone in being saved from slavery: the Syrians, Cushites, and Philistines, too, have been redeemed by God.

50. See Mal. 1:11. God judges all nations; Damascus, Philistia, Tyre, Edom, Moab are not immune (Amos 1–2). For universal peace, Isa. 11:6-9, 2:4; Mic. 4:3, mimicking and reversing Joel 3:10.

51. Isaiah 2:3, 11:6; Maimonides, *Code*, Book of Judges: Kings and Wars, 11–12, trans. A. Hershman (YJS), 238–42.

52. Genesis Rabbah 27; Maimonides, *Guide* I 46, II 38, ed. Munk, 1.49b–53, 2.82–83b.

53. *Shabbat* 92a, *Nedarim* 38a; *Guide* II 36; III 18, ed. Munk 2.80, 3.38–39.

54. For the Rabbis' technique of making biblical themes explicit, see Max Kaddushin, *The Rabbinic Mind* (New York: JTS, 1952); *A Conceptual Approach to the Mekhilta* (New York: JTS, 1969).

55. "Halakhah in general could function as a legal system only by authority of the state. Lacking recognition, Halakhah became a system of morality and entirely lost its legal character. Take, for example, the abolition of Jewish criminal jurisdiction by the Roman administration, even before the destruction of the Temple. As a result, most of the rules of tractate Sanhedrin became social conventions of the rabbis and their followers, and were no longer law. This was a decisive step in the privatization of Halakhah" (Falk, 100; cf. 115).

56. "How did they order the matter in the days of fasting? They used to bring out the Ark into the open space in the town and put wood ashes on the Ark and on the heads of the President and the Head of the Court; and each one took ashes and put them on his head. The eldest of them then uttered these words of admonition: 'Brethren, it is not written of the men of Nineveh (Jonah 3:10) that God saw their sack cloth and their fasting, but that "God saw their deeds, that they turned away from their evil way," and in the Prophets, "Rend your heart, not your garments" (Joel 2:13)'" (Mishnah *Ta'anit* 2.1). Safrai remarks (110): "The essence of repentance is to leave the path of sin and to decide not to return to it. . . . fasting is considered only a means of awakening man to repentance."

57. See Jacob Neusner, *Judaism: The Evidence of the Mishnah* (Chicago: University of Chicago Press, 1981); *Avot* 2.13; Safrai, 126, 129.

58. Safrai, 84.

59. See Mishnah *Yoma* 1.6; cf. the advisory role of the *parhedrin* (palhedrin) toward the High Priest, *Yoma* 1.1, a projection of the Rabbinic role. For the disciples of Aaron, see *Yoma* 91b; Mishnah *Avot* 1.12; E. E. Urbach in Baron, Wise, and Goodman, 89–90; Safrai, 103.

60. See Safrai, 11, 15. Hillel died ca. 10 C.E.

61. Safrai, 50 for the humanism of the Rabbinic tradition, see Myer S. Lew, *The Humanity of Jewish Law* (London: Soncino, 1985); cf. S. T. Lachs, *Humanism in Talmud and Midrash* (Rutherford, N.J.: Fairleigh Dickinson University Press, 1993).

62. Safrai, 50.

63. Novak, *Jewish Social Ethics*, 37.

64. Tanḥuma, Ki Tissa 16; cf. Falk, 132.

65. Safrai, 51; cf. *Avot* 2.11–12; as Safrai explains, the "flowing spring" spoken of there is a metaphor of creativity.

66. Y. *Sanhedrin* 4, 22a; Safrai, 49.

67. *Religious Law and Ethics*, 118, citing *Avodah Zarah* 19a.

68. See Safrai, 146–68; cf. 124: even in the "well-grounded" laws of purity, immense legislative structures were cantilevered well beyond the scriptural givens.

69. Cf. *Shabbat* 135a, *Bava Batra* 110b, *Ḥagigah* 1, 75d, *Soṭa* 3a, Y. *Soṭa* 3, 18d. Safrai (51) explains Hillel's comment "He who increases Torah increases life" (*Avot* 2.7; cf. 1.13, 5.22) as an encomium of creativity.

70. *Avot* 1.3, 4.5, 6.1, *Avot de Rabbi Nathan* 28.10, *Sifre* to Deuteronomy 41, 48.

71. Mishnah *Peah* 1.1, trans. Danby, p. 10; Avot, 6.1, 2.9; but cf. 1.17, 2.2.

72. Eccles. 1:17–18; 6:8, 12; cf. 2:15–23; with Avot 2.21.

73. See I. Heinemann, *Ta'amei Ha-Mitzvot* (Jerusalem: Histadrut, 1949), vol. 1; Solomon Ibn Adret of Barcelona (1235–1310), the Rashba, Responsum no. 94; Louis Jacobs, *Theology in the Responsa* (London: Routledge, 1975), 64. But the Rashba's positivism, targeting a rationalism he feared was reductionistic, did not exclude spiritual or mystical rationales of the intrinsic value of the *mitzvot*.

74. *Genesis Rabbah* 8.8–9; 1.1; 13; cf. *Berakhot* 55a; Philo, *De Opificio Mundi* 4, 15–16, LCL 1.15; Maimonides, *Guide* II 6, ed. Munk, 2.16–18. The imagery is reversed but the theme held constant in *Avot* 4.10: only God can judge alone.

75. *Sanhedrin* 33b–34a, 81b, 84b. For the procedural protections in capital cases, Mishnah *Sanhedrin* 4.1 (which also bans reversal of acquittals in capital cases); for the ban on hearsay, 4.5; trans. Danby, 387. For the exclusion of circumstantial evidence, *Tosefta* to *Sanhedrin* 8.3; cf. *Baba Kamma* 73a: "Evidence voided in part is voided altogether." Cf. Urbach in Baron, Wise, and Goodman, 104–8.

76. Rava in *Sanhedrin* 96; cf. Mishnah *Ketubot* 2.9, trans. Danby, 247; Maimonides, *Code* XIV, *H. Sanhedrin* 18.6, YJS 14.52–53: "Perhaps he was one of those who are in misery, bitter in soul, who long for death. . . . The principle that no man is to be declared guilty on his own admission is a divine decree." Yet, as Urbach notes (Baron, Wise, and Goodman, 107), "in a civil case the admission of fault or liability had the power of one hundred witnesses."

77. The Rabbis demand warning by the husband before two witnesses, naming the suspected third party, overt ignoring of the warning, again certified by two witnesses other than the husband, and consent by the wife to the ordeal. Her refusal made her subject to divorce without return of the marriage settlement. But insufficient warning or inadequate testimony left divorce the only remedy, *with* return to the wife of her marriage settlement. Cases under this law could come only before the full Sanhedrin of seventy-one high court judges in Jerusalem. Renewed sexual relations of the married couple between the warning and the ordeal voided the procedure and required their divorce with return of the settlement. So did the husband's relenting in his demand for the ordeal. Any premarital or extramarital affairs on his part nullified his demand; so did any significant physical handicap in either party; Mishnah *Soṭah* 1–5, trans. Danby, 293–98; Maimonides, *Code* IV, *Soṭah*, ed. I. Klein, YJS, 341–64; Abraham Chill, *The Mitzvot* (Jerusalem: Keter, 1974), 322–24. The requirement of consent ensured that the ordeal would be little practiced. It was magical from the outset—the only commandment, Naḥmanides remarks, that depended on a miracle—and the Mishnah treats its practice as legendary: the ordeal was expected to produce identical effects on the lover as on the woman who drank the waters. Maimonides is rather casual about the composition of the waters themselves: "some bitter ingredient such as wormwood or the like" (356); he implies (358) that the ordeal's efficacy rested on popular belief. In Second Temple times, following a hint in Hosea (4:14), the Sanhedrin abolished the ordeal completely, arguing that adultery was too widespread to allow the required presumption of a husband's innocence.

78. The oath is expressed euphemistically, suppressing the word "never."

79. The same talmudic passage pictures a judge instructing a witness in a case like Shimeon's: "If that is what you saw, you saw nothing." Shimeon saw enough to call the aggressor "villain" but cannot charge him with murder. He invokes God's punishment on the murderer, not verbally presuming the guilt of the man before him. The Muslim jurist Ibn Khallikan (1211–1282) reports several similar stories in his *Biographical Dictionary*, trans. B. Mac Guckin de Slane (Paris and London, 1842; reprint, Beirut: Librairie du Liban, 1970), 4.276.

80. See Urbach in Baron, Wise, and Goodman, 109.

81. Safrai, 131. The Talmud is not reporting that the Torah legislates for a null class but voicing the Rabbis' determination that no case will ever meet the Torah's standard for capital punishment in this matter: the statute will be of regulative value only, as penal laws today are sometimes used to make possible therapeutic and social interventions. As Falk renders the dictum of R. Simon: "Why should he be executed for having eaten a quantity of meat and drunk a measure of wine? This case should therefore not be understood as an actual ruling; it never happened in the past nor will it happen in the future, but was meant as a theoretical paradigm" (*Religious Law and Ethics*, 119).

82. Cf. Deut. 5:30; 6:3, 18; 4:40; 5:26. If quality of life is understood to include preservation of communal and sacred values, then preservation and enhancement of life may be called *the* cardinal principles.

83. Mishnah *Yoma* 8.6, trans. Danby, 172, and *Yoma* 84a, 85ab; cf. Mishnah *Shabbat* 2.5, trans. Danby, 102, and *Shabbat* 30, 32a, *Kiddushin* 39b. Babies are delivered normally on the Sabbath and boys are circumcised even if the day of circumcision falls on the Sabbath; a sick child is not circumcised until recovered; Mishnah *Shabbat* 18.3, 19.5.

84. Mishnah *Yoma* 8.5–6, trans. Danby, 172, and Gemara ad loc.

85. *Pesaḥim* 72b, *Ketubot* 105a; see Ben Zion Bokser in M. Konvitz, ed., *Judaism and Human Rights* (New York: Viking, 1972), 151–52.

86. As George Fletcher notes, Jewish law generalizes the defense of human life from one's own to that of others, and stiffens it from an option to an obligation, pegged to the rule "Neither shalt thou stand idly by the blood of thy neighbor" (Lev. 19:16); "Talmudic Reflections on Self-Defense," in *Crime, Punishment and Deterrence: An American Jewish Exploration*, ed. Robert Gordis (Los Angeles: Wilstein Institute, 1989), 71. Fletcher writes: "However challenging it might be to think of self-defense in the talmudic mode as a duty of concern for others, this way of thinking strains the capacity for solidarity in modern society. It is surely possible to adapt the talmudic communitarian mode of thinking to contemporary problems, but one should not be surprised that the influential thinkers in Western law (e.g. Kant, Hegel, and Blackstone) found it necessary to focus not on rescue but on the aggressor's threat to the legal order" (72).

87. Mishnah *Terumot* 8.12, trans. Danby, 62; Israel Lipschutz (1782–1860), *Tif'eret Israel* quoted by Danby, ad loc.

88. *Pesaḥim* 168a, 173b, *Bava Metzia* 48b, *Sanhedrin* 24b; Safrai, 83.

89. *Bava Metzia* 59b, citing Deut. 30:12. God, they said, rejoiced at this citation: "My children have triumphed over Me." Medieval anti-Jewish polemicists made this dictum a scandal; see Marc Saperstein, *Decoding the Rabbis* (Cambridge, Mass.: Harvard University Press, 1980), 4. James Rachels's response to Abraham's intercession for the Cities of the Plain parallels this medieval response to the Judaic appropriation of God's Law.

90. See S. R. Hirsch's meditation "Do Not Destroy!" trans. I. Grunfeld in *Judaism and Human Rights*, 259–64; Novak, *Jewish Social Ethics*, chap. 6.

91. Exod. 23:19, 34:26; Deut. 14:21; Mishnah *Ḥullin* 8, trans. Danby, 524–25.

92. Mishnah *Ḥullin* 1, trans. Danby, 513–15; Maimonides, *Guide* III 26, ed. Munk, 3.58.

93. *Yevamot* 62b–63a ad Gen. 5:2; Midrash *Tanḥuma* 12.

94. E.g., Mishnah *Sanhedrin* 3.3, *Avot* 1.10.

95. Mishnah *Sanhedrin* 4.5, trans. Danby, 387–88.

Chapter 5

1. *Guide* III 17.5: "No denial of this axiom has ever been heard in our religion, thank God"; cf. I 71, ed. Munk, 94ab.

2. For *kavod nivrah*, *ED* II 12, ed. Kafih, 109, trans. Rosenblatt, 130. Maimonides does not directly contradict Saadiah but proposes his own as the more sophisticated approach; *Guide* I 54, 27, 19. For the pellucid lens, "Eight Chapters," 7; *Rambam*, 240–42; cf. A. Altmann, "Saadya's Theory of Revelation," (1943), reprinted in *Saadya Studies*, ed. E. I. J. Rosenthal (New York: Arno, 1980), 23.

3. *ED* IV, Exordium; *Guide* III 13.

4. *Guide* III 13 introduces the critique of Saadiah with the words "Often perfect minds grow perplexed inquiring after the object of existence"; *Rambam*, 262–77; cf. *The Book of Theodicy*, 41–42, 91–92, 114–16, 303–4, 362–63.

5. *ED* II 1, ed. Kafih, 83, trans. Rosenblatt, 96; *Guide* I 75.

6. See "Eight Chapters," 6; cf. *Guide* III 17.4, etc.

7. *ED* X 1, ed. Kafih, 288–89; Rosenblatt's rendering (359) is not very lucid.

8. *ED* X 17, glossing Eccles. 1:15.

9. *ED* X 3, ed. Kafih, 291, trans. Rosenblatt, 361–62.

10. *ED* X 18; contrast Plotinus, *Enneads* I 6.1.

11. *Kitāb al-Tibb al-Rūḥānī*, in *Razis Opera Philosophica*, ed. Paul Kraus (Cairo, 1939; Pars prior, all published), 1–96; trans. A. J. Arberry as *The Spiritual Physick* (London: John Murray, 1950); see my essay "The Epicurean Ethic of Rāzī."

12. See al-Kindī, "Essay on How to Banish Sorrows," ed. in H. Ritter and R. Walzer, "Uno Scritto inedito di al-Kindi," *Studi su al-Kindi II* (Rome: Academia dei Lincei, 1938); cf. al-Rāzī, *Spiritual Physick* xii, trans. Arberry, 68–74.

13. *ED* X 4, ed. Kafih, 293, trans. Rosenblatt, 365.

14. *ED* X 17, trans. Rosenblatt, 400; cf. Israel Efros, *Studies in Medieval Jewish Philosophy* (New York: Columbia University Press, 1974), 128–33.

15. *ED* X 4, ed. Kafih, 292, trans. Rosenblatt, 364.

16. *ED* X 4, ed. Kafih, 295, trans. Rosenblatt, 367.

17. *ED* X 5, ed. Kafih, 296, trans. Rosenblatt, 369–70. Plato's argument (*Gorgias* 493; cf. *Republic* 585–87; *Philebus* 27e, 31–32) was central to Epicurus and well known to al-Rāzī, probably via Galen. Saadiah links the argument to Isa. 28:8 and Prov. 23:8, read as allusions to bulimia and thus as counterparts to Plato's images of the cormorant and the legendary sieve of the Danaids, which Ibn Tibbon's translation of Saadiah's text seems to try to suggest.

18. *Vatican Fragments* 33; cf. 42, *KD* 9.

19. *KD* 8; cf. *Vatican Fragments* 16.

20. *ED* X 7, trans. Rosenblatt, 373 n. 26.

21. See Lois Giffen, *Theory of Profane Love Among the Arabs* (Albany: SUNY Press, 1971); J. N. Bell, *Love Theory in Later Hanbalite Islam* (Albany: SUNY Press, 1974); my "Sacred and the Secular: Rival Themes in Arabic Literature"; R. Scheindlin, *Wine, Women and Death* (New York: JTS, 1986); cf. al-Rāzī's polemic in "Spiritual Physick," chap. 5. For further discussion of the conventions Saadiah rejects here, see Georges Vajda, "Saadia Gaon et l'amour courtois," *Mélanges d'Islamologie dédiés à la mémoire de A. Abel* (Brussels, 1975),

reprinted in *Saadiah Gaon*, ed. Steven Katz (New York: Arno, 1980), unpaginated, and the earlier studies cited there, by Jacob Guttmann and Henry Malter.

22. Giffen, *Theory of Profane Love*, xvi.

23. His synonym for *jimāʻ*, coupling, is *ghashyān*, orgasm, a term used by al-Rāzī and other authorities, medical and literary; see Kraus, ed., *Razis Opera* 23 line 1.

24. *Guide* III 33, ed. Munk 3.73a: "the boor (*al-jāhil*) makes pleasure alone an end to be sought for its own sake"; cf. "Eight Chapters," 4, trans. Gorfinkle, 26.

25. *ED* X 6, ed. Kafih, 298–99, trans. Rosenblatt, 371. Folklore deems coitus a fine remedy for melancholy; cf. Shakespeare's *Taming of the Shrew* and such popular romances as *Gone with the Wind*. The notion both underwrites and is underwritten by medical notions, ancient, medieval, and modern, and by psychoanalysis.

26. *ED* X 6, ed. Kafih, 299–300, trans. Rosenblatt, 372–73.

27. *ED* X 6, ed. Kafih, 299, trans. Rosenblatt, 372; the verse goes on: "and she conceived and bore a son."

28. Plato, *Symposium* 189–93; Saadiah *ED* X 7, ed. Kafih, 300–301, trans. Rosenblatt, 374.

29. *ED* X 7, ed. Kafih, 301, trans. Rosenblatt, 374: "They go even further, treating it as a duty, saying that it is but a discipline by which God's worshippers learn the humility of love, to prepare them for the abasement they will show in worship of their Lord."

30. *ED* X 7, ed. Kafih, 301, trans. Rosenblatt, 375.

31. *ED* X 7, ed. Kafih, 301, trans. Rosenblatt, 375. Fascinated by the tragic pathos or farcical irony of unrequited love, romantics cherish the notion of star-crossed lovers. But Saadiah argues that astral determinations should affect lovers symmetrically, making unrequited love impossible. Maimonides discredits star-destined love on moral grounds, as an apologue of adultery and fornication; "Eight Chapters," 8, trans. Gorfinkle, 88. But he omits Saadiah's dialectical reductio.

32. *ED* X 7, ed. Kafih, 302, trans. Rosenblatt, 376–77.

33. Epicurus, *KD* 10, 14, 17; *Vatican Fragments* 7, 51; Lucretius, *De Rerum Natura* IV 1122–91, esp. 1185ff.; *ED* X 7, ed. Kafih, 303, trans. Rosenblatt, 377.

34. See Exod. 21:10 and *Mekhilta* ad loc., ed. Lauterbach, JPS 3.27–29; Y. Ketubot V 6; Ketubot 47b, 48a, and Tosafot; David Feldman, *Marital Relations*, 60–80.

35. *ED* X 7, ed. Kafih, 303, trans. Rosenblatt, 377. I follow Saadiah's rendering; the context addresses the joys of love and bitterness of adultery; the preceding verse: "Find joy in the wife of thy youth."

36. *ED* X 7, ed. Kafih, 301, trans. Rosenblatt, 374.

37. *ED* X 7, ed. Kafih, 303, trans. Rosenblatt, 377; cf. W. H. Masters and V. E. Johnson, *The Pleasure Bond* (Boston: Little, Brown, 1975).

38. "Eight Chapters," 5.

39. See *The Case of The Animals vs. Man*.

40. "Eight Chapters," 5.

41. *ED* X 11, ed. Kafih, 309, trans. Rosenblatt, 386; cf. Plato, *Republic* 329a.

42. "Eight Chapters," 5.

43. Ibn Ṭufayl, *Ḥayy Ibn Yaqẓān*, trans. Goodman, 143–48; cf. Plotinus: "Cut away everything."

44. Saadiah refuses simply to instrumentalize life, arguing that we live to *earn* our place in the hereafter and can do so only by living through this life, with all its sufferings and doubts. Since earned rewards are far more precious than sheer gifts of grace, this life has intrinsic value not in its pleasures, which are always outweighed in the end by pains, but in its authenticity, the fact that our choices and commitments here are always our own.

45. Maimonides in some measure imbibes Aristotle's elitism, but he transmutes the Peripatetic idea that some men are natural slaves from a rationale to a warning: those who do not lift their eyes above material gain are, in effect, mere instruments of others' aims. The shift is telling, for the Law treats all its subjects as ends in themselves when it makes holiness their proper goal.

46. *ED* X 14, ed. Kafih, 316, trans. Rosenblatt, 394.

47. *Philosophical Life*, trans. A. J. Arberry, as "Rhazes on the Philosophic Life," *The Asiatic Review* 45 (1949): 703–13.

48. Cf. Baḥya Ibn Pakuda, *Kitāb al-Hidāya ʾilā Farā'id al-Qulūb* (The Book of Direction to Duties of the Heart) IV, ed. A. S. Yahuda (Leiden: Brill, 1912), trans. M. Mansoor (London: Routledge, 1973); al-Ghazālī, Iḥyāʾ *'Ulūm al-Dīn (Revival of Religious Studies)* XXXV, and his source, al-Makkī, *Qūt al-Qulūb* (Sustenance for the Heart) II on *tawakkul*, trust (Cairo, 1310 A. H.) 2.4, citing Ps. 118:8 and Matt. 6:27; cf. al-Ḥujwīrī, *Kashf al-Maḥjūb* (The Unknown Unveiled), trans. R. A. Nicholson (1911; London: Luzac, 1967). Hujwīrī and al-Makkī depend ultimately on al-Junayd and on pietist readings of the Hebrew, Christian, and Muslim scriptures.

49. Cf. the Socratic unity of the virtues.

50. *ED* X 17, 2, ed. Kafih, 319, 289–90, trans. Rosenblatt, 400–401, 360.

51. *ED* X 17, 19, ed. Kafih, 319, 323–24, trans. Rosenblatt, 400, 405–6.

52. "Eight Chapters," 31; Gorfinkle (69) translates misleadingly.

53. For *ittiṣāl*, see my *Avicenna*, 163–72.

54. Cf. Ibn Bājjah on unity in diversity: what gives unity to the many volumes of al-Ṭabarī's history is not simplicity but organicity; see my "Ibn Bājjah" in Nasr and Leaman, *History of Islamic Philosophy*. For Maimonides' appreciation of Ibn Bājjah's thoughts on this topic, see *Guide* I 74.7, ed. Munk 1.121–22.

55. Herbert Davidson, "The Middle Way in Maimonides' Ethics," *PAAJR* 54 (1987): 31–72, quotation on page 33.

56. *Guide* I 46, ed. Munk 1.50a.

57. *Guide* I 46, ed. Munk 1.50, lines 6–8. "The Arabic word *sulṭan* [cf. the Hebrew *shilton*] is an abstract noun meaning authority or rule, and was used from early times to denote the government. In a society where state and ruler are more or less synonymous terms, it came to be applied to the holder, as well as the function of political authority, and was used informally to refer to ministers, governors, and other rulers" (Bernard Lewis, *The Legacy of Islam*, 2d ed., ed. J. Schacht and C. E. Bosworth [Oxford: Oxford University Press, 1974], 169).

58. *Guide* II 40, ed. Munk 2.86ab.

59. *Guide* II 38, 40; cf. "Eight Chapters," 3–4, ed. Gorfinkle 17, 51.

60. "Eight Chapters," 4, ed. Gorfinkle 24, trans. 63; Maimonides' Neoplatonic gloss is confirmed in the balancing hemistich: "The testimonies of the Lord are sure, making wise the simple"; cf. *Guide* III 13, ed. Munk 3.25a line12.

61. *Guide* II 39, 40, ed. Munk 2.84b *l.* 9, 86a; *Code*, I, introduction.

62. *Guide* III 34, ed. Munk 3.74b–75a

63. "Eight Chapters," 7; cf. *Guide* III 23, ed. Munk 3.48b–49a.

64. As Moritz Lazarus noted, the biblical imperative to holiness is always addressed in plural.

65. So *Guide* I 2: the Torah is not to be read simply as history or literature.

66. Maimonides on Avot 1.4, trans. David, 4–5, esp. p. 5, lines 3–4.

67. Eleven of the thirteen hermeneutical rules of R. Ishmael (*Sifra*, introduction) directly address the relations of generality and particularity in biblical dicta.

68. "Eight Chapters," 7; *Guide* II 40.

69. M. Hyamson, *The Book of Adoration*, prefatory note; *Guide* III 35.1, 35.3.

70. "Eight Chapters," 6, ed. Gorfinkle 36, trans. 77; *Guide* III 26–27. See also Chapter 6.

71. Maimonides adopts the word *de'ot* from the usage of *Avot* 5.14; see Ray Weiss, "Language and Ethics: Reflections on Maimonides' 'Ethics,'" *JHP* 9 (1971): 425–33, quotation on page 430; Herbert Davidson, "The Middle Way in Maimonides' Ethics," *PAAJR* 54 (1987): 31–72, see p. 39 n. 28. In *Avot* 5.13, *middot* means traits; *de'ot*, characters. Thus *Avot* 5.14: "There are four traits (or dispositions) of character. Following Aristotelian usage, Maimonides applies the term to psychological temperaments in general.

72. "Eight Chapters," 3; cf. Plato, *Republic* 431, *Gorgias* 479, *Timaeus* 86; Baḥya ibn Pakuda, *Duties of the Heart*, introduction and chaps. 1 and 2; Herbert Davidson, "The Study of Philosophy as a Religious Obligation," in *Religion in a Religious Age*, ed. S. D. Goitein Proceedings of conferences held at Brandeis and UCLA, April 1973 (Cambridge, Mass.: Association for Jewish Studies, 1974).

73. *Code* I, ed. Hyamson, 47a.

74. Maimonides stresses the parallel between the commandment to love the stranger and that (Deut. 6:5) to love God. As we have seen, the commandment to love the stranger models the purity of the ethical motive, which is of a piece with the love of God.

75. *Code* I 55a, lines 7ff.

76. *Code* I 54b, lines 23ff.

77. See Daniel Frank, "Humility as a Virtue," in *Moses Maimonides and His Time*, ed. Eric Ormsby (Washington: Catholic University of America Press, 1989), 89–99; "Anger as a Vice," *HPQ* 7 (1990): 269–81.

78. We see here the conceptual synthesis underlying R. Horowitz's homiletic gloss of Hillel's dictum; see chapter 3, n. 21.

79. *Code* I 48a, citing Deut. 28:9, Gen. 18:19.

80. *Code* I, *Hilkhot De'ot* 3.1, ed. Hyamson, 1.49a–50a; "Eight Chapters," 4.

81. "Eight Chapters," 5; *Guide* III 54.

82. *Code* I 49b–50a.

83. *Code* I 55b.

84. *Code* I 57a.

85. "Eight Chapters," 4, ed. Gorfinkle 26–27, trans. 65; Exod. 23:5; Deut. 22:4; cf. Pythagoras ap. Iamblichus, *Protr.* 21 = DK 58C 6. See chap. 4, n. 14.

86. *Code* I 55ab, citing Arakhin 16b.

87. *Guide* I 46, 52–59, II 38; cf. my "Ordinary and Extraordinary Language." See also M. Halbertal and A. Margalit, *Idolatry* (Cambridge: Harvard University Press, 1992), 151–59.

88. *Code* I 34b, lines 15ff.; "Eight Chapters," 5; *Guide* II 40, III 23, ed. Munk 3.48b.

89. *The Book of the Commandments*, item 1 of the positive and negative commandments, respectively, trans. Chavel, 1.1, 2.1; *Guide* II 48.

90. *Guide* III 27.

91. *ED* X 13 ad fin. and III 1, IX 1.

92. *Guide* Ill 43; Aristotle, *Politics* III 9, 1280b 35–39; cf. Novak, *The Theology of Naḥmanides*, 7–8; and my "Friendship in Aristotle, Miskawayh, and Ghazālī."

93. *Guide* III 28, ed. Munk 3.62a.

94. Code X *Hilkhot Tum'at 'Okhlin*, 16:8.

95. *Code* XIV 5, *Hilkhot Melakhim*, 2.4.

96. *Guide* III 48–49; cf. "Eight Chapters," 3–5.

97. *Guide* I 15, ed. Munk 1.22; Pines's translation here is not perspicuous.

98. Maimonides uses the Arabic *Amr* for the Logos; for this usage, see my "Judah Halevi," in Frank and Leaman, *History of Jewish Philosophy*.

Chapter 6

1. See Alexander Altmann, "Ḥalukat ha-Mitzvot le-Rasag," in *Rasag: Kovetz Torani*, ed. J. L. Fishman (Jerusalem, 1943); "Saadya's Conception of the Law," *Bulletin of the John Rylands Library* 28 (1944): 320–39; reprinted in *Saadiah Gaon*, ed. Steven Katz (New York: Arno, 1980), unpaginated; Yoav Elstein, "Torat ha-Mitzvot be-Mishnat R. Saadiah," *Tarbiz* 38 (1969): 120–35; Haggai Ben-Shammai, "Ḥalukat ha-Mitzvot u-Musag ha-Ḥokhmah be-Mishnat Rasag" *Tarbiz* 41 (1972): 170–82.

2. In the previous verse, David alludes to all God's commandments. The context confirms Saadiah's reading.

3. As Rashi, Ibn Ezra, and Rashbam note, the context links the lying here to theft and fraud.

4. See my *On Justice*, chap. 1; also "Toward a Jewish Philosophy of Justice."

5. Saadiah, *ED* III 1, Kafih, 119–20, Rosenblatt, 140.

6. See Saadiah, *The Book of Theodicy*, 128; cf. 82 n. 181, 94, 103–4, etc.

7. Rosenblatt, 140–41; the square brackets are his.

8. *The Book of Theodicy*, trans. Goodman, 156–57.

9. See *ED* III Exordium, 1; IX 1, 7–9; *The Book of Theodicy*, 357.

10. See *The Book of Theodicy*, trans. Goodman, 224 n. 1; 409 n. 7, etc.

11. *ED* III 6, ed. Kafih, 130, trans. Rosenblatt, 155.

12. *Makkot* 10b, *Shabbat* 104a, *Yoma* 39a, *Berakhot* 7a, *Sanhedrin* 27b; Saadiah on Lev. 26:39, at Job 21:19; cf. Prov. 11:3, 11; *On Justice*, 137–38.

13. Compare the increasing otherworldliness of the last remaining Marxists, who increasingly insist that the *real* teachings of Marx were never really tried.

14. *ED* III 3, Kafih, 120–21; Rosenblatt, 145–46. The Rabbis recognize that sanctions, warnings, exceptions, parallels, and the like belong to the interpretive penumbra without which laws would not be operative; see *Midrash ha-Gadol Deuteronomy*, ed. S. Fisch (Jerusalem: Mosad Ha-Rav Kook, 1972), 705; cf. *Sifre* to Deuteronomy, 313, trans. Reuven Hammer (New Haven: Yale University Press, 1986), 320; Safrai, 59–60.

15. Cf. Kant's similarly pietist treatment of reverence for the moral law.

16. *ED* IV 5, trans. Rosenblatt, 192; cf. Maimonides, "Eight Chapters," 8, ed. Gorfinkle, 92.

17. *ED* V 1, ed. Kafih, 169, Rosenblatt, 205. I translate the biblical passages in keeping with Saadiah's rendering. For example, he translates Lev. 5:1, "If any person sin by hearing the sound of a voice that crieth for help, of which he is a witness, or seeth such a thing, or knoweth of it, and doth not report it, he shall bear his iniquity." Saadiah understands "they set their soul on their iniquity" (Hos. 4:8) as an idiomatic transposition; cf. his glosses of Lev. 14:3 and Job 6:7, 15:22, 18:7, 19:20. Just as Saadiah glosses the trope of God's searching the heart and trying the kidneys by reference to the impact of our actions on our ethos, Maimonides takes "a seeing eye and hearing ear" in terms of accountability. This moral reading of providence is corroborated in the Psalms: When "the fool saith in his heart there is no God," it is his actions that speak, and what they deny is accountability.

18. See n. 12.

19. *ED* VI 4, ed. Kafih, 203, trans. Rosenblatt, 246.

20. See *On Justice*, esp. chaps. 3–4.

21. See *ED* IX 5; *The Book of Theodicy*, trans. Goodman 129, and on Job 33:28–30, 15:34, 20:26, 22:20.

22. *ED* VII 5 (variant), trans. Rosenblatt, 424–26.

23. See my "Saadiah's Interpretive Technique."

24. *The Book of Theodicy*, trans. Goodman 359–60.

25. Marvin Fox, "On the Rational Commandments in Saadia's Philosophy," in *Modern Jewish Ethics*, 174. The recovery of fragments from a lost work of Saadiah's means that we are not in the dark as to his motives for singling out a category of positive, or literally "received" or "traditional" commandments (cf. the Islamic duality of *'aql* and *naql*). See Moshe Zucker, "Ḳeṭa'im me-*Kitāb Taḥṣīl al-Sharā'i al-Sam'iyya*" ["Fragments from the *Book on the Comprehension of the Positive Commandments*"] *Tarbiz* 41 (1972): 373–410. The target here is the Karaite view that the received or traditional laws can be deduced, that is, derived by "analogy" (*qiyās*). Saadiah's suitably Rabbanite denial of that view does not entail his abandonment of the less ambitious rationalistic promise of his title, that such commandments can be made in some measure comprehensible to us.

26. Fox, "Rational Commandments in Saadiah's Philosophy," 175.

27. Fox, "Rational Commandments in Saadiah's Philosophy," 175.

28. *The Book of Theodicy*, trans. Goodman 127.

29. *The Book of Theodicy*, 129.

30. *The Book of Theodicy*, 126–27.

31. Fox, "Rational Commandments in Saadiah's Philosophy," 176.

32. Spinoza, *Ethics* IV prop. 18, schol.

33. Spinoza, *Ethics* IV, props. 24, 37, 46, 70, 72, 73.

34. Fox, "Rational Commandments in Saadiah's Philosophy," 176.

35. Fox, "Rational Commandments in Saadiah's Philosophy," 176.

36. Fox, "Rational Commandments in Saadiah's Philosophy," 177.

37. *The Book of Theodicy*, 123–24.

38. See my "Saadya on the Human Condition."

39. *ED* IX 1, ed. Kafih, 262, trans. Rosenblatt, 324. Saadiah argues further that human anxiety and insecurity express our underlying awareness of the inadequacy of this life and the superiority of the life of perfection reserved to us in the hereafter.

40. *The Book of Theodicy*, trans. Goodman 123.

41. See *The Book of Theodicy*, 383, and my discussions, 41–42, 114–16, 139, 143, 254, 362–63.

42. Fox, "Rational Commandments in Saadiah's Philosophy," 178.

43. See Saadiah on Job 2:4 in *The Book of Theodicy*, trans. Goodman 173.

44. Fox, "Rational Commandments in Saadiah's Philosophy," 178.

45. See *ED*, introduction, 5.

46. Saadiah critiques radical empiricism in his epistemological introduction to *The Book of Critically Chosen Beliefs and Convictions*; see A. J. Heschel, *The Quest for Certainty in Saadiah's Philosophy* (New York: Feldheim, 1944), originally published in *JQR* 33–34 (1942/43, 1943/44); Georges Vajda, "Autour de la théorie de la connaissance chez Saadia," *REJ* 126 (1967): 135–89, 375–97; Israel Efros, "Saadiah's Theory of Knowledge," in his *Studies in Medieval Jewish Philosophy* (New York: Columbia University Press, 1974), 7–36.

47. For Mu'tazilite objectivism and its modern counterparts, see George Hourani, *Islamic Rationalism: The Ethics of 'Abd al-Jabbār* (Oxford: Clarendon Press, 1971). G. E. Moore, like Saadiah, was objectivist, almost Platonizing, in ethics; and Kant finds rational intuitions in morals, although none are to be countenanced elsewhere.

48. Fox, "Rational Commandments in Saadiah's Philosophy," 180.

49. Rosenblatt, 181–82.

50. See Ikhwān al-Safā', Goodman, 200–202.

51. For my own attempt, see chapter 7.

52. Fox, *Interpreting Maimonides*, chap. 6, first published in *Dinei Yisrael* 3 (1972): 5–36. In republishing this essay Fox cites his 1975 critique of Saadiah, reprinted in 1977, as "an

extended discussion of this topic." He remarks, "Critics have disagreed with my views on this subject, but I have seen no counterarguments that are persuasive" (129 n. 12).

53. Even Leibniz, Spinoza, and Descartes held no such view: Leibniz used the principle of sufficient reason to discriminate sharply between the demands of logic and the determinants of reality. Descartes made similar use of divine volition. Spinoza, the most intellectualist of the three, held that all facts are in principle deducible from knowledge of God. But the relevant premises included adequate ideas of the natures of things—ultimately, all things.

54. Fox, 182–83.

55. See chap. 3, n. 58.

56. *Bava Batra* 12a; cf. Y. *Berakhot* 1.4; *Makkot* 22b.

57. See Ben Sirah 39:1; cf. Maimonides, *Guide* II 40, III 29.

58. In Islamic law, major river courses are public; see EI_2 5.870. The claim is voided by its terms of reference.

59. *Guide* I 23, II 47; *Guide* I 36, as we have noted (chap. 1, n. 61), glosses the anthropomorphism of ascribing wrath to God as referring consistently to logical repugnance: "only that which is false angers Him."

60. David Novak elegantly describes legal positivists by their penchant for making authority prior to right, where natural law theorists derive authority from right; *Jewish Social Ethics*, chap. 1. When authority derives from power, there is always the risk that right will collapse into power. Natural law theory fosters a corresponding denial of power where there is no right.

61. As Mary Douglas sagely notes, the *motives* of positivists are rarely positivistic. That is as true of Yeshayahu Leibowitz as it is of Kelsen, Perlman, Holmes, or the Vienna Circle.

62. Fox, *Interpreting Maimonides*, 127–28.

63. The reason for levirate marriage is stated three times in the five verses. It gains near-cosmic import in the story of Onan (Gen. 38:8–9; 46:12) and vivid social application in the case of Zelophehad's daughters (Num. 27:1–11, 36:1–12)—although the Torah's general rule places a brother's wife within the penumbra of his privacy (Lev. 18:16), so that release is ultimately preferred (*Yevamot* 109a), and Israel's Chief Rabbinate has dissolved the levirate obligation.

64. *ED* III 2, ed. Kafih, 120, trans. Rosenblatt, 142.

65. Saadiah's reference to Epicureans is clear from their description of optimal pleasure as *ataraxia*, repose or undisturbedness.

66. *ED* III 2, ed. Kafih, 123, trans. Rosenblatt, 142.

67. See Exodus Rabbah 30.11; *The Book of Theodicy*, 178–79, 182 n. 1.

68. See my introduction to *The Book of Theodicy*, 5–16.

69. So Saadiah understands the term, since he categorically rejects the myth of fallen angels; see *The Book of Theodicy*, on Job 1:6, trans. Goodman 154–57.

70. Urbach, *The Sages*, 2.846 n. 90; cf. *Avot* 5.26.

71. Naḥmanides ad Deut. 22:6.

72. Cf. the Stoic-influenced Midrashic images of the potter who fires only the best wares, the farmer who yokes his strongest ox, improves his flax by braking, or harvests the ripe figs before they breed worms: Genesis Rabbah, 32.3, 34.2, 55.1–2; Song of Songs Rabbah 1.16.2.

73. Cf. *Guide* III 26; II 6, 10, 12; *On Justice*, 107–10, 247 n. 50, 249 n. 67.

74. See Urbach, *The Sages*, 1.366.

75. *The Sages*, 1.366–67.

76. Cf. my *On Justice*, esp. chap. 3, and chap. 5 of the present book.

77. See *The Book of Theodicy*, 155–59, 168 n. 31; *Pirke De Rabbi Eliezer* 22.

78. Maimonides, "Eight Chapters," 6, ed. Gorfinkle, 36–37; 75–78 English.

79. *Guide* III 26.

80. See my "Rational and Irrational in Medieval Jewish and Islamic Philosophy."

81. See page 164.

82. See *Guide* III 29, ed. Munk, 3.64b: "The meaning of many of our laws became clear to me and their grounds became known to me only when I studied the schools, views, practices, and forms of worship of the pagans. . . . The greatest book on this subject is *The Nabataean Agriculture*, translated by Ibn Waḥshiyya." As Pines notes, "Ibn Waḥshiyya seems to have been the author of this work, which he passed off as a translation from the Chaldean. The work appeared in 904."

83. *Guide* III 26. Maimonides' Ghazālī-influenced voluntarism is in play here; see Joseph Stern, "The Idea of a *Ḥoq* in Maimonides' Explanation of the Law," in *Maimonides and Philosophy*, ed. S. Pines and Y. Yovel (The Hague: Nijhoff, 1986), 92–130. But in God will and wisdom are one: what seems arbitrary at one historical moment proves rational in a broader perspective.

84. *On Justice*, 2, 235 n. 1.

85. Cf. *Guide* III 35: "Every command or prohibition whose purpose is to inculcate a certain moral trait, instill an idea or improve behavior exclusively with reference to the individual's personal development is classed as between-man-and-God by the Sages, even if it actually does affect relations between man and man—for this may result only after numerous intermediate stages."

86. *Guide* III 31–32; cf. Ikhwān al-Ṣafā, trans. Goodman 108–15.

87. *The Book of Theodicy*, trans. Goodman, 393–96.

88. Maimonides, "Eight Chapters," 4.

89. Cf. Spinoza, *Ethics* IV, preface, ed. Gebhardt 2.208, line 16.

90. See Charles Stevenson, *Ethics and Language* (1944; New Haven, Conn.: Yale University Press, 1950), chap. 9.

91. See Maimonides, *Guide* I 46.

92. See my "Ordinary and Extraordinary Language."

93. David Shatz rightly calls attention to the evocative power of rituals.

94. Much that Lévi-Strauss says in *The Raw and the Cooked* about the shifting symbolisms of mythic motifs applies equally to rituals, which, as anthropologists have long taught, provide a socially visible counterpart of mythic motifs.

95. Mary Douglas, *In the Active Voice* (London: Routledge, 1982), 34–38.

96. See Moshe Greenberg, *Biblical Prose Prayer as a Window to the Popular Religion of Ancient Israel* (Berkeley: University of California Press, 1983), 38–39, 55–57. The thematic of these early prayers, in the most general terms, is ethical—nonmagical—intimate, social, and personal.

97. Mary Douglas, *Natural Symbols* (London: Barrie and Jenkins, 1973), 60–62; see 21–76.

98. John D'Amato, "The Wind and the Amber: Notes on Headhunting and the Interpretation of Accounts," *Journal of Anthropological Research* 35 (1979): 62; Gregory Bateson, *Naven: A Survey of the Problems Suggested by a Composite Picture of the Culture of a New Guinea Tribe Drawn from Three Points of View* (1939; reprint, Stanford: Stanford University Press, 1958), 1–33, 38–39, 98, 107, 123–41, 161–77, 229–30, 286–89.

99. See *On Justice*, chap. 2.

100. Herbert Fingarette, Presidential Address, *Proceedings and Addresses of the American Philosophical Association* 50.6 (1977): 499–525.

101. Fingarette, "The Meaning of Law in the Book of Job," *Hastings Law Journal* 29.6 (1978): 1581–617.

102. Personal letter, Nov. 12, 1979; cf. Soṭah 35a; but contrast *ARN* 34.9.

103. See *On Justice*, chap. 1.

104. Bernard Jackson, "The Concept of Religious Law in Judaism," in *Aufstieg und Niedergang der Römischen Welt*, ed. H. Temporini and W. Haase (Berlin: De Gruyter, 1979), 2.33–52, quotation on page 43.

105. For the Christian doctrine that the Torah's judicial and ceremonial laws lapsed with the death of Christ, leaving only the moral law, which belonged to the law of nature, see Heb. 7:12 and Lev. 26:10 per Gratian, *Commentary on Gregory's Homily* and *Decretum*, pt. II, xxiii, question iv, chap. xv, ed. Friedberg 1.903–4, ed. Lancelotti 1.787–88.

106. Edna Ullmann-Margalit, "On Presumption," *Journal of Philosophy* 80 (1990); cf. "Revision of Norms," *Ethics* 100 (1989); *Iyyun* 39 (1983): 139–50.

107. Cf. Maimonides, *Guide* III 34.

108. See Moshe Greenberg, "Some Postulates of Biblical Criminal Law"; Chaim Grade poignantly frames the theme in *My Mother's Sabbath Days*, trans. Channa K. Goldstein and Inna H. Grade (New York: Alfred Knopf, 1986).

109. Mary Douglas, *In the Active Voice*, 34–35.

110. Richard Lienhardt, *Divinity and Experience: The Religion of the Dinka* (Oxford: Clarendon Press, 1961); Douglas calls this "the most important book in anthropological studies of religion, because it broke the impasse foisted on anthropology by the confusion of ritual with religion and the rigid separation of religion from ordinary life" (*In the Active Voice*, 36).

111. Douglas, *In the Active Voice*, 35.

112. See Henry Skaja "*Li* (Ceremonial) as a Primal Concept in Confucian Spiritual-Humanism," *Chinese Culture* 25 (1984): 1–26.

113. Søren Kierkegaard, *Concluding Unscientific Postscript to the Philosophical Fragments* (1844), trans. David F. Swenson and Walter Lowrie (Princeton, N.J.: Princeton University Press, 1941, 417–49; cf. Andrew Burgess, *Passion, "Knowing How," and Understanding: An Essay on the Concept of Faith* (Missoula, Mont.: Scholars Press, 1975), 46–47.

114. Halevi, *Kuzari* 3.20–21, trans. Hirschfeld, 158–60.

115. It is as much a ritual law to make flag burning a protected act as it is to ban it.

116. Indeed, it is an important corollary of the underdetermination of the expressive commandments by their moral thematics that apart from those thematics one cannot (as is commonly presumed among many social groups) judge a person's character by expressive style, degree, or kind of devotional practice.

Chapter 7

1. *Guide* II 38, 40; *Republic* VIII–IX; cf. *Laws* I 625d, VII 796b.

2. *Republic* III 398–403; *Laws* II 654–60; John Wild, *Plato's Modern Enemies and the Theory of Natural Law* (1953; reprint, Chicago: University of Chicago Press, 1971), 53–56.

3. Mary Douglas, *Purity and Danger*, 2–3.

4. Plato, *Laws* VII 796b, II 660b, 666e, I 625dff., IV 705d.

5. Lev. 19:30; cf. Deut. 18:10, Exod. 22:17.

6. Douglas, *Purity and Danger*, 29ff.

7. Spinoza, *Ethics* IV, Definitions of the Emotions 38, ed. Gebhardt 2.201.

8. See Ps. 119:20; Amos 6:8; Num. 11:34; cf. the cognate *t'v*.

9. Deep in mourning for Moses, the Midrash has it, Israel forgot the Halakha. When new problems placed the people in a quandary, they asked Joshua to seek guidance from the *Urim ve-Tummim*, but he refused, since the Torah "is not in heaven" (Deut. 30:12). Othniel ben Kenaz then reconstituted the Halakha using dialectics (*Temurah* 16a). So the Law needed constant reinvention, from the start, not by oracles but by thought, and the Rabbis are "disciples of Aaron"—whose descendants used no magic in diagnosing "leprosy."

10. For this rare sense of *ḥesed*, see N. Glueck, *Ḥesed in the Bible* (Cincinnati: HUC, 1967), 107; cf. Prov. 14:34, 25:10.

11. See Hertz, ad loc., 507. The new JPS renders the prohibition in terms of marriage! But what is forbidden is *taking* one's sister, whether or not one marries her.

12. See Lévi-Strauss, *The Raw and the Cooked.*

13. See Goodman and Goodman, *The Sexes in the Human Population*, 72–78.

14. Thus the force of *ʿezer ke-negdo* (Gen. 2:18).

15. See Talcott Parsons et al., *Family, Socialization, and Interaction* (Glencoe, Ill.: Free Press, 1955), 101–3, 113, 305–6, 356; *Social Structure and Personality* (Glencoe, Ill.: Free Press, 1964), 3–8, 43–46, 51, 57–77, 97–101, 264; *Societies, Evolutionary and Comparative Perspectives* (Englewood Cliffs, N.J.: Prentice-Hall, 1966), 36; cf. D. M. Schneider and R. T. Smith, *Class Differences and Sex Roles in American Kinship and Family Structure* (Englewood Cliffs, N.J.: Prentice-Hall, 1973), 9–11, 16–17, 54–55; D. M. Schneider, *American Kinship: A Cultural Account* (Englewood Cliffs, N.J.: Prentice-Hall, 1968), 37–40, 49–54, 57–62, 114–17.

16. Kenneth Clark, *The Nude: A Study in Ideal Art* (London: Murray, 1957), 1ff.; cf. 2 Samuel 11:2.

17. Cf. Eric Voegelin, *Israel and Revelation*, 111–14ff.

18. Parsons, *Societies*, 59–60.

19. *On Justice*, chap. 6 argues that the Torah's rejection of an afterworld and lack of interest in funerary laws reflect the Mosaic response to the culture of Egypt.

20. See R. A. Wasserstrom, "Is Adultery Immoral?" in *Today's Moral Problems*, ed. R. A. Wasserstrom (New York: Macmillan, 1979), 288–300.

21. For the transactional aspects of what is sometimes deemed a form of free love, see Charles Varni, "An Exploratory Study of Spouse Swapping," in *Beyond Monogamy*, ed. J. R. Smith and L. B. Smith (Baltimore: Johns Hopkins University Press, 1974), 247–59.

22. See, e.g., J. Delaney et al., *The Curse: A Cultural History of Menstruation* (New York: Dutton, 1976); S. Weitz, *Sex Roles* (New York: Oxford University Press, 1977), 161–63.

23. *Niddah*, to begin with, is sprinkling, as in our clinical use of the term "spotting"; see Num. 19:9, 13, 20; 31:23. The "spattering" of Lev. 20:21 is transitional to the moral sense used in the Prophets (cf. the Latin *maculata*). That sense, as Milgrom notes in the JPS Leviticus commentary, stems from the image of Israel as a faithless bride.

24. The Sabbath day *is* God's praise. Thus the liturgy, playing on Ps. 92:1, "a song of the Sabbath day," playfully ascribes God's praises to the day itself; Birnbaum, 341.

25. See Deut. 7:15, 28:60; Lam. 5:17, 1:13; Ps. 41:4; Isa. 1:5; Jer. 8:18.

26. Cf. Lev. 12:2: A woman who has just given birth to a son is "unclean for seven days, as many days as for her period of infirmity"—that is, for as long as it would be impure to approach her sexually on account of her menstrual period. "She shall be impure as long as the impurity of her sickness" would be unmeaning; "as in the days of the period of her impurity" yields a tautology. If we take the two together, we get "she shall be unclean as long as the uncleanness of her uncleanness"—a double tautology engendered by anachronism. *Niddah* here is the period, *devotah* is her infirmity; only *ṭam'ah* and *titmaʾ* denote impurity—of the time, not the woman; thus, of the intercourse and the ethos it fosters.

27. See Jacob Milgrom, Anchor Bible, Leviticus; Noam Zohar, "Repentance and Purification . . . in the Pentateuch; *JBL* 107 (1988): 609–18.

28. Saul's consulting a necromancer (1 Sam. 28) violates the Law and the king's own decree (vv. 9–12); his desperate quest is clearly not prescriptive; the ghost's appearance reveals no more of the author's beliefs about ghosts than does the ghost in Hamlet. The story does reveal Saul's state of mind: he knows Samuel, the old voice of his conscience, by no more hint than that the apparition is robed and stands erect.

29. Douglas, *Purity and Danger*, 41–57.

30. Douglas, *Purity and Danger*, 56, is misled by a note in Danby's translation of the *Mishnah*, 722, which explains that frogs are not *ritually* defiling.

31. For the unsoundness of the totem-taboo idea, see Lévi-Strauss, *Totemism*.

32. The Talmud (Y. *Berakhot* 2) reasons that swine's wallowing made them a symbol of filth, but their physical impurity bore moral overtones (Prov. 11:22; cf. Isa. (65:4, 66:3, 66:17), heightened by their use in pagan sacrifices and by the persecutions of Antiochus Epiphanes, the Seleucid ruler of Syria, whose attempts to impose cultic conformity on the Jews of his empire included a ban on circumcision. His defiling of the altar at Jerusalem with the sacrifice of swine (1 Macc. 1:47) inflamed the Hasmonean Revolt of 165–63 B.C. When Eleazar, a venerable scribe, refused pork, his mouth was forced open to admit it: "Welcoming a glorious death in preference to a life of pollution," the handsome old man "went up of his own accord to the torture wheel" (2 Macc. 6:18–20). His martyrdom helped make pork a paradigm of impurity and disloyalty. By Rabbinic times, even the word for pigs was avoided, and one who raised them was considered accursed (*Menaḥot* 64b). Jews were forbidden to trade in swine or derive any benefit from them. Again the symbolic, hygienic, social, and aesthetic dimensions map and underscore one another's messages.

33. Isa. 66:3 symbolizes hypocrisy in worship as the sacrifice of dogs and swine.

34. Cf. Ikhwān al-Ṣafā, *The Case of the Animals vs Man*, Goodman, 87–89, for the association of domestic scavengers with waste and corruption.

35. Cf. the parataxis of Exod. 20:22 and 20:23.

36. Maimonides, *Code* II, Hilkhot Milah, and I, introduction, ed. Hyamson 2.161b–65a, 1.18b. The *Guide* (III 32, 33, 35.14) invokes (a rather proximate) teleology; the *Yad* is topically organized, like its model, the Mishnah. So circumcision is *codified* as an expression of devotion; cf. Isadore Twersky, *Introduction to the Code of Maimonides* (New Haven, Conn.: Yale University Press, 1980), 283–84, 300–302.

37. See W. H. Masters and V. E. Johnson, *Human Sexual Response* (Boston: Little, Brown, 1966), 189–91; cf. Alex Comfort, *The Anxiety Makers* (1967; reprint, New York: Delta, 1970), 106, etc.

38. We have evidence that circumcision is prophylactic against penile cancer and infection and possibly against cervical cancer and infection, although the latter effect is difficult to differentiate from the benefits of monogamy.

39. Bar Mitzvah, correspondingly, marks puberty not with sexual but with moral, spiritual, and intellectual celebrations.

40. *Birḥat ha-mazon*; cf. Berakhot 48 with Gen. 17:7–8.

41. See Kant, *Groundwork*, trans. Paton, 74–75.

42. See Moses Isserles' (ca. 1525–1572) glosses on the *Shulḥan Arukh*.

43. See Gen. 28:12 and Maimonides, *Guide* I 15.

Chapter 8

1. John Eccles, *The Human Mystery*, Gifford Lectures of 1977–1978 (Berlin: Springer, 1979), 12–13.

2. See Goodman and Goodman, "Creation and Evolution."

3. See C. W. Misner "Cosmology and Theology," in *Cosmology, History and Theology*, ed. W. Yourgrau and A. D. Breck (New York: Plenum, 1977).

4. *Science News*, August 3, 1985.

5. *ED* I, Exordium, ed. Kafih, 33, trans. Rosenblatt 38–39.

6. Eric Voegelin, *Order and History*, vol. 4: *The Ecumenic Age, Order and History*, 112–13.

7. See al-Ghazali, Jerusalem Letter in *Iḥya' 'Ulūm al-Dīn*, Qawa'id al-'Aqā'id (Bastions of Convictions), Fasl 3; ed. and trans. A. L. Tibawi in *Islamic Quarterly* 9 (1965): 78–122; and my "Ghazālī's Argument from Creation."

8. For al-Ghazali, as for Maimonides, this life's goodness is critical in the argument for creation. Thus al-Ghazālī's claim that "Nothing in the realm of possibility is more wondrous than what came to be" qualified theistic subjectivism and was criticized by purist Ash'arites; see Eric Ormsby, *Theodicy in Islamic Thought: The Dispute Over al-Ghazālī's 'Best of All Possible Worlds'* (Princeton, N.J.: Princeton University Press, 1984), and my review in *JHP* 25 (1987), 589–91. Joseph Stern questions the world's goodness. I find its denial coherent internally but radically incoherent with the other judgments of those who propose it. Puzzled by the obscurantist readings of Maimonides popularized in the 1950s, Stern also asks if Maimonides didn't want us to believe (1) that God is unknowable and (2) that there is no relation of any kind between God and nature. But (1) is refuted by Maimonides' elaborate discussion of the Torah's use of indirection to convey positive knowledge of God, as the all-perfect Being (*Guide* I 1–63); (2) fails internally and textually. For if we take "relation" abstractly, as in current usage, no two things are unrelated; even unrelatedness is a relation. And Maimonides specifically countenances descriptions of God as Creator. Textually the Arabic term (*nisba*), commonly translated "relation," has a more restricted reference. Like the Latin *ratio*, it denotes relations of proportion; see Munk, ed., *Guide des Égarés*, 1.200 n. 1. There is no proportion between us and God's perfection. For proportion requires a common measure. Yet there are structural symmetries, the basis of what Thomists will call analogy, not in the sense of a qualitative similarity but in the sense of a structural symmetry. Thus Maimonides can say that we become godlike by perfecting our humanity. We realize our affinity to God by perfecting what is best in us, and what is most perfect in our humanity links us to God's perfection. As Narboni notes, the *Guide* opens by identifying human understanding as our affinity with God. The reason, we must understand, is not that divine intelligence is like our own, but rather that what is highest to us has, for that very reason, an affinity to that which renders God the Highest.

9. Al-Rāzī, for one, thought *formatio mundi* afforded the only viable argument "against the eternalists," because it found an origin for the world but not for time, space, or matter. See my "Rāzī's Myth of the Fall of the Soul."

10. *Guide* I 73.10, II 17; cf. Francis Oakley, "Christian Theology and Newtonian Science: The Rise of the Concept of the Laws of Nature," *Church History* 30 (1961); reprinted in *Creation: The Impact of an Idea*, ed. D. O'Connor and Oakley (New York: Scribners, 1969), 54–83; and my "Maimonides and Leibniz."

11. *TF* XVII; cf. my "Did al-al-Ghazālī Deny Causality?"

12. al-Ghazālī, *Munqidh*, ed. Jabre, 50–51; cf. 35, 42; trans. Watt, 78–79; cf. 55, 64–68.

13. M. B. Foster, "The Christian Doctrine of Creation and the Rise of Modern Natural Science," *Mind* 43 (1934); repr. in O'Connor and Oakley, *Creation*.

14. Ibn Ṭufayl, *Ḥayy Ibn Yaqẓān*, trans. Goodman, 130–33.

15. al-Ghazālī, *TF* I 4 corresponding to ed. *TT*, Bouyges 102. Cf. Hume in *Dialogues Concerning Natural Religion* IX; but contrast Hume's account of necessity in relation to liberty and al-Ghazālī's comparable theistic determinism.

16. Would perfect knowledge be deductive? Such perfection could belong only to God, in whom the distinction between induction and deduction is meaningless, since God is timeless. In God, determination of what shall be done (God's will) and what is so (God's understanding) are one and the same; the distinction between necessity and contingency dissolves.

Indeed, that distinction is irrelevant even to us insofar as we act; it is relevant only insofar as we are acted upon.

17. Saadiah, *Book of Theodicy*, trans. Goodman 126; *ED* IX 4, trans. Rosenblatt, 333–34.

18. Saadiah, *ED* IV Exordium; cf. III Exordium.

19. Chrysippus ap. Porphyry *De Abst.* III 20, "God mingled soul, as if it were salt, with the flesh of this animal." Also Cicero, *De Natura Deorum* II 160.

20. Spinoza, *Ethics* I, appendix; cf. II 18 Scholium; Hume, *Dialogues Concerning Natural Religion*, II–III, ed. Kemp Smith 143, 146; cf. VI–VIII.

21. See Foster, "The Christian Doctrine of Creation," 46.

22. Maimonides, *Guide* II 6, citing Plato, *Timaeus* 28a and Sanhedrin 38b, which glosses Gen. 1:26 as an allusion to God's "consulting" his heavenly retinue.

23. See my "Matter and Form as Attributes of God in Maimonides' Philosophy."

24. See H. A. Wolfson, *Philo* (Cambridge, Mass.: Harvard University Press, 1962), 1.200ff.; David Winston, *Logos and Mystical Theology in Philo of Alexandria* (Cincinnati: HUC Press, 1985).

25. "Therefore everyone must say, 'For my sake was the world created.'"

26. *Guide* III 13; cf. II 6 and Mishnah *Avot* 6.11. For Maimonides each natural being has its own imparted essence to fulfill; thus the delegation of free will, Code I, *Hilkhot Teshuvah*, 5.1–4; contrast al-Ghazālī, *Munqidh*, trans. Watt, 37.

27. Mishnah *Avot* 2.17; see chap. 5.

28. Here I part company with Foster. My understanding of induction is Socratic, like Aristotle's, not Humean.

29. Spinoza, *Short Treatise on God, Man and His Well-Being*, trans. Curley, 1.84.

30. Aristotle, *De Partibus Animalium* I 5, 644b 26–645a 25, after J. Barnes, ed., W. Ogle, trans., *Revised Oxford Translation of the Complete Works of Aristotle* 1.1003–4. Aristotle's artificer is immanent, thus allegorical. Refusing to make the divine a deus ex machina, Aristotle avoids resolving Plato's imagery, retaining the metaphor of an artificer: there is no better description of the effect than as a product of design—yet the design is the work of natural causes.

31. It is no part of our project, however, to seek to choose between volition and intelligence as models of God's creativity. For Maimonides showed us that these two aspects should not be too sharply dichotomized.

32. Mishnah *Avot* 5.9; cf. Genesis Rabbah 5.5. The imagery supports naturalism by treating miracles as stipulations in God's original covenant with nature. Also in support of naturalism Maimonides (*Guide* II 29) cites Eccles. 1:9 and *Avodah Zarah* 54b: "There is nothing new under the sun," and "The world runs in its accustomed course."

33. Emergence does not imply discontinuity ("saltation") and is not confined to the differentiation of levels (e.g., the biological from the chemical). It does imply that prior givens are insufficient to determine outcomes, since subjects active in the present also play their roles. Emergence is critical not only in evolution but in learning, invention, discovery—all forms of creativity. See my "Determinism and Freedom in Spinoza, Maimonides and Aristotle."

34. From the blessings before the Shema: *U-meḥadesh be-tuvo be-khol yom tamid ma'aseh bereshit, ka-amur: "le-'oseh orim gedolim, ki-le-'olam ḥasdo,"* glossing Ps. 136:7, by stressing the imperfect verb and linking eternal and continuous grace (*ḥesed*) with the ongoing creation of the "great lights" of the heavens.

35. Charles Hartshorne, "Bergson's Aesthetic Creationism Compared to Whitehead's," in *Bergson and Modern Thought*, ed. Andrew C. Papanicolaou and Pete A. Y. Gunter (Chur, Switzerland: Harwood, 1987), 372.

36. Plotinus, *Enneads* V 7.1–2; for the Stoic view, see Nemesius 309.5, 311.2.

37. For Bergson's reflections on Zeno, see his *"L'Intuition philosophique," Revue de*

Métaphysique et de Morale 19 (1911); reprinted in *La Pensée et le mouvant* (Paris: F. Alcan, 1934). Bergson came to Zeno's paradoxes and thus to the problem of time with the background of a promising mathematics student. Of his school days he writes: "It was at Condorcet that I experienced the first and perhaps the only hesitation of my life. I was attracted equally by science and by letters; I felt an equal aptitude for mathematics and philosophy. And then, when I had decided for letters, my teacher of mathematics came and made a scene before my parents, telling them I was about to commit an irremediable act of folly." For the impact on Bergson's thought of the ideas of Jules Tannéry, Jules Lachelier, Emile Boutroux, and others in subverting the claims of mechanistic science and the geometrical modeling of nature, see Ben-Ami Scharfstein, *Roots of Bergson's Philosophy* (New York: Columbia University Press, 1943), 8–19.

38. Augustine, *Confessions* XI 19–37.

39. Hume, *Treatise*, bk. I, pt. II, sec. II, ed. Selby-Bigge, 31.

40. Cf. Albert Éduard Michotte, *The Perception of Causality*, trans., T. R. Miles and Elaine Miles (1946; reprint, London: Methuen, 1963), 256: "If Hume had been able to carry out experiments such as ours, there is no doubt that he would have been led to revise his views on the psychological origin of the popular idea of causality"; see D. C. G. Macnabb's fictive dialogue between Hume and Michotte, "Michotte and Hume on Mechanical Causation," in *Hume and the Enlightenment: Essays Presented to Ernest Campbell Mossner* (Edinburgh: Edinburgh University Press, 1974). The Bergsonian critique of Hume rests not, of course, on the immediacy of any impression of causal force but on the relationality, and thus temporality, in the sense of duration, implicit in the Humean idea of succession. This relationality is concealed when Hume treats succession as the mere occurrence now of one sensum, now of another.

41. My physicist friend David Yount has argued (in an unpublished paper) that the temporal moment should be envisioned "as an arbitrarily short interval" and duration as "the sum or integral over a number of such intervals." The profit is that the Laplacean fiction of a point instant that is still somehow pregnant with the future (indeed, with all possible pasts and futures) dissolves, and the causal efficacy of events at a given moment is not reduced to their *logical* relation to all other events via a set of ontologically mysterious "laws."

42. Leibniz, *Discourse on Metaphysics*, 13; cf. to Arnauld, March 23, 1690; to John Bernoulli, February 21, 1699; all in L. E. Loemker, ed. *Leibniz: Philosophical Papers and Letters* (Dordrecht: Reidel, 1976), 310, 360, 513. Cf. my "Leibniz and Futurity: Was It All Over with Adam?"

43. See M. Čapek, "Leibniz' Thought Prior to the Year 1670: From Atomism to a Geometrical Kinetism," *Revue Internationale de Philosophie* 20 (1966): 249–56.

44. G. Lemaître, *The Primeval Atom: An Essay on Cosmology*, trans. after B. Korff and S. Korff (New York: Van Nostrand, 1950), 18–19.

45. Cf. Augustine, *Confessions*, XI xxviii 38: "I am about to repeat a Psalm that I know. Before I begin, my expectation is extended over the whole; but once I have begun, whatever I pluck off from it and let fall into the past enters the realm of memory. So the life of this action of mine extends in two directions, my memory of what I have repeated and my expectation of what I am about to repeat. But all the while, my attention is present with me, so that through it what was future may be conveyed over to become past."

46. See Johannes Itten, *The Art of Color*, trans. E. van Haagen (New York: Van Nostrand, 1973); Errol Harris, *Hypothesis and Perception* (London: Allen and Unwin, 1970), 237–92. Bergson remarked trenchantly in his Huxley Lecture at the University of Birmingham, May 29, 1911: "When I open and close my eyes in rapid succession, I experience a succession of visual sensations each of which is the condensation of an extraordinarily long history unrolled in the external world. There are then, succeeding one another, billions of vibrations,

that is a series of events which, even with the greatest possible economy of time, would take me thousands of years to count. Yet these momentous events, which would fill thirty centuries of a matter become conscious, occupy only a second of my own consciousness, able to contract them into one picturesque sensation of light" (quoted in Milič Čapek, "Bergson's Theory of the Mind-Brain Relation," in *Bergson and Modern Thought*, ed. Andrew C. Papanicolaou and Pete A. Y. Gunter (Chur, Switzerland: Harwood, 1987), 139–40.

47. Hume, *Enquiry*, sec. II, 16, ed. Selby-Bigge, 20–21; cf. *Treatise*, bk. I, pt. I, sec. I, ed. Selby-Bigge, 6. Hume candidly allows that one who had never seen a particular shade of blue would still notice its absence from a continuous progression of the remaining shades and would be able to supply it. He infers: "the simple ideas are not always, in every instance, derived from the correspondent impressions." But he evades the implication, that "simple ideas" and even "simple impressions" may be simple only superficially. And he treats the case as "so singular, that it is scarcely worth our observing, and does not merit that for it alone we should alter our general maxim." Hume does not see how typical the case really is, that all simple percepts are the achievements of integrative activity, their supposed simplicity merely emblematic of their phenomenal givenness or all-at-onceness. Physiologically, even phenomenally, all sensations will be complex. They must be, if they are temporal. Their givenness is not indicative of an underlying atomicity but only reflects our attending to the integrated product, which is itself, in part, an outcome of that very attending.

48. Milič Čapek, *Bergson and Modern Physics* (Dordrecht: Reidel, 1971), 30–39.

49. See Čapek, "Bergson's Theory of the Mind–Brain Relation," 141–42.

50. It was a device of Hume's to assign the elements of a natural event different names, so as to accentuate their logical discreteness, but this was achieved only by ignoring the ontological unities and continuities. When medieval philosophers called cause and effect "correlatives," they were canonizing in logic the same natural linkage that Hume canonically concealed.

51. Čapek, "Bergson's Theory of the Mind–Brain Relation," 140.

52. Čapek urges that "the volume of the present, or what may be called 'the mnemic span,' is *variable*." But he applies the point strictly psychologically; "Bergson's Theory of the Mind–Brain Relation," 141–42.

53. Cf. Ali Dashti, *In Search of Omar Khayyam*, trans. L. P. Elwell-Sutton (London: Allen Unwin, 1971).

54. See Čapek, *Bergson and Modern Physics*, 226–36.

55. Henri Bergson, *A Study in Metaphysics: The Creative Mind*, trans., Mabelle L. Andison (Totowa, N.J.: Littlefield Adams, 1965), 211.

56. Bergson, *The Creative Mind*, 83; cf. Čapek, *Bergson and Modern Physics*, 129–30. Memory for Bergson (like 'perception,' in Leibniz) was not confined to the mental; it had something of the sense that metallurgists give the term.

57. Hartshorne, "Bergson's Aesthetic Creationism," 372.

58. It is somewhat disingenuous for Hartshorne to rely on the logical contrast of potentiality with actuality to ground the claim that the potential is nothing actual. In fact, the ontic status of potentialities is quite varied. Aristotle cannot have been entirely wrong to locate some in matter. Surely dispositions, talents, and capacities are not virtual. A disposition may govern several possibilities, and these are virtual. Masa harina can be made right in the kitchen into a tortilla or a tamale but not into a chili relleno. There must be something real that allows the one and not the other.

59. See A. N. Whitehead, *The Concept of Nature* (Cambridge: Cambridge University Press, 1920), 71, and the discussions led by Margaret Masterman and Dorothy Emmet in "The Pardshaw Dialogues: Sense Awareness and the Passage of Nature," in *Process Studies* 16.2 (1987): 91–92, 103–4. Under the influence of quantum discoveries, Whitehead came in the

end to quantize time; I think that in so doing he lost some of the value of his original, more Aristotelian and Spinozistic approach that regards occasions as differentiated more by the relations of their active constituents than by isolation from their environment.

60. Whitehead, *Essays in Science and Philosophy* (New York: Philosophical Library, 1947), 117; Dorothy Emmet "The Pardshaw Dialogues," 126. What Hartshorne values most in Bergson is the theological grounding of this point of Whitehead's: "But Bergson is consistent in taking preservative becoming as the paradigm of reality. This was a great step" ("Bergson's Aesthetic Creationism," 373). True, Bergson sees the living presence of past acts. But what mattered to him most was the taking up of the past in life, not the embalming of its pastness.

61. "Bergson's Aesthetic Creationism," 377. For a more balanced reading of Whitehead, see Donald Sherburne, "Some Reflections on Sartre's Nothingness and Whitehead's Perishing," *Review of Metaphysics* 48 (1994) 3–17: "Whitehead's notion of perishing, and the concepts which cluster around it, provide for disconnection, for cutting off, and yet at the same time allow for connectedness, for relatedness, and for the kind of predictive regularity required by science in those areas where science requires predictive regularity. . . . for Whitehead, to be is to be in relation." p. 7.

62. Cf. Bergson's letter of March 25, 1903: "The more I try to grasp myself by consciousness, the more I perceive myself as the totalization or *Inbegriff* of my own past, this past being contracted with a view to action. 'The unity of Self' of which philosophers speak, appears to me as a unity of an apex, of a summit to which I narrow myself by an effort of attention—an effort which is prolonged during the whole of life, and which, as it seems to me, is the very essence of life."

63. "Bergson's Aesthetic Creationism," 372.

64. See my *On Justice*, esp. chaps. 4–5.

65. Under the rubric "The creativity of the past," F. Bradford Wallack writes: "There is nothing passive or static about objects, the antecedent occasions which are the data of prehensions. Endowed with creativity, they are in fact very forceful and energetic, aspects of the efficient causation of new subjects. . . . Objects are not simply the passive recipients of the actions of subjects but the very activity fueling the subjects" see *The Epochal Nature of Process in Whitehead's Metaphysics* (Albany: SUNY Press, 1980), 140.

66. Cf. David Burrell, "Why Not Pursue the Metaphor of Artisan and View God's Knowledge as Practical?" in my *Neoplatonism and Jewish Thought*; Joseph Incandela, "Aquinas' Lost Legacy: God's Practical Knowledge and Situated Human Freedom" (Ph.D. diss., Princeton University, 1986).

67. See, for example, al-Ghazālī, *TF*, ed. Bouyges, 2d ed. 57, rem. 30, and my "Maimonides and Leibniz."

68. Spiritualism shows its materialist roots, as we have noted, in its pictorialism and unceasing efforts to physicalize the "spirit world"—to make it squeak in answer to the sensuous demands of mechanism; and again, in the conventional appearance of some fetish or sign from the "Beyond" at the climax of a chilling tale—in attempts to photograph ectoplasm or use "state of the art engineering equipment" to validate psychokinesis and "precognitive remote perception"; see R. G. Jahn and B. J. Dunne, "Consciousness, Quantum Mechanics, and Random Physical Processes," in *Bergson and Modern Thought*, ed. Andrew C. Papanicolaou and Pete A. Y. Gunter (Chur, Switzerland: Harwood, 1987), 271–307.

69. "Bergson's Aesthetic Creationism," 373–74.

70. "Bergson's Aesthetic Creationism," 373. The idea of duration originates in Plotinus's project of discovering a temporality that would not be the mere measure and correlate of motion. Plotinian duration, the temporality of the hypostatic Soul, is psychic rather than physical; it mediates the transition from pure, timeless thought to temporal nature via the dialectic of discursive thinking. Monotheist creationists like Philo, Saadiah, Maimonides, Crescas, al-

Tabrīzī, and Albo adapted Plotinian duration as the archetype of (created) time, anticipating Bergson's discovery that real duration is not confined to the realm of thought. See *Enneads* III vii 8; H. A. Wolfson, *The Philosophy of Spinoza: Unfolding the Latent Process of His Reasoning* (1934; reprint, New York: Schocken, 1969), 1.331–46. The object was not to engage God in temporality but to derive temporality from God. Quite the contrary with the new tradition. Wallack writes: "The time spans of actual occasions are subject to many a curious calculation. . . . Lewis Ford has produced a diagram which . . . 'standardizes the temporal length of an occasion, which may be considered to vary considerably, perhaps between 20 milliseconds for a human occasion and 20^{-24} seconds for subatomic occasions.' . . . There is even a debate as to the exact specious present, the exact duration of the time-span of God. . . . Apparently God is to become and perish faster than any earthly actual occasion." Hartshorne and Cobb worry over just how short the divine specious present must be for God to attend the start and finish of each worldly occasion to give it a subjective aim and receive it as objectively immortal; see *The Epochal Nature*, 197.

71. See Émile Meyerson, *Identity and Reality*, trans., Kate Loewenberg (London, 1930; *Identité et Réalité*, Paris, 1908); and Bergson's 1909 review, in *Écrits et Paroles*, ed. R. M. Mossé-Bastide (Paris: Presses Universitaires de France, 1959); Čapek, *Bergson and Modern Physics*, 108, 368–97.

72. Čapek, *Bergson and Modern Physics*, esp. 375.

73. Philo, *De Opificio Mundi* vii 26; Philoponus, ap. Simplicius *On Aristotle's Physics*, 1169c: "Time co-exists with the heavens and the world . . . so the assumption of the eternity of time is refuted" in *Philoponus Against the Eternity of the World*, trans., Christian Wildberg (Ithaca, N.Y.: Cornell University Press, 1987), 140; al-Ghazālī: "Duration [*al-mudda*] and time according to us are created" (*TF* 56); cf. 66; Maimonides, *Guide* II 13. Averroës reports: "Most people who hold the world originated hold time to be originated with it," *TT*, ed. Bouyges, 32.

74. Čapek, *Bergson and Modern Physics*, 238–56.

75. Eliot Deutsch, "On the Being of Time," in his *Personhood, Creativity and Freedom* (Honolulu: University of Hawaii Press, 1982), 92–99; "Time is uniquely *performed* in art" (99).

76. Qur'ān 28:88; cf. 2:115: "Whithersoever you turn, there is the face of God"; see Emil Fackenheim, "The Possibility of the Universe in al-Fārābī, Ibn Sīnā, and Maimonides," *PAAJR* 16 (1947): 39–70; reprinted in *Essays in Medieval Jewish and Islamic Philosophy*, ed. A. Hyman (New York: Ktav, 1977), 303–34.

77. Maimonides, *Guide* II 19, 21; al-Ghazālī, *TF*, 58–59.

78. Nineteenth-century anti-Darwinism did not defend Biblicism but hid behind it to guard the Aristotelian essentialism in which Victorian theism was invested. But the real quarrel of today's anti-Darwinists is with a kind of neo-Spencerian triumphalism suspected of taking aid and comfort from evolutionism; see Goodman and Goodman, "Creation and Evolution."

79. Biblical history adopts a universal perspective by taking the creation as its starting point and situating Israel within the history of the nations. All nations are blood relations (Gen. 3:20), all cultures and languages spring from a common source (Gen. 10, 11) and coalesce (Zeph. 3:9) to a common end. All are subject to the same moral laws. Hence God's concern for Noah's lawless generation (Gen. 6:11-13), his visitation of liberations and punishments on all nations (Gen. 13:13, 15:14; Deut. 27:16–26; Amos 1:3–2:9, 9:7). Biblical history is objective in that its goal is not to celebrate the nation, and still less its kings, but to record the insights, acts, and failings of a people and its leaders, setting out an emerging order of meaning. See Eric Vogelin, *Order and History: Israel and Revelation*, 116–87; Paul Merkley, *The Greek and Hebrew Origins of Our Idea of History* (Lewiston, Ont.: Mellen, 1987).

80. Bergson did not share the positivist penchant for equating meaning with verifiabil-

ity or falsifiability, but he saw the risk of vacating metaphysical judgments by making them independent of all possible evidence. He proudly and truthfully stated: "I have constant recourse to scientific argumentation" (M. Grémil, Report of a Visit to Bergson, *Mercure de France* 108, (1914), 397, cited in Scharfstein, 10.

81. "Bergson's Aesthetic Creationism," 374—a rather limp-wristed phrasing of Popper's falsifiability test!

82. See Popper's Peterhouse Lecture of summer 1953, in *Scientific Knowledge*, ed. Janet Kourany (Belmont, Calif.: Wadsworth, 1987), 139–57.

83. Robert Neville, *Creativity and God: A Challenge to Process Theology* (New York: Seabury Press, 1980), 44–45.

84. Neville, *Creativity and God*, 50.

85. Neville, *Creativity and God*, 8–9.

86. Paul Weiss, *Beyond All Appearances* (Carbondale: Southern Illinois University Press, 1974), 169.

87. See my "Matter and Form as Attributes of God in Maimonides' Philosophy."

88. See my "al-Ghazālī's Argument from Creation"; Maimonides, *Guide* II 2–21.

89. See Shmuel Sambursky, *The Physical World of Late Antiquity* (London: Routledge, 1962), 154–75; Richard Sorabji, ed., *Philoponus and the Rejection of Aristotelian Science* (Ithaca, N.Y.: Cornell University Press, 1987), esp. the chapters by Michael Wolff and Lindsay Judson.

90. "Bergson's Aesthetic Creationism," 374.

91. "Bergson's Aesthetic Creationism," 374.

92. Neville writes: "Apart from the relative nature the divinity gives itself as creator in creating the world, God is utterly transcendent" (*Creativity and God*. 8); cf. Maimonides: "Every predicate we assign to Him either designates His act or, if intended to apply to Him rather than His work, its significance is in denying the privation of such a character"—that is, affirming his perfection; *Guide* I 58.

93. See Milton Munitz, *The Mystery of Existence* (New York: Appleton-Century-Crofts, 1965), esp. 145–46, where Bergson's (ultimately Parmenidean) argument that the idea of nothingness is somehow logically flawed is shown to be not only psychologistic but dependent on the limited capabilities of the imagination.

94. Agus, "If God Be the *Élan Vital*," in Jacob B. Agus, *Jewish Identity in an Age of Ideologies* (New York: Ungar, 1978), 249–51; cf. C. F. von Weiszsäcker, *The Relevance of Science*, Gifford Lectures of 1959–1960 (New York: Harper and Row, 1964), 3.

95. Cf. Agus, "If God Be the *Élan Vital*," 251–52, 255–57.

96. Teilhard de Chardin, *The Phenomenon of Man* (London: Collins, 1966), 257–61; *The Appearance of Man* (New York: Harper and Row, 1965), 271–73.

97. *Sof ma'aseh be-mashavah tehilla*. The phrase in *Lecha Dodi* (Birnbaum, 245; cf. Isa. 46:10) is a poetic excursus on the Talmud's (*Shevu'ot* 20b) homiletic gloss of the distinct wordings of the commandment to "observe" or "remember" the Sabbath; Exod. 20:8 and Deut. 5:12.

98. Cf. Maimonides, *Guide* II 36–37, III 17–18; and *Tikkunei Zohar*, ed. R. Margaliot (Jerusalem: Y. A. Hendler, 1964), 17a, trans. in Louis Jacobs, *Jewish Ethics, Philosophy and Mysticism* (New York: Behrman House, 1969), 115–20.

99. The Whiteheadian idea of co-creation resonates with the idea found in Saadiah, Leone Ebreo, and Spinoza that God delights *"in"* creation and loves himself through it.

100. Quoted in Jacques Maritain, *Ransoming the Time* (New York: Scribners, 1941), 101 n. Maritain in his youth was a Catholic Bergsonian. But he wrote: "Bergsonism can never be 'baptized.'"; See his *Bergsonian Philosophy and Thomism*, trans., M. L. Andison (New York: Philosophical Library, 1955), 19.

101. Agus, "If God Be the *Élan Vital*," 238.

102. See George Wald, "Cosmology of Life and Mind," in *Los Alamos Science* 16 (1988), 3–12; "Life and Mind in the Universe," in *Essays on Creativity and Science*, ed. D. DeLuca (Honolulu: Hawaii Council of Teachers of English, 1986), 1–14; "Consciousness and Cosmology: Their Interrelations," in *Bergson and Modern Thought*, ed. Andrew C. Papanicolaou and Pete A. Y. Gunter (Chur, Switzerland: Harwood, 1987), 343–52.

103. Wald, "Life and Mind in the Universe," 2–3.

104. Wald, "Life and Mind in the Universe," 3–4.

105. Wald, "Life and Mind in the Universe," 4.

106. Wald, "Life and Mind in the Universe," 5–7.

107. Wald, "Life and Mind in the Universe," 10.

108. Thus the Nasadiya Hymn of the Rgveda (10:129, trans. Walter Maurer, *Journal of Indo-European Studies* 3 (1975): 234.

> Not non-existent was it nor existent was it at that time;
> There was not atmosphere nor the heavens which are beyond.
> What existed? Where? In whose care?
> Water was it? An abyss unfathomable?
> Neither mortal was there nor immortal then;
> Not of night, of day was there distinction:
> That alone breathed windless through inherent power.
> Other than That there was naught else.
> Darkness it was, by darkness hidden in the beginning:
> An undistinguished sea was all this.
> The germ of all things which was enveloped in void,
> That alone through the power of brooding thought was born.

109. Teilhard de Chardin, *The Phenomenon of Man*, 258.

110. Harold Morowitz, "Modern Science and Pantheism," in *Essays on Creativity and Science*, ed. D. DeLuca (Honolulu: Hawaii Council of Teachers of English, 1986), 203.

111. Morowitz, "Modern Science and Pantheism," 209.

112. Morowitz, "Modern Science and Pantheism," 203.

113. Cf. his *Mayonnaise and the Origin of Life* (New York: Scribners, 1985); *Cosmic Joys and Local Pain: Musings of a Mystic Scientist* (New York: Scribner's, 1987); *The Wine of Life and Other Essays on Society, Energy, and Living Things* (New York: St. Martin's, 1979).

114. Morowitz, "Modern Science and Pantheism," 209.

115. Eccles, *The Human Mystery*, 28; J. A. Wheeler, "The Universe as a Home for Man," *American Scientist* 62 (1974): 683–91; "Genesis and Observership," in *Basic Problems in Methodology and Linguistics*, Robert E. Butts and Jaakko Hintikka, eds., University of Western Ontario Series in the Philosophy of Science (Boston: Reidel, 1977).

116. Wheeler (1977), cited in Eccles, *The Human Mystery*, 29.

117. Eccles, *The Human Mystery*, 30–31. As Čapek shows, Bergson, read in the light of de Broglie's 1928–1953 outlook, undercuts the popular subjectivist readings of quantum phenomena: indeterminacy would reflect not the mere involvement of the observer but the impossibility in principle of fixating the ultimacy of change in a single, instantaneous velocity and location; *Bergson and Modern Physics*, 284–99; page 300 cites an appreciation of Bergson by Einstein on this point. Čapek's fine argumentation would hardly satisfy those who seek a free pass for subjectivism in the findings of science, but physics itself is hardly relevant to their quest: if subjectivism holds, physics (including the indeterminacy principle) lacks the

authority they seek to build on. For further development of de Broglie's approach in a realist direction, see David Bohm, *The Undivided Universe* (London: Routledge, 1993).

118. *Guide* III 13; cf. *Rambam*, 262–77.

119. Saadiah, *ED*, introduction, 5; ed. Kafih, 21; trans. Rosenblatt, 23–24.

120. See his *Born to Sing: An Interpretation and World Survey of Bird Song* (Bloomington: Indiana University Press, 1973).

121. *The Leibniz-Arnauld Correspondence*, trans., H. T. Mason (Manchester, England: Manchester University Press, 1967), 14; cf. 26.

122. *Arnauld Correspondence*, 19.

123. F. Dyson, *Infinite in All Directions* (New York: Harper and Row, 1989), 296.

124. Dyson, *Infinite in All Directions*, 119; cf. 295.

125. Errol Harris, *Nature, Mind and Modern Science* (1954; reprint, London: Allen and Unwin, 1968), 398.

126. Adolf Grünbaum revives that hoary argument in "The Pseudo-Problem of Creation in Physical Cosmology," *Philosophy of Science* 56 (1989): 373–94.

127. Rensch's idea of the *Rassenkreis* gave evolutionary significance to racial variations among biological strains. His 1928 paper and 1929 monograph on the subject were bellwethers of German biology for the 1930s. Introduced to American readers by Theodosius Dobzhansky as one of the century's most penetrating theorists of evolution, Rensch was taken up by the racist anthropologist John Baker, who used the *Rassenkreis* to argue that it is "absolutely necessary" for scientists to obliterate "all distinction between races and species." See Bernhard Rensch, *Evolution Above the Species Level* (New York: Columbia, 1974), and Dobzhansky's preface; *Das Prinzip geographischer Rassenkreise und das Problem der Artbildung* (Berlin: Borntraeger, 1929); John Baker, *Race* (New York: Oxford University Press, 1974), 83 and nn. 891–94.

128. *Homo Sapiens: From Man to Demigod* (New York: Columbia University Press, 1972), 158–61.

129. Václav Havel, "Anti-Political Politics," in *Civil Society and the State*, ed. John Keane (London: Verso, 1988), 381–98; 383, 386, 389–90.

130. An old Hasidic story tells of the sage who instructs a young man to look out the window. "What do you see?" he asks. "People," the young man answers. Turning the youth around to face a mirror, the sage asks, "Now what do you see?" "Only myself." "And what made the difference?" Silver. Even as I wrote the preceding lines in the text, the newly liberated republic that Václav Havel helped to found and rose to lead, now divided into its Czech and Slovak parts, debated selling off its excess tanks to Syria—ironic proof of Havel's words that the smokestack staining the horizon is no mere aberration but almost an outgrowth of the land, more a cancer to be cut out than a blemish to be salved or masked.

131. Spinoza, *Ethica*, pt. I, def. 6; props. 9, 10.

132. *Enneads* VI 9.2, 25–45; cf. I 7.1, 8.2.8, V 1.5; cf. Plato, *Republic* 509B.

Bibliography

Baron, S., G. Wise, and L. E. Goodman, eds. *Violence and Defense in The Jewish Experience*. Philadelphia: JPS, 1977.

Bergson, Henri. *Two Sources of Morality and Religion*. Translated by R. A. Audra and C. Brereton. 1935; reprint, Westport, Conn.: Greenwood Press, 1977.

Birnbaum, Philip, ed. and trans. *Ha-Siddur ha-Shalem*. New York: Hebrew Publishing Company, 1949.

Carmichael, Calum. *Women, Law, and the Genesis Traditions*. Edinburgh: Edinburgh University Press, 1979.

Cicero. *De Finibus*. Edited by H. Rackman. Cambridge, Mass.: Harvard University Press, 1971.

Cohen, Hermann. *Religion of Reason Out of the Sources of Judaism* (first published posthumously in 1919). Translated by Simon Kaplan. New York: Ungar, 1972.

Danby, H., trans. *The Mishnah*. Oxford: Oxford University Press, 1977; 1933.

Dodds, E. R. *The Greeks and the Irrational*. Berkeley: University of California Press, 1964; 1951.

Douglas, Mary. *Purity and Danger: An Analysis of the Concepts of Pollution and Taboo*. London: Routledge, 1978; 1966.

Fackenheim, Emil. *Encounters Between Judaism and Modern Philosophy*. Philadelphia: JPS, 1973.

Falk, Ze'ev W. *Religious Law and Ethics: Studies in Biblical and Rabbinical Theonomy*. Jerusalem: Mesharim, 1991.

Feldman, David. *Marital Relations, Birth Control, and Abortion in Jewish Law*. New York: Schocken, 1975; 1968.

Fox, Marvin, ed. *Modern Jewish Ethics: Theory and Practice*. Columbus: Ohio State University Press, 1975.

———. *Interpreting Maimonides: Studies in Methodology, Metaphysics, and Moral Philosophy*. Chicago: University of Chicago Press, 1990.

al-Ghazālī. *Al-Munqidh min al-Dalal* (Deliverance from Error). Edited by F. Jabre. Beirut: Unesco, 1959. Translated by William Montgomery Watt in *The Faith and Practice of al-Ghazali*. London: Allen Unwin, 1963; 1953.

———. *Tahāfut al-Falāsifa* (The Incoherence of the Philosophers). Edited by M. Bouyges. Beirut: Catholic Press, 1962; 1927.

Ginzberg, Louis. *Legends of the Jews*. Translated by Henrietta Szold. 1909; reprint, Philadelphia: JPS, 1968.

Golding, Martin. *The Nature of Law*. New York: Random House, 1966.

Goodman, Lenn E. "Ghazālī's Argument from Creation," *International Journal of Middle East Studies* 2 (1971): 67–85, 168–88.

———. "Ibn Khaldūn and Thucydides," *JAOS* 92 (1972): 250–70.

———. "Rāzī's Myth of the Fall of the Soul: Its Function in His Philosophy." In *Essays on Islamic Philosophy and Science*, edited by George Hourani, 25–40, Albany: SUNY Press, 1975.

———. *Rambam*. New York: Viking, 1976.

———. "Equality and Human Rights, the Lockean and the Judaic Views." *Judaism* 25 (1976): 357–62.

———. "Saadya on the Human Condition." *JQR* 67 (1976): 23–29.

———. "Did Ghazālī Deny Causality?" *Studia Islamica* 47 (1978): 83–120.

———. "Maimonides' Philosophy of Law." *Jewish Law Annual* 1 (1978): 72–107.

———. "Maimonides and Leibniz." *JJS* 31 (1980): 214–36, with Leibniz's reading notes on *The Guide to the Perplexed.*

———. "The Greek Impact on Arabic Literature." In *The Cambridge History of Arabic Literature: Arabic Literature to the End of the Umayyad Period*, edited by M. J. C. Young, 460–82, Cambridge University Press, 1984.

———. "Matter and Form as Attributes of God in Maimonides' Philosophy." In *A Straight Path: Essays in Honor of Arthur Hyman*, edited by R. J. Long, and C. H. Manekin, 86–97, Washington, D.C.: CUA Press, 1987.

———. "Determinism and Freedom in Spinoza, Maimonides and Aristotle." In *Responsibility, Character and the Emotions*, edited by F. Schoeman, 107–64, Cambridge: Cambridge University Press, 1987.

———. "Ordinary and Extraordinary Language in Medieval Jewish and Islamic Philosophy," *Manuscrito* 11 (1988): 57–83.

———. "Context," *Philosophy East and West* 38 (1988): 307–23.

———. "The Rational and Irrational in Jewish and Islamic Philosophy." In *Rationality in Question*, edited by Shlomo Biderman and Ben-Ami Scharfstein, 93–118, Leiden: Brill, 1989.

———. "Saadiah's Interpretive Technique in Translating the Book of Job." In *Translation of Scripture,* edited by D. Goldberg, *JQR Supplement* (1990): 47–76.

———. *On Justice: An Essay in Jewish Philosophy.* New Haven: Yale University Press, 1991.

———. "Six Dogmas of Relativism." In *Cultural Relativism and Philosophy*, edited by M. Dascal, 77–102, Leiden: Brill, 1991.

———. "The Trouble with Phenomenalism," *APQ* 29 (1992): 237–52.

———. *Avicenna*. London and New York: Routledge, 1992.

———. "Maimonidean Naturalism." In *Neoplatonism and Jewish Thought*, edited by Lenn E. Goodman, 157–94, Albany: SUNY Press, 1992.

———. "Abortion and the Emergence of Human Life: Maimonides and the Judaic View." In *Bits of Honey: Essays for Samson H. Levey*, edited by S. Chyet and D. Ellenson, 163–90, Atlanta: Scholars Press, 1993.

———. "Mythic Discourse." In *Myths and Fictions*, edited by Ben-Ami Scharfstein and Schlomo Biderman, 51–112, Leiden: Brill, 1993.

———. "Leibniz and Futurity: Was It All Over with Adam?" In *Leibniz and Adam*, edited by M. Dascal and E. Yakira, 301–24, Tel Aviv: University Publishing, 1994.

———. "Crosspollinations: Philosophically Fruitful Exchanges between Jewish and Islamic Thought." In *The Jews of Islamic Lands*, edited by Jacob Lassner, Detroit: Wayne State University, forthcoming.

———. "Judah Halevi." In *History of Jewish Philosophy*, edited by Daniel Frank and Oliver Leaman, London: Routledge, 1995.

———. "Toward a Jewish Philosophy of Justice." In *Commandment and Community*, edited by D. Frank, 3–53, Albany: SUNY Press, 1995.

———. "Ibn Bajjah." In *History of Islamic Philosophy*, edited by S. H. Nasr and Oliver Leaman, London: Routledge, forthcoming.

———. and M. J. Goodman. "Creation and Evolution: Another Round in an Ancient Struggle," *Zygon* 18 (1983): 3–43.

M. J. Goodman and L. E. Goodman. *The Sexes in the Human Population*. Los Angeles: Gee Tee Bee, 3rd ed., 1984.

———. *Sex Differences in the Human Life Cycle*. Los Angeles: Gee Tee Bee, 7th ed., 1987.

Greenberg, Moshe. "Some Postulates of Biblical Criminal Law." In The *Jewish Expression*. Edited by Judah Goldin, 18–37. New Haven: Yale University Press, 1976.

Halevi, Judah. *Kitāb al-Radd wa-'l-Dalīl fī 'l-Dīn al-Dhalīl* (The Book of Rebuttal and Evidence in Behalf of the Scorned Faith, Known as the Kuzari). Edited by David Baneth. Jerusalem: Magnes Press, 1977. Translated by Hartwig Hirschfeld. 1905; reprint, New York: Schocken, 1964.

Hume, David. *A Treatise of Human Nature* (1739). Edited by L. A. Selby-Bigge. 1888; reprint, Oxford: Oxford University Press, 1968.

———. *An Enquiry Concerning Human Understanding* (1777). Edited by L. A. Selby-Bigge. 1902; reprint, Oxford: Clarendon Press, 1982.

———. *Dialogues Concerning Natural Religion* (1779; completed ca. 1751–1755). Edited by Norman Kemp Smith. Indianapolis: Bobbs Merrill, 1947.

Ikhwān al-Safā' (ca. 970). *The Case of the Animals vs Man*. Translated by L. E. Goodman. Boston: Twayne, 1978, reissued, Gee Tee Bee, 1984.

Jacobs, Louis. *Religion and the Individual: A Jewish Perspective*. Cambridge: Cambridge University Press, 1992.

Josephus. *Antiquities*. Edited by Louis Feldman. Cambridge, Mass.: Harvard University Press, 1965.

Kant, Immanuel. *Lectures on Ethics* (1775–1780). Translated by Louis Infield. New York: Harper, 1963; 1930.

———. *Critique of Pure Reason* (A = 1781/B = 1787). Translated by Normal Kemp Smith. London: St. Martin's, 1965; 1929.

———. *Groundwork of the Metaphysic of Morals* (1785). Translated by H. J. Paton. (New York: Harper, 1964.

———. *Religion Within the Limits of Reason Alone* (1793). Translated by T. M. Greene and H. H. Hudson. New York: Harper, 1960; 1934.

———. *The Metaphysics of Morals* (1797). Translated by Mary Gregor. Cambridge: Cambridge University Press, 1991.

Kellner, Menachem, ed., *Contemporary Jewish Ethics*. New York: Sanhedrin, 1978.

Kirk, G. S., J. E. Raven, and M. Schofield. *The Presocratic Philosophers*. Cambridge: Cambridge University Press, 1985.

Lévi-Strauss, Claude. *Totemism*. Translated by Rodney Needham. Boston: Beacon, 1963.

———. *The Savage Mind*. Chicago: University of Chicago Press, 1966; Paris, 1962.

———. *The Raw and the Cooked*. Translated by John Weightman and Doreen Weightman. New York: Harper and Row, 1970.

Lucretius. *De Rerum Natura*. Translated by Rolfe Humphries. Bloomington: Indiana University Press, 1968.

Maimonides, Moses. *Guide to the Perplexed. Le Guide des Égarés*. 3 vols. Edited by S. Munk. Osnabrück: Zeller, 1964; Paris, 1856–1866.

———. *Code. Mishneh Torah* II–XIV. Translated by various hands. New Haven: Yale University Press, 1949–. YJS.

———. *Code*. The Book of Knowledge, The Book of Adoration. Edited by Moses Hyamson, Jerusalem: Feldheim, 1974.

———. *The Eight Chapters*, edited by Joseph Gorfinkle. New York: AMS, 1966; 1912.

———. *Commentary to Mishnah Avot*. Translated by Arthur David. New York: Bloch, 1968.

———. *Book of the Commandments*. Translated by C. B. Chavel as *The Commandments*. London: Soncino, 1967.

Midrash *Tanḥuma*. Edited by S. Buber. Wilna: The Widow and Brothers Ram, 1913.

Milgrom, Jacob. *The JPS Commentary: Leviticus*. Philadelphia: JPS, 1989.

Naḥmanides, Moses. *Commentary on the Torah*. Edited by C. B. Chavel. Jerusalem: Mosad ha-Rav Kook, 1959–1963. Translated by C. B. Chavel, New York: Shilo, 1971.

Novak, David. *Jewish Social Ethics*. New York: Oxford University Press, 1992.

———. *The Theology of Nahmanides Systematically Presented*. Atlanta: Scholars Press, 1993.

Philo. *Works*. Edited by F. H. Colson and G. H. Whitaker. Cambridge, Mass.: Harvard University Press, 1929–53.

Quine, Willard V. O. *From a Logical Point of View*. Cambridge, Mass.: Harvard University Press, 1961.

Rosenzweig, Franz. *The Star of Redemption* [begun in 1918]. Translated by William Hallo. Boston: Beacon Press, 1971; from the 2d ed. of 1930.

Ibn Rushd. *Tahāfut al-Tahāfut* (The Incoherence of the Incoherence). Edited by M. Bouyges. Beirut: Catholic Press, 1930. Translated by Simon Van Den Bergh. London: Luzac, 1954.

Saadiah Gaon al-Fayyūmī. *K. al-Mukhtār fī 'l-Amānāt wa-'l-'I'tiqādāt*, The Book of Critically Chosen Beliefs and Convictions, known in Hebrew as *Sefer ha-Nivkhar ba-Emunot ve-De'ot*. Edited by J. Kafih. Jerusalem: Sura, 1970. Translated by S. Rosenblatt. New Haven: Yale University Press, 1948.

———. *The Book of Theodicy* (Commentary on the Book of Job). Translated by L. E. Goodman. New Haven: Yale University Press, 1988.

Safrai, Shmuel. *The Literature of the Sages*. Assen: Van Gorcum, 1987.

Sarna, Nahum. *The JPS Commentary: Genesis; Exodus*. Philadelphia: JPS, 1989.

Norman Kemp Smith. *A Commentary on Kant's "Critique of Pure Reason."* New York: Humanities Press, 2d ed., 1962.

Spinoza, Baruch. *Ethica Ordine Geometrico Demonstrata* (1677). Edited by Carl Gebhardt, *Spinoza Opera*. 4 vols. Heidelberg: Carl Winter, 1925. Translated by Edwin Curley in *The Collected Works of Spinoza*, vol. 1. Princeton: Princeton University Press, 1985.

Ibn Tufayl. *Ḥayy Ibn Yaqzan* (ca. 1180). Translated by L. E. Goodman. New York: Twayne, 1972. Reprint, Los Angeles: Gee Tee Bee, 1984.

Urbach, Ephraim. *The Sages: Their Concepts and Beliefs*. 2 vols. Translated by Israel Abrahams. Jerusalem: Magnes Press, 1975.

Voegelin, Eric. *Order and History*. 1956; reprint, Baton Rouge: LSU Press, 1976.

General Index

Index of Citations

HEBREW BIBLE

Genesis

Exodus

Leviticus

Joshua

Judges

1 Samuel

2 Samuel

Joel

Amos

Jonah

Micah

Zephaniah

Zechariah

Malachi

Psalms 126

Proverbs

Romans

1 Corinthians

Galatians

Colossians

Hebrews

James

OTHER SCRIPTURES

Qur'ān 63

Rgveda

Chandogya Upanishad

MISHNAH

Peah

Shevi'it

Terumot

Shabbat

Yoma

Ḥagigah

Yevamot

Ketubot

Soṭah